THE PAPACY
AND THE CHURCH

By the Same Author:

PASCAL ET NIETZSCHE. ÉTUDE HISTORIQUE ET
COMPARÉE.
Thèse pour le Doctorat de l'Université [Paris-Sorbonne, 1965]
New York: Burt Franklin & Co., 1974.

THE PAPACY
AND THE CHURCH

*A Study of Praxis and Reception
in Ecumenical Perspective*

J. Robert Dionne

Philosophical Library
New York

Library of Congress Cataloging in Publication Data

Dionne, J. Robert (James Robert), 1929-
  The papacy and the church.

  Bibliography: p.
  1. Popes—Teaching Office.   2. Authority
(Religion)   I. Title.
BX1806.D49   1985   262'.13   85-9319
ISBN 0-8022-2494-6

IN MEMORY OF MY MOTHER
MARGARET MARY SCHACHNER DIONNE

"Clearly as in all my writings I would desire not only a kind reader but a free corrector, more especially do I do so in this where would that the very vastness of the matter could have as many inquirers as it has gainsayers. But just as I do not wish my reader to favor me, so I do not wish my corrector to favor himself. Let the former not love me more than he loves Catholic faith; let not the latter love himself more than he loves Catholic truth."

"Sane cum in omnibus litteris meis non solum pium lectorem sed etiam liberum correctorem desiderem, multo maxime in his, ubi ipsa magnitudo quaestionis utinam tam multos inventores habere posset quam multos contradictores habet. Verumtamen sicut lectorem meum nolo mihi esse deditum, ita correctorem nolo sibi. Ille me non amet amplius quam catholicam fidem, iste se non amet amplius quam catholicam veritatem."[1]

---

[1]   Aurelius Augustinus, *De Trinitate*, Preface to Book III, no. 2, in Patrologiae Cursus Completus, ed. J[acques]-P[aul] Migne. *Patrologia Latina*, 221 vols. (Paris: n.p., 1844-64), 42 (1845): 869. Migne notes that the majority of mss. read *deditum* rather than *debitum*.

CONTENTS

PART ONE
ROMA LOCUTA

PREFACE

Is there, it may be asked, any place within authentic Catholicism for respectful and responsible "talking back" to its Petrine ministers, commonly called the Popes? The exact sense of this question should be carefully noted. For there is no doubt that "talking back" occurs.[1] The question is whether it is fundamentally compatible or, in the last analysis, radically inconsistent with the nature of Catholicism. As the Christian world, Catholic, Orthodox and Protestant, continues to evaluate the aftermath of the Second Vatican Council, a frank assessment of certain underlying issues yet to be resolved still seems called for.

The central thrust of this book has been an *arrière-pensée* for well over a decade. Indeed, its pivotal conclusion expressed in Chapter VII[2] was stated a number of years ago in another related context,[3] thus antedating similar but somewhat broader views.[4] Though its earliest form had to do with doctrinal development within a wider spectrum, it occurred to me for the first time when in January 1971 I read Hans Küng's provocative study,

11

Unfehlbar? Eine Anfrage.[5] It seemed to me then, and it has seemed to me ever since, that Küng's approach to problems of this kind constitutes *inter alia* a serious mistake in method. Further reflection suggested that my findings may be relevant to the problem posed by those I have called maximalists.[6] Shortly before going to the University of Chicago in the autumn of 1975, I began to see that the results of my inquiry may have much to say not only about the nature of the ordinary papal magisterium but also about the nature of the Catholic Church itself, and in addition significantly contribute to the ongoing ecumenical dialogues inasmuch as they have to do with the issue of authority. The reader who perseveres to the end will realize that I have not set out to refute Küng but to face, as squarely as I can, a matter far deeper than the infallibility question. However, the question raised by Küng (inasmuch as it has to do with what I have called the minimalist stance[7]) had something to do with the genesis of this book. In this regard, Küng and I cannot both be right.

Subsequent administrative posts held prior to my studies at the University of Chicago prevented me from attending to these matters as soon as I would have liked. The present inquiry was originally a doctoral dissertation presented in June 1981 to the Field of Christian Theology in the Divinity School and has been published with some small but significant revisions. In regard to the book in its dissertation form, I wish to thank in particular Professors Bernard McGinn and David Tracy, who were my co-advisors, and Professor Martin E. Marty, who graciously consented to serve as reader.

The staffs of a number of libraries must be mentioned for greatly facilitating my work: those at the Catholic Theological Union in Chicago and the Lutheran School of Theology there, together with those at Harvard Divinity School, the Episcopal Divinity School in Cambridge, Massachusetts, St. John's Seminary in Brighton, Massachusetts, The Catholic University of America, The University of Notre Dame, St. Mary Seminary in Cleveland, Ohio, and the incomparable Bibliothèque nationale in Paris.

The reader will note my use of a device not usually encountered elsewhere; viz., the more important texts cited have been identified alphabetically in those chapters—and that is in most chapters—where the procedure seems called for. The main reason is the fact that many of the documents are virtually unidentifiable except by their opening words and dates. The viability of my argument depends not only on an accurate analysis of this material and its context but also on the path which development seems to take as one document is compared with another. It will become apparent that the documentation is frequently rather complex. Though some readers may find the device initially distracting, I hope that in the end most will have found it helpful in quickly spotting those texts around which my argument in a given chapter is primarily oriented.

The manuscript went through a number of revisions which, though they did not turn out to be major, were nonetheless time-consuming, given its length. The task would not yet be complete had not my teaching load during my first two years at Case Western Reserve University been significantly reduced. I am grateful in this regard to the late Dr. Bernard Martin who in 1981 invited me there as the Archbishop Paul J. Hallinan Visiting Professor of Catholic Studies.

Special acknowledgments should be made to three publishers. I wish to thank America Press, Inc. (106 West 56th St., New York, N.Y., 10019) for permission to use material from the Abbott-Gallagher edition of *The Documents of Vatican II*; the Crossroad Publishing Company, for allowing me to quote passages from two of Karl Rahner's articles in *Theological Investigations* (published in England by Darton, Longman and Todd); and the editors of *Theological Studies* for use of articles chiefly by John Courtney Murray, S.J. All of the above were exceptionally cooperative.

Finally, whatever strengths the reader may discern in the pages that follow are due in no small measure to the persons mentioned above; whatever defects he or she may come upon remain, of course, my own.

J. Robert Dionne
Framingham, Massachusetts
September 17, 1986

PRINCIPAL ABBREVIATIONS

AAS	*Acta Apostolicae Sedis.* Rome: Typis Polyglottis Vaticanis, 1908-.
Acta Syn	*Acta Synodalia Sacrosancti Concilii Oecumenici Vaticani Secundi.* 4 vols., 26 tomes. Rome: Typis Polyglottis Vaticanis, 1971-78.
ADOC I	*Acta et Documenta Concilio Oecumenico Vaticano Secundo apparando.* Series I (Antepraeparatoria). 5 vols., 16 tomes. Rome: Typis Polyglottis Vaticanis, 1960-61.
ADOC II	*Acta et Documenta Concilio Oecumenico Vaticano Secundo apparando.* Series II (Praeparatoria). 3 vols., 7 tomes. Rome: Typis Polyglottis Vaticanis, 1964-69.
AER	*American Ecclesiastical Review.*
AG	*Documents of Vatican II.* Edited by Walter M. Abbott and Joseph Gallagher. New York: America Press, 1966.
AGP	*Acta Gregorii Papae XVI.* 4 vols. Rome: Ex Typographia Polyglotta S.C. de Propaganda Fide, 1901-4.
ASS	*Acta Sanctae Sedis.* 42 vols. Rome: Ex Typographia Polyglotta, 1865-1908.
CDD	*Sacrosanctum Oecumenicum Concilium Vaticanum*

15

DS

DTC

HD

LCD

MPM

P

PIXA

SDNL

Secundum: Constitutiones, Decreta, Declarationes. Rome: Typis Polyglottis Vaticanis, 1966.

Enchiridion Symbolorum Definitionum et Declarationum de Rebus Fidei et Morum. Edited by Henricus Denziger and Adolfus Schönmetzer. 26th corrected ed. Barcelona, Freiburg im Breisgau, and Rome: Herder, 1976.

Dictionnaire de Théologie catholique. 15 vols., 22 tomes. Paris: Letouzey et Ané, 1909-.

Petitiones de Assumptione Corporea B.V. Mariae in Caelum Definienda ad Sanctam Sedem Delatae. 2 vols. Edited by G[uilhemus] Hentrich and R[udolfus] G[ualterus] De Moos. Rome: Typis Polyglottis Vaticanis, 1942.

Lutherans and Catholics in Dialogue. Vol. 1: *The Status of the Nicene Creed as the Dogma of the Church.* Vol. 2: *One Baptism for the Remission of Sins.* Vol. 3: *The Eucharist as Sacrifice.* Edited by Paul C. Empie and T. Austin Murphy. Minneapolis: Augsburg Publishing House, n.d. Vol. 4: *Eucharist and Ministry.* N.p.: 1970. Vol. 5: *Papal Primacy and the Universal Church.* Edited by Paul C. Empie and T. Austin Murphy. Minneapolis: Augsburg Publishing House, 1974. Vol. 6: *Teaching Authority and Infallibility in the Church.* Edited by Paul C. Empie, T. Austin Murphy and Joseph A. Burgess. Minneapolis: Augsburg Publishing House, 1978. Vol. 7: *Justification by Faith.* Edited by H. George Anderson, T. Austin Murphy and Joseph A. Burgess. Minneapolis: Augsburg Publishing House, 1985.

Sacrorum Conciliorum Nova et Amplissima Collectio. 53 vols. Arnheim and Leipzig: Société nouvelle d'édition de la collection Mansi curantibus Ludovico Petit et Ioanne Baptista Martin, 1748-1927.

Pareri dell' Episcopato cattolico, di Capitoli, di Congregazioni, di Università, di Personaggi ragguardevoli. 11 vols. Rome: coi tipi della Civiltà Cattolica, 1851-54.

Pii IX Pontificis Maximi Acta. 9 vols. Rome: Ex Typographia Bonarum Artium, 1854-78.

Sanctissimi Domini Nostri Leonis Papae XIII: Allocutiones, Epistolae, Constitutiones, Aliaque Acta Praecipua. 7 vols. Bruges and Lille: Desclée de Brouwer et Soc., 1887-1906.

GLOSSARY

ASSENT OF FAITH. The judgment that a particular doctrine has the Godhead as its guarantor. The person making the judgment believes first in some*one* (i.e., the Godhead as unfailingly trustworthy) before he or she believes in some*thing* (the particular doctrine). In this latter case, the assent is not to the proposition but to the reality which the proposition expresses.

AUTHENTIC AND AUTHORITATIVE. Though in themselves these terms apply to legitimate doctrinal or dogmatic decisions taken by the Roman Bishop on the level of his ordinary and extraordinary magisteria (q.v.) respectively, as used in this book they pertain only to the ordinary. The term *authentic* is used primarily in the sense of the Latin *authenticum* and connotes both the notion and the judgment that the task to be acquitted by one holding a particular office in the Church, and the office itself, are rooted in the Christ event (q.v.). But since the Latin term as used by some of the medieval canonists denotes the authenticity of a particular ecclesiastical decree, *authentic* is coupled with *authoritative*. The phrase *authentic and authoritative doctrinal position(s) taken by the ordinary papal magisterium* thus refers to the kinds of doctrinal decisions which the Pope has the right to make by virtue of his exercising the Petrine function within Catholicism, but it does not connote the notion that such decisions are necessarily unerring. See *Ordinary Papal Magisterium*; *Extraordinary Papal Magisterium*; *Infallibility*.

CASTI CONUBII. An encyclical directed to Catholics and promulgated by Pius XI on December 31, 1930. Therein the Pope affirmed in rather strong terms that any use whatsoever of matrimony which deliberately frustrates the generation of life is an offense against the law of God and nature; that those who indulge in such are considered guilty of grave sin. The papal argument was essentially a natural law argument based on the primary purpose of the conjugal act. See *Humanae vitae.*

DEFINED DOCTRINE. Some authors limit the use of the verb *to define* to making a solemn judgment; i.e., a judgment made by a Pope teaching *ex cathedra* (see *Extraordinary Papal Magisterium*) or by an ecumenical Council approved by him.[1] I differ from this tendency in that I see no reason why defining may not under certain circumstances come under the aegis of the ordinary universal magisterium (q.v.), a usage which one encounters elsewhere.[2] Though some may not agree, I further differ in that like others[3] I regard anything pertaining to the substance of the faith (q.v.) as definable, *positis ponendis.* In this book, therefore, *defined doctrine* means:

1. Teaching pertaining to faith or morals and proposed by the ordinary universal magisterium when concurring in one viewpoint as the one *to be held definitively as pertaining to the substance of the faith.*
2. Teaching pertaining to faith and morals and proposed by an ecumenical Council (approved by the Roman Bishop) when that teaching is presented in such a way that henceforth to reject it is to fall away from the Catholic and apostolic faith.
3. Teaching pertaining to faith or morals and proposed by the extraordinary papal magisterium (q.v.).

If the doctrine is defined as revealed, it is called dogma. Thus every dogma entails infallibility but not every infallibly taught doctrine is a dogma, for the latter may pertain to the secondary object of infallibility.[4]

DEI FILIUS. The dogmatic constitution *On Catholic Faith* approved by the First Vatican Council on April 24, 1870 and on the same day confirmed by Pius IX.

DEPOSIT OF FAITH. Revealed truth about God, Jesus Christ, the Church and the ultimate destiny of the human race. Grounded in the Christ event, the Church through the assistance of the Holy Spirit gradually but infallibly comes to understand this revealed truth in a measure increasingly approaching but never actually achieving fullness. In Catholic theology, growth in understanding does not result in a new truth but in a deeper and more accurate understanding of the same unchanging truth.

DOCTRINA CATHOLICA IN SCHEEBEN'S SENSE. A particular doctrine revealed by God or so closely connected with a revealed truth that to deny or call into question the latter logically leads to denying or calling into question the revealed truth itself. See *Substance of the Faith*; *Primary* and *Secondary Objects of Infallibility*.

DOCTRINE. Any teaching on a theological matter. The Church does not teach univocally; some doctrines are proposed as safe, others as probable, still others as theologically certain, etc. See the *Scale of Theological Notes*.

DOGMA. Doctrine considered to have been revealed by God and rooted in the Christ event (q.v.).

EXCOMMUNICATUS VITANDUS. Probably the most severe kind of excommunication in that the person under censure would not be allowed even to be present at the celebration of the Eucharist. If he or she insists on being present, the officiating priest is instructed to leave the altar and finish the Mass privately in the sacristy.

EXTRAORDINARY PAPAL MAGISTERIUM. Synonymous with papal infallibility. In terms of Catholic theology, this occurs when, under the conditions mentioned below, the Pope in solemn fashion (*ex cathedra*) declares that a particular docrine belongs to the substance of the faith (q.v.) and that henceforth to reject that doctrine is to fall away from the Catholic and apostolic faith. There is however a hierarchy of truths even among dogmas, as Vatican II affirmed. Thus it is more important to believe in the dogma of the divinity of Christ than to believe in the dogma of papal infallibility—these two dogmas having been defined by a General Council, not by the extraordinary papal magisterium. The Pope does not possess charism (gift, grace) of infallibility as a personal prerogative—on this point, Vatican I rejected the opinion of Pius IX—but by reason of his office. Thus, if he resigns, there is no way in which the former Pope can possess the charism. The Pope enjoys the charism only at the moment of the definition of a doctrine and only under certain conditions:

1. He must address the whole Church, not just a part of it.
2. He must address the whole Church on a matter of faith or morals.
3. He must make it clear that he is defining, and make it clear that thereafter to reject the doctrine defined is to fall away completely from the Catholic and apostolic faith.

Note that the charism is negative (i.e., protection from error) and has nothing to do with inspiration. The Pope must do his homework like anyone else, and that includes, in a special way, the prior consultation of the rest of the Church. There is room for complementary (as distinguished from contradictory) pluralism.

EXTRAORDINARY UNIVERSAL MAGISTERIUM. Bishops in an ecumenical council acknowledging the ultimately final authority of the Roman Bishop under the Christ and his Spirit. See *Defined Doctrine*.

HUMANAE VITAE. An encyclical directed not only to Catholics but to all men and women of good will. Promulgated by Paul VI on July 25, 1968. The essential stand of Pius XI in *Casti conubii* is reaffirmed but in language less strong. Taking account of demographic problems and those not infrequently encountered by married couples, the Pope pleaded with the scientific world-community to find a reliable method of birth control based on natural biological rhythms. The Pope's fundamental argument remained a natural-law argument but of a kind different from that of Pius XI; i.e., to make use of conjugal love while respecting the laws of the generative process means to acknowledge that one is not the arbiter of the sources of human life.

INFALLIBILITY. The Church's inability to err theologically whenever it makes a definitive judgment about the Deposit of Faith or truths necessary to defend it; hence, not to be confused with impeccability. While the charism resides primarily in the whole Church, it is exercised with certainty only with the concurrence of its magisterial officers. The infallibility of these officers, including that of the Roman Bishop as he exercises the Petrine ministry within Catholicism, is not an infallibility separate from that of the Church. Its source, however, particularly in regard to the Roman Bishop, is not the Church but a special disposition of Divine Providence in and for the Church. See *Ordinary Universal Magisterium*, *Extraordinary Universal Magisterium*, *Extraordinary Papal Magisterium*.

LOCUS THEOLOGICUS. In Catholic theology, the term denotes the sources of theological knowledge; e.g., scripture, tradition, the magisterium, Fathers of the Church, writings of major theologians, especially those who have been declared Doctors of the Church; the liturgy, and Canon Law.

MAGISTERIUM. "The Church's active competence, juridicially embodied, to prolong by its witness God's self-communicative revelation in Christ . . . and which demands obedience."[5]

MODERATE INFALLIBILIST. One who judges and believes that Divine Providence, having brought about an authentic revelation in Jesus Christ, has also provided the means of preserving it and/or of growing in understanding it; that the Church, ultimately through its magisterial officers, is preserved from error in this regard if it makes an irrevocable judgment. Such a judgment is considered *certainly relatively adequate* in terms of the question asked; i.e., it is sufficient to dispel speculative and practical doubt about the reality affirmed but not necessarily sufficient to remove the desirability of a subsequent better (hence complementary as opposed to contradictory) expression of the same truth. See *Extraordinary Papal Magisterium, Extraordinary Universal Magisterium, Ordinary Universal Magisterium, Philosophico-Cultural Limits of a Definition.*

MOTU PROPRIO. Papal treatment (usually of a doctrinal matter) undertaken at the Pope's initiative.

OCCULT HERETIC. One who has ceased to believe in one or more truths contained in the Deposit of Faith and whose disbelief is unknown to the rest of the Church, perhaps even to the heretic himself or herself.

ORDINARY PAPAL MAGISTERIUM. The exercise of the papal teaching office in the context of doctrine. The Pope indicates the seriousness of the matter by the kind of document he issues. Thus a doctrine taught in an *allocution* (for example, a speech to a particular group visiting or consulting the Pope) would not have the same weight as the same doctrine taught in a letter to a national hierarchy; the same doctrine taught in a letter to a national hierarchy would not have the same weight as the same doctrine taught in an *encyclical* (a letter to the whole Catholic Church), etc. This kind of teaching is called *authentic and authoritative.* These terms as defined above mean that a Catholic is bound to assent to the doctrine internally and externally unless his or her own learning is such that he or she feels he or she must disagree. In those cases, he or she expresses his or her disagreement through the appropriate channels. There is thus room for contradictory pluralism.

ORDINARY POWER. The competence a person has by reason of his or her position in the Church. Such power or competence is not delegated but arises from the very nature of the person's office. Thus the competence of residential bishops is one they have by reason of their ordination as bishops; it is not a power they receive from the Roman Bishop. What comes from the Pope, besides acceptance into the college of bishops, is the determination of the diocese or territory where the bishop or bishops will exercise their competence.

ORDINARY UNIVERSAL MAGISTERIUM. Bishops dispersed throughout the world and who, in union with the Roman Bishop under the Christ and his Spirit, teach a particular doctrine relating to faith and morals. According to *Lumen gentium,* the charism of infallibility (not to be confused with inspiration) is operative under certain circumstances.[6] (The Conciliar position is not however without inherent, unresolved problems.[7]) See *Defined Doctrine*.

PAPAL INFALLIBILITY. See *Extraordinary Papal Magisterium*.

PASTOR AETERNUS. The dogmatic constitution in which the definition of the doctrine relating to the infallibility of the Roman Bishop is to be found. It was promulgated on July 18, 1870.

PHILOSOPHICO-CULTURAL LIMITS OF A DEFINITION. On an elementary level, what this phrase implies is quite easy to grasp. Suppose that the question is: *In an economic set-up in which money is not productive, is it a moral good to charge interest on money?* Here the Catholic Church has always answered in the negative. But let us suppose the question is: *In an economic set-up in which money IS productive, CAN it be a moral good to charge interest on it?* Here the answer of the Catholic Church came to be affirmative. On a deeper level, however, the matter is more complex. Suppose that the Christian Gospel went toward India before it went toward Greece. In that case, the faith centering on and/or resulting from the life, death and resurrection of Jesus as the Christ of God and the sending of his Spirit would be clothed in a very different garment. Could the Christian doctrine of the Trinity be expressed in terms of Hindu culture? Perhaps, *if* it is true that Ísvara bears to Brahman essentially the same relation as the *Logos* (as Word) bears to *Theos*. Other problems would arise, however, *if* it is true that in Hindu culture God is not conceived as personal because "person" implies limitation. There may, of course, be solutions to these "problems." My purpose is not to solve them but to hint at their complexity. Thus the Hindu "equivalent" of the Creed of Nicea-Constantinople recited every Sunday morning in Catholic Churches would sound very different. For in Hindu culture almost certainly different kinds of questions would have arisen creating a situation where, if the question changes, one must not be surprised if the "answer" changes accordingly. The problem then becomes how the papal magisterium would cope (without falling into sheer relativism) with the kind of pluralism where *simultaneously* seemingly antithetical doctrinal positions are held by people in different cultures.

PRELATE NULLIUS. A priest, not necessarily a bishop, in charge of a territory having its own clergy and laity but which is outside the jurisdiction of any diocese. The prelature *nullius* is in effect a "diocese" within a diocese.

PRIMARY OBJECT OF INFALLIBILITY. The Deposit of Faith; i.e., those truths revealed by God through Jesus Christ.

QUANTA CURA. See *Syllabus of Errors.*

RESIDENTIAL BISHOP. The bishop of a diocese as distinguished from a vicar apostolic. The latter is the bishop of a mission territory still under the supervision of the Roman Bishop.

SECONDARY OBJECT OF INFALLIBILITY. A truth which in itself is not revealed but so closely connected with revealed truth that to call into question the former logically entails calling into question the revealed truth itself.

SENSUS FIDELIUM. As used by most theologians prior to Vatican II, the term denoted a spiritual instinct which the so-called laity possesses and which enables it, under the guidance of the Holy Spirit, to discern whether a particular doctrine is true and/or whether it belongs to the substance of the faith (q.v.). As used in this book, the term is functionally equivalent to the *sensus fidei*; i.e., the same instinct possessed by the whole Church.

SUBSTANCE OF THE FAITH. The Deposit of Faith and/or those truths so closely connected with it that to call into question the latter amounts to calling into question the Deposit itself.

SYLLABUS OF ERRORS. A series of eighty theses which Pius IX had earlier condemned in various pronouncements ranging from allocutions to encyclicals. The Syllabus was promulgated with the Encyclical *Quanta cura* on December 8, 1864, and raised a storm of protest especially in France where Bishop Félix Dupanloup (later among the minority at Vatican I) attempted to explain it benignly. Thus no. 80 had condemned the thesis that the Pope must reconcile himself with and adjust himself to modern civilization. But the context Pius IX had been speaking of was that envisaged by the allocution *Iamdudum cernimus* of March 18, 1861. Therein the Pope was objecting to those government-supported groups of Piedmontese clergy who were resisting the Pope's position on the closing of monasteries. In *La Convention du 15 septembre et l'Encyclique du 8 décembre*, Dupanloup was able to dissipate much of the bad feeling which the Syllabus had stirred up.

THEOLOGICAL NOTES. Theological notes are an assessment of the weight or importance to be attached to a particular doctrine as taught in the Catholic Church. They are judgments by theologians and occasionally by the magisterium. As such, they state the degree of certainty with which a particular doctrine may be said to be in harmony with revealed truth. As he goes about his work each theologian makes his own assessment; the theological note that a particular doctrine enjoys is the result of a consensus on the part of theologians in the case where the hierarchical magisterium is not directly involved.

Theological notes are both positive and negative; there is no systematized or authoritative list. As used in these pages they are herewith presented in descending order according to the following scale:

Scale of Theological Notes

de fide divina	The doctrine is clearly contained in the sources of revelation.
de fide divina et catholica	The same doctrine is also taught by the hierarchical magisterium.
de fide ecclesiastica	The doctrine is not directly revealed but is infallibly taught by the hierarchical magisterium.
fidei proximum	The doctrine is commonly considered revealed but not yet clearly and definitely taught as a truth of revelation.
doctrina catholica in the generic sense	It is not clear whether a doctrine has been taught only authentically or whether it has been defined by the ordinary universal magisterium
doctrina catholica in the strict sense	The doctrine is authentically taught by the universal or papal magisterium.
theologice certum	The doctrine is not yet explicitly declared to be true or necessarily connected with revelation but, *in the more or less unanimous opinion of theologians,* its denial would involve denial of a truth of faith or indirectly threaten it.
sententia communis theologorum	Most theologians consider the doctrine true.
probabilis	The doctrine is probably true.
tuta	It would not be imprudent to believe this doctrine.

Though at the beginning of the nineteenth century the doctrine of papal infallibility was considered *probabilis* in the sense subsequently defined by the First Vatican Council (so that since 1870 its proper theological note has been *de fide divina et catholica*), a particular doctrine does not automatically ascend on the scale of theological notes, for some doctrines become psychologically irrelevant or are discarded. Two examples will suffice. It was once *doctrina catholica* in the strict sense that collecting interest on money loaned to others in need is immoral; but when the economic system changed and money became productive, that doctrine ceased to be taught. And it was once *sententia communis* that hell is a *place*, whereas today most theologians hold that hell is a state of being, the possibility of which exists for any creature that makes itself into an absolute.

Negative theological notes are the "censure" attached to the deliberate denial of a particular doctrine. For example, to reject a doctrine taught *de fide* would be *an error in divine faith*; to reject a doctrine taught *de fide divina et catholica* would be formal heresy; but to deny a truth taught as *theologice certum* would be *temerarius*. It is a matter of dispute whether the rejection of a doctrine taught as *de fide ecclesiastica* is formal heresy.

Theological notes are an attempt on the part of a community of some eight hundred million people to have, primarily through their theologians, some order in their theological reflection. Their ultimate purpose "... is both to safeguard the faith and to prevent any confusion between real divine revelation and theological opinion."[8]

VIRTUALLY REVEALED. One of several kinds of truth that constitute the secondary object of infallibility (q.v.). The truth itself is not revealed but follows as the conclusion of a syllogism in which one of the premises is revealed, while the other is a truth naturally known.

INTRODUCTION

We shall have made no small advance in ecumenical relations once praxis is allowed not only to illumine theory but also to transform it. Though that fact applies to the function of authority in all Christian churches including, in a surprising way, those built on a Free Church model,[1] it surely applies with greater urgency to the Catholic Church, given its immense responsibility in the present ecumenical endeavor. Hence it is with the function of authority in relation to doctrinal and dogmatic development in the Catholic Church, defined herein as the Roman Church and those other local Christian churches in union with it, that the following study is principally concerned. Since, inasmuch as it has to do with doctrine I shall approach the matter within the wider perspective of reception, it will become apparent that certain interconfessional disputes are intimately linked with a persistent malaise within Catholicism.[2]

For it cannot have escaped even the casual observer that more than twenty years after the Second Vatican Council the Catholic Church so defined is still beset by two central problems, the one internal, having to do with its authority structure, the other external, concerned with a slowdown in the ecumenical dialogues.[3] Both problems are at least generically related to the tensions Ernst Troeltsch saw inherent in Christianity. Indeed, if one takes an overall view of its almost two-thousand-year history, one may discern in the Christian movement two very different orientations. In the first, the Church as a universal, sacramental institution takes up in itself secular institutions, groups, and values;[4] the second takes as its specific norm the *Sermon on the Mount* and is characterized by a tendency either not to recognize or at best quietly to tolerate institutions, groups, and values outside it.[5] Troeltsch called these two ways the "Church-type" and the "sect-type" respectively.[6] He saw both rooted in the Christian gospel and therefore, not surprisingly, existing (though in different ways) in Christianity before and after the Reformation. The two differ in many ways. Most directly related to our inquiry are the divergent views on the nature of *Christian κοινωνία*,[7] which become, in turn, the source of divergent views on the function of authority within Christianity:

> . . . in the first instance [the Church-type] it [Christian κοινωνία] is conceived as an institution, not dependent on individualism, possessing a *depositum* of absolute truths and wonderful civilizing sacramental powers; in the second instance [the sect-type] it is conceived as a society whose life is constantly renewed by the deliberate allegiance and personal work of its individual members.[8]

Though Troeltsch was writing of the ways in which Christianity relates itself to the world,[9] his analysis is relevant to the function of authority and its relation to doctrinal and dogmatic development within Catholicism. In that more limited context, it may be said that the Church-type tends to exercise authority from the top down, whereas the sect-type tends to exercise it from the bottom up.[10] For the purpose of the critical and constructive argument advanced below, I shall on the one hand refer to the Church-type as the institutional model and on the other to the sect-type as the associative,[11] asking the reader to bear in mind that no one concrete model manifests perfectly the characteristics of any one ideal type.

The issue I shall deal with is the exercise of authority in doctrinal and dogmatic matters within the Catholic Church. The Catholic Church is here considered as the most fully developed form of the institutional model in that it ultimately concentrates its authority in one bishop. Given the central position it occupies in the contemporary quest for Christian unity, I shall ask whether a revised view of authority within that body may not incorporate more explicitly some of the elements of the associative model, thereby not only resolving the conflict between minimalists and maximalists as described below, but also narrowing the gap between itself and other Christian churches.

I shall attempt to ground an affirmative answer to that question. At this point let me simply remark in passing that I fully agree with Giuseppe Alberigo who some years ago pointed out that history should not be pursued for purely ecumenical concerns. Such an endeavor can lead to an unsatisfactory reconstruction of historical events wherein doctrine is watered down in the name of ecumenism.[12] While this constitutes a danger to be avoided at all costs, nothing, I believe, can or should prevent the theologian and/or historian from presenting his colleagues with those findings he deems relevant to the ecumenical cul-de-sac in which the Christian churches presently find themselves. Before proceeding further, however, let me describe in more detail what I take to be Catholicism's internal and external problems, state my central argument more precisely, and indicate the method I shall employ. I shall then clarify the meaning of certain terms, acknowledge some fundamental methodological assumptions and sketch the perspective both from which the reader might approach this study as well as that from which I shall proceed.

Unresolved Difficulties

THE INTERNAL PROBLEM

The tensions that Troeltsch saw as inherent in Christianity resurface in Catholicism in another form, for Catholicism's internal problem seems to be the result of a tension between Church as institution and Church as association. On the one hand, there are those—let us call them *maximalists*—who argue that the ordinary papal magisterium (the way the Roman Bishop goes about his work in the day-to-day shuffle of events) may, under certain circumstances, enjoy the charism of infallibility; on the other, there are those—let us call them *minimalists*—who maintain that modification, change and/or subsequent rejection of papal teaching is an argument against papal infallibility. This latter group sees authority anchored not simply in papal primacy (which some minimalists acknowledge to be of divine design[13]) but much more broadly based. Quite clearly, while maximalists accentuate Church as institution, minimalists stress Church as association. Both tendencies should be considered in greater detail.

The Minimalists

With the excommunication of Johannes Joseph Ignaz von Döllinger in 1871 and with the Old Catholic schism resulting from *Pastor Aeternus* (q.v.), minimalist tendencies seemed until recently to have died out within Catholicism. Their resurgence was antedated slightly by the revival of conciliarism some twenty years ago.[14] Perhaps the most widely read among those I have called minimalists is Hans Küng, who in his book *Infallible? An Inquiry*, wrote:

> The assertion of an "infallibility" of the teaching office in the Catholic Church has always been unacceptable to non-Christians and to Christians outside that Church. In recent times, however, it has become to a surprising extent at least questionable even within the Catholic Church . . .
>
> It is easy to understand why the question is urgent. The errors of the ecclesiastical teaching office are numerous and serious: today, when frank discussion can no longer be forbidden, they may not be denied even by the more conservative theologians and Church leaders. What might be called classical errors of the ecclesiastical teaching office, now largely admitted, may be listed as follows: the excommunication of Photius, . . . the prohibition of interest at the beginning of modern times, . . . the condemnation of Galileo and the measures adopted as a consequence of this action . . .[15]

Küng cites other instances, e.g., the condemnation of new forms of worship in the Chinese Rites Controversy and much earlier the case of Pope Honorius I, a question much discussed by the Fathers of the First Vatican Council.[16] Despite the sometimes devastating criticism to which it has occasionally been subjected,[17] Küng's position remains unchanged in the 1983 edition of his book,[18] and it had earlier enjoyed a favorable reception among some Catholics. Thus in the *Journal of Ecumenical Studies*:

> Perhaps even more damaging than the arguments in the areas of philosophy and Scripture have been the arguments against infallibility in the area of history. Just the plain facts of history have proved to be the most intractable obstacles to calm acceptance of infallibility by many sincere Catholics. The facts are that fully authoritative papal *definitions* and condemnations have

often been reversed. And it is appropriate to use here the word *reversed* rather than *developed*.[19]

Among the examples given by the author as illustrative of his thesis are the doctrinal positions taken by Gregory XVI and Pius IX in the context of religious freedom. I shall address this issue in some detail in Chap. IV. For the moment, it may be remarked in passing that none of the examples given by Küng and his followers have to do with what since the latter part of the nineteenth century came to be called with increasing frequency the extraordinary papal magisterium.[20] As in the case of those I have called maximalists, so in that of the minimalists I am concerned not so much with these theologians and / or historians as I am with those who in the postconciliar Church tend to identify with their views.[21]

The Maximalists

The counter-current to the minimalist is characterized, as I have said, by an exaggerated concept of papal infallibility.[22] Apparently still or almost motionless for a few years after the First Vatican Council (which, in the promulgated *Pastor Aeternus*, spoke of papal infallibility only in the context of *ex cathedra* definitions), maximalist tendencies seem to have been initially revived by Alfred Vacant,[23] one of the co-founders of the justly famed *Dictionnaire de Théologie catholique*, and received fresh impetus after the Second World War at least partially as a consequence of a complaint by Pius XII in *Humani generis*.[24] Although it is not entirely clear whether the maximalist thesis should have been considered refuted as a result of *Pastor Aeternus*, certain factors suggest an affirmative response to this question. I am referring to two important paragraphs in a speech given on July 11, 1870, by Vincenz Ferrer Gasser, bishop at Brixen[25] and a member of the Committee on Faith (*Deputatio de rebus ad fidem pertinentibus*) at the Council:

> *Text A.* ... by reason of the authority of the papacy the Pontiff is always supreme judge in matters pertaining to faith and morals and the Father and Teacher of all Christians; but only then [*solummodo tunc*] does he enjoy the divine assistance promised him, by which he cannot err, when he truly [*reipsa*] and actually acquits himself of his task as the supreme judge and universal teacher of the Church in controversies pertaining to the faith.[26]

> *Text B.* Hence the opinion, the Roman Pontiff is infallible, must not, to be

sure, be considered false, since Christ promised it to the person of
Peter and to the person of his successor; but it is only incomplete
*since the Pope is infallible only when in a so mn judgment he
defines a matter of faith and morals for the universal Church.*[27]

In the Mansi-Petit-Martin edition of the council documents, Text B
follows immediately upon Text A, a fact which serves to highlight an
important point frequently overlooked by those who would identify
Gasser's view with the maximalist.[28] Text B suggests that Gasser's *solummodo tunc*, as expressed in Text A, had to do with a solemn judgment
(hence with what in the promulgated *Pastor Aeternus* is referred to as an *ex
cathedra* definition), not with the exercise of the ordinary papal magisterium. Within the limits of the caution I have suggested below,[29] it may be
said it was Gasser's view that carried the day at the First Vatican Council,
not that, say, of Bartolomeo d'Avanzo, bishop at Calvi and Teano (Italy)
or that of the counter-current represented by Félix-Antoine-Philibert
Dupanloup, bishop at Orléans (France). But the promulgated *Pastor
Aeternus* did not expressly state that the Popes in the exercise of their
ordinary papal magisterium were *not* unerring or *not* infallible in doctrinal
matters. These lacunae left open the possibility of an unfortunate
development—beginning with Vacant and followed by theologians of no
less stature than the Marist, Edmond Dublanchy and the Jesuits, Louis
Billot and Joaquín Salaverri de la Torre.[30] As there are various currents
that flow into the stream of maximalist thinking,[31] attention will be
focused on three which have been more widespread during the past generation or so: those represented by Salaverri, Paul Nau together with Fidelis
Gallati, and Arthur Peiffer.

Joaquín Salaverri de la Torre

Salaverri's position seems to have gone through at least two phases, the
first being that expressed in a well-known treatise on the Church published
in the early 1950s.[32] At that time, he held that the ordinary papal magisterium is infallibly exercised whenever the Roman Bishop in a doctrinal
matter makes known his intention to bind the whole Church to absolute
assent,[33] an example subsequently given as illustrative of this thesis being
that of Pius IX in *Quanta cura* and its accompanying Syllabus.[34] Salaverri
derived this view from speculative theological reasoning based on what he
saw implied in the documents of the First Vatican Council. Thus, if the

Roman Pontiff possesses that infallibility with which the Divine Redeemer wishes his Church to be endowed, and if that Church is endowed with an infallibility which it exercises in an ordinary as well as an extraordinary manner, then the Roman Pontiff must be likewise endowed.[35] Or again, so Salaverri argued, if one maintains that the ordinary universal magisterium of the Church can be infallibly exercised under certain circumstances but that the ordinary papal magisterium cannot be, then the supreme power of infallibility, at least in its exercise, is more restricted in the Roman Pontiff who holds the primacy over the whole Church than it is in the whole Church over which he holds the primacy.[36] Though he differentiated his position from those advanced by Vacant and Billot, Salaverri's earlier view paralleled at least in part that propounded by the Marist, Dublanchy.[37]

It is not surprising that Salaverri's thesis was subjected to intense criticism by fellow Catholic theologians.[38] Nonetheless, it remained essentially unchanged as late as the fifth edition of his treatise (1962).[39] For reasons that are not entirely clear, there seems to have been a shift in his stance as it entered what I have called its second phase. Thus, in an article in the English edition of *Sacramentum Mundi*, he stated:

> The doctrine of an encyclical is ultimately an authentic pronouncement of the magisterium. In theory, the Pope could use an encyclical for his infallible magisterium. Four conditions would then have to be verified: a) the Pope would have to speak as supreme teacher of the Church, b) in virtue of his supreme apostolic authority, c) on a matter of faith or morals, d) pronouncing a final and binding definition. An encyclical does not normally fulfill the fourth condition, but could do so if the Pope clearly expressed his intention of defining *ex cathedra*. The Pope decides at his discretion whether to give a "solemn definition," as at canonizations and at the proclamation of the dogma of Mary's bodily assumption into heaven, or a simple one, as is customary in encyclicals.[40]

From this it seems one may conclude that in its second phase Salaverri's view is functionally equivalent to that expressed much earlier by J. Bellamy;[41] that is, that the Roman Bishops can speak *ex cathedra* on two levels, that of their ordinary and extraordinary magisteria. The difference between Salaverri's opinion in its first and second phases comes down, then, to this: In the former, it was sufficient that in the exercise of his ordinary magisterium the Pope intend to bind the whole Church to absolute assent and so express that intent, whereas in the latter he must manifest his intention of speaking *ex cathedra*, the actual form in which that intention is expressed being somewhat flexible. Short of that, the teaching of the ordinary papal magisterium is merely authentic. Though the second phase may not be germane to the problem posed by maximalists in the context of some of the issues discussed in this book, I have come upon no evidence that Salaverri has explicitly modified his judgment that in *Quanta cura* and the Syllabus (q.v.) the charism of infallibility was operative,[42] a matter especially pertinent to the questions explored in Chaps. III and IV. There are, to be sure, additional reasons why his earlier view is still pertinent to the issues I intend to examine. For despite what happened at Vatican II, some have continued to uphold the infallibility of the ordinary papal magisterium in a sense very much similar to Salaverri in the early 1950s.[43] And though direct reference to the Spanish theologian is not always made, some writers continue to advance arguments that presuppose that Salaverri's thesis in its first phase remains viable,[44] while still others have embraced (and as far as I have been able to ascertain, never explicitly abandoned) a position which, despite difference of language, is ideologically reducible to that propounded by Salaverri in 1950.[45] Thus though Salaverri has since changed perspective, the question raised by Vacant almost a hundred years ago paradoxically still finds an affirmative answer along the lines suggested by Salaverri in his first phase.

Paul Nau and Fidelis Gallati

The perspective from which the Dominican, Fidelis Gallati, approached the matter[46] is similar to an earlier view embraced by the Benedictine, Paul Nau.[47] That is to say, the teaching of a series of Roman Bishops expounding the same doctrine on faith and morals to the universal Church is infallibly true. Though Gallati may have arrived at his conclusions independently of Nau, the former's thesis, ideologically speaking, may be regarded as a more developed version of Nau's initial argument. For Gallati, the ordinary like the extraordinary papal magisterium is included in the primacy of the Apostolic See and is a component in papal jurisdiction. Gallati was at pains to point out that, as such, it can make even non-definitive doctrinal decisions binding in conscience.[48] Hence, for him, these decisions must have special reliability (*Wahrheitsbürgschaft*).[49] Because they are not definitive, they are not infallible taken individually, but they have a high degree of truth that in general surpasses the certainty offered by purely human disciplines.[50] Nevertheless, one must distinguish degrees of reliability. Assent to doctrinal pronouncements of this kind is not an assent of faith (q.v.).[51] Indeed, it can happen that for weighty reasons the believer may legitimately withhold it. Very different however are those doctrinal pronouncements which, in contrast to an individual occurrence, begin to form a chain. Here Gallati advanced his central thesis:

> But when several Popes constantly over a longer period of time make non-definitive doctrinal pronouncements [*nicht-endgültige Lehrkundgebun-gen*] which from their matter and content proclaim the same teaching, a tradition of the Apostolic See begins [*entsteht*]; this is a clear rule for the faith of the whole Church. Such a tradition has therefore the unconditioned pledge of truth and is infallibly true. Thus under the stated conditions not only the extraordinary but also the ordinary magisterium of the Apostolic See is equipped with the charism of infallibility.[52]

Though doctrinal pronouncements by the Roman Bishops may be binding in the sense that they are to be obeyed, they do not necessarily command the assent of faith, for in making such pronouncements the Roman Bishops do not necessarily possess the charism of infallibility. Thus Gallati emphatically disassociated himself from Vacant, Dublanchy and Salaverri. He saw infallibility coming into play only when the teaching of the Popes on a particular doctrinal matter has been of long standing, a perspective which, from a Catholic point of view, is not without initial plausibility.

Thus far it may be said that the positions of Nau and Gallati are virtually indistinguishable. A fact that should not be overlooked is that Nau's reflections subsequently published in book form[53] seem to have been favorably but cautiously received by one of the greatest Catholic ecclesiologists of the century.[54] But Nau was to refine his view even more.[55] Made in response to a dissertation defended at Louvain by Marc Caudron (who, basing himself on an analysis of *Dei Filius* [q.v.] and the debates surrounding it, had argued that the Fathers of the First Vatican Council seem to have expressly intended to exclude as theologically viable the thesis that the ordinary magisterium can be personally exercised infallibly by the Roman Bishop[56]), Nau attempted to ground his stance on a closer study of the relevant conciliar documents. He now claimed that his 1962 analysis was in harmony with what Gasser had meant when, in response to the question of whether the Roman Bishop, prior to a definition, is dogmatically obliged to consult the rest of the Catholic Church, Gasser replied that the Roman Bishop had other ways of ascertaining the faith of the Church, among which ways is " . . . *illa traditio ecclesiae romanae . . . ad quam perfidia non habet accessum . . . .*"[57] Gasser was paraphrasing Irenaeus and clearly meant the local Roman Church.[58] Nau interpreted Gasser as having held the same opinion as that of a fellow member of the same committee, Bishop Bartolomeo d'Avanzo, who in a speech on June 20, 1870, had in effect argued that in the exercise of his ordinary magisterium the Pope is infallible.[59] Nau concluded this phase of his article:

> Their conclusion is also the same: If the Pope may and must sometimes have recourse to consulting the bishops, this consultation cannot be made a condition for the exercise of infallibility on the part of the sovereign magisterium. One criterion is sufficient and it is always at the disposition of the Pope, Bishop Gasser reminded the Council Fathers . . . the sole of tradition of the Church of Rome.[60]

Nau distinguished between an *infallible judgment* and a *teaching faithful to revelation*, suggesting that the former is more appropriately used of an *ex cathedra* definition while the latter describes more accurately what is (or at least can be) involved in the teaching of the ordinary papal magisterium.[61] The two terms, however, are functionally equivalent in Nau's exposition.[62] His conclusion from all this was that (1) d'Avanzo and Gasser meant the same thing, that (2) what they meant was that the teaching of the ordinary papal magisterium could be infallibly exercised under certain circumstances, that (3) though the promulgated *Pastor Aeternus* refers only to *ex cathedra* definitions, the thinking of d'Avanzo and Gasser was typical of a considerable number of the Council Fathers, and that (4) according to this opinion the teaching of a series of Roman Bishops in proclaiming a particular doctrine pertaining to faith and morals was to be judged as certainly faithful to revelation and hence functionally equivalent to being infallibly true.

However tendentious Nau's interpretation of Gasser may have been,[63] if Nau's position was substantially correct in its main thrust, then Caudron's, of course, was wrong. The fact that as late as 1969 Nau's 1962 article along with Caudron's was included in an important collection of monographs meant to prepare for the one-hundredth anniversary of the First Vatican Council is illustrative of the seriousness with which his thesis was still being taken in the years immediately after the Second Vatican Council.[64] Despite the nuance that Nau's later writing on this subject comprises, his view remains essentially unchanged from his first sally on these controversial waters. We have seen that Gallati's is fundamentally the same. I shall henceforth refer to this current of maximalist thinking as the Nau-Gallati position.

Arthur Peiffer

Another contributory to the maximalist stream is the monograph by Arthur Peiffer presented (1962) to the Theological Faculty at the University of Freiburg (Switzerland).[65] Unfortunately, Peiffer's dissertation was not published until 1968 and seems to have been neglected in the aftermath of *Humanae vitae*. He envisages the situation where *p*, having been taught by the majority of Catholic bishops over some time, is subsequently declared by the Roman Bishop to be *doctrina catholica* in Scheeben's sense.[66] As in the case of the aforementioned, it seems best to allow the author to speak for himself:

> In this *testimonium* of the teaching office lies the particular [and] thus so eminently important significance of the Encyclicals for knowledge about the Faith and theology insofar as they make what is a material dogma clearly and plainly recognizable as a formal dogma and authentically attest [to the fact] that a definite teaching is grounded in revelation and through the living teaching office is unanimously [*übereinstimmend*] proclaimed to the whole Church. In this more declarative transmission of doctrine, it is naturally not yet a question of a genuine [*eigentliche*] and *specific decision of Faith*. Yet one may say that with it the last phase of dogmatic development antecedent to a definition is closed . . .
>
> We have a very recent example of such a knowledge of the Faith deepened through an Encyclical in that of *Mystici corporis* of Pius XII. . . .[67]

There can be no doubt that for Peiffer, in this last phase prior to a definition, infallibility comes into play, for he states that such teaching in encyclicals is a more sure theological source and possesses an absolute degree of certainty.[68] The example to which he subsequently points is the teaching of Pius XII that the Mystical Body of Christ and the (Roman) Catholic Church are one and the same thing.[69] To paraphrase Peiffer's position more precisely: It is not a question of the majority of Catholicism's magisterial officers teaching *p* as, say, probable, and the Roman Bishop teaching it as *doctrina catholica* in Scheeben's sense (q.v.), thereby making the doctrine *de fide* (but not *de fide definita*). Rather what was materially a dogma becomes formally so from the confluence of two circumstances; namely, (1) the vast majority of the world-wide episcopate teaching *p* as *doctrina catholica* (in Scheeben's sense) and (2) the Roman Bishop concurring with them, so expressing himself to the whole Church, clearly stating that *p* is indeed the teaching of the Church.[70] Peiffer's view is thus quite distinct from Salaverri's position (in its first phase) on the one hand and that of Nau-Gallati on the other, both of which Peiffer rejects.[71] In the former case, it may be one particular Roman Bishop who clearly teaches *p* with the manifest intent of binding the rest of the Catholic Church to absolute assent; in the second, it is a question of a series of Popes who teach the same doctrine, but in each instance there is not necessarily an intent of binding the rest of the Catholic Church. The effect is simply cumulative. What both the Salaverri and the Nau-Gallati views have in common is the fact that initially only the Roman Bishop(s) are involved. The case proposed by Peiffer differs in that the whole episcopacy comes into play when the movement flows from the bishops to the Roman Bishop and thence from the Roman Bishop to the rest of the Catholic Church. The proper theological note is henceforth *de fide*.[72] Though one might question whether the circumstances envisaged by Peiffer might not more properly be considered an exercise of the ordinary universal magisterium (q.v.), it is obvious from the very title of his book that he was thinking in terms of the ordinary papal magisterium. I shall return to this point in Chap. IX.

Finally, as with the minimalists, I am concerned not so much with individual thinkers as I am with those currents of thought which, within contemporary Catholicism, tend to be sympathetic to maximalist thinking. For the waters have by no means settled.[73] And one sometimes comes upon what appears to be a maximalist tendency where one least expects to find it. Thus, if one may judge from the internal logic of his thought, Heinrich Stirnimann, one of Salaverri's severest critics, may have been open to a view similar to that propounded by Nau-Gallati.[74]

Previous criticism of maximalist claims seems to have been limited primarily to analyses of the Dogmatic Constitutions of the First Vatican Council. It is certain that not a few of those who voted for *Pastor Aeternus* were at heart maximalists (for example, Bartolomeo d'Avanzo) and that they may have voted for it as a *pis-aller*. Therefore all that can be maintained from a study of the documentation presently accessible is that, while the officially promulgated texts do not support the thesis that the ordinary papal magisterium is infallibly exercised, nothing rules out the possibility that many Council Fathers thought it was—but settled for leaving the matter open for discussion. Garibaldi's troops were, after all, advancing, and under the circumstances some Council Fathers may have thought half a loaf of bread was better than none. But those who sided with what Gasser actually said on July 11, 1870 (as distinguished from the internal logic of some of his statements, which could be interpreted in the sense of Nau-Gallati) may be supposed to have thought that the judgment of the Roman

Bishop in the exercise of his ordinary magisterium is not infallible. I shall return in Chap. VIII to other aspects of Gasser's important contribution. In the meantime, while I do not wish to anticipate here the detailed conclusions which—on this and other matters—I shall draw in Chaps. VII and IX, nothing, I suggest (*pace* Caudron), can be definitively settled on the basis of documentation so far emanating from the First Vatican Council. The ultimate test for the maximalist (and, as we shall see, *mutatis mutandis*, for the minimalist) will be whether any current of maximalist thinking can continue to flow once it comes up against Catholicism's praxis.

THE EXTERNAL PROBLEM

While maximalist and minimalist tendencies constitute Catholicism's internal problem, a primary factor in the external is, as in the case of maximalists and minimalists, a certain tension between Church as institution and Church as association. This tension manifests itself in apparent authoritarianism on the part of the Roman Bishop:

> A third area of controversy centers on the practical consequences drawn from these prior disagreements. Roman Catholics have tended to think of most aspects of papal structure and function as divinely authorized. The need or possibility of significant change, renewal, or reform has generally been ignored. Most important, it has been argued that all ministry concerned with fostering unity among the churches is subject—at least in crisis situations—to the supervision of the bishop of Rome. His jurisdiction over the universal Church is . . . "supreme," "full," "ordinary," and "immediate." This authority is not subject to any higher human jurisdiction . . . . This view of the exercise of papal power has been vehemently repudiated by Lutherans and viewed by them as leading to intolerable ecclesiastical tyranny.[75]

In an important address to Jesuit ecumenists given a few years ago, Karl Rahner highlighted Roman authoritarianism as one of the reasons why ecumenically oriented Protestants hesitate about eventual reunion with the Roman Church.[76] And though Anglican members of the Anglican-Roman Catholic International Commission acknowledge that, in any future union, a universal primacy such as that described in their joint statement should be held by the Roman See, they express the fear that papal claim to universal, immediate jurisdiction might lead to its illegitimate or uncontrolled use.[77]

A secondary but nonetheless important cause of the block to further ecumenical progress is substantially the same as the minimalist charge. In the address mentioned above, Karl Rahner alluded to this problem when he said that Protestant Christians find the Catholic concentration of the sure charism of truth in a specific papal act an example of the temptation to objectify and juridicize that charism. One of the reasons why Protestants find this emphasis unworthy of belief is the fact that ". . . the ordinary teaching office of the pope, at least in its authentic decisions, often contains errors, even up to our own day . . . ."[78] Nonetheless, not a few ecumenically minded Protestants and Orthodox Christians will recognize Catholicism's external problem as in some sense their own and thus, while external to them, as somehow internal to Christianity. However, if relevant conclusions stated below have been adequately grounded, careful study of Catholicism's praxis will be seen to dissipate the illusions of both maximalists and minimalists, and paradoxically to suggest that, within Catholicism, Church as association is part of Church as institution. Thus it may be possible to contribute both to a new perspective on the papal magisterium and to a partial removal of anxiety expressed by non-Catholic Christians seeking Christian unity.

The Argument

I shall claim that the Catholic Church can best face its responsibility by settling its internal problem relative to the role, status, and authority of its Petrine minister, the Roman Bishop. From a revised view of authority as exercised within itself, it should then make certain deductions conducive to the at least partial solution of its external problem. These considerations will lead to the following conclusions, which constitute my central argument:

I.   *The way doctrine has developed within the Catholic Church beginning with the Petrine ministry of Pius IX (1846) up to the end of the Second Vatican Council (1965) requires a correction of the understanding of how the ordinary papal magisterium functions within Catholicism.*

II. *Associative elements present in the process that culminated in the definition of the dogmas of the Immaculate Conception and the Assumption may provide a partial solution to the ecumenical impasse brought about by the common understanding of so-called papal infallibility.*

The first and second parts of the argument have to do with doctrine and dogma respectively, but I shall be more concerned with the former than with the latter. Hence, except for Chap. IX wherein the cumulative results of my inquiry are stated, matter pertaining to dogma will be limited chiefly to Chap. VIII, whereas considerations pertaining to doctrine will comprise Chaps. I-VII. As the additional findings indicated in Chap. IX attest, these two principal conclusions do not exhaust my total argument. They do, however, form its nucleus. As I proceed, I shall occasionally touch upon matters (e.g., pertaining to the ordinary universal magisterium), which are not the primary object of my inquiry. But the questions are nonetheless sufficiently important to justify at least passing comment. Thus in the conclusions stated in the final chapter I shall distinguish between areas of indirect and direct concern.

Method

Except for a few parenthetical remarks made in the final chapter, this inquiry has to do with but a brief span of some 119 years, from the election of Giovanni Maria Cardinal Mastai-Ferretti as Pope in 1846 to the end of the Second Vatican Council in 1965. In regard to doctrine, I will focus on seven issues and the modalities of their reception by the rest of the Catholic Church. The phrase *modalities of reception by the rest of the Catholic Church* thus recurs with some frequency. While in itself it surely applies to the so-called laity, in the study of reception, as pursued herein, I have had to restrict myself primarily to bishops and theologians or else be faced with an impossible task. Hence the reader should normally understand the phrase in that limited sense. In regard to dogma, attention to the function of authority will be confined to certain aspects of the process that culminated in the definition of the two Marian dogmas.

The reader should thus take careful account of what I am about, for I shall not treat the issue of infallibility itself, a fact reflected in the limited bibliographical selections on this topic. That is to say, though I write as a Roman Catholic with everything that implies both in principle and in fact, I shall not in this book address myself to questions such as whether the concept of infallibility is itself viable and, if so, whether there can be circumstances under which whoever exercises the Petrine ministry within Christianity can and should be judged to be endowed with that charism. Thus while I shall be concerned *inter alia* with whether modification and/or reversal of the teaching of the papal magisterium constitutes a valid argument against so-called papal infallibility, my conclusions, if correct, do not ground that dogma. They merely show that the minimalist argument, as defined herein, is without substance. I shall therefore not deal here with other issues that Küng raised in *Infallible? An Inquiry*.[79] A thorough exploration of the infallibility question itself must await a subsequent book. Hence in Chap. VIII, in dealing with the two Marian dogmas, I shall be occupied mainly with praxis as it illuminates theory. Nor do I wish to deal here with conciliarists who, inasmuch as they are strict conciliarists, must logically reject *Pastor Aeternus*.[80] That some minimalists be conciliarists is irrelevant as far as my present objectives go. Thus while I shall not be taken up with the problem discussed by Francis Oakley,[81] I shall nonetheless proceed with an eye to that brought up by Brian Tierney.[82]

As I have stated, I shall examine seven issues of doctrine, six of which have more to do with belief than with morals. A word must therefore be said about the principle of selection. At least two questions arise, the first being, *why only one issue relating to morals?* It is true that in this period, Pius XII frequently spoke about medico-moral problems but, though his positions have been largely well received by the rest of the Catholic Church, they did not on the whole attract widespread international attention. The fact of the matter is that in the period under discussion there are, other than the doctrinal issues raised by *Rerum novarum* (1891) and *Casti conubii* (1930), no highly significant doctrinal issues having to do with morals as such. Since it is impossible to discuss *Casti conubii* without considering its aftermath in *Humanae vitae* (1968), and since (except for an occasional aside) extended comment on it would go beyond the historical limits I have imposed upon myself, *Rerum novarum* remains the only relevant moral issue.

The second question that might be asked is, *why only seven issues?* To this, of course, I might respond that one must stop somewhere. But there are additional reasons. If one were to include decisions of the Biblical Commission, most of which have been tacitly revoked because of the modalities of their reception, one would indeed have a much broader terrain in which to operate. In principle, these decisions, as well as those of what was formerly called the Holy Office, are relevant to my task since, when setting up the Commission, Pius X indicated that each of its decisions was to be regarded as a *motu proprio* (q.v.) of the Pope. Yet, it is possible to make a technical distinction and to claim that such decisions do not, properly speaking, constitute the teaching of the ordinary papal magisterium. In view of the theory of doctrinal development I intend to sustain, I have judged it wiser to limit myself for the most part to those issues that are clearly doctrinal stances taken, or doctrinal pronouncements made by the Roman Bishop himself in exercising the Petrine ministry within the Catholic Church. The one exception is the brief discussion of the *Monita ad Missionarios* in Chap. II. On that basis, decisions by the other Roman congregations must be excluded for similar reasons. Nonetheless, I suggest that the seven cases around which my inquiry is principally oriented are sufficient to document my case inasmuch as it has to do with doctrine.

The results of the analysis of the function of authority in relation to development of doctrine and dogma are the two pillars on which the bipartite argument stated above rests; the same results ground most of the remaining conclusions with the exception of the seventh and eighth of Chap. VII, where I am concerned to show how my findings parallel certain data in the New Testament.

Initial Clarification of Language, Methodological Assumptions and Perspectives

TERMINOLOGY

The reader will no doubt be struck by at least three divergences from conventional English usage. The first has to do with my use of the term *human being* and is merely an attempt to avoid sexist language as much as possible; the second, with my use of the verb *realize*: I frequently use it in the sense of the French *réaliser* or the German *verwirklichen*; the third I have already alluded to. At the suggestion of one of the Fathers of Vatican II, I prefer to speak of the bishop *at* rather than *of* a particular place.[83] This usage smacks less of lordship and brings out more forcefully Catholicism's traditional but presently obscured stress on the importance of the local Church.

By the *Church*, I mean the Catholic Church. And by the Catholic Church I mean, as stated above, the Roman Church and those local Churches in union with it. But in making this distinction I do not wish to imply that, say, Protestant or Orthodox Churches are not Christian Churches, as will be clear from my treatment of this question in Chap. V. It is simply that, whether he or she agrees with me or not, the reader has a right to know what I mean by certain terms. Hence the term *Roman Catholic* rarely occurs unless that particular emphasis seems called for. By the *Petrine function and/or ministry* is meant the ministry of teaching, governing, and sanctifying as presently exercised by the Roman Bishop as the chief magisterial officer within Catholicism.[84] The term *conciliar documents* embraces a number of collections.[85] Contrary to usage current before Vatican II, I use the term *sensus fidelium* as synonymous with the term *sensus fidei* in *Lumen gentium*;[86] that is to say: Since every real member of the Church is a *fidelis*, I use that term as pertaining to the whole Church.[87]

Since I am writing not only for Catholics but also for a Christian readership that overflows the boundaries of the Catholic Church, I shall, whenever a technical term occurs, offer in parentheses a working definition and/or write *q.v.*, which means that the reader is invited to consult the Glossary. Thus I use the term *theological note* (q.v.), which refers to the degree of certitude with which a particular doctrine is taught and/or believed within Catholicism. Though some Catholic theologians at present tend to eschew this kind of language, I find it useful provided it is not used rigidly. I also use the term *infallibility* (q.v.), though I would prefer to use another to express what Catholic dogma is meant to convey relative to so-called papal infallibility.

The phrase *pertaining to the substance of the faith* deserves special attention. I use it to include what is called both the primary and secondary objects of infallibility, the former meaning a truth revealed by God in Jesus Christ, the latter a doctrine not directly revealed but nonetheless so intimately connected with the revealed truth that to call this doctrine into question amounts to calling into question the revealed truth itself. But a speculative doubt remains even for the Catholic who fully accepts the concept of magisterial officers who cannot err theologically whenever they make a judgment in matters pertaining to faith and morals, if that judgment is binding on the whole Church in such a way that henceforth to reject it is to fall away from the fullness of the Catholic and apostolic faith. In the case of the primary object, where one is dealing with a revealed truth and hence with dogma, the proper theological note may be *de fide divina* or *de fide divina et catholica* (q.v.); in the case of the secondary, matters are not so certain. Is the proper theological note in the case of the secondary object *de fide ecclesiastica* (q.v.)? A minor point, perhaps, since for the traditional Catholic the charism of infallibility is considered operative in both cases.[88] At the risk of some oversimplification, I use the phrase *pertaining to the substance of the faith* to refer to both primary and secondary objects.

METHODOLOGICAL ASSUMPTIONS

It is obvious from the foregoing that I consider the distinction between doctrine (q.v.) and dogma (q.v.) to be valid. I thus find unconvincing the view proposed some years ago to the effect that if ". . . we continue to use dogma in its theological sense, it is an uncertain unity, an unserviceable category."[89] *Dogma* I understand to be a binding judgment made by Catholicism's magisterial officers to the effect that a particular doctrine has been revealed by God in Jesus Christ and that henceforth to reject it is to fall away from the fullness of the Catholic and apostolic faith.[90] It is not my purpose here to state why I find these counter-positions inadequate; my purpose is simply to alert the reader to some of the bases which my argument presupposes.[91]

I likewise assume that within Catholicism, doctrine and dogma develop.[92] That is to say: From a Catholic point of view, the Church of Christ grows in understanding the meaning of Jesus Christ as God's revelation. But I do not thereby understand development to mean continuous growth in the sense that the appropriate model to which it corresponds is organic.[93] Development may indeed be "episodic."[94] Though I would be prepared to admit that a modified structuralist approach may be viable, I consider unsustainable any view that purports to explain growth in understanding of the kerygma as development of structures but not of doctrine or dogma.[95]

PERSPECTIVES

Lest the somewhat detailed analysis of certain chapters obscure the forest for the trees, the reader should grasp at the outset the general sweep of my argument. The first part of the book (Chap. I) deals in summary fashion with positive modalities whereby the teaching of the ordinary papal magisterium has been received by the rest of the Catholic Church, particularly by bishops and theologians; the second (Chaps. II-VI) with certain doctrinal issues wherein modalities of reception led to development, modification, and/or reversal of its teaching.[96] The reason for detailed attention to the latter as distinguished from the global treatment of the former will become clear from what follows. The data may be compared to theses, antitheses, and syntheses. These terms, as is well known, are not frequently found in Hegel as compared with, say, Fichte; but the corresponding concepts recur repeatedly throughout the whole Hegelian enterprise. The attentive reader discerns in Hegel's work multiple triads, some minor and subordinate, others major and tending to dominate. It is much the same with this book. The reader is left for the most part to sort them out for himself or herself, if he or she so desires. The principal synthesis emerging from the data, however, is the tenth conclusion of Chap. VII in part three.[97] Though that *Aufhebung* adds nothing new but merely discloses the Catholic Church for what it is, it should nonetheless be highlighted from the very beginning. For it affirms on the basis of an inductively grounded argument pursued from Chaps. I through VII that regarding the function of authority in relation to doctrinal development the Catholic Church exhibited characteristics of the Church as κοινωνία on the level of word.[98] That finding, which has to do with doctrine and the ordinary papal magisterium, provides the perspective from which to approach the question of dogma and the extraordinary papal magisterium. Such is the burden of Chap. VIII. The concluding Chap. IX speaks for itself. If that be the case, however—if indeed, in the development both of doctrine and of dogma the Church manifested characteristics of the Church as κοινωνία on the level of word—then perhaps it behooves official Catholicism, with the vast ecumenical implications this may involve, to ask itself whether its theory on the function of authority within Christianity is fully in harmony with its praxis. Indeed, that ambiguity still seems evident in its most recently promulgated code of Canon law.[99]

I shall proceed from the standpoint of the teaching of the papal magisterium as "over against" the rest of the Catholic Church. This distinction however, is purely methodological, since the data assessed in Chaps. VII and IX suggest that the Roman Bishops served the Catholic Church from within. Nonetheless, while on the one hand my conclusions, when carefully weighed, can in no sense be taken as endorsing the kind of ecclesiology representative of the recently founded (in the United States) Association for the Rights of Catholics in the Church, on the other they will surely if not sorely vex those on the right of the Catholic spectrum. In this regard, I can only refer eventual Catholic critics to the words of Augustine quoted at the very outset of this study.

I hope that my findings may be helpful not only in charting a course between what many regard as the Scylla and Charybdis of contemporary Catholic ecclesiology but also in providing a means of proceeding further on the sea of broader ecumenical horizons. For my concerns are not only Catholic. As the ongoing ecumenical dialogues attest, they are the concerns of other Christian churches as well.

As is frequently the case in matters of great theological moment, an appropriate place to begin is with a passage from Augustine. During the Pelagian crisis, the great African Doctor is reported to have given the following advice, often quoted, sometimes misquoted, ever since:

> My brothers, suffer along with me. When you meet such [who share the Pelagian view] do not dissimulate; let there not be in you a warped kind of mercy; wherever you find such people, do not dissimulate. Talk back and argue against them and bring those who resist to us. For two councils have been sent to the Apostolic See from which written answers have come back. *The case is closed.*[100]

PART ONE
ROMA LOCUTA

Chapter I
THE TEACHING
OF THE ORDINARY PAPAL
MAGISTERIUM: POSITIVE
MODALITIES OF RECEPTION

On the eve of the Second Vatican Council, few things within Catholicism seemed more secure than the self-sufficiency of the ordinary papal magisterium. Had John XXIII looked not forwards but backwards over the waters across which the Catholic Church had sailed from the time of Pius IX, he would have seen that, though the distance was short in terms of Catholicism's long history, the logs that told the ship's story contain impressive comments on the record of the Roman Bishops during this period. In the political order, the Catholic Church had had to face a number of catastrophes, two of which were worldwide in their scope. In the intellectual order, it had had to deal with the aftermath of the Enlightenment, soon to be followed by the Modernist crisis. In the spiritual order, it had had to cope with the severe hampering of its missionary effort as the result of the First World War. Through all of this the Roman Bishops had chartered a fairly steady course for the Catholic Church.

My principal concern however is with the modalities whereby their teaching was received. I shall argue that *within Catholicism reception of papal teaching from the time of Pius IX up to the end of the Second Vatican Council was largely positive.*

This central thesis is so historically obvious that no effort need be made to ground it. But it must be illustrated, for the history of this period contains an occasional surprise. My attempt to do so is divided into three sections. I shall begin by describing the broad spectrum of reception, using as an index two drafts prepared for but never discussed by the Fathers of Vatican II; I shall then approach the matter from the viewpoint of two particular doctrinal issues, namely, papal pronouncements as they relate to Catholic social teaching and statements by Pius XII as they relate to collegiality. Of these two issues, special attention will be given to the second not only because of its overriding ecclesiological importance but also because as compared to the influence of papal social teaching, which was merely integrated into conciliar documents, papal teaching in the latter context was influential in plotting a new course, thus providing evidence for positive modalities of reception in a way different from any of the preceding cases. There is a third outstanding possibility in this period, namely the teaching of Pius XII on truth or good in non-Christian religions; but I have left it for Chap. II. Finally, I shall close with an overview.

Positive Modalities Of Reception In General

The drafts to which we now turn our attention are two that until now have received little attention. I shall therefore summarize their contents before I proceed to suggest the sense in which both documents show that on the whole papal teaching during the period under discussion was well received by the rest of the Catholic Church. It should be borne in mind that neither draft was intended as a finished product but only as a point of departure for debate.

Sancta Vaticana Synodus

The *Schema Constitutionis Dogmaticae de Deposito Fidei Pure Custodiendo* had for its opening words *Sancta Vaticana Synodus* (henceforth referred to for the most part as *SVS*), whence its title as used in these pages.

In the *Acta Synodalia Sacrosancti Concilii Oecumenici Vaticani Secundi* it comprises forty-one pages and about 10,000 words.[1] Its obvious purpose was to inculcate a particular theological perspective intended to keep error from creeping into the deposit of faith. Besides its preface, which explained in more detail what its authors had in mind,[2] the draft was divided into ten chapters that constituted an updated Syllabus of Errors.[3] SVS was notably different in at least one respect. Whereas the document promulgated by Pius IX had been largely negative in that it listed condemned propositions and a bibliography of one or more pontifical documents from Pius IX's writings and addresses intended to show the meaning of each condemnation, *SVS* usually began with an explanation of the truth of the faith and only then went on to reprove certain tendencies in current Catholic theologizing. The language used was not severe. It was nonetheless firm.

The protection (*custodia*) of the deposit of faith, the preface states, is incumbent not only upon individual pastors who must render an account before God but especially on all bishops gathered together under the Roman Pontiff.[4] Fidelity to the truth of the gospel is thus not the business of Pope and bishops alone. Chap. I is almost entirely epistemological in scope. A human being by its very nature is able to know truth, for certain fundamental principles pertaining to knowing cannot really be put into serious doubt.[5] Because of the Fall, however, knowledge of the truth especially as it pertains to religious and moral matters is rendered more difficult. These are areas where a human being's fundamental disposition of mind can prevent him or her from correctly discerning the way things are. Chap. II states that the existence of the invisible God can be (like the Dogmatic Constitution *Dei Filius* of Vatican I, the text says *posse* not *debere*, a distinction that seems to have escaped the notice of not a few commentators) known (*cognosci*, not *sciri*) as certain and demonstrated both from degrees of perfection in the world and the imperfection of creatures.[6] Chap. III takes up a number of related issues: The world had a beginning; the notion of creation is to be preserved.[7] There can never be a real conflict between faith and reason; apparent contradiction has its origin in an inadequate understanding of the dogmas of faith or in cases where mere opinions are taken as statements of fact. Thus science is worthy of the name when it prudently investigates the origin of the world and in no way damages what faith teaches.[8] It must however be maintained that a human being is composed of body and spirit and that body and spirit are essentially different; likewise, it must be held that the individual soul of each human being is directly created by God. The human soul is not the product of any other vital principle.[9]

In Chap. IV revelation (i.e., that revelation which is the object of Catholic faith and is hence called public revelation) is defined as a speaking (*locutio*) by which the Godhead, formerly through the prophets but very recently through His Son (Heb 1:1), bears witness to itself, the mysteries of salvation and the truths connected with it, demanding from everyone the obedience of faith.[10] Revelation is not simply a series of events, for such events have nothing to do with revelation unless the truths hidden in them or connected with them are declared by God's legates to be matters of faith. The fullness of revelation is in Christ. At this point numbers 22-28, about which I shall make a passing comment below, outline what is in effect a basic apologetics. In Chap. V the draft states that the deposit of faith, once the apostolic age came to a close, could not be increased in itself; what increases is knowledge (*cognitione*) of what is contained in it.[11] In Chap. VI, it is mentioned that private revelation cannot become the object of Catholic faith but only of human faith within the limits of prudence.[12] Chap. VII takes up a matter controverted in the late 1940s. That human beings have been raised to the order of graced human nature is a gratuitous gift of God; hence, those are to be reproved who hold that human beings' call to grace and glory is somehow due to human nature.[13] Original sin, Chap. VIII states, is a real sin; its reality is a dogma of faith, whose scrutiny by human reason will not suffice to understand it completely. It is not a defect flowing from the limitations of human nature but is transmitted through procreation in such a way that the human race in both body and soul has been affected for the worse.[14] This chapter comes down solidly on the side of monogenesis. Chap. IX has to do with eschatology in the generic sense of that term. The authors reject anything that smacks of reincarnation; they affirm the traditional doctrine of heaven or hell as a human being's ultimate state but avoid such notions, once the *sententia communis theologorum* (q.v.) that hell is a place.[15] Finally, in Chap. X, the framers of the draft maintained that sin is a real offense against God and that satisfaction brought about by Christ was real satisfaction, as over against the opinion of those who were beginning to hold that the sacrifice of Christ on the cross had only exemplary but not efficacious value.[16]

Such was the general bearing of *SVS*, summarized here perhaps only too briefly. It is clear that its authors embraced a number of positions that betrayed a certain philosophical and theological innocence. Thus in the first chapter, where they spoke of a human being's ability to discern the truth, one would have expected some suggestion that there is a sense in which the human mind also shapes it, an orientation that could have been integrated into a transcendental—as distinguished from a neo-Thomist—

epistemology. And numbers 22-28 of Chap. IV, which present in effect an apologetics in outline, could have been written at the turn of the century. One discerns no indication that the authors were aware of what the application of form criticism and redaction criticism have done to traditional apologetics. It is not my purpose however to analyze this draft's strengths and weaknesses. My interest in it lies in showing the manner in which the teaching of the ordinary papal magisterium had been blended into it. The position of Pius IX, not that of Vatican I, is appealed to first when it is a question of affirming a human being's ability to know that God is;[17] that of Pius XII is referred to in regard to the kind of dispositions required to discern religious and moral truths;[18] that of Pius X in rejecting the notion, later somewhat attenuated by the Second Vatican Council, that all religions have brought forth (*protulisse*) some revelation, though in a way less perfect than the religion of the Old and New Testaments;[19] that of Pius XI is quoted in the context of labeling as blindness the denial of God's existence.[20] These instances however are somewhat exceptional in the sense I shall indicate below. The teaching of some Roman Bishops prior to Pius IX is of course used as a witness for some statements; in the period with which we are dealing, that of every Pope with the exception of Benedict XV is referred to in one question or another either as an indication of what the authors meant or as "proof texts" for a particular theological view. But of all these Popes, it is clear that the dominating influence is that of Pius XII and the encyclical *Humani generis* (1950), in which particular philosophical and theological orientations of the *nouvelle théologie* were reproved.

In Chap. I, Pius' teaching was used to show what the draft meant when it stated that the human mind is capable of coming to a knowledge of the truth;[21] that there are certain fundamental principles (e.g., those of identity, contradiction, efficient and final causality) that are so obvious that they are, as it were, known (*cognosci*) spontaneously.[22] What faith teaches is built upon those principles; hence their importance. The reader of both *Humani generis* and *SVS* realizes that the influence of that encyclical on the draft is even greater than the numerous explicit references to it suggest. Thus in Chap. VII, though he—unlike others[23]—is not explicitly mentioned, the opinion of Father Henri (now Cardinal) de Lubac was explicitly condemned.[24] The parallel between *Humani generis* and *SVS* on this point is simply too close to be accidental. In general, despite the exceptions noted above, the authors tended first to appeal to older Catholic tradition as reflected in conciliar positions and the great doctors of the past; they then tended to refer more frequently to the ordinary papal magisterium whenever it was a question of problems that earlier Catholic tradition did not address or of which it had been only dimly aware. In this latter context, the influence of Pius XII and *Humani generis* was simply all-pervasive.

DEUS INFINITE BONUS

Entitled *Schema Constitutionis Dogmaticae de Ordine Morali Christiano*, this draft, whose opening words are those of the heading above and which is henceforth referred to herein for the most part as *DI*, was intended to correct erroneous teaching in contemporary moral theology. A document of some 850 words and in the *Acta Synodalia Sacrosancti Concilii Oecumenici Vaticani Secundi* comprising twenty-two pages,[25] *DI* consisted of five chapters,[26] the brunt of which was an insistence on the objectivity of the moral law as distinguished from situation ethics (the exact Latin equivalent of which term does not appear in the document). Human freedom is a gift; the ultimate norm for its proper use is none other than the eternal law.[27] Knowledge of the moral law is to be had from the natural law and from revelation. Because human nature has been weakened by the effects of original sin, it needs the help of revelation in order to discern some of the precepts of the natural law.[28] And the magisterium of the Church, though not a vehicle of revelation, can nonetheless be decisive in discerning what the natural law requires. The authors of the draft go on to summarize contemporary errors, rejecting especially the opinion of those who hold that the moral law is subject to development even in its fundamental concepts.[29] Conscience, if rightly formed according to objectively valid norms, indicates at the moment of choice what the will of God is in a particular course of action. But the duty to follow even an erroneous conscience remains, a duty not founded in subjectivity but in the objectively unassailable fact that a human being does not have a moral right to sin.[30] Yet, because the way human beings act affects the common good of society, Christians may not be indifferent to the way others form their conscience.[31] An erroneous conscience does not change the objective moral law.

Implicit in the document is the distinction between two notions of freedom. Freedom in the psychological order (the ability to do what one likes) is rejected as the norm for freedom in the moral order (the ability to do what one ought). The authors of the draft place heavy emphasis on the role of the Gospel in ruling out anything that smacks of moral relativism.[32]

This does not mean that in the application of the moral law there are no gray areas. The draft does not speak of probabilism, which when correctly used is one of the ways for Catholics to deal with conflicting moral obligations. Instead, it refers to *prudentia*, the Thomistic notion of which is a way of making difficult moral decisions with integrity.[33] The Catholic faithful are to be warned of the dangers of ethical relativism. If sincerity before God is the sole norm of human conduct, then certain effects may be expected to follow. Among these consequences are religious indifferentism, divorce, abortion, refusal to obey legitimate authority, directly willed suicide.[34] By anticipation the draft rejected what in the post-conciliar period was to become the theology of fundamental option.[35]

Having stressed objective norms, the authors maintained that serious sin remains a real possibility. To sin mortally, it is not necessary to have a hatred of God; it is sufficient that a human being embrace a particular course of action with full consent and with full awareness that it is completely (*omnino*) inconsistent with friendship with God and that it neglects the means which are truly (*per se et absolute*) necessary to attain his or her last end.[36] For in the psychological order a human being remains free; the Church has always defended that freedom against any innovating heresy.[37] But it is one thing to say that various circumstances can diminish freedom (and consequent moral responsibility); it is quite another to say that freedom (and consequent responsibility) are non-existent.[38] (The document speaks of "normal" human beings; it does not directly envisage the case of those who are so psychologically impaired that freedom in the psychological order [and consequent moral responsibility] are virtually destroyed.)

The final chapter contains a number of loosely connected concepts. The dignity of the human person consists in this: That a human being is made in the image and likeness of God and is directly related to its creator from whom it receives the light of reason, power of free choice, the fire of love (*amoris*) and dominion over material (*corporalium*) things.[39] A number of paragraphs later the authors of the draft speak of the dignity of the human person as consisting in divine sonship and the Godhead as companion (*consortioque divinae naturae*). The link between the source of a human being's dignity and its real freedom is not explored. Instead, the document points out that a human being should not indiscriminately submit to medical and scientific experimentation that may be inconsistent with its dignity as person. The document comes close to stating but does not explicitly say that freedom is grounded in the dignity of the human person. Similarly, the authors of the draft praise scientific and cultural enterprises which build up the earthly city, provided human beings do not forget that the earthly city is not the kingdom of God.[40] The authors suggest but they do not explicitly state that the building up of the earthly city should be the result of the right use of freedom. Indeed, they take positions which will later find their way into other conciliar texts promulgated by Paul VI; e.g.:

> It is entirely foreign to the mind of the Church to say that because of their hope and love of things eternal Christians may not love the things of time, as one should; that as regards physical evil, pain, famine and war, they work with a certain false indifference.[41]

This will be one of the principal themes of *Gaudium et spes*. But progress in matters moral and religious does not of its very nature follow from progress in science and culture. Hence the closing statement of *DI*: "If you are risen with Christ, seek the things which are above, not the things which are of the earth" (Col. 3:1-2).[42]

After the Council, some of the positions embraced by the authors were to become matters of debate.[43] What concerns us here is the manner in which the teaching of the ordinary papal magisterium had been integrated into the draft. Thus for the notion of the Godhead as the foundation of the natural law, the authors referred to Pius IX's statement in *Maxima quidem* and to that of Pius XII in *Summi pontificatus*.[44] On the complementary relation between the revelation and the natural law, they appealed to the teaching of Pius XI in *Divini illius Magistri* and that of Pius XII in *Humani generis*.[45] When treating the difference between true and false freedom, the authors did not hesitate to refer to Gregory XVI who, in the context of what he considered a false freedom of conscience, had called such freedom madness (*deliramentum*), as though a human being could be free against God.[46] When the authors stated that the Christian cannot remain indifferent to the manner in which others form their conscience, they were quick to point out that the act of faith may not be forced, basing their views here on the teaching of Leo XIII.[47] But the teaching of Pius IX, Pius XI and Pius XII was that most frequently referred to. In the case of the last mentioned, abundant use was made of lesser known addresses (*allocutiones*), especially as they had to do with medico-moral problems.[48] Upon analysis the same pattern emerges as that detected in *SVS*: appeal to older Catholic tradition, especially to the Councils, to Augustine, and to Aquinas whenever possible, and, as was to be expected, increasing dependence on the teaching of the ordinary papal magisterium whenever it was a question of more recent problems.

In regard to the matters discussed in both *SVS* and *DI*, it is obvious even upon a cursory reading of the relevant documentation that the teaching of the ordinary papal magisterium as reflected in these documents was disputed neither by the authors of the drafts nor by the Preparatory Commission nor by the Council in session. The question does not of course end there, for *Humani generis* had caused not a little grumbling, especially in France, where it met the *"nouvelle théologie"* head on. Yet to the extent that reception has to do with obedience, positive reception was the rule rather than the exception. The impression conveyed by *Sancta Vaticana Synodus* and *Deus Infinite Bonus* is by no means deceptive and fully substantiates the argument stated above.

Particular Doctrinal Issues

PAPAL SOCIAL TEACHING

It is a fact well known to the historian of nineteenth-century Christianity that Catholic social teaching did not begin with *Rerum novarum* of Leo XIII.[49] Socially concerned Catholics like Wilhelm von Ketteler, Bishop at Mainz, and Gaspard Mermillod, auxiliary at Lausanne (and later Cardinal of the Roman Church), had long been pressing the issue by their study of the theory grounding acceptable social conditions and by their insistence on the necessity of changing the structure of society as then constituted. Though a relevant passage of *Quanta cura* by Pius IX (whose personal library is said to have contained a significant number of books related to the social question[50]) could be interpreted as suggesting a middle course between outright socialism and unbridled capitalism, nonetheless the initial move toward a Catholic thesis on these matters came from others in the Catholic Church before it came from the Roman Bishops. But had the latter not sifted through these gropings and presented them synthetically to the Catholic Church, there would be today no official Catholic teaching on socio-economic issues. Initial emphasis came from others, but from May 15, 1891 onwards, when Leo XIII promulgated *Rerum novarum*, it was henceforth the Roman Bishops who at least in theory became within Catholicism the undisputed champions of social justice.

General Scope of Papal Teaching

Sometimes called the Magna Carta on which all Catholic activities in social matters are based,[51] the content of *Rerum novarum* (henceforth, for the most part, *RN*), which in its official Latin text was expressed in something close to six thousand words, is so well known that a summary of its message here may be dispensed with.[52] If, however, one digs deep for the constants of Leo's position and for those of his successors, those constants are perceived as rooted in two fundamental principles. Leo recognized that there are natural differences in human talent and that these differences are intrinsically related to the reward which a particular human being might expect from his or her labor. Thus Leo maintained that wise government consists not in dealing with "subjects" as though they were equal in talent but *in devoting to all equal care in spite of de facto inequality*.[53] The first is related to everything the Pope was to say about the right to private property; the second, with what he was to say about its responsible use. The trunk growing from these roots was to provide the basis for avoiding the extremes of capitalism on the one hand and those of socialism on the other.

Subsequent Popes not only insisted on but developed Leo's position. In *Quadragesimo anno* (henceforth, for the most part, *QA*), written to mark the fortieth anniversary of *Rerum novarum*, Pius XI admitted that Leo's doctrine had been looked upon with suspicion even among Catholics.[54] Yet the benefits due to it were undeniable. Pius highlighted the individual and social character of property, steering a course between "individualism" (Leo's capitalism) and "collectivism" (Leo's socialism), and inveighed against the unjust claims of both capital and labor. He said there had to be a just distribution of profits, and went so far as to argue for modifying the wage contract by instituting a partnership between capital and labor, a partnership that would result in wage earners becoming sharers in ownership.[55] For just as property had individual and social implications, so did labor. Writing at a time when the Great Depression was approaching its height, the Pope called for a reconstruction of the social order.

Since the fiftieth anniversary of *Rerum novarum* occurred in the midst of World War II, Pius XII had other concerns; but for all that he did not fail to address the issues.[56] The next encyclical endorsing the doctrine of Leo XIII is to be found in John XXIII's *Mater et Magistra* (henceforth, for the most part, *MM*).[57] John began by summing up the context in which Leo's manifesto had appeared and the developments up to the Petrine ministries of Pius XI and Pius XII.[58] He then proceeded to explain and enlarge upon the position of Leo XIII. The principle of subsidiarity as set forth by Pius XI must not be infringed upon.[59] The basic rights of the human person were to be preserved inviolate. Included among these rights were "...the right and duty of each individual *normally* to provide the necessities of life for himself and his dependents."[60] Yet where "...appropriate activity of the state is lacking or defective...there occurs the exploitation of the weak by the unscrupulous strong who flourish, unfortunately, like cockle among the wheat, in all times and places."[61]

John noted carefully the increased complexity of social structure but refused to see therein simply the blind drive of natural forces. Human beings could still progress provided there was a balance between the freedom of individual citizens and suitable regulation by the state, something which *mutatis mutandis* was to apply to international relations.

There is no need to dwell on the particulars of John's argument as he analyzed the changed conditions wherein the right to private property is exercised as well as the social obligations to which it is related. Suffice it to say the Pope was especially concerned about the needs of the agricultural segment of society.[62] Nor is there need to take up his analysis of the imbalance between population, land, and economic development. The constants of papal teaching that have their roots in the principles stated above are all there but are developed in terms of the cultural changes whose full impact is even now not apparent. In *Rerum novarum*, the constants and the roots from which they grow had to do essentially with the right of the working person wherever he or she might be; in *Mater et Magistra*, they had to do with entire peoples.[63]

Modalities of Reception

Rerum novarum stunned the Catholic world. Given the socio-political situation of the day in which *laissez-faire* capitalism was the dominant ethos, it is not surprising that the Roman Bishop's stance was opposed by many Catholics.[64] The wealthy were fully in agreement when Leo insisted that the right to private property is a natural right and not one that results from human convention. But they were distressed when he went on to say among other things that a just wage was not simply one to which employer and employee agree but one which allows a man to provide for his wife and children with some measure of comfort. In other words, he was saying that through thrift the worker should be able to acquire some little wealth and thus plan for the future; that children should not be allowed to do the work befitting adults only; that labor has a natural right to organize. These and other orientations in *Rerum novarum*, too well known to require more extensive commentary, went directly against socio-economic theory and practice then current in the United States and Europe. When *Rerum novarum* was read from the pulpit in some Catholic Churches, many otherwise loyal Catholics are reported to have walked out.

Yet despite initial rejection the full extent of which has never been fully documented, there can be no doubt that papal social teaching has "taken" within the Catholic Church, at least in principle. Besides a seemingly almost unending number of studies that could be cited in support of this assertion,[65] it is sufficient to examine the influence of papal social encyclicals in some of the documents emanating from Vatican II. Among them a key document is *Gaudium et spes*, particularly Chapter III of part two. When it came to the basis of a just wage, it is the teaching of Leo XIII in *RN* and Pius XI in *QA* which is affirmed along with that of John XXIII in *MM*.[66] John's encyclical was cited then especially when it was a question of the economics of society conceived as a cooperative enterprise.[67] As with Leo, the right to private property is restated together with its social obligations.[68] A cursory reading allows one to conclude that every major position of the Roman Bishops on socio-economic matters has been integrated into this conciliar document.

And yet, as one surveys the ninety-some years that have elapsed since *Rerum novarum* shook the Catholic world, certain ironies unforeseen at the time, remain. On its fortieth anniversary Pius XI stated that there are those who abuse religion itself, cloaking their own unjust position under its name. He then went on to add:

> Such men are the cause that the Church, without deserving it, may have the appearance and be accused of taking sides with the wealthy, and of being little moved by the needs and sufferings of the disinherited.[69]

The irony is that in seeking to take to heart John XXIII's advice in *Mater et Magistra*—Observe, Judge, Act—Catholic priests, religious, and militant lay persons in a number of Central American countries are subjected to increasingly systematic violence because, siding with the poor, they are now portrayed as crypto-communists. Papal social teaching, initially rejected by some otherwise loyal Catholics, is still resisted by a powerful, often nominally Catholic minority, a resistance that affects the material and spiritual well-being of millions. But therein lies a lesson for those concerned with the theory of doctrinal development within Catholicism. The teaching of the ordinary papal magisterium in *Rerum novarum* and its trajectory through Pius XI, Pius XII and John XXIII is undoubtedly one of the glories of the ordinary papal magisterium; nonetheless, initial, even persistent long-term rejection of a doctrinal stance taken by the Roman Bishops says nothing in itself about whether or not the same doctrinal stance will eventually prevail. No adequately informed Catholic today doubts that papal social teaching is here to stay or that it forms part of authentic Catholic heritage.

PAPAL TEACHING AND COLLEGIALITY

"...each bishop in the act and by force of his ordination begins to be a member of the episcopal body [*corpo episcopale*] and as a result receives the right to govern and administer the whole Church whenever he is in union with all the others and constitutes a body with them...."[70]

In the passage just cited, the term *collegio* does not occur, but *corpo episcopale* means the same. Words of Vincenzo Bolgeni, approvingly quoted by Mauro Cappellari who in 1831 became Gregory XVI, they suggest that collegiality, understood as the supreme and full power of the body of Catholic bishops over the whole Catholic Church, a power coming from Christ and not from the Pope, was an emphasis rather than the discovery of Vatican II.[71] Indeed, a careful study of papal documents relating to this concept in our period would reveal that, in regard to the nature of their authority, the attitude of the Roman Bishops was largely collegial at least in theory long before the question of collegiality was placed before the Fathers of Vatican II.[72]

Such an inquiry would however lead me away from my present purpose, which is to illustrate the central thesis stated at the outset of this chapter.[73] As suggested in the heading of this section, I shall approach the matter from a new direction. I shall first examine the teaching of Pius XII in *Fidei donum* (henceforth, for the most part, *FD*) as it relates to the concept of collegiality. But since during the Second Vatican Council there was a tendency to see in some statements of *Mystici corporis* an argument against the idea, I shall then proceed to explore the Pope's teaching in that document. Finally, I shall indicate in bold strokes how the teaching of *Fidei donum* was a significant factor in the development that took place at the Council. The effort to illustrate the positive modalities whereby the teaching of the ordinary papal magisterium was received in our period will thus take a different turn. In this case, those who, as I shall show, incorrectly thought the Pope's teaching militated against collegiality as well as those who thought that his teaching pointed toward it, were both, though in different ways, witnessing to the positive manner in which they themselves had received it.

Fidei Donum

Promulgated on August 21, 1957, and addressed to the Catholic hierarchy, *Fidei donum*, which in the *Acta Apostolicae Sedis* comprises twenty-three pages and some five thousand words, was intended to alert the episcopacy about the difficulties, challenges and opportunities of the nascent African church.[74] Part of the context, though the exact equivalent of the Latin term does not occur in the document, was the process of decolonization then underway. There was every reason to rejoice over the progress made by the Gospel on that continent.[75] But there were too few missionaries. And while some elements were spreading atheistic propaganda, other religious persuasions, not those of Jesus Christ, were enticing many.[76] Whereas on the one hand hundreds of thousands still worshipped idols, on the other, technology was making headway and was almost becoming the object of a new cult.[77] It was the duty of the Church to spread the Gospel among these peoples. Those who have received the gift of faith—here the Pope alluded again to the words with which he had begun—ought to show their gratitude especially by spreading it and helping the missionary effort. There was danger in delay.[78]

The Pope then applied the doctrine of the Mystical Body of Christ to the existing situation. It is no part of Catholic doctrine that members of the Church go off by themselves; they come to each other's aid. Joined so closely to Christ and his Vicar, the bishops desire to participate in the care of all the churches,[79] which, the Pope states, "...weighs on our shoulders."[80] Pius thereupon made the following statements not infrequently discussed in the context of collegiality as put forth by the Council:

Text A.   Beyond doubt, to the Apostle Peter alone and to his successors, namely the Roman Pontiffs, Jesus Christ entrusted his whole flock: "Feed my lambs; feed my sheep."[81]

Text B.   But if each bishop is the sacred shepherd of that part only of his flock which has been entrusted to him, nevertheless inasmuch as by divine ordinance and precept he is a legitimate successor of the Apostles, together with the rest of the bishops he becomes responsible [*sponsor*] for the apostolic task of the Church, according to those words which Christ addressed to the Apostles: "As the Father has sent me, I also send you." This mission which embraces all nations...until the end of the world by no means ceased when the Apostles left this mortal life; nay, it still continues in the bishops in communion with the Vicar of Jesus Christ.[82]

Text B follows immediately upon Text A; they are separated here merely to illustrate a difference of perspective. Pius then stated that this concern (*prospicientia*) for the needs of the Church universal highlights its Catholic nature and in the penultimate section of the encyclical suggested concrete ways of prayer, financial help and means for increasing missionary vocations.[83] Here he laid the foundation for what was to become the lay missionary movement.[84] In the concluding paragraphs the Pope turned his attention briefly but affectionately to the efforts of those laboring in mission fields other than Africa.[85]

Two matters should here be emphasized. First, in regard to Text A, nothing that Vatican II stated about collegiality modified what Pius had stated. Collegiality for the Council Fathers did not mean that any other bishop besides the Roman Bishop has jurisdiction over the whole Church. The fullness of the Pope's jurisdiction is affirmed; what is stressed is that he has it as *head* of a *college*. Equally stressed is that the college without its head is no longer a college but a collection of bishops. Second, in regard to Text B, it cannot be maintained that Pius fully anticipated the direction Vatican II was to take; but it can be affirmed that his thinking was along those lines. When the Pope maintained that each bishop "...apostolici muneris Ecclesiae una cum ceteris Episcopis *sponsor* fit..."[86] he was using language that in the context of the conciliar debates some years later was to become highly suggestive; they led directly into the position that the Council was to adopt. For to say in Latin that someone is *sponsor* connotes the idea that he or she is guarantor or surety for someone else. There were some however who maintained that violence was being done to the Pope's thinking and who pointed to *Mystici corporis* as proof.[87]

Mystici Corporis *as Counter-Evidence?*

Before showing how those who were opposed to the concept of collegiality could use one of Pius' statements against it, I shall first summarize Catholic teaching as it relates to my question. Catholic theology distinguishes between the priesthood of all (baptized) believers and the ministerial priesthood of priests and bishops; the role of the latter is to serve the former. As for the latter group, two further matters must be distinguished; namely, the power of orders (the ability validly to administer sacraments besides baptism) and the power of jurisdiction (which includes the ability validly to teach and govern in the name of Christ). It is considered that the former is received as the direct result of valid ordination. The First Vatican Council left open for theological debate the question whether the jurisdiction of bishops is conferred through the Pope (*mediante Summo Pontifice*) or directly (*immediate*) by God. It thus becomes clear that though collegiality is not reducible to jurisdiction *tout court*, the two concepts are so closely connected that they may be considered two sides of the same coin.

Now during the Council some were to cite the encyclical *Mystici corporis* as a basis for ruling out the concept of collegiality. In the *Acta Apostolicae Sedis* in which it was promulgated, this encyclical (henceforth, for the most part, *MC*) comprises fifty-five pages and totals approximately fifteen thousand words.[88] From a merely cursory reading it is clear that the Pope's purpose as stated in the opening pages was pastoral. On the doctrinal level, he attempted to face what he considered false positions on the nature of the Church;[89] on the existential, he remarked that the Catholic Church (the encyclical was published in 1943 at the height of the Second World War) was passing through a raging tempest—many of its members (together with their Protestant counterparts) were in concentration camps by reason of their opposition to National Socialism.[90] Pius was to state elsewhere in the document that when one member of the Body which is the Church suffers, all the members do because of their mutual union in Christ.[91]

Mystici corporis will occupy our attention at greater length in part two. I shall not summarize its content further since, unlike the two conciliar drafts discussed above, and unlike some of the encyclicals and addresses of Pius IX, its message is well known or is at least easily accessible. The following quotation is relevant:

> *Text C.*   ...Bishops must be considered as the more illustrious members of the universal Church, for they are united by a very special bond to the divine Head of the whole Body ...*moreover, as far as his own diocese is concerned, each one as a true Shepherd feeds the flock entrusted to him and rules it in the name of the Lord.*[92]

> *Text D.*   Yet, in exercising this office, they are not altogether independent, but are subordinate to the lawful authority of the Roman Pontiff, *although enjoying the ordinary power of jurisdiction, which they receive directly from the Supreme Pontiff.*[93]

Text D follows immediately upon Text C and is separated here for the purpose of clarification. *Ordinary power* (Text D) is a technical term meaning that the power envisaged is one that its possessor uses as his own by reason of his office or position. The Pope was therefore implicitly saying with Pius IX in 1875 what Catholic doctrine has always maintained; namely, that bishops qua bishops are not the Roman Bishop's delegates.[94] The difficulty arises from the fact that the Pope stated that bishops receive their ordinary power of jurisdiction directly (*immediate*) from the Pope. The extent to which such a statement could be used as an argument against the concept of collegiality depends on what he meant by jurisdiction. Did Pius mean (1) jurisdiction over a particular diocese? Or (2) the jurisdiction of the college of bishops over the whole church? In regard to (1), Text C clarifies the frame of reference: Pius was speaking of the relation of a bishop to his diocese; in regard to (2), he did not raise the question. Hence, the attempts of a number of Council Fathers to use passages like Texts C and D as an argument against the concept of collegiality as it was then evolving in the Council seems gratuitous.

Shortly before he died some fifteen years later, Pius again wrote in a related context, a careful examination of which further clarifies his intent in *MC*. In *Ad Apostolorum Principis sepulchrum*, promulgated on June 29, 1958, he began by noting that Pius XI thirty-two years earlier had ordained a number of Chinese bishops, thus hinting at the Roman ties which linked the Catholic Church in China to the See of Rome. He then proceeded to address the situation of the Catholic Church in China where the communist government had been attempting to set up a national Church, an enterprise involving the ordination of bishops without the Pope's approval. This is the frame of reference for the following remark:

> *Text E.* ....For it is clearly and expressly laid down in the sacred canons that it pertains to the Apostolic See alone to judge whether or not anyone is suitable for the dignity and office of bishop and that it belongs to the Roman Pontiff freely to appoint bishops ....This having been established, the result is that bishops who are neither appointed nor confirmed by the Apostolic See, nay, who are chosen and consecrated contrary to its express wishes [*ordinationes*] do not enjoy any power to teach nor to govern [*nulla fruantur potestate magisterii et iurisdictionis*] since jurisdiction falls to bishops through the Roman Pontiff alone, as we have advised in our encyclical *Mystici corporis*....[95]

Pius then quoted the italicized sentence of Text C and the whole of Text D, citing *Ad Sinarum gentem* in which several years earlier (October 7, 1954) he had stated essentially the same position. Text E is therefore useful in that it throws light on what Pius meant in *Mystici corporis* (Texts C and D). It should be noted that in Text E Pius did not question the validity of episcopal ordination from the point of view of the power of orders, his one concern being to point out to Chinese Catholics that bishops ordained without the consent of the Pope do not enjoy the power to teach and to govern in the Catholic Church. The obvious implications were that no Catholic was obliged to obey them.

On close reading, however, Text E is more revealing. Pius did not say that such illicitly ordained bishops have no jurisdiction at all in the sense that jurisdiction was simply non-existent. He said, "... efficitur, ut...nulla *fruantur* potestate magisterii et iurisdictionis..."[96] The choice of *fruantur* may be taken as suggesting the possibility that jurisdiction is conferred in some radical sense (what a neo-Thomist might call *in actu primo*[97]) by episcopal ordination but that its exercise (*in actu secundo*) is null and void until the Pope freely and without constraint through appropriate channels puts a bishop in charge of a diocese or territory. Since it is highly doubtful that in a document of this kind every word used by the Pope, who himself was a skilled canonist, was not carefully weighed with a view to all its connotations, considerations of this kind cannot be lightly dismissed.

Whatever be the intent behind these and other passages which have been adduced from the teaching of the ordinary papal magisterium as an argument against collegiality, I have found therein no evidence to support such a view. That is to say: Statements of Pius XII (and other Popes) on the source of general episcopal jurisdiction (which is as we have said the other side of the coin in the question of collegiality of bishops) are at best inconclusive. *Mystici corporis* cannot therefore be legitimately put forth as militating against the thesis that the thinking of Pius XII on collegiality was conducive to the position which Vatican II was to develop. Everything suggested above concerning the implications of what the Pope said in *Fidei donum* when he spoke of the concern for all the Churches ("...participare studete sollicitudinem illam omnium ecclesiarum..."[98]) as part of the duty of bishops retains its force. It remains to examine the modalities of its reception at Vatican II.

The Trajectory of Fidei Donum at Vatican II

Here we have to do with essentially five documents, which are as follows:

(1) *Aeternus Unigeniti* (*AU*-a) discussed by the Preparatory Commission on May 8 and 9, 1962.[99]

(2) *Aeternus Unigeniti* (*AU*-b) presented to the Council Fathers on November 23, 1962.[100]

(3) *Lumen gentium* (*LG*-a) to be transmitted to the dispersed Council Fathers as of April 22, 1963.[101]

(4) *Lumen gentium* (*LG*-b) to be transmitted to the dispersed Council Fathers as of July 3, 1964.[102]

(5) *Lumen gentium* (*LG*-c), the Dogmatic Constitution on the Church promulgated by Paul VI on November 21, 1964.[103]

My remarks will be limited to three phrases of development.

The Preparatory Period

The relevant paragraph from *AU*-a stated:

> *Text F.* The episcopal body or the College of bishops which succeeds the College of the Apostles in teaching and pastoral government, nay, in which the apostolic body continues without interruption [*continuo*], together with its head, the Roman Pontiff and never without this head, is believed to be one [*unum*] subject having full and supreme power over the whole Church. Nevertheless the power of this body is not exercised except in an extraordinary way at the command of its sole head and the good pleasure [*ad nutum exclusivum*] of the same.[104]

The qualifying phrase "...nonnisi modo extraordinario...exercetur,"[105] when read in the context of the preceding number seems to indicate that the college of bishops, when not united in an ecumenical council, are a college only by reason of their concern for all the local Churches; hence, for the authors of the draft, the question of jurisdiction over the whole Church is not affirmed. It is in that sense that in the critical apparatus the authors refer to *Fidei donum*.[106] This is clear from a reading of number 3; it is also clear from the report that, as given by Cardinal Ottaviani, was intended to explain the meaning of the draft.

Ottaviani began by pointing out that the draft was limited to bishops of residential sees; it did not have to do with Vicars apostolic, i.e., with bishops who govern a particular mission territory in the name of the Pope.[107] He then explained that although the draft did not state that jurisdiction is given immediately by the Pope—the term *immediate* was susceptible of various interpretations—that opinion nevertheless was excluded by which it is claimed that a bishop receives his power to govern a diocese (*gregem particularem*) in the same manner in which the Pope receives his power over the whole Church. That is to say: Designation by the Pope merely as a *conditio sine qua non* is excluded as an explanation of how a bishop-elect receives jurisdiction.[108] And quite clearly, he said, the care of the bishops for all the churches is not a matter of jurisdiction, for one must distinguish between a power (*potestas*) and its exercise (*exercitium*). Thus Ottaviani's brief commentary was thoroughly consistent with the phrase "...nonnisi modo extraordinario...exercetur" of Text F. It was this perspective which, within the limits imposed by the *Nota explicativa praevia*, the Fathers of Vatican II were to overturn, as I shall demonstrate below.[109]

The inadequacy of *AU*-a was highlighted from the very beginning, Cardinal Frings stating that the expression "...from the command of the head and the exclusive good pleasure of the same..."[110] did not seem to fit either the dignity or the importance of the episcopal college. But it was Paul Cardinal Richaud, Archbishop at Bordeaux, who gave the most incisive critique during the debates of May 8 and 9. He was disappointed with those chapters (III and IV) that had to do with the episcopacy. He, along with many other bishops, had hoped that the Council would take up the unfinished work of the First Vatican Council. It was not sufficient to say that the bishops at the discretion of the Pope have power over the universal Church—Richaud quoted the telling phrase "... nonnisi modo extraordinario ex iussu solius Capitis et ad nutum exclusivum eiusdem."[111] There was another ordinary power (q.v.) which comes truly though indirectly from consecration (*ordinatione sacra*) and radically calls for (*postulat*) a juridical mission. If this were not the case, Pius IX could not have written the way he did to the German bishops in 1875.[112] And:

> ...Pius XI in *Rerum Ecclesiae* and Pius XII in *Fidei donum* could not have referred to the obligation on the part of the bishops in the work of evangelization. Aside from the matter of authority it is not only a question of concern [*sollicitudinis*] but also of responsibility....[113]

As the debate during the Preparatory Session continued, the creeping centralism exhibited by the draft was successively criticized by Cardinals König, Döpfner, Bea and Lienart, to mention only a few.[114] Cardinal Browne's attitude seems to have been fairly representative of those who favored chapter IV of *AU*-a as it stood. His remarks seemed directed against the line of reasoning that had been developing:

> As for Chap. IV, par. 3: Likewise I note that all Bishops ought to have responsibility and concern for the whole Church but I do not see what the jurisdiction of the College of Bishops could consist in even under the Roman Pontiff, outside an ecumenical Council.[115]

The opening lines of this quotation indicate that Browne was unwilling to go beyond what Pius XII had explicitly maintained in *FD* (Text B); his remark in the latter part of this sentence was to find at least ideological continuity in number 4 of the *Nota explicativa praevia* to which we shall turn our attention below. (With that *Nota* the defenders of an exaggerated papal centralism were to attempt to curtail the "new" concept as it had evolved in the Council.) In this context, the words of Giovanni Battista Cardinal Montini, the future Paul VI, are significant. Montini said he was not entirely happy with chapter IV (*placet iuxta modum*) and that account should be taken of the remarks made by Cardinals Richaud, König, Döpfner, Bea and Patriarch Maximos IV.[116] Montini then added:

> Let there be an exact and orderly doctrine on the episcopacy in one draft which hangs together better and which is complete. The Council cannot be silent about this matter, for the expectation of the whole Catholic Church and of the dissident brethren has its attention on this argument especially.
> Let neither this gathering be ashamed nor the Council tomorrow be afraid to treat this doctrine which integrates and crowns that of the primacy and pontifical infallibility defined by the First Vatican Council....
> Finally, it seems to me that Cardinal Confalioneri's wish possesses great authority....[117]

A review of the speeches of each one named by Montini would suffice to show that he was clearly on the side of those who wished to correct the one-sided emphasis of Vatican I. Indeed, Maximos IV's critique of chapter IV, to which Montini approvingly alluded, is the most scathing criticism of exaggerated papal centralism which I have ever seen written by a Catholic;[118] but it is too long to reproduce here. And Cardinal Confalioneri was one of those relatively few Italian Cardinals who were in favor of the "new" concept, maintaining that the jurisdiction that a bishop has is the result of ordination (hence, by implication, Confalioneri was saying that it was not from the Pope); only the application to a particular diocese depended on the Roman Bishop.[119] It should be noted that in referring to Richaud, Montini was implicitly endorsing the former's line of argument that had been based on the internal logic of Pius XII's statement in *Fidei donum* (Text B). (It may be noted in passing that Cardinal Siri, who was later to become the implacable foe of the concept of collegiality as it evolved concretely during the Council, manifested at this point some sympathy for the idea.[120])

My purpose here however is an analysis not of the critiques given by various members of the Commission but of the increasing frequency with which the line of argument pursued by Richaud—with explicit reference to *Fidei donum* (Text B)—was used. When the draft came to a vote, at least twenty-two out of sixty-two explicitly referred to it.[121] Unfortunately, these criticisms did not produce the desired changes. The following draft (*A U*-b) not only retained the offensive phrase "...nonnisi modo extraordinario...exercetur..." but seemed, as we shall see, deliberately to exaggerate it.[122]

Critique By The Council In Session

The modifications made in the subsequent text (*A U*-b) were only slight. The amended text read as follows:

> *Text G.* The College of Bishops, which succeeds the College of the Apostles in teaching and pastoral government, nay, in which the College of the Apostles continues without interruption and in which it constantly bears witness to the mission of Jesus Christ as well as to his teaching and laws, together with its head and never without its head, is believed to be one subject having full and supreme power over the whole Church. Nevertheless, the power of this college, although ordinary as inherent in the office, is legitimately exercised only in an extraordinary way and in devoted submission to the Vicar of Jesus Christ on earth when, how and for as long as in the Lord it seems expedient to the same [Vicar of Christ].[123]

Instead of incorporating the suggestions of Richaud and others who had followed his lead, the authors of this section of the new draft, almost certainly at the direction of Ottaviani, seem to have taken a hardened position. They also seemed to have emphasized those very nuances which the so-called progressives found so objectionable. The offending phrase "...nonnisi modo extraordinario...exercetur..." is not only repeated but the adverb *legitime* is added. The *ad nutum exclusivum* of Text F is removed but the concept behind it is repeated even more strongly: The College does not exercise its power qua college except when, how, and for as long as it seems expedient to the Pope. The sentence following immediately upon both Texts F and G suggests that only residential bishops (q.v.) belong to the College.

What was at issue was an exaggerated papal centralism resulting in a diminished concept of the episcopacy, a one-sided orientation that Karl Rahner, Joseph Ratzinger and others had already attempted to redress.[124] Having its roots in the Ultramontane movement prior to Vatican I and on the increase since 1870, this perspective was not to prevail. And in the corrective process under way at Vatican II, a minor but significant factor in the development was certain statements by the ordinary papal magisterium, particularly of Pius XII in *Fidei donum* (Text B), with which among the various pontifical statements I am principally concerned here.

One must however be careful of the manner in which one assesses the data. A distinction must be made between what the Pope had stated explicitly on the one hand and the internal logic of his position on the other. In regard to the former, Pius XII in *Fidei donum* cannot be said to have espoused the evolved concept of collegiality that the promulgated *Lumen gentium* (*LG*-c) in numbers 21 and 22 was to embrace. For Pius to have done so would have required (1) his interpreting the *sollicitudo omnium ecclesiarum* of the bishops as involving episcopal jurisdiction over the whole Catholic Church and not merely (2) jurisdiction of an individual bishop over his diocese along with (3) a necessary willingness to further, as best as the individual bishop can, the global mission of the Catholic Church. Pius explicitly taught (2) and (3); it would be stretching the evidence to say he explicitly taught (1). Yet, though the quotation from Bolgeni as cited by the future Gregory XVI was known,[125] those Council Fathers who in subsequent conciliar debate tended to interpret *FD* (Texts A and B) as affirming no more than (2) and (3) were undoubtedly correct only if the matter may be said to have ended with what Pius XII had explicitly stated. But the internal logic of what the Pope had taught was something else again.

It is in this wider context that the analyses of Richaud, Léger, and Montini must be considered entirely valid.[126] Recall that the key concept in *FD* was that the bishop is *sponsor* (along with the other bishops) of the apostolic task (*muneris*) of the Church; that the obligation is not merely from ecclesiastical law but from divine ordinance and precept. In an analysis more penetrating than that presented some months earlier in the Preparatory Commission, Cardinal Richaud argued during the first session that from the moment of his consecration a bishop has a radical power of governing the Mystical Body in union with the other bishops and in submission to the Sovereign Pontiff.[127] It is true, he said, that no one can be accepted into the college without the at least implicit consent of the successor of Peter.[128] But once the assent is given, beyond the jurisdiction over his own diocese some general jurisdiction for the good of the Church is given by the very fact of consecration. This general jurisdiction precedes particular jurisdiction (i.e., over a diocese) and is considered as the source of episcopal power.[129] Otherwise (here Richaud appealed again to the internal logic of *FD*), bishops cannot be said to have any responsibility— the connotation suggested by the word *sponsor*—as Pius XII "...had solemnly declared to be the case in *Fidei donum*, after the manner of other pontifical documents."[130]

Consequences Of Critique

It was this turn to the internal logic of papal teaching, particularly as discernible in the position of Pius XII, that constituted an important factor in development. Richaud's remarks here had to do with the concept of collegiality as expressed in *AU*-b. As a result of criticism by him and others, the offending phrase "...nonnisi modo extraordinario...exercetur..." was removed from the subsequent draft on the Church, *LG*-a. The concept of collegiality as found in number 16 of the new document was to prove to be basically satisfactory:

> *Text H.*   Just as in the Gospel, by the Lord's decree, Saint Peter and the other apostles constituted an apostolic college, in the same way Peter's successor, the Roman Pontiff, and the bishops, as successors of the Apostles, are joined together.
>
> The Roman Pontiff has in the Church by himself [*per se*] full and universal power; however, the College of Bishops, which succeeds the college of the apostles in teaching and pastoral government, nay, in which the apostolic body continues without interruption, together with its head and never without its head, is believed to be an undivided subject having full and supreme power over the whole Church.[131]

It seemed that the essential battle had been won. Nevertheless, sustained attention continued to be given to Texts A and B. A diminishing minority tended to use *FD* as confirming indeed a necessary *sollicitudo omnium ecclesiarum* on the part of the bishops but as excluding anything like jurisdiction over the Church universal;[132] they appealed to *FD*'s explicit statements. Others, a minority too but a growing one, tended to see in *FD* the confirmation of the kind of collegiality affirmed in Text H.[133] Cardinal Léger, Archbishop at Montreal, in the Preparatory Period had favored the concept as it was to evolve in the Council, but at that time he did not— though he was sympathetic to Richaud's reasoning—argue from the teaching of Pius XII. However, he now expressed the hope that reference to that encyclical would not be limited simply to the critical apparatus. The draft on the bishops had an exceptional importance in the Constitution on the Church, for it was a doctrinal question that in the current circumstances seemed decisive for the strong and stable renewal of the Church's pastoral activity.[134] He was happy about what the draft said concerning the sacramentality of the episcopacy.[135] He then took up the specific matter of collegiality. His third observation is directly relevant to my analysis:

> Finally, and always in the context of collegiality, I would like to propose that the task of the bishops as it relates to the universal Church be expressed more accurately. On page 28, line 15, the draft [*LG-a*] defines this task by saying that the bishops "as a result of their office" must have "concern" for the whole Church. I would wish that the draft not only in note 39 but in the very text itself recall the stronger and profound words of Pope Pius XII used in his encyclical *Fidei donum*, at least in regard to their meaning. In this document the individual bishop is presented as *sponsor* of the whole Church along with the other bishops.[136]

Léger's remark had to do with number 17 of *LG*-a of which the relevant part may be translated as follows:

> *Text I.* But as a member of the sacred College he [i.e., the individual bishop] by reason of his office is bound to have for the whole Church that care which, though not an act of jurisdiction, is however conducive to the advantage of the whole Church.[137]

The following draft reflected this suggestion of Léger and others when it inserted such phrases as "ex Christi institutione et praecepto."[138] While the report indicated that the intent behind the change was none other than to incorporate into the text the perspective to be found in *FD*,[139] the authors of *LG*-b did not use the very wording of the encyclical; the term *sponsor* does not occur in the text. Nonetheless, it is clear that the trend begun largely by Richaud as early as the Preparatory Period had caught on and that it is reflected in the promulgated text:

> *Text J.* Just as, by the Lord's will, St. Peter and the other apostles

constituted one apostolic college, so in a similar way the Roman
Pontiff as the successor of Peter, and the bishops as the successors of the apostles are joined together.[140]

Text K.   Together with its head, the Roman Pontiff, and never without
this head, the episcopal order is the subject of supreme and full
power over the universal Church.[141]

Text L.   This sacred Synod teaches that by episcopal consecration is
conferred the fullness of the sacrament of orders...But episcopal
consecration, together with the office of sanctifying also confers
the offices [*munera*] of teaching and of governing.[142]

Texts J and K are part of number 22 and in the Latin text are separated
by five sentences the omission of which here in no way affects the meaning
of Texts J and K.[143] The two sentences that constitute Text L form part of
number 21, in the Latin text are to be found in the same paragraph, and are
contiguous.[144] Nowhere in these texts, indeed nowhere in the promulgated
Lumen gentium (*LG*-c) does the phrase "...nonnisi modo extraordinario...exercetur..." occur nor does its equivalent in the context of collegiality. Beyond all doubt, the vast majority of the Council Fathers, as is
evident in Text K, embraced collegiality as a doctrine.

At this point, an unfortunate event occurred. In a moment of weakness,
Paul VI, who in the Preparatory Period was, as we have seen, clearly on the
side of the progressives, seems to have allowed himself to be pressured into
approving the so-called *Nota explicativa praevia* to which I referred above.
I shall limit myself here to number 4 of the same, which stated in part:

Text M.   While the College always exists, it does not for that reason
permanently operate through *strictly* collegial action, as the
tradition of the Church shows. In other words, it is not always
"in full act"; indeed, it operates through collegial actions only at
intervals and only *with the consent of its head*.[145]

Text N.   In every instance, it is clear that the union of the bishops with
their head is contemplated, and never any action of the bishops
taken independently of the Pope.[146]

The intent behind Text N seems to have been to ward off the spectre of
conciliarism. If that be the case, then as far as I am concerned, there need
be no further comment from an authentic Catholic point of view.[147] The
problem as I see it has to do with Text M, which in the Latin text is to be

found three sentences before Text N. Though the term *ecumenical council* does not occur, the phrase *only at intervals* may be an indirect allusion to it. For the sense of Text M seems to be that bishops dispersed throughout the world are not actually a college. In the Neo-Thomist terms used above, the College would be said to exist *in actu primo*, not *in actu secundo*, unless the Pope called it into action.[148]

Two questions must be distinguished: (A) *Is the episcopal order, together with its head, the Roman Pontiff and never without this head, the subject of full power over the universal Church?* and (B) *When is this power operative?* The Council Fathers answered Question (A) affirmatively (Text K); but in approving the change from "...collegialem nexum servantes..."[149] of *LG*-b to "....communionis nexum inter se et cum Successore Petri servantes..."[150] of *LG*-c they refused to take a position on whether the exercise of the ordinary universal magisterium (including, therefore, the situation where the majority of bishops teach authentically a doctrine pertaining to faith or morals as the one which is to be held definitively by the whole Church) constitutes an act of collegiality. They were thus less than fully coherent in their answer to Question (B). The *Nota explicativa praevia* however goes a step further, for the phrase "nonnisi per intervalla..."[151] and "...nonnisi consentiente Capite..."[152] suggests that collegiality is non-operative (which is not to say non-existent) except in the equivalent of a general council. Given the statement in the *Nota* and its timing (the eve of the final vote, thus preventing the majority from having the chance to organize themselves) it is difficult to escape the impression that the majority of the Council Fathers had been outmaneuvered by powerful members of the Roman Curia.[153]

There are fundamentally two ways of viewing the matter: If one looks primarily at the *Nota explicativa praevia*, then there is a sense in which the notorious phrase "...nonnisi modo extraordinario...exercetur..." of Texts F and G lingers on, though not explicitly stated in those words; it has been transformed into "...nonnisi per intervalla actu stricte collegiali agit et nonnisi consentiente Capite";[154] if one looks at the promulgated *LG*-c as over against the *Nota* (which is *not* part of the text but which forms part of the *Acta* of the Council), then the perspective presented by the Theological Commission in May and November of 1962 (Texts F and G) was completely overturned. In any case, from a Catholic point of view and for the reason suggested above, number 4 of the *Nota* (Text M) probably cannot stand the test of long-term Catholic scrutiny; it is only a question of time before it becomes purely a matter of history. For the essential point has been made: Bishops united with the Roman Bishop constitute a college in the true sense of the word even when dispersed throughout the world and together *with* (but not *from*) him have full power over the Churches. The *munus regendi* does not come from the Pope; it comes from being incorporated into a college that, with the Roman Bishop at its head, succeeds to certain functions of the apostles of whom Peter was the head.[155] Though the term does not occur in numbers 21 and 22 of *LG*-c as applied to collegiality, it is clearly a question of jurisdiction, as is evident from Text L. Finally, the *Nota explicativa praevia* notwithstanding, the doctrine of collegiality as found in the promulgated *Lumen gentium* (*LG*-c) seems at least *fidei proximum* (q.v.) and could be defined by the Roman Bishop at any time.

However that may be, in light of the development culminating in Text K, it would be misleading to suggest that most of the bishops who espoused the "new" concept as it evolved in the Council explicitly appealed to the teaching of Pius XII in this regard. But no amount of counter-appealing to alleged papal teaching in *Mystici corporis* was to win out as evidence against it. The Popes as distinct from their curial aids had long been on the side of collegiality as far as the theory of their authority was concerned, a lesson learned, perhaps, from the Council of Constance and its aftermath.[156] In the process of clarifying Catholic doctrine during the Second Vatican Council there can be no doubt that the teaching of Pius XII in *Fidei donum* had been a highly significant influence, a fact that, in a totally unexpected way, is further evidence of the overall positive modalities whereby the teaching of the ordinary papal magisterium had been received during this period.

Overview

Evidence for positive modalities of reception has been approached from two different angles. There was first the broad basis provided by *Sancta Vaticana Synodus* and *Deus Infinite Bonus*. Second, sharper focus centered on two particular issues, papal teaching as it related to Catholic doctrine on the social question and the concept of collegiality. Papal teaching in both instances was reflected in the promulgated conciliar documents, the difference between the two being that in the former case papal social teaching prior to the Council was merely repeated in the relevant sections of *Gaudium et spes*, whereas in the latter case the teaching of Pius XII in *Fidei donum* seems to have been conducive to a "new" emphasis in Catholicism. That is to say: The evidence suggests that the concept of collegiality as found in *Lumen gentium* (*LG*-c) might have had more difficulty in gaining acceptance had it not been shown that the internal logic of the Pope's teaching pointed in the direction that the Council ultimately took. *Sancta Vaticana Synodus* and *Deus Infinite Bonus* having served their purpose, I shall not refer to them again except in passing. Of the issues discussed above, only (1) papal social teaching and (2) the teaching of Pius XII in *Fidei donum* relative to collegiality constitute two of the seven issues around which this study is oriented inasmuch as it has to do with doctrine. In order of treatment, the remaining doctrinal issues are (3) Catholicism and non-Christian religions, (4) the Church-state and (5) religious freedom issues, (6) the Church and (7) her members.

To this general survey there are of course an indefinite number of other instances that might be adduced as illustrative of the central argument stated at the beginning of this chapter. One thinks for example of *Pascendi* whereby in 1907 Pius X condemned modernism, the synthesis, as he called it, of all heresies. Despite the fact that by hindsight it seems the Pope overreacted; despite the fact that the atmosphere that followed upon *Pascendi* seems to have somewhat inhibited Catholic scholarship for at least a generation, many Catholics today would admit that the Pope's action probably saved the Catholic Church from a number of unsound positions relating particularly to the theology of revelation and Christology. Though there was some resentment, especially in France, the modalities whereby *Pascendi* was received within Catholicism were on the whole positive. Indeed, some would be prepared to argue that, inasmuch as modernism had to do with scriptural exegesis, obedience by Catholics bore fruit some thirty-six years later when Pius XII promulgated *Divino afflante Spiritu* and thereby revolutionized Catholic exegesis. The ship's log, inasmuch as it reflects the captain's performance, is not only instructive; it is also impressive, given the troubled waters through which the ship had sailed. Positive reception of papal teaching during this period needs no further documentation. Any lingering doubt will be fully dissipated by a reading of Lucien Choupin's *Valeur des Décisions doctrinales et disciplinaires du Saint-Siège*, to which we shall return in part two.

And yet, the discerning student of history senses that things are more complex; that though there is a level of theological discourse in which the old adage *Roma locuta est, causa finita est* will always apply for the authentic Catholic, there are still other levels in which automatic and unquestioning acceptance of doctrinal pronouncements by the Roman Bishop can not only be inappropriate but at the deepest level mask a consummate infidelity. The ship's log contains matters other than the beneficent results of the captain's decisions stretching back over the past 119 years. These data we must now scrutinize, allowing the results of our inquiry to lead us where they will.

PART TWO
"BUT WHEN CEPHAS CAME TO ANTIOCH..." (GAL. 2:11)

Chapter II
CATHOLICISM AND NON-CHRISTIAN RELIGIONS

In *Evangelii praecones*, Pius XII stated that though human nature is tainted with original sin it nonetheless has in itself something that is naturally Christian, an indirect reference to Tertullian's *Apology*.[1] The Pope further said that this "something," if illumined by divine light and nourished by grace, can eventually be changed into true and supernatural virtue.[2] Indeed, insistence on unity-in-diversity of cultures that builds up the "something naturally Christian" was so frequent in Pius XII's writings and speeches that it may well constitute a principal theme in a Petrine ministry the positive features of which have yet to be evaluated.[3] Thus *The Declaration on the Relationship of the Church to Non-Christian Religions* (*Nostra aetate*), which exhibits a similar outlook, seems at first sight to suggest that the teaching of the Second Vatican Council on truth and good in non-Christian religions is in continuity with that of the ordinary papal magisterium; for, as we shall see, the thinking of Pius XII in this regard seems to have embraced not only individuals but also non-Christian religions as such.

Yet matters are not so simple. While the condemnation in number 16 of the Syllabus might upon superficial examination indicate that all Pius IX wished to reprove was religious indifferentism, a careful reading of the pertinent documents uncovers a clearly taken doctrinal stance exactly contrary to that of the Second Vatican Council. For in *Qui pluribus* of November 9, 1846, Pius IX seems to have denied in principle any truth or good in non-Christian religions. In order to discern the context of the discussion more clearly, at least four questions should be carefully distinguished at the outset:

(A)   Is there any truth or good in non-Christian religions?

(B)   What is the source of that truth or good?

(C)   Is that truth or good salvific?

(D)   If the answers to (A) and (C) are affirmative, what happens to the axiom *extra Ecclesiam nulla salus*?

It should be noted that Question (A) has to do not simply with truth or good in non-Christian cultures and/or solid traits of character among a given people, but with truth or good in non-Christian religions as such. Indeed, that distinction constitutes the central point of my inquiry in this chapter. I shall advance the following argument:

I.   *The internal logic of Text A as quoted below from* Qui pluribus *of November 9, 1846 suggests that Pius IX would have been logically constrained to answer Question (A) negatively.*

II.   *At least from the time of* Quanta cura *(1864) to the late twenties or thirties of this century the cumulative evidence indicates that reception of the doctrinal stance discernible in Text A was almost with no exceptions essentially positive.*

III.   *Favorable reception seems further confirmed by the fact that Pius IX's outlook as discernible in Text A seems to have been reflected in subsequent papal documents up to but excluding the Petrine ministry of Pius XII.*

IV.   *Vatican II reversed standard papal teaching as found in Text A in that the Council reaffirmed ancient Catholic positive tradition.*

V.   *The path to reversal and the reaffirmation of ancient Catholic positive tradition seems to have been cleared first by the work of missiologists, then by the teaching of Pius XII, and subsequently by the bishops in conciliar debate.*

This chapter is divided into six sections, the first five of which run parallel to the first five parts of my argument as stated above, the sixth being an overview. Though I shall touch upon the concerns reflected in Questions (C) and (D), I will focus attention principally on Questions (A) and (B).

Two words of caution before proceeding further. First, as a sequel to the Declaration on non-Christian Religions (*Nostra aetate*) and to some extent while that document was in preparation, research into the relation between Christianity and non-Christian religions intensified.[4] But the interest among Catholics was not always as sharp as in the decades immediately preceding the Council. The temptation to read back into the data and to make the Roman Bishops affirm what in fact they denied or were not explicitly aware of is something that must be avoided at all costs. Second, as stated above, I shall argue below that Pius IX would have been logically constrained to answer Question (A) negatively. But that does not mean he thought non-Christians could not be saved; it means he thought they could not be saved through a non-Catholic religion. For implicit in *Quanto conficiamur moerore* of August 10, 1863 is the admission that divine grace operates outside the boundaries of the Catholic Church.[5] Thus the thinking of this Pope contains an unresolved tension between two polarities, a point that should not be forgotten in what follows.[6]

The Teaching Of Pius IX

In number 16 of the Syllabus, Pius IX condemned the proposition that *in the practice of any religion at all human beings can find the way to and attain eternal salvation.*[7] At first blush, it seems that determining the contradictory of the condemned proposition would suffice in order to understand what the Pope was trying to get at. Yet despite Dupanloup's suggestion, such a method is insufficient in the case of the Syllabus.[8] The bishops—or anyone else who deals with it—were and are expected to read the documents listed under each condemned proposition in order to grasp precisely what was being affirmed and what was being reproved. In the

present case, the relevant documents are the encyclical *Qui pluribus* of
November 9, 1846, the allocution *Ubi primum* of December 17, 1847, and
the encyclical *Singulari quidem* of March 17, 1856 (not to be confused with
the allocution *Singulari quadam* of December 9, 1854).

Qui pluribus, addressed to the world-wide Catholic hierarchy, is about
five thousand words long and in the Bonarum Artium edition comprises
twenty-one pages.[9] The Pope begins by saying that several years ago he had
been like his brother bishops himself a bishop tending his flock when the
papacy in the inscrutable design of Providence was unexpectedly thrust
upon him.[10] If this ministry had always been fraught with danger, it was all
the more so now in these perilous times. God however chooses the weak
both to show his power and to demonstrate that it is God who rules the
Church. Nothing would please the new Pope more than to be able to speak
to the bishops; for that reason, the present letter was being sent without
delay. His brother bishops constituted no small consolation in his new
task. One notes in these opening pages an additional unresolved tension,
that between the Petrine function and the episcopacy.[11]

Pius then points out the difficulties through which the Church of Christ
is passing. There seems to be a plot *contra catholicam rem universam*
according to which the Catholic Church is presented as being founded
upon a lie and as opposed to the good of society.[12] Since those involved in
this plot extol human reason, the Pope goes on to show that faith is not
opposed to reason but is above it; indeed they have the same source. A
right use of reason grounds faith while faith preserves reason from the
errors to which reason is prone.[13] The enemies of the Church pit reason
against her as though Catholic religion were the work of a human being
and not of God. The Pope then outlines a fundamental theology. Paradoxically, he insists reason must examine the Catholic claim carefully, for a
responsible use of reason affirms that the Catholic religion has its foundation not in human reason but in God's action perceived in the life, death,
and resurrection of Jesus;[14] in the fulfillment of the prophecies that
announced His coming; in the miracles He wrought; in the constancy of the
martyrs; in the holiness of the saints; in the survival of the Church through
persecution in every century, with no other weapon but the Cross.[15] This
was the old eighteenth-century apologetic that Nietzsche was to attack
violently some thirty-five years later in *Morgenröthe*. However inadequate
such an apologetic may be from the standpoint of modern scholarship, it
was sufficient for the Pope to say in his first encyclical that divine revelation, which a right use of reason grounds as credible, is infallibly preserved
from error through the exercise of the Petrine ministry within Catholicism.

Hence, the faithful should be warned not to be taken in by the errors of the day.

There are other monstrous errors, Pius continues, by which the world seeks to do battle against the Catholic religion, its divinely established authority and its laws, trampling under foot the rights of both Church and state. Such is the purpose (*huc spectat*) of plots against the Holy See;[16] such the purpose of secret societies; such that of so-called Bible groups that circulate inaccurate translations of the scriptures interpreted according to private judgment. It is at this point that the Pope states:

> *Text A*. This is the purpose [*huc spectat*] of that dreadful system of religious indifference repugnant even to natural reason itself; with the blurring over [*sublato*] of every distinction between virtue and vice, between truth and falsehood, and between goodness and filth, these crafty people pretend that human beings may be saved by practicing any religion, *as if there could ever be any participation of justice with iniquity, any mixing* [societas] *of light and darkness, and any agreement* [conventio] *of Christ with Belial*.[17]

This last phrase is a quotation of 2 Cor. 6:14-15. A clear distinction must be made between (1) the scriptural passage and (2) its use by the Pope. As to the latter, Text A is the specific context in which 2 Cor. 6:14-15 occurs; *Qui pluribus* is its general context; and *Qui pluribus* itself is but one of the three *loci* which the Pope asked the rest of the Catholic Church to read in order to understand his intent in condemning number 16 of the Syllabus. As to the former, the larger context (2 Cor. 6:14-7:1) in which the cited passage occurs may be a fragment from a lost Pauline letter (e.g., that mentioned in 1 Cor. 5:9-11) and inserted here. More probably 2 Cor. 6:14-15 is a non-Pauline interpolation.

Whatever the case may be, at least two matters are clear. First, the Pope does not employ 2 Cor. 6:14-15 to characterize relations between Catholicism and other Christian churches (though perhaps some Protestant groups may be what he had in mind when just previously he referred to so-called Bible groups) but to reject a specific kind of religious indifference. Second, the tension between Christianity and non-Christian religions is not the creation of the papacy but has an initially plausible but ultimately unfounded basis in the New Testament. For Paul is portrayed in Acts 17:23 as attempting to establish a rapport with the Athenians on the basis of an altar dedicated to an unknown god. Be that as it may, the fact that the offending phrase in Text A is a quotation of 2 Cor. 6:14-15 suggests that Catholic tradition in this regard is not all of a piece. That is to

say: Alongside and perhaps even anterior to the notion of possible truth or
good in non-Christian religions as propaedeutic to the Gospel, there
existed a contrary view. It is thus possible to isolate two viewpoints, both
ancient, the one being negative, the other positive. Pius IX's perspective
seems to have been along the lines of the former; Vatican II was to reaffirm
the latter.

To continue with the Pope's analysis—the battle against the Church was
the purpose of other evils described in some detail: opposition to priestly
celibacy,[18] erroneous orientation in philosophy courses which deceive a
younger generation unable to sift truth from error; the rise of communism;
the proliferation of unwholesome reading material and an indiscriminate
(*effrenata*) freedom (*licentia*) of thought, of speech, and of the press;
disdain of the Christian religion; infringement on the rights of bishops,[19]
and assaults on the holiness of the married state.[20] Having sounded the call
to battle, the new Pope pledges himself to do all in his power, telling the
bishops to stand firm in the faith, united with the Catholic Church, *outside
of which there is no salvation.*[21] These bishops are to expose the errors of
the day, bidding the faithful above all to keep clear of secret societies. Let
the bishops never grow weary of preaching the gospel, combining with that
a certain gentleness in dealing with those who have strayed from the
straight path. The bishops are to seek the things which build up love
(*caritas*) and peace, instilling in the people respect and obedience due to a
legitimate state. In all this a well trained and highly disciplined clergy is
essential, a theme on which the Pope dwells at great length. The bishops
should go forward cheerfully and confidently, ready to lay down their lives
if necessary. The Pope hopes that heads of state will recall that their power
is given them not only for the sake of an earthly kingdom but also for the
protection of the Church.

The Pope's language is often florid and highly emotional in tone. His
treatment is not systematic; he merely lists the evils of his day without
attempting to show how they are logically interconnected. Thus religious
indifferentism is merely one of many errors that the Pope sees as part of the
world in which the Church of Christ is incarnate. Some of them may have
been exaggerated—the exact extent of a Masonic plot, which Leo XIII
himself seems to have considered worldwide, is difficult to document.[22] An
assessment of the Pope's accuracy in diagnosing ills and prescribing reme-
dies is not however my purpose. It is sufficient to note here that in terms of
the whole document, the statement made in Text A seems to have been
made parenthetically.

The next document listed as illustrative of the Pope's meaning in condemning number 16 is *Ubi primum* of December 17, 1847, a private address (*allocutio*) given to the Cardinals in consistory and later communicated to the other bishops. It is brief (about two thousand words and in the Bonarum Artium edition comprising eight pages) and somewhat rambling, reflecting as explicitly stated near the end of the discourse those concerns uppermost in the Pope's mind on that particular day. He first discusses the state of the Church in Spain and Portugal, especially the appointment of suitable bishops.[23] He then comments on a recently published book written by an ecclesiastic who maintained therein that the ecclesiastical positions in the latter's country (*regiminis*) could be had for a price. Pius takes the occasion to say that he will never deviate from the policies of his forebears (*majorum*) nor from defending the rights of the Holy See. His attention then takes a different turn, focusing on the question of indifferentism. He then complains that because of changes he had introduced in the governance of the papal states, some had misconstrued his mind, saying that:

> *Text B.* ...we have such feelings of benevolence toward the whole human race that not only the sons of the Church but also *others who remain estranged from Catholic unity as individuals are equally on the way to salvation and that we think they can be saved.*[24]

Pius states that he does indeed love all human beings but that he loves them with the love of Christ. Let those who wish to be saved come to the column and foundation of truth that is the Catholic Church. Pius will do all in his power to bring this about but—and here he becomes somewhat oratorical—all should bear in mind that heaven and earth will pass away before he will permit any change in the teaching of Christ or in the doctrine entrusted to the Church.[25] He then changes the subject, complaining of lack of sensitivity—in the city of Rome itself—to recent events in Switzerland and consequent harm to the Catholic cause. But the difficulties through which the Church was passing were offset by the success of the missionary effort.[26]

Singulari quidem of March 17, 1856, is about 5,300 words long and in the Bonarum Artium edition comprises twenty-one pages.[27] Addressed to the Austrian hierarchy who had been organizing a forthcoming episcopal conference to be held at Vienna, the Pope takes the occasion to express his concern. The region that would be touched by its decisions was vast.

Hence, if the bishops had any difficulty, they should (in terms of the concordat [*Conventionis*] between the Church and the Emperor) consult the Holy See.

Pius' remarks may be considered under two general categories: (1) discussion of two general evils affecting the Church as a whole and (2) practical orientation that the decrees of the forthcoming episcopal conference should take. The latter—reformation and education of the clergy, the education of youth, evangelization of the people through missions, ongoing formation of the clergy, efficiency of pastors on the local scene—do not concern us here. The former, the *maux du siècle* to which the Pope directs the bishop's attention, are indifferentism and rationalism. It is from these two sources that other difficulties besetting the Church take their origin.[28]

As to rationalism, the Catholic Church does not impugn true learning—on the contrary (!), wrote the Pope. What the Church condemns is that abuse of reason that pits itself against the authority of God. Against this prevalent tendency the Pope advances several arguments that purport to show as in *Qui pluribus* that not only do faith and reason not contradict, rather do they complement each other. This part of the Pope's discussion closes with an insightful statement on the development (*profectus*) of Christian doctrine, a point frequently overlooked by his critics.[29]

As to indifferentism, the Pope first distinguishes a general kind of indifferentism which affects the common good both of Church and state; from this flows neglect of one's duty toward God and the commonwealth. At this point he states:

> *Text C.* From which obviously sordid form of *indifferentism* is by no means far removed that system of religious *indifference* born [*eruptum*] of darkness. According to this, human beings, having become estranged from truth, hostile to true profession [of faith], forgetful of their salvation, teaching opposing positions and having no unshaken opinion of anything, admit *no difference between various professions of faith, are at peace with whomever they meet, and defend the position that the port which leads to eternal life is open to all, no matter what one's religion.*[30]

The Pope then insists that there is only one revealed truth, one divine faith that is the beginning of salvation, the foundation of all justification, a faith by which the just man lives and without which it is impossible to please God.[31] And there is, he says, only one holy, Catholic, apostolic and Roman Church founded upon Peter "...outside of which neither true faith nor eternal salvation is to be found."[32] In an obvious reference to Jewish temple worship, the Pope said that whoever eats lamb outside this house does so as one outside the temple (*profanus*); if anyone is not in Noah's Ark, he or she will perish at the height of the flood (*regnante diluvio*).[33] The Pope is careful to say, as he does later in the same letter, that all this is true "...*citra invincibilis ignorantiae excusationem*...."[34]

Text C seems concerned with religious indifferentism but in the more narrow sense of inter-Christian relations; Text B is logically applicable to the negation of truth or good not only in non-Catholic Christian but also in non-Christian religions; Text A is directly relevant only to the latter. Thus an examination of the documents listed in the Syllabus as illustrative of the meaning behind the condemned proposition 16 leads to the conclusion that in regard to truth or good in non-Christian religions, it is Text A that constitutes the primary text of reference. It is around the history and fate of that text, including its prima facie and ultimate modalities of reception, that my remarks will henceforth be primarily centered.

Before proceeding further, however, Text A should be situated within a wider frame of reference. In the three documents we have examined, it is possible to discern a constant as contrasted with variables. In *Qui pluribus*, the fundamental bulwark against the errors of the day is the Catholic Church, outside of which, the Pope affirms, there is no salvation. In *Ubi primum*, those who wish to be saved are to come to the column and foundation of truth, which is the same institution. In *Singulari quidem*, the Pope stated that there is only one faith by which the just man lives and there is only one Catholic and apostolic Church, the Roman Church founded upon Peter, outside of which there is neither true faith nor eternal salvation. That there is only one mediator between God and man, the man Christ Jesus, that there is only one true Church is not the variable but the constant that in turn becomes the source of the Pope's insistence on the axiom *extra Ecclesiam nulla salus*. It is the affirmation of what the Pope takes to be that truth that requires the condemnation of what he considers to be the falsehood condemned in number 16; namely, *that in the practice of any religion at all a human being can find the way to and attain eternal salvation*. And it is that constant that leads the Pope, parenthetically it is true but unabashedly, to the doctrinal slant manifest in Text A.

That he may have been unconsciously victimized by the aftermath of the Chinese Rites controversy cannot be denied; but there is no way of proving it. What seems clear from the documents is that, given the first of the unresolved tensions I have previously mentioned, the proximate cause of his outlook seems to have been a one-sided insistence on the constant isolated above. Obviously, the issue of the source of possible truth or good in non-Christian religions (Question [B]) can arise only if the answer to Question (A) (namely, is there any truth or good in non-Christian religions?) is affirmative. If the answer to Question (A) is affirmative, but that to Question (B) is anything less than *the Godhead,* then of course the answer to the question whether truth or good in non-Christian religions is salvific (Question [C]) must be negative. For if there is one thing that the whole of authentic Catholic tradition stands firm on, it is the negation of salvation by works. However, if the answer to Question (C) is *Verbum* or *Veritas* or *Logos spermatikos* or their equivalents, then an ancient Catholic positive tradition having its roots in the Johannine Prologue and blossoming in Irenaeus, Justin Martyr, Origen and Augustine is affirmed, and there is no intrinsic reason why the answer to Question (C) cannot be affirmative, with consequent modification of the axiom *extra Ecclesiam nulla salus* (Question [D]).[35] But the Pope's narrowness of vision prevented him from explicitly asking Question (A); hence, Question (B) did not arise, and Question (C) would have been meaningless. What remained was a rigid interpretation of the axiom *extra Ecclesiam nulla salus* (Question [D]). Though Pius did not always speak in such stark terms—in a context where the Latin word *infideles* does not have the negative connotations of its English cognate he sometimes simply referred to the necessity of converting the infidels[36]—his attitude toward possible truth or good in non-Christian religions can hardly be described as positive. It is true that he nowhere explicitly asks Question (A); but I submit that the internal logic of Text A as quoted from *Qui pluribus* of November 9, 1846 suggests that Pius IX would have been logically constrained to answer it negatively.

Prima Facie Modalities of Reception

Now it may be argued that since the doctrinal perspective of Text A had been taken parenthetically, it was therefore not typical of the position articulated by the ordinary papal magisterium. Comment on that hypothesis will be made below. At this point, it may be helpful to explore the modalities whereby Text A was received, a decidedly more difficult matter, for direct reference to it is comparatively rare. Negatively, in the whole period subsequent to that document's appearance, I have come upon no single author who *ex industria* challenged the Pope's teaching, although oblique criticism is sometimes, though rarely, detectable.[37] Positively, direct references that one does find seem to confirm the second part of my argument as stated above.[38]

An early reference to Text A is to be found in the *Dublin Review* (1865) wherein an unsigned article followed by both the Latin text and an English translation of *Quanta cura* and the Syllabus contained a commentary on various condemned propositions. As regards number 16 the author stated somewhat too succinctly:

> But misbelievers here denounced profess that the Hindoo can gain salvation by offering human victims and practising foul impurities no less than the Catholic by fasting and prayer; as though, well may the Pope add, "there could be any participation or any agreement of Christ with Belial." So much then on proposition XVI.[39]

It should be remarked in passing that the author's ignorance of Hinduism was almost as great as his misunderstanding of Catholic dogma as clarified by the Council of Trent; no informed Catholic claims *tout court* that salvation is attained by fasting and prayer, for in Catholic theology neither the grace of initial justification nor the grace of final perseverance can be merited. Indeed, whatever merit a justified human being may have before God is the result not of human endeavor but is and remains God's gift. More directly relevant to the point of our inquiry, however, is the fact that the author of the unsigned article in translating number 16 of the Syllabus accepted Text A of *Qui pluribus* with unquestioning approval, thus probably reflecting the teaching already current in the manuals.[40]

Positive modalities of reception find more significant confirmation in an unexpected place. I refer to *Supremi pastoris*, the first draft on the Church prepared for debate at the First Vatican Council.[41] The fifteen chapters that comprise it contain two kinds of notes, the first being scriptural, patristic, or other references at the bottom of each column; the second, entitled *Adnotationes*, to be found at the end of the draft. The latter are lengthy theological explanations of what the author intended to affirm.[42] Besides additional scriptural passages and selections from the Fathers, the *Adnotationes* make abundant use of papal documents, including those promulgated by Pius IX in the context of the Syllabus. Such was especially the case with Chap. VII, entitled *"Extra Ecclesiam salvari neminem posse."*[43] Thus the *Adnotationes* should have been a clear guide to understanding what the author, probably the Jesuit, Klemens Schrader[44] (one of the principal architects of the scholastic revival[45]), intended to present to the Council Fathers as a point of departure for debate.

The reader approaching the documents with that expectation will come away confused. For the quotation from 2 Cor. 6:14-15, which in the Latin Vulgate is the same as the quotation to be found in Text A of *Qui pluribus*, appears in two places, with two meanings rendered divergent because of their contexts. The first is to be found in the body of *Supremi pastoris* itself, the second, in the *Adnotationes*; the former without, the latter with, direct reference to the encyclical of November 9, 1846. While the first clearly but not deliberately distorts the Pope's intent, the second is similar to but not identical with it. Let me quote *Supremi pastoris*:

> *Text D.* Furthermore, it is a dogma of faith that no one outside the church can be saved....[46] That is why we reprove and abominate the impious teaching of religious indifference equally repugnant to reason itself, by which teaching people [*filii*] of this generation [*saeculi*], with the blurring over of the distinction between truth and error [*veritatis et erroris sublato discrimine*] say that from any religion at all the port of eternal life is open to all human beings ....And likewise we reprove the indifference [*impietatem*] of those who close human beings off from the kingdom of heaven[47] by stating on false pretexts that it is unbecoming or that it is by no means necessary for salvation to abandon a religion, even a false one, in which one has been born, educated and formed; and who blame the Church herself for professing herself to be the only true religion and moreover for censuring and condemning all religions and sects not in communion with her, *as if there could ever by any participation of justice with iniquity, any mixing of light and darkness, and any agreement of Christ with Belial.*[48]

Several remarks seem called for. First, in Chap. II the author had earlier paraphrased John 1:9 referring to the Word that enlightens every human being coming into this world, but did not seem to see that Text D could not encompass the wider Johannine horizon. This may have been due to the fact that he was at pains to quote approvingly statements made by the reigning Roman Pontiff. Indeed, it would be obvious to anyone who reads both documents in the Latin that several sentences in Text D are almost verbatim quotations of certain others in *Qui pluribus* which lead up to Text A. Second, but paradoxically, the use of 2 Cor. 6:14-15 is not *a pari* with that of Pius IX. In the papal statement, the parallel between light and darkness, Christ and Belial, etc., had to do with Catholicism and non-Christian religions whereas in Text D the focus is broadened, the parallel now being between Catholicism and non-Catholic religions, respectively. While the former orientation is contrary to Pius IX's in *Qui pluribus*, that in the *Adnotationes* does less violence to the Pope's thought. Therein the author states that the purpose of Chap. VII was to reprove religious indifferentism, which, with the risk of some oversimplification, may be reduced to two kinds. The first was concretized by any attitude which either in principle or in practice tended to deny the Catholic dogma that there is only one Church rooted in the Christ-event and that that Church is the Catholic Church, not the Church catholic, whatever be the defects of the former body;[49] the second rejected the notion that it matters little what religion one practices provided one lives an upright life.[50] The former kind of indifference had to do with post-Reformation polemics, the latter with the post-Enlightenment situation in which Catholicism found itself. An important transitional paragraph in the *Adnotationes* clearly differentiates between both, stating that "...from the specific indifference toward *all bodies* [societatum] *of the Christian religion* very many have fallen into a general indifference toward *all religions as such* [simpliciter]...."[51] Here the modified Cyprianic axiom is affirmed: *extra Ecclesiam nulla salus.* It is, however, in the context of the second, not the first, that the quotation from *Qui pluribus* (Text A) itself is introduced,[52] the author of the draft indicating that one of its main concerns was indifference to *dogma.* Whereas the same parallels between injustice and iniquity, light and darkness, Christ and Belial are affirmed, their usage in the *Adnotationes* is closer to the intent behind their use in the *Qui pluribus.*

Now if the Council Fathers were to find fault with *Supremi pastoris*— and they did in their written critiques, the draft not having been submitted to formal debate in the aula—it was not because they were dissatisfied with the use of 2 Cor. 6:14-15. Of the fifty-five bishops who commented on Chap. VII, not one suggested that the use of 2 Cor. 6:14-15 was contrary to the scope of John 1:9 (paraphrased, as we have seen, in Chap.II) and that therefore the possibility should be explored that some non-Christian religions might in principle contain some truth or good.[53] It was not, as I have stated, for reasons such as this that the bishops were dissatisfied. They were unhappy because, for example, the draft gave insufficient attention to the role of bishops, an issue which, like that of the relation of Catholicism to non-Christian religions, was to be faced head-on almost one hundred years later at Vatican II. What might have been the fate of Chap. VII of *Supremi pastoris* had it been subjected to full conciliar debate? Conjecture is difficult. Perhaps the Council Fathers would have noted the unresolved tension mentioned above and insisted that, if as stated in the *Adnotationes* the target of Chap. VII was indifference to dogma, then the draft should be recast accordingly and not be allowed to suggest an implicit parallel

between justice/light/Christ/Catholicism on the one hand and iniqui-
ty/darkness/Belial/non-Catholic religions on the other. In any case,
though the author's task had been merely to draw up an instrument for
conciliar debate, relevant paragraphs of his work contain both implicit
(Text D) and explicit (the *Adnotationes*) appeal to Text A. While the
former tends to betray the Pope's thought, the latter approximates it and
testifies to its favorable reception.

Further evidence of positive reception emerges some six years later,
when in explaining the condemned propositions of the Syllabus, a certain
Monsignor Maupied quoted Text A directly, using it however not in the
sense of the *Dublin Review* article but in the sense of the Text D in *Supremi
pastoris*.[54] In a chapter entitled "La Clef du Syllabus et la Restauration
sociale," Maupied drew a parallel between Christ and Belial not as applicable to Christian as distinguished from non-Christian religious values but
as applicable to Catholicism as opposed to heresy.[55] In using Text A in this
manner, the author read into it rather than out of it. For the relevant texts
applicable to non-Catholic Christians are Texts B and C. But there the
parallel of Christ versus Belial does not occur. Though there is no evidence
of direct dependence on the unpromulgated *Supremi pastoris*, Maupied's
understanding of Text A was strikingly similar. For if there is a parallel
between Christ/Catholicism and Belial/non-Catholic religions (something that Pius IX never implied), then a fortiori there is one between
Christ/Catholicism and Belial/non-Christian religions (something that
the Pope would have been logically constrained to affirm on the basis of
Text A). Thus Maupied's use of Text A, though partially inaccurate,
constitutes an additional example of favorable reception.[56]

Though as we shall see below, initial positive reception of Text A is
misleading, evidence that it increased rather than diminished in the first
decades of this century seems unmistakable, a fact that finds additional
confirmation in *L'Ami du Clergé*. Therein the authors of a book (*L'Apo-
logétique chrétienne*, by A. Moulard and F. Vincent) complained about the
way their work had been reviewed in the pages of *L'Ami*.[57] They had
maintained that in order to understand what Pius IX meant by the condemnation of a particular proposition in the Syllabus, it was necessary to
read the pontifical documents listed as illustrative of his meaning, for to
take certain propositions of the Syllabus in the raw would be to affirm a
falsehood. Try to interpret number 16 of the Syllabus in the raw, they said,
and see whether or not your interpretation does not go directly contrary to
theological teaching relative to the soul of the Church.[58]

The editors of *L'Ami* were quick to point out in an extended footnote that number 16 of the Syllabus was precisely one of the condemned propositions that needed no explanation.[59] Whether human beings belonging to a false cult can be saved is not the question. The question is: Do those saved human beings belonging to a false cult find therein the path to salvation and the possibility of attaining it? The answer, the editors said, must be negative.[60] Human beings in such a situation are saved by divine providence; the false cult in which they are involved is only an obstacle.

Moulard and Vincent were correct in maintaining that in the case of the Syllabus it is necessary to read the pontifical documents listed after each condemned proposition in order to understand the Pope's intent; on that point, the editors of *L'Ami* were unquestionably wrong. But had Moulard and Vincent followed through with an analysis of the pontifical documents, they would have discovered that the attitude of Pius IX toward truth or good in non-Christian religions was undoubtedly negative and that the Pope's attitude in this matter in no way militated against Catholic doctrine on the soul of the Church. As for the editors of *L'Ami*, had they simply said that truth or good in non-Christian religions is not salvific, they would have taken a position in consonance with Catholic doctrine as then almost universally understood, provided the source of truth or good is not simultaneously perceived as the eternal and Incarnate Word of God. But the editors did not take that position; basing themselves precisely on number 16 of the Syllabus, they affirmed that a false cult is *only* an obstacle to salvation.

Essentially the same modality of reception is to be found in Lucien Choupin's *Valeur des décisions doctrinales et disciplinaires du Saint-Siège*, but with an important difference.[61] Whereas the editors of *L'Ami* did not consider that for number 16 a reading of pontifical documents supporting it was necessary—the condemnation was said to be clear *dans son sens naturel*—Choupin was almost scrupulous in his analysis and had clearly read all the relevant documents. His work is important for the additional reason that from 1908 to the early thirties, it went through several editions, a fact that attests to its wide appeal. Of the several parts that comprise *Valeur*, only the fifth (*Commentaire du Syllabus*) interests us here, for therein Choupin commented on each of the eighty condemned propositions. About number 16 he stated:

> Without doubt, it can happen that a human being belonging to a false cult can be saved. That is not the point. But, yes or no, is that false cult the *way that leads to eternal salvation*?
>
> As long as he or she belongs to a false religion, does that human being find

therein the road to eternal salvation and the means of attaining it? Certainly not. The false cult in which the human being is involved, far from being a help, *is only an obstacle*.[62]

Now what is involved in this interpretation as well as in that just noted in *L'Ami* must be considered in all its implications. *L'Ami du Clergé* was read widely not only in France but abroad; and Choupin's book was influential well into the second generation of this century. In admitting that those outside the confines of the visible Church can be saved, the editors of *L'Ami* and Choupin in *Valeur* along with the dominant Catholic theologizing up to *Mystici corporis* had recourse to the so-called doctrine on the soul of the Church, a matter that need not detain us here.[63] At first blush, their comment seems pertinent only to whether truth and good in non-Christian religions are salvific (Question [C]), which is answered negatively. One could indeed hold that nothing in non-Christian religions is salvific without being logically constrained to say there is nothing true or good in them. But the statements by the editors of *L'Ami* and Choupin are at least indirectly relevant to whether there is any truth or good in non-Christian religions (Question [A]). For in the very context of commenting on number 16 of the Syllabus they clearly mean not simply that the non-Christian cult—and they mean *any* non-Christian cult—is false; they also affirm that it is *only an obstacle* to salvation. And that is tantamount to answering Question (A) negatively while simultaneously testifying to the positive manner in which they had received the Pope's teaching as found in *Qui pluribus* of November 9, 1846. Though in part three of his work Choupin had admitted that the theological note given to *Quanta cura* and the Syllabus was not *de fide* (q.v.),[64] nonetheless, like that of the editors of *L'Ami* to whom he refers, his attitude and manner of receiving the Pope's teaching was unquestioning.

Choupin's book along with *L'Ami du Clergé* was widely read—it is necessary to draw attention once again to the fact.[65] At least from the time of *Quanta cura* (1864) to the late twenties or early thirties of this century, the cumulative evidence indicates that reception of the doctrinal stance discernible in Text A was with almost no exceptions essentially positive.[66] It was essentially positive in that on the one hand no bona fide Catholic seems explicitly to have subjected it to serious criticism and that on the other those who did explicitly refer to it seem to have acquiesced in the Pope's pejorative view.

The Papal Magisterium Prior to Pius XII

Favorable reception seems further confirmed by the fact that Pius IX's outlook as discernible in Text A seems to have been reflected in subsequent papal statements up to but excluding the Petrine ministry of Pius XII. There is, however, an apparent exception, that to be found in the *Monita ad Missionarios* published by the former Sacred Congregation for the Propagation of the Faith. I shall deal first with the official papal documents.

THE ENCYCLICALS

That there is in the documents promulgated by Pius IX no observable positive attitude on possible truth or good in non-Christian religions is beyond serious dispute.[67] The trend continued under his successor. Thus *Sancta Dei civitas*, promulgated by Leo XIII on December 3, 1880, had to do principally with two matters; namely, material and spiritual assistance to Catholic foreign missions.[68] The question of truth or good in non-Christian religions is not approached; the closest the Pope comes to it is an oblique reference to Isa. 9:1.[69] But six years later the Pope's negative view seemed evident in *Humanae salutis*, an apostolic letter dated September 15, 1886, whereby the Catholic hierarchy in India was established.[70] He reports how his predecessors had constantly tried to see to it that missionaries (*apostolici viri*) keep Christian doctrine holy and inviolate in all of India and that missionaries never in any way be open to being stained (*inquinari*) with vestiges of ethnic superstition.[71] No one was unaware of how vigilant the Pope's predecessors had been radically to root out the weeds of empty observances and rites abhorrent to Christian faith.[72] The Pope nowhere hints that somewhere in these rites and cultures there may be a ray of that Truth which to some extent might be piercing the darkness. Finally, in *Tametsi*, an encyclical on Christ the Redeemer promulgated on November 1, 1900, about three years before his death, Leo took as his principal theme Jesus the Way, the Truth, and the Life. Despite abundant use of John's gospel and the theme around which the Pope's remarks were organized, one finds no reference to the Word which enlightens every human being coming into this world (John 1:9). Instead when speaking in the context of knowledge of religious truth outside Catholicism, the Pope uses another Johannine passage, "You shall know the truth and the truth shall make you free" (John 8:32).[73] Though Leo does not explicitly raise the question of truth or good in non-Christian religions, nothing suggests that his attitude differed from that of his predecessors.

Lacrimabili statu Indorum, directed to the Latin American hierarchy, had to do with the deplorable conditions of Indians in that region.[74] Promulgated by Pius X on June 7, 1912, the encyclical suggested steps that should be taken by various governments to prevent further cruelty—the Pope describes it in stark terms—and stated that the Catholic Church would do its part by sending missionaries. The document seems to be the closest Pius X came to dealing with Catholic missionary activity and was concerned, not with the theory of the missionary apostolate in general, but with a concrete problem in a continent where the Church, having its own hierarchy, technically was no longer a missionary territory. Despite this limited context, a negative attitude toward possible truth or good in non-Christian religions is discernible when the Pope states that is why he thought it necessary "...to use the more abundantly these helps which, because of the divine goodness, are at hand for Us, *in order to free the Indians from the slavery of Satan* and wicked men."[75] Nothing in the Pope's attempt to stop oppression of the Indians in South America indicates that the missionaries were to pay due attention to those elements in indigenous religions that with due caution might serve as stepping-stones to the Gospel.

With the exception of one passage in *Maximum illud* promulgated by Benedict XV on November 30, 1919, with the purpose of invigorating missionary effort severely hampered by the results of the First World War, the attitude of Pius X's successor seems even more closely akin to that of Pius IX.[76] The one statement that prima facie suggests a positive view on non-Christian religions is that wherein the Pope admonishes each missionary to so conduct himself that everyone "...can recognize in him a minister of a religion which embraces all men that adore God in spirit and truth, is a stranger to no nation, and 'where there is neither Gentile nor Jew, circumcision nor uncircumcision, Barbarian nor Scythian, bond nor free. But Christ is all in all.' "[77] The phrase "all men that adore God in spirit and truth" does not seem to refer to truth or good in non-Christian religions but to a natural disposition of mind, for the Pope in the same encyclical refers to numberless heathen still sitting in the shadow of death, and to the task of opening the gate of heaven to those who rush to their destruction. When missionaries have completed their task in one region they should be transferred to some other nation, "*...to snatch it from Satan's grasp.*"[78] In referring to the necessity of financial assistance for the missions, Benedict notes how much more sacred becomes the law of charity when it is not only a question of relieving poverty but also and especially "*....of reconquering from Satan's dominion* to the liberty of the children of God an incalculable number of souls."[79]

While upon closer analysis Benedict's stance on possible truth or good in non-Christian religions turns out to be negative, there seems at first sight to have been a slight shift in attitude under Pius XI. *Rerum Ecclesiae*, promulgated on February 28, 1926, was a major articulation of Catholic missionary theory.[80] Among its significant recommendations was the introduction of contemplative orders into the mission fields, "...since the inhabitants, especially in some regions, although mostly pagans, tend naturally to solitude and to prayer and to contemplation."[81] Taken as it stands, that statement might suggest possible truth or good in a given non-Christian religion. But as one ponders the drift of the Pope's reflection, the light that momentarily seemed to flicker is snuffed out. For earlier he had asked whether, since Christ commanded his disciples to love one another, we can "...vouchsafe to our neighbors a greater love or more signal charity than that of having them *withdrawn from the darkness of superstition* and instructed in the true faith of Christ?"[82] One is still far from the all-embracing warmth that was to characterize the thinking of Pius XII.

THE *Monita ad Missionarios*

Certain data may seem to suggest, however, a more nuanced conclusion. Among the directives occasionally published by the former Sacred Congregation for the Propagation of the Faith[83] are to be found statements that are at best puzzling when compared with the optic under which the Popes of the period seemed to have seen things. A striking example is to be found in the *Monita ad Missionarios* of 1840:

> *Text E.* In proposing these fundamental [truths] let the missionary beware of using subtle arguments rather than reasons and homely examples derived from the common sense of all human beings; [the missionary] being certainly convinced he is in the religious school of God who teaches interiorly; that God gives both intellect and

understanding. *Let him beware lest in treating with these Gentiles he seem to bring a new doctrine but let it be known that they are imbued with some knowledge of these truths* [the missionary] *discoursing on their beauty...*[84]

This *monitum* which at first blush seems to have appeared for the first time during the Petrine ministry of Gregory XVI, was repeated twice during the Petrine ministry of Pius IX (1853 and 1874), once during that of Leo XIII (1886) and again well into the twentieth century, in the time of Pius XI (1930). A close reading of the context in which this highly suggestive advice is given shows that it was precisely religious truth or good that the authors had in mind. It seems, then, that during the period when the Roman Bishops were taking a decidedly negative attitude on the matter, the Sacred Congregation for the Propagation of the Faith, as it was then called, was encouraging a directly contrary outlook among Catholic missionaries. It is true that routine decisions by the Roman Congregations are not explicitly approved by the Popes; but they must be presumed to be implicitly approved. In that sense, Text E from the *Monita* of 1840 onwards may seem to militate against the argument advanced in this section.

A closer look at the origin of Text E diminishes that likelihood. Contrary to what the *Monita* of 1840 seem to suggest, it dates not from the nineteenth but from the seventeenth century and is French, not Roman in origin. The outgrowth of a little known Synod of Ajuthia (Siam [Thailand]) and of early missionary effort in what was later to be called French Indochina,[85] the path to Text E seems to have been blazed in three stages: (1) While waiting for clarification of their missionary situation, six French missionaries in Siam met (1664?) to discuss their common apostolic endeavor; (2) on the basis of their lived experience, they composed a document entitled *Instructiones ad munera Apostolica rite obeunda perutiles*, a work that, depending on the edition, numbered from about two hundred fifty to some three hundred pages in 12°; (3) in 1669, the *Instructiones* with slight changes, won the support of the Sacred Congregation for the Propagation of the Faith.[86] Text E is to be found in Chap. V, "Quomodo Missionario vacandum sit gentium conversioni."[87]

Now it has been claimed that the *Instructiones* and their subsequent appearance as *Monita* became the Magna Carta of the Sacred Congregation for the Propagation of the Faith.[88] It is strange, however, that this Magna Carta seems to have been systematically ignored by every Roman Bishop during the period with which we have been dealing up to but excluding Pius XII (upon whom, as we shall see, influence in this regard was German rather than French). It is even more strange that Text E does not appear in modern editions of the *Collectanea*, though there was, as I have noted, another edition of the *Monita* in 1930.

A number of different questions arise for which there are no clear-cut answers. Was Text E omitted from the *Collectanea* simply because of the sheer length of the original document in which it is found? But the *Collectanea* contain many an excerpt; hence, an excerpt or two from the *Monita* could have been included. Metzler notes[89] that in a handwritten copy found in the Archives of the same Congregation, the first five chapters, with the notation "*...utpote nobis non necessaria...*"[90] were omitted. Recall that Text E was to be found in Chap. V. Was it omitted because it might seem to favor the religious indifferentism that the Popes of the period were attempting to combat? Hence, might not Text E as found in the *Monita* and published twice during the Petrine ministry of Pius IX tend to confirm the view of those who held that in number 16 of the Syllabus all the old Pope had wished to reprove was religious indifferentism? If that be the case, then why did his successors up to but excluding Pius XII exhibit the same negative attitude toward possible truth or good in non-Christian religions? Furthermore, there is no evidence that scholars like Choupin, whose work was widely known and who explicitly interpreted number 16 of the Syllabus as meaning that non-Christian religions were only an *obstacle* to salvation, were ever admonished by the Holy See for misinterpreting the thought of the Pope.

What Text E as used in the *Monita* suggests is that not all the candles reflecting the ancient tradition of John 1:9 had been extinguished within Catholicism. However dimly, that light was still discernible. But it is not discernible in the documents published under the direct aegis of the Roman Bishops before the time of Pius XII.[91] Hence, to argue that Text E represents their real thinking during the nineteenth and early twentieth centuries but that the view that permeated their officially promulgated encyclicals does not, would surely be tendentious. Given its origin and trajectory, I suggest that Text E does not militate against my argument as thus far advanced but rather tends to confirm it.[92]

Reversal By Vatican II

In regard to possible truth or good in non-Christian religions, two ancient traditions, the one negative, the other positive, were identified above. It is now possible to advance to the fourth part of my argument. *The Second Vatican Council*, I have claimed, *reversed standard papal teaching as found in Text A in that the Council reaffirmed ancient Catholic positive tradition.* It is not however immediately apparent that such was the case, for in the documents promulgated by Paul VI there seems to be a certain ambivalence. On the one hand, *Nostra aetate* states:

> *Text F.* ...other religions to be found everywhere strive variously to answer the restless searchings of the human heart by proposing "ways," which consist of teachings, rules of life, and sacred ceremonies.
>
> The Catholic Church rejects nothing which is true and holy in these religions. She looks with sincere respect upon those ways of conduct and of life, those rules and teachings which, though differing in many particulars from what she holds and sets forth, nevertheless *often* reflect a ray of that Truth which enlightens all men....[93]

On the other hand, *Ad gentes* has a somewhat different orientation:

> *Text G.* ...whatever truth and grace are to be found among the nations, as a sort of secret presence of God, this [missionary] activity frees from all taint of evil and restores to Christ its maker, *who overthrows the devil's domain and wards off the manifold malice of vice.* And so, whatever good is to be found sown in the hearts and minds of men, or in the rites and cultures peculiar to various peoples, is not lost. More than that, it is healed, ennobled, and perfected for the glory of God, *the shame of the demon,* and the bliss of men.[94]

Upon a closer reading, the difference between Texts F and G turns out to be one of nuance. The former stresses the positive features of non-Christian religions and highlights them in stronger hues. Yet it gives no blanket approval: Those ways of conduct and life, those rules and teachings do not *always* reflect a ray of that Truth but they *often* do. Text G is more cautious: It admits that truth and grace are to be found among the nations but sees them as sometimes under the devil's sway.

This difference in emphasis originated however neither in the Declaration on non-Christian Religions nor in the Decree on Missionary Activity; it is first detectable in the early drafts on the Church. The concept of truth or good in non-Christian religions occurs as early as Chapter X of *Aeternus Unigeniti* and again in the first draft of *Lumen gentium* (LG-a).[95] The shift toward a more nuanced view, i.e., to the admission of possible error and/or demonic influence occurs not in *Ecclesia Christi* (a reworked

Chapter IV of the draft on ecumenism and now called *declaratio altera*, the nucleus of the subsequent declaration on non-Christian religions) but in the second draft of *Lumen gentium* (LG-b), though both drafts were to be transmitted to the dispersed Council Fathers as of July 3, 1964.[96] Of the two documents sent out (it may be presumed) simultaneously between sessions, the former admits truth or good as such, while the latter contains the important modifier: Such truth or good may be tainted with error and evil. It was thus the draft on the Church that, chronologically speaking, constitutes the frame of reference wherein both themes are first worked out.

Though this is true chronologically, it is not the major context in which to determine the sense in which the position of Vatican II evolved. I shall concentrate first on the *Declaration on the Relationship of the Church to non-Christian Religions* (*Nostra aetate*) and secondly on the *Decree on the Church's Missionary Activity* (*Ad gentes*). What is important is not so much the shift in perspective as the theological reasoning whereby possible truth or good in non-Christian religions is affirmed at all.

ON THE WAY TO *Nostra Aetate*

In dealing with the evolution of this Declaration (*Nostra aetate*), we have to do essentially with five documents:

(1) *In hoc apparuit* (*IHA*). This document comprises five chapters, the first of which pertain to ecumenism, the fourth to the relation of Catholics to non-Christians, especially to Jews, while the fifth had to do with religious freedom.[97] As of April 22, 1963, the first three chapters were to be transmitted to the dispersed Council Fathers. The fourth was distributed to them on November 8, 1963, while the Council was in session; the fifth, eleven days later. Only the fourth concerns us here.[98]

(2) *Unitatis redintegratio* (*UR*). As of April 27, 1964, the three chapters on ecumenism and the draft on religious freedom (now called *declaratio prior*) were to be sent to the dispersed Council Fathers. But the draft on the relation between Catholics and non-Christians (now called *declaratio altera*), beginning with the words *Ecclesia Christi* (henceforth *EC*) was to be sent, as decided on July 3, 1964, some months later.[99]

(3)   *Nostra aetate* (*NA*-a). This was the draft on the relation between Catholics and non-Christians, distributed to the Council in session (November 18, 1964). It contains the former draft (*EC*) now called *Textus prior* and an amended text (*Textus emendatus*) of which the opening words are *Nostra aetate*.[100]

(4)   *Nostra aetate* (*NA*-b). This was an amended *NA*-a (now called *Textus approbatus*), the new *Nostra aetate* (*NA*-b) being called *Textus emendatus*.[101]

(5)   *Nostra aetate* (*NA*-c) as promulgated by Pope Paul VI on October 28, 1965.[102]

Except for its opening paragraph of forty-six words, the five paragraphs that constitute Chap. IV of *IHA* were devoted almost entirely to the relation between Catholics and Jews. Nothing therein suggests a positive attitude toward truth or good in other non-Christian religions.[103] Subsequent debate through the various stages of development of the drafts listed above was to result in the broadened horizon of the promulgated text (Text F). The crucial shift came in *EC*:

> *Text H.* Urged on by this love [*caritate*] toward our brothers, let us look with great respect [*observantia*] on their views [*opiniones*] and doctrines which, although differing from ours in many respects, *reflect nevertheless a ray of that Truth which enlightens every man coming into this world*.[104]

The first six paragraphs of *EC* having dealt with the relations between Catholics and Jews, the authors of the new draft went on to show that all human beings have God as their Father, and this being the case, asked how anyone could despise his or her brother. This commandment we have from the Lord, they continued, that anyone who loves God love his brother as well. It is at this point that Text H occurs and is followed by a brief paragraph of twenty-four words on relations with Moslems. This change made by the authors of the draft reflects previous critiques by the Council Fathers, whose thought was obviously evolving and was to continue to do so in the successive drafts leading to *NA*-c. There is no need to trace the evolution of Text H throughout the different modifications culminating in the final form that we find in Text F. It is sufficient to understand the reasoning behind the change of orientation in *IHA*, which had made no mention of possible truth or good in non-Christian religions. In Text H modification was made on the basis of John 1:9 and thus by implication on the basis of a kind of *praeparatio evangelica* antecedent to the explicit hearing of the Christian Gospel. The appeal was thus made to Catholic tradition having in this case its roots in the Johannine Prologue.

During the second session, most of the discussion on *IHA* had to do with Chapters I, II, and III; i.e., with inter-Christian ecumenical concerns. Yet, because the discussion at this stage was on ecumenism in general, many Fathers made observations that logically had to do with Chapter IV. Some were to say that the matter should be handled elsewhere; others were to voice the necessity for extensive treatment.

Thus, in the meeting of November 18, 1963, Peter Tatsuo Cardinal Doi of Tokyo (in addition to the written critique that he submitted during the interim and to which I shall turn my attention below) said the draft *IHA* should make some mention of the great non-Christian and ethical systems—he mentioned specifically Buddhism and Confucianism.[105] It should be briefly shown, he said, that "...the Catholic Church esteems in a fitting way the seeds of truth contained in the same; namely, those by which according to the designs of Providence, they seem to prepare for Christ."[106] The Church by the preaching of the Gospel intends to fulfill their profoundest yearnings.[107] The following day, Lawrence Cardinal Rugambwa, Bishop at Bukoba (Africa), after having indicated that humility befits those who have the gift of faith, said that all human beings are to be treated with respect and reverence; that is to say: If there is to be a prejudgment, it should be exercised in their favor, and that without any suggestion of false irenicism.[108] This is already done in the missions, he said; it is indeed a norm dating from the beginning of the Church and can be found in Justin and other Fathers of the Church: "*Whatever truth, whatever good there is on the earth and in the human heart belongs to Christ and is the seed of the Word*, and we may add, *has already been brought in by Christ as part of the heritage of the Church*."[109] But Bishop Fortunato da Veiga Coutinho, coadjutor in the diocese of Belgaum (India), articulated the most advanced view when he said:

> Three things should be determined in drafting this text: (1) there is only one way [*oeconomiam*] of salvation for the whole human race; (2) *all the religions of the human race are included in this way of salvation*; (3) these religions, especially of those oldest cultures, are an evangelical preparation for the completed revelation of God in Christ.[110]

Though other Fathers were to make statements less strong than that made by da Veiga Coutinho, all were far removed from the negative outlook of Pius IX. Some of the written critiques submitted during the interim continued in much the same vein. No less than twenty-five submitted reports on *IHA* in general; no less than seven addressed one or more of the concerns expressed in the four questions I set at the beginning of this chapter. And of that number, most of the comments came from non-Western, indigenous bishops.

Thus Stanislaus Lokuang, Bishop at Tainan (Taiwan), wrote that the relation between Catholics and non-Christians cannot be based on anything but love (*caritas*), for in every religion there are always some doctrinal elements that are both true and good, are conducive to the true religion, or can be a preparation for coming to know Christ.[111] We cannot condemn all religions as all bad or superstitious. In times past, there were those who wrote in that vein. Since Lokuang went on to exempt the Holy See from that charge, it is doubtful that he was aware of the doctrinal slant manifest in Pius IX's thought or of the generally negative attitude of succeeding pontificates. Speaking in the same frame of reference, Peter Tatsuo Cardinal Doi of Japan suggested an addition to Chap. IV to the effect that the Church esteems the religious mind that manifests itself under different forms; that the grace of God, who wishes all human beings to be saved, is operative among non-Christians in various ways. In religious, ethical and cultural traditions the Church gladly acknowledges that there are seeds of truth by which non-Christians are disposed to a higher knowledge of God given through his Son; that the Church, while conscious of the command to proclaim the Gospel of Christ to the human race, at the same time discerns whatever truth or good is found among non-Christian peoples.[112] Bishop (later Cardinal) Colombo wrote that the draft could not be approved as it stood because in practice it was concerned only with relations with Jews; something must be said about other religions—Islam, Hinduism, Buddhism. Indeed in these religions positive elements may be found perhaps, not without the influence of the grace of Christ that touches the whole human race. These elements invite the motherly consideration of the Church and should be considered as the innate foundation of the missionary and social enterprise.[113] But it was Bishop Alfred Ancel, then auxiliary in the Archdiocese of Lyons, who wrote the most penetrating critique of Chap. IV.

Ancel's argument consisted of three parts, only the first two of which need concern us here. The first was negative in that it was concerned with dangers to be avoided. Discovery of values in non-Christian religions can indeed lead to indifferentism, the position that all religions are equally good.[114] But this danger, however real, should not be used as an excuse to disdain what is true or good in these religions, for such an attitude would be against both truth and love.[115] A further danger to be avoided is the confusion of evangelization with proselytism. The second part of Ancel's critique was positive in that it explained that the attitude of Catholics to non-Christian religions should be based on faith. Because of faith, Catholics are able to rejoice over any moral or religious value to be found either in doctrine or in persons themselves. For every truth and every good come from God.[116]

As no bishop in reference to *IHA* seems to have expressed a contrary opinion, it is not surprising to find appropriate change introduced into the following draft (*EC* [Text H]). From that point on, the perspective of the drafts' authors increasingly broadened, reflecting the various critiques made by the bishops in the aula.[117] Thus in regard to the modification made in *EC* (Text H), Lawrence Satoski Nagae, Bishop at Urawa, spoke in the name of the entire Japanese episcopate. The relevant parts of his remarks centered on a theological argument and a discussion of a concrete way for Catholics to conduct themselves with non-Christians:

> And thus fortunately there is rejected [in the draft, *EC*] that manner of judging and condemning a priori and under the label "paganism" everything found in non-Christian religions...and there is positively affirmed our disposition sincerely to embrace the attempts of non-Christians who seek, to be sure, the Truth itself [and there is positively affirmed our disposition] to find traces of the Truth which they possess as a kind of preparation for the Gospel. What our draft lacks is any mention of how Christians can and should concretely live and cooperate with non-Christians....[118]

Joseph Parecattil, then bishop (later Cardinal) at Ernakulam (India), made a similar point:

> It seems we can go further [than *EC*] and find in the sacred books of non-Christians real foundations which call for [*postulant*] the revelation of Christ....
> This is especially true of sincere and devout followers of the major religions, such as Hinduism. Their sacred books document their calling out [*gemituum*] for Christ....[119]

It may be said in summary that a careful analysis of the documents reveals that the tone with which the Council Fathers speak of possible truth or good in non-Christian religions becomes increasingly positive from *EC* onwards and that by way of reference to John 1:9, to Irenaeus and Justin Martyr, or in some other appropriate manner, appeal is made to an ancient Catholic positive tradition that sees in that detectable truth or good a kind of propaedeutic to the Gospel. Indeed, that appeal was to become a dominant motif. In the document on the missions the evolution of the same theme was to be significantly different.

On the Way to *Ad Gentes*

Aside from the drafts discussed in the Preparatory Period,[120] the evolution of *Ad gentes* went through at least five stages:

(1)   *Christus Jesus (CJ)*. A position paper to be transmitted to the dispersed Council Fathers as of January 17, 1964.[121]

(2)   *Ecclesia cum finem habeat (ECF)*. A drastically revised draft of the former, to be transmitted to the dispersed Council Fathers as of July 3, 1964.[122]

(3)   *Ad gentes (AG*-a). To be transmitted to the dispersed Council Fathers as of May 28, 1965.[123]

(4)   *Ad gentes (AG*-b). Distributed to the Council in session on November 9, 1965, the former being called *Textus prior*, the new, *Textus emendatus*.[124]

(5)   *Ad gentes (AG*-c). The document as promulgated on December 7, 1965.[125]

Ideologically, aside from the draft of the Preparatory Period where the notion of possible truth or good in non-Christian religions does not occur at all, the earliest draft on the missions submitted to the Council Fathers once the Council was in session begins where *NA*-c was to leave off. Thus in *CJ*, the idea of truth or good occurs at least five times:

Text I.   The ministry of truth which frees individual persons the Church renders to peoples also, since Christ whom she serves is the "desire of the nations," "what creation is waiting for," and the fulfillment of all things.[126]

Text J.   Since the Church has the strength and capacity of assuming everything human, sin excepted, and of transforming it into Christ, everything true, everything holy, and everything lovable must be integrated into Christ himself.[127]

Text K. They shall strive rather intimately to know [*callere*] the religious and cultural heritage, the language and customs of a given people to be evangelized, and they shall recognize in their great variety God's providence, which prepares the way for the Gospel....[128]

Text L. To those minds which are well disposed, Christ as Savior of the world must be proclaimed as one who completes their culture and spiritual needs; indeed, he exceeds them by far.[129]

Text M. Indeed, the Church of Christ, inasmuch as it is catholic, must appear as foreign to no people or nation but as in harmony with the way of life of any people, in such a way that "whatever is gracious, if there is any excellence, if there is anything worthy of praise" ...may be absorbed for building up the people of God, who causes all things to be summed up in Christ....[130]

Texts I and J occur in Chap. I where the authors of the draft discussed doctrinal principles in general. After having described the mystery of Christ, the ministry of the Church and the necessity of the missionary apostolate, they successively speak of the manner of preaching the gospel and the building up of the Church, the respective contexts in which Texts I and J are to be found. Texts K, L and M occur in Chap. II which expands upon a theme touched upon in Chap. I, namely, the manner of going about missionary work. Text K bears upon the Gospel spirit, Text L upon the work of the missionary, and Text M upon adaptation to new cultures. In the following draft (*ECF*) in which the former (*CJ*) was almost entirely reworked and drastically reduced in length, the notion of truth or good in a non-Christian religion is reduced to a sentence of twenty words.[131] Nowhere in the first two drafts is the possibility directly raised that, in some cases at least, truth or good in non-Christian religions may be mixed with error and evil. The shift occurs in *AG*-a, most notably in number 9:

Text N. [Missionary activity] does not only make Christ present through the word of preaching and the celebration of the sacraments *but sets free from the contagion of evil and restores to Christ, its Author*, whatever truth and grace as the hidden presence of God were already to be found among the peoples, that through Him it may become known and loved by all, and that *whatever good is found sown in the minds and hearts of human beings or in the peoples' own rites and cultures not only not be lost but be healed, raised up, and completed for the glory of God, the confusion of the demon, and the happiness of humankind.*[132]

This range of vision was to remain in the promulgated text and far from being weakened was to be highlighted even more, as I shall point out below. For the moment, it is sufficient to note that the phrase "...quidquid veritatis et gratiae iam apud gentes quasi secreta Dei praesentia invenie-batur...."[133] logically includes not simply non-Christian culture(s) but also non-Christian religion, otherwise the universal "...*whatever* truth and *grace* were already to be found..." makes no sense, an interpretation confirmed further on in the text when it refers to rites. The shift of perspective wherein truth and good in other religions are seen as some-times mixed with demonic influence is entirely foreign to the orientation of the earlier drafts *CJ* and *ECF* and is, as we have seen, nowhere to be found explicitly stated in the various drafts of *NA*. One may ask, Why this change in outlook? It would be tempting to propose the hypothesis that in the course of the development of *NA* those who pointed out truth or good in non-Christian religions were primarily indigenous bishops, whereas in the case of the successive drafts of *AG*, the significant shift (Text L) was introduced through the interventions of non-indigenous missionary bishops. Such a view however is entirely simplistic and is not justified by a careful examination of the data.

Thus in a written report pertaining to *CJ*, Valerian Cardinal Gracias, Archbishop at Bombay, was quite blunt:

> There seems to be a sort of nervousness to state that the Church is the divinely instituted and necessary "medium salutis."
> With the modern talk of "dialogue" between religions, there is the danger of regarding the dialogue as between equals. Some progressive missiologists seem to exaggerate the supernatural "bona" in non-Christian religions, as if these were "per se" sufficient for salvation, "*sine Ecclesia.*"[134]

Yet Gracias did not intend to play down truth or good in non-Christian religions. Recall that Chap. II of *CJ* (Texts K, L and M) along with Chap. I (Texts I, J) of the same draft had been entirely positive. Gracias commented:

> The description of the missionary work (Chap. II), lengthy and rather general, does not sufficiently face up to the *concrete situation*:
> We bring the salvation of Christ to the "gentes," but we might remember that the *grace of Christ has already been active in* all men of John 1:9. Presumably, many "good pagans" are in the state of grace. *But all grace calls for visible incorporation into the Church.* We must reveal Christ to them and give them a chance to become conscious Christians.

> Not only do individuals receive grace, but the non-Christian religions contain religious elements which constitute a real *praeparatio...evangelica*, and which we must study in order to build on it, and this poses many problems. Why is it that we have made no impact among the great religions?[135]

When the preceding quotation is kept in mind as part of the same written report submitted by Gracias, the key to understanding the Cardinal's critique seems to be that, though as an indigenous bishop he does not hesitate to signal out truth or good in non-Christian religions, nonetheless such truth or good is of no value without the Church, for as he says elsewhere in the same report, "The schema does well to give positive recognition to the real '*bona*' [spiritual values] to be found in non-Christian religions...but it is necessary to point out that without the ministry of the Church these values and '*bona*' are doomed to distortion and are precarious."[136]

The draft *CJ*, to which Gracias' comments were directed, had contained, as we have seen, several allusions to positive cultural and religious values in non-Christian religions and in the succeeding paper (*ECF*) had been drastically reduced in length. It was to that subsequent draft that Cardinal Léger of Montreal spoke when he complained of lack of sufficient attention to truth or good in non-Christian religions.[137] It was of the same draft that Cardinal Rugambwa of Bukoba spoke when he signaled out the good, sacred, and the beautiful to be found in the moral and religious treasury of every people. Bishop John Baptist Velasco, exiled from Xiamen (China) seems to have been one of the first in the context of *ECF* to suggest the change in perspective (Text N, along with Bishop Lokuang of Tainan [Taiwan]).[138] The latter pointed out that in order for a non-Christian to come to faith, it is not necessary that he or she renounce his or her culture as such, but only those things in the culture that are erroneous, inauthentic, and irreconcilable with his or her new life in Christ.[139]

By far the most powerful defense of truth and good in non-Christian religions was given by Bishop Elias Zoghby, Melchite vice-Patriarch for Egypt. For centuries, he said, the Eastern churches have regarded the mission of Christ as a kind of epiphany; i.e., as a kind of divine light breaking into the work of creation.[140] The mission of the Church is to perpetuate that epiphany and to prepare for the coming of the Kingdom. Another notion dear to the hearts of the Eastern Fathers is that the mission of Christ and the Church has to do with humanity as made pregnant by the divine "*spermata tou logou*," the Bishop said, using the Logos-language of Justin, Clement of Alexandria, and Origen. The same Fathers describe the progressive preparation of the world for the coming of the Savior as a divine pedagogy.[141] From these two considerations two fitting conclusions flow:

> The first consists in this, that there is no rupture between the Word as Redeemer and the Word as Creator, or between the human race as redeemed and the human race as created. In the mission [of Christ] described as epiphany, there breaks into the work the very divine light which was communicated to human beings with the life they received in creation: "In the beginning was the Word...in him was life and the life was the light of humankind...."[142]
> The second fitting conclusion of the Fathers' description of the mission [of Christ] consists in this, that the missionary Church is invited to give the utmost importance to the seed of the Word planted [*condita*] in every human being..... In evangelizing peoples, the Church must uncover the first divine seed and the natural riches which the same seed has produced.[143]

Not all the bishops showed the enthusiasm of Bishop Zoghby, as I have been at pains to indicate, some perceiving truth or good in non-Christian religions as not always unmixed with error and evil. Indeed, somewhat later, one Father asked that words pertaining to possible good in pagan rites be removed from *AG*-b.[144] And to the penultimate draft there was made a highly significant addition, the phrase "...qui imperium diaboli evertit et multimodam scelerum malitiam arcet."[145] When somewhat later an account was given of suggested amendments, it was stated by the Commission that one of the Council Fathers had asked that this phrase be removed. The Commission decided to stand by the addition, giving as its reason that the addition was placed in the text in response to the request of several Fathers.[146] In the report (*relatio*) itself, the intent behind reference to possible Satanic influence in some non-Christian religions was described as the attempt to forestall any kind of false optimism in the preaching of the Gospel.[147]

Despite an occasional disclaimer, it cannot be denied that most of the Council Fathers who said that not everything in non-Christian religions is positive nonetheless insisted each in his own way on at least partial truth or good therein. Thus the difference between the debates in the successive stages of development of *NA* and *AG* is primarily a difference of tone. In the evolution of the latter, many of those who admitted discernible truth or good in non-Christian religions felt simultaneously obliged to add that it was to be purified and perfected. This must not be taken to mean that the Council Fathers' conviction was less when they voted the final text of *AG*-c as compared with *NA*-c. It merely means that, the essential point having been made in the document on the Church—which in the new numbers 13 and 17 of *LG*-b had anticipated the positive outlook of *NA*-c and *AG*-c, respectively—there was less need in the debates surrounding the successive stages of development of *AG*-a to insist further.[148] The emphasis in the development is thus perceptibly different. In the case of the document on the relation between Catholicism and non-Christian religions (*NA*-c), the movement begins with a positive outlook (*EC*) and progressively broadens; in the case of the document on the missions (*AG*-c), the initial thrust is just as open (*CJ*) but gradually narrows, a discreet check on inculturation theory discussed below. Yet both affirm possible truth or good in non-Christian religions. If one may judge by the debates, there can be no doubt the theological reasoning behind this position was based on an appeal to the early apostolic Fathers, a fact confirmed in the report given by Cardinal Bea. Though it pertains directly only to number 2 of *NA*-a, it is nonetheless for the reason indicated below relevant to the development of *AG*. Bea stated:

> (1) The fundamental principle is proposed that other religions are not to be disdained *tout court* [*simpliciter*] but that whatever ethical and religious value is found in them is to be acknowledged and preserved. (2) This relation has its foundation in the mystery of Christ, which may be considered from two points of view: Christ is the complete [*tota*] truth and universal revelation of the Father; He is the way, the truth and the life; He comes in such a way, however, that the creature is not destroyed but raised up [*assumatur*] and is reconciled to God. (3) Hence the Church, according to an ancient tradition, of which Irenaeus is produced as a witness, in taking stock of religions and in her practical relations with them, first takes into consideration those things which are false; in their positive values, she acknowledges the truth which has its origin from God, namely, the ray of eternal light which enlightens every human being.[149]

Four matters should be noted about this text. First, its purpose was (as I have stated) to explain the rationale behind the amendments incorporated into number 2 of *NA*-a. Second, unlike the various drafts through which *NA* evolved, the paragraph cited contains a direct allusion to de facto falsehood in non-Christian religions. Third, the rationale behind number 2 of *NA*-a is explicitly described as an appeal to a tradition found in Irenaeus. Fourth, the report was given on November 20, 1964, well before *AG*-a was to be sent to the dispersed Council Fathers (i.e., as of May 28, 1965), and hence well before the voting on the penultimate text of *AG*. This means that the report, though given in the context of *NA*-a, probably exercised an influence on the thinking of the Council Fathers when much later they came to vote on *AG*-b. It thus remains to determine the sense in which Vatican II modified the papal position and the relevance that the conciliar teaching has for the four questions placed at the outset of this chapter.

IN WHAT SENSE, REVERSAL?

On the basis of the foregoing discussion, there can be no doubt that the Council Fathers not only answer Question (A) affirmatively but also that they answer Question (B) by "*Verbum*" or "*Veritas*," thus reaffirming an ancient Catholic positive tradition. In taking this tack, the Council Fathers reversed the doctrinal stance of Pius IX as it is reflected in Text A and as maintained by his successors up to Pius XII. But they do not seem to have referred to the problem of Text A of *Qui pluribus*. I have come upon no clear evidence that indicates that they were aware of what the perspective of a much earlier ordinary papal magisterium had been.[150] Thus it cannot be argued that the orientation relative to possible truth or good in non-Christian religions that Vatican II was to take constitutes a modality with which the position reflected in Text A of *Qui pluribus* was received, a point to which I shall return in Chap. VII.

Though my concern has been principally with Questions (A) and (B), a brief comment must be made on Questions (C) and (D). The Council Fathers in the promulgated texts do not raise the question of the salvific value of non-Christian religions (Question [C]) but the internal logic of their thinking seems to suggest that they could have answered it affirmatively.[151] Indeed, much post-conciliar writing has been in that vein.[152] As to Question (D), the Council Fathers explicitly affirm the necessity of the Church for salvation—and by that they mean the Catholic Church. And though as we shall see in Chap. V they modified the Pope's teaching on the questions of identity and of membership, the truth behind the axiom *extra Ecclesiam nulla salus* remains intact. But it is highly nuanced, very different from the one-sided emphasis to be found in the writings and speeches of Pius IX, whose obsession with the constant isolated above led him to miss the relevance of and consequently to contribute to the obscuring of Catholic doctrine.[153]

The Rediscovery of Catholic Tradition

Concomitant with the manner wherein the teaching of Pius IX was being received, another movement, and a contrary one to be sure, was developing and was eventually to constitute a significant factor in the rediscovery of authentic positive tradition. Chronologically, the new development, the result of probing by missiologists whose work as a discipline was then in its infancy, seems to have preceded any marked shift of perspective on the part of the papal magisterium. I shall here touch upon the work of two authors whose thought contributed to a gradual change in view; I shall then close this section with a brief glance at the fresh outlook emanating from the Petrine ministry of Pius XII.

MISSIOLOGICAL SCIENCE

In the early years of this century, those concerned with a more adequately grounded Christian approach to mission work were beginning to lay the foundation of *Akkommodation* or inculturation. An article of Alois Knöpfler's, one of the more learned historians of the day, is particularly illustrative.[154]

At first sight, Knöpfler seems to have provided a merely historical analysis of missionary adaptation discernible in Church praxis culminating with Gregory the Great. *Akkommodation* is thus rather broadly defined. As regards a particular people to be evangelized, Knöpfler understood it to embrace their political, social, ethico-religious characteristics, their art and their level of education. In brief, inculturation had to do not simply with subjective but also with objective compatibility with the Christian Gospel;[155]that is, of non-Christian religions as such with the kerygma. Knöpfler made it clear that *Akkommodation* had from earliest times been a dominant characteristic of much of the Church's missionary effort. Whereas Gregory's initial advice to missionaries among the Anglo-Saxons had been much more negative, his subsequent directives regarding customs of the people allowed much of the external ritual to remain provided its meaning be changed. Yet Gregory did not refer to the need to look for a hidden *praeparatio evangelica* where it might exist; his reasoning was simply that one could not take everything away from difficult temperaments at once. In climbing to a high place one proceeds step by step, not by leaps.[156] Thus in the end, Gregory's attitude, the point where Knöpfler's study leaves off, seems to have remained somewhat negative. Knöpfler's suggestion was not however that it should be imitated without qualification but that *Akkommodation*, already part of a forgotten Catholic tradition, should be investigated further and applied to contemporary missionary effort.

That challenge was fully accepted in Johannes Thauren's dissertation, *Die Akkommodation im katholischen Heidenapostolat*, of which Joseph Schmidlin was a co-director.[157] Thauren's work represents a milestone. While the concept of inculturation itself was rather broadly defined as was the case in Knöpfler's article, Thauren devoted five sections—the whole of part two—to exploring five generally different kinds of missionary adaptation.[158] Only the tenor of his remarks on ethico-religious inculturation is relevant here.

Thauren's treatment was remarkable for its balance. The Christian missionary will not always find in a given religion elements with which he can fully empathize. Thauren cites as an example the social status of women in Islam.[159] These are aspects of a given religion which the missionary must rather tolerate. Despite the fact that the very nature of Christianity presupposes some built-in limits, the emphasis of Thauren's approach to truth or good in non-Christian religions was essentially positive. In speaking of intellectual *Akkommodation*, Thauren had already referred to the *Logos spermatikos* of Justin Martyr and when taking up the matter of specifically religious matters did not hesitate to apply the same principle. If it was indispensable in modern missionary effort to investigate and evaluate non-Christian philosophizing, the same holds true of religious values. Given that at the time Thauren's book was published, the popularity of Choupin's study with its positive reception of Text A of *Qui pluribus* was still at its height, Thauren is worth quoting:

> With a more direct observation of the religious element in paganism we discover even among primitives much light and truth. In all pagan religions one still traces the essence of the *Logos spermatikos*. In this sense, the words of Christ also apply: "I have not come to take away the law but to fulfill it." Christianity should not nor does it desire to separate the pagan from his whole historical and religious past. It is a mistake if the missionary takes the one-sided stand that he brings to the people something *absolutely* new, whence he draws a sharp line of demarcation between his own religious domain and paganism.[160]

One recognizes here an indirect reference to the improperly documented

Monita ad Missionarios to which I referred above (Text E).[161] Much more explicitly than Knöpfler before him, Thauren answers Question (A) affirmatively and by this reference to the *Logos spermatikos* affirmatively answers Question (B) as well. What one does not seem to find in this period but which has become an orientation taken with increasing frequency since Vatican II, is an affirmative answer to Question (C) with consequent modification but surely not abandonment of the truth behind the axiom *extra Ecclesiam nulla salus* (Question [D]).

It should be noted in passing that nowhere in his dissertation did Thauren refer to Text A of *Qui pluribus*. Yet, he was careful to enlist papal support whenever he could in order to rest his case. In that context, it is further noteworthy that he was unable to cite a single positive statement of the ordinary papal magisterium throughout the whole period from Pius IX up to and including Pius XI, thus indirectly confirming my conclusion as stated above. Indeed, if Thauren was correct, an important cause of the breakdown of the inculturation idea may have been the result of the so-called Chinese Rites controversy.[162] The decision of the Holy See, fully approved by Benedict XIV, made with the intention of preserving the truth of the faith "delivered once for all to the saints," turned out to be a very serious mistake because it was based on insufficient examination of the data. Though the decision in itself had to do only with China, it nonetheless had far-reaching effects, causing the inculturation theory to cease being a significant catalyst in Catholic missionary endeavor.

Some of the documentation in Thauren's work would today be considered dated;[163] but that fact does not affect its substantive quality. His dissertation was a significant contribution on the way to *Nostra aetate* and *Ad gentes* and, like Knöpfler's analysis, is illustrative of the kind of work mission theorists were doing. It would be possible to mention others along the way, most notably the work of Thauren's mentor, Joseph Schmidlin.[164]

There is no need however to trace the whole development of inculturation theory throughout this period, for the evidence uncovered seems sufficient to establish as fairly probable that the lead toward reversing the negative outlook of Pius IX was not, chronologically speaking, taken by the ordinary papal magisterium. But on the way to Vatican II, the missiologists had not stood alone. As early as 1939, in the first year of his Petrine ministry, a former papal nuncio to Germany and one thoroughly familiar with German thought both within and without Catholicism was to embrace a similar point of view, thus officially acknowledging their contribution.

The Contribution of Pius XII

Pius XII's implicit acceptance of the inculturation principle is to be found in an unexpected place. *Summi pontificatus*, his first encyclical, promulgated on October 20, 1939, had to do essentially with world order seriously threatened by the recent German invasion of Poland on September 1, 1939. Comprising thirty-nine pages and some 10,900 words in its official Latin text, the new Pope's message, while acknowledging the role played by economic injustice, attempted to analyze the ideological causes of current difficulties.[165] The most important was the denial and rejection of a universal norm of morality for individual and social life as well as for international relations. In briefer terms, the Pope was concerned with disregard for the natural law itself, a disregard that he seems to have seen as originating in the sixteenth century; i.e., in the "abandonment of that Christian teaching of which the Chair of Peter is the depository and exponent," [166] for "...cut off from the infallible teaching authority of the Church, not a few separated brethren have gone so far as to overthrow the central dogma of Christianity, the Divinity of the Savior, and have hastened thereby the process of spiritual decay."[167] But Pius does not dwell on the remote causes of what he called disorder, and in another place in the same encyclical he extends to non-Catholic Christians a friendly hand surprising in those pre-ecumenical days.[168]

Denial of the natural law leads chiefly to two effects directly connected with international tension: (1) forgetfullness of that law of human solidarity and love that is found in the human being's common origin and in the quality of rational nature, and (2) the divorcing of civil authority from dependence upon the Supreme Being.[169] These are the headings under which the Pope's further remarks are organized. Thus on the one hand and under the heading of human solidarity Pius quotes Col. 3:10-11, which refers to putting on the new man ($\alpha\nu\theta\rho\omega\pi o\nu$, not $\alpha\nu\delta\rho\alpha$) "...whence there is neither Gentile nor Jew, circumcision or uncircumcision, Barbarian nor Scythian, bond nor free. But Christ is all and in all,"[170] an indirect attack upon Nazi persecution of the Jews; while on the other, and under the heading of dependence on the Supreme Being, the Pope lashes out against the "...formation of youth that is misdirected towards a goal that alienates from Christ and leads to open or hidden apostasy...."[171] from Him, an indirect reference no doubt to the *Hitlerjugend*. At first sight, this reference to Christ seems far removed from concerns about the natural law, until one remembers that the Popes' traditional position had always been that the primary duty and right to educate children belongs not to the state but to the family, the rights of which in this regard were being violated in Germany and in Italy. The terms fascism and Nazism do not occur in the encyclical; it is nonetheless apparent that the Pope had for his target not interconfessional disputes of the past but fascist Italy and Nazi Germany.

I shall not proceed further with an analysis of *Summi pontificatus* and the orientation the Pope attempted to give the Catholic Church before the onslaught of a war which he correctly foresaw as only widening.[172] Sufficient for my purpose here is the Pope's indirect allusion to the work of missiologists whose contribution he discussed under the heading of human solidarity. He stated:

> *Text O.* Pioneer research and investigation, involving sacrifice, devotedness and love on the part of her missionaries of every age, have been undertaken in order to facilitate the deeper appreciative insight into the most varied civilizations and to put their spiritual values to account for a living and vital preaching of the Gospel of Christ. All that in such usages and customs is not inseparably bound up with religious errors will always be subject to kindly consideration and, when it is found possible, will be sponsored and developed.[173]

The "distance" between Text A of *Qui pluribus* and Text O of *Summi pontificatus* is assuredly vast not only chronologically but also psychologically and theologically. Openness to non-Christian cultures was to be an enduring characteristic of Pius' ministry. The words, "All that in such usages and customs is not inseparably bound up with religious errors...," may have been intended to include even religious values. Indeed, this concern may be said to have intensified, so that twelve years later in *Evangelii praecones* the Pope developed the theme more broadly:

> *Text P.* The Church from the beginning down to our own time has *always* followed this wise practice: let not the Gospel on being introduced into any new land destroy or extinguish *whatever its people possess that is naturally good, just or beautiful.* For the Church, when she calls people to a higher culture, and a better way of life, under the inspiration of the Christian religion, does not act like one who recklessly cuts down and uproots a thriving forest. No, she grafts a good scion upon the wild stock that it may bear a crop of more delicious fruit.[174]

> *Text Q.* Although owing to Adam's fall, human nature is tainted with original sin, yet it has in itself something that is naturally Christian;

and this, if illumined by divine light and nourished by God's grace, can eventually be changed into true and supernatural virtue.[175]

Text R. That is the reason the Catholic Church has neither scorned nor rejected the pagan philosophies. Instead, after freeing them from error and all contamination she has perfected and completed them by Christian revelation.[176]

Comprising thirty-one pages and some 8,400 words in the *Acta Apostolicae Sedis, Evangelii praecones* was, unlike *Summi pontificatus*, devoted entirely to Catholic missionary effort; hence, in contradistinction to the latter, there is no need to explain the context in which the passages just quoted occur. Text R follows immediately upon Text Q as does Text Q upon Text P. In the first cited, the Pope seems forgetful if not somewhat naive in not at least indirectly acknowledging the effects of the Chinese Rites controversy, the results of which according to Thauren were to cause the thrust of inculturation theory to lie dormant for several generations.[177] One is dealing with a period of about one hundred sixty years, from *Ex qua singulari* of July 5, 1742, to efforts in the early twentieth century to re-awaken the ancient positive tradition. Yet on the whole the Pope's assessment was correct, as evidenced in 1679 by the directives of the Congregation for the Propagation of the Faith[178] and the *Monita ad Missionarios* discussed earlier. Text Q as it stands does not refer to anything more than traits of character and so by itself does not suggest a horizon broader than that in *Maximum illud* or *Rerum Ecclesiae*, an interpretation seemingly confirmed by Text R. One could therefore argue on the basis of these texts that Pius had in mind only cultural values and/or solid traits of character among indigenous peoples, not truth or good in non-Christian religions as such.

Yet, the case seems quite otherwise. I have found nothing in Pius' writings that suggests that the "whatever its people possess" of Text P might not include religious values. Thus as one continues on in *Evangelii praecones*, one sees the Pope quoting directly from a Latin translation of *Ad adolescentes* of Basil the Great:

Text S. Certainly the essential function of a tree is to produce fruit in season; still the foliage that its branches also bear serves to adorn it. In the same way the primary fruit of the soul is truth itself; but the garb of natural culture is a welcome addition, just as leaves provide shade for the fruit and add to its beauty. *Thus Moses, a man of the greatest renown for his wisdom, is said to have come to the con-*

> templation of Him Who Is, only after having been trained in
> Egyptian lore. So later the wise Daniel is said to have been first
> schooled in Babylon in the wisdom of the Chaldeans, and only then
> to have come to know Divine Revelation.[179]

Although in neither encyclical does the Pope refer to the Word that
enlightens every human being coming into this world (John 1:9) and
though there is no reference to the *Logos spermatikos* of Justin Martyr and
its equivalent in Irenaeus, nonetheless the very least that may be said about
Text S is that the Pope seems to have envisaged non-Christian lore and
wisdom as constituting in some cases a kind of *praeparatio evangelica*. But
he may have intended much more, for immediately after this passage he
referred to Text O of *Summi pontificatus*, thereby suggesting that the
orientation of *Evangelii praecones* was to be considered continuous with
his statement made much earlier in a different frame of reference.[180] The
phrase "to put their spiritual values to account" of Text O (which in the
Latin text reads "...sua ipsorum animi [not *mentis*] ornamenta ac dotes
...colere ac provehere..."[181]) may have been intended to include religious
values, since "*all* that is not inseparably bound up with religious
errors..."[182] will always be subject to kindly consideration and, when
possible, developed. The Pope's explicit reference to Text O in *Evangelii
praecones* suggests that what he said therein be seen in that earlier context.
Those who had striven to reawaken within Catholicism its ancient thrust
toward inculturation were receiving strong endorsement from its Petrine
minister.

In these texts from Pius XII, one deviation from normal practice is
noteworthy. Usually the Popes in making an important point use such
phrases as "As our predecessor of venerable memory said...." But when
Pius XII speaks of truth or good in non-Christian religions, no such
phrases are to be found. It is not, of course, that there was absolutely no
previous papal precedent—within limits he could have made reference to
Gregory the Great. But he could in no way have appealed to the *Monita ad
Missionarios* from 1840 onwards. For contrary to what a superficial
reading of the data might suggest, that document did not originate with the
Roman Bishops nor even with the former Sacred Congregation for the
Propagation of the Faith; it originated with French missionaries in the
field. The scope of Leo XIII's *Sancta Dei civitas* along with the thinking of
his successors up to the time of Pius XII did nothing to diminish the
negative outlook of Pius IX: They tended rather to confirm it. Thus in the
whole period under discussion there is as a matter of brute fact not a single
statement by a Roman Bishop to which Pius XII could have referred as

precedent. No, the fresh invigorating attitude that surfaced at Vatican II had originated elsewhere. For as stated earlier, the path to reversal of the doctrinal stance exhibited in Text A and the reaffirmation of ancient Catholic positive tradition seems to have been cleared first by the work of missiologists, thence by the teaching of Pius XII, and subsequently by the bishops in conciliar debate.

Overview

The narrow horizon of *Qui pluribus* relative to possible truth or good in non-Christian religions was destined to widen as subsequent events demonstrate. But while the work of the missiologists preceded any marked shift of emphasis on the part of the ordinary papal magisterium, Pius' contribution was nonetheless invaluable. Had it been lacking; had the Council been obliged to debate the issue with a slant not much different from that of Pius IX, Leo XIII, Pius X, Benedict XV and Pius XI, its success in restoring positive Catholic tradition on a conciliar level might have been longer in coming. For one of the first concerns of an authentic Catholic theologian and/or bishop in conciliar debate is to determine what the Roman Bishops have held on a particular theological matter, not because the latter's teaching on the level of their ordinary magisterium is itself decisive, but because for the authentic Catholic it constitutes a *locus theologicus* (q.v.). But in the present case, one would have met only a stumbling block. Thus the importance of Pius XII's antecedent urging the Church to a positive attitude cannot be underestimated. Contrary to the situation that, as we shall see, was to obtain in the debates on Church-state relations, religious freedom, and the Church, no one seems to have noticed, or at least did not seem to think he had to point out, that the tack the Council was taking relative to possible truth or good in non-Christian religions was contrary to the earlier teaching of the ordinary papal magisterium. The role of Pius XII had indeed been crucial.

Though sheer intellectual probity calls for such an admission, it should not be allowed to obscure what had happened, for the sequence of developments masks the ultimate modalities whereby the teaching of Pius IX had been received; it also masks an important lesson both for theory of doctrinal development within Catholicism and for official Catholicism's claims relative to the ordinary papal magisterium. That is a tale yet to be told: We shall leave it for the concluding chapters.[183]

Chapter III
THE CHURCH-STATE ISSUE

Whatever the degree of ambiguity that in the end attaches to the preceding question, the teaching of the ordinary papal magisterium on Church-state relations was not one that had been made parenthetically. For it constituted, along with the correlative matter of religious freedom, a central position of that magisterium stretching back at least seven generations prior to the Council, a fact of which, in contrast to the question of truth or good in non-Christian religions, the Council Fathers were fully aware.

However, at first sight, it does not appear that the Church-state issue merits treatment separate from that of religious freedom, the two being so intimately related that it is rarely possible given the actual historical developments to speak for long of one without having to allude to the other. Yet it is ideologically possible to hold that a human being does not have an objective right to worship God in a way different from the way God has established (and that consequently religious freedom granted to those who do not follow that way is granted on the basis of toleration of error for the common good) without one's being logically constrained to hold that the true religion must in principle be the religion of the state. Conversely, one might hold that where Catholics are in the majority Catholicism must be the religion of state without one's being logically obliged to deny that religious freedom enjoyed by non-Catholics is based upon the dignity of the human person. Though doubtless in the minds of the Popes the two issues were two sides of the same coin and thus insepara-ble, they are nonetheless logically distinct. For that reason, and the addi-tional reason that the treatment of the religious freedom issue in the following chapter will itself be sufficiently complex, I shall here treat separately of the Church-state issue with occasional reference, when neces-sary, to the correlative issue of religious freedom.

I shall advance the following argument:

I. For Pius IX, (1) the ideal relation between Church and state seems to have entailed a union in which (a) Catholicism was the officially recognized religion (b) protected by the state; (2) such a union seems to have been perceived by him as necessitated on the basis of doctrine, and did not seem envisaged merely as a matter of policy.

II. The teaching of Leo XIII on Church-state relations as put forth in Immortale Dei may be regarded as the development and syste-matization of the doctrine of Pius IX and remained the official position of the ordinary papal magisterium up to and probably including John XXIII.

III. Despite vigorous critique during the Preparatory Period, the teaching of the ordinary papal magisterium on the ideal relation between Church and state during the same period was modified chiefly in regard to its tone. Thus the stance of the ordinary papal magisterium on ideal Church-state relations as exhibited by Pius IX and developed and systematized by Leo XIII remained the official position of the ordinary papal magisterium well after the opening of the Council.

IV. The position of the ordinary papal magisterium on ideal Church-state relations was in the end reversed by the Council.

This chapter comprises four sections corresponding to each of the four parts of my argument. The last section will be particularly brief, since the following chapter may be regarded as a continuation of the same theme considered from the viewpoint of its correlative.

The Teaching of Pius IX

Before proceeding directly to the matter at hand, it may be helpful to dispose of two questions different from those discussed above:

(A)   Does union between Church and state necessarily imply that ideally Catholicism should be, whenever possible, the official state religion?

(B)   If Catholicism is the official state religion, is it ideologically necessary that Catholicism's magisterial officers insist that Catholicism be the state religion to the exclusion of all other religions *as state religions?*

In regard to the first, the concept of Catholicism as the official religion of state entails the concept of union between Church and state, but the contrary does not necessarily obtain. Though it remains to be seen whether it obtained in the mind of Pius IX and his successors within the period with which I am dealing, union between Church and state might mean nothing more than Catholicism's enjoying favored status. But that does not in itself imply that the state qua state must worship as the Catholic Church does. The distinction may be a fine one, but it is nonetheless real. Regarding the second question, the answer from the perspective of official Catholicism must be affirmative, the statement in number 6 of *Dignitatis humanae* notwithstanding.[1] It is true that, within the nuances highlighted in Chap. V, *Lumen gentium* does not, as was formerly the case, put an equal sign between (Roman) Catholicism and the Church of Christ; but the Fathers of Vatican II did not, on that account, consider the Catholic Church to be merely one among equals, even in relation to other Christian Churches.[2] Thus an affirmative answer to Question (B) is simply another aspect of the religious freedom debate discussed below.[3]

Initially, the position of Pius IX does not seem so clear-cut. It may be helpful, then, first to contrast the issues and then determine the extent to which the data shed light on them. Thus the historian will ask at least four additional questions:

(C)   Why can and should one judge that it was the teaching of Pius IX that a union between Church and state was both desirable in principle and an ideal for which Catholics should strive?

(D)   Did such a union as envisaged by Pius IX seem to imply that ideally Catholicism should be, whenever possible, the official state religion?

(E)   Why can and should one judge it was the teaching of Pius IX that union
between Church and state meant that the Church should be protected
by the state?

(F)   Why can and should one judge that the teaching of Pius IX relative to
union between Church and state was proposed by him as a matter of
doctrine and not merely as one of policy?

Any attempt to clarify these issues had best begin with number 55 of the
Syllabus wherein the Pope condemned the proposition "*The Church is to
be separated from the state and the state from the Church.*"[4] The document
listed as illustrative of his meaning is *Acerbissimum*, an allocution given to
the Cardinals in a private meeting (*consistorio secreto*) on September 27,
1852.[5] The speech comprises approximately 2,900 words and in the Bonarum Artium edition is thirteen pages long. On that occasion, the Pope was
concerned with one problem, namely, the persecution of the Church in
Nuevo Grandes Casas, a prelature suffragan to the diocese of Chihuahua
(Mexico).[6] This open harassment was a sorrow for the Pope and came as a
complete surprise, given the previous attempt of both Gregory XVI and
Pius himself to remove the causes of difficulty.[7] A law of 1845, for example
had required bishops and priests under the threat of exile to abstain from
the exercise of their ministry. Gregory XVI had protested against this law;
Pius himself had even contacted the President, complaining also about
tithes to be collected without the consent of the Holy See and about the fact
that anyone entering that territory was allowed to practice any religion he
or she chose.[8] Pius had hoped some good would have come from his
intervention. Yet, the situation had only worsened. The past year, the Pope
said, a law had been promulgated against religious congregations. The
Jesuits themselves had been expelled, while the government extended its
help to anyone who would leave his or her congregation. The Archbishop
had been forbidden to visit religious houses. Cases which belong to the
Church to decide were being referred to a civil court. The *Cabildo parro-
quial* had assuméd the function of naming pastoᴦs.[9] The census, upon
which previous support of the Church by the state had depended, had been
abolished. There was unlimited freedom of the press. And Catholics who
resisted the new laws were in danger. The authority of the bishops had been
repressed, pastors had been inhibited from performing their duties: The
best were in prison, while the rest were reduced to indigence.

The Pope then dwelt at some length on the heroism of the Archbishop of
Bogotà,† Emanuel José de Monsquera, and on the state's attempt to

---

†   The diocese to which the Pope refers was erected on March 22, 1564. See José
Bravo Ugarte, *Diocesis y Obispos de la Iglesia Mexicana 1519-1939* (Mexico, D.F.:
"Buena Prensa," 1941), p. 17.

reinstate competitive examinations of the clergy for the placement of pastors. The Archbishop had been imprisoned, and later, despite frail health, had been banished. After stating that he would omit the description of further laws enacted against the Church, the Pope said:

> *Text A.* Thus we say nothing about those intended [*conceptis*] *decrees by which it was proposed that the Church be separated from the State*; that the property of the Regular Orders and of Church [*piorum*] legates be completely subjected to the burden of providing loans; that all laws having to do with protecting the status of religious congregations [*Familiarum*], their rights and duties, be repealed; that the civil authority there be given the right of erecting and limiting dioceses as well as Church-related schools [*Canonicorum Collegia*]; that ecclesiastical jurisdiction be given to those nominated by the government.[10]

The Pope goes on to discuss other evils in the present upheaval. What the state was doing relative to marriage laws disturbed him. It was not simply that the state was granting divorces in the strict sense of the term. The theology of marriage itself was being distorted by heretical views: Marriage was being considered as nothing more than a civil contract.[11] Despite everything, the Pope was consoled by the fortitude of the Archbishop and of the people themselves. In all this, Pius had not ceased to try through diplomatic channels to rectify the situation. In the meantime, he wanted no one to doubt that the Holy See condemned these developments, hoping that those perpetrating these outrages would have a change of heart, touched by grace to take the path of justice and truth.

From the Pope's manner of speaking, one would not have gathered that the persecution had been occasioned at least in part by significant abuses in the Church; yet there seems little doubt that all the right was not on one side.[12] Be that as it may, the cause of the disturbance is not my concern. My attention is centered on *Acerbissimum* because as cited in the Syllabus it allows one to discern the raison d'être of the condemned number 55. But the help it affords is only partial, it must be completed by a careful reading of *Quanta cura* itself:

> *Text B.* These false, perverse opinions are all the more to be detested in that they aim above all to inhibit and remove that saving power which the Catholic Church from the institution and command of her divine Author must until the end of the world freely exercise not less in relation to individuals than in relation to nations, peoples, and their highest rulers. . . .[13]

Text C. [These opinions are all the more to be detested in that they aim]...
to remove from society [de medio] that intermingling [mutua...
societas] and harmony of considerations between the Sacerdotium
and the Imperium, which have always been so auspicious and
salutary both for church and state.[14]

Text C follows immediately upon Text B; they are separated here only
for the purpose of clarifying the issues. One might hold (as in Text B) that
the mission of the Church is the result of a divine command, that that
mission extends not only to individuals but also—I take the words summos
Principes of the text as an equivalent to it—to the state without being
thereby obliged to hold that such a mission, though rooted in a command
from the Savior, necessarily entails a union between Church and state. But
the same cannot be said of the following passage (Text C). For if the phrase
mutua illa inter Sacerdotium et Imperium consiliorum societas et concordia does not imply a union between Church and state, then words have lost
all meaning.

Let us return to the as yet unanswered questions distinguished above. It
is the condemnation of number 55 of the Syllabus, Acerbissimum (Text A)
and Quanta cura itself (Text C) which establish the basis for affirming that
for Pius IX a union between Church and state was desirable in principle
and an ideal for which Catholics should strive (Question [C]). The answer
to Question (D), whether such a union implied that Catholicism should be,
whenever possible, the official state religion, is less easily determined. I
know of no explicit statement in the whole corpus of Pius IX's promulgated encyclicals and allocutions which grounds an unequivocally affirmative answer. However that may be, I suggest that scrutiny of Quanta
cura (Text C) permits one to make a legitimate inference. When speaking
of the mutua illa inter Sacerdotium et Imperium consiliorum societas et
concordia, Pius IX was looking not only to the present and future but
above all to the past as an ideal. And he seems to have looked at it with a
kind of yearning, for he says fausta semper exstitit.

Now I have come upon no case in the centuries prior to Pius IX in which
union between Church and state meant that Catholicism was to be other
than the official state religion. It must not be forgotten that the perspective
from which we are looking at things is the theology of the Roman Bishops,
not that of a particular Holy Roman Emperor who may have had thoughts
to the contrary. And even if in the centuries between Constantine and Pius
IX there be a rare exception, the evidence flows overwhelmingly in the

reverse direction. The implications relative to the Pope's intent should be obvious.

In regard to Question (E), the answer is more easily detectable and is implied, I suggest, in *Acerbissimum*. There (Text A), when speaking of laws intended to separate Church from state, the Pope complains of the proposed repeal of laws protecting religious congregations and the property belonging to them. The fundamental question, however, is the issue involved in Question (F). Let us continue with *Quanta cura*. After the last passage quoted above (Text C), there follows a sentence of fifty-four words in which religious indifferentism as a doctrinal system is condemned. The Pope then reverts to the Church-state question and says:

> *Text D.* ... *contrary to the doctrine of the scriptures, of the Church and the Holy Fathers,* these people do not hesitate to assert that the "best set-up [*conditionem*] of society is that in which the duty of coercing with sanctions and punishments those who violate the Catholic religion is not recognized, except inasmuch as the public peace demands it.[15]

One notes in passing that Text D provides additional information relative to Question (E) and the duty of the state to protect the Church. But the phrase " ... *contrary to the doctrine of the scriptures, of the Church and the Holy Fathers* ... " suggests that whatever Pius IX propounded on Church-state relations was intended as doctrine. That distinction is crucial for my argument, as the *intégriste* of the post-conciliar period invariably attempts to avoid the ecclesiological implications of what happened at Vatican II and in regard to the matter under consideration (one might add that of religious freedom) frequently does so by attempting to show that what the Popes taught was never really meant as anything more than policy. However superficially appealing that contention may be, it cannot withstand the test of sustained analysis. For despite the rambling manner in which Pius IX tended to approach theological questions, the data suggest that he propounded to the universal Church as ideal a union between Church and state in which Catholicism is the official religion protected by the state. It is no less certain that he taught this as Catholic doctrine. I submit that any lingering doubt is fully dissipated by the study of subsequent papal teaching and the modality of its reception, not to speak of diplomatic practice.

Development, Systemization, Continuity

LEO XIII

The encyclical *Immortale Dei* of November 1, 1885, the document perhaps most frequently referred to in the context of a theoretically ideal relation between Church and state as conceived by the more recent Roman Bishops, may be regarded as the development and systemization of the position exhibited by Pius IX and his immediate predecessors.[16] Indeed, with an indirect reference to *Quanta cura* and the Syllabus and in one footnote a direct reference to number 55 of the latter document,[17] Leo XIII put forth the claim in *Immortale Dei* that his teaching was in direct continuity with that of Pius IX. For Leo maintained that the state qua state must worship God, not according to a religion which might happen to strike the state's fancy but according to that religion which God has shown to be his will.[18] As Pius in *Quanta cura*, so Leo in *Immortale Dei* declared that it cannot be difficult to discern which is the true religion, for proofs are abundant and striking—fulfillment of prophecies; miracles in great number; rapid spread of the faith in the midst of enemies and of over-whelming obstacles; the witness of martyrs.[19] Form criticism, not yet clearly on the horizon of Christian thought, together with incipient studies in comparative religion, was to remove much of the ground from under this apologetic-in-outline. Whatever the extent to which a more self-disciplined and informed apologetic might throw some light in the approaching twilight, Leo's unexplicitly stated but unmistakable point was that the true Church of Christ is the Catholic Church and no other, despite the defects of that body. Its authentic signs being manifest to any sincere inquirer, the state might not legitimately proceed with indifference to that fact.[20] Between Church and state there must exist a certain orderly connection (*colligatio*) which may be compared to the union (*coniunctio*) of soul and body in a human being.[21]

Thus far Leo's thought is in complete continuity with that of Pius IX in *Quanta cura*, the condemned number 55 of the Syllabus, and *Acerbissimum*. Where Leo seems to go beyond Pius and his predecessors—at one point Leo says his position is in continuity with *Mirari vos* of Gregory XVI[22]—are those sections of *Immortale Dei* wherein the Pope attempts to ground the rationale behind a union between Church and state at least as an ideal. Without a single direct reference to Gelasius I, Leo nonetheless appeals to the doctrine of *Duo sunt* as developed by John of Paris: God has appointed the charge of the human race between two powers, the ecclesiastical and the civil, the one being set over things divine, the other over things human.[23] Each in its own way is supreme, each has fixed limits, each is defined by its nature. But these two powers have authority over the same persons; hence, for the sake of these persons, there must exist a certain harmony between them. The issue is clear in principle:

> *Text E.* Whatever therefore, in things human is of a sacred character, whatever belongs either of its own nature or by reason of the end to which it is referred, to the salvation of souls, or to the worship of God, is subject to the power and judgment of the Church. Whatever is to be ranged under the civil and political order is rightly subject to the civil authority. Jesus Christ has Himself given the command that what is Caesar's be rendered to Caesar, and that what belongs to God be rendered to God.[24]

What Leo, his predecessors and successors up to and including John XXIII did not apparently see is that, in order for harmony to exist between these two powers, a *coniunctio* between Church and state in Leo's terms, or a *mutua consiliorum societas et concordia* in Pius IX's was *not* necessary even as a matter of policy. The Fathers of Vatican II, however, were to see this and affirm it. Nonetheless, it is the perspective of Leo XIII, with its teaching on the two powers (and the necessary harmony between them), that is most frequently referred to in the first two drafts on Church-state relations as prepared by the Theological Commission. But Leo's doctrine as a development and systematization of the position of Pius IX—and of Pius' predecessors—is only one of the sources quoted in these documents. In the first of the drafts, Pius IX is referred to at least seven times,[25] in the second, at least eight,[26] there being in each case several direct references to *Quanta cura* and/or the Syllabus. Leo XIII's position on ideal Church-state relations constitutes a more logical presentation of what Pius IX had held in a more loosely construed if not somewhat confused fashion.

LEO'S SUCCESSORS

Special attention to the teaching of Leo XIII was necessary because it has frequently been maintained that Leo represents a turning away from the perspective of Pius IX, whereas in fact he developed and systematized the position of his predecessor.[27] As regards Leo's successors up to and probably including John XXIII, no attempt will be made here to document the obvious, which may be found in *Vehementer Nos* of Pius X, *Quas primas* of Pius XI, and *Mediator Dei* of Pius XII.[28] Indeed, in contrast with the correlative matter of religious freedom, I am aware of no serious attempt to show that the position that Vatican II took on ideal Church-state relations (Text F)[29] was in any way continuous with the teaching of the previous ordinary papal magisterium. The whole controversy between John Courtney Murray, S.J., Francis Connell, C.SS.R., and Joseph Clifford Fenton in the early fifties of this century, a controversy that ended in Murray's being silenced, makes no sense if the doctrine of the papal magisterium at the time were significantly different from that of Pius IX and Leo XIII.[30] I found in the documents nothing that indicates that ideal Church-state relations perceived as a doctrine by Pius IX had in any one of his successors become merely a matter of policy. That includes John XXIII. Unlike his somewhat ambivalent stance on religious freedom in *Pacem in terris*,[31] there is no indication that on the correlative matter of ideal Church-state relations John's teaching differed noticeably from that of his predecessors.

Early Conciliar Drafts

In this section, we shall deal essentially with three documents:[32]

1. *Homo a Deo destinatus* (*HAD*-a) submitted as Chap. IX of *Aeternus Unigeniti* (*AU*-a) which was concerned with the theology of the Church, and submitted by the theological Commission.[33]
2. *In nova salutis oeconomia* (*INS*), which constituted Chap. III of the draft *De Libertate religiosa* submitted by the Secretariat for Christian Unity.[34]
3. *Homo a Deo destinatus* (*HAD*-b) submitted as Chap. IX of *Aeternus Unigeniti* (*AU*-b) presented to the Council Fathers on November 23, 1962.[35]

Both *HAD*-a and *INS* were presented to the Preparatory Commission to be discussed on June 19 and 20, 1962; *HAD*-b was never formally discussed by the Council Fathers. I shall first summarize the relevant content of the first two documents, proceeding thence to illustrate the main thrust of the debate by the Preparatory Commission. I shall then indicate the extent of the changes reflected in the second draft of *Homo a Deo destinatus*, my purpose being the grounding of the third part of my argument as stated at the outset of this chapter.

DRAFTS PRESENTED
TO THE PREPARATORY COMMISSION

The First Draft Homo a Deo Destinatus

I have referred to this document by its opening words. But its title as presented by the Theological Commission was "*De Relationibus inter Ecclesiam et Statum necnon de Tolerantia religiosa*," the latter term itself suggesting that its framers were still within the worldview of Pius IX and Leo XIII. For though the Latin equivalent of the term *union* does not explicitly occur in the draft, nonetheless certain statements made by its authors make no sense unless Pius IX's position as developed and system-atized by Leo XIII was considered still to obtain. Number 1 of the draft simply describes the distinction between Church and state, saying that both are supreme in their own sphere and not subject one to the other. But since the two societies, though distinct, exercise their power in regard to the same persons, they cannot be indifferent to each other but must proceed in harmony. One recognizes at once the reasoning of *Immortale Dei*. Hence the purpose or end that civil society endeavors to attain must not be pursued in such a way that the last end of a human being is excluded or infringed upon (*laeso*). Thus, as stated in number 2, temporal affairs are not *per se* the concern of the Church. However, in those matters that regard both Church and state—marriage, the education of children—the power of the state should be exercised in such a way that, in the judgment of the Church, higher goods of the supernatural order suffer no detri-ment.[36] In other matters, provided the divine law is kept intact, the Church should not embroil itself in the affairs of state. It is in number 3 however that the position of Pius IX as developed by Leo XIII is adamantly retained. Its salient points may be summarized as follows:

1. Not only individuals but also the state (*potestas civilis*) must do their duty toward God[37]
2. That duty includes the public worship of God[38]

3. In the present economy of salvation, the way in which God is to be worshiped is none other than the way of the true Church of Christ[39]
4. From manifest signs of its divine foundation (*institutionis*) and the mission with which the Church has been provided by its Founder, it is possible for the state to come to know the true Church[40]
5. It is therefore incumbent upon the state, and not simply upon individual citizens, to accept the revelation proposed by the Church[41]
6. Hence the state must exclude from law, government, and the public domain (*actione publica*) anything that the Church judges to be prejudicial to the attainment of a human being's last end[42]
7. Indeed, the state must direct its efforts to facilitating life built upon Christian principles and conducive to that sublime purpose for which God created human beings in the first place[43]
8. The Church has always acknowledged that the relation between Church and state depends on the extent to which the state (*potestas civilis*) as representing the people comes to know Christ and the Church founded by Him[44]

Thus the draft makes clear that all this is possible only in that situation wherein the citizens of the state, and the state inasmuch as it represents the citizens, have made the judgment that a revelation has in fact been given.[45] These principles having been explained, the authors of the draft proceed to show how they are to be applied in a Catholic versus a non-Catholic state. I shall return to that aspect of the question when I take up the matter of religious freedom.

For my present purpose, it will be sufficient accurately to understand what the authors of the draft did and did not state. They did not find acceptable any situation wherein Catholicism is forced upon those who in good conscience feel they must reject it. In fact, the draft explicitly excludes any such attempt, its reason being that the act of faith by its very nature must be a free act.[46] Nor did the framers of *HAD*-a see its principles as applicable in a context where the majority of citizens, though baptized Catholics, do not in fact practice the faith. What the authors envisaged was a situation wherein the vast majority of citizens *freely* accept Christ as preached by the Catholic Church; at that point, and at that point alone, the authors maintain that such citizens have the right to insist that the state, which represents them, do its work in the light of Catholic principles. Quite clearly the authors thought on the level of abstract theory. Still on the level of principle, they intended much more: (1) and (5) require a particular ideological stance on the part of the state over and above that which its members have already given as individuals. In that way, the authors involved themselves in a faulty logic, for the state is not really distinct from the individuals who compose it. Thus the authors failed adequately to distinguish, as John Courtney Murray eventually came to do, between state and society, and that despite the fact that *potestas civilis* and *societas civilis* are used for state and society respectively. It is however especially in (6) and (7) that the perspective of the ordinary papal magisterium is manifest. For it is difficult to see how that kind and degree of cooperation between Church and state could obtain or be envisaged to obtain without a veritable union between these two bodies. Thus though the document does not say *ipsissimis verbis* that ideally there must be a union between Church and state in which Catholicism, as the official religion, is protected by the state, nonetheless it is difficult to make any sense out of it unless one presupposes that such was the intent of its authors.

The Draft on Religious Freedom: In nova salutis oeconomia

Compared to *HAD*-a, Chapter III of *De Libertate religiosa* (*INS*) reflected obvious differences of views. Where the former had been entitled "*De Relationibus inter Ecclesiam et* **Statum** *necnon de* Tolerantia religiosa," the latter was called "*De Relationibus inter Ecclesiam et* **Societatem** *civilem.*" A fundamental difference of thrust was apparent at once. Its essential characteristics may be highlighted as follows:

1. Civil *society*, just as every human community, is obliged to worship God. This it will do according to its nature; i.e., by attending in its legislation to divine law and by faithfully fulfilling its mission received from God. By protecting in a befitting legal way the dignity of the human person and by promoting civic virtue, civil society will prepare the way for all things to be restored in Christ.[47]

2. A theocracy befitted the Chosen People of the Old Testament; it does not befit the Church, which precisely as universal, transcends the temporal order. Whence civil society must keep to its own affairs and grant freedom to the Church, not excluding the propagation of the faith.[48]

3. The Catholic Church has never admitted that the *state* (*statum*) may (*potest*) positively (*modo positivo*) propagate a doctrine of religious indifference by which all *religions* are affirmed as being equal. But the Church does approve of those modern civil societies which in practice decide that religious freedom and political equality be granted to the *followers* of any religion.[49]

4.   Religious freedom acknowledged as the right of individuals must be granted to religious communities that citizens set up, because of the social nature of the human person, as long as these activities are consistent with public order and the common good.[50]

5.   Lest such freedom in the constitutions of civil society be considered a passing concession (*concessio fluxa*) it ought (*debet*) to be sanctioned by the forces of law (*iure firmo*) and to be expressed by the *civil equality of cults.*[51]

6.   Although the juridical statute that makes religious freedom sacred may take on various forms according to diverse historical circumstances, it is nonetheless to be hoped that the Catholic Church in those of its activities that serve the common good from the point of view of civil society, will receive financial help (*subsidiaria*) inasmuch as the nature of the said civil constitution permits. This financial help, in due proportion and within the limits of the common good, should be granted likewise to those communities that are not Catholic.[52]

From Cardinal Bea's report, to which I shall turn below, it seems that the term *societas civilis* was chosen deliberately in order to distinguish *society* from *state*.[53] Hence, Bea was to say that the *potestas civilis* (not to be confused with *societas civilis*) synonymous with *state* must serve God, which is not the same as to say that it must participate in a cult (*exercere cultum*), something that is the task of the Church alone.[54] It is noteworthy that this document, the salient features of which I have sketched above, contains no critical apparatus but only a series of remarks (*Adnotationes*) that precede Bea's report. There is no reference to the teaching of the ordinary papal magisterium; there could not be: The whole tone of the document takes a note directly contrary to it.[55] Yet, the authors in (3) attempt to safeguard what they considered of enduring value in what the magisterium had indeed taught. It is further noteworthy that Bea pointed out that the draft presented by the Secretariat for Christian Unity was essentially in agreement with numbers 1 and 2 of *HAD*-a but differed from it in numbers 3-8, especially in those matters pertaining to the mission and competence of civil authority (*auctoritas civilis*).[56] The position of the Secretariat was that civil authority is concerned only with the common *human* good and that this is manifest through reason, for the state (*Status*) qua state knows nothing of the supernatural.[57] This is a sociological problem, Bea said, not a theological one. It is not laicism; it is the application of the words of the Lord, "Render to Caesar the things that are Caesar's, and to God the things that are God's."[58] Quite clearly the Secretariat had taken a position not unlike that which John Courtney Murray had defended some years earlier.[59]

Debate by the Preparatory Commission

The document submitted by the Secretariat for Christian Unity had been separate from that presented by the Theological Commission because, as Bea complained in his report, the Theological Commission (under Ottaviani) had refused to cooperate with the Secretariat for Christian Unity (under Bea). The discussion within the Preparatory Commission on June 19 and 20, 1962 related to both documents; but I shall here emphasize those aspects of the exchanges that bear on Church-state relations. It will be seen that the critique of both drafts resulted in the shelving of the draft on religious freedom (*INS*) and in making merely cosmetic changes in Chap. IX of *Aeternus Unigeniti (HAD*-a).

Besides Ottaviani and Bea, there were twelve speakers, of whom at least seven were clearly against the draft as presented by the Theological Commission. Cardinal Frings was the first to speak and among other things said that, whatever may have been the situation in the past, the Church never needs the arm of the state to protect the Catholic faith or to prevent the spread of religious error.[60] Cardinal Léger stated that the draft presented for discussion merely repeated the position that had obtained a century ago; namely, that the thesis is applied whenever the State is Catholic but is suspended whenever it is not.[61] While *HAD*-a personified certain abstractions or functions such as *potestas civilis non catholica* as though they had a separate existence, the term *civitas catholica* was itself very ambiguous (*confusa*). What, he asked, is a *Catholic* state?[62] Furthermore, the logic of the draft, if the majority of citizens in a state are Protestant, or, say, Buddhists, would lead to a situation of totalitarianism into which Catholicism could not penetrate.[63] It will be seen that in his reply at the end of the debate Cardinal Ottaviani missed the real thrust of Léger's point.

Cardinal Döpfner raised further difficulties.[64] Reducing the argument of the draft as he understood it to its simplest terms (both Church and state each has its own purpose, but the purpose of the Church is a higher one, from which fact certain conclusions follow . . .), he said that the argument is valid and has indeed been confirmed by the authority of the Sovereign Pontiffs, especially Leo XIII. But today it must be completed: Leo XIII was speaking of another situation, that of rationalistic individualism.[65] Circumstances now are different, for today, with the exception of Communism, there is a new kind of humanism that has developed not without the influence of the social doctrine of the Church and that in many respects corresponds to the Catholic concept. That is to say, the new humanism

admits *social* values on which the *polis* can be founded.[66] Döpfner then
indicated, without pointing out (as Archbishop Hurley was to do later) the
intrinsic contradictions in the draft, that according to *HAD*-a the purpose
of the state is restricted to the pursuit of an earthly good; that it would be
better to take up the matter from the point of view of the *common* good to
be derived from the *social* nature of the human being; that in the draft
many rights and duties are ascribed to the state whereas in fact they pertain
to the Church.[67] Döpfner's next remark was highly significant:

> ... among the duties of the state [*potestatis civilis*] there are recounted many
> about which Catholic authors have hitherto been in doubt . . . thus, for
> example, Catholic theologians do not agree whether every state [*civitas*]
> absolutely and per se, by reason [*vi*] of the common good, is obliged to
> perform civil acts of public worship, explicitly to defend the Catholic faith,
> or to limit the freedom of worship of non-Catholics. Among those who hold
> a negative opinion, there are to be found men who are both highly intelligent
> [*clarissimi*] and who, in regard to social doctrine, have served the Church
> well, such as Gundlach, Pavan, Lecler, De la Brière, Rouquette, Murray, A.
> Hartmann, M. Pribilla. It does not seem opportune to decide in Council
> these matters which up to the present have been disputed.[68]

Perhaps the most vigorous attack on the internal logic of the document
came from Archbishop Denis Eugene Hurley, O.M.I., of Durban, South
Africa. The crux of the question, he said, came down to this: The state must
worship God in the manner in which God has indicated, and that, in the
present economy of salvation, can be done only in the true Church of
Christ. If this doctrine cannot be changed, then we have done with the draft
presented by the Secretariat for Christian Unity and we must stand by the
draft, "De Relationibus inter Ecclesiam et Statum necnon de Tolerantia
religiosa."[69] But, he went on, there are problems with the traditional
doctrine. I limit myself here to two of Hurley's central points:

1. On the one hand, the traditional doctrine as put forth in the
   draft asserts that the end of civil society is the common good of
   the temporal order; on the other hand, it asserts that in the
   present economy of salvation the state must worship the God of
   the supernatural order.[70]
2. On the one hand, the traditional doctrine as put forth in the
   draft says that the state, as a perfect society, has the means of
   attaining its end; on the other hand, the traditional doctrine
   contends that the state cannot do this adequately without having
   recourse to the Church.[71]

Behind these inconsistencies lay a whole Augustinian-Thomistic theology of grace unstated in the draft but commonly accepted by Catholic theologians; namely, that though human nature in a state of estrangement after the Fall remains essentially good, it does not always rightly discern the true and the good and therefore needs the help of revelation. It is for that reason that a human being needs the help of the teaching Church, not because the Church is the author of revelation but because she is its authentic custodian and faithful interpreter. For in certain religio-moral matters where a human being is left to his or her own devices pure and simple, he or she is likely to choose a path inimical to true happiness. But it was not this theology that was the cause of the inconsistencies noted by Hurley. In Lonergan's terms, the cause was the failure to ask further relevant questions. Must help from a biblically based revelation come about through a union of Church and state, or through reasonable debate in society? If one says it must come about through a union between Church and state, does one not ultimately presuppose that the state is really distinct from those who compose it?

At this point in the debate, Hurley said he did not see how these contradictions could be resolved without some change in the traditional doctrine. He added further:

> I do not see why this change cannot be made. *For the doctrine concerning the obligation of the state to worship God in the Catholic Church has not been infallibly defined.* And in the past, the very theological argument was able in some way to proceed in a less correct manner.[72]

It is quite clear from the context that Hurley was suggesting that the teaching of the ordinary papal magisterium over the past four generations—and earlier—might be changed by the Council. He then continued with his argument. Human beings, he said, have a social nature and must, not only as individuals but also as individuals who constitute a society, render worship to God. About that there can be no doubt. But the conclusion that both as citizens (*in societate civili*) and through the state (*per potestatem civilem*) human beings must worship God is not justified. Why should this be the case? There exists another society in which human beings as a society may worship God. And that society is the Church.[73]

Others such as Bishop Cooray were to attack the position of *HAD*-a with arguments more philosophical than theological, though nonetheless probing.[74] Still others stood by the draft, the most outstanding being, perhaps, Cardinal Browne.[75] His remarks deserve special attention because they stand in polarity with those of Hurley:

In regard to doctrine, the first draft [*HAD*-a] is almost impeccable, as far as I know. And in no way can I understand how the encyclical *Immortale Dei* which was written by Leo XIII to protect the philosophy and theology of the present question can ever be changed. It seems somewhat infantile to suppose that the doctrine expounded in the encyclical *Immortale Dei* was an affair of the moment.[76]

However, the concrete situation in which the Church finds herself is a fact of life that must be reckoned with.[77] Let the Pope decide whether he wants a draft in which Catholic principles are clearly enunciated, or whether he wants a draft more pastorally oriented.[78] In the latter case, Browne suggested that Bea's draft be rewritten according to the principles expounded in *HAD*-a, not in any cut and dried way but in a way befitting current circumstances.[79] Thus nothing would be lost of the doctrine put forth by Leo XIII in *Immortale Dei*. The truth does not have to be stated out of due season (*in omni instanti*).[80]

At the end of this two-day discussion, Cardinal Ottaviani said that the length of the debate showed how important the issue was. Hence he wished before the actual voting to say how necessary it was to distinguish between the two drafts (*HAD*-a and *INS*). This was essential, he said, in order to know what direction to take.[81] The fundamental question, as the Archbishop of Durban (i.e., Archbishop Hurley) had pointed out, is whether the state has the obligation to worship God or not. That it does had always been the teaching of the magisterium.[82] He then praised the remarks of Archbishop Alter of Cincinnati, who had shown that in the United States separation of Church and state does not mean that the state is ex officio atheistic. But Ottaviani objected strenuously to what he considered a misinterpretation of his position: We do not want, he insisted, a situation where, when Catholics are in the majority, we merely tolerate other religions; or a situation wherein, Catholics being the minority, we opt for equality (*paritatem*).[83] The principle involved is a democratic one: In a state where Catholics are in a majority, they may insist that the state act according to the principles laid down by the citizens. But let us suppose a situation as in Yugoslavia, there being about fourteen million Catholics, fourteen million Orthodox, and fourteen million Mohammedans. In such circumstances, the Church opts for equality (*pro paritate cultuum*).[84] In a situation where the vast majority are non-Catholics, only toleration is called for. Here Ottaviani missed the point of Léger's objection, for logically, according to Ottaviani's democratic principle, in a state wherein the vast majority are atheistic, the people may decide that the law of the land be enacted according to atheistic principles. Hence, if the majority of

Russian citizens really accepted the official atheism of the Union of Soviet Socialist Republics, no logical objection could be made. One would have to initiate another kind of argument; that is to say, one would have to ask whether atheism takes fully into account the facts of human experience. But that is another question and one that the framers of *HAD*-a obviously presupposed must be answered in the negative.

I pass over here Ottaviani's remarks relative to Protestantism in Latin America and the difficulties that a change in the traditional doctrine would entail in that region.[85] His concluding remarks are especially significant:

> Therefore, it is useless to say, as one bishop said, "with due respect to the ecclesiastical magisterium": The ecclesiastical magisterium has been what it has been, and we cannot say we have due reverence for it and then proceed to act against it.[86]

With that remark, as with the challenge set by Archbishop Hurley along with others who thought the traditional teaching of the ordinary papal magisterium might and should be changed in this regard, the tone of the debate to be continued during the Council was set. On the day of the vote, there were sixty-six present, not counting Ottaviani and Bea. As the former had requested, when the actual voting took place most members of the Preparatory Commission explicitly distinguished *HAD*-a from *INS*. There was one abstention (Roberti).[87] Eighteen were clearly in favor of *HAD*-a, fifteen were equally opposed to it. Twenty voted *iuxta modum* (i.e., with qualified acceptance). Of the remaining number, it is impossible to say from the documentation presently accessible to me how many votes of qualified acceptance meant that *HAD*-a was to be reworked in the sense of *INS*, or vice versa. Thus, for example, Cardinal Ciriaci simply stated, in the context of *De Libertate religiosa*, "Placeret de concordia inter Commissionem Theologicam et Secretariatum ad christianam unitatem fovendam,"[88] and Cardinal Traglia, referring apparently to *HAD*-a, "Placet, iuxta observationes in foliis adnexis expositas."[89] In regard to the document prepared by the Secretariat for Christian Unity, fifteen voted in its favor, seven were clearly opposed, twelve expressed qualified acceptance. The intentions of the remaining number are uncertain. Though there was undoubtedly a very strong sentiment in favor of rejecting the document prepared by the Theological Commission, I have so far come upon no evidence to suggest that Ottaviani was given a mandate to change its central theses. Thus for the moment at least the draft on religious freedom (*INS*) with its quite different orientation on Church-state relations seemed doomed to oblivion. Yet it is interesting to note in passing that Cardinal

Montini, the future Paul VI, voted against the document prepared by the Theological Commission. His expressed sympathies were along the lines of the critique made by Léger, Döpfner, Alfrink and Hurley, all of whom he explicitly cited.[90]

Homo a Deo Destinatus
(*Second Draft*)

That changes in the first draft on ideal Church-state relations were only cosmetic is clear from even a cursory reading of the second. Chap. IX of *Aeternus Unigeniti* as presented to the Council Fathers on November 23, 1962, was at once distinguishable by its modified title, wherein the document no longer made reference to religious tolerance but read simply, "De Relationibus inter Ecclesiam et Statum."[91] Though drastically reduced in length, sentences remained that suggested a union between Church and state such as Pius IX and Leo XIII seem to have conceived it. Thus the new draft presented no changes which made it in any way substantially different from its antecedent. Even the state, *HAD*-b asserts, must worship God, although liturgical cult is the business of the Church alone.[92] The state will do its duty if it sees to it that laws established by God for this economy of salvation are observed.[93] And that means, so continued the draft, that full freedom having been given to the Church, there be excluded from law, government and the public domain whatever the Church judges inimical to a human being's last end.[94] The state of course cannot be expected to do this, the draft stated in the manner of *HAD*-a, unless the citizens, whom the state represents, have come to accept revelation as a fact.[95]

Though *HAD*-b is less direct in its approach, its stance on the ideal relation between Church and state remained essentially the same as that of *HAD*-a. Its doctrine was to be applied with great moderation, but the Council, the new draft stated, could not permit the principles underlying the proper relation between Church and state to be obscured by a false laicism and that under the pretext of the common good.[96] It is impossible to read sentences like "And these duties toward God are to be performed not only by individual citizens but also by the state [*a Potestate civili*], which in acts of polity acts as a person [*Societatis civilis personam gerit*]"[97] without realizing that nothing much had changed between the discussion of *HAD*-a by the Preparatory Commission on June 19-20, 1962, and the presentation of *HAD*-b to the Council Fathers on November 23 of the same year. The spirit and indeed the letter though not of course the *ipsissima verba* of Pius IX's position on ideal Church-state relations developed and systematized by Leo XIII and continuing in their successors, were thus presented to the Council Fathers for what was doubtless expected to be their approval. Papal teaching on ideal Church-state relations thus lasted well after the opening of the Second Vatican Council.

Reversal

That doctrine was unambiguously overturned by the Council:[98]

> *Text F.* If, in view of peculiar circumstances obtaining among certain peoples, special legal recognition is given in the constitutional order of society to one religious body, it is at the same time imperative that the right of all citizens and religious bodies to religious freedom should be recognized and made effective in practice.[99]

The text does not speak specifically of Church-state relations but such is its obvious intent. Reflecting a few minor changes as compared with its first appearance in *Dignitatis humanae personae* (*DH*-a),[100] a draft on religious freedom to be distributed (as of May 28, 1965) to the dispersed Council Fathers, this paragraph constitutes an undeniable reversal of the official papal position on ideal Church-state relations. Recall that the teaching of Pius IX and Leo XIII and its continuance in their successors had been presented not merely as policy but as doctrine. The *if* with which Text F begins transforms their *must-in-principle* to a *may-under-certain-conditions*.

The change was not made without a struggle. One has only to think of the critiques of a Cardinal Browne, a Cardinal Quiroga y Palacios and a Cardinal Meouchi, to mention only three, at whose insistence the earlier versions of Text F were introduced into the drafts in the first place, but in a form much attenuated.[101] The possibility of a union between Church and state in which Catholicism is acknowledged as the official religion protected by the state remains but it is no longer presented as necessary in principle.[102] Though as I have said the issues are ideologically distinct, it had been an outmoded papal position on ideal Church-state relations that historically speaking had led the Popes to a partially erroneous doctrine on religious freedom. In this case, the Council did not first develop the papal teaching and from that development perceive that aspects of the papal position had to be dropped or changed in the name of consistency; in this case, the Council quite simply reversed it. That the reversal, discreet but unmistakable, occurred not in the document on the Church (where *HAD*-a and *HAD*-b had originally appeared) but in the Declaration on Religious Freedom is itself symbolic. As an issue, the question of ideal Church-state relations simply faded away and was replaced by another on which the full weight of the ordinary papal magisterium had rested for well over one hundred fifty years. Such is the burden of the following chapter.

Chapter IV
THE RELIGIOUS
FREEDOM ISSUE

The notion of development, not the notion of religious freedom, was the real
sticking-point for many of those who opposed the Declaration [on Religious
Freedom] to the end. The course of development between the *Syllabus of
Errors* [1864] and *Dignitatis Humanae Personae* [1965] remains to be
explained by theologians. But the Council formally sanctioned the validity
of the development itself; and this was a doctrinal event of high importance
for theological thought in many other areas.[1]

This assessment by John Courtney Murray, one of the principal architects of the Declaration on Religious Freedom, may in the end prove to be
an understatement. But if it does, it will not be primarily because of the
notion of development itself. At least from the time of Bossuet, Catholic
theologians have admitted that in a very real sense doctrine does indeed
develop.[2] The only further questions for Catholic theologians concern
criteria for distinguishing authentic from inauthentic growth in under-

147

standing the Gospel and what it requires.[3] In the latter context, the underlying issue at the Council was not the notion but the process by which the teaching that culminated in *Dignitatis humanae* was taking place. For in at least one significant respect it involved the reversal of the position of the ordinary papal magisterium.

The fact is not, however, immediately obvious. In *Pacem in terris* John XXIII listed among the rights of every human being the right ". . . to honor God according to the sincere dictates of conscience and therefore the right to practice his [or her] religion privately and publicly."[4] That right, along with the duties from which it flows, is based on the dignity of the human person. Indeed, the term *dignitas humanae personae* and its synonyms occur so frequently in *Pacem in terris* that the uninformed reader might be led to conclude from the opening words of the promulgated Declaration on Religious Freedom (*Dignitatis humanae*, henceforth referred to, for the most part, as *DH*-d) that the teaching of the Council is continuous with that of the papal magisterium, an alleged fact that some commentators both during and after the Council have been at pains to point out.[5] I find their view oversimplified.

Before proceeding further, however, it may be helpful to note that the term *religious freedom* is an umbrella concept and that as such it has a number of built-in ambiguities. At least six different questions must be distinguished within the complex "religious freedom":

(A)   In religious matters especially, does a human being have an objective duty to seek the truth and adhere to it once it has been found?

(B)   Does a human being have an objective duty to inform his or her conscience honestly and responsibly?

(C)   Does a human being have an objective duty to follow his or her conscience, even if that conscience be erroneous?

(D)   May the assent of faith be forced?

(E)   Does a human being in the present economy of salvation have the *objective* right to worship God in the manner in which a responsible use of intellect indicates he or she should?

(F)   Does a human being have an objective right to worship God in a way other than the way God is worshiped in the Roman Church and those other local Christian churches in union with it?

These questions do not occur in the documents to be examined below; they are presented here merely as a heuristic device. The reader is asked to keep them in mind as we proceed. Note that Questions (A) and (B) are intimately related but that the thrust of the former is sufficiently different to justify its being placed as a separate question. Note also that Question (A) is closely connected with Question (F). For not only in the minds of the Popes but also for most informed Catholics the pursuit of religious truth leads per se to the Catholic Church as defined in the introduction to this book. The term *religious freedom* as used in these pages embraces all these nuances but the question with which I am more directly concerned is Question (E), an affirmative answer to which constitutes the distinctive contribution of *Dignitatis humanae*.

That answer, when seen within the broader context of Catholic "tradition" seems to constitute a tension between a Thomistic and a Suarezian notion of *conscientia recta*. For Aquinas, a person has a "right conscience" when he or she, in deciding that a particular act is to be done or to be avoided, forms an antecedent judgment in conformity with objectively valid norms.[6] For Suarez, a distinction having its roots in Scotus is to be made between objective and subjective truth. The former is roughly equivalent to the Thomistic notion of *conscientia recta*; the latter comes about in the mind of a person who, though mistaken about the legitimacy of a particular course of action, is nonetheless motivated by the will to know the true and to do the good.[7] Paradoxical as it may seem, however, the development that terminated in *Dignitatis humanae* did not come about from an affirmative answer to Question (C) but from an affirmative answer to Question (A), which in the minds of those who insisted on it was necessitated by a negative answer to Question (F). Thus the distinctive contribution of *Dignitatis humanae* is incompatible with a Suarezian definition of subjective truth *tout court* in that the conciliar declaration insists on the objective duty to seek the truth; on the other hand, contrary to previous papal teaching, the Council does not accept a Thomistic definition of *conscientia recta* as a condition for religious freedom as an objective right.

I shall not pursue this investigation however in terms of norms for *conscientia recta* but shall by and large keep to the six heuristic questions listed above. I shall argue:

> I. Despite John XXIII's alleged attempt in Pacem in terris *to correct the teaching of his predecessors, papal doctrine on religious freedom as enunciated by Pius IX and as systemized by Leo XIII prevailed in the*

Catholic Church well into the beginning of the Second Vatican Council.

II.   *The position of Vatican II on the nature of religious freedom seems to constitute both a development and a reversal of papal teaching previous to* Pacem in terris.

This chapter consists of two principal parts corresponding to the above statements respectively. Each is composed of four sections. In the first, I shall begin by determining the teaching of Pius IX, showing in the second that, contrary to what has sometimes been affirmed, it was (like the matter of ideal Church-state relations) systematized by Leo XIII. Since a significant minority at Vatican II argued that the doctrine that found its way into *DH*-d was indeed continuous with the teaching of the previous papal magisterium, I shall in the third section assess the extent to which such an assertion may or may not be probable. In the fourth, I shall indicate how the position of Pius IX as continued by Leo XIII prevailed well into the beginning of the Second Vatican Council. My purpose in and the general thrust of the second part of this chapter will be clarified below. The third part is a brief assessment.

Finally, just as in the preceding chapter in dealing with Church-state relations it proved impossible not to refer on occasion to the correlative issue of religious freedom, so in treating the latter it will sometimes be difficult not to touch upon Church-state relations.

The Lasting Consistency of the Papal Position

THE TEACHING OF PIUS IX

The doctrine on religious freedom as enunciated by Pius IX was quite obviously based on that of his immediate predecessors. One has only to think of *Mirari vos* (August 17, 1832) by Gregory XVI or still earlier of *Diu satis* (May 15, 1800) by Pius VII. Regarding Pius IX, three *loci* are central: the letter *Multiplices inter* of June 10, 1851, the allocution *Maxima quidem laetitia* of January 6, 1862, and the encyclical *Quanta cura* with its attached Syllabus of Errors of December 8, 1864.

Multiplices inter is a brief letter of about 950 words comprising five pages in the Bonarum Artium edition—the *Acta Sanctae Sedis* as the official organ of the Holy See was still fourteen years in the future.[8] Addressed to Catholic Bishops, the letter advises them of the Holy See's action relative to a book published three years earlier. Entitled *Defensa de la autoridad de los Gobiernos y de los Obispos contra las pretenciones de la Curia Romana*, written by Francisco de Paula and published by G. Vigil in Lima, the book contains, according to Pius, a number of very serious errors.[9] Its author denies that the Church has the power to define as dogma that the Catholic Religion is the only true one;[10] he further teaches that marriage is to be preferred to virginity;[11] that the power of the Church to set up diriment impediments to marriage in the Church flows from the secular power that the Church simply assumed for itself;[12] that the immunity of the Church from the civil power has its origin not in the divine foundation of the Church but in civil law.[13] It is unnecessary to continue the list of errors Pius and his advisors say they found in the book; it is sufficient for our present purpose to note the general context in which Pius lists among the errors in de Paula's book the fact that its author claims "... anyone is free to embrace and profess that religion which the light of reason leads him to consider true."[14] Pius tells his fellow magisterial officers that the book has been condemned; that anyone who, after this public admonition, reads it or even has it in his possession, incurs excommunication; and that anyone possessing a copy of the book must turn it in to the Inquisition.[15]

Maxima quidem laetitia is an allocution delivered to the cardinals and bishops assembled in Rome for the canonization of twenty-seven Japanese martyrs. In the Bonarum Artium edition, it is eleven pages long and contains about 2,600 words.[16] The meeting is one of joy, but the Pope takes the occasion to speak to the bishops and cardinals about the difficulties through which the Church of Christ is presently passing. He intends to point out errors and give some pastoral advice as to how they may be met. A fundamental cause of tumult in both Church and state is a highly organized attempt to establish the theoretical and practical foundations of a lay state in which the supreme value is unaided human reason.[17] Such a perspective results in the denial of divine revelation. The Pope goes on to say:

> *Text A.*   Since they [i.e., this highly organized conspiracy] dare to derive all religious truth from the innate strength of human reason, they then attribute to each man a certain primitive right to think and speak

as he likes about matters religious, to worship God as he thinks best.[18]

Two years later these two documents will become the basis of the condemned proposition number 15 of the Syllabus of Errors, which states it is an error to say a human being may ". . . embrace and practice that religion which by the light of reason he [or she] thinks true."[19] But the emphasis of *Maxima quidem* is different from that of *Multiplices inter*. In the earlier document, the Pope's stricture on religious freedom occurs with reference to an ideological conflict in Church-state relations; in the later document, the stricture appears in the context of exposing and refuting a pretended basis for a lay state in which reason is proposed as the ultimate and self-sufficient norm not only for private morality but also for government.

The third *locus*, the encyclical *Quanta cura*, not only combines the different perspectives of the two former documents but, with some probing, provides the means of discerning the internal logic of the Pope's position. For at first blush, the Pope's thought appears somewhat confused. In this document, which comprises some three thousand words and in the Bonarum Artium edition exactly fourteen pages, Pius explicitly mentions *Maxima quidem laetitia* as one of the occasions whereon he had previously dealt with the errors he sees as menacing the Church.[20] Whereas the question of religious freedom is linked in *Quanta cura* not with the supremacy of unaided human reason as in *Maxima quidem laetitia* but with an ideological conflict on separation of Church and state as described in the earlier (but unmentioned in the *Quanta cura*) document, *Multiplices inter*, the drive for separation of Church and state itself is the result of *naturalism*, a term that does not occur in the two previous documents.[21] By *naturalism* the Pope means the exaltation of unaided human reason as the principal source of the evils of his day.[22] The real enemy of Catholicism is thus the Enlightenment and its aftermath, though the Pope does not use the term. In the same paragraph in which the criticism of unaided human reason as an absolute norm occurs, he makes a direct connection between the move to separate the Church from the state and what he considers an erroneous view on the nature of religious freedom; namely, that

Text B. . . . the freedom of conscience and/or worship is the inalienable right of each individual, a fact which must be proclaimed and affirmed by law in every duly constituted society . . . .[23]

The Pope then goes on to mention other errors and/or evils flowing from the same source henceforth called naturalism. Thus for example public opinion or the will of the people once manifested has by that fact alone the force of law;[24] religious congregations are now persecuted;[25] the clergy are no longer allowed to have anything to do with the education of youth.[26] Pius suggests the means for coping with what he sees as a deteriorating situation, laying considerable stress on a collegial approach (surprising, perhaps, given Pius' reputation as an autocrat) to the constant teaching of pure doctrine.[27] What interests us here, given the purpose of this inquiry, is discerning the logical link between the perception of the various errors. For Pius IX, whatever other qualities he may have possessed, did not possess the logical mind of a Leo XIII. It is not clear from the documents we have examined whether what the Pope condemns as a false notion of religious freedom expressed in Text B is condemned as an objective right or as a subjective one. From other sources, however, we know he meant the former.[28] And from the different emphases of *Multiplices inter* and *Maxima quidem laetitia*, which span a period of some eleven years and come together in *Quanta cura*, the somewhat blurred logic of the Pope's thought may be summarized as follows: (1) religious freedom as an objective right is an error; (2) its proximate cause is to be attributed to the impetus to separate Church from state; (3) its remote cause is the exaltation of unaided human reason as a norm in itself sufficient for both private and public morality, whence the denial of divine revelation. It should be noted that Pius' concerns are directed not toward Catholicism as it was being lived in the United States but toward the situation in European or South American states where the majority of citizens were Catholics. It should further be noted that in these three documents, the Pope rarely argues from the intrinsic viability of his position but rather from the consequences of its contradictory. He tells Catholics and their bishops in these nations to look about them and to see what is happening: Morals are deteriorating; there is revolution everywhere. A tree that produces this kind of fruit cannot be good.

Yet the Pope sometimes essays a positive argument as in his very first encyclical, *Qui pluribus* of November 9, 1846, summarized in the preceding chapter on non-Christian religions. However inadequate his apologetic may be from the standpoint of modern scholarship, it is clear for the Pope that, since God's revelation is manifest in the Catholic Religion, a human being is not objectively free to take a contrary stance, much less a contradictory one. Reduced to syllogistic form, Pius' argument might be stated as follows:

A human being must worship God according to God's will.
But God's will is that He be worshiped as He is in the Roman Church and those local Christian churches united with it.
Therefore a human being must worship God as He is worshiped in the Roman Church and those local Christian churches united with it.

This is the principle that had to be maintained at all costs, as a man in the wilderness must hang on to his compass. In Catholic polemical language of the time, it was frequently called the *thesis*, in the light of which to speak as though a human being had an objective right to do as he pleased in matters religious was for Pius to speak theological nonsense. But even an officially Catholic state may tolerate for the common good (as Pius did in the papal states as long as they were his) other cults even publicly manifested. In Catholic theological language of the time, this concession to concrete reality was frequently called the *hypothesis*.[29] Though the terms do not appear in the above mentioned documents, *thesis* and *hypothesis* (or theory and practice) constitute the perimeter of the Pope's thinking.

In regard to that statement the data suggest a certain caution. At least three different but closely connected uses of the terms *thesis*/ *hypothesis* must be distinguished:

thesis	(α)	timeless principle
hypothesis		applied to circumstances
thesis	(β)	ideal situation
hypothesis		mitigated by circumstances
thesis	(γ)	accommodation elevated to principle
hypothesis		accommodation to circumstances

Thesis/hypothesis (α) is at least as old as Quintillian;[30] its difference from (β) is subtle but perceptible. In the former, one is dealing with an abstract principle (Human beings should marry) as opposed to the concrete question (Should Cato marry?). In the latter one is not dealing with the timeless truth of the Gospel, which cannot be mitigated, but with an ideal socio-political setup were it possible to put the Gospel fully into effect.[31] The movement in (α) and (β) is from the top down, as it were; that in (γ) from the bottom up.

There can be no doubt that the principal target of Pius IX's condemnations (and one may add those of his successors up to but possibly excluding John XXIII) had to do with thesis/hypothesis (γ). As Aubert has powerfully demonstrated, Pius had no difficulty with the Belgian Constitution (*indifférentisme pratique*) as distinguished from efforts of certain French liberal Catholics (*indifférentisme théorique*).[32] The latter tended to justify in theory what was admissible only as a *pis-aller*. Scholarly discussion however centers more closely around thesis/hypothesis (β). Some have maintained that in condemning thesis/hypothesis (γ) Pius IX (and his successors) did not think in terms of thesis/hypothesis (β) because they did not say what the ideal situation was.[33]

I find this view insufficiently attentive to the data. In regard to Church-state relations, it has been shown in the previous chapter that the Popes of the period considered a viable union between Church and state as doctrinally necessary in principle; what was negotiable was the concrete form government might take. Regarding the correlative issue of religious freedom with which we are principally concerned here, Pius IX held a view that the religious freedom of non-Catholics was to be granted on the basis of toleration of error for the common good. In terms of thesis/hypothesis (β), the ideal situation is one in which everyone is Catholic. Thesis/hypothesis (β) is the logical result of thesis/hypothesis (α) where the abstract principle is that a human being does not have an objective right to worship God in a way other than that willed by God. Thus though thesis/hypothesis language seems to have entered Catholic theological discussion only in the nineteenth century,[34] and though the terms as such appear but rarely in the pontifical documents, the concepts themselves were and had long been the frame of reference within which the papal position was being affirmed. What must be kept in mind is that the concepts constitute a constant admission of at least three variables.

Religious tolerance for Pius IX, I have said, was not a subjective right; for him as for his immediate predecessors it was the concession of a Catholic state for the common good. In the political and religious upheaval that surrounded him, Pius IX overlooked the implications of the answers he would undoubtedly have given to Questions (A), (B), (C) and (D), four of the contexts in which the issue of religious freedom must be discussed, as I indicated above. The implications of the answers to these foundational questions were to remain dormant in Catholicism and were to go largely undetected by the papal magisterium at least up to the time of John XXIII. But to the extent that John intended to innovate, *Pacem in terris* did not prevail. What did prevail in the matter of religious freedom was a variant of the thesis/hypothesis view. To ask whether a human being has the objective right to worship God in the manner that a responsible use of intellect indicates was for Pius IX a question without meaning, because there was only one stance that a responsible use of intellect could ultimately take. In that sense, religious freedom was for him, as for his immediate predecessors, if not madness, then at least a kind of mental delirium.[35]

SYSTEMIZATION BY LEO XIII

The doctrine put forth by Pius IX in the documents examined above was in no way diminished by his successor; on the contrary, it may be said that Leo XIII did nothing less than to systematize it.[36] In *Libertas praestantissimum*, promulgated on June 20, 1888, and comprising in the Latin text twenty pages and some 7,500 words,[37] the Pope's primary concern was freedom in the moral order. But he was obliged first to discuss natural freedom (*libertas naturalis*) by which he seems to have meant what the scholastics called *libertas contradictionis* (the ability to place or not to place an act) and *libertas contraietatis* (the ability to choose between a number of courses of action in order to achieve an end). Such ability is what differentiates human from merely animal being.[38] *Libertas naturalis* is present only in those endowed with intelligence and reason, by the use of which a human being is rightly held to be responsible for its acts.[39] Freedom in that sense, says the Pope, has always been defended by the Catholic Church against any innovating contradiction—the Pope mentions for example the Manichean and Jansenist heresies.[40] Christianity is thus the implacable foe of anything that smacks of fate.

Whereas a human being, because of factors ultimately due to its fallen state, does not always rightly discern the truth and/or do the good, God and the blessed in heaven have no such limitation. Hence, as Augustine argued against the Pelagians, if the possibility of defection from the true and the good belongs inherently to freedom, then God, Jesus and the saints in heaven could not be said to be free.[41] But as it is, they are so preeminently. In making this remark that seems at first blush unrelated to his purpose, the Pope approaches his major concern, which is freedom in the moral order (the ability to do what one *ought* to do) as against freedom in the psychological order (the ability to do what one would *like*). It is at this point that one discerns the threads that will constitute the warp and woof of the Pope's argument. Though he does not here quote John 8:32 as he will later in the same encyclical, the liberating power of truth is what he is getting at. Leo quotes Aquinas to the effect that, when a human being acts according to reason, it acts of itself and according to its free will (which is real freedom) but that when a human being sins it acts in opposition to reason and is moved by another (which is slavery). The Pope then adds: "Even the heathen philosophers clearly recognized this truth, especially those who held that the wise man *alone* is free . . ."[42] Later on, when discussing academic freedom, Leo will affirm with the evangelist, "The truth shall make you free . . . ." (John 8:32). Since the well-known papal position was (and is) that the fullness of religious truth is to be found only in the teaching of the Catholic Church despite the defects of that body, it is not difficult to foresee that the Pope's position on religious freedom will result from an essentially negative answer to Question (F).

But for the moment, Leo proceeds with his analysis. A human being, prone to error and sin, needs light and strength to direct its action and restrain it from evil, hence the necessity of law.[43] This law is an ordinance of reason, by which ordinance reason prescribes to the will what it should seek and avoid in order to attain a human being's last end. There is first of all natural law, which the Pope here speaks of in terms of its primary principle; namely, that good is to be done and evil to be avoided.[44] But since all prescriptions of human reason have the force of law only inasmuch as they are the voice and interpretation of some higher power on which they all depend, then it follows for the theist that the higher power is ultimately the eternal reason of God himself. What applies to individuals applies *mutatis mutandis* to civil society.[45]

The Pope's immediate target is rationalism, by which he means the ". . . supremacy of the human reason, which, refusing due submission to the divine and eternal reason, proclaims its own independence and constitutes itself the supreme principle and source and judge of truth."[46] As one follows along with the Pope, one sees that in the process of his analysis he has made a subtle transition from *libertas naturalis* to *libertas moralis*. From saying that (1) ". . . the eternal law of God is the sole standard and rule of human liberty, not only in each individual man but also in the community and civil society . . ."[47] to maintaining some pages later that (2) a human being must take its ". . . standard of a loyal and religious life from the eternal law . . . and from all and every one of those laws *which God . . . has been pleased to enact and to make known to us by such clear and unmistakable signs as leave no room for doubt* . . ."[48] the logical distance is short indeed. Those clear and unmistakable signs point, in Leo's thinking as in that of his successors, to the Catholic Church and to no other.

After having briefly shown the relevance of his position to Church-state relations—an issue with which *Immortale Dei*, it will be recalled, had dealt more at length—the Pope comes to the discussion of the so-called modern freedoms, of which he enumerates four: (1) freedom of worship, (2) freedom of speech, (3) academic freedom and (4) freedom of conscience. I shall here be concerned only with the first and the last.

Regarding (1), Leo's reasoning closely parallels that of Pius IX:

> *Text C.* And if it be asked which of the many conflicting religions it is necessary to adopt, reason and the natural law unhesitatingly tell us to practise that one which God enjoins, and which men can easily recognize by certain exterior notes, whereby divine Providence has willed that it should be distinguished, because, in a matter of such moment, the most terrible loss would be the consequence of error.[49]

A human being is morally free to worship God in that way only that God has established. Regarding (4), the Pope explicitly states, "If by this is meant that everyone may, as he chooses, worship God or not, it is sufficiently refuted by the arguments already adduced."[50] Leo then takes up the real meaning of freedom of conscience; I shall return to it below in Text E, it being sufficient here to note that, just as the so-called thesis is obvious in Text C, so the so-called hypothesis is evident in Text D:

> *Text D.* Yet, with the discernment of a true mother, the Church weighs the great burden of human weakness, and well knows the course down which the minds and actions of men are being borne in this age. For this reason, while not conceding any right to anything save what is true and honest, she does not forbid public authority to tolerate what is at variance with truth and justice, for the sake of avoiding some greater evil, or of obtaining or preserving some greater good.[51]

A few sentences later Leo explicitly states that the common good is the *only* legitimate reason for the toleration of evil.[52] There is in *Libertas praestantissimum*, as in *Quanta cura* and its accompanying documents, no indication that such toleration was perceived as based on a subjective (as distinguished from an objective) right. Besides the peripheral matter of Leo's superb Latinity, the only perceptible difference between the position of Pius IX and that of Leo XIII is that the latter systematizes the teaching of the former, thereby giving it an internal coherence that the rambling, somewhat confused mind of Pius IX could not. [53]

AN EVOLVING PAPAL POSITION?

Now a small but significant minority at the Second Vatican Council argued that the doctrine that culminated in the promulgated *Dignitatis humanae* was in fact continuous with the teaching of the previous papal magisterium.[54] That stand and its alleged bases must now be faced.

That in the published *Acta* of Pius IX there is no foundation for such an argument is absolutely beyond dispute. But certain passages in the writings and speeches of succeeding pontiffs make the claim initially plausible. Let us then return to *Libertas praestantissimum.*

Immediately after having eliminated a false notion of freedom of conscience, Leo makes the following statement:

> *Text E.* But it [i.e., freedom of conscience] may also be taken to mean that every man in the State may follow the will of God and, from a consciousness of duty and free from every obstacle, obey his commands. This, indeed, is true liberty, a liberty worthy of the sons of God, which nobly maintains the dignity of man [*quae humanae dignitatem personae honestissime tuetur*], and is stronger than all violence or wrong—a liberty which the Church has always desired and held most dear.[55]

As it stands, this passage could well be taken to mean that a human being in the present economy of salvation has the objective right to worship God in the manner that a responsible use of intellect indicates, and therefore the statement seems to constitute an affirmative answer to Question (E). Yet one must proceed cautiously, for the question at once arises: If such be the case, how can the Pope's position be harmonized with Texts C and D of the same encyclical? This, upon analysis, turns out to be only an apparent problem. Immediately following Text E, the Pope states:

> *Text F.* This is the kind of liberty the apostles claimed for themselves with intrepid constancy, which the apologists of Christianity confirmed by their writings, and which the martyrs in vast numbers consecrated by their blood. And deservedly so; for this Christian liberty

bears witness to the absolute and most just dominion of God over
man, and to the chief and supreme duty of man towards God.[56]

If Text F is meant to illustrate the meaning of Text E, as it must, given its
place in the document, then the true freedom spoken of in Text E has to do
not with what the individual sincerely takes to be the truth (the *conscientia
recta* of Suarez) but with the objective truth of the Christian Gospel (the
conscientia recta of Aquinas) that, for the Pope, (it hardly need be
repeated), is found in its fullness only in the Catholic Church. While the
Pope does not here say anything that amounts to a negative answer to
Question (F), nothing he says, when examined in its total context, implies
an affirmative answer to Question (E).

The next relevant passages occur in two encyclicals of Pius XI, *Non
abbiamo bisogno* of July 29, 1931, and *Mit brennender Sorge* of March 14,
1937. The former dealt with the fascist attempt to curtail the influence of
Catholic Action, the latter with the intensification of hostilities of the
Hitler regime toward the Catholic Church in Germany. In *Non abbiamo
bisogno*, which in the *Acta Apostolicae Sedis* comprises about ten thousand words and twenty-seven pages, the Pope is concerned with exposing
the nature, extent and ultimate purpose of fascist militancy against
Catholic influence, especially over the young.[57] In that frame of reference
he refers to two rights: the rights of souls to procure for themselves the
greatest spiritual good according to the teaching and formation of the
Church, and the right of souls so formed to bring the treasury of the
redemption to others. It is precisely at that point that the Pope states:

> *Text G.* And in consideration of this double right of souls, we are, as we
> stated above, happy and proud to wage the good fight for the
> liberty of consciences [*libertà delle coscienze*] not indeed (as some-
> one, perhaps inadvertently, has quoted Us as saying) for the liberty
> of conscience [*libertà della coscienza*] which is an equivocal
> expression too often distorted to mean the absolute independence
> of conscience, which is absurd in a soul created and redeemed by
> God.[58]

If this distinction between the freedom of consciences and the freedom
of conscience had occurred in an encyclical of the general orientation of
Pacem in terris, still thirty-two years in the future, it might be argued that
Pius XI was here taking a position along the lines that Vatican II was later
to adopt. But *Pacem in terris* is itself, as I shall show, problematic. And in

the case of *Non abbiamo bisogno* the basis for such an interpretation, for the reasons I shall suggest below, seems weak.

The second document frequently urged to show that the thinking of Pius XI was at least not contrary to that of *Dignitatis humanae* is *Mit brennender Sorge*. Comprising in the official text about 7,900 words spanning twenty-two pages, this encyclical had both a primary and a secondary purpose.[59] The latter had to do with a defense of the religious values found in the Hebrew scriptures and was probably an indirect attempt to express disapproval of growing Nazi harassment of the Jews, who, however, are not explicitly mentioned.[60] The primary purpose had to do with the problems the Catholic Church was facing and, without a direct mention of National Socialism, consisted of a critical exposure of blatantly false philosophical principles upon which Pius considered Nazism to have been based,[61] along with encouragement and advice not simply to the German bishops but to the whole Catholic Church in Germany.[62] Such is the general context in which the following much cited sentence occurs:

> *Text H.* The believer has an inalienable right to profess his faith and put it into practice in the manner suited to him. Laws that suppress or make this profession and practice difficult contradict the natural law.[63]

Nothing in *Mit brennender Sorge* indicates that this sentence was written with any intent other than defending the rights of Catholics. Indeed, in those pre-ecumenical days, one finds in this encyclical nary a reference to other Christians who along with Catholics were paying a heavy price for fidelity to their own understanding of the Gospel. Yet Text H, like Text G, was frequently quoted in the debates of Vatican II as a "proof text" that the doctrine on religious freedom as evolving in the Council and as culminating in *Dignitatis humanae* was in fact continuous with the teaching of the previous papal magisterium.[64]

In the case of both *Non abbiamo bisogno* and *Mit brennender Sorge*, several factors militate against this interpretation. First, as already suggested, both encyclicals had to do with the religious freedom of Catholics, not with religious freedom in general. Second, while Pius was issuing these encyclicals, the error-has-no-rights theory as propounded by the then Don Alfredo Ottaviani continued unchallenged.[65] Third, Pius XII himself in his published writings and speeches never interpreted his predecessor as having put forth the religious freedom of non-Catholics as an objective right, a fact difficult to understand if Pius XI had done so in two highly significant official documents. Fourth, and this is decisive, it will become clear below that the position of Pius IX as systematized by Leo XIII persisted in official Catholicism well into the beginning of the Second Vatican Council.

The penultimate source not infrequently put forward as evidence of continuity between *Dignitatis humanae* and the teaching of the ordinary papal magisterium consists of two documents emanating from the pen of Pius XII.[66] The first is the radio address of December 24, 1942; the second is the allocution *Ci riesce* of December 6, 1953. A comparison of the orientation in each document seems initially to betray a contradiction in the Pope's thinking, or at least a change of mind.

The former document, comprising in the *Acta Apostolicae Sedis* some five thousand words and a total of sixteen pages, was a Christmas message to a world torn by war.[67] Nourishing hope for better days, the Pope was even more concerned with the principles on which a lasting peace could be built. The preceding Christmas address had dealt with the relations *between* nations and peoples; the present was to take up the matter of relations *within* them.[68] The former (external relations) were intimately connected with the internal: It would be impossible to have real peace without a proper balance between the two. Of this address, that part is especially relevant which had to do with the five principles the Pope laid down for healthy internal relations within a people or nation. Only the first concerns me here, and may be cited in part as follows:

> *Text I.* Whoever wishes the star of peace to appear and stop over society, let him [or her] concur for his [or her] part to give back to the human person that dignity given it by God from the very beginning. . . .
>
> Let him [or her] sustain the respect and the practical implementation of the following fundamental rights of persons: the right to maintain and to develop bodily, intellectual, and moral life, especially the right to worship God privately and publicly, including charitable works of a religious nature. . . .[69]

Pius goes on to mention other rights—the right to work, the right to choose one's station in life—but they are not relevant to my inquiry. Taken as it stands, Text I seems to be an unequivocally affirmative answer to Question (E) and as such seems in direct continuity with the development that terminated with *Dignitatis humanae*. It was passages such as these that led some Council Fathers, and much earlier John Courtney Murray himself, to see as already posited in the speeches and writings of recent

Popes—at least in principle—the very foundation of human freedom as it bears on matters religious.[70] Indeed, if texts like Text I were all that existed, it would be difficult to gainsay their argument. As I shall point out below, however, the fundamental error in this regard consisted in confusing the internal logic of certain papal positions with their explicit statements, insufficient attention being given to the total context in which both the former and the latter occur.

For matters are indeed more complex. Eleven years later, in a document that caused some discussion at the time,[71] the same Pius XII could be seen holding a position not essentially different from that of Pius IX and Leo XIII. This is the much cited *Ci riesce*, an allocution given to the Fifth National Congress of Italian Jurists. A relatively brief speech comprising barely three thousand words and only eight pages in the *Acta Apostolicae Sedis*, this document exhibits the Pope's concern for a hypothetically new international situation in which each state, while retaining its individual sovereignty, would choose to join a union with other states, thereby constituting a supranational community.[72] The Pope readily admitted that the possibility seemed utopian, yet the desire to avoid the conflicts of the past seemed to be tending in the direction of such an international arrangement. The possibility of an international order of this kind raised questions, he said, that cannot be answered by a simple yes or no.

Pius mentioned a number of problems and suggested a norm for their solution: As much as possible promote what unites, remove what divides, tolerate (*sopportare*) that which cannot be smoothed out without bringing the community of peoples to the shoals. This principle, the Pope conceded, is only too obvious; the difficulty lies in its application.[73] He then centered his attention on a particular problem: In this new international order, should it ever materialize, how, practically speaking, would Catholic communities exist together with non-Catholic ones? Pius' reasoning should be followed closely as he gives his answer.

A supranational community of states will almost inevitably be composed of Christians, non-Christians, the religiously indifferent, and so on. Most likely their mutual relations in this context will be governed according to the following rule: Internally, each state will regulate religious and moral matters with its own laws; nonetheless, within the community of states the citizens of each member state will be permitted to practice their own religious and ethical beliefs inasmuch as these do not contravene the penal law of the state in which they happen to sojourn.[74] Can Catholic jurists consent to such an arrangement? Pius asked.

Two different questions should be distinguished. The first concerns objective truth and the obligations of conscience to pursue the objectively true and the objectively good.[75] The second has to do with the actual behavior (*contegno*) of the community of peoples toward the individual state and of the individual state toward the community of peoples.[76] The answer to the question placed above is stated in a twofold principle:

> *Text J.* First, that which does not correspond to truth and the moral norm *has objectively no right to exist, to be propagated,* or *to be put into practice.* Second, not to prevent it by legal means of state and coercive measures can nonetheless be justified in the interests of a higher and wider good.[77]

This twofold principle evoked by the Pope is nothing less than a variant of the old thesis/hypothesis model applied to a hypothetical situation. That the Pope's thought is seemingly in direct contradiction with that expressed in Text I is clear from what follows in *Ci riesce*. At that point in his discourse, the Pope's thinking takes a turn in no way logically linked to the point he had raised with the Italian Jurists. He begins to compare the hypothetical international community with the Catholic Church.

The problems that an eventual community of sovereign states would experience are not unlike those Catholicism has long had to deal with. But there are differences: In Catholicism the movement is from the top down (because of its divine foundation by Christ) while unity already exists; in the hypothetical community of states, the movement is from the bottom up while unity remains to be created.[78] What is particularly relevant here, however, is not the comparison as such but rather the Pope's application of the twofold principle stated in Text J. There can be no reasonable doubt whatsoever that both principles enunciated in Text J are meant to apply to the question of religious freedom as it affects the relation of the Catholic Church with other Christians, and as the case may be, with non-Christian religions.[79] The only perceptible differences are that (1) whereas Leo XIII stated that the common good is the *only* basis on which toleration of religious error may be exhibited, Pius XII speaks not simply of the common good but also of toleration ". . . per riguardo a coloro che in buona coscienza (sebbene erronea, ma invincibile) sono di diversa opinione . . ."[80] and (2) toleration in Leo is a *may* but in Pius it is tantamount to a *must*.[81] Yet the old thesis/hypothesis is not only operative in *Ci riesce* but in one telling phrase the term *thesis* itself occurs, an event exceedingly rare in an official papal document.[82] Given the data, one could say that the position of the papal magisterium was evolving; one might also admit that in due course it might have come to an affirmative answer to Question (E). But if one takes the explicit statements as they are found in the documents, to say that the position of the Popes prior to John XXIII was along the lines of the distinctive contribution of *Dignitatis humanae* seems gratuitous.

What, however, is to be made of Text I cited from the Christmas message of 1942? Did the Pope contradict himself or change his mind when eleven years later he took the position unambiguously affirmed in *Ci riesce*? For the astuteness of a mind like that of Pius XII such a possibility does not seem likely, as an examination of internal and external factors that constitute the total context of Text I tends to confirm. Internally, Text I occurs within the frame of reference of the first of five principles set down as the basis for lasting peace. The five principles are as follows:

1. Dignity and rights of the human person[83]
2. Defense of social unity, especially of the family[84]
3. Dignity and prerogative of work[85]
4. Reintegration of the juridical system (*ordinamento*)[86]
5. Christian conception of the state[87]

Text I is part of what the Pope has to say in grounding the first principle. When one looks at the remaining four, it becomes obvious at once that all without exception are in harmony with traditional Catholic doctrine. Unless one wishes to presuppose that in establishing the first principle the Pope wished to depart from traditional Catholic doctrine—in which case Pius could hardly have been unaware that he was departing from the teaching of Pius IX and Leo XIII—then most probably the assertion of religious freedom made under the heading and in the context of the first principle must likewise be interpreted in a traditional sense. That is to say: Only those who profess the true religion have an *objective* right to religious freedom; freedom granted to others is based on toleration of error for the common good. Thus Text I does not betray a momentary aberration on the part of the Pope but is fully consistent with his position in *Ci riesce*.

External factors tend to confirm this interpretation. In the Roman faculties, the error-has-no-rights theory continued to be taught. If in Text I Pius had indeed intended to innovate, his attempt is not only incomprehensible (if not completely unsustainable in light of both internal and external factors), but would involve the Pope in self-contradiction. Only they saw the possibilities in texts like Text I (and Text G of *Non abbiamo bisogno*) who were beginning to argue that the *internal logic* of papal teaching led to conclusions quite different from its official position. But that is another matter; I shall return to it below.[88]

I come now to the more sensitive matter of John XXIII in *Pacem in terris*. Measured by standards usual for encyclicals, this document is rather long, comprising in the official text forty-seven pages and well over twelve thousand words. Its content is too well known to require even a brief summary, it being sufficient to recall that John's purpose was an elucidation of the principles whereby a secure international order might come about. One of the bases of such an order is a properly grounded religious freedom. Hence the Pope as quoted above states that among the rights of every human being must be counted the right ". . . to honor God according to the sincere dictates of conscience and therefore the right to practice his [or her] religion privately and publicly."[89] Does that statement constitute an innovation and hence a departure from the teaching of Pius IX and Leo XIII?

A perusal of the Latin text reveals a nuance not reflected in the English translation. I am obliged to quote it directly:

> *Text K.* In hominis iuribus hoc quoque numerandum est, ut et Deum, ad rectam conscientiae suae normam, venerari possit, et religionem privatim publice profiteri.[90]

Those who maintain that John held a position that in effect amounted to an affirmative answer to Question (E) seem to have been misled by the various translations into the vernacular, many of which read as though the Latin text were (1) *ad rectae conscientiae suae normam* instead of (2) *ad rectam conscientiae suae normam*. The difference in nuance is considerable, for the *right norm* of conscience is not synonymous with the norm of a *right conscience*, the latter (2) pertaining to objective truth (Aquinas), the former to subjective sincerity (Suarez).[91] Does the wider context of *Pacem in terris* permit one to say conclusively that John's view was in fact broader than a close reading of the Latin text suggests?[92]

The answer must be negative, for in the end John's perspective remains somewhat enigmatic. On the one hand, one cannot read this encyclical in one sitting, as it were, and come away without the impression that John intended more than he actually stated. The phrase *dignity of the human person* or its equivalent simply occurs too frequently. And there is no reference to toleration of religious error on the basis of the common good. On the other hand, a careful reading of the document suggests that John in fact did not textually depart from the teaching of his predecessors. Immediately after Text K occurs, the Pope appeals to Lactantius, who in Book IV of the *Divinae Institutiones* was concerned with the defense of religious freedom of Christians, not with the defense of religious freedom in general.[93] And following upon this direct quotation, John quotes *Libertas praestantissimum* of Leo XIII, ironically the very passage I have quoted above (Text F), the context of which is meant to support the traditional papal teaching on religious freedom.[94] When one adds to these considerations, as one must in the case of *Non abbiamo bisogno*, *Mit brennender Sorge* of Pius XI and the 1942 Christmas Message of Pius XII, the fact that the error-has-no-rights theory continued to hold sway even after *Pacem in terris* was promulgated, one remains somewhat perplexed regarding the Pope's intentions.[95] Was John simply biding his time?

To what extent, then, may it be said that the papal position on religious freedom evolved from the time of Pius IX to John XXIII? To say that the development was more than minimal is to distort the evidence; to suggest that the doctrine of the ordinary papal magisterium at least near the end of this period was developing along the lines that culminated in *Dignitatis humanae* is to make a statement that in the end cannot be sustained. The most that one could say is that while the Popes, as does Vatican II itself, remained adamant in a negative answer to Question (F), there was a growing tendency to base the toleration of religious error not simply on the common good but on a common good that includes regard for the human person as such. Thus Cardinal Ottaviani at one phase of the conciliar debates admitted that the right that a person in religious error has to religious freedom is a *subjective* right,[96] a term however that as far as I am aware is one that the Popes in their official statements did not use. The teaching enunciated by Pius IX and systematized by Leo XIII remained intact. That is to say: To ask whether a human being in the present economy of salvation has the *objective* right to worship God in the manner that a responsible use of intellect indicates (Question [E]) remained until the end a meaningless question. Within the limits of the possible exception that *Pacem in terris* may constitute, official papal teaching, as I am about to show, lasted well into the opening of the Second Vatican Council.

The Papal Position
in the Early Drafts on the Church

Chapter IV, "*De Relationibus inter Ecclesiam et Statum*," of the draft on the Church presented to the Council Fathers on November 23, 1962 (*HAD*-b) contains a description of what the proponents of the draft considered an adequate relationship between Church and state. As I have in the preceding chapter summarized its general thrust, there is no need to repeat it here.

After describing the limits of each power, the draft in number 42 turns its attention to the religious duties of the state (*potestas civilis*). The good of the state requires that the civil power not be indifferent toward religion, for the state is not to be concerned with the temporal order alone. Rather must the state bring about a situation where spiritual good(s) can more easily circulate. Among those goods, nothing is more highly to be esteemed than to know that God exists, to acknowledge that fact, and to fulfill one's duties toward Him. Such is the foundation of private and even public morality (*virtutis*).[97] Thus far, the description of the ideal relation between Church and state is not far removed from the thought of, say, a Benjamin Franklin. But then the draft adds:

> *Text L.* And these duties toward God are to be performed not only by individual citizens but also by the state [*a Potestate civili*] which in acts of polity acts as a person [*societatis civilis personam gerit*]. For God is the foundation [*auctor*] of civil society and the source of all those benefits [*bonorum*] which through it overflow onto all its members. Although in this particular order willed by Christ, liturgical cult is the concern only of the true Church of God, also the civil community must, in some social way, worship God. Thus, with due regard toward its character, the state will acquit itself of its duty if in faithfully providing for the common good, it keeps the laws of God established for the economy of salvation. And this demands before everything else that, while the Church enjoys the fullness of its freedom, there be excluded from public law, government and public action all those things which the Church might judge as prejudicial to its purpose. . . .[98]

The paragraph following the above quotation speaks indeed of the application of these general principles to concrete situations: The state obviously cannot be expected to do what in principle it ought to do unless its citizens and the state that represents them have previously come to accept revelation as something that has indeed happened. And the fact that the state does come to recognize Christ and the Church He founded does not in itself presuppose any one system of government in preference to another. But the citizens have full freedom to decide that public life (*vita civilis*) be ordered according to Catholic principles.

It was shown in the previous chapter that attenuation of the papal position on ideal Church-state relations was only apparent in this and the following draft. But regarding the issue of religious freedom, neither the paragraph quoted in Text L nor those that follow it go so far as explicitly to affirm the doctrine of Pius IX and Leo XIII. Did the authors of the draft intend at least implicitly to correct the previous papal magisterium?

It is true that *HAD*-a as proposed by the Theological Commission contains whole paragraphs omitted in *HAD*-b.[99] Not only did number 3 of *HAD*-a explicitly state that the way God is to be worshiped in the present economy of salvation is none other than that which God himself has determined in the true Church of Christ (number 7 of Chap. I of the same draft had pointed out that only the Roman Catholic Church is rightly [*iure*] called a Church, an orientation that the Council was subsequently to change), but also number 5 enunciated two principles that seem to stand in polarity. Distinguishing the situation in a Catholic state from that of a non-Catholic one, the document stated on the one hand, that in a Catholic state the civil power is in no way permitted to coerce the assent of faith, for the act of faith by its essence must be a free act; on the other hand (still within the context of a Catholic state), *HAD*-a stated:

> *Text M.* This does not prevent the state from bringing about those intellectual, social and moral conditions by which the less educated of the faithful might more easily persevere in the faith they have received. For this reason, as the state does not think that safe guarding of public morals is none of its business, then in order to protect its citizens from seductive error and to preserve the government [*Rempublicam*] in the unity of faith . . . the state can set limits to [*temperare*] the public display of cults and defend its citizens against the spread of false doctrines which in the Church's judgment can endanger their eternal salvation.[100]

But when it is a question of applying these principles in a non-Catholic state, number 7 of *HAD*-a affirms that the Catholic Church is to be granted full freedom to pursue its mission. It is thus clear that the thought-patterns behind *HAD*-a reflect the thinking of Pius IX and his successors up to but perhaps excluding John XXIII. We are dealing here with the old thesis/hypothesis ideology without its explicit label.[101]

Was that ideology removed from *HAD*-b distributed to the Council Fathers after the Council was in session? While a superficial examination of the data would incline one to think so, such is by no means the case. It is important to realize that, though the offending paragraphs from *HAD*-a were removed from that of *HAD*-b, in each draft there is a reference to a significant work by the Jesuit, Luigi Taparelli d'Azeglio. Therein the double standard of how a Catholic state may curtail the religious freedom of non-Catholic religions as distinguished from the fullness of freedom that the Catholic Church demanded for itself when the state was not Catholic is explained and defended at some length.[102] This is again a variant of the old thesis/hypothesis model without the name. Taparelli d'Azeglio's work is cited along with others in the critical apparatus of both drafts, not, to be sure, as part of the text to be voted on, but to illustrate its meaning for the Council Fathers who had to study it prior to voting. In the end it should be quite clear that despite John XXIII's alleged attempt in *Pacem in terris* to correct the teaching of his predecessors, papal doctrine on religious freedom as enunciated by Pius IX and as systematized by Leo XIII prevailed in the Catholic Church well into the beginning of the Second Vatican Council.

But the position of Pius IX and Leo XIII was not replaced without a struggle. A careful reading of the conciliar debates illustrates that, as the Council continued, their teaching consistently lost ground and was corrected in the sense I shall indicate below. This issue was central: whether in affirming religious freedom as an objective right the Council was not also rejecting the papal teaching of several generations. The struggle was to last well into the third session and even beyond. The first and most obvious clue that something very significant had been afoot is the fact that, whereas both in the *HAD*-a and *HAD*-b references to Pius IX and Leo XIII are frequent, in the text finally promulgated by Paul VI all references to Pius IX have been removed. Those to Leo XIII remaining in the promulgated document are not those pertaining to a variation of the old thesis/hypothesis model. And so the question arises: What precisely is the relation between the teaching of *Dignitatis humanae* and that of the ordinary papal magisterium prior to John XXIII?

The Declaration on Religious Freedom: Continuity with the Teaching of the Ordinary Papal Magisterium?

Did, in fact, *Dignitatis humanae* reverse the position of Pius IX and his successors prior to John XXIII? Any attempt to ground an affirmative answer faces an immediate hurdle of no small proportions. For the council document explicitly claims to speak in continuity with the teaching of earlier generations:

> *Text N.* The truth cannot impose itself except by virtue of its own truth, as it makes its entrance into the mind at once quietly and with power. Religious freedom, in turn, which men demand as necessary to fulfill their duty to worship God, has to do with immunity from coercion in civil society. *Therefore it leaves untouched traditional Catholic doctrine* on the moral duty of men and societies toward the true religion and toward the one Church of Christ.[103]

The context in which the phrase ". . . immunity from coercion in civil society . . ." occurs includes the previous sentence, namely, that truth cannot impose itself except by virtue of its own truth; hence, a further meaning of the phrase is that a human being may not be coerced to the assent of faith. If the six questions I have distinguished at the outset are truly distinct, however closely interrelated, then the Council oversimplifies matters when in Text N it states that religious freedom has to do with immunity from coercion in civil society. This relates to the context of Question (D) and is indeed one of the aspects of the issue. But the Council itself implicitly affirms more than that when, as I shall show, the inner logic of *Dignitatis humanae* suggests an affirmative answer to Question (E). Indeed, however one assesses the role of the Popes in the various phases of the Inquisition, it has consistently been their teaching, at least in principle, that a human being may not be coerced to the assent of faith. If, then, freedom from coercion by civil society is all that is meant by religious freedom, why the need of a declaration by the Council? The answer is that the Council intended to develop the traditional teaching of the Church, including that of the papal magisterium, to bring forth new things that are in harmony with those that are old. Are the *nova* in harmony with the *vetera*? *Dignitatis humanae* affirms:

> *Text O.* Provided the just requirements of public order are observed, religious bodies rightfully claim freedom in order that they may govern themselves according to their own norms, honor the Supreme Being in public worship, assist their members in the practice of the religious life, strengthen them by instruction and promote institutions in which they may join together for the purpose of ordering their own lives in accordance with their religious principles.[104]

Is that statement in agreement with the doctrine of Pius IX and his successors? The attempt to answer that question brings me to the second part of my argument, which comprises four steps:

A.   *An analysis of the successive drafts culminating in the promulgated* Dignitatis humanae *reveals that the Council's deliberations began with traditional regard for the rights and duties of conscience and ended with traditional insistence on the duty to seek the truth.*

B.   *That development was concomitant with increasing concern for continuity with the teaching of the ordinary papal magisterium.*

C.   *Analysis of the oral and written critiques of the drafts reveals at least four different ways of facing the issue of continuity with the teaching of the ordinary papal magisterium.*

D.   *Despite efforts to ground continuity, the distinctive contribution that* Dignitatis humanae *made to the theology of religious freedom is not continuous with the teaching of the ordinary papal magisterium prior to John XXIII in* Pacem in terris.

My argument at this point comprises four additional sections corresponding to each of these four steps, the second and fourth of which are the most significant. For of all the debates at the Council, the central issue during that four-year period (and indeed the major shoals against which the maximalist position as described in the Introduction runs aground) was the question of religious freedom and the correlative matter of ideal Church-state relations. The importance of what happened cannot be underestimated. It will be helpful to begin by examining closely the manner in which the conciliar position developed.

Evolving Doctrine

Here we have to do essentially with eight documents,[105] the first seven of which are successive drafts, the eighth being the promulgated text. They are as follows:

(1)   *Mater Ecclesia* (*ME*), the first two chapters of the document *De Libertate religiosa* as prepared by the Secretariat for Christian Unity and as presented to the Preparatory Commission in June, 1962.[106]

(2) *Huius capitis momentum* (*HC*), Chapter V of the draft on *De Oecumenismo*, distributed to the Council Fathers on November 19, 1963.[107]

(3) *Huius declarationis momentum* (*HD*), the *Declaratio prior De Libertate religiosa*, appended to the draft *Unitatis redintegratio*, to be sent to the dispersed Council Fathers as of April 27, 1964.[108]

(4) *Dignitatis personae humanae* (*DP*). This is the so-called *Textus emendatus*. Together with the former text now called *Textus prior*, it was distributed to the Council on November 17, 1964.[109]

(5) *Dignitatis humanae personae* (*DH*-a), the *Textus reemendatus*. Together with the former, now called *Textus emendatus*, it was during the interim to be distributed as of May 28, 1965.[110]

(6) *Dignitatis humanae personae* (*DH*-b). This is the *Textus recognitus*. Along with the former text, it was brought to the Roman residences of the Council Fathers on October 22, 1965.[111]

(7) *Dignitatis humanae personae* (*DH*-c). This is the *Textus denuo recognitus*, distributed to the Council Fathers on November 17, 1965.[112]

(8) *Dignitatis humanae personae* (*DH*-d), the promulgated text.[113]

The number of drafts was considerable, itself an indication that the Council Fathers were wrestling with no small difficulty. Though each dealt with a whole range of issues pertaining to religious freedom—the right of assembly, the education of children, freedom to publish and preach one's faith openly, to mention only three—my approach must be more modest and will be limited to an attempt to discern how the thinking reflected in the drafts provides the basis for affirmative (or negative) answers to the six questions I have listed above, my attention being focused primarily on how the right to religious freedom is grounded in reason as distinguished from its grounding in revelation.

ME consisted of three chapters of which the third (*INS*) has to do with the relation between Church and society; I have treated it briefly in the preceding chapter.[114] Religious freedom, defined as "immunitas ab externa coactione,"[115] is said to have its source in the right (*ius*) to follow one's conscience and, with the later addition of the phrase *in societate civili*, remains constant throughout the drafts. The value behind a negative answer to Question (D) is thus affirmed. Within a frame of reference deeply rooted in the scriptures, the authors maintain that although the disciples of Christ have the duty to preach and defend the truth, something that relates to the concerns reflected in Question (F), they also have the obligation to deal lovingly, prudently, and patiently with those who have not come to the full knowledge of the Gospel.[116] The person erring about the faith is worthy of esteem; His or her right to religious freedom is always defended by the Church. Given the church's earlier involvement with various phases of the Inquisition, such has surely not always been the case; hence the authors here wisely use the present tense (*vindicatur*). Regard for the values reflected in a negative answer to Question (F) is present but minimal, while concern for those of Question (E) dominate. In fact at least three paragraphs of over two hundred words are given over to that and related values. While the draft alludes briefly to the prudent formation of conscience, the duty to do so is not mentioned explicitly. Nor is there mentioned at all the fact that there are objective norms according to which conscience is responsibly formed. And the values behind an affirmative answer to Question (A) are barely touched upon.

HC preserves much of the orientation of *ME* but broadens its argument. Like *ME*, it appeals to mankind in general: Given the present circumstances of culture and mores, the Catholic Church exhorts all to direct their efforts toward defending the honor of God and the dignity of the human person.[117] Human beings should esteem and promote truths and values that they have in common, attending not only to objective truth and the rights of God, but also to the rights and duties of persons.[118] Religious freedom is said to have its source in conscience (Question [C]). But one discerns a subtle shift of emphasis. In *ME*, a person was said to have the *right* (*ius*) to follow conscience; in *HC*, the authors come close to stating that religious freedom has its source in the *duty* (*officium*) to do so, whence the right (*ius*) to religious freedom. At this point, the minds of the authors, having begun with the concerns reflected in Question (C), seem unclear about whether the following of conscience is primarily a duty or a right.

HC makes a definite advance over the preceding document in that its authors perceive the solution to the problem as the tension between two poles; namely, (1) the fact that there is only one truth, God himself, to whose holy will all must submit (Question [F]) and (2) the fact that God wills a submission that is free (Question [D]).[119] Thus the writers begin to give more attention to the concerns reflected in Question (F) while developing those of Questions (C) and (D). Attention to the values illustrated by an affirmative answer to Question (E) is abundant, as in *ME*, and tends to dominate. Up to this point, the concerns reflected in Question (A) are touched upon but not developed.

The following draft (*HD*) represents a further advance. Religious freedom seems to have its roots in the duty (*officium*) to follow (even an erroneous) conscience, from which fact flows the right (*ius*) to religious freedom as defined in the preceding documents (Question [C]).[120] The authors make the additional move of portraying the dignity of the human person as grounded in a divine vocation, a view not explicitly maintained in the following drafts.[121] This vocation is a divine law: eternal, objective, absolute, universal. It is obvious that greater attention is being given to the concerns reflected in Questions (A) and (F). Everyone must seek out that law and freely conform to it.[122] But a human being cannot do this without prudently forming conscience and sincerely following it. The values behind an affirmative answer to Question (C) are still present as are those behind an affirmative answer to Question (E).[123]

DP is much more highly developed and more carefully nuanced, consisting of four parts: (1) the general notion of religious freedom, (2) its source in reason, (3) practical consequences of that fact, and (4) the grounding of religious freedom in revelation.[124] The right to religious freedom is described as that right according to which "... human beings must be free or immune from coercion on the part of others or of any human power, not only in forming their conscience in religious matters but also in the free exercise of religion."[125] That right was to be understood in a twofold sense; namely, (1) no one is to be compelled to act against his or her conscience; and (2) within due limits, no one is to be prevented from acting according to it.[126] Freedom of religion has its source in the duty (*officium*) and right (*ius*) to seek the truth, the role of conscience being described as in the preceding drafts. The innovation of *DP* consisted in the attempt to show how the dignity of the human person has its roots in revelation itself; e.g., in the conduct of Christ.[127] After illustrations from the Gospels, the draft states that the apostles followed his example and so does the Church when today she protects *religious* freedom and favors it by her pastoral concern for *human* freedom.[128]

While most of these concepts are at least seminally present in the earlier drafts, the direction that the development takes is striking. From an initial concern with the values behind an affirmative answer to Questions (B), (C) and (E), the authors give increasing attention to a negative response to Question (F) and an affirmative to Question (A). Furthermore, while there can be little doubt that the solution to the problem of religious freedom as grounded in reason emerged from an affirmative answer to Question (A), that development itself seems to have been preceded and initiated by a negative answer to Question (F).[129]

That fact is perhaps best illustrated by *DH*-b, which borrows heavily from *Lumen gentium*. A whole new section appears in which the authors affirm that God himself has shown to the human race those paths (*vias*) through which human beings may be saved and attain happiness.[130] The authors affirm their belief in the one true religion that subsists in the Catholic and apostolic Church. Since all human beings are bound, especially in those matters that pertain to the worship of God (". . . praesertim in iis quae cultum Dei respiciunt . . ."), to seek the truth and embrace it once it has become known (*agnitam*) to them,[131] the authors insist that human beings are also bound to embrace and profess the Catholic faith in the measure that human beings have come to recognize it as true (". . . prout eam agnoscere potuerunt . . .").[132] These duties bind the human conscience; yet the truth cannot impose itself except by the force of truth itself, which quietly and at the same time forcefully finds its way (*illabitur*) into the human mind.[133] The document then states as in the passage quoted above:

> *Text P.* Therefore, since the religious freedom human beings demand in acquitting themselves of duty to worship God . . . has to do with immunity from coercion by civil society, it is evident that it leaves untouched the Catholic doctrine concerning the one true religion, the one Church of Christ, and the moral obligation human beings have toward it.[134]

That emphasis did not arise, as it were, out of nowhere. When one examines the previous draft (*DH*-a), affirmation of the values behind a negative answer to Question (F) occurs at least five times, while affirmation of those behind a positive answer to Question (A) occurs at least twice and in one paragraph is logically connected with those of Question (F).[135] The difference between *DH*-a and *DH*-b consists precisely in this, that in the latter the emphasis on a negative answer to Question (F) is so highly developed that it has no exact parallel in any preceding draft. While in *DH*-a the values behind an affirmative answer to Questions (A) and (B) are quite frankly affirmed, in *DH*-b (Text P) the same affirmation is used to say what freedom of religion, defined as immunity from coercion in civil society, does *not* mean. Quite obviously, the authors of *DH*-b were attempting to do justice to the concerns of the minority.

Though this orientation as it here pertains to the values reflected in a negative answer to Question (F) remains the same in the promulgated document (*DH*-d), a perceptible "tightening" of the draft becomes evident. The *vias* of *DH*-b become the *viam* of *DH*-c and *DH*-d, the implication being that there is only one path just as there is only one true religion and one Church of Christ.[136] And the *praesertim in iis quae cultum Dei respiciunt* of *DH*-b will become the *praesertim in iis quae Deum Eiusque Ecclesiam respiciunt* of *DH*-c and *DH*-d. In these two last documents *agnitam* is changed to *cognitam*: The true Church of Christ is known, not merely acknowledged. And from *DH*-c onwards, the adjective *traditionalem* is added to *doctrinam*.[137] In this way, the traditional doctrine about a human being's obligations toward the true religion remains unchanged. And the obligation is incumbent not upon the state to be sure—the use of *societatem* in place of *statum* or *potestatem civilem* reflects the tone of the debate as it had borne upon the Church-state issue—but upon society.[138] Finally, in contrast to *DH*-b, *DH*-c and *DH*-d add *recentiorum* to *Summorum Pontificum*: It is the teaching of the more recent Popes that the Council explicitly undertakes to develop, the traditional doctrine remaining intact.[139]

From the earliest document (*ME*), where concerns reflected in a negative answer to Question (F) were but minimally attended to, to the much firmer stance from *DH*-b onwards, the difference is assuredly great. Indeed, while the values reflected in the traditional answers to Questions (C) and (D) are progressively clarified and affirmed, increased insistence on those behind appropriate answers to Questions (A) and (F) is unmistakable. It is not that the values behind an affirmative answer to Question (E), so clearly the orientation of *ME*, have been lost sight of; it is that a fundamental change of perspective has evolved as illustrated by a significant paragraph from *DH*-b:

Text Q. For according to their dignity, all human beings, because they are persons, endowed with reason and free will and therefore enriched with personal responsibility, are impelled by their nature and bound by moral obligation to seek the truth, that truth especially which has to do with religion. They are also bound to adhere to the truth when known and to organize their whole life according to its exigencies.[140]

Text R. However, human beings cannot satisfy this obligation in a way which befits their own nature unless they enjoy psychological freedom as well as immunity from external compulsion. *Religious freedom does not however have its foundation in a subjective disposition but in the very nature of the human person.* For that reason the right to immunity continues even in those who do not fulfill the obligation to seek the truth and adhere to it, provided that, lawful public order being preserved, they do not hinder [*laedant*] the rights of others.[141]

Text R follows immediately upon Text Q and as translated here from *DH*-b remains the same in the promulgated document (*DH*-d), with the exception of minor changes that in no way affect its substance.[142] Text Q affirms the values behind an affirmative answer to Question (A) and as such stands in tension with Text R, which insists on the necessity of freedom both psychologically and socially (Question [D]). To be sure, the obligation to follow even an erroneous conscience (Question [C]) remains, but it no longer occupies, as in an earlier draft, the center on which the right to religious freedom rests. In this regard, the *obligatio veritatem quaerendi* has replaced the *officium conscientiam sequendi*.

The changes made by the authors of the successive drafts were made, of course, at the insistence of the Council Fathers either while the Council was in session or during the interim. In regard to grounding in reason, which is my primary interest here, a clear stream of development is discernible and may be described as a transition from traditional regard for the rights and duties of conscience to traditional insistence on the duty to seek the truth. More concretely and by way of summary, the general thrust of the current may be described as follows. In the beginning, the dignity of the human person is hardly more than baldly asserted, with little or no hint as to the axes that support it. The effort to establish the right to religious freedom is first oriented primarily around the rights and then the duties of conscience (Questions [C] and [B] respectively). While increasing attention is given to the values behind a negative answer to Question (F), the attempt to base the right to religious freedom on a divine vocation, whence the dignity of the human person, fails, and is ultimately replaced by the affirmation that all human beings have the duty to seek the truth (Question [A]). It is this that in the end establishes the dignity of the human person. Since a human being cannot seek the truth unless it is free both psychologically and socially (Question [D]), the right to religious freedom is at last perceived as flowing from the very nature of the human person. The conciliar position seems in the end to hover midway between a Thomistic as over against a Suarezian concept of *conscientia recta*.

CONCERN FOR CONTINUITY

That development, as I have said, was concomitant with an increasing concern for continuity with the teaching of the ordinary papal magisterium, as is evident in one of the drafts itself. The so-called *Quaestio historica* as number 2 of the draft *DP* consisted of some 380 words divided into four paragraphs, the first of which may be translated as follows:

> *Text S.* It is clear therefore that religious freedom today is not considered in the same way as formerly. Indeed, in the nineteenth century in many nations there began to prevail an ideology called laicism. It rested on rationalistic opinion concerning the absolute autonomy of individual human reason, according to which opinion a human being is a law unto itself and is in no way subject to God. From this philosophic opinion there was derived a certain notion of religious freedom in which was concealed every kind of relativism and indifferentism in religious matters. The Church condemned this notion of religious freedom and its philosophic premise: It cannot be reconciled with human dignity which consists in this especially that a human being, made to the image of God, should know the living and true God and serve Him alone.[143]

Throughout the draft the authors speak of the Church whereas they really meant the ordinary papal magisterium. The second paragraph went on to describe political aspects of this nineteenth-century situation, namely the notion that the state was supreme over matters of religion.[144] That position the Church likewise rejected: Total autonomy of the state (*potestatis publicae*) without limit and without the restraint of law cannot be harmonized with the freedom of a human being in society.

The third paragraph stated:

> *Text T.* Each of these condemnations pronounced of old today remain complete and unchangeable. But times and ideologies change. Indeed, in our own day, the raw kind of rationalism which characterized the nineteenth century has almost made room for yet more serious errors. What is more, from that time, state totalitarianism, so entirely inimical to human freedom, has begun to dominate in many parts of the world. Furthermore, when new problems arise and are examined, the Church, drawing from her treasure new things and old, at once develops *from principles which remain ever the same in their meaning and in their purport* a wider doctrine on matters social and civil. In this doctrine, the human person is every day more strongly declared to be . . . the foundation, purpose and subject of the whole of social life. Likewise, it is brought to light that a human being, as a person, is bound by duties and enjoys rights which have their source in its very nature. This holds true in all walks of life and human activity, especially in those matters

which have to do with religion. Finally, it is affirmed more clearly every day that the principal task of the state consists in this, that it protect, cultivate, and defend the natural rights of all citizens.[145]

The fourth and final paragraph stated that with the flow of history a new question had arisen about religious freedom. Today it was a question of regard for the dignity of the person and of protecting human rights, the first of which in matters pertaining to religion is a human being's right to be free from coercion, especially by the state.[146]

The *Quaestio historica* had been added in response to the growing objections of an increasing number of Council Fathers that the doctrine put forth in the drafts previous to *DP* departed from the traditional position of the ordinary papal magisterium.[147] The *Quaestio*'s central theme was to be found in the notes appended to the earlier drafts but here incorporated into the text itself.[148] It is difficult to see why anyone who had carefully read all the relevant pontifical documents from the time of Pius IX on should challenge the essential accuracy of Text S. The principal intent of the Popes had in fact been to protect the values behind a negative answer to Question (F): All talk of religious freedom notwithstanding, a human being was not for them objectively free to worship God in a way different from that whereby God is worshiped in the Catholic Church. What the Popes of the period meant in the first place was that freedom makes no sense if it means freedom from the will of God. But the same Popes meant much more, as we have seen. Concretely the central problem concerned the explicitly made assertion in Text T and implicitly in the notes of the previous drafts; namely, that the position that the authors of the successive drafts were taking was a development from principles that remain ever the same *in suo sensu et sua sententia*.[149] I shall indicate below that such was probably not the case. For the moment, the *Quaestio historica*, though ultimately discarded, is sufficient to show the Council's concern for continuity.

ATTEMPTS TO DEAL WITH THE ISSUE

Two of the ways in which efforts were made to solve the problem have to do with the manner in which the Council Fathers reacted to the new paragraphs that constituted the *Quaestio historica* itself. Typical of one current of thought was Manuel Moll y Salord, Bishop at Tortosa (Spain), who concluded his critique as follows:

> A new chapter would be desirable: "*The Doctrine on Religious Freedom in the Light of the Magisterium of the Sovereign Pontiffs.*"
> How, namely, did Leo XIII, Saint Pius X, Benedict XV, Pius XI and Pius XII feel about religious freedom? That there is no will to consider the doctrinal aspect with appropriate study is indeed amazing. Is it because the said Pontiffs do not admit and reject religious freedom of the kind put forth in the draft? An Ecumenical Council cannot condone this silence about the constant teaching of the Sovereign Pontiffs of our time.[150]

Now it is clear from the foregoing that the authors of *DP* had in the *Quaestio historica* already addressed themselves to the very point Moll y Salord brought up in the text I have just quoted. The key to understanding the Bishop's remarks lies, then, in his use of the term *debito studio*: Despite the addition of number 2 in *DP*, the matter for Moll y Salord had not yet been adequately treated. For earlier in his long analysis he had stated:

> As to number 2 . . . This number is to be omitted entirely. In the first place, these historico-doctrinal *excursus* are very dangerous and open to subjective interpretation. . . .
> Furthermore, because—though it is not expressly so stated—the intention behind this number is directed toward weakening the force of the magisterium of the Church, or rather of the Roman Pontiffs, especially of Leo XIII, attributing a value to his teaching that is merely passing.[151]

Moll y Salord seems to have been one of that persistent minority for whom departure from the teaching of the ordinary papal magisterium was in itself sufficient either for rejection or at least for significant revision of a particular draft. However, a number of those for whom the position of the ordinary papal magisterium seems not to have been ultimately decisive in itself were of a different view. Among those was Cardinal König, who wrote:

> As to number two: Either omit the whole text from the words of number two, page four, "patet igitur libertatem" up to the words "colat, vindicet" near the end of page five; let the rest of the number be adapted according to what will be said below. Or, on page four, line five of number two, in place of the words "laicismus nuncupata," let it be said in this or a similar way, "which also contained indeed seeds of truth but which finally led into the error which is called laicism." On page five, after "ideologiae," let the words be added: "The

Church, however, new questions having arisen, has been moved to seek out
from the Gospel as a source a more profound understanding of religious
freedom and to express in a more fitting way her teaching on this freedom.
My reasons: Historical continuity, which the survey exhibited in number two
intends to show, does not as a matter of fact exist in the manner [described].
The position as given cannot be sustained [teneri]*historically.* Indeed, historical truth both for Catholics and for non-Catholic readers is of the utmost
importance and is the pastoral duty of the Church. *The apologetic intent of
safeguarding the principle of continuity should not lead us to adapt historical facts according to our good pleasure.*[152]

These words, though measured, were strong and to the point. It is not
surprising, then, that along with those of Moll y Salord and of others like
him, they resulted in the suppression of the *Quaestio historica.*[153] Together
they illustrate two of the tendencies at the Council, the one seeing non-
continuity with the papal magisterium as sufficient for rejection or revision, the other seeing that fact as not ultimately decisive in itself. It was that
latter view that came to dominate. But for the moment it was merely one of
the currents flowing into the stream of development.

Meanwhile other currents were contributory. Very different from the
aforementioned was the argument that the doctrine evolving in the Council was in fact continuous with the teaching of the ordinary papal magisterium. An outstanding example is the speech given by Pedro Cantero
Cuadrado, Archbishop at Saragossa. His remarks concerned *DH*-a, poste-
rior to the draft in which the *Quaestio historica* had appeared.

Cantero began by saying that a distinction was to be made between the
various meanings that the term *libertas religiosa* might have.[154] It was one
thing to speak of religious freedom *coram Caesare*; it was quite another to
speak of it *in materia religiosa.* It is the former that is proclaimed by the
Council, not the latter. Thus in his own way Cantero initially distinguished
between a negative answer to Question (F) and an affirmative answer to
Question (D). But more was involved. It is true, he said, that the civil order
(*ordo iuridicus civilis*) is not independent but is indeed an integral part of
the moral law. To grant that however does not affect the distinction
between the two orders but only the relation of the civil order to positive
law. When this distinction is made, there arises the further question that
pertains to the legal and theological foundation of the aforesaid religious
freedom. Cantero then stated:

These explanations having been set down, and always with due regard for the
Catholic doctrine on the one true religion and the one Church of Christ, it is

my humble opinion that not on the level of mere toleration but on that of civil law an acknowledgment and positive affirmation of an objective civil right of persons and communities to the limited exercise of the aforesaid religious freedom can be defended as a true proposition in harmony with . . . the fundamental principles of the ecclesiastical magisterium, which principles in their orientation and doctrinal development are fully coherent, beginning with the encyclical *Mirari vos* up to *Pacem in terris*, and *Ecclesiam suam* of Pope Paul VI.[155]

Cantero then went on to give his reasons. It is logically impossible to ground the right to religious freedom on the claims of conscience because of absurd consequences that flow from such an attempt.[156] Nor is it sufficient to posit as basis the dignity of the human person without saying why that dignity requires the right to religious freedom.[157] In saying that within the limits legally established by society, human beings have the civil freedom to profess their religion—and that they have this freedom precisely because of their religious responsibility before God and society, and because of the nature and the transcendence of the religious act itself—Cantero clearly affirmed the values behind a positive answer to Question (E). It should thus be remarked in passing that not all Spaniards argued for the traditional position. And his phrase ". . . propter responsabilitatem religiosam personalem coram Deo . . ."[158] came close to affirming the values behind a positive answer to Question (A). My main interest in his speech, however, is that as of September 17, 1965, and hence as late as the last session, some were willing to argue that the evolving doctrine on religious freedom was fully in harmony with the teaching of the ordinary papal magisterium.

The tendency exhibited by Cantero had however been there all along, as earlier speeches by Archbishop Garrone of Toulouse and Lawrence Cardinal Shehan of Baltimore attest.[159] But they, like those who argued that the evolving doctrine was not continuous with the teaching of the ordinary papal magisterium and should therefore be discarded or corrected, seem to have constituted a minority. Thus there were at least two minority views, the larger and more persistent being that of the Moll y Salord faction; and the lesser but theologically somewhat naive being that of the Cantero Cuadrados.

An additional way of dealing with the issue and one that in the end turned into a major current contributory to the stream of development is represented by those who attempted to ground religious freedom as an objective right *while simultaneously refraining from any direct comment on the matter of continuity*. Such was the approach, for example, of a

Montini and a Wojtyla, one of the speeches of the latter being especially interesting in retrospect.[160] Karol Wojtyla, then Archbishop at Cracow, arguing on September 25, 1964, with regard to *HD*, distinguished two contexts or meanings of the term religious freedom.[161] The first pertained to its use in an ecumenical frame of reference. Here, he said, the relation between truth and freedom ought to be more clearly highlighted. On the one hand, freedom exists because of truth; on the other, it cannot be made perfect except by truth.[162] It is the truth that makes a human being free, Wojtyla had said earlier,[163] just as he was later to say that religious freedom reaches its climax in a human being's responsibility.[164] But in this speech in the third session of the Council, he stated that in an ecumenical context the right to freedom cannot be based on toleration alone, a position directly contrary to that of the previous papal magisterium prior to *Pacem in terris*.[165] What is to be desired is progress together (*simul*) in truth. However, when one is dealing with religious freedom in the civic as distinguished from the ecumenical context, toleration does indeed come into play. At this point, Wojtyla's speech reflected the situation of the Catholic Church in Poland. Atheists tend to see in every religion the alienation of the human mind, from which, with means sometimes proper to the state, they wish a human being to be liberated. Relying on materialism, they say that liberation must come about through scientific, especially economic, progress.[166] By contrast:

> The human person must appear in the real loftiness of his or her rational nature, and religion as the culmination of that nature. Indeed, it [religion] consists in the free clinging of the human mind to God, a clinging which is entirely personal and related to conscience, *having its origin in the desire for truth*.[167]

A human person so conceived earnestly demands (*expostulat*) freedom and does not stop until he or she obtains it. No secular power has the right to come between the relation between God and humankind. The Council therefore in the light of faith and reason must profess the fullness of human freedom. A human being is perfected, not alienated, by religion.[168]

Wojtyla's argument closely resembled remarks made by Montini in the first session just as the speech made by Colombo later that morning was along the same lines as that of Wojtyla,[169] with the difference that Colombo seemed at least indirectly concerned with the issue of continuity.[170] Neither Montini nor Colombo in the respective speeches I have so far referred to tended to ground religious freedom on the *duty* to seek the truth; they approached the matter more from the *right* to do so. Yet the distance from the right to the duty is assuredly short, especially once it is seen that duties are the source of the former, not vice versa. By contrast, Wojtyla early on in the debates made suggestions along the line of the duty to seek the truth. The question that concerns us here, however, is not the relative success of Wojytla's argument but whether he realized the position he was embracing ran counter to the previous teaching of the ordinary papal magisterium. As in the matter of Pius XII's doctrine on the relation of the Catholic Church to the Mystical Body of Christ, an issue that constitutes the principal burden of a subsequent chapter, Wojtyla seems to have been silent about continuity. He seems to have been equally silent about the *Quaestio historica*. Meanwhile, a persistent minority was constantly bringing the issue to the attention of the Council Fathers. It is possible of course that Wojtyla belonged to that other minority who claimed that the doctrine evolving in the Council was in fact continuous; but the sharpness of his mind tends to minimize that possibility.

The effort to face the problem of continuity as exhibited by a Wojtyla was surely divergent from that exhibited by the Moll y Salords and the Königs, and those in turn were different from the manner of the Cantero Cuadrados. Thus it is possible to discern at least four ways of dealing with the issue. I must approach the close of this section, however, with a note of caution. I have not attempted a day-by-day description of the debates in the Council, nor the chronology of events and the substance of all the arguments put forth, not to mention the maneuvers that led up to the notorious "Black Week" as they affected the draft (*DP*) on religious freedom.[171] As one reads the debates and written critiques in the *Acta Synodalia Sacrosancti Concilii Oecumenici Vaticani Secundi*, it is clear that continuity was not the only concern even of the Moll y Salords. For example, the attempt to ground the dignity of the human person in a divine vocation, whence the right to religious freedom, was removed from the drafts not because of lack of continuity with the teaching of the ordinary papal magisterium but because of a *reductio ad absurdum*.[172] As one bishop touched upon one aspect of the question of religious freedom and others in turn concentrated on still others, the issue of continuity was not always relevant. Thus anyone arguing from the point of view of following even an erroneous conscience as the proximate norm of morality and hence the basis of the right to religious freedom may have had a problem with the internal coherence of his argument, but he had none whatever with the ordinary papal magisterium and was therefore not likely to allude to the problem. Provided this larger context is kept in mind, there is little danger of distortion.

Yet the issue remained alive even to the end, a fact borne out by a remark of Bishop De Smedt almost on the very eve of the final vote:

> Some Fathers affirm that the Declaration does not sufficiently show how our doctrine is not opposed to the Church documents up to the time of the sovereign pontiff, Leo XIII. In the last report, we have already said that this question will have to be opened up completely [*in plena luce ponenda*] in future theological and historical studies.[173]

The vote was to be on whether the Commission had handled the suggested amendments satisfactorily. When it came to a vote on the document (*DH*-c) as a whole, the vote was 1,954 in favor and 249 for complete rejection out of a total of 2,216 voting (there being seven for qualified acceptance, and six invalid votes).[174] A persistent minority seems to have held out until the end.

What then is to be made of these facts? With the exception of the two minorities it may be said that the majority, realizing that they were in some way departing from the teaching of the ordinary papal magisterium, left it up to the future research of historians and theologians to determine precisely what had happened. And the minority who, in the name of continuity, had opposed the "new" doctrine came forward, once the debates were over, and, one by one, signed the document promulgated by Pope Paul VI. Thus the various currents of thought relative to the issue of continuity in the end flowed into one stream. And that, in the last analysis, was not an attitude of *laissez-faire* but of *laissez-approfondir*.

But the crucial question remains: In what sense is the doctrine of *Dignitatis humanae* continuous with that of Pius IX and his successors up to John XXIII in *Pacem in terris*? That is the *point nerveux* of the whole discussion and the matter to which I must now direct the reader's attention.

DEVELOPMENT AND REVERSAL

Before I complete the last step in my attempt to ground the second part of my argument, a final hurdle must be faced. To that number of Council Fathers who maintained that the teaching of *Dignitatis humanae* as it was evolving in the Council was in fact continuous with the teaching of the previous ordinary papal magisterium must seemingly be added the name of Canon Roger Aubert, at this writing perhaps the greatest living authority on the Catholic Church in the nineteenth century.[175] Since Aubert's remarks are better understood when seen against the background of Bishop De Smedt's first report, I shall begin there. We are thus back in the second session of the Council and the sixty-ninth meeting (November 18, 1963) of that session.[176]

Bishop De Smedt's Initial Attempt to Maintain Continuity

After explaining why the declaration was necessary—ecumenical reasons predominated—and the three steps that constituted the argument of *HC*, De Smedt came in the fourth and fifth parts of his presentation to the sensitive question of continuity. In part four he began with *Pacem in terris*; in part five, he ended with it. Although John's position was in fact problematical in the sense I have indicated, De Smedt (and the Secretariat for which he presumably spoke) did not seem to understand this. He seems to have seen in John's encyclical a development according to a twofold principle or norm, of continuity on the one hand and progress on the other.[177] Continuity, in that the doctrine of the Church remains ever the same; progress, in that the questions arising out of the concrete situation in which the Church finds herself prompt her to examine her teaching more deeply and to understand it more clearly. Thus John could distinguish false philosophies on the one hand and make a clear distinction between error and the errant on the other. Errors are always to be rejected, but the errant never loses his or her dignity as a person.[178]

With due attention to the caution I have suggested above, it may be granted that De Smedt's interpretation of *Pacem in terris* was not entirely lacking in prima facie plausibility. The problems begin with De Smedt's turn to Pius IX, *Quanta cura* and the Syllabus. From that point on, it appears that De Smedt and the members of the Secretariat for Christian Unity were reading into history rather than out of it. Applying the norm of continuity, De Smedt interpreted Pius IX as meaning that the ultimate foundation of human dignity consists in the fact that the human being is a creature of God. From that absolute dependence flows every right and duty—the Council was later to see that rights flow from respective duties, not vice versa—to establish a claim to religious freedom worthy of the name.[179] Therefore, a human being is *subjectively* bound to worship God according to the right norm of conscience (*iuxta rectam conscientiae suae normam*) because *objectively* a human being depends absolutely on God. It is clear that De Smedt's and the Secretariat's thinking was becoming increasingly murky. Thus—still in the context of Pius IX—De Smedt concluded: "By taking up the battle, therefore, against the philosophic as well as political tenets of laicism, the Church for excellent reason was contending for the dignity of the human person and for its true freedom."[180] From this it follows according to the norm of continuity ". . . that the Church yesterday [olim] and today is clearly consistent with herself, however changed circumstances might be."[181] It should be noted that De Smedt (and the Secretariat) said "Church" whereas he should have said "ordinary papal magisterium," the same inaccuracy seen in the *Quaestio historica*. In so doing he obfuscated the problem, for if my conclusions stated below are correct, the Church—understood according to an extended concept of κοινωνία—was groping for a better notion of religious freedom during all this period while simultaneously the ordinary papal magisterium was fully consistent only in its adamant stand on a value still fully shared by most Catholics; namely, that a human being does not have an *objective* right to worship God in a way other than He is worshiped in the Roman Church and those other local Christian churches united with it.

De Smedt then maintained that Leo XIII developed the Church's position, but this is true only in the context of the related question of Church-state relations, not in that of religious freedom. This alleged development was said to be the result of the norm of progress.[182] Leo distinguished more clearly than his immediate predecessors between the Church, which is the people of God, and civil society, which is the people as temporal and of the earth, opening the way to affirm in a new manner the legitimate autonomy that belongs to the civil order. It is true that for Leo modern freedoms, including religious freedom, were to be tolerated. But that was because Leo saw them as still infected with laicism; hence, there was always the danger they might end up harming the dignity of the human being and his true freedom.[183]

Coming to Pius XI and Pius XII, De Smedt next referred to the documents I have examined above and in the fifth part of his presentation cited again *Pacem in terris*.[184] The Bishop then made the explicit claim that the draft (*HC*) being presented to the Council was in continuity with John's encyclical.[185] But even though at that point studies by de Broglie and Janssens had not yet appeared, a careful reading of the text should have suggested that claiming continuity with *Pacem in terris* solved nothing since John's thought on the issue of religious freedom as expressed in that document is ambiguous. De Smedt then said:

This text [*HC*] we now submit to your judgment [*cogitationibus*]. In the historical survey of this doctrine we have shown that, besides the fact that the doctrine has continuity [with the past], the doctrine becomes more and more clear. It is obvious that certain pontifical quotations that materially have a different ring can be placed as objections to our draft. But I beseech you, venerable Fathers, not to make the texts speak outside their historical and doctrinal context, lest you make a fish swim out of water.[186]

Now manifestly if my analysis of the doctrine of Pius IX—as systematized by Leo XIII and, with the possible exception of *Pacem in terris*, as reflected in subsequent pontifical documents—is reasonably correct, then at the very least De Smedt's account was oversimplified, if not tendentious. For upon analysis the papal statements on the issue of religious freedom as it affected non-Catholics can hardly be said to have been only materially different from the position being presented in *HC* or any later conciliar draft. The difference between the two orientations regarding Question (E) is unquestionably formal. It was De Smedt and the Secretariat for Christian Unity who were taking a fish out of water. Only in that way could the teaching of Pius XI and Pius XII, not to mention Pius IX and Leo XIII, be interpreted as being primarily concerned with the dignity of the human person. The Popes were primarily concerned with what they perceived to be an unalterable truth; in terms of thesis/hypothesis (α), that truth was the same as a negative answer to Question (F), a view that the Enlightenment, the French Revolution and its aftermath had challenged far more radically than had the Protestant Reformation. It was because the Popes of the period thought they perceived an organized attempt to answer Question (F) affirmatively (not simply because they perceived modern freedoms as tainted with laicism) that they maintained religious freedom for non-Catholics could at best be tolerated, non-toleration being a greater evil. They held this position as a consequence (albeit unnecessary) of a negative answer to Question (F). Thus few seemed even mildly astonished that De Smedt's hermeneutics were ultimately interpreted by the majority as a maneuver, as the removal of the later *Quaestio historica* attests.[187] And in the end, that maneuver, real or alleged, did not work.

Canon Aubert's Argument

The analysis in De Smedt's first report seems to have been based in large measure on an earlier article (1951) by Roger Aubert, though De Smedt does not say so in the report itself.[188] In a later article Aubert seems to have lent support to De Smedt's interpretation and to have argued at least indirectly for continuity between the doctrine evolving in the Council and the teaching of the previous ordinary papal magisterium.[189]

"La Liberté religieuse du Syllabus de 1864 à nos jours" described in stark terms the problem before the Council. Referring to the thunderous applause that at the end of the previous session followed upon De Smedt's report on the draft to be approved the following year, Aubert stated:

> But then a rather serious question arises at once: Has the Church changed her doctrine after a century? Was the magisterium which gave the faithful the Syllabus in error? And in touch with the facts or under the pressure of opinion, has it since been obliged to reverse its position? . . .[190]

After admitting that such a hypothesis was not impossible, Aubert continued:

> One could then declare that upon examination it constitutes a mistake on the part of the Holy See, without the bases of the Catholic system being shaken any more than they are when historians prove to us that in the monophysite period Pope Honorius fell into heresy or something very much like that. But is it really necessary to go that far? I believe the answer is more nuanced....[191]

Aubert refers to the monophysite period whereas in fact he must have meant the monothelite. His article appeared in. March 1965, several months before the opening of the last session of the Council. The difficulties the Council Fathers had in coming to a consensus on the draft on religious freedom were well known and were, as we have seen, in great measure due to concern for continuity with the previous ordinary papal magisterium. It cannot but be that Aubert's article, along with the others of Cahier 50 of *Recherches et débats du Centre Catholique des intellectuels français* were meant to help dissipate the difficulties. The last sentence from the above passage quoted from the beginning of Aubert's article does not, as it stands, imply that its author claimed continuity between the doctrine evolving in the Council and the teaching of the previous ordinary papal magisterium. However, the whole movement of his analysis, culminating in the passage I shall quote below, leads the reader to surmise that such indeed was Aubert's intent. This interpretation seems confirmed, I suggest, not only by Aubert's analysis but also by the fact that Aubert refers to and seems uncritically to accept the general thrust of De Smedt's first report.

In order to understand a Church document, Aubert said, it is indispensable to put it in its historical perspective. When the Syllabus reproves liberalism it is not so much the essence of liberalism that is condemned as the concrete form that the liberal system was taking at the time.[192] Despite certain equivocations in Montalembert, the expression "A Free Church in a Free State" with him did not have the ring of statism (subjection of the Church to the state) that the same expression had on the lips of Cavour. Pius IX was well aware of the difference.[193] It was the latter kind of liberalism that the Pope was getting at. Yet, it cannot be denied, Aubert admits, that Pius IX, in the name of a particular anthropology current among the theologians of his day, struck at a certain liberal organization of society that today seems much more respectful of the individual than was the *ancien régime*.[194] Though many a condemned proposition of the Syllabus has to do with a position no longer regarded as relevant by anyone, one proceeds with complete integrity when one tries to understand why Pius IX took the stand he did.

Aubert then described in bold strokes the search for a properly grounded religious freedom, tracing its history from the Syllabus up to John XXIII and touching upon the documents I have discussed above. What the Popes condemned was especially a relativism and indifference elevated to the dignity of principle (*un relativisme et un indifférentisme théorique*) more than an indifference that in practice was limited to respect for free personhood (*personalité libre*) even when it was mistaken (*indifférentisme pratique*). What the Popes from Gregory XVI to Leo XIII affirmed was that there is only one true religion, that willed by God. Therefore a human being is not free to set up another at its good pleasure.[195]

In his attempt to help resolve the dilemma facing the Council, Aubert, whose immense erudition is beyond dispute, tended to oversimplify certain problems. The comparison between the ordinary papal magisterium from the time of Pius IX (up to but possibly excluding John XXIII) and Honorius I was not entirely apposite. Whereas the position that Honorius embraced and that was subsequently rejected by the Third Council of Constantinople was expressed in a private letter to a patriarch,[196] the consistent teaching of the Popes for at least one hundred fifty years had been that religious freedom for non-Catholics was the result of toleration of error for the common good. Furthermore, it is inaccurate to suggest that in the Syllabus errors condemned under the heading "Errors pertaining to *contemporary* liberalism" was meant to apply to number 15, which deals with the extent of religious freedom as with an immutable truth.[197] As I have conceded, Text I from Pius XII's 1942 Christmas Message can, until it is balanced by Text J from *Ci riesce*, lend some support to the idea that the papacy was indeed evolving toward the position on religious freedom ultimately embraced by Vatican II. Nonetheless, those statements regarding religious freedom from Pius IX to Pius XII, when examined in their context, have to do with religious freedom of Catholics, not with that of human beings in general. Yet, Aubert in 1965 left his reader with the impression that the doctrine on religious freedom as maintained by the Popes up to the opening of Vatican II and the doctrines evolving in the Council were in essential continuity:

> This interpretation of the pontifical documents of the nineteenth century, which I had sketched a good ten years ago . . . has since been taken up by various parties in order to show that there is no fundamental objection from that point of view, notably by Cardinal Lercaro in a noteworthy speech and more recently by Bishop De Smedt in 1963 in the first report intended to present to the Fathers of the Second Vatican Council the chapter on religious freedom. Furthermore, Bishop De Smedt could henceforth invoke the very clear affirmation of John XXIII in his encyclical *Pacem in terris*.[198]

John's stance remains, as we have seen, somewhat uncertain, but in the article of 1965 Aubert did not seem to have been aware of the ambiguity. Nonetheless, while the fact that a historian of Aubert's stature seems to have been willing to argue for essential continuity surely must give one pause, I must state quite candidly that I find his position tendentious.[199]

Assessment

It is time to take up again the six heuristic questions placed at the beginning of this chapter and to draw up the balance as it emerges from the data. That a human being in religious matters especially has the duty to seek the truth and to adhere to it once it is found; that a human being has an objective duty to inform his or her conscience honestly and responsibly; that he or she has the objective duty to follow even an erroneous conscience, and that the assent of faith may not be forced: These answers to Questions (A), (B), (C), and (D) respectively were fully shared by the Fathers of Vatican II and the Popes who preceded them. As a result of drawing the logical conclusions from these shared values, the Council Fathers, conscious of the problem of continuity, developed the distinctive contribution of *Dignitatis humanae*. Continuity with the Popes from Pius IX onward was further enhanced by a unanimously negative answer to Question (F): For the Council Fathers as for the previous ordinary papal magisterium, a human being does not have an objective right to worship God in a way other than the way God is worshiped in the Roman Church and those other local Christian churches in union with it. There the Council Fathers stood shoulder to shoulder with the Popes.

But there is a sense in which the Council Fathers reversed the teaching of the ordinary papal magisterium, for the distinctive contribution of *Dignitatis humanae* amounts to an affirmative answer to Question (E): Does a human being in the present economy of salvation have the *objective* right to worship God in the manner in which a responsible use of intellect indicates he or she should? If the official documents of the papal magisterium from Pius IX up to and including Pius XII held to variations of the old thesis/hypothesis model (though usually without its explicit label), in which religious freedom in the sense of Question (E) is officially meaningless, then the Council in affirmatively answering in its own way that same question asserts that the Question is *not* meaningless but a fundamental human right. Though *Dignitatis humanae* (*DH*-d) does not use the terms subjective versus objective, it undoubtedly meant the latter. For the Council affirms that the right to religious freedom is based on the dignity of the human person and is grounded in revelation itself. In that sense, there can be no doubt whatever that the Council reversed the position of Pius IX and his successors, with the possible exception of John XXIII. To use in a reverse sense the terms of Bishop Cantero, the Popes simply did not teach that everyone has the right to religious freedom *coram Caesare*; what they taught was that Caesar could tolerate the public expression of non-Catholic cults in order to avoid a greater evil. And that is very, very different. Thus, if the term *religious freedom* is taken according to its meaning in the context of Question (E), then *pace* Aubert and perhaps at one point John Courtney Murray himself,[200] it must be conceded that the distinctive contribution of *Dignitatis humanae* is not continuous with the doctrine of Pius IX and his successors prior to John XXIII.[201]

That the papal magisterium could have answered Question (E) affirmatively if it had been more attentive to the inner dynamic of its answers to Questions (A), (B), (C), and (D) is one thing; in that sense, the Council developed the teaching of the previous papal magisterium, bringing "new" things out of "old." That the same magisterium at least prior to *Pacem in terris* did not in fact address itself to the values behind an affirmative answer to Question (E) and was indeed corrected by the rest of the Church is something else again, a fact highly relevant to the theory of doctrinal development that I intend to sustain.[202] Thus it is not merely the course of development that has yet to be accounted for. Of even greater significance are its implications for Catholic ecclesiology and contemporary ecumenical endeavors.

In the meantime, two more doctrinal issues and their trajectories at the Second Vatican Council must be examined. I shall thus be dealing with the Petrine ministry of Pius XII and his teaching on two closely related matters pertaining to the theology of the Church. But here, as I shall show, modalities of reception were ultimately very different from those whereby *Fidei donum* along with its meaning for the doctrine of collegiality had been received.[203]

Chapter V
THE CHURCH AND HER MEMBERS

Since the Mystical Body of Christ, that is to say, the Church, is like the physical body, a unity, a compact thing closely joined together, it would be false and foolish to say that Christ's Mystical Body could be composed of separated and scattered members. Whoever therefore is not united with it is not a member of it nor does he communicate with its Head Who is Christ.[1]

These words from *Mortalium animos* of Pius XI suffice to show that the identification of the Mystical Body of Christ with the Church—and Pius clearly meant the (Roman) Catholic Church—did not, regarding the ordinary papal magisterium, originate with the teaching of Pius XII in *Mystici corporis* (henceforth, for the most part, *MC*). Enough has been said above about the latter encyclical for me to proceed at once to the matter at hand; that is, to an examination of how the Fathers of Vatican II received the teaching of Pius XII concerning the identity of the Mystical Body of Christ with the (Roman) Catholic Church and the correlative question of who belongs to it, the two poles around which the analysis undertaken below is oriented. I shall attempt to establish the following conclusions:

I.   *Explicit statements in* Mystici corporis, *when seen in the context of* Humani generis, *which followed it, indicate that Pius XII taught that the relation of the Mystical Body of Christ to the (Roman) Catholic Church was one of identity. The internal logic of other statements in the same encyclical suggest that regarding the correlative question of membership, the Pope's position was not inconsistent with the older Catholic theory that considered non-Catholic Christians as belonging to the Soul of the Church. The theory of Church membership subjacent in that document is perhaps best described as a stratification theory* (Schichtentheorie).

II.   *Conciliar data indicate that the Decree on Eastern Catholic Churches* (Orientalium Ecclesiarum) *as well as the early drafts of the Dogmatic Constitution on the Church (*Lumen gentium), *respectively, preserve and preserved the orientation of* Mystici corporis *both on the identity question and the correlative question of membership.*

III.   *The data surrounding the genesis of* Lumen gentium, *however, further reveal general dissatisfaction with the position of Pius XII on the identity question as well as its reversal, the Council Fathers being explicitly aware of what was happening. Paradoxically, careful reading of the documents suggests that the Council Fathers were unwilling totally to depart from the teaching of Pius XII on the correlative question of membership.*

IV.   *Despite the inconsistency which* Orientalium Ecclesiarum *constitutes it is the thrust of* Lumen gentium, *not that of* Orientalium Ecclesiarum, *that must be considered the normative index of the Council's thinking on both questions.*

This chapter is divided into five sections corresponding to the four parts of my argument as stated above, followed by an overview. The first attempts to clarify the complexity of the Pope's teaching by distinguishing between explicit statements and their internal logic. It then determines what is involved in a stratification theory of membership (*Schichtentheorie*) as over against a theory of degrees or levels (*Stufentheorie*), and closes with a preliminary synthesis. The second and third sections deal with what happened to the Pope's teaching at the Second Vatican Council. Since a close reading of the documents uncovers a fundamental inconsistency in the promulgated texts, these sections become increasingly complex until the last, where the difficulties noted earlier are finally resolved. The ground is thus cleared for my claim relative to the manner in which the teaching of Pius XII was received by the Fathers of Vatican II. Finally, it would have been logically more neat in the second and third sections to treat first of the identity question and then of the correlative question of membership. This however has proved to be an impossible task because in the conciliar debates the Fathers rarely spoke of the one without alluding to the other. I shall therefore write of one or the other as found in the data, stating my conclusions at appropriate points as I proceed.

The Teaching of Pius XII
EXPLICIT STATEMENTS

The teaching of Pius XII on the identity question, but even more so on the correlative question of membership, is more involved than has sometimes been supposed. Indeed, in *Mystici corporis* his stance on the former is itself not without a certain ambivalence:

> *Text A.* The doctrine of the Mystical Body of Christ, which is the Church, was first taught us by the Redeemer Himself...[2] If we would define and describe this true Church of Jesus Christ—which is the One, Holy, Catholic, Apostolic and Roman Church—we shall find nothing more noble, more sublime, or more divine than the expression "the Mystical Body of Jesus Christ"...[3]

This text, composed of two paragraphs occurring in different parts of the encyclical, does not, as it stands and without reference to *Humani generis*, which followed it, exclude the possibility that in *Mystici corporis* the Pope taught that though the (Roman) Catholic Church is the Mystical Body of Christ, the Mystical Body of Christ is not absolutely coextensive with the (Roman) Catholic Church. This possibility, difficult to document given the total context of the encyclical and the tradition from which it flowed, must nonetheless be allowed in principle. Yet those who thought such might have been the case seemed later to have been victims of a delusion, for seven years subsequently in *Humani generis* the Pope complained:

> *Text B.* Some say they are not bound by the doctrine, explained in Our Encyclical Letter of a few years ago, and based on the sources of

revelation, which teaches that the Mystical Body of Christ and the
Roman Catholic Church are one and the same thing. Some reduce
to a meaningless formula the necessity of belonging to the true
Church in order to gain eternal salvation.[4]

While it is not clear from the document itself just what the Pope's target
was, those familiar with the theological scene at the time had no difficulty
in identifying the theological horizon to which he was addressing himself.[5]
Particularly in Germany certain excesses in ecclesiological reflection had
been manifesting themselves. On the one hand, there were those who
maintained a real identity between Christ and the Christian; on the other,
there were those who judged that the expression *body of Christ* was simply
one in a whole nomenclature and could in no way be used as a definition of
the Church. Still others manifested a tendency toward quietism. It was in
this latter context that the tendency on the part of many ecumenically
minded Catholics sometimes expressed itself; namely, that, provided one
belonged to the Mystical Body of Christ, it was of no import what one's
relation to the Catholic Church was. In this context, Pius XII had two
alternatives; either abandon all talk of the Church as the Mystical Body of
Christ and thereby do away with these tendencies, or give a more exact
description of the biblical notion of the Church as the Body of Christ such
that it would exclude the above-mentioned positions.[6] Pius XII chose the
second alternative and in so doing seems to have overlooked some of the
implications of baptism. Thus to those who thought that through baptism
one may not necessarily belong to the Catholic Church but that one could
nonetheless belong to the Mystical Body of Christ, Pius in Texts A and B
was saying in effect that for him and Catholicism such a view was not
theologically viable. Though the question is more complex, as the debates
at Vatican II were to show, they explain a second major emphasis in
Mystici corporis, the correlative question of membership:

> *Text C.* Actually [*reapse*], only those are to be included as members of the
> Church who have been baptized and profess the true faith, and who
> have not been so unfortunate as to separate themselves from the
> unity of the Body, or have been excluded by legitimate authority
> for grave faults committed.[7]

The conditions for membership as seen by the Pope were three: (1)
baptism, (2) profession of the true faith and (3) communion with the rest of
the Church. Thus the Church includes sinners. "For not every sin, however
grave it may be, is such as of its own nature to sever a man from the Body of

the Church, as does schism or heresy or apostasy."[8] For human beings may lose *caritas* and divine grace through sin but they are not deprived of all supernatural life "...if they hold fast to faith and Christian hope, and if illuminated from above, they are spurred on by the interior promptings of the Holy Spirit to salutary fear and are moved to prayer and penance for their sins."[9] Though the Pope implies there are some sins so grave that of their very nature they would remove those guilty of them from membership in the Mystical Body, it is clear nonetheless that for him schism, heresy, or apostasy constitute the chief obstacles to membership. Thus in the end it is profession of the true faith that is crucial for Pius' argument on membership; for baptism by most non-Catholic Christian Churches is regarded as valid by the Roman Church. And it could be argued that most present-day non-Catholic Christians have not deliberately separated themselves from the unity of the Catholic Church, that they are material, not formal, heretics, to use the language current in Catholicism before Vatican II.

But during the Council some were to argue that Pius did not really intend to teach that non-Catholic Christians are not members of the Church of Christ. A notable example of this tendency was Giacomo Cardinal Lercaro, Archbishop at Bologna. Lercaro's argument should be carefully considered not simply because, if correct, it puts in doubt my own position as expressed above, but also because during the conciliar debates many were to adopt a similar view, especially as it related to Canon 87 of the *Codex Iuris Canonici* and Canon 16 of *Cleri sanctitati*, a corpus of 558 canons promulgated (1957) for the Eastern Catholic Churches.[10] Lercaro based his argument on four sources:

1. The *Bulla Unionis Armeniorum*
2. Canon 2, *De Paenitentia* of the twenty-fourth session of the Council of Trent
3. Canon 87 of the *Codex Iuris Canonici*
4. Canon 16 of *Cleri sanctitati*[11]

It must be said at once that none of the above documents supports Lercaro's claim. Thus *Exsultate Deo*—from the *Bulla Unionis Armeniorum*, promulgated on November 22, 1439 during the Council of Florence—when discussing baptism refers to it as the door of the spiritual life and states that the baptized are made members of Christ and of the body that is the Church.[12] This statement is in no sense incompatible with the subsequent teaching of Benedict XIV in *Singulari nobis* discussed below.

The reference to Canon 2 of *De Paenitentia* of the twenty-fourth session of the Council of Trent seems to have been inaccurate, since the Sacrament of Penance was treated in the fourteenth session, its canons not pertaining to the point under discussion. Lercaro probably meant the fourth canon on Baptism of the seventh session. That canon rejected the notion that Trinitarian baptism performed by a heretic is not valid, under the usual conditions.[13] Only Canon 87 of the *Codex Iuris Canonici* and Canon 16 of *Cleri sanctitati* are relevant, and may be translated respectively as follows:

> By baptism, a human being is constituted a person in the Church with all the rights and duties of Christians *unless regarding rights there be an obstacle impeding the bond of communion with the Church* or a censure pronounced by the Church.[14]

> 1⁰ By baptism, a human being is constituted a person in the Church of Christ.
> 2⁰ A person in the Church of Christ enjoys all the rights of and is bound by the duties of Christians, unless, *regarding rights, there be an obstacle impeding the bond of communion with the Church.*[15]

It will be seen at once that there is little difference between the text from *Codex Iuris Canonici* and that from *Cleri sanctitati*. Lercaro's argument seems to have been based especially on the first paragraph of Canon 16 (*Cleri sanctitati*) and the first half of the second, where the rights and duties of Christians, not simply of Catholics, flowing from the personhood conferred by baptism are affirmed. But Lercaro seems to have overlooked completely the proviso expressed by the clause "...*nisi obstet obex*..." which in the Latin text is the same both in Canon 87 and in Canon 16 of *Cleri sanctitati*. The *obex* in this case would not come from a censure that had been incurred—from a Catholic point of view, non-Catholic Christians are material, not formal, heretics—but from the fact that from the same Catholic point of view, non-Catholic Christians do not profess the true faith, at least not in its fullness. Thus nothing in these canons is incompatible with the conditions for membership that Pius XII had described (Text [C]). It is therefore incorrect to construe these conditions to mean that Pius XII could not really have thought, and consequently could not have taught, that non-Catholic Christians are not members of the Church of Christ. On the contrary, the teaching of Pius XII in *Mystici corporis* is fully in agreement with traditional papal teaching in this regard.

I limit myself here to one example. Benedict XIV in *Singulari nobis* (February 9, 1749) mentioned that whoever received baptism from a heretic, by that very reason (*vi*) becomes a member of the Catholic Church, but ceases to be a member when he or she accepts the heresy of the baptizer.[16] Since in *Singulari nobis* Benedict did not distinguish between material and formal heretics, the implications are that an infant baptized in a non-Catholic Christian religion is a member of the Catholic Church until later he or she explicitly embraces the tenets of a non-Christian or a non-Catholic Christian religion. Such is the traditional papal stance; Canon 87 of the *Codex* and Canon 16 of *Cleri sanctitati* are fully in accord with it, as is the statement made in the much earlier *Bulla Unionis Armeniorum*. Lercaro's point that Canon 16 of *Cleri sanctitati* belongs to a corpus of law promulgated in 1957, well after *Mystici corporis* (1943) and hence a better index of Pius' thinking, was consequently irrelevant.

Yet, though Lercaro's documentation was inadequate, surely his instincts were right, for Vatican II was indeed to modify the position of Pius XII on the question of membership. Lercaro had put his finger on a problem that Pius XII in his own way had attempted to face. In order to see this, it may be advantageous to explicate the teaching of Pius XII in all its starkness. By identifying the Mystical Body of Christ with the Catholic Church—and Pius XII like Pius XI meant by that the (Roman) Catholic Church—Pius XII was affirming that the Church of Christ is the (Roman) Catholic Church and no other. This meant that non-Catholic Christians were not *ecclesia* but *vestigia ecclesiae*, Calvin's term in the *Institutes* turned around in the other direction. Certainly the Church as a visible institution has its precedent in Aquinas back through Irenaeus and Ignatius of Antioch. But extended emphasis on the Church of Christ as a concrete, organized, social entity to which one can point is the result of post-Reformation polemics and has its roots in Robert Bellarmine. Now if that is the case—if the Church of Christ and the Catholic Church defined as the Roman Church and those other local Christian Churches in union with it are interchangeable concepts—and the Pope's teaching in *Mystici corporis* must ultimately be interpreted in that sense—then Christians who are not in union with the Roman Church are not members of the Church of Christ so defined. The logic of Pius' equation, once the premise is admitted, is inescapable.

Were non-Catholic Christians then simply to be dismissed because, according to the logic flowing from the Pope's identification of the Mystical Body of Christ with the (Roman) Catholic Church, they could not be called *members* of the Church? By no means. Pius had his own way of facing the problem and stated that while non-Catholic Christians are not members of the Church as he understood it, they are nonetheless related to it:

> *Text D.* For even though [*licet*] by an unconscious desire and longing [*inscio quodam desiderio ac voto*] they have a certain relationship [*ordinentur*] with the Mystical Body of the Redeemer, they still remain deprived of those many heavenly gifts and helps which can be enjoyed only in the Catholic Church. [17]

The fact that, for Pius, non-Catholic Christians remained deprived of many heavenly gifts and helps should not be allowed to obscure what he granted in the antecedent concessive clause (*licet...ordinentur...*). For they have indeed a certain relation to the Church of Christ. And it is because of that relation that they are, or at least can be, saved. Thus Text D may be regarded as an attenuation of the statement made by Pius XI in *Mortalium animos*, which, in an excessively harsh manner, claimed that whoever is not united with the Mystical Body is not a member of it nor does he or she "...communicate with its Head Who is Christ."[18] Compared with the position of his predecessor, that of Pius XII on the correlative question of membership is highly nuanced and, as we are now about to see, is probably not inconsistent with an older Catholic doctrine.

INTERNAL LOGIC

Non-Catholic Christians and the Soul of the Church

While it must be admitted that speaking of non-Catholic Christians (and for that matter of non-Christians in the context of the axiom *extra Ecclesiam nulla salus*) as belonging to the Soul of the Church fell into disuse after *Mystici corporis*—the tendency thereafter became to distinguish between actual and potential members, or between membership *in re* and belonging *in voto*—there was no intrinsic reason why the older approach had to be dropped. Indeed, at one stage of the Preparatory Period of the Second Vatican Council, Cardinal Bea suggested that its use be taken up again.[19] Nothing in *Mystici corporis* had explicitly ruled out its viability.[20] Thus, though speaking in a frame of reference not directly pertaining to the question of membership, Pius made a statement whose internal logic, upon close examination, is directly relevant to the point at issue. He began by quoting Leo XIII:

Text E. "Let it suffice to say that, as Christ is the Head of the Church, so is the Holy Spirit her soul."[21]

Text F. If that vital principle, *by which the whole community of Christians* is sustained by its Founder, be considered not now in itself but in the created effects which proceed from it, it consists in those heavenly gifts which our Redeemer, together with His Spirit, bestows on the Church, and which He and His Spirit, from whom come supernatural light and holiness, make operative in the Church.[22]

Text F opens a new paragraph following immediately upon Text E, which is a quotation from Leo XIII's encyclical, *Divinum illud munus.* The general context in which Texts E and F occurs is the manner and completeness whereby Christ through the Holy Spirit is present in all the members of His Body. Immediately preceding Text E the Pope had said, in speaking of the role of the Holy Spirit, that "... while by His grace he provides for the continued growth of the Church, He yet refuses to dwell through sanctifying grace in those members that are wholly severed from the Body."[23] Thus the frame of reference in which Text E occurs is that of sanctifying grace.

Up to this point in *Mystici corporis* the fundamental analogy functioning in that document had been as follows:

Analogy (A)

(a) Holy Spirit   (c) soul

                                    ::

(b) Church (*Gesellschaft*)   (d) body

Like every analogy, this one also limps. It limps because, though the neo-Thomist theologizing out of which the Pope was speaking affirms a substantial union between (c) and (d), one cannot predicate the same of (a) and (b) without falling into something very close to pantheism, a danger to which Pius shows himself to have been particularly sensitive. But Text F introduces a new analogy, which at first blush seems to be inconsistent with everything the Pope had hitherto maintained. For logically speaking, according to Analogy (A) the Pope in Text F should have referred to that vital principle by which the whole community of *Catholics* is sustained by its founder; instead, he speaks of the whole community of *Christians*. The Pope must be read carefully, for the new analogy is not

Analogy (B)

(e) Holy Spirit   (g) soul
                                          ::
(f) community of Christians   (h) body
    (*Gemeinschaft*)

Analogy (B) would at once suggest a theological position entirely unacceptable to official Catholicism; namely, that the Church of Christ is the whole community of Christians, whence the implication that the Church of Christ is simply the sum of Christian sects. Instead, what the Pope seems to be getting at in Texts E and F and their larger frame of reference may be expressed in terms of another analogy dependent upon the first:

Analogy (C)

(i) Holy Spirit   (k) divine life
                                          ::
(j) Christians as community   (l) grace
    (*Gemeinschaft*)

That this is what Pius seems to have had in mind seems clear not only from the immediate context in which Texts E and F are found but also from the broader one. Christ, the Pope had just finished teaching, is the support of the body (*Gesellschaft*) not only by reason of its juridical mission but also by reason of his Spirit. "If we examine closely the divine principle of life and power given by Christ, insofar as it constitutes the very source of every gift and created grace," the Pope says, "we easily perceive that it is nothing else than the Holy Spirit..."[24] But the Holy Spirit has a relation to Christians not only as *Gesellschaft* (σῶμα, *corpus*); the Holy Spirit has a relation to them as *Gemeinschaft* (κοινωνία, *communio*). Once one perceives that in Analogies (A) and (C) the first terms (a) and (i) are the same, it becomes clear that Christians as *Gemeinschaft* have a relation to the Holy Spirit who is the soul of Christians as *Gesellschaft*, i.e., the Church. It is this third analogy (C), when seen in the context of the first to which it is subordinate, that allows the careful reader of *Mystici corporis* to conclude that the Pope's position on the correlative question of membership was not inconsistent with the older Catholic theory, which envisaged non-Catholic Christians as belonging under the usual conditions to the Soul of the Church, a condition applicable *mutatis mutandis* to non-Christians. But like Analogy (A), Analogy (C), from the point of view of Catholic theology, has its own built-in caveat. Serious divisions among Christians are not the result of grace but of its refusal, and that on the Catholic side as well as on the Orthodox and Protestant.

To speak however of non-Catholic Christians as somehow belonging to the Soul of the Church implies, as we are now about to see, a particular theory of Church relationship, a further conclusion drawn from Pius' internal logic.

Schichtentheorie

The encyclical clearly envisages at least two possible situations regarding membership in the Mystical Body of Christ:

(1) Those who are in a state of grace and who are also members of the visible Church

(2) Those who are not in a state of grace but who are nonetheless members of the visible Church

I have already touched upon both possibilities when commenting on Text C. The Pope himself is more direct when he says that one must not imagine that the Body of the Church, just because it bears the name of Christ, "...is made up during the days of its earthly pilgrimage only of members conspicuous for their holiness..."[25] or "...only of those whom God has predestined to eternal happiness."[26] For it is due to "...the Savior's infinite mercy that place is allowed in his Mystical Body here below for those whom, of old, He did not exclude from the banquet."[27] It is true that in Catholic theology one may speak of degrees or intensities or gradations of grace that distinguish the heroic sanctity of the saints from their contemporaries. Yet the difference between (1) and (2) as described above is not a difference of degree or level; it is not a question of gradation of being (*Stufentheorie*). The difference is one of graced human being (*esse; sein*) as against non-graced human being (*esse; sein*). Since, in the context of Catholics as members of the Church, two different states of being come into play in one and the same reality, *stratification theory* (*Schichtentheorie*) seems the most suitable term to express what the Pope was getting at.

May one go a step further and say that *Schichtentheorie* is applicable to non-Catholics also? Certainly another stratum is suggested when the Pope in Text D speaks of those who are not members of the Church but who are nonetheless related to it by an unconscious desire and longing. And in the same text, he speaks of non-Catholic Christians as being deprived of many—he does not say *all*—heavenly gifts and helps which can be enjoyed only in the Catholic Church. When one considers that a human being may have an unconscious desire and longing for the Church of Christ and still be in a state of serious sin or, as the case may be, in a state of grace, then at least two further strata seem suggested. In these cases one is again dealing with grace or its absence within the same reality, which is not the Catholic Church but the larger Christian community. Therefore it is not a question of *degrees* or *levels* of being (*Stufentheorie*) but of different kinds of being. *Schichtentheorie* better conveys the nuance. The various strata discernible from the foregoing analysis may now be restated in the following sequence:

(1) Those who are in a state of grace and who are members of the visible Church

(2) Those who are in a state of grace but who are not members of the visible Church

(3) Those who are not in a state of grace but who nevertheless are members of the visible Church

(4) Those who are not in a state of grace and who are not members of the visible Church

Stated somewhat differently, (1) all who are in a state of grace belong to the Soul of the Church; (2) bona fide Catholics in a state of grace belong both to the Soul and Body; (3) bona fide Catholics in a state of serious sin belong under the usual conditions (Text [C]) to the Body of the Church but not to its Soul; (4) non-Catholics in a state of serious sin belong to neither. Of the strata just mentioned, it is (1) and (2) that constitute an ontological union between all Christians. When one joins to these reflections those pertaining to the sacraments, then one perceives that the union between those baptized in Christ is greater than that between those not so baptized. Thus, logically speaking, Pius XII could have included non-Catholics, especially Christians, within the stratification theory of membership subjacent in *Mystici corporis*. Unfortunately, it is precisely considerations of this kind to which he does not seem to have given sufficient attention. In *Mystici corporis*, the sacramental system (at least among Protestants) has to do with degrees approaching fullness (*Stufentheorie*) whereas stratification theory (*Schichtentheorie*), as the Pope seems actually to have envisaged it, has to do with different kinds of being (*esse*; *sein*).

Since Vatican II, however, there have been attempts at a revisionist interpretation of Pius in this regard. Thus while he admits that the orientation of *Mystici corporis* is different from that of Vatican II and that one may ask whether Pius had taken with full seriousness the thesis that baptism makes one a member of the Church, Michael Schmaus nonetheless saw in the *reapse* of Text C the possibility that Pius understood non-Catholic Christians as belonging *in some sense* to the Catholic Church.[28] Such an interpretation is unassailable in itself; what seems open to dispute is Schmaus' claim that the Pope's approach must be seen not in the context of *Schichtentheorie* but in that of *Stufentheorie*. Schmaus sees Pius as embracing the latter and scuttling the former.[29]

Factors both extrinsic and intrinsic seem incompatible with Schmaus' suggestion. Extrinsically, if Schmaus is correct, it is difficult to see why in the debates on *Aeternus Unigeniti* (*AU*) and *Lumen gentium* (*LG*-a), which I shall analyze below, the Council Fathers found the position of Pius XII so much of a hurdle. Intrinsically, from the foregoing discussion it should at the very least be clear that the teaching of Pius XII on the correlative question of membership was not inconsistent with the older Catholic theory on the Soul of the Church; it should further be clear that the Pope does not seem to have thought in terms of degrees or gradation of membership.

One would have to agree with Schmaus if a stratification theory necessarily entailed the notion of an invisible Church explicitly excluded by Pius as a viable possibility for Catholicism:

> *Text G.* ...they err in a matter of divine truth, who imagine the Church to be invisible, intangible, a something merely "pneumatological" as they say, by which many Christian communities, though they differ from each other in their profession of faith, are united by an invisible bond.[30]

Though the first two of the strata isolated above imply an ontological union of Catholics in a state of grace with non-Catholics who are so too, they do not suggest an invisible Church since they do not entail the notion of belonging to the Soul of the Church *while simultaneously not being related to the Catholic Church as to a visible body*. For of the two principal analogies uncovered in *Mystici corporis*, it is Analogy (A) that is fundamental; Analogy (C) is subordinate to it. The fundamental fact regarding membership as Pius seems to have seen it was *Gesellschaft*, not *Gemeinschaft*. *Gesellschaft* does not exist as the result of *Gemeinschaft*; *Gemeinschaft* exists as a result of *Gesellschaft* ($\sigma\tilde{\omega}\mu\alpha$) part of the paradox of Catholicism that, inasmuch as it bears on the means of grace, has to do with instrumental causality and lies, as Troeltsch correctly pointed out, at the heart of the division between Catholicism and Protestantism.[31]

I am forced, then, to conclude that Schmaus' interpretation of *Mystici corporis* as embracing *Stufentheorie* as over against *Schichtentheorie* seems, in the end, not to be supported by the data. The position of Pius XII seems to have been much more nuanced. The difference between that and what Schmaus has suggested is subtle but nonetheless real and should be borne in mind when below I take up the manner in which the Council Fathers received the Pope's teaching.

Preliminary Synthesis

Mystici corporis was the anticlimax of a movement that was to terminate with *Lumen gentium* of the Second Vatican Council. From the lectures of Klemens Schrader at the Gregorian University,[32] the notion of the Church as the Mystical Body of Christ eventually found its way into the first draft on the Church (*Supremi pastoris*) at the First Vatican Council and, though much diminished in scope, into the second draft prepared by Josef Kleutgen.[33] Neither draft was ever promulgated. But the theme did not die. Taken up by a number of outstanding theologians after the Council, the doctrine was developed with greater consistency especially in the period between the two World Wars. Many a theme in this encyclical of Pius XII was thus the result of reflection by others in the Church before it was taken up by the Pope, a fact not always noted by his critics.

Regarding the membership question and *Supremi pastoris*, the age-old maxim *extra Ecclesiam nulla salus* had been drafted in the form of a projected solemn definition.[34] But as the consultant theologians could not agree on the modalities of membership, the distinction between those who belong to the Church *in re* as against those who belong to it *in voto* was not worked into the text. Pius XII incorporated that distinction (the *reapse* of Text [C] and the *inscio quodem desiderio ac voto* of Text [D]) into his encyclical. As a result, theologians for the most part ceased to approach the question of non-Catholics' status from the point of view of their belonging to the Soul of the Church, a development perhaps as unfortunate as it was unnecessary. The trend was certainly unnecessary; it seems to have been unfortunate in that ceasing to speak of belonging to the Soul of the Church tended to obscure the ontological union existing between all human beings in a state of grace.

Regarding the identity question, a methodological distinction must be made between (1) an equation between the one true Church and the Catholic Church on the one hand, and (2) an equation between the Catholic Church and the Mystical Body of Christ on the other. Part of the reasoning behind the rejection of the second equation, as expressed in the draft *Supremi pastoris* of the First Vatican Council, was, perhaps, that the notion as described therein smacked of German idealism.[35] To be sure, Schrader, whose influence on the draft was everywhere apparent, tended to begin from the idea of the Mystical Body of Christ and work his way to the Catholic Church. Pius XII reversed the movement, beginning with the Catholic Church and working his way to the Mystical Body of Christ. Pius did not innovate in regard to equation (1); its roots are clearly within Catholic tradition and, within the nuance of *Lumen gentium* discussed below, remain so after Vatican II. The "innovation" was in the sharpness of his focus on equation (2). But it would not be correct, as Rahner suggests,[36] to consider that focus the peculiarity (*Eigenart*) of *Mystici corporis*, for that of Pius XI in *Mortalium animos* was essentially the same if not more narrow.

It seems best to see the effort of Pius XII as the attempt to pursue two different objectives. Positively, he aimed to bring to partial completion the unfinished ecclesiology of Vatican I; negatively he sought to meet head-on what he considered certain errors, one of which was the notion that the Mystical Body of Christ was analogous to an invisible Church.[37] In the exercise of the Petrine ministry as he saw it, Pius thought he had to pull the proponents of that view up short.

Mystici corporis was thus the penultimate moment in a process. With the promulgation of that document, the doctrine of the Church as the Mystical Body of Christ ceased to be the private opinion of theologians; it became the authentic, authoritative teaching of the ordinary papal magisterium. The Fathers of Vatican II were to agree in principle with Pius' objectives; they were in the end to find their focus theologically too constraining.

Conciliar Data
Relative to *Orientalium Ecclesiarum* and the Early Drafts on the Church
ORIENTALIUM ECCLESIARUM

Any attempt to show that the teaching of Pius XII was both developed and reversed by the Second Vatican Council must face a considerable hurdle. Without direct reference to *Mystici corporis*, the Decree *Orientalium Ecclesiarum* (*OE*) repeated in its own way the very position of Pius XII on both questions. For the opening words of number 2 read:

> *Text H.* That Church, Holy and Catholic, which is the Mystical Body of Christ, is made up of the faithful who are organically united in the Holy Spirit through the same faith, the same sacraments, and the same government and who combining into various groups held together by a hierarchy, form separate Churches or rites.[38]

It is clear from the following number that the word *Catholic*, as used in the Council documents, means those local Christian Churches that are in communion with the Roman Church. For such churches "...are nevertheless equally entrusted to the pastoral guidance of the Roman Pontiff, the divinely appointed successor of St. Peter in supreme governance over the universal Church."[39] Thus because of the frame of reference in which it occurs, the phrase "That Church, Holy and Catholic, which is the Mystical Body of Christ..."[40] means nothing else than the Roman Catholic Church and constitutes a puzzling inconsistency with the thrust of *Lumen gentium* (*LG*).

That inconsistency, all the more enigmatic in view of the chronology and development of both *OE* and *LG*, may be described as going through five phases. The documentation here is particularly complex; hence the reader is asked to exercise more than the usual forbearance. First, the original draft, *Conditor et Redemptor* (*CR*)[41] of which the promulgated decree is an almost entirely reworked replacement, was distributed to the Council Fathers on November 26, 1962, three days after the original draft *Aeternus Unigeniti Pater* (*AU*-b) on the Church.[42] Both documents take the position of Pius XII relative to the identity and membership questions, but *CR* does so without direct reference to *Mystici corporis*. Thus, in the debates on *CR* one finds little direct criticism of Pius' equation, whereas, as will be seen below, negative criticism of *AU*-b was immediate. Despite that fact, the position of Pius XII reappears in the following draft on the Eastern Churches, *Sancta Oecumenica Synodus* (*SO*) of April 23, 1963 (the second draft of *CR*),[43] and in the draft *Lumen gentium* of April 22, 1963 (*LG*-a).[44] Third, Pius' teaching on identity is removed from the following draft on the Church (*Lumen gentium* of July 3, 1964 [*LG*-b]) while his position on membership is not affirmed in that document.[45] In the third draft on the Eastern Churches (*Orientalium Ecclesiarum* [April 27,1964], from which the promulgated decree was to take its name), Pius' position on identity is stated clearly while his position on membership is affirmed in substance.[46] Fourth, on the questions of identity and membership, the perspectives of *Orientalium Ecclesiarum* of April 27, 1964, and *Lumen gentium* of July 3, 1964 (*LG*-b) remain unchanged from that point onwards.[47] Fifth, both the Dogmatic Constitution on the Church and the Decree on the Eastern Catholic Churches are promulgated on the same day, November 21, 1964.

It is striking that no one seems directly to have alluded to the inconsistency between the two documents (*OE* of April 27, 1964, and *LG*-b of July 3, 1964). That there was no direct, immediate reaction to the identity and membership question in *CR* may perhaps be explained from the general tone of that document and from the fact that the teaching of Pius XII on both questions was not highlighted. With epistles from the Pauline corpus and Ephesians as its principal focus, the document began by stating that the one and true God, founder and restorer of the human race, chose us in Christ before the constitution of the world that in His sight we might be holy and without spot in Christ; that those who love God have from Him the command to love their brothers.[48] Through sin, which is the opposite of love, human beings became separated from God and from each other. By the death and resurrection of Jesus Christ, a new creation (*creatura*) has been made wherein there is neither Gentile nor Jew, neither slave nor free, but Christ is all in all. Putting on Christ as the new being (*Novum Hominem*) through baptism, the faithful are made new in oneness with Christ and each other. They become the Body of Christ and members of each other (*membra de membro*).[49]

This last sentence, a reference to 1 Cor. 12:27, immediately precedes number 2, which in the Latin text is a cryptic sentence of fifteen words: "This Body of Christ is the Church, the society of elect who are united with Christ and who receive salvation from him."[50] As it stands, that sentence is not far removed from Calvin's definition in the *Institutes*.[51] But the text goes on to state that salvation is not yet complete, that Christ's faithful are still subject to sin and death, the world not yet having been loosed from its bonds (*absolutus*) through the second coming.[52] That is why the Church has a twofold way of being (*status*). On the one hand, it is already made perfect with Christ in heaven; on the other, it is still confined (*constricta*) in this world and must be made into a holy temple of the Lord and grow as a body (*corpus*) into the fullness of Christ.[53] For that reason the Church uses the structures of human society and is linked with the temporal order, struggling against worldly elements. The text then describes the hierarchical nature of the Church and its visible unity under Peter and his successors.[54] The Church cannot be divided. Yet paradoxically, the text then goes on to state that divisions have wounded and still wound the Church.[55] It is precisely at that point, near the end of the long paragraph constituting number 7, that the position of Pius XII on the identity question is distinctly stated:

> *Text I.*   Therefore, in fidelity to the will of Christ, we profess and declare that there is only one Church, even in its earthly condition, and this true Church is the one governed by Peter's successor. For that reason no other Church may [*valeat*] proclaim itself the one true Church. Communion with the See of Peter is necessary in such a way that any Church on earth separated from this See certainly [*certe*] does not really [*vere*] belong in the same way [*eodem modo*] to the invisible and heavenly Church.[56]

With that paragraph, the momentary echo of the *Institutes* in the sentence quoted above dies out completely. Though there is no explicit reference to Pius XII in *CR*, its position on the identity question is the same as his. The question of membership surfaces obliquely much later in the document. Whereas the Decree on Ecumenism was largely directed to the division between Protestants and Catholics and the promulgated *Orientalium Ecclesiarum* was concerned with matters pertaining to Eastern Catholics, it should be recalled that *CR* was destined primarily for the separated Eastern Churches. And that was the frame of reference in which the draft spoke of membership:

> *Text J.*   ...no one is unaware that all those who in good faith live in separated Churches, who materially only and as it were by tradition are separated from the Vicar of Christ, in a certain way are not strangers to the true Church. But they are deprived of many means of salvation to be found in the true Church....[57]

And later, when stating conditions for reunion:

Text K. First, let nothing more be required from those who return than what is truly necessary in order that they *actually* [*reapse*] become members of the one, holy, catholic and apostolic Church of Christ....[58]

From those who had been separated in good faith, nothing more was to be required than a simple profession of faith, especially concerning those matters that pertain to the unity of the Church. The situation of those who had become separated through their own fault was different.[59] Such matters do not concern us here. What does concern us is first the fact that through the adverb *reapse* (which is the term used in *Mystici corporis*) to distinguish those who are actually members of the Church from those who are so only by desire (*voto*) *CR* clearly maintained the position of Pius XII on membership but did so without explicit mention of *Mystici corporis*; second, that the critique of *CR* did not directly take up that point as did the debates on *AU*-b. A partial explanation of this apparent oversight, which with few exceptions was to continue all through the Council and which remains in the promulgated *Orientalium Ecclesiarum*, may be suggested by the foregoing analysis. The position of Pius XII, though unmistakable upon a careful reading of *CR*, was less directly stated in that document. Furthermore, though distributed three days previously, it could have been supposed that the proper place to approach the question was in the context of *AU*-b. And it was indeed in that frame of reference, as I shall show below, that the position of Pius XII on the identity question and its correlative was debated.

Though the general inadequacy of *CR* was pointed out,[60] nothing on November 26, 1962 was reported as spoken against the draft's statement on the identity question; consequently, in the following draft, *Sancta Oecumenica Synodus* (*SO*) of April 22, 1963, the first sentence of number 3 (which was the first sentence of number 2 of the former draft) is, with the exception of the words *et ritibus*, the same as in Text H of the promulgated *OE*. (I shall not quote the text again here.) On the question of membership, *SO* retained the orientation of *Mystici corporis* and the closing words of number 52 are virtually the same as in Text K of *CR*:

Text L. Finally, this ecumenical Synod, weighing the fact [*animo considerans*] that the difference by which Easterners are separated is not great, and seeing that they find daily new and worthy [*justa*] motives for drawing near to Catholic unity and sharing in the fullness of Revelation, commands that from those who do [*ab iis convenientibus*] there be no more required than what is necessary

in order for them actually [*reapse*] to become members of the one,
holy, catholic and apostolic Church of Christ....[61]

The distinction Pius XII implied by the adverb *reapse* appears again.
But as a sufficient number of Council Fathers in the context of the draft on
the Church had criticized the position of Pius XII and *Mystici corporis* on
the identity question and its correlative with, it may be presumed, the
understanding that whatever changes were to be made in the draft on the
Church would be reflected in relevant sections of other conciliar documents, it is perhaps not surprising that only a few thought it advisable to
pay particular attention to Text L. That is to say: Relatively few brought
up the problem in the context of the discussion of *SO* during the second
session and the written critiques submitted in the interim. What is difficult
to explain is the fact that, once Pius' equation had been removed from the
draft *LG*-b of July 3, 1964, no one seems to have explicitly pointed out the
inconsistency with number 2 of *Orientalium Ecclesiarum* several months
previously (April 27, 1964). It was not that there was no indirect criticism
of the position of Pius XII in the context of that document; it is that, in the
debates of the Council and in the suggested amendments, no one seems to
have alluded to the fact that the orientation of the two positions on the
identity question was inconsistent. That is to say: From the moment the *est*
was changed to *subsistit in* in the corresponding section of *LG* (the draft
that was to be distributed to the Council Fathers as of July 3, 1964—see
Text O below),[62] an appropriate adjustment should have been made in *OE*
as it was evolving through the Council.

It was not that there were no critiques. Cardinal König pointed out that
in *OE* of July 3, 1963, non-Catholic Eastern Churches were not honored as
churches; that Eastern churches were identified, as it were, with those
united with the Holy See and that relations with the Orthodox were
considered from the point of view of conversion to Catholicism. He said
the draft should be made to harmonize with the third chapter of the draft
on ecumenism.[63] Maximos IV Saigh, Patriarch of the Melchites (Antioch)
stated that in speaking of the East, one should not think only of those who
humbly represent it today within Catholicism, an indirect reference to the
role of the Uniate Eastern Churches.[64] Those who came closest to pointing
out the inconsistency between *LG* of July 3, 1963, and *OE* of the previous
April were Bishop Maurice Baudoux (who in reference to *SO* of April 22,
1963, had suggested that the term *Corpus Ecclesiarum* be substituted for
the term *Corpus Christi mysticum*)[65] and Joannes Hoeck of the German
Benedictines (who in the same context offered a substitute draft in which
number 3 of *SO* was almost completely removed).[66] In a subsequent

critique of *OE* of April 27, 1964, Baudoux suggested that the phrase *quae est Corpus Christi mysticum* be omitted because the context was simply a reference to the Church.[67] Nor was the phrase sufficiently sensitive to Eastern theology. These and other criticisms may no doubt be considered oblique references to the doctrine of Pius XII. But strangely, neither Baudoux here nor Hoeck in his post-conciliar commentary on the promulgated *OE* pointed to the underlying inconsistency between number 2 of that document and number 8 of *Lumen gentium*.[68]

Thus on October 21 and 22, 1964, a vote was taken on the several sections of the amended text in which the only change in the first sentence of number 2 was the addition of the words *et ritibus*. The vote on numbers 2-4, which are the only numbers that concern us, indicated a general acceptance (*placet*) by 1,373, qualified acceptance (*placet iuxta modum*) by a large minority of 719, and outright rejection (*non placet*) by 73.[69] Of the 719 who would have accepted the text if amended, only one asked for the suppression of number 2 because it contained material already mentioned either in the draft on the Church or in that on Ecumenism, because it smacked of Latin ecclesiology—the suggested amendment, according to the commission, explicitly referred to the expression *Corpus Christi mysticum*—and because the expression *eodem regimine* did not fully correspond to the truth. This was brought to the attention of the full assembly, along with the account of the other suggested amendments. To the suggested amendment that number 2 be removed, the commission answered: "The commission took this expressly into consideration and its position is to be accepted."[70] The Council was free to reject this decision of the commission but despite the fact that at the next voting there were forty-one fewer present than on October 21 and 22, full acceptance of the *modi* rose to 1,841, and qualified acceptance decreased to one. But outright rejection (283) increased by 210.[71] It is impossible to say whether this change reflected a growing awareness of the inconsistency between the orientation of *OE* and *LG*-b. If it did, those concerned failed to rally support. The final voting was 1,964 for full acceptance, 135 for outright rejection, and one for qualified acceptance. There were four invalid votes.[72] Thus the data establish beyond doubt that the promulgated Decree on the Eastern Catholic Churches (*OE*) preserves the orientation of *Mystici corporis* both on the identity question and the correlative question of membership. Yet the data surrounding the genesis of numbers 8 and 14 of *LG*-c, promulgated along with *OE* on the same day (November 21, 1964), require a more nuanced conclusion about the judgment of the Council Fathers on both questions and lay the groundwork that will subsequently enable us to clear the hurdle placed by *Orientalium Ecclesiarum*.

EARLY DRAFTS ON THE CHURCH

In their masterly presentation of the drafts that culminated in the promulgated *Lumen gentium*, Giuseppe Alberigo and Franca Magistretti list seven complete and four partial drafts as having preceded it.[73] Throughout the remaining pages of this chapter, only four concern us:

(1) *Aeternus Unigeniti Pater* (*AU*-b) distributed to the Council Fathers on November 23, 1962.[74]

(2) *Lumen gentium* (*LG*-a), to be sent to the dispersed Council Fathers as of April 22, 1963.[75]

(3) *Lumen gentium* (*LG*-b), to be sent to the Council Fathers as of July 3, 1964.[76]

(4) *Lumen gentium* (*LG*-c), as promulgated by Paul VI on November 21, 1964.[77]

On the question of identity, *AU*-b and *LG*-a stated respectively:

Text M-1.   Therefore this Sacred Synod teaches and solemnly professes that there is only one true Church of Jesus Christ, that namely which in the Creed [*Symbolo*] we celebrate as one, holy, catholic and apostolic, which the Savior acquired on the Cross and united to himself as a body to the head and spouse to a husband, and which after his resurrection he handed over to Peter and his successors, the Roman Pontiffs, to be governed by them. Therefore, only the Roman Catholic Church is rightly [*iure*] called a Church.[78]

Text N-1.   Moreover, this Sacred Synod teaches and solemnly professes that there is only one Church of Jesus Christ which in the Creed [*Symbolo*] we celebrate as one, holy, catholic and apostolic, which the Savior after his resurrection gave to Peter, the apostles and their successors to be fed by them. On them he set up the column and support of truth for the mystery [*sacramentum*] of salvation. This Church, therefore, the real [*vera*] Mother and teacher of all, organized [*constituta*] and set up [*ordinata*] in this world as a society, is the Catholic Church governed [*directa*] by the Roman Pontiff and the bishops in communion with him, although outside the totality of that body [*compaginem*] many elements of salvation may be found, which, belonging to the Church of Christ, are a driving force toward catholic unity.[79]

Text M-1 identified the Church of Christ with the (Roman) Catholic Church—which alone, it stated, is rightly called a Church—and in the critical apparatus identified this with the Mystical Body of Christ. Thus in its own way, the text implied that non-Roman Catholic churches are no more than footprints (*vestigia*) of where the Church had once been.[80] Text N-1 is less direct in its claim. Governing of the Church is expressed in more collegial terms. And in *AU*-b, as later in *LG*-c, elements of sanctification are acknowledged outside the confines of the (Roman) Catholic Church. But for all that, the claim advanced in the second of these texts is fundamentally the same as in the first. The Church of Christ is a society organized in the world; it is the one governed by the Roman Pontiff and the bishops in communion with him. Any elements of salvation outside the (Roman) Catholic Church are to be taken as the result of having once been part of it, otherwise the phrase *ut res Ecclesiae Christi propriae* makes no sense. Because these elements of salvation belong to the Church of Christ, already identified with the (Roman) Catholic Church, they are a driving force toward catholic unity. Though somewhat attenuated in the second text, the doctrine put forth is in complete harmony with *Mystici corporis*, directly referred to in footnotes 49 of *AU*-b and 20 of *LG*-a and that precisely in the context of the identity Pius had taught between the Mystical Body of Christ and the (Roman) Catholic Church.[81]

On the correlative question of membership the orientation is essentially the same in both documents. Thus in *AU*-b:

Text M-2. Although many real links [*relationes*] exist in the juridical, sacramental, nay they can even exist in the mystical order by which absolutely [*omnino*] every baptized person is joined to the Church, nevertheless, from the earliest tradition only those in a true and proper sense [*vero et proprio sensu*] are called members of the Church, from whom the Church itself, inasmuch as it is one, and indivisible, indefectible and infallible, is made up [*coalescit*] of a unity of faith, sacramental life [*sacramentorum*] and government. Therefore, those are truly and properly [*vere et proprie*] called members of the Church who, washed in the sacrament of rebirth, professing the true faith and acknowledging the authority of the Church, are joined in the visible body [*compagine*] of the same Church with Christ its head who rules them through its Vicar and who are not because of grave faults separated from the company [*compage*] of the Mystical Body.[82]

And in *LG*-a:

Text N-2.   Actually [*reapse*] and strictly speaking [*simpliciter loquendo*] there are incorporated into the Church as society those only who acknowledge its full way of life [*ordinationem*] and all the means of salvation that have been instituted in it, and who with

(*A*)   Christ, who rules it through the Sovereign Pontiff and the bishops, are, in the visible company [*compage*] of the same Church, united by the bonds, namely, of professed faith, sacramental life [*sacramenti*], Church government and communion....

United with the Church by desire [*voto*] are prospective converts [*catechumeni*] who, under the influence of the Holy Spirit, after due consideration explicitly ask to be incorporated into

(*B*)   it...In its own way the same holds for those who, unaware that the Catholic Church is the one true Church of Christ, with the help of grace sincerely seek to do the will of Christ, or if they lack a definite awareness of Christ, seek to do the will of God the Creator....

With all the baptized, who are honored by the name Christian, but who do not profess the fullness of faith or the the unity of

(*C*)   communion under the Roman Pontiff, the Church, loving Mother of all, knows itself for many reasons to be united [*coniunctam*]....[83]

The opening lines of Text M-2 contain in the relevant footnotes references to *Regnans in excelsis*, directed against Elizabeth I of England, and paradoxically to speeches and letters of John XXIII.[84] The same lines also hint at the implications of baptism whose development, as will be shown, were to lead the Council Fathers to depart from the position of Pius XII on the identity question. After the phrase "...acknowledging the authority of the Church..." ("...*Ecclesiae auctoritatem agnoscentes*...") footnote 8 (not presented as part of the draft itself but as an illustration of its meaning) stated that the words of Pius XII in *Mystici corporis* had been changed (Pius had used the phrase "...*neque a corporis compage semet ipsos misere separarunt*...") because among the baptized there are very many (*perplures*) who have never personally separated themselves from the (Roman

Catholic) Church, as Baptists do when they are baptized. [85] Thus even before *A U*-b was presented to the Council for debate, there was some attempt on the part of the Commission to soften the Pope's position. This attempt, as subsequent debate in the Council testifies, was really only a token gesture since membership in the Church of Christ was still excluded on other grounds laid down by Pius, namely, the profession of the true faith. This slight nuancing of Pius' teaching is not however emphasized, nor are the possible implications of valid baptism adequately explored either in *A U*-b or in *LG*-a. Instead both texts embrace the position of Pius XII, *A U*-b coming more closely to the actual wording of *Mystici corporis*. And in both *A U*-b and *LG*-a the lines immediately following Texts M-2 and N-2, respectively, state how those who are not bona fide Roman Catholics are nonetheless related to the (Roman) Catholic Church. But neither *A U*-b nor *LG*-a admits that any but Roman Catholics are under the usual conditions really (*vero et proprio sensu* in *A U*-b; *reapse et simpliciter loquendo* in *LG*-a) members of the Church of Christ. Though the language is nonetheless irenic when compared to the polemics of the sixteenth and seventeenth centuries, the early drafts on the Church, like the promulgated Decree on Eastern Catholic Churches, preserved the orientation of *Mystici corporis* regarding both the identity question and the correlative question of membership.

But though the draft *LG*-a did not adequately reflect the criticism aimed at *A U*-b in the first session, nonetheless it cannot be said that the Commission had been completely impervious to suggested criticism when it presented the draft *LG*-a for discussion and debate. The sentence "...only the Roman Catholic Church is rightly called a Church," with which Chapter I of *A U*-b had closed, is absent in *LG*-a. But more important, where the Prologue of *A U*-b had referred to those redeemed in both the Old and New Testaments (in the context of saying that no one is saved as an individual but only as one of a group [*ex multitudine*], a theme Vatican II was later to develop as the People of God), Chapter I of *LG*-a is more explicit: "This congregation of those justified is called by the Holy Fathers the universal Church, 'gathered together beginning with Abel the Just up to the last of the elect,' " the reference being to Gregory the Great.[86] That holy Church, already prefigured from the origin of the human race and marvelously prepared in the Chosen People, has been made manifest in more recent times.[87]

Despite this somewhat broadened horizon, the Council was not to find that of *LG*-a wide enough, for the latter, like *A U*-b, identified with insufficient nuance the Church of Christ with the (Roman) Catholic Church

(Text M-1). There is some evidence that one of the reasons the Commission had difficulty taking the step that the majority of the Council Fathers were to insist it take lay in its initial inability to give *Mystici corporis* its proper theological note. Though on the question of membership it seems that the Commission which had prepared *A U*-b had entertained some doubt,[88] on the identity question it seems to have been content to take the position that there was no real distinction between the Mystical Body of Christ and the Catholic Church.[89] But the actual draft that the Commission presented (*A U*-b), like both *A U*-a before it and the encyclical *Mystici corporis*, equated the two.[90] The logical first step toward modification was to explore all the images of the Church in the Scriptures and thence to see that the Church as the Body of Christ, however powerful, was only one among many images. The second step, logically speaking, was to explore the implications of baptism. But as of December 1, 1962, the early drafts on the Church, like the promulgated Decree on Eastern Churches, were both solidly within the confines of *Mystici corporis*. The debate on the Church had hardly begun.

Conciliar Data
Relative to Subsequent Drafts

Negative reaction to *Aeternus Unigeniti* (*A U*-b) was immediate and, as will be seen in the following chapter, had been anticipated in the Preparatory Period. Cardinal Liénart of Lille said he was happy that the draft, like the one proposed but never promulgated by Vatican I, began with a chapter on the Mystical Body of Christ.[91] (Actually, explicit reference to the concept of the Church as the Mystical Body of Christ occurred for the first time in *A U*-b only in number 4 of Chapter I.) But in the strict sense, he said, the Church remains a mystery that exceeds the mind's grasp.[92] The decree should attempt not to explain the mystery but to present it according to the data of revelation. This revelation exhibits both an invisible and a visible element, though there is only one Church, just as in speaking of Christ one confesses two natures and one person.[93] Liénart went on to say that any way of speaking that might corrupt that mystery was to be avoided, e.g., any identification of the Roman Church with the Mystical Body, as if the Mystical Body were confined within the boundaries of the Roman Church. The Roman Church—Liénart obviously meant the

Roman Catholic Church—is indeed the Body of Christ but does not exhaust it.[94]

Nowhere in the speech of December 1, 1962, did Liénart explicitly refer to Pius XII. Yet, in its fourth paragraph he did in the very aula of St. Peter's what Pius XII had complained of in *Humani generis*: He openly questioned the equation that the Pope had made between the Mystical Body of Christ and the (Roman) Catholic Church.[95] He then proceeded to speak of what I have called the correlative question of membership. Since there is no grace given to a human being that is not the grace of Christ, and since no one is justified without being incorporated into Christ, all those who are justified pertain to the Mystical Body.[96] Only those belong to the Roman Church who are validly baptized, are joined to it (*aggregati*), and have not renounced the bonds of faith and communion with it.[97] Thus it appears that our Church, he continued, though the visible manifestation of the Mystical Body of Jesus Christ, cannot be absolutely identified with it in the sense explained in the draft.

Important though Liénart's speech for setting the tone for respectful critique, the Council Fathers by no means followed through by accepting all of his suggestions. Though it cannot be held that *ipsissimis verbis* Liénart espoused a doctrine of an invisible Church—his intent was quite the contrary—his manner of speaking left something to be desired from a Catholic point of view. As will become increasingly clear, a route that the Council Fathers as a whole refused to take in order to produce a more theologically accurate description of the identity of the Catholic Church and correlative criteria for membership was that which might suggest an invisible as over against a visible Church.

Quite clearly others were concerned with the issue. José Cardinal Bueno y Monreal, Archbishop at Seville, was the third speaker and brought this point to the attention of the gathering: That Mystical Body is from the will of its founder a social body held together by one principle, Peter, and by the bishops subject to him; and it is a living body, kept alive by grace and the Holy Spirit.[98] If the draft had lacked either of these principles, it would have proclaimed a false doctrine (*mendosum esset et falsum*). On this point, Bueno y Monreal said the draft emphasized the mystical aspect more than the social. He then took the occasion to ask some questions about the Church as the Mystical Body. What value, he asked, did the Council wish to give its doctrinal decisions?[99] Two things have been taught by the ordinary (papal) magisterium: (1) the Spirit is the Soul of the Church and (2) the Roman (Catholic) Church is the Body of Christ. The first was taught by both Leo XIII and Pius XII, the second by Pius XII in

Mystici corporis and *Humani generis*, which rejected contrary positions.[100] He then asked: Is the approval of these formulations by the Council to be an act of the *solemn* magisterium?[101] With that question, Bueno y Monreal obliquely indicated what was for him the proper theological note of these doctrines as proclaimed by the ordinary papal magisterium. The Cardinal apparently did not foresee at the time that the Council would not simply not repeat the doctrine of Pius XII on this matter, much less define it, but that it would actually modify it. But his question, addressed to the full assembly of the Council, demonstrated a sensitivity to the perceived relation between the ordinary (papal) magisterium and an ecumenical Council. The role of the Council was clearly not to act as a rubber stamp.

While others gave more incisive critiques, still others exhibited a growth in perception of the issue. Thus Bernard Cardinal Alfrink, who in his report to the Holy See in the Antepreparatory Period, did not question the teaching of Pius XII either on the identity question or on the correlative criteria of membership,[102] and who, in the debate on *A U*-a in the Preparatory Period, had begun to change his mind on the latter issue, [103] stated in the debate in the Council itself that *A U*-b was too narrow on the question of membership.[104] Two opposed positions seemed to be forming. The first was represented by a sizable and articulate minority that was not only satisfied with the orientation of *A U*-b but was also inclined to defend it; the second by a growing majority who thought the theology of the draft was to some extent inaccurate from the point of view of authentic Catholic doctrine. Representative of the first was Luigi Carli, Bishop at Segni; representative of the second was Alexandre Poncet, Vicar Apostolic of Wallis and Futuna (Oceania).

In the context of the discussion concerning *A U*-b, Carli said quite frankly that he considered some speakers excessively preoccupied with ecumenism to the point where certain fundamental Catholic doctrines were being passed over in silence.[105] But since at that point discussion was on the draft in general and not on its particular numbers, Carli said he was satisfied with the draft because it treated of things that although of the greatest importance, had received little attention from other Councils; e.g., the doctrine on the Mystical Body, the sacramentality of the episcopacy, etc.[106] Carli was later to present a detailed critique in the context of *LG*-a.[107] Since that draft in number 7 of Chap. I maintained the equation between the Church (militant) and the (Roman) Catholic Church, Carli had no substantial criticism. But his remark on line 22 of the same number was significant: Why say *many* elements of sanctification are found outside

Catholicism? Say *some*, not *many*: God knows whether there are many or few![108] His dissatisfaction concerned especially number 8 where he wished the text amended so that it would read: "The Holy Synod teaches...that *only* the Catholic Church, founded by God through Jesus Christ, and *built upon Peter*, is an institution necessary for salvation...,"[109] because one should clearly say it was a question of the *Roman* Catholic Church, otherwise the Orthodox might say the same of their Church.[110] As for the correlative question of membership, the meaning of *simpliciter loquendo* was not clear. Carli suggested the removal of the phrase and that the adverb *plene* be put in its place, a point Cardinal Lercaro was later to take up in his attempt (described below) to mediate between the two opposing tendencies discussed above.[111]

Carli did not explicitly refer to *Mystici corporis* of Pius XII in numbers 7 and 8 of *LG*-a (Texts M-2 and N-2) but he did so in another context of the same chapter. Just as in his general account on *AU*-b the theology of the Mystical Body in that draft seemed satisfactory to him, so when commenting on number 5 of *LG*-a, where the faithful are spoken of before the bishops (*praepositos*), Carli pointed out that according to the encyclical *Mystici corporis* it should be the other way around.[112] Quite clearly, on this point of our inquiry, Carli was one of a significant minority who were following *Mystici corporis* to the letter.

Alexandre Poncet, was, as I have said, representative of a broader view. The relevant part of his written critique of *LG*-a concerns number 8, line 2, of page 12 (Text N-2).[113] Poncet suggested that he text be changed to read as follows:

> For that reason, all those who are validly baptized and who have not withdrawn from the Church by a formal sin which excludes them from communion with her are truly incorporated into the Church as a society just as they are to Christ himself, although perhaps because of invincible ignorance they do not know that the Roman Catholic Church alone is the true Church of Christ and belong in good faith to another Church or community honored by the name Christian but which is separated from the Roman Church....
>
> In practice, however, since only the Lord sees into the heart (1 Kings 16:7), among baptized adults those alone may be externally considered incorporated into the Church as a society who acknowledge the full way of life [*ordinationem*] of that Church and all the means of salvation which it possesses [*in ea constituta*] and in the visible body [*compagine*] of this same Church, by the bonds, namely, not only of baptism but by those of an external, explicit profession of faith and the external sign [*sacramenti*] of

Church rule and union [*ecclesiastici regiminis ac communionis*] are joined to Christ who rules over it through the Sovereign Pontiff and the bishops.

However, he or she who does not live a life of faith, hope and charity but sins, remaining in the Church [*in sinu Ecclesiae*] "physically" indeed but not "in his or her heart," is not saved, whatever be the manner in which he or she pertains to the Church.[114]

Though Poncet did not in this passage refer explicitly to *Mystici corporis*, there can be little doubt he was wrestling with it. The "*In Praxi*" with which the second of the three paragraphs quoted above begins, suggests that he was approaching the problem on two levels, that of principle and that of practice. On the former he drew the conclusion that all baptized Christians are incorporated into Christ and his Church unless they exclude themselves from communion with it by a real (*formale*) sin. On the level of practice however Poncet seemed to mean that only (Roman) Catholics who fulfill the conditions he enumerated may be accounted members of the Church. Those conditions are essentially the same as those stated by Pius XII in *Mystici corporis*. What Poncet had done in effect was to preserve the teaching of Pius on the level of practice while expanding it on the level of principle. Poncet's final paragraph was even stronger:

The reasons for this suggested amendment are as follows: When it is said that human beings [*homines*] enter the Church through baptism as through a door, every valid baptism, whether of an adult in good faith or of someone who lacks the use of reason, leads into the true Church of Christ. How therefore can one so baptized leave the Church without real [*formali*] fault on his or her part? He or she always remains a member of this Roman Church even if he or she is unaware of the fact.[115]

Like Liénart, Poncet said "*Ecclesia Romana*" whereas he meant "*Ecclesia Catholica et Romana*." The Council was ultimately to adopt a view somewhat similar to that suggested by Poncet's critique. Poncet, like Carli at the other end of the spectrum, was after all only representative of different tendencies at the Council. But though the view illustrated by Poncet's written critique was eventually to win out in large measure, the Council was not to adopt it totally. The Council was to admit that most non-Catholic Christian churches are rightly (*iure*) honored by the name Christian—something the post-Tridentine Roman Church had refused to do. But as in the case of suggestions made by Liénart, so in those made by Poncet, the Council was to go only part way. It was to admit the implications of validly conferred baptism—it incorporated into Christ—but it was not to follow through with an affirmation that valid baptism incorporated into his Church, which it described as subsisting in the (Roman) Catholic Church.[116] But to make this move, the Council Fathers were to find themselves obliged to pass from *Schichtentheorie* to a *Modalitättheorie* of relationships to the Catholic Church.

Carli's and Poncet's remarks had been submitted in writing, and, according to a note in the *Acta Synodalia*, concerned *LG*-a.[117] A kind of theological deadlock seems to have been setting in along with various attempts to break it.[118] The Dutch Conference suggested that number 9 (Text N-2 [C]), which spoke of the links of the Church with non-Catholic Christians, be brought forward so that it immediately follow the description of the mode whereby the relation of Roman Catholics to the Church had been described (Text N-2 [A]), and that the part of the text referring to those who are united with the Church by desire (Text N-2[B]) be put last. The reason for this suggested change was that non-Catholic Christians are more closely joined to the Church than non-Christians. Thus one is not obliged to settle in precise terms just how they belong to the Church. It would be better too if instead of saying *reapse et simpliciter loquendo* (Text N-2 [A]) one were to say simply *simpliciter loquendo*.[119]

The remarks of the Dutch Conference, like those of Carli and Poncet, had been submitted in the interim and concerned *LG*-a. Critiques along the lines of those suggested by Poncet and the Dutch Conference had little effect on the following draft. During the second session, a turning point seems to have been reached with the speech of Giacomo Cardinal Lercaro, Archbishop at Bologna. The *Acta Synodalia* lists it as having been given on October 3, 1963 in the Context of *LG*-a.[120] Lercaro stated at the outset that he spoke in his own name—in order to economize on time, it had become the custom whenever possible or desirable for one bishop to speak in the name of a group. First, he said, it is true to affirm that the Church is a visible society and that the Mystical Body of Christ constitutes one reality (not two), which can be understood in both an existential and a historical way. These ways are not always co-extensive; they give rise to dispute (*contentiones*) even now, and they always will until history has run its course, when finally the identity and equality of the Church and the Mystical Body will be brought to perfection (*consummata*) and made manifest.[121] For that reason Lercaro said he agreed with what the Bishop at Haarlem had proposed in the name of the Dutch Conference,[122] but that if that position was not accepted, he would be ready to affirm the identity of the Church with the Mystical Body of Christ, but not without distinction

226 THE PAPACY AND THE CHURCH

(*non secundum eamdem rationem*).[123] To affirm it without further data
(*simpliciter*) could result in excessive conclusions being drawn, as is clear
from the teaching of some theologians after the encyclical *Mystici corporis*. Second, regarding membership in the Church, Lercaro said he was in
agreement with suggested amendments and that he approved the formula
Bishop Carli had proposed; namely, that for the terms *reapse et simpliciter*
there be substituted the words *plene et perfecte*.[124] Lercaro went on to say
that he advanced this argument not especially for ecumenical reasons, but
for reasons that pertain to the concept of validly conferred baptism.[125] For
that doctrine—that baptism validly accepted in the Church joins a human
being once and for all into a visible body (*compage*)—is a Catholic doctrine that has always obtained. He then cited four sources, among them
what he called the recent Code of Canon Law for the Eastern Churches
(*Cleri sanctitati*), which so far, he said, he had heard no one quote and
which settled the question because it was put into operation (*sancitam*) in
1957, after *Mystici corporis*.[126] (It will be recalled that I discussed Lercaro's
argument above and was forced to reject it as based on the documents
adduced.)

The failure of the redactors to incorporate into *LG*-a the critiques that
had been made against *AU*-b represented an impasse. Lercaro felt it was
caused not by the proposition definitely affirmed by Pius XII (Mystical
Body of Christ = [Roman] Catholic Church) but by the excessive conclusions drawn by some theologians.[127]

Even a cursory glance at the notes appended to *AU*-b (which were
carried over virtually unchanged to *LG*-a) should have sufficed to show
him that the Commission itself interpreted *Mystici corporis* as excluding
non-Catholic Christians. Nonetheless, from Lercaro's references to the
Canon Law for the Eastern Churches promulgated during the pontificate
of Pius XII, one might argue that Lercaro himself thought (incorrectly, in
my view) that exclusion of non-Catholic Christians from membership in
the Mystical Body of Christ was not Pius' intent. But that is only one aspect
of the matter and concerns membership. It seems that regarding the other
aspect—the question of identity as distinct from that of membership—
Lercaro was urging, while being too shrewd to say so openly on the
Council floor, a departure from the authentic, authoritative, non-infallible
position of a previous papal magisterium. For there are at least two things
that could not have escaped the attentive listener's notice. First, Pius XII in
Mystici corporis had equated the Mystical Body of Christ with the
Catholic Church, by which he meant the *Roman* Catholic Church.
Second, Lercaro in effect was saying he could not accept that position

without adding a distinction, a distinction not found in *Mystici corporis*. In appealing to what he called the recent Canon Law for Eastern Churches, which Pius XII had ratified and put into operation, Lercaro thought he was appealing to the internal logic of the Pope's teaching. Had Lercaro proceeded to show that the teaching of Pius XII in *Mystici corporis* was not inconsistent with the older Catholic theory on the Soul of the Church (which discloses an ontological union among all human beings in a state of grace, a fortiori among those baptized in Christ), and that consequently the perspective of Pius XII, however much an improvement over that of Pius XI in *Mortalium animos*, had to be modified, he would have stood on much firmer ground, not on the identity question, to be sure, but quite clearly on that of the correlative question of membership.

The issue and its relation to *Mystici corporis* was thus becoming less obscure, as is evident from a study of a critique submitted by Antonio Jannucci, Bishop at Penne-Pescara (Italy). Jannucci's report was submitted during the intersession, before the Council Fathers received the draft *LG*-b. Writing in Italian, Jannucci asked, "Who is a member of the Church?" and suggested the following answer:

> In homage to the fruitful encyclical *Mystici corporis*, the concept "member of the Church" ought to be better expressed in the draft.
>
> Certainly Bellarmine's concept, justified by Protestant polemics, is respected therein, a concept which emphasizes the visible, social, and juridical element of the Church, that unequivocal sign of full, true incorporation into the Church.
>
> At the same time, however, one ought to bring out the ontological element, which makes one really a member of the Church, and that is valid baptism, however received.[128]

Jannucci's remarks seem to parallel those of the Pontifical Theological Faculty of Milan as discussed in the following chapter. He then went on to speak of non-Christians, a point that does not concern me here. There followed a suggestion that the amended draft speak in terms of degrees of membership:

1. The Catholic is a member in a real, full, and true meaning of the term.
2. The non-Catholic Christian is a member of the Church in a real sense, but not in the full and true meaning of the term.
3. A human being of good will in search of salvation...is a member of the Church in a real but rudimentary sense.[129]

It is not clear from the text on what basis Jannucci would have distinguished real (*reale*) from true (*vero*). Probably, *real* was meant to refer to the effects of baptism while *true* referred to matters of doctrine. If such was the basis of Jannucci's distinction, non-Catholic Christians would really be members of the Church if they are validly baptized but they would not be truly members of it because they do not profess the true faith. Whatever be the basis of the distinction, the importance of Jannucci's critique consisted not so much in its content—others had said the equivalent—but in its being another attempt directly to grapple with the doctrine of *Mystici corporis*. Unlike Lercaro, he avoided the identity question entirely; like both Poncet and Lercaro, he approached the question of membership from the perspective of the implications of valid baptism. But he did not, like Poncet, confine the explicit statements of Pius XII to the level of practice while expanding their internal logic on that of principle. Instead, Jannucci seems to have considered membership in the Church to be a matter of degree, and if my understanding of the teaching of Pius XII in *Mystici corporis* is correct, Jannucci departed from it when he said that non-Catholic Christians are members of the Church in a real sense.

The need for a perspective broader than that of *Mystici corporis* had been apparent ever since the speech of Liénart in the first session. It was becoming increasingly clear that a more theologically accurate expression of Catholic doctrine required a partial departure from the position of Pius XII in *Mystici corporis*. It is therefore not surprising that *LG*-b entailed a number of changes. On the question of identity the new draft stated:

> *Text O.* This Church, constituted and set up [*ordinata*] in the world as a society, subsists in [*subsistit in*] the Catholic Church governed by the successor of Peter and the bishops in union with him, although outside its company [*compaginem*] many elements of holiness and truth may be found, which as gifts belonging to the Church of Christ, are a driving force [*impellunt*] toward catholic unity.[130]

It is obvious from Text O that the equation set up by Pius XII in *Mystici corporis* between the Mystical Body of Christ and the (Roman) Catholic Church had been changed.[131] The change remains in the promulgated text. The second sentence of number 8 (*LG*-a) had identified the Church of Christ with His Mystical Body; number 8 of the following draft (*LG*-b) does not do so *tout court* but adds an important nuance. This Church, the latter document states, constituted and set up (*ordinata*) *in this world as a society* (here the Council Fathers state again—obliquely this time—that the Church is not an invisible but a visible reality), *subsists* in the Catholic Church governed by Peter's successor and the bishops in union with him. That is to say: The Church of Christ *subsists* in the (Roman) Catholic Church. This modification of the teaching of Pius XII, less immediately obvious in the change in the use of footnotes referring to sections of *Mystici corporis* and *Humani generis*, is unmistakable in the change from the *est* of the previous drafts to the *subsistit in* of *LG*-b. The report on the particular numbers of that draft explains that the change was made in order to be in better harmony with the affirmation that Church elements (*elementis ecclesialibus*) are present elsewhere (*alibi*).[132] Sixty-three voted for the text on the condition that it be amended (*iuxta modum*).[133] And of those, thirteen expressed a wish for a return from the *subsistit in* of *LG*-b to the *est* of the previous drafts.[134] The Commission decided to stand by the text, and the change was subsequently adopted by the overwhelming majority of the Council.

On the identity question there can be no doubt that the position of Pius XII in *Mystici corporis* had been reversed. But matters on the correlative of membership are not so clear, for at first blush the Council seems to have spoken in terms of degrees of membership (*Stufentheorie*):

> *Text P.* Those are fully [*plene*] incorporated [*incorporantur*] into the Church as a society who, having the Spirit of Christ, accept its full [*integram*] way of life [*ordinationem*] and all the means of salvation instituted in it, and in the same visible company [*compage*], by the bonds of the same professed faith, the sacraments and Church government are united with Christ who rules it through the Sovereign Pontiff and the bishops...Let all the sons of the Church remember, however, that their exalted position is not to be ascribed to their own merits but...to a particular grace of Christ.[135]

The same number proceeds to speak of those under instruction (*catechumeni*). These, because of their express will to be incorporated into the Church, are joined to it by reason of that desire (*voto*). Non-Catholic Christians are spoken of in the following number:

> *Text Q.* The Church knows for many reasons it is joined with all those who, as baptized, are honored by the name Christian, but who do not profess the fullness of faith [*integram...fidem*] or who do not preserve the *unity of communion under the successor of Peter*. [These Christians]...are signed with baptism, by which they are joined [*coniunguntur*] to Christ....[136]

The difference of language in Text P and Text Q is striking. When speaking of Catholics, the former speaks of their full incorporation (*plene...incorporantur*) into the *Church* as a society (thus hinting at degrees of belonging), while the latter, speaking of non-Catholic Christians, speaks of their being *joined* (*coniunguntur*) to *Christ* by reason of their baptism. Does this mean that the thought of the Council Fathers was that all baptized Christians are members of the Church but that Catholics, due not to their own merits but to a special grace of Christ, are fully so? It will be seen that in the last analysis the Council, while avoiding the word *member-*(*ship*) as such, thought not in terms of degrees but of modalities.

That such is the case does not at once strike the reader. In the earlier meetings of the third session, the report on specific changes introduced into *LG*-b indicated that the adverb *plene* (Text P) was used in place of *reapse et simplicater* of *LG*-a (Text N-2 [A]). *A U*-b had used the terms *vere et proprie*; and the word *membra* had occurred as such (Text M-2). In order not to exclude children and less well-educated Christians, *LG*-b read *plene* but omitted *tantum*.[137] Since the Commission as of the third session had carefully honed its choice of words, the term *Christiani* may be taken in its strict sense as referring to non-Catholics who, as *rudiores*, could not be expected adequately to understand what the dispute between Catholics and other Christians is about. This is not merely a question of the papacy but, as Troeltsch pointed out, touches upon much deeper matters.[138] That the term *Christiani rudiores* was meant to include at least some baptized non-Catholics seems confirmed by the reporter's allusion to the fact that regarding the choice of *coniunguntur* (Text Q), some Fathers had asked that the verb *incorporantur* be used instead. The reporter answered that the Commission felt it had satisfied this request, presumably because of the general context in which that verb was being used.[139] It is obvious from the context that the Commission thought it was dealing precisely with the question of membership (though the term does not occur in Texts P and Q).[140] From the tone of these remarks made by the reporter in order to explain the changes introduced into *LG*-b, one might deduce that on the question of membership the intent of the draft was to speak in terms of degrees (*Stufentheorie*). Given the lack of any significant number of negative votes or votes *iuxta modum* in the final voting, it would not be unreasonable to conclude that the Council Fathers were implicitly accepting the meaning of the text as suggested by the Commission.

Yet matters are more complex. A draft on Ecumenism (*Unitatis redintegratio*) had been prepared and, as decided in a note dated April 27, 1964, was sent to the dispersed Council Fathers several months before the opening of the third session, indeed before *LG*-b. A relevant paragraph stated:

> *Text R.* Those who believe in Christ and have validly received baptism are constituted in a certain [*quadam*] union [*communione*] with the Catholic Church, although that union is not perfect. Indeed, because of differences existing in various ways between them and the faithful of the Catholic Church both in doctrinal, sometimes even disciplinary matters and the structure of the Church, not a few obstacles are placed in the way of full ecclesiastical union. The ecumenical movement attempts [*tendit*] to overcome these obstacles which are sometimes rather serious [*graviora*]. Nonetheless, *those who are justified by faith and who are baptized* are *incorported into Christ* and therefore are rightly [*iure*] honored by the name of Christian and deserve to be acknowledged as brothers in the Lord by the Sons of the Catholic Church.[141]

Much later during the same session the Commission gave an account of several suggested amendments of the wording of this text. The account of the reporter is worth quoting because the reason given for the amendments contained an explicit reference to *Mystici corporis*:

> *Text S.* On page 7, lines 27 and 28, in place of "Christo incorporantur" let the phrase read "Christo uniuntur" instead, lest there be an appearance of contradicting the teaching of Pius XII in *Mystici corporis* and those theologians who maintain that profession of the true faith is required in order that anyone become in fact [*reapse*] a member of the Mystical Body which is the Church. Appeal to the Decree for the Armenians is doubtful.[142]

Six Council Fathers had requested the amendment and twenty-two had proposed that the phrase "Christo incorporantur" be omitted. The reply of the Commission was succinct and revealing:

> *Text T.* In the text, it is said only that they are incorporated into Christ, not into the Mystical Body of Christ which is the Church. *In that way, the controversial question about who is a member of the Church is avoided.*[143]

If *LG*-b as quoted in Text P were all one had to go on, then given the text and the report of the Commission on why the changes had been introduced, one might argue that in voting for the text the Council had intended to reverse the position of Pius XII on the question of membership. For if those who fulfill the conditions of Text P are fully incorporated into the Church as a society and the adverb *plene* is introduced in order *not to exclude* less well-educated non-Catholic Christians (*Christiani rudiores*), then it might be concluded that some non-Catholic Christians were incorporated into the Catholic Church as a society; i.e., into the Church as a visible, organized body. But while Text R of the April 1964 draft on Ecumenism, if taken in isolation, tends to confirm that interpretation, the reply of the Commission to the request of several Fathers (Text T) removed much of the ground from under that possibility.

Given the tenor of the debates as reflected in the various changes in the texts, the data suggest several conclusions regarding our two central questions. At the very least the data indicate general dissatisfaction with the position of Pius XII on the identity question as well as its development and consequent reversal, the Council Fathers being explicitly aware of what was happening. But a study of the conciliar documents further reveals that the Council Fathers were paradoxically unwilling to depart totally from the teaching of Pius XII on the correlative question of membership.

This is not clear from a cursory reading of the texts, for at first blush they seem to betray a certain ambivalence. In number 14 of the *LG*-b (Text P) the writers of the drafts speak in terms of those who are fully (*plene*) incorporated into the Church as a society, words that hint at degrees, levels, or gradation of membership (*Stufentheorie*). But this suggestion is more apparent than real. A new number (13) precedes number 14 and is not to be found in the preceding documents. Number 13 states:

> *Text U.* All human beings are called to be part of this Catholic unity of the People of God, a unity which is harbinger of the peace it promotes. And there belong to it or are related to it in various ways [*variis modis*] the Catholic faithful as well as all who believe in Christ and indeed the whole of mankind. For all men are called to salvation by the grace of God.[144]

Text U suggests that in the end the Council Fathers thought in terms of modalities whereby various people are related to the oneness (*unitatem*) of the Church. This is the frame of reference in which the *plene* of the following number 14 (Text P) must be read. Thus, in the context of being related to the unity of the Church of Christ, the modality whereby a Catholic who has his Spirit and fulfills the other conditions mentioned in number 14 belongs to the Church is one of fullness. According to the

Council document, the same cannot be said of non-Catholic Christians even when they are in a state of grace. For in number 14, the Council Fathers describe the bona fide Catholic as being fully incorporated into the Church of Christ;[145] in number 25, they affirm that the Catholic Church acknowledges its link with all who are baptized and who consequently are rightly (*iure*) honored by the name Christian; [146] in number 16, they speak of those who have not yet received the Gospel but who nonetheless are related to the Catholic Church *in various ways*.[147] Thus the *plene* of number 14 may not be taken as an oblique indication that the Council Fathers thought in terms of *degrees* of membership.

In what sense, then, may it be maintained that the Council Fathers manifested an unwillingness to depart totally from the teaching of Pius XII on the question of membership? While the initial drafts (*A U*-b and *LG*-a) presuppose *Schichtentheorie* because they do not depart from the teaching of Pius XII, and the later and promulgated drafts embrace *Modalitättheorie*, the Council Father refused to endorse *Stufentheorie*. Recall that the position of Pius XII seems to have been (*pace* Schmaus) on of *Schichtentheorie*. It then becomes apparent that in refusing to say that non-Catholic Christians are members of the Church and in refusing to say they differ from Catholics only in degree or level of membership, the Council manifested an unwillingness to differ completely with Pius on this point.

It has been suggested that the Council Fathers did not wish to affirm that non-Catholic Christians are members of the Church because they did not wish to go against the teaching of Pius XII in *Mystici corporis*.[148] Indeed, while Text T seems to lend some support to that view, all it truly reveals is that the Council Fathers refused to speak in terms of membership. But this cannot be because they did not wish to go against the teaching of Pius XII: They had already modified it considerably on the identity question. I suggest the reasons lie far deeper. Though I shall not attempt to demonstrate it here—to do so would require another chapter, unnecessary given my limited purpose—there is abundant evidence in the documents to show that two of the abiding concerns of the Council Fathers were to avoid anything that would imply either that the Church is the sum of Christian sects or that the Church of Christ is essentially invisible. One is already on the way to the first if one hints that profession of the true faith, including union with the Roman Church, whose head presently exercises the Petrine function, is not an integral requirement for membership. One is on the way to the second if one implies that all that really matters is that one be in a state of grace. Since only the Godhead really knows who is and who is not, the Church conceived as an invisible reality begins to loom on the horizon of one's thought. One would then have a further problem. Why should baptism, which is a *visible rite*, be a condition for membership in an *invisible Church*? In both cases, one could fittingly speak of degrees of membership—there are, after all, degrees of holiness. These are moves that the Council Fathers refused to make. For them, as for John Courtney Murray some years earlier, the Church of Christ is a "Thing." *Semper reformanda*, it has its sinners as well as its saints; but it is a sociological reality to which one can point. For the Council Fathers it was in the end a matter of fullness: Either one has it or one does not. But if one does not, they say, there are various ways of being related to it, among which are the means of grace found in non-Catholic Christian Churches. These means, as *res propriae* of the Church of Christ, are a driving force toward unity. To express that reality, the Council Fathers could move from *Schichten-theorie* to *Modalitättheorie*; they could not embrace *Stufentheorie*. And they could not embrace *Stufentheorie* because of its implication relative to the nature of the Church as they understood it. When that was at stake; when it was a question of departing from an aspect of what they considered to be the truth delivered once for all to the "saints," they budged not an inch from the teaching of the ordinary papal magisterium. When it was a matter of doctrine there could be contradictory pluralism if need be; when it was a matter of dogma, complementary pluralism circumscribed the limits beyond which they would not go.

Orientalium Ecclesiarum Versus *Lumen Gentium*

It is time to take up once again the problem posed by *Orientalium Ecclesiarum* and to determine more precisely the sense in which the Council Fathers, developed, reversed, or as the case may be, modified the teaching of Pius XII. *Orientalium Ecclesiarum* is clearly inconsistent with *Lumen gentium*. As stated above, I intend to argue that it is the thrust of *Lumen gentium*, not that of the former document, which must be considered the normative index of the Council's thinking on the identity and membership questions. It will be recalled that the Decree on Eastern Catholic Churches (Text H) has to do with both matters.

On the level of principle, it must be conceded that a fundamental inconsistency remains in the promulgated documents as distinguished from the debates that produced them. Both *Orientalium Ecclesiarum* and

Lumen gentium are documents of an Ecumenical Council within Catholicism; one is not more conciliar than the other. Yet, on the level of practice, it was from the latter, not the former, that most of the remaining Council documents were to take their cue in matters pertaining to ecclesiology. And in *Lumen gentium* the Council Fathers proceeded to reverse the teaching of the ordinary papal magisterium on the identity question while on the correlative question of membership they modified it by moving from *Schichtentheorie* to *Modalitättheorie*.[149] Now if all one had to go on were the promulgated documents as such, one could not without further proof claim that the Council Fathers really meant to do this, for the thrust of *Orientalium Ecclesiarum* as manifested in Text H is nothing other than a restatement of the position of Pius XII in *Mystici corporis*, though without direct reference to it. One could only claim that in *Lumen gentium* the Council Fathers departed from the teaching of Pius XII and in *Orientalium Ecclesiarum* they affirmed it. The crucial factor is the evidence of the debates. From the foregoing discussion, it is beyond doubt that the Council Fathers were explicitly aware of moving away from the teaching of Pius XII on both questions. That fact throws light on everything else and removes the hurdle placed by Text H. I suggest, then, that to the extent that *Orientalium Ecclesiarum* is inconsistent with *Lumen gentium*, the discrepancies be considered as oversights.

Overview

My argument as stated at the outset of this chapter has now come full circle. There remains to say a word on the sense in which the Council Fathers reversed the teaching of Pius XII. I would like to be able to affirm that the change came from an insight into the Pope's teaching on the Holy Spirit as the Soul of the Church. For the Council Fathers along with Leo XIII and Pius XII before them unquestionably affirm it. But though they come close to doing so, the Council Fathers do not go further and explicitly embrace the older Catholic theory.[150] No, the fundamental thrust of the conciliar position both on the identity question and the correlative issue of membership seems to have come from an insight into the implications of baptism, to which the Pope did not seem to have been sufficiently attentive. Hence his uncritical acceptance of the theologizing manifested in the unpromulgated drafts of the First Vatican Council, which in turn reflect the perspective of Bellarmine's *Disputationes*, the first volume of which was published about thirty years after Protestantism had become an established fact. Yet the implications of valid baptism are seminally present in *Mystici corporis*. Thus one might maintain that the Council developed the internal logic of the Pope's thinking.

To allow matters to rest at that, however, would amount to dissimulating the truth. The concept of the Church as the Mystical Body of Christ remains in the promulgated texts of the Second Vatican Council; but it is no longer central to Catholic ecclesiology. For manifestly on the identity question, perhaps less clearly on the correlative question of membership, the Council Fathers not only developed they also reversed and modified the authentic, authoritative teaching of the Roman Bishop and they did so with increasing awareness of precisely what they were doing.

Schmaus may well be correct in his assessment that without *Mystici corporis* the Dogmatic Constitution *Lumen gentium* might not have been possible.[151] For as will be shown in the following chapter, *Mystici corporis* caused the Catholic Church to reflect and debate within itself long before Vatican II was even a dream.

Chapter VI
PRIOR MODALITIES OF RECEPTION

While the foregoing pages constitute an attempt to determine the modalities whereby papal teaching was received during the Council, this chapter has for its principal object the illustration of the manner in which papal teaching was received before its opening. In part two we have been concerned with five issues. The way papal teaching on the possibility of truth or good in non-Christian religions was received has already been indicated.[1] A final problem remains; I shall take it up in Chap. VII.[2] We shall therefore be concerned here with the remaining four issues; viz., those of religious freedom and the identification of the Mystical Body of Christ with the (Roman) Catholic Church, each with its closely connected correlative.

I shall regroup them as follows: the religious freedom/Church-state issues and the identity/Church membership questions. This chapter is thus divided into three sections, the first two of which correspond to these groupings respectively; the third comprises a general overview. Detailed attention will be given to the work of Bishop Dupanloup and John Courtney Murray in the first section and to that of Valentin Morel, P. Michalon, and Karl Rahner in the second, as concrete instances of what was involved in the years antecedent to the Council. Each section contains in addition an examination of the reports of the bishops and theological faculties in the Antepreparatory Period. Regarding the role of the theologians as such in the years before John XXIII, attention to the work of John Courtney Murray will be more detailed than that given to any other, not only because the issue with which he dealt is by far the most important of those treated in this book, but also because Murray himself best incarnates—at least for most American readers—that "loyal opposition" that has always been a part of traditional Catholicism.

As for the Preparatory Period, the reader will note a difference between the analyses. In the context of Church-state and religious freedom issues, debate in the Preparatory Period was not so much about the latter as about the former. That discussion, it will be recalled, was reported and commented on in Chap. III.[3] But no such analysis was given of the debate surrounding the identity/membership questions in the Preparatory Period. To complete the picture of what happened prior to the opening of the Council, I will summarize that debate below. In reference to the Antepreparatory Period, I shall from time to time deal with comments by those theologians whose reception of papal teaching was largely positive; however, I shall be more taken up with those who received it with critical attention. The reason for the difference is the fact that within authentic Catholicism, full and unequivocating reception of a Pope's teaching is the rule rather than the exception. Hence the task I have undertaken in this book requires that it be the role of the "loyal opposition" that is highlighted, rather than the reverse. For the import of that kind of criticism has never been acknowledged by official Catholicism. And it is that kind of criticism that paradoxically constitutes the more significant factor in that praxis which illumines and transforms theory within the context of the issues explored in this study.

Church-State and Religious Freedom Issues

From the beginning, modalities of reception of the papal position as described above[4] were widely divergent. On the one hand, the so-called Ultramontane party welcomed *Quanta·cura* and its attached Syllabus,[5] particularly those sections referring to Church-state relations and religious freedom; on the other hand, many Catholics were simply stunned.[6] Thus the need to assign to the papal doctrine a proper theological note. For once the theological note due to *Quanta cura* had been determined, then the proper theological note of the individual condemnations in the Syllabus could be clarified. And so began the process, long in terms of a human life but short when measured against the previous 1,900-year history of the Catholic Church, of the formation of a kind of collective awareness whereby the rest of the Church, primarily through its theologians, both developed and reversed the doctrine of religious freedom as enunciated by Pius IX and his successors. The process took almost exactly 101 years— from *Quanta cura* and the Syllabus, promulgated on December 8, 1864, to *Dignitatis humanae*, promulgated by Paul VI on December 7, 1965. The questions were: Had the Pope truly defined this doctrine? Or was his position "merely" the authentic, authoritative teaching of the Roman Bishop? And if it was "merely" that, was it a faithful expression of the truth of the Gospel?[7] What weight must be assigned to the Holy Father's teaching? A final assessment was to take several generations.

I cannot hope to give a full account of that intricate process. Indeed, a definitive study of the role of *sensus fidelium* in the evolution of the doctrine on religious freedom as culminating in the distinctive contribution of *Dignitatis humanae* and Vatican II's position on the correlative issue of Church-state relations remains to be written. I shall confine myself here to three periods of reception, one at the beginning of the process, the other near its end, and still another almost on the eve of the Council. *At this point of my inquiry I merely want to show how common reflection on the part of the rest of the Catholic Church led to the gradual realization that the papal position on Church-state relations and religious freedom should be changed, something in which a subsequent papal magisterium was to acquiesce fully.*

BISHOP DUPANLOUP AND THE SYLLABUS

Within the period with which we are dealing, certainly the most notable modality of reception was by far that of Félix-Antoine-Philibert Dupanloup, Bishop at Orléans. Though I shall here bracket the question of Dupanloup's own views on Church-state and religious freedom, and hence his relation to the de Montalemberts on the one hand and the Louis Veuillots on the other, Dupanloup's manner of receiving *Quanta cura* and the Syllabus was crucial.[8] It provided a focal point whereby succeeding generations were to put the encyclical and its condemnations into a broader context, thus clearing the path for further theological reflection on the part of the rest of the Church. I am referring to one of the most widely read pamphlets in the second half of the nineteenth century; it was entitled *La Convention du 15 septembre et l'Encyclique du 8 décembre*.[9]

This document, which appeared in late January of 1865, comprises in the edition published by Charles Douniol approximately 35,000 words in rather small print spread over seventy-five pages and shows signs of having been written in great haste.[10] Dupanloup deliberately conjoins two very disparate events, (1) the *Agreement* (*convention*) of September 15, 1864, between the Emperor Napoleon III and King Victor Emmanuel (whereby France within a period of two years would withdraw from Italy its forces stationed there for the protection of the Pope) and (2) the publication of the papal encyclical *Quanta cura* some eleven weeks later. Dupanloup says he is proceeding this way because the enemies of the Church were distorting the meaning of *Quanta cura* in order to justify the *Agreement*. Who, after all, would wish to protect a Pope so opposed to modern times? The withdrawal of French troops could then be made with no qualms of conscience on the part of the French people. Thus Dupanloup's pamphlet is divided into two parts, one pertaining to the *Agreement*, the other to the true meaning of *Quanta cura* and its attached Syllabus. It is the latter, not the former, which is of interest here.

Part two of *La Convention* is divided into seven sections; namely (1) Mistranslations and misinterpretations,[11] (2) The character of the pontifical document, (3) True and false principles of interpretation, (4) Philosophy and reason, (5) Progress and modern civilization, (6) Freedom of religion (*liberté des cultes*) and (7) Political freedom. After pointing out in (1) serious errors of translation in the Latin text as published by the anticlerical press,[12] Dupanloup states in (2) that the Encyclical was in fact a very courageous act on the part of the Pope.[13] What is especially interesting is (3), for therein Dupanloup enumerates the general rules for interpreting pontifical documents, part of the process whereby one assigns, as a later generation was to call it, a fitting theological note. Dupanloup's rules for interpretation may be reduced to three:

(1) *It is not the contrary of a proposition which is condemned but its contradictory.*[14]
(2) *Distinguish the sense in which a proposition is condemned. Is it condemned because if universalized and made absolute it would be unacceptable?*[15]
(3) *Carefully determine the meaning of all terms used.*[16]

He then mentions other rules but they are not really different; they are in fact a combination of the three stated above:

> In the interpretation of condemned propositions, all terms and the slightest nuances must be noted because the chief mischief of a proposition often consists in a nuance or a word which itself makes the proposition erroneous. One must distinguish absolute from relative propositions, *for what could be admitted by way of hypothesis is often false if affirmed as thesis.*[17]

The last four sections of part two concern those parts of the encyclical and Syllabus that were causing a storm of protest in France. Only the sixth, freedom of religion (*liberté des cultes*) concerns us here. Dupanloup complains:

> Must we say it for the hundredth time? What the Pope condemns is religious indifferentism...that absurdity which is perhaps more absurd than lacking in piety and which is constantly clanging in our ears, namely that God, the soul, truth, virtue, the Gospel, the Koran, Buddha or Jesus Christ, truth and falsehood, good and evil, are all the same [*égal*].[18]

In the second of these quotations there is no mention of a thesis/hypothesis frame of reference. Dupanloup explicitly uses the terms chiefly in describing general rules for interpreting pontifical documents. But elsewhere the idea hovers very much in the background.

> Never have the Popes intended to condemn those governments which have believed themselves obliged, according to the demands of the time, to include this tolerance and freedom [*liberté des cultes*] in their constitutions. What

shall I say? The Pope himself practices it in Rome...That is what Pius IX meant when he told me last winter: "Jews and Protestants," he said, "are free and at peace here [*chez moi*]; the Jews have their synagogue in the ghetto and Protestants have their church at the disposition of their people."[19]

The former quotation represents an effort to explain what the Pope was really trying to get at when he seemingly condemned abruptly freedom of religion in number 15 of the Syllabus. The argument Dupanloup advances therein is more relevant to number 16 of the same document than it is to number 15.[20] Nonetheless, in this third quotation the thesis/hypothesis model (in which religious freedom is not founded on right but on the legitimate tolerance of error for the common good) is still there by implication. It will be noted that at least in *La Convention* Dupanloup seems to agree with it, one reason why, perhaps, he received a guarded letter of praise from Pius IX and a note of thanks, written in careful but somewhat stilted French, from the Archbishop at Perugia, the future Leo XIII.[21] It should further be noted that Dupanloup's method in general is not an analysis of the documents from which and on which the eighty condemned propositions of the Syllabus were based, but an interplay of the application of the three general principles of interpretation mentioned above plus a *reductio ad absurdum*. Regarding the latter, he must be considered successful; regarding the former, he is not always consistent, revealing himself to be more of an orator than a logician.[22]

The intrinsic value of Dupanloup's argument however is not my immediate concern. What does concern me is this question: If in *La Convention* Dupanloup seems to approve of a variable of thesis/hypothesis language, in what sense may it be said that he kept open the door for future discussion? I suggest the answer is that Dupanloup's rules for interpreting pontifical documents in effect give to the thesis/hypothesis argument its proper theological note. All discussion was not therefore closed forever.[23] Thus to the antagonists who were using *Quanta cura* and its attached Syllabus as a pretext for justifying the previous governmental *Agreement* of September 15, Dupanloup could say, "Learn how to read!" ("*Sachez donc lire!*"[24]) while to the rest of the Church he could say with the phrase that constitutes the subtitle of his conclusion, "*Sursum corda!*"

Obvious limitations of space do not permit me to describe here the efforts of the next four generations to responsibly assign for themselves a theological note proper to the teaching of Pius IX in *Quanta cura* and the Syllabus. Suffice it to say that Dupanloup's master stroke both calmed the storm of unreasonable protest against the Pope and at the same time kept open the possibility of future debate, particularly in regard to so-called ideal Church-state relations and the correlative issue of religious freedom for non-Catholics. In the eventual resolution of that debate, which culminated at Vatican II, an important, some would say almost indispensible factor was the work of an American Jesuit.

THE CONTRIBUTION OF JOHN COURTNEY MURRAY

My treatment of Murray's contribution will be limited principally to the nine-year period 1945-54, near the end of which he was, in effect, silenced by the Roman authorities.[25] I shall not attempt a blow-by-blow account of the so-called Church-state controversy between Murray and his antagonists at the Catholic University of America. I shall therefore proceed in summary fashion, using as a heuristic device the three suggested planes or levels on which Murray thought the Catholic doctrine on religious freedom had to be explored.[26] I shall not be concerned so much with the chronological development of his thought as with its logical sequence, leaving my critical remarks to an occasional *obiter dictum* and to a few general observations below.

As far as I am aware, Murray's first *ex professo* treatment of religious freedom was a review of a book and statement on that subject sponsored by the Joint Committee on Religious Liberty of the Federal Council of Churches and the Foreign Mission Conference of North America. Murray's remarks appeared under the heading "Current Theology" in the March 1945 issue of *Theological Studies*. Regarding the *Statement on Religious Liberty* itself (set forth in a pamphlet published by the Joint Committee under the title "Religious Liberty, Its Meaning and Significance for Our Day"), Murray's critique was in substance that the *Statement*, though intended to be based on natural law, was in fact inconsistent with its premise and betrayed, upon further analysis, preoccupation with narrow Protestant sectarian interests.[27] But Murray acknowledged the need for a clarification of the Catholic position on the question and in the following issue of *Theological Studies* took the first step toward a solution. That attempt at clarification was to occupy much of Murray's energy for the next ten years and more. The value of this article (henceforth referred to as *the second 1945 article*) lay in its pregnant suggestion that a Catholic contribution to the discussion must distinguish three different planes or levels of discourse, listed here in an ascending order of concern:

3.   *The political plane*. This is the problem of constitutional provisions for the rights of conscience both in the international community as such and particular national religio-social contexts.

> Principles of solution are the light of revelation completing the light of reason plus the precepts of political prudence with regard to the achievement of the common good of the political community. Factors entering into the problem are God and the moral law; Christ and the Gospel; the Church and Catholic conscience; the churches and the synagogues; the consciences of their adherents; perhaps the secularists and their "conscience" (if they have any); and the state.[28]

2.   *The theological plane*. This is the problem of Church and state.

> The principle of solution is the light of revelation completing the light of reason. Factors entering into the problem are God, the moral law, the Church and the Gospel, the Church, the Catholic conscience, and the state.[29]

1.   *The ethical plane*. This is the problem of freedom of conscience.

> The principle of solution is the light of reason. Factors entering into the problem are God, the moral law, the human conscience, the state.[30]

Considered in an ascending order, it is clear that the problem becomes increasingly complex but that a solution on the ethical plane constitutes the foundation upon which subsequent solutions on the theological and political planes will rest. If one abstracts from the actual chronological development of Murray's thought and considers it *in globo*, then it may be said that on the ethical plane Murray was to locate a Catholic solution to the problem of religious freedom in the rights of conscience rooted in the natural law; on the theological plane he was to urge that Catholic consciousness of being the one true Church does not logically require setting up Catholicism as a state religion and that the Church may not enlist the arm of the state in the repression of heresy; and finally, on the political plane, that the inner logic of the papal position as enunciated especially by Leo XIII led to a conclusion quite different from that of official Catholicism. In my schematic summary of Murray's contribution, I shall follow the division suggested by these three planes, asking the reader to bear in mind that, although they are distinct, the three planes tend to overlap, and that such is especially the case regarding the theological and political planes.

The Ethical Plane

Murray dealt with the ethical foundation of religious freedom in the remaining pages of the second 1945 article, approaching it from the point of view of natural law. "...the ensemble of things to be done and things not to be done which follow of necessity from the sheer fact that man is man."[31] This is the first law to which the question of religious freedom is related, the second being human law rooted in the social nature of a human being. The primary demand in human society is that human society be a cooperating unity wherein, in pursuit of a common good, free human beings associate themselves under authoritative guidance. The role of the state is not only to protect the common *good* (not simply material but also moral in scope, civic virtue being its primary component) but, too, to provide for the *common* good.[32] Within the sphere of its competence, the state has true moral authority and can oblige in conscience.[33]

The first duty of conscience (that "...practical judgment of reason, whereby in the light of the known law, a man judges of the morality of a concrete act..."[34]) is to educate itself. For an erroneous conscience (that "...practical judgment...formed in ignorance of the full realities of the case and [which], as a matter of fact, is wrong..."[35]) does not create rights against legitimate authority within the competence of that authority. Thus, one who sincerely believes that all senile people should be destroyed because they are no longer useful to society does not by reason of his or her conscientious judgment have a right to proceed to eliminate them.[36] If he or she attempts to carry out his or her conscientious judgment, the state may prosecute. And when it does so, the state violates no right of conscience because there is no right to violate. Here Murray deserves to be quoted at some length:

> The individual is also involved in a whole system of social relationships, and his beliefs and acts have social repercussions. And when he projects himself into society by his actions, he finds himself in an order, a social and juridical order, based on law and vindicated by law. His "liberty" to act according to conscience comes under the control of the legitimate demands of this juridical order; and an erroneous conscience creates no rights, as against a legitimate order of law. It is a valid principle of liberty only in the internal forum of private morality, where there is also another law to be considered. *The State cannot, indeed, permit itself to make mere religious or moral opinion a crime; on the other hand, it cannot permit others to make crime a mere matter of religious or moral opinion.*[37]

Expressed in other terms, an erroneous conscience does not have an objective right against the common good. After enumerating the *obligations* of conscience before God and state *versus* those of the state before God and conscience,[38] Murray comes to the *rights* of conscience, distinguishing its immunities (or inviolabilities) from its positive empowerments (rights).[39] From this list I shall select those more directly relevant to religious freedom and enumerate them as follows. Conscience has the right to:

1. Immunity from force and from the pressure of organized propaganda that would undermine belief in God or obstruct the search for religious and moral truth;[40]

2. Immunity from force, legal enactments, governmental action, and the pressure of social institutions that would hinder obedience to conscience in private and domestic life.[41]

Conscience has as positive empowerment the:

3. Right of free association with others for religious purposes, especially for the purpose of social worship; [42]

4. Right to propagate belief in God and the precepts of morality, by education and by the spoken and written word.[43]

These rights do not, for Murray, include the right to irreligious propaganda nor the right of association for anti-religious purposes. These are not natural rights but may become civil rights whose origin is *lex tolerans*.[44] There will ultimately be for Murray no parallel here with the law of the supernatural order.[45]

In the second 1945 article, his first major step in clarifying the Catholic position on religious freedom, Murray believed that on the ethical plane he had found common ground on which Catholics and Protestants might stand shoulder to shoulder. That common ground is the natural law wherein both parties prescind from all realities of the present, historical, supernatural order certified only by revelation and known only by faith.[46] The essential part of the problem remains, indeed, the manner of harmonizing claims legitimately made on the ethical plane with those which may be legitimately made on the theological. But "...the process of harmonizing these two solutions [on the ethical and theological plane] into an organic synthesis is not, and cannot be accomplished at the cost of destroying one of them. Concretely, this means that the rights of conscience as determined by the natural law retain their full validity under the Christian law."[47]

A reading of the second 1945 article reveals that Murray's thought had by no means attained the maturity it was to have attained by the end of the next decade. A fundamental distinction between the state and society is lacking in these pages, a distinction that will be crucial for his attempt to solve the problem on the theological and political planes. And in a revealing footnote, he maintained at this time that the absolute obligation of the state to acknowledge God as its author, to worship Him as He wills, and to subject its official life and action to His law, "...includes also the hypothetical obligation of accepting a higher belief, law and mode of worship, if God reveals them as His will."[48] Nonetheless, by distinguishing the three planes on which the problem of religious freedom must be discussed, and by insisting that, whatever be the solutions effected on the theological and political planes, nothing on these higher levels can be allowed to invalidate what has been established on the ethical, which is the foundation of all the others, Murray had at least cleared the ground for meaningful discussion.

The Theological Plane

Perhaps the best *locus* wherein to begin to grasp Murray's understanding of religious freedom on this higher plane is a paper delivered at the 1948 meeting of the Catholic Theological Society of America. Entitled "Governmental Repression of Heresy," the paper contained besides the development of its main theme a fundamental distinction between the state and society.[49] That distinction, joined with its more highly refined and expanded nuances in an article published some three years later,[50] allows us, at Murray's suggestion in 1948,[51] to set up the following analogy:

(a)"matter"	(c) population	(e) society	(g) state
::	::	::	
(b)"form"	(d) people	(f) state	(h) government

It is important to bear in mind that whereas in Aristotelian philosophy matter is really distinct from form, these concepts are only virtually distinct, or in neo-Thomist terms, they are logically distinct *cum fundamento in re*. For the people are the population as cultured, the state is society as organized for the common good, the government is the ruler(s) in relation to the ruled and the ruled in relation to the ruler(s). A popula-

tion is a mere collectivity and simply inhabits the soil; a people is the result
of varied forces—environment, national consciousness, temperament, the
inheritance of common experience.[52] "*We the People* is made of flesh and
blood, ensouled by a community of ideals and purposes."[53] Thus the
people include both civil society whose scope is as broad as civilization
itself and the body politic (synonymous with political society).[54] But the
state is not the body politic; rather is it the particular functional organization of the body politic whose purpose is the good of the whole.[55] Among
these terms, it is especially the distinction between the state and society that
will be pivotal for what Murray will have to say. For obviously the
Catholic Church is the warp and woof of any truly Catholic society. To say
this, however, is to raise two distinct but closely related questions; namely:

(1)   In such a society; i.e., in a society in which at least the vast
      majority are Catholics, does Catholic consciousness of being
      the one true Church logically entail the setting up of Catholicism
      as the state religion?

(2)   In such a society, may the Church enlist the arm of the state
      in the repression of heresy?

Both questions Murray was to answer negatively. It is important to see
why, for the path to these negative answers cleared the ground still further
in the wilderness of fluctuating Catholic practice on the subject of religious
freedom. The common ground for the answers to each of these questions is
found in an analysis of the indirect power. Indeed, the theory of indirect
power as elaborated by John of Paris (d. 1306) and based upon the *Duo
sunt* of Gelasius I (492-496) is the source of the perennial though frequently
obscured Catholic position.[56] Compared to a theory of direct power as
represented by, say, Hugh of St. Victor and a theory of indirect power as
elaborated by Bellarmine (Bellarmine's theory, for Murray, is really a
theory of direct power susceptible to exceptional use), Murray found the
Gelasian-John of Paris approach to the question of Church-state relations
to be, if not entirely without reproach, at least seminal for a development
able to guide the thought and actions of the Church in its relation to the
state in contemporary society.[57] This development, as we shall see, had
important implications for the question of religious freedom considered on
the theological plane. Briefly stated, John of Paris' theory rested on two
principles: (1) the *regnum* (which in our society would be functionally
synonymous with the state) is a natural institution for human and tem-

poral ends; (2) the unity of the Church is supernatural; its power is exclusively spiritual.[58] This dyarchy of power(s) has its origin in God, a common origin that necessitates their mutual harmony. But if the prince (and in contemporary terms, the state) becomes a *peccator*, the Church may not enlist the secular arm. Her only weapons are spiritual. She can declare that the people are no longer obliged to obey the prince (or in my terms, the state) in a particular matter. The Church may even excommunicate those who do.[59] The rest is in the hands of the people. They may proceed to depose the prince (or in my terms, to change the government [understood in Murray's sense as indicated above]), which would in turn modify or remove the offending decree of the state. Thus in the Gelasian-John of Paris theory of the two powers, the power of the Church over the state is indirect.

Such is the basis from which Murray proceeded to ground the negative answers to each of the questions stated above. I shall briefly consider each separately.

Catholic Society and the Confessional State

Here we must lay aside, for the moment, the paper delivered to the Catholic Theological Society of America in 1948. In a subsequent article (1949) Murray was to contend that Leo XIII restated and developed the Gelasian thesis and that it was completed by Pius XI and Pius XII.[60] The situation that the contemporary Church faced was very different from that which challenged it in the past. What was in the time of Gelasius a balance to be established between *sacerdotium et* **imperium** and in the time of Boniface VIII an ill-fated and misguided attempt to find a balance between *sacerdotium et* **regnum** had become today the attempt to find a balance between *sacerdotium et* **civis**. Murray admitted it is questionable whether Leo XIII fully realized the modern problematic but considered nonetheless that, by some manner of genius, Leo put forth the principle of a solution. In saying that one and the same human person and his integrity as citizen and Christian is the end and object of the harmony that must exist between Church and state, Leo was implicitly saying that a human person by his or her action as Christian and as citizen ought to be the instrument and agent of establishing this harmony in actual fact. More important is Murray's interpretation of Leo's statements on the necessity of a confessional state. These, for Murray, did not belong to Leo's doctrinal contribution to the Church—this is limited to his restatement and development of the Gelasian doctrine—but to the polemical aspect of his work; i.e., to Leo's attack on the monism of the state, most notably in France. The internal logic of the two powers as described by Gelasius, its continuation in John of Paris, its restatement and development by Leo XIII enabled Murray to conclude:

> There is first the *free* obedience of the Christian conscience to the magisterial and jurisdictional authority of the Church; there is secondly the *free* participation of the citizen, as a Christian, in the institutions whereby all the processes of temporal life are directed to their proper ends.[61]

That, in sum, said Murray, is the Catholic thesis as it relates to democratic society.[62] A lay state is not a laicized state that sets itself up as the norm of All That Is, the situation of Continental Liberalism against which the nineteenth-century popes fought. A lay state is fully in harmony with the older Catholic tradition, the internal logic of which would point the way out of the cul-de-sac wherein contemporary Catholicism found itself on the issue of religious freedom. Murray could therefore conclude by saying "...in these perspectives and in the logic of these [i.e., especially Leonine] premises, one need not, and indeed cannot, go on to the constitutional situation characteristic of the confessional state."[63] One notes that Murray had changed the position he had espoused in a footnote in the second 1945 article four years earlier; he had therein held the hypothetical obligation of the state to worship God as God wills if God reveals the way He wishes to be worshipped.[64] But Murray had since learned to distinguish between the state and society and on that basis could, as he did later, say the state *qua* state knows nothing of the supernatural. Thus on these grounds, summarized perhaps all too rapidly, Murray could answer negatively the first of the questions placed above.

The Church, the State, and the Repression of Heresy

The Gelasian *Duo sunt*, its continued use in the work of John of Paris, and its subsequent restatement and development by Leo XIII constitute the foundation of a negative answer to the second question just as it did to the first. But the emphasis is different. Here we take up again the paper delivered at the meeting of the Catholic Theological Society of America (1948). First, the state accepts its definition of the Church not from above but from below; that is to say: The state takes its definition from its citizens who, in a society of Roman Catholics, are directly subject to the magisterium in matters pertaining to faith and morals, but with the important nuance mentioned below.[65] Second, the state aids the Church only in the exercise of the state's own inherent power, human in origin and temporal in purpose. The state cannot act outside these limits, and even when it acts in alliance with the Church, it acts only for its own ends, the ordering of what is already "there" in society.[66] The aid that the state owes to the Church "...consists in the full performances of its own political duty of creating, or assisting in the creation of those conditions in society—political, social, economic, cultural—which will favor the ends of human personality, the peaceful enjoyment of all its rights, the unobstructed performance of all its duties, the full development of all its powers."[67] Thus the basic right of the Church, as of the human person, is the fundamental right to be recognized for what it *is*. And that right the Church can no more renounce than the human person can renounce his or her essential dignity.[68] But there is an important difference. Whereas the juridical statute of the human person directly and necessarily enters into the constitution of the state and government and is consequently an essential part of the public order, the Church does not stand in the same relation. For the Church is not an intrinsic exigency of the human person in the manner that the state is (because of a human being's social nature).[69] The statute of the Church does not rest on reason and natural law but on faith and divine law. Consequently, says Murray, "...the statute of the Church does not enter into the constitution of the state directly, necessarily, and *per se*";[70] it is not part of the definition of public order, the order of justice, that would "...have its own consistency, even if there were no Church.... The relationship (between Church and state) is established through the members of society, the citizens, that the state organizes."[71]

But precisely because of that fact it may be urged that, if a society is predominantly Catholic, subject to the magisterium in matters pertaining to faith and morals, then at least logically it is the duty of that society to repress, through the state that said society has set up, significant expressions of religious doctrine different from that of Catholicism held by that society to be the one true Church. It is here that what Murray had established on the ethical plane must be borne in mind. It is true that Catholic society is "subject" to the magisterium in matters pertaining to faith and morals, but it is also true that no small part of those morals is the natural law, the basis, as we have seen, of religious freedom on the ethical plane. *The Church has no right to demand of the state that which the state by its nature is not empowered to give.* What, then, is the duty of the state in a Catholic society wherein heretical doctrine is being disseminated? Murray's answer was unequivocal:

If, for instance, there are individuals or groups within society that deny the exclusive right of the Church, as the true Church of Christ, to preach the Gospel, and undertake to preach a gospel of their own, the state has no empowerment from the only source from which its empowerments come (the natural law) to forbid them, provided the tenets of their gospel are not incompatible with the order of justice and the manner of their preaching is not in prudent judgment a threat to the public peace.[72]

But the fact that the Church may not enlist the arm of the state does not mean that the Church is withdrawn from society. The judgment of the Church will be that, in terms of divine law, these heretical groups do not have a right to preach "another gospel." And a truly Catholic society will do well to take note of that publicly expressed judgment. The Church's judgment however is not so binding that the state, even in a Catholic society, is obliged to enforce it on those citizens not prepared to accept it. Thus did Murray address the second of the two questions placed above. For as he stated elsewhere, the state can punish a thief but it can hardly wring the neck of an idea.

The Political Plane

The ground for a solution to the question of religious freedom on the political plane has already been largely cleared on the theological and ethical. I shall therefore proceed in more summary fashion.

Murray's analysis of the *Duo sunt* of Gelasius, its trajectory in John of Paris and its restatement and development by Leo XIII led him to the startling conclusion that the internal logic of Leo's position on Church-state relations, as perfected by Pius XI and Pius XII, presents some striking similarities to the problematic envisaged by the American Constitution.[73] On several occasions, Murray insisted that the older Catholic doctrine, though stifled over several generations of religious persecutions in England, had nonetheless survived in English common law.[74] It was upon that tradition, not on the monism of the state (as All That Is) as the aftermath of the French revolution and the basis of Continental Liberalism, that the American experiment was founded.[75]

Why did a mind possessing the qualities of Leo XIII's not see this? The reasons were fundamentally twofold. First, Leo thought he saw a gigantic conspiracy afoot to rob his people of their faith.[76] Thus he was addressing a practical situation. Second, Leo could restate the two-power theory of Gelasius and still miss further aspects of the older medieval tradition. Of the two great canons of human legislation that the scholastic tradition had elaborated, Leo adverts to only one, the moral law or the canon of justice; the other canon, that of consent by the people, is omitted.[77] For the medieval king had to have the consent of the governed.[78] By contrast, the questions Leo asked himself were *quid sit potestas*, not *quid sit lex*. Leo's great weakness was that he gave relatively little attention to the nature of law.[79]

Murray's breakthrough, already apparent in the early 1950s, had important implications for religious freedom on the political plane. For it meant that the inner dynamic of Catholic doctrine on religious freedom, as elaborated at least *from* (not *by*) Pius IX onward, was in substantial agreement with the original intent (as distinguished from a secularist interpretation) of the American Constitution.[80] Murray was of course thoroughly aware that even Leo XIII officially held a view contrary to that which Murray proclaimed as the core of Catholic doctrine long obscured by the concrete political situations in which the Church was to find itself. His point was that the official teaching of the Popes in this matter was no necessary part of Catholic doctrine and was in fact maintained contrary to an older and more authentic Catholic position. What in fact had been only policy had slowly been elevated to the status of doctrine.

Murray's contribution on the path to reversal and development was one of the modalities wherein the papal doctrine on religious freedom was received. Between Dupanloup at the beginning of this process and Murray near its end, a number of concerned Catholics in each generation of that period grappled with the issue. I have renounced above any attempt in these pages to describe that long process.[81] As to Murray's contribution itself, he was sometimes, though rarely, mistaken, as when he maintained that motivation to repress heresy could not find support in Catholic political philosophy.[82] He was, to be sure, probably right about Leo; he was certainly wrong about others. One has only to point to the work of the Jesuit, Luigi Taparelli d'Azeglio, mentioned above.[83] And Murray so emphasized the inner logic of the Leonine position and its development by Pius XI and Pius XII that he tended to obscure the fact that the official position of the Popes was directly opposed to that which Murray said was really theirs by reason of the inner dynamic of their principles.[84] Thus I find nowhere in Murray's writing on Leo XIII any mention of the famous statement in *Longinqua oceani* wherein the Pope, after praising the progress made by Catholics in the United States, says in no uncertain terms that Church-state relations in this country are not to be thought ideal.[85] And both in *Immortale Dei* and *Libertas* itself, variables of the old *thesis/hypothesis* frame of reference, with everything they imply on tolerating materially and/or formally heretical doctrine for the common good, are undeniably affirmed as they are even in *Ci riesce* of Pius XII.[86] Murray was surely aware of these matters. His obscuring of the continuity between Pius IX through Pius XII was not deliberate but a by-product of his thesis; namely, that the inner logic of the papal position, especially as developed by Leo XIII, led to quite different conclusions, as could that of Pius IX if, as I have pointed out above, Pius had been more attentive to the implications of the traditional Catholic answers to the first four of the heuristic questions placed at the outset of Chap. IV.[87] But Murray's analysis of the *Duo sunt* of Gelasius, its continuation in John of Paris and its creative use by Leo XIII, coming near the end of this long period of soul searching on the part of the rest of the Church was a brilliant stroke unmatched by most of his contemporaries.[88] Despite the fact that the position of Pius IX prevailed well into the first session of Vatican II (and beyond), Murray's contribution was in the long run to prove decisive in reversing the official Catholic position as maintained by the Popes from Pius IX up to *Pacem in terris*. It is therefore not surprising that already on the eve of the Council—that is, in its Antepreparatory Period—even some bishops were beginning to voice their misgivings about the official Catholic position.[89]

THE ANTEPREPARATORY PERIOD

Murray, of course, had not been a lone pioneer in the effort to clear new ground. A complete assessment of how the *sensus fidelium* was operating, particularly as it was reflected in the work of theologians, would have to include preconciliar spade work by Yves Congar, E. Guerrero, J. Leclercq, T. Jiménez-Urresti, J. Lecler, M. Pribilla and Yves de Montcheuil, to mention only a few.[90] Dupanloup near the beginning of this development and Murray near its end have been presented in some detail merely as examples of how responsible Catholics go about the work of giving to a particular papal teaching its proper theological note (Dupanloup) or of "talking back" to the ordinary papal magisterium, not by taking a defiant stance as did Lamennais much earlier in the controversy,[91] but by digging deeper into the sources (Murray). The efforts of Murray and his peers were to be reflected a few years later in the reports of bishops and theological faculties just prior to the opening of the Council. Here the data are somewhat sparse, for the questions, though a matter of some concern in some local Churches, had not yet developed into the burning issues they were to become once the Council was in session.

The Bishops Divided

It is well known that most bishops of Hispanic and Italian provenance were opposed to any significant change in the official position of the Catholic Church as enunciated by the ordinary papal magisterium and that, precisely in view of recent controversy, they desired confirmation of the traditional doctrine.[92] But one did not have to be a bishop of Hispanic origin in order to take that or a similar stand, a fact not difficult to document.[93] I shall not concentrate however on those who in their reports to the Holy See relative to the agenda of the coming Çouncil suggested that the long-standing position of the Church (or, more precisely, of the ordinary papal magisterium) be maintained. Instead, I should like to draw attention to the fact that certain bishops raised serious questions about the viability of the traditional doctrine.

Thus Emile Guerry, Archbishop at Cambrai, suggested that the public law of the Church be better adapted to modern circumstances.[94] The old doctrine of the "perfect state" was outmoded not in the sense that, as Leo XIII pointed out, Church and state were not complete each in its own sphere but in the sense that interdependence was the order of the day. But how achieve this interdependence? Times had indeed changed: A lay state that subjects conscience to itself is to be condemned; but a lay state as an autonomous state may (*potest*) be accepted.[95] This does not mean that Guerry was arguing for separation of Church and state in the nineteenth and early twentieth-century sense. To show what he meant, he pointed to the then current situation in his native France in the time of De Gaulle. If the worship of God (presumably by the state) does not take place in some states as in France after the separation, it is still important that religion (*religiosum factum*) there not go unnoticed (*ignoratum*) and that, not simply from the point of view of the individual but also from that of institutions and society.[96] French law after the separation affirms freedom of both conscience and worship. Guerry concluded this part of his report:

> This positive notion of a lay state [*laicitatis*] in a nation divided regarding the faith appears then [*tunc*] as salvific and, although it does not seem to be completely in conformity with the teaching of the Church, in the name of the common good seems to have reverence for freedom of conscience and [for freedom of] forms of faith.[97]

This situation, which seems to have impressed Guerry as entirely viable, is one that prompted him to suggest that the traditional position of the Church be re-examined. Two extremes were to be avoided: the error of separation of the two powers (*regionum*) as the philosophies of liberalism and laicism wished on the one hand and the error of mixing (*confusionis*) them on the other.[98] It was of great importance, Guerry said, to determine the mission of the Church regarding the tasks of the earthly city (*civitatis terrestris*). The position Guerry seems to have embraced near the end of his report seems to have been one in which the Church accomplishes her mission of salvation not by confirming the efficiency of the state regarding its direct temporal purpose but one in which the Church, simply by accomplishing her mission of evangelization, provides human beings with the means of salvation.[99] Quite clearly the Archbishop at Cambrai was ahead of his time, his thought reflecting, without direct reference to it, the best theological thinking of the day. If I have grasped Guerry's intent correctly, the Archbishop's position may be paraphrased as follows: Separation of Church and state in the sense urged by many of its nineteenth and early twentieth-century proponents was one thing; "separation" in which the state simply provides the means for religion to do its work, without officially favoring any one religion, is something else again.[100] It is to be noted, however, that Guerry, in the report of August 17, 1959, the date that his report carries, did not suggest that the de facto situation that he found viable be elevated to acceptance in principle; it was sufficient for him to suggest that the official view was not beyond question.

I shall limit myself here to one further example, that of Richard Cardinal Cushing, Archbishop at Boston, who in his report stated:

> Very troubling controversies have arisen on the relation between the Church and the modern, secular state, as it is called, and the power and competence of each as regards the various spheres [*provincias*] of human life. And that these [*controversiae*] be stopped [*dirimantur*] in practice, an insightful explanation of those fundamental principles, both theological and juridical, which would provide a new concept of that relation, would be useful, since the old concepts which have been in vogue up to now have their roots in a political order which no longer exists.[101]

Quite clearly Cushing's suggestions reflected the Church-state controversy between John Courtney Murray and his antagonists, most of whom were professors at the Catholic University of America. Cushing was here obviously siding with Murray who, it will be remembered, through his Jesuit superiors had been silenced by the Holy See. Other American bishops were to express similar concerns, some stressing those aspects of the case that pertained to Church-state relations, others those having to do with religious freedom of non-Catholics.[102]

It is not to be thought that in the Antepreparatory Period most of the bishops raised the issue of ideal Church-state relations and/or the correlative matter of religious freedom. But among those who did, a clear pattern emerges in that there was a tendency to argue not from principle but from the existential situation in which they found themselves. Thus the Hispanic and Italian element, who had found a union between Church and state (with religious freedom granted to non-Catholics as a result of toleration) viable for their people, were inclined to suggest that the traditional doctrine be confirmed, while those who, like the French and the Americans, had come to see that "separation" actually worked to the advantage of the Church, tended to argue that it should be reviewed. Few of them at the Antepreparatory stage of the Council seemed to have approached the matter as had Murray and his European peers from the point of view of the intrinsic viability or non-viability of papal teaching. That had been and was still to be the work of the theologians. At the time of the Antepreparatory Period, even a cursory comparison of Italo-Hispanic as over against French-American views indicated that the Catholic episcopacy was beginning to show evidence of a sharp division on the issues.

The Theological Faculties

Unexpectedly both the Holy Office itself, as it was then called, as well as what was the Sacred Congregation for Extraordinary Affairs suggested that the traditional doctrine be re-examined by the forthcoming Council.[103] The wording of these reports however is so succinct that it is impossible to tell from the document as such whether re-examination was suggested with a view to confirming or to changing the long-standing position of the papacy. However, at least in regard to the former Holy Office, confirmation rather than change seemed to have been what was intended, since Cardinal Ottaviani was its sub-prefect (the Pope himself being the prefect of that particular congregation). But as to the intent of their authors, I shall pass that over, turning my attention to the reports of the theological faculties.

By and large these reports reflect a spectrum of views similar to those discernible in the suggestions sent in by the bishops. Among the faculties that desired to see the traditional doctrine reaffirmed, that of the Angelicum (the present-day University of Saint Thomas) may be taken as representative. That faculty stated:

> In these last years, many authors have departed from the doctrine contained in the ecclesiastical documents of the Magisterium and published by the approved authors, which doctrine pertains to the religious duties of a Catholic state. To them this doctrine does not seem to flow from the essential purpose of each society but seems nothing else than a theoretic synthesis of relations formerly existing between Church and monarchy "during the period when holy Christianity flourished." A solemn affirmation [*affirmatio solemnis*] of this doctrine seems opportune, provided that along with it there be proposed the doctrine of legitimate tolerance, the elements of which are to be found in the encyclicals of Pope Leo XIII and the speeches of Pope Pius XII.[104]

The Angelicum, with which Cardinal Browne, whom I have quoted in a preceding chapter, had long been associated, approached the matter from the point of view of ideal Church-state relations and perhaps desired a dogmatic definition, since it spoke of an *affirmatio solemnis* as being opportune. The Catholic University of Louvain took a contrary stance, but approached it from the point of view of the correlative question of religious freedom for non-Catholics. Its suggestion was expressed in one long sentence of approximately 135 words:

> For the same reasons as those which have been reported in the preceding chapter, with regard furthermore not only to contemporary conditions in which there is hardly a homogeneously Catholic nation, and with regard to those conditions in which how Catholics behave toward non-Catholics in a nation where Catholics constitute the greater part of the citizenry influences how non-Catholics behave toward Catholics in nations where non-Catholics are more numerous, but with regard also and especially to Catholic principles concerning the obligation of conforming to a conscience of good faith and the freedom and supernatural character of faith: It is hoped that the Council publicly and solemnly will proclaim that the Catholic faith cannot be imposed or preserved by any coercion which harms the integrity of conscience and the freedom of faith, so that it be evident the dignity of the human person, which Our Lord Jesus Christ through his Incarnation fully revealed to the world, is perfectly acknowledged by the Catholic Church in all human beings.[105]

Much the same was said more succinctly by the theological faculty of the Institut Catholique de Paris, but its reference to the 1953 Discourse of Pius

XII to the Italian Jurists (*Ci riesce*) does not support the orientation it suggested. It has been shown that nothing in that document, when examined in its total context, may be properly understood as grounding anything but the traditional Catholic position.[106]

Cushing's suggestion which favored re-examination of the traditional stand and that of the Angelicum which stood by the existing doctrine both reflect the theological controversies that had been seething sometimes below the surface or that, as in Murray's case, had come to a hard boil. The same documents, along with others which might be adduced, attest to the fact that the work of the minority was having its effect on the thinking of the rest of the Church, if not as a position that might be embraced, then certainly as a challenge that had to be met.

PRELIMINARY OVERVIEW

When one scans the prolonged debate within the Catholic Church as it attempted to wrestle with these problems, it is clear that initially those who thought the official papal position inadequate were in the minority. Yet as the actual opening of the Council drew near, the view of the minority was gaining momentum. For it was no longer the opinion of an individual theologian here and there; it was a critique reflected in the reports of bishops and whole faculties of theology. It is not surprising then that in the Preparatory Period the document presented by the Theological Commission came under severe attack, the main thrust of which has been indicated above.[107] For the *sensus fidelium* had been operative since the time of Dupanloup's famous pamphlet (and before) and, as has been shown, was eventually to come to the climax described in Chaps. III and IV.

My purpose, of course, has not been to write the history of the Catholic Church from the time of the Syllabus to the opening of the Second Vatican Council. Adequate treatments are available elsewhere, as the bibliographical material utilized in the foregoing chapters suggests. My purpose has simply been to describe the kind of respectful and responsible "talking back" that led to the development, reversal, and/or modification of papal teaching on these important questions, with eventual confirmation by the ordinary papal magisterium itself. Much the same obtains regarding the two remaining issues. But there the twists and turns of reception and doctrinal development were somewhat less tortuous.

The Identification of the Mystical Body of Christ with the Catholic Church and the Question of Church Membership

As in the case of Church-state and religious freedom issues, so in that of the theology of the Church and her members the changes introduced by Vatican II were not the product of a moment. For since its promulgation on June 23, 1943, *Mystici corporis* (henceforth, for the most part, *MC*) had initiated a quiet debate within the Catholic Church. From the uncritical acceptance by Joseph Clifford Fenton at the Catholic University of America to the refined analysis and development of Karl Rahner,[108] four distinct phases of discussion stand out prior to the opening of the Council. There is first the time from its promulgation to *Humani generis* (1950; henceforth, for the most part, *HG*) wherein, among other things, the Pope restated with some insistence his position on the identity question; second, from *Humani generis* to the convocation of Vatican II (December 25, 1961); third, from the convocation to the end of the Antepreparatory Period; and fourth, from the Preparatory Period to the opening of the Council on October 11, 1962. I cannot hope to summarize even in bold strokes much less to analyze in detail all that happened in even one of these phases. Hence, regarding the first two, I shall be obliged to limit myself to the critique of only two theologians, leaving observations on others for occasional remarks in the notes.[109] Regarding the third, I shall deal only with the reports submitted by Bishops and Theological Faculties and the important contribution of Karl Rahner; regarding the fourth, I shall treat only the debates on the preliminary draft. The last two phases have to do with the Antepreparatory and Preparatory Periods, respectively.

From the Promulgation of *Mystici Corporis* (1943) to *Humani Generis* (1950)

Outstanding in this period was the article of Valentin Morel, O.F.M. Cap., Professor at the Capuchin scholasticate in Izegem, Belgium. Its opening lines illustrate well what Roman Catholic theologians do when they assign a proper theological note to a particular thesis proposed either by the ordinary papal magisterium, the ordinary universal magisterium, or theologians. For the benefit of those less familiar with this process, it is worthwhile quoting Morel in full:

> In the strict sense, does the Mystical Body on earth comprise no others than the members of the Roman Catholic Church? The following pages are given over to a solution of this problem. The encyclical *Mystici corporis* of His Holiness, Pius XII currently identifies, it is true, the Catholic Church and the Mystical Body. But it is incumbent on theology to scrutinize, in a spirit of complete submission to the magisterium of the Church, the teachings of this very magisterium, and to translate them into technical theological language: regarding the case in point, to determine the meaning and degree of the above-mentioned identification.[110]

Morel first examined the meaning of the term *Mystical Body* and, after having shown its basis in scripture, concluded against Sébastien Tromp but with Emile Mersch that the term *Body of Christ* refers to anyone who lives the life of Christ, something that admits of degrees. Morel went on to say that whoever fulfills that condition as founded in biblical theology is, in the strict sense, a member of the Mystical Body.[111] But the term *strict sense* can be further distinguished. Thus one might speak of being a member in the simple sense (*sens simple*) as over against being a member in the eminent and perfect sense (*sens parfait et éminent*), a distinction of utmost importance in order to harmonize the data of Scripture with the key concepts of *MC*.[112]

What difference does it make to belong to the Mystical Body in the simple sense distinguished from the perfect and eminent sense? It is important to realize that Morel's distinction was made in the context of those who are habitually united with the Redeemer by sanctifying grace and/or supernatural faith. His basic analogy was, in my terms, the distinction between essential and integral being. Just as any being with a body and intellectual soul is a human being in an essential sense (Morel's *sens propre et simple*), so everyone in a state of grace, or failing that, anyone with supernatural faith is a member of the Mystical Body in an essential sense (Morel's *sens simple*). But just as, in my terms, a human being who is ill or maimed is not a human being in an integral sense (*sens parfait et éminent* in Morel's terms), so it is possible to be an ill or maimed member of the Mystical Body. Integral being is then lacking, for however statistically frequent illness or injury may be, it is not *normal* for human beings to be ill or to have, say, only one arm.

Morel's distinctions may be summarized as follows:

1. *Members of the Mystical Body of Christ in a perfect and eminent sense*: Roman Catholics
2. *Members in a proper and simple sense*: All who are in a state of grace or who have supernatural faith; material heretics, etc.
3. *Related to the Mystical Body by desire*: All who have not yet made a supernatural act of faith but, receiving actual graces from time to time, are on their way to justification by faith
4. *Not members in any sense*: Apostates, formal heretics, etc.

Morel seems to have espoused a theory of degrees of membership (*Stufentheorie*) and to that extent deviated from Pius' teaching which in *Mystici corporis* was one of stratification (*Schichtentheorie*). Morel's next step was to examine the relation between the Mystical Body and the (Roman) Catholic Church; he then went on to ground the following theses:

1. The Mystical Body of Christ does not constitute a complete [*stricte*] definition of the (Roman) Catholic Church[113]
2. Ontologically [*sur le plan réel*] the Mystical Body on earth overflows the boundaries of the Roman Catholic Church[114]
3. Only the Roman Catholic Church is rightly [*de droit*] called the Mystical Body of Christ *par excellence*[115]

After establishing these theses, Morel proceeded to give them their proper theological note. In a remark that presumably referred to the third thesis, Morel stated that it had the status of dogma (in Salaverri's terms, *de fide divina et catholica*, q.v.);[116] in a remark that presumably referred to the first and second, Morel said he could not admit it was heretical to affirm them, if one understands the fundamental meaning (*sens primordial*) of scripture and the magisterium.[117] This last phrase ("le sens *primordial* de l'Ecriture et *des documents du magistère*") I take to mean that the inner logic of scripture and of the magisterium might lead to conclusions different from those officially drawn by the magisterium itself.

Morel's article was a substantial contribution to the discussion but was somewhat weakened by three factors. First, it failed clearly to distinguish degrees of belonging to the Mystical Body from modalities, the former referring to different existential circumstances of the same reality, the latter to ontologically different relations. Second, the above distinctions, though at the base of what Morel was doing, were somewhat inconsistent in their application. Third, and related to the second, was Morel's failure to follow through with his analogy. For as he takes leave of his reader, nothing Morel had said definitely eliminated the possibility that a Roman Catholic in a state of serious sin still remained a member of the Mystical Body in a perfect and eminent sense, something maintained not even by Pius XII.[118] A logically grounded distinction between essential and integral being (to revert for the moment to my terms) would have allowed Morel to affirm that no one can be in a state of serious sin and *simultaneously* a member of the Mystical Body in a perfect and eminent sense (integral being). Nonetheless, Morel's article remains an outstanding example of "talking back" to the ordinary papal magisterium in a generally competent, thoroughly responsible, entirely respectful manner.

From *Humani Generis* (August 12, 1950) to the Convocation of the Second Vatican Council (December 25, 1961)

On August 12, 1950, Pius XII promulgated *Humani generis*, in which a number of theological positions considered as threatening the purity of Catholic doctrine were reproved. It was a powerful document and dominated, as has been seen, much of theological reflection up to the very eve of the Council. Among the errors that the Pope attempted to correct was the fact that some did not feel obliged to accept his teaching that the Mystical Body of Christ and the (Roman) Catholic Church are one and the same thing.[119] Though the Pontifical Theological Faculty of Milan and Karl Rahner, to mention only two instances, were later to give a benign interpretation of Pius' teaching,[120] others attempted more directly to show its inadequacy. Among them may be mentioned a brief but significant article (1952) by the Sulpician, P. Michalon.[121]

Michalon argued that in the plan of God there is a necessary connection between cross and triumph, that redemption is full only when glorification has occurred.[122] For it is the Christ as glorified who is the head of the new humanity. Indeed, Pauline realism presents σῶμα τοῦ χριστοῦ as being on the same plane as the resurrected Christ.[123] If in regard to the person of Christ, the Church is the zone of his fulfillment (*épanouissement*), it stands in this respect in the same relation to Christ as his glorified body stands in relation to his person.[124] Now this triumphant reality has a tangible side: the Church, the Body of the glorified Christ.

Michalon's method resulted in grounding the Mystical Body of Christ as the Body of the glorified Christ. The Body of the glorified Christ consti- tutes the primary datum; the visible Church is its tangible manifestation. But Pius XII—indeed Pius expressly conceded the fact in *MC*—limited his discussion almost entirely to the visible Church and left inadequately treated its relation to the Church suffering and triumphant. Michalon concluded: "We see from that how much this would falsify our vision if the visible organism of the Church is considered as something apart. One would surely misunderstand it and disfigure it."[125] Then with an indirect reference to *Mystici corporis* he added:

> Perhaps the reader will grasp also why the Roman Catholic Church affirms itself as being strictly speaking the Mystical Body because of the amplitude of the bonds which link her with the members of that Body. But I emphasize as well that, for the Roman Church, all non-Catholics are related to this Body, invisibly, yes, but also *by certain visible elements* which, from a Catholic viewpoint, manifest their relative belonging to the one Church and makes of them, from a perspective of eventual union, potential members of this Body.[126]

Pius' statement on the identity of the Mystical Body of Christ and the Roman Catholic Church had been unmistakably clear, but its purpose had not been. That purpose, as the Pontifical Faculty at Milan and Karl Rahner were later to point out, was to ward off an error that Pius saw creeping into Catholic thinking; namely, *that one could attain salvation no matter what one's relation to the (Roman) Catholic Church*. Though Michalon did not seem to have grasped what Pius was getting at, he was correct in divining, as Rahner was later to say, that even after *MC* a wider use of the term *Mystical Body of Christ* was legitimate. And Michalon advanced the argument somewhat by showing that the relation of non- Catholics to the Catholic Church is a visible one and exceeds a relation merely *inscio quodam desiderio ac voto* as stated in *MC*. Michalon's article remains a further example of appropriate response to the teaching of the ordinary papal magisterium.

FROM THE CONVOCATION OF VATICAN II (DECEMBER 25, 1961) TO THE END OF THE ANTEPREPARATORY PERIOD

Given the negative but loyal critique of the Pope's position on the identity question and the correlative question of membership as illustrated by Morel and Michalon, among others, as opposed to its uncritical acceptance chiefly by American theologians, it would not be surprising in the years immediately preceding the Council to find indications of the two mutually opposed views. I refer to the suggestions of bishops and theological faculties in what is largely co-extensive with the Antepreparatory Period. Their reflections are abundantly documented in the conciliar texts.

The Bishops' Reports

No less than 115 bishops reported to the Holy See the necessity, in their view, of an apostolic Constitution on the Catholic Church as the Mystical Body of Christ and as the one and only means of salvation;[127] no less than forty spoke of the necessity of explaining and confirming the teaching on the Mystical Body;[128] and no less than eleven thought the doctrine on the Mystical Body should be defined as dogma.[129] Though in these reports the encyclical *MC* is not always mentioned explicitly, the context of the bishops' remarks allows one reasonably to presume that most of them meant the doctrine contained in that encyclical, particularly the position of Pius XII on the identity question and the correlative question of membership. These figures represent indeed a relatively small minority among the bishops in the preconciliar Church.[130] But it was not an insignificant one. Thus Gabriel Garrone, then Archbishop at Toulouse, suggested that it be shown by a solemn and more ample explanation that the (Roman) Catholic Church is the Mystical Body of Christ, the grounds for which had already been laid, he said, by the encyclicals of Leo XIII and Pius XII.[131] And Bernard Cardinal Alfrink, who was to play a central role in the vicissitudes of the postconciliar Dutch Church, suggested that, since in the previous Vatican Council the explanation of the doctrine on the Church had been left unfinished, the forthcoming Council should deal with it more amply, the standard being the encyclical *Mystici corporis*.[132] But strangely, Achille Liénart, Archbishop at Lille, so outspoken a critic of *AU*-b on this point, as we have seen, did not raise the question in his written report sent to the Holy See in the Antepreparatory Period.[133]

Yet while most of the bishops did not allude to it, a number thought the inadequacy of the position set forth in *Mystici corporis* should be treated by the Council. Thus Cardinal König, Archbishop at Vienna, suggested that the dogmatic constitution on the Church begun at Vatican I be concluded, for since *MC* theologians had sufficiently reflected on the matter and therefore the question could be drawn to a close and defined.[134] It is not to be thought however that König was suggesting a blanket endorsement of Pius' teaching. In the third paragraph of his written report, after quoting in the Latin Pius' position on membership, König went on to say many found it too severe; that much more frequently today people were wont to quote the phrase pertaining to or belonging to the Mystical Body of the Redeemer by desire.[135] And Cardinal Frings of Cologne raised the question of the relation of non-Catholic Christians with the one true Church, since in good faith they are outside it, a question some thought had been answered in *Mystici corporis*.[136]

Highly significant in retrospect was the report of Karol Wojtyla, then an auxiliary bishop in Krakow. His report reflected a number of concerns.[137] Those pertaining to the present point of my inquiry are as follows:

With the greatest eagerness the Council is awaited by all, especially by those separated from the unity of the Church by reason of heresy or schism. They also seem to have some love of Christ the Lord, whence there is hope of their reconciliation with the true Church of Christ, for love begets unity. In nothing else is the unity of the Church set forth than in the doctrine of the Mystical Body of Christ: If the Church is the Body of Christ, it cannot be otherwise than the one and only, for the Body is also the one and only.[138]

And in this Body there are various members, both healthy and ailing—and this by reason of heresy also, a sin against faith, and schism, a sin against charity. *But ailing members do not cease being members of the Body of Christ in some way*, [a Body] which is glorious only in heaven but which on earth was wounded and given over to death, whence its similarity to the Mystical Body ailing on earth and wounded. *Its wounds are in us all*, whence we are all obliged to be solicitous for its well being.[139]

The second quotation follows immediately upon the first. Nowhere in this section of his report does Wojtyla refer explicitly to *MC*. In the former quotation he implicitly agrees with Pius on the identity question but in the latter he seems to part company with him on the correlative question of membership. It is highly unlikely that a mind of Wojtyla's astuteness did not realize what he was doing. He concluded:

> The Council and the whole theology of the Church can explain all these matters, putting less emphasis on those that divide while being on the lookout for those which unite. Thus perhaps a change of attitude will be prepared for....[140]

But before the Council was to do so, the Antepreparatory Commission had yet to hear from the various theological faculties. The majority of the bishops in the Antepreparatory Period did not bring up the problem of Pius' position on the identity question and the correlative of membership. Of those who did, modalities of reception varied along a spectrum from unquestioned acceptance on the one hand to dissatisfaction on the other. Many of the latter had found Pius' position simply too facile.

Reports from the Theological Faculties

In the city of Rome itself the Faculty of the Oriental Institute and the theological Faculty of the Gregorian exemplify two divergent views. The former suggested the forthcoming Council explain again the concept of the Mystical Body in the light of (*ad normam*) the draft proposed in the First Vatican Council and the encyclical *Mystici corporis*.[141] The reason given by that Faculty is significant. After the publication of *MC* a number of (presumably) Eastern Orthodox theologians (*dissidentes boni nominis theologi*) of some repute had written to the effect that, in their view, differences on the Primacy of the Roman Pontiff might be removed on the basis of the orientation provided by that encyclical. Nothing in the report suggests that the Faculty had a problem with either the identity question or the correlative question of membership.

On the other hand, the theological Faculty of the Gregorian exhibited some uneasiness on the correlative question of membership, stating it might be useful clearly to teach that heretics and schismatics by that very fact cannot actually (*actu*) be members of the Church; that if however they are in good faith, they are not simply members of the Church by desire (*voto*) but in some way (*aliquatenus*) are part of the communion of saints (*gaudere communione sanctorum*);[142] that the reply of the then Holy Office to the Archbishop at Boston (the context being the so-called Feeney case) might serve as a better approach.[143]

These differences of perspective as shown in the reports of two presti-gious institutions both staffed by the Society of Jesus were to find their counterparts in other theological faculties. On the positive side, the Facul-ties of the Catholic University of America and St. Patrick's University in Ireland may be taken as illustrative of that tendency.[144] But it was the Faculty of the Discalced Carmelites in Rome who seemed to exhibit the most unbending position. In a report of ninety-nine pages dated April 28, 1960, and signed by Father Philip of the Trinity, O.C.D., Superior General, no less than twelve pages were devoted to the theology of the Mystical Body.[145] Each of the main doctrinal affirmations of *MC* was presented in the form of a suggested draft for the forthcoming Council. At the end of the appropriate sections each of the principal doctrinal stances of *MC* was to be defined under anathema. Thus on the identity and membership questions, the first, second and sixth suggested definitions read as follows:

1. If anyone should affirm that the Mystical Body of Christ (which is the holy, apostolic, Catholic and Roman Church) is not one and undivided; let him be anathema.[146]

2. If anyone should affirm that the various groups of Christians although divided in faith and government among themselves are to be numbered among the members of the Mystical Body of Christ; let him be anathema....[147]

6. If anyone should affirm that among the members of the Church are not truly [*reapse*] to be counted those only who have received baptism [*lavacrum regenerationis*], who profess the true faith and who are subject to the same rule of government; let him be anathema.[148]

It is difficult to imagine stronger language. On the right side of the spectrum, i.e., on the side of positive acceptance of the doctrine of *MC*, theological reflection went from mild endorsement of the Oriental Insti-tute to the vibrantly affirmative stance of the Discalced Carmelites; on the left; i.e., on the side of negative but loyal criticism, similar shades of opinion were to be found. The theological Faculty of the Catholic Univer-sity of Lublin, where the future John Paul II had been a professor—we have seen above his comment as bishop—asked for an explanation of how non-Catholics who have supernatural faith or even the grace of charity are joined to the Catholic Church, since it is said that though they do not belong to the group (*compaginem*) they are nonetheless by an unconscious desire and longing related to the Mystical Body of the Redeemer.[149] And though Cardinal Alfrink in his own report had given general endorse-ment of Pius' position, the Catholic Faculty of Nijmegen demurred somewhat, asking that the mystery of the Church be defined in the context of the biblical idea of the Kingdom of God so that the spiritual (*pneumaticus*) character of the Church as well as its sacramental or visible nature (*indoles*) might be put in a brighter light. And it stated that since non-Catholics are no longer truly (*reapse*) among the faithful, it would be better to speak of degrees (*gradus*) of incorporation into the Church so that the concept of what a member is might be made clear.[150] The University of Ottawa (subsequently renamed Saint Paul University) stated that according to *MC* and *HG* the Mystical Body of Christ and the Catholic Church are one and the same thing but on this matter theologians had not yet reached a consensus.[151] On the correlative of membership, the faculty stated that the term "member by desire" (*membrum voto*) seemed too harsh, that it had been dropped from the proposed draft *De Ecclesia Christi* of Vatican I.[152] And how could it be harmonized with the Letter of the then Holy Office to the Archbishop of Boston (another indirect reference to the so-called Feeney case)?[153] The Faculties of Bonn and Fribourg issued similar demurrers.[154] But it was the Pontifical Faculty of Theology of Milan that took the most nuanced approach to the problem. In a report of twenty-nine pages, dated May 11, 1960, and signed by Father Carlo Figini, the Faculty devoted six penetrating pages to the theology of the Church.[155] In an oblique reference to Pius XII's position on the identity question, the Faculty said a more fitting explanation of revealed doctrine on the Church should focus on its inner nature (*intima natura*) rather than on its visible and external form.[156] And that would come about if attention were paid to the biblical images of the Church as body, spouse, and temple.[157] Here the Faculty anticipated the logically first step the Council was to take in departing from Pius on the question of identity; the biblical image of the Church as body, however powerful, was only one among others. And in an important footnote on the following page the Faculty said that the purpose of the magisterium in identifying the visible Church and the Mystical Body of Christ was to make obvious the dignity of the former. For if the two were not the same, the visible Church would run the risk of being considered a strictly (*simpliciter*) juridical reality.[158] That is why it cannot be said, so continued the note, that the justified who do not belong to the visible Church can attain salvation because they are, for all that, still members of the Mystical Body (or because they pertain to the Soul of the Church).[159] It was not however the intent of *MC* to deal harshly with non-Catholics. Much more significantly, in a longer footnote pertaining directly to the correlative on membership (*aggregatio*) the Faculty distinguished between legal membership (*secundum ius*) and membership in fact (*secundum rem*).[160] The latter is ontological or real and occurs whenever there is a link with the visible Church. Ideally each kind of membership calls for the other. It can however happen that they do not always coincide (*adaequari*), and then legal membership (*cooptatio*) can exist without the ontological reality or the ontological reality without the legal relationship.[161]

Departure from the teaching of Pius XII was obvious in this report. While it interpreted benignly his teaching on the matter of identity, the Faculty departed from it on the question of membership. In fact, on this latter point, it turned the papal position around completely. It was not those who had a legal relationship who were really (*reapse*) members of the Church but rather those who had an ontological one.

Such in general was the tone of the reports submitted in the Antepreparatory Period. To some extent, those from the theological faculties parallel those submitted by the bishops in that, just as the majority of bishops, so the majority of theological faculties did not bring up the problem of the identity question and the correlative of membership as affirmed in *Mystici corporis*. It is striking that few French bishops, who were to become such outspoken critics as early as the Preparatory Period and more so in the aula of St. Peter's, registered few negative comments.[162] Perhaps even more striking is the fact that neither the Institut Catholique de Lyon nor the Institut Catholique de Paris brought the matter up in the Antepreparatory Period. A number of factors might explain this reticence. Because the critique of *Mystici corporis* went back over a number of years, they may have considered the question as more or less settled. And they had yet to see an actual draft of a conciliar document. *Aeternus Unigeniti* (both *AU*-a and *AU*-b) was still in the future.

It is clear that *Mystici corporis* had caused a persistent debate within the Catholic Church and that critique of that document ranged from positive, at times uncritical acceptance to negative but loyal criticism. Manifestly, both bishops and theologians considered—and subsequent events were to vindicate them—that they were lending a helping hand to the ordinary papal magisterium and the coming Council. An outstanding example, the consideration of which I have had to postpone because of the apparent date of its publication, was the work of a German theologian whom some in Rome had begun to regard as dangerous.

Karl Rahner's Contribution

The German original of Rahner's article, translated under the title "Membership of the Church According to the Teaching of Pius XII's Encyclical '*Mystici corporis Christi*,'" appeared approximately six months before the opening of the Council.[163] It is not clear to me whether the article had been composed some years before and published only later or whether it had been written as a response to some of the problems voiced on the eve of the opening of the Council. In any case, Rahner's article is an excellent example of acceptance of the teaching of the papal magisterium combined with a faithful interpretation of its meaning *and* the suggestion of a solution to some of the problems *Mystici corporis* had raised on the identity question and the correlative of membership.

Rahner set out to answer three questions:

1. What does the encyclical say about conditions for membership in the Church?
2. What does it say about the possibility of union with Christ through grace for those who are not members of the Church, as determined in the answer to the first question?
3. In the context of the Church's nature, what further facts and what indications for further inquiry can be gleaned from the answer to the first two questions?[164]

As to the first question, the method consisted in determining what had been the teaching of the Church prior to *MC* and what *MC* had in fact intended to teach. Here he dealt essentially with the question of membership. Rahner inferred that if one prescinds from the question of the *excommunicatus vitandus* (q.v.), the explanation given by the encyclical of what it means to belong to the Church did not create a new situation in Catholic theology. Regarding the second question, he concluded that the encyclical said nothing beyond what had already been Catholic doctrine, for *MC* did not exclude the possibility of justification and salvation for those who, through no fault of their own, do not belong to the Church in the full and strict sense. The peculiarity (*Eigenart*) of *MC* lay in its predication of Church and Mystical Body of Christ as synonymous, thus using those terms in a less equivocal way (*eindeutiger*) than they had been used hitherto in Catholic theology.[165] Rahner, like the theological Faculty of Milan, here interpreted the Pope's intention benignly, saying that the encyclical wished to remove an error that in the context of discussions of reunion had been insinuated among Catholics; the error, namely, that a human being may belong to the Church or at least to the Mystical Body of Christ *no matter how he or she stands in relation to the Catholic Church.*[166] But, continued Rahner, *Mystici corporis* as a whole makes the visible Church on earth, not the Mystical Body of Christ, the subject of its declarations. That fact was to give Rahner the opening he needed in order to approach the third of the questions listed above, the one most relevant to the kind of dissatisfaction that has been noted among certain bishops and theological faculties.

Here Rahner's starting point was the recognition of two problems: (1) the notion of the Church at the root of the encyclical and (2) the tension between two polarities, (a) the necessity of the Church for salvation and (b) the possibility of salvation for those outside it.[167] He here noted a tension within *MC* itself, for it defined membership in the Church in juridical terms while stating unequivocally that it would be a rationalistic error to see nothing more in the Church than a purely juridical, social entity.[168] A solution to this apparent contradiction should provide the possibility of a better understanding of the Church's nature. Here Rahner took up again an analogy he had touched upon earlier, namely, that between Church and sacrament. I shall call it Analogy (A); its fundamental concepts may be diagrammed as follows:

Analogy (A)

(a) sacrament   (c) Church
                              ::
(b) the grace of the sacrament   (d) grace of full membership

It is essential to grasp the full import of Rahner's presuppositions. The above analogy is one of proportion—the term does not occur in Rahner's article—in the sense that the first ratio is meant to disclose the meaning of the second. The term which is heuristically prior to all the others is the Catholic notion of sacrament. At least indirectly traceable to the Christ-event, a sacrament is not merely a symbol that points to a reality; under certain conditions it brings that reality about. That is to say: A sacrament signifies what it effects and effects what it signifies unless the recipient places an obex (e.g., by way of unworthy dispositions). Thus sacrament functions on two levels, that of sign (*sacramentum*) and that of grace conferred or conferrable (*res sacramenti*). Hence, just as it is possible to receive the sign without receiving the grace signified, so it is possible to receive the grace without receiving the sign. The basis of these possibilities is that though the Godhead is always faithful—those who receive the sign with proper dispositions by that very fact (*ex opere operato*) receive the grace signified—the Godhead cannot be bound or limited by that which is creaturely. In the present economy of salvation, a human being is meant to receive both the sign and the grace; but from that one cannot argue that those who through no fault of their own do not receive the sign are therefore bereft of grace. With these theological presuppositions in the background, Rahner's analysis should be read carefully, for to the twofold notion of sacrament corresponds a twofold notion of Church (which is not the same as a notion of two Churches):

> The Church is in a certain sense the Proto-Sacrament; this means, how- ever, that she is, in her whole concrete, visible and juridically verifiable appearance, a real sign and embodiment of the salvific will of God and of the grace of Christ. That is, she has a bodily nature which as such possesses an unmistakable, fully determined and juridically determinable form, and which actually causes the grace which it renders present in the historical here and now; *and yet that bodily nature remains essentially different from this divine grace which will always be the sovereign mystery of God's freedom and can never be subdued by man.*[169]

The phrase, "...and which can never be subdued by man...," is of immense importance. For after having explained the difference between a fully valid sign and *a fully valid sign which is also an (instrumental) cause of grace*, Rahner says, after having pointed out earlier the parallel between sacrament and Church:

> The ultimate reason for this distinction of the two notions of "Church" is easy to understand; only if there are Sacraments which really cause grace, can there be a genuinely "incarnational" presence of God and of his grace in the world of man here below where he is imprisoned in space and time and in the "flesh." *Only if there are (in principle) also merely valid Sacraments which are Sacraments and yet are empty of grace, can the grace of God remain free and beyond the ravishing grasp of man which would turn it into magic.*[170]

Within the framework of Rahner's highly refined language the classical objection *nihil finiti infiniti capax* or its variant *nothing relative can contain the absolute* becomes not simply irrelevant but constitutes *ignoratio elenchi*. In classical Thomistic terms, what Rahner was getting at is that an instrumental cause is essentially different from an efficient cause and does not embody (if *embody* means *limit* or *contain*) the efficient cause that uses it. This is the notion of *sacramentum* that lies at the root of *MC*. The encyclical does not explore it but presumes awareness of it on the part of Catholic readers.

How did Rahner's analysis advance the argument and move beyond *Mystici corporis* thereby "correcting" its perspective? A sacrament is a visible sign just as the Church is a visible Church. Before there was the Church, there was the people of God; and before there was the people of God, there was the human race. With due regard for problems flowing from a theory of polygenesis, Rahner stated that the human race constitutes a visible oneness.[171] A given human being does not freely will its condition but he or she can freely will to accept it. Hence, a clear distinction must be made between what can be *freely willed* and what can be *freely done*:

> Insofar as the finite freedom of man presupposes nature as its condition of possibility, the expression of man's act of freedom in his historical visible nature implies always essentially an acceptance of "impressions." It means that what is his very own always reveals itself essentially also by accepting what is alien, *by accepting the imposed determination of his nature.*[172]

The real oneness of the human race, which Rahner had emphasized as a *visible* unity, is determined in the concrete also by the Incarnation of the Word of God.[173] Hence, to the extent that a human being as a spiritual person accomplishes his or her "nature" by the total decision about himself or herself; i.e., to the extent that he or she freely accepts or freely does not accept the full reality of the human condition whatever that may be, to that extent a human being therefore implicitly takes or does not take a position for or against his or her supernatural calling to a participation with the triune Godhead itself.[174] Thus:

> By the fact that the word of God became man humanity has already in advance become ontologically the real sanctification of individual men by grace and also the people of God...[175] In as far as mankind thus "consecrated" is a real unity from the very start there already exists a "people of God" which extends as far as humanity itself...[176] This people of God exists before its juridical and social organization into what we call "Church," somewhat as a definite historical people exists before its organization into a state on the plane of this world.[177]

Both the people of God and the Church lie on the visible, historical plane of reality that precedes the free decision of each human being. That is why whenever a human being totally accepts the concrete reality of his or her nature, in a free act of supernatural justification of faith and love, "...membership of the people of God becomes the expression of this justifying act."[178] That act is oriented toward the *votum Ecclesiae*, a (usually) unconscious desire to be a member of the Church. And precisely "...because man as a concrete, bodily human being is a blood-relation of the Christ, the *votum Ecclesiae* does not at all take place in a purely extra-sacramental and invisible interiority of grace."[179]

The analogy that Rahner had developed in the first part of his answer to the third question had thus been broadened:

Analogy (B)

(a) sacramentum	(c) People of God	(e) Church
::	::	
(b) res sacramenti	(d) human nature graced by the Incarnation	(f) grace of full membership

Just as when one receives a sacrament, one receives the grace of the sacrament provided one does not place an obstacle to grace, so if one accepts fully one's human condition, one is already involved in sacrament. One's link with human nature graced by the Incarnation constitutes a visible sign that, precisely because of a blood relation with Christ, is a source of grace to those who place no obstacle. Oneness with graced human nature whereby one belongs to the people of God contains at least implicitly the *votum Ecclesiae*. At this point, a distinction must not be overlooked. "For whenever man is consciously and freely guilty of excluding this membership of the Church in the proper sense from his intention, he opposes himself to his membership of the people of God, so that even the latter no longer profits him for salvation but only for damnation."[180] According to the same analogy, it is possible to be a member of the Church and simultaneously be in a state of serious sin. But for Rahner it is equally clear "...with regard to the full notion of the Church as giving grace, that the sinner does not belong to the Church to the same extent and in the same sense as the justified member of the Church."[181]

Rahner's analysis of the second problem in the light of *MC* made comprehensible and at the same time maintained a tension between two apparently contradictory Catholic dogmas: the possibility of being saved outside the Catholic Church and the necessity (by a contingent necessity of means) of the Church for salvation. Rahner's solution implies a theory of stratification (*Mehrschichtigkeit*) of membership within the nature of the Church as sacramental sign.[182] The stratification is between the Church as something visible as a sign of union with God, and the Church as humanity consecrated by the Incarnation. Rahner claimed that *MC* dealt only with the first and left to the theologians the elaboration of the second.

On the identity question Rahner concluded that nothing in *MC* indicated it was no longer possible to use the term *Mystical Body of Christ* in a sense wider than that used in that encyclical, for the purpose of the identification between the Mystical Body of Christ and the Catholic Church had been to ward off the error mentioned above.[183] On the membership question, two factors must be borne in mind. First, Rahner agreed that non-Catholics are not members of the *visible* Church—membership in the visible Church pertains to the Church as valid sign. Second, if Rahner was correct, then his reflections amounted to an implicit correction of *MC*. For it would no longer be accurate to say that those who are justified and who are in a state of grace are *merely related* to the Mystical Body of Christ *inscio quodam desiderio ac voto* as Pius XII had maintained. One would have to say that "...the justified person who belongs [or is 'referred'] to the Church without being a member of it, belongs 'invisibly' to the *visible* Church by grace and has a *visible* relation to this Church."[184] That is a very different nuance and recalled a point Michalon had made ten years previously.[185]

FROM THE PREPARATORY PERIOD TO THE OPENING OF THE COUNCIL

Within apparently a matter of weeks after the appearance of Rahner's article, the Preparatory Commission received for discussion *Aeternus Unigeniti* (*AU*-a) antecedent to the same document distributed to the Council Fathers in late November 1962 (*AU*-b).[186] On May 8, 1962, the Preparatory Commission discussed its first two chapters, which alone are relevant here. Regarding the question of identity, the wording of the draft was, with one slight exception, the same as that discussed during the first session; [187] regarding the correlative question of membership, its wording was substantially the same as that of *MC*. Thus there is no need to reproduce the texts here.

Prior to the beginning of the discussion, the Jesuit, Sébastien Tromp, read the report of Cardinal Ottaviani.[188] It was stated that two fundamental principles had guided the Commission in preparing the draft. The first was that Christ wills salvation through the union of each individual with the person of Christ (in the light of postconciliar Christological controversy, the word used in Ottaviani's report is interesting: He spoke of the *theandric* person of Christ).[189] He went on to affirm that on earth such union does not take place except in a social organism that Christ had called his Church. The second principle was that there is no real distinction between the Catholic Church and the Mystical Body of Christ.[190]

Since the *Acta et Documenta* indicate that Tromp read Ottaviani's opening address, it is not known whether Ottaviani was there at the beginning. Present were no less than thirty-nine Cardinals, twenty bishops, two Eastern Patriarchs, and three priests. Of these, eight Cardinals, three bishops, and one priest addressed the issues. No less than six Cardinals voiced dissatisfaction with the way the draft addressed the identity and/or the membership question; two of the three bishops did likewise, as did Father Sépinski, the only priest who spoke. It is unnecessary to analyze in detail the remarks of each speaker. I shall here limit myself to three.

Cardinal Liénart was the first to speak. He began by noting that the definition of the nature of the Church was, in his opinion, the most important matter to be treated in the Council.[191] It was his firm belief that the Church, by its nature, is the Mystical Body of Christ. He added that he believed with all his heart the (Roman) Catholic Church is the true Church founded by Jesus Christ upon the Apostles and Prophets as a visible society, one, holy, universal and apostolic; intended (*destinatam*) for the careful guarding and spreading of revelation and the bestowal of the fruits of redemption to all human beings.[192] But, so it seemed to him, the Council could not "solemnly profess" that the Roman Church and the Mystical Body of Christ are one and the same thing.[193] The rest of Liénart's critique was substantially the same as that given some months later in the aula of St. Peter's. I have summarized it above.[194]

The most incisive speech was that by Cardinal Bea. He too noted that of all the questions to be treated by the forthcoming Council those pertaining to the Church were of the greatest importance. The Secretariat for Christian Unity had treated them in a very accurate manner and had several times, he said, asked the Theological Commission that a mixed commission be set up, but the request had always been denied.[195] Nevertheless, his commission had turned over its finding to the Theological Commission whose draft—the very one before the Preparatory Commission—had indeed reflected some of its orientations (Bea was grateful) although many others had not been considered. Hence Bea felt obliged to treat them more fully now.[196]

Bea touched on a number of isues but did not directly confront the question of identity. Regarding the correlative of membership, he said the draft before the Commission gave the impression that the term *member* was the decisive element in the whole affair, something that was surely not the case.[197] It would be better first to speak of the necessity of the Church for salvation, and to show *how* the Church is necessary: Most people today attain salvation outside it.[198] Furthermore, a non-Catholic professor of systematic theology had told him it was difficult to understand how, when teaching about the confines of the Church, the Pope (Pius XII) could neglect the salvific force of valid baptism as though it did not exist: How could baptism be valid and at the same time inefficacious in incorporating into Christ? (We have seen how the Commission was later to treat this objection.) That author, said Bea, was only one of many who regretted the manner of speaking that had been adopted.[199]

Bea suggested that a distinction be made between salvation as *gift* and salvation as *means*.[200] Salvation as *gift* is the grace of God given to those who are properly disposed. For salvation in this sense at least one thing is required, namely, that a human being believe in God and that God rewards those who seek him (Heb. 11:6). Salvation as *means* is faith, the sacraments, the precepts, the pastors and the community of the brethren, in brief, all those things that make the Church an instrument of salvation.[201] The Catholic Church, as a means of salvation, is not *absolutely* necessary in the sense that God in his kindness and wisdom did not wish to impose on human beings the unjust yoke of having to accept in fact something of which they have not even heard.[202] What is required is the disposition to accept the Church if one knows about it and is aware that it is the ordinary means of salvation.

With this as background, it could now be asked, said Bea, just who are members of the Church. It is to be noted that the Church in the New Testament is not presented only as a "body" that has "members" but that it is also spoken of as kingdom, vine, family, house, people, etc.[203] These are metaphors but it is better to go to the reality itself. That reality is the fact that each religious community and each human being is related to the Church in a *different* way (*vario modo*). The alternative ("*in voto*," "*in re*") recently introduced because of discussions after the encyclical is disputed and even now authors are not in agreement.[204] Hence that alternative is not suitable for a dogmatic constitution. To speak in terms whereby non-Catholics, in one general formula, are members of the Church by desire is in fact rather jejune. It is true, but it is like saying that humanity is divided into Americans and non-Americans: Those who do not have American citizenship may aspire to it![205] Therefore, Bea suggested the following as a working text:

> "Those who completely and in fact adhere to the Catholic Church as the means of salvation may be said to be its members in a full and proper sense." But those elements, those by which one is constituted a member of the Church according to the full meaning of the term do not belong exclusively to Catholics. For many non-Catholics have been cleansed in the waters of baptism and profess the true faith though not in a complete manner and they are even subject to pastors, according to the ministry which to them appears legitimate...All those who live in divine grace and profess theological faith, hope and charity remain in the same Spirit which is the soul of the Mystical Body of Christ. They are therefore rightly called our "brothers" though "separated" from us, and "sons" of the Church, as the Sovereign Pontiff calls them in the Apostolic Constitution *Humanae salutis*.[206]

Father Sépinski, Superior General of the Order of Friars Minor, is the next speaker to whom I would turn my attention.[207] In regard to the question of membership, he said that the meaning of the term *truly (reapse) members* was members in a full sense (*integraliter*).[208] What the encyclical dealt with was full and absolute membership in the Church; it did not deal with the further problem of an invisible or visible way of belonging to the Church, although to some extent the matter could be discussed.[209] In Sépinski's opinion, it would be better to speak more clearly and more urgently of the various categories by which human beings may be more or less fully members of the Church.[210]

At the end of this discussion, Cardinal Ottaviani spoke personally, in contrast to the beginning of the meeting when his report had been read by Sébastien Tromp. After summing up most of the points that had been made and of which he approved, he launched into a critique of Liénart's observations, saying that the latter's remarks proceeded, perhaps, from a certain misunderstanding: When in the draft it was stated that the Mystical Body of Christ is the Catholic Church, the Church was to be understood in its fullness; that is, as embracing the Church militant—a possibly better mode of expression might be the "Pilgrim Church," the Church suffering, and the Church triumphant, in which last were certainly to be found those who, though not completely (*perfecte*) members of the Church militant, died nonetheless in the grace of God.[211] It would be false to say that the draft identified the Church militant with the Mystical Body of Christ. He then expressed agreement with much that Cardinals Léger, Spellman, and Ruffini had said, as well as Cardinals König and Döpfner, and with much that had been said by Cardinal Bea.[212] But some of Bea's remarks impressed him as being dangerous, though he appreciated Bea's zeal. It would be dangerous to say, as it had been said in a particular Conference, that as soon as one is baptized one is a member of the Mystical Body of Christ, though not a member of the Church. To say that from the pulpit (*coram massa populi*) would be extremely dangerous. The Catholic Church and the Mystical Body of Christ are the same thing. The separated brethren should not be misled on this point. At the same time, they should not be given the impression that remaining where they are is a matter of indifference.[213] That outside the Church there is no salvation is after all a point well taken, in the sense, of course, in which that maxim was explained in the letter of the Holy Office to the Archbishop at Boston.[214]

As far as I can see, Bea's suggestion (that non-Catholic Christians in a state of grace may be said to belong to the Soul of the Church) is fully in harmony with what I understand to be the internal logic of *Mystici corporis*.[215] But he did not expressly state that he was basing this suggestion on the inner logic of that encyclical. That he was in fact doing so however seems implied by his reference to *Humanae salutis* with which Pope John XXIII officially convoked the Council.

In the voting that followed, no less than fifty-three members of the Preparatory Commission voted with qualified acceptance (i.e., *iuxta modum*) for the draft as discussed on May 8, 1962; i.e., they would accept it on the condition that certain changes were made in it. The suggestions made by Liénart, König, Döpfner, Léger, and Bea were those most frequently mentioned. Of the six Cardinals who had voiced dissatisfaction with the draft's perspective, only two, Liénart and Léger, had faced the identity question head-on, the others limiting their remarks primarily to various aspects of the membership question. It is interesting to note that Cardinal Montini, the future Paul VI, had not spoken. But when the time came to cast his vote, he said that matters brought up by Liénart, König, Döpfner, Bea, Brown and Ottaviani ought to be examined more fully: The draft should therefore be sent back for revision.[216] And Cardinal Siri, an implacable foe of collegiality, was surprisingly open on this matter.[217]

Since most of the discussion of the two points around which this part of my study is oriented had turned on the membership question rather than on that of identity, it was to be expected that on November 23, 1962, in the draft *Aeternus Unigeniti* (*A U*-b) then presented to the Council Fathers for debate, numbers 7 and 2 of chapters I and II respectively would be almost entirely rewritten. But only the wording was to be changed. Both on the identity question and the correlative question of membership the orientation of *AU*-b remained essentially that of *Mystici corporis*.

Hence the debate; hence the drama that, as we have seen, was to follow.

General Overview

It should be obvious that in the issues under discussion the more significant modalities of reception seem to have been those by Catholic theologians who, out of deep concern for the Church and not infrequently without a personal price to pay from the point of view of obedience when they were silenced, had submitted the teaching of the ordinary papal magisterium to careful scrutiny. Had such work not preceded, it is doubtful that the reports of a minority among the bishops and theological faculties in the Antepreparatory and Preparatory Periods would have been what they in fact were. It is clear that in these matters appropriate criticism led to development, reversal and/or modification of papal teaching. Paul VI in exercising the Petrine function within Catholicism confirmed his brothers in almost every case.[218]

The modalities as a whole covered a rather wide spectrum. On the one hand, they were dominated by uncritical acceptance by most of the Catholic Church, a statement so historically obvious it would be tedious to document it. On the other hand, a small, well-informed minority provided the wedge that in the end succeeded in opening the windows of the Catholic Church at Vatican II. On the surface of things, the critiques of the minority appear to be negative; in the end, they stand revealed as consummate loyalty. At times, as in the case of Dupanloup, whose move was crucial, they took the form of attempting to assign to papal teaching its proper theological note; at others, as in the case of John Courtney Murray, they took the additional form of demonstrating that the internal logic of the papal position led to conclusions quite different from those officially held by the Popes; at still other times, as in the case of Morel and Michalon, they took the form of showing the inadequacy of the papal position, or as in the case of Rahner, of broadening and discreetly "correcting" it. No amount of unfair criticism could ever succeed in casting Dupanloup or these theologians and their peers as rebels. Quite clearly, they saw themselves involved in a cooperative enterprise with the ordinary papal magisterium. In Troeltsch's terms there can be no doubt that in the generations prior to the opening of the Second Vatican Council, *Church as association* was an intimate part of *Church as institution*. The implications for Catholic ecclesiology can no longer be overlooked.

PART THREE
THE CHURCH AS *KOINŌNÍA*
ON THE LEVEL OF WORD

Chapter VII
PRELIMINARY SYNTHESIS

It is time for a partial assessment. Though I cannot at this point delineate those conclusions with which my inquiry will terminate, the historical analysis pursued in the foregoing pages suffices to make certain initial inferences that flow from the data therein. I am thus dealing with the results of my findings in parts one and two.

This chapter is divided into three sections. The first states the frame of reference and terminology used; the second the conclusions themselves; the third discusses the sense in which the Catholic Church in the context of the seven issues I have analyzed seems to have manifested the marks of κοινωνία. Whenever appropriate, I shall indicate the basis of my conclusions in tradition and/or their parallels in the New Testament.

Frame of Reference and Terminology

Our task may perhaps be facilitated by adapting an image from Schleiermacher.[1] Let us think of a number of concentric circles of which the center represents Christ; the first concentric circle, the ordinary papal magisterium; the second, the bishops; the third, ministerial priests; the fourth professional theologians (ordained or lay); the fifth, Catholics who consistently make whole-hearted efforts to understand and live the faith; the sixth, Catholics whose commitment to Christ and his Church is less than total. Movements from the first concentric circle I shall call *eccyclic*; those from the periphery toward the first concentric circle, *eiscyclic*.[2] Looking at the data from this perspective, one discerns eiscyclic movements approved by the ordinary papal magisterium. Examples are the exploration of inculturation theory taken up by Pius XII and Catholic reflection on social questions that found its way into *Rerum novarum*. In these two cases, the movement was eiscyclic before it was eccyclic. Such was largely the case also with the theology of the Mystical Body of Christ, one of the differences being that Pius XII, in attempting to purify the concept of some of its excessive expressions (particularly in Germany), ended up like Pius XI in identifying the Mystical Body of Christ with the (Roman) Catholic Church. In two cases, the movement was essentially eccyclic. Such was the case with papal teaching on religious freedom and ideal Church-state relations. Paradoxically, papal teaching on the episcopal office in *Fidei donum* was an eccyclic movement with little eiscyclic basis for it prior to 1957. In the area of doctrinal development as reflected in most of the seven issues explored above, the laity with the exception of Montalembert do not seem to have played a predominant role. Hence my attention in what follows will be focused on the first, second and fourth concentric circles (i.e., on the interplay between the Roman Bishop on the one hand and bishops/theologians on the other).

When one looks at the data within a modified phenomenological perspective, eccyclic and eiscyclic movements may be further distinguished from the point of view of their original thrust. Thus, though the position of Pius IX on the relation between Catholicism and non-Christian religions presents a problem that I shall continue to bracket for the moment, there is a great difference between eiscyclic movements like those taken up in *Rerum novarum* and *Evangelii praecones* as over against an eiscyclic movement like that taken up in *Mystici corporis*. For in the former, papal teaching was eventually well received and found its way into the Council documents whereas in the latter it was modified *by the rest of the Church and with the full approval of the Roman Bishop* only as modified found its way into the council documents. The seven doctrinal issues with which I have been dealing may therefore be subdistinguished according to the following schema:

eccyclic α: the teaching of Pius XII on the role of bishops and its influence on the development of collegiality

eccyclic β: papal teaching on religious freedom and ideal Church-state relations

eiscyclic α: papal social teaching and the teaching of Pius XII on possible truth or good in non-Christian religions

eiscyclic β: papal teaching on the identity question and the correlative of membership

In a cooperative enterprise that would attempt to analyze completely the manner in which doctrine had developed in Catholicism not only throughout its history but even within the limited period with which we are concerned, further distinctions, inasmuch as the papacy was directly involved, would have to be made. Thus there are eiscyclic movements that, upon reproval by the Holy See, simply seem to have died out.[3] For my present purpose, which is to deal with the data uncovered in parts one and two, the above distinctions will suffice. In all cases we have to do with the teaching of the ordinary papal magisterium and the modalities' of its reception. The terms *alpha* and *beta* serve to distinguish modalities of reception of eccyclic movements or of eiscyclic movements once they have become eccyclic, while the terms *eccyclic* and *eiscyclic* are used to highlight the thrust from which a movement originated. As a rule of thumb, the reader may simply recall that a *beta* movement, whether eccyclic or eiscyclic, means that the teaching of the ordinary papal magisterium in a particular instance had been modified and/or reversed because of the manner in which it had been received and that the same or a subsequent Roman Bishop approved the change. The reader will note that the case of Pius IX and non-Christian religions is not listed above. I shall take it up below.

Initial Findings

The following conclusions seem justified on the basis of the analysis made in parts one and two:

First, *one of the ways in which doctrine seems to have developed within the Catholic Church from the time of Pius IX up to the end of the Second*

Vatican Council was through the interplay of two forces; namely, (1) *the authentic, authoritative, non-infallible doctrinal pronouncements of the ordinary papal magisterium on the one hand and* (2) *the modalities whereby these pronouncements were received by the rest of the Catholic Church on the other.* This conclusion I shall henceforth refer to as *pivotal* because around it revolve most of those stated below. It will of course come as no surprise to the working Catholic theologian. What differentiates it from more general positions embraced elsewhere[4] is its relevance to the minimalist and maximalist questions and the fact that its consequences for Catholic ecclesiology in today's ecumenical setting have never, as far as I am aware, been explicitly drawn. I shall have more to say in this regard in Chap. IX. For the moment, it may be noted that while the pivotal result of my inquiry does not mean that dissent from doctrinal positions taken by the Roman Bishops should be the usual pattern, it nonetheless does suggest something about the nature of the Church as expressed below.[5]

This is the proper context in which to face the initially perplexing problem which the negative outlook of Pius IX on possible truth or good in non-Christian religions constitutes. It will be recalled that in Text A of *Qui pluribus* the Pope seems to have excluded the possibility of at least some truth or good in non-Christian religions as though there could ever be any participation of justice with iniquity, light with darkness, or Christ with Belial (2 Cor. 6:14-15). The problem is precisely this: Though the data suggest that one may speak of modalities of reception in the sense that the manner in which the teaching of Pius IX was received seems to have been essentially positive,[6] how may one do so in the context of eventual correction of the papal position if neither the missiologists in the development of inculturation theory nor the Fathers of Vatican II manifested any explicit awareness of papal teaching prior to Pius XII?[7] From the solution of this enigma emerges, I suggest, a parenthetical but no less important lesson for theorists of doctrinal development within Catholicism. It is true, as I argued in Chap. II, that the manner of receiving Text A of *Qui pluribus* seems to have been one of uncritical acceptance, for the force of that stance had not been lost on succeeding generations, as the *Dublin Review*, *L'Ami du Clergé*, Père Choupin and others attest. These constitute, as I have said, prima facie modalities of reception; they were not, however, ultimate. Favorable reception of Text A seems to have extended at least from the time of *Quanta cura* and the Syllabus up through the first quarter of this century. Without explicit reference to Text A, a contrary movement headed by the missiologists, confirmed by Pius XII, and culminating in the reaffirmation of an ancient Catholic positive tradition by Vatican II takes place and does so with seemingly little difficulty. However pervasive antecedent conditioning by the manuals; however widely read the *Dublin Review*, *L'Ami du Clergé* and Père Choupin's book, positive reception that one finds there and elsewhere seems to have been insufficient to make the view propounded by Pius IX "take."

Therein lies, I suggest, the ultimate manner wherein Text A of *Qui pluribus* had been received. How else explain the fact that the missiologists, in their efforts to reinvigorate *Akkommodationsprinzip*, were either unaware of, or at least did not consider themselves bound by, the doctrinal thrust perceptible in Text A of *Qui pluribus*? May one simply argue that they felt Pius IX's position on truth or good discernible in non-Christian religions had been taken parenthetically and hence was not to be considered relevant? The evidence seems to diminish that likelihood. That the teaching of Pius IX had not really "caught on" despite superficial indications to the contrary seems, with due regard for the difference of emphasis between *Ad gentes* and *Nostra aetate*, to be the best explanation of why the Council Fathers had no significant problem with the idea of possible truth or good in non-Christian religions. At the very most it may be said that they suggested some restraint in the application of *Akkommodationsprinzip*.

But why, it may be asked, did not the teaching of Pius IX "take"? Something much deeper seems to have been operative all along. Catholic instincts reaching back to Irenaeus and Justin Martyr were simply too profound and succeeded in eradicating from official Catholicism the stance of 2 Cor. 6:14-15 as interpreted by Pius IX in *Qui pluribus* and reflected in subsequent papal documents up to but excluding Pius XII. Catholic instincts that the Church's attitude should be positive in this regard were dormant, not dead. And the Council Fathers had for years been reciting the Johannine Prologue as the scripture reading with which the old Tridentine Mass usually ended. In that passage, John 1:9 may have constituted a *lex-orandi lex-credendi* experience that could hardly have been harmonized with the perspective of Text A. Despite the gray in an area of Church history still to be adequately researched[8] (for which the pages that constitute Chap. II, it hardly need be repeated, are in no way intended to substitute even in outline), this ultimate, less easily documented way in which the teaching of Pius IX seems to have been received constitutes the basis of the lesson to be gleaned from the history and fate of Text A. At the very least that lesson amounts to this: *Initial, even relatively long-term positive reception of a papal stance on a doctrinal matter is insufficient to cause it to prevail if it is contrary to a deeply imbedded*

Catholic tradition. The ultimate modalities whereby Text A of *Qui pluribus* was received amount in the end to its implicit rejection. Thus, while providing an important lesson, the trajectory of Pius IX's teaching in this regard not only does not detract from the pivotal conclusion stated above but rather confirms it.

Second, *neither acceptance of eccyclic movements by the rest of the Catholic Church nor acceptance of eiscyclic movements by the Roman Bishop resulted in defining these doctrines as dogma.* (This applies *mutatis mutandis* to the doctrines of the Immaculate Conception and the Assumption on their way to becoming dogmas. There the process was, as we shall see in Chap. VIII, somewhat different.)

Regarding eiscyclic movements that subsequently found their way into the teaching of the ordinary papal magisterium, approval by the Roman Bishop did no more than establish their viability as *doctrine.* That is to say: These movements were no longer merely the teaching of theologians but now enjoyed official status within the Catholic Church. Their theological note was henceforth at least *doctrina catholica* in the strict sense (q.v.). Yet the difference between the fate of *alpha* and *beta* movements was assuredly vast, though both were once *doctrina catholica* in this narrower sense. Regarding acceptance of eccyclic movements by the rest of the Catholic Church, the same *mutatis mutandis* applies.

The basis for these realized (*réalisé; verwirklichtet*) possibilities has its roots in the tradition. The fact that the Roman Bishop teaches a particular doctrine (henceforth, for the most part, p) and that the universal episcopate takes up the same teaching in union with him does not in itself mean that p belongs to the substance of the faith. Conversely, that Catholicism's magisterial officers from appropriate interchange with their people teach p; that subsequently the Roman Bishop(s) approve the teaching of their brother bishops in this regard does not necessarily mean that the charism of infallibility has been operative in the ordinary universal magisterium. *For the Church does not teach univocally.* Some doctrines it teaches as safe or probable; others as the common opinion of theologians. And still others as *doctrina catholica* in the strict sense or, say, as *de fide divina et catholica.*[9] I shall return to this point in Chap. IX where I shall offer a brief comment on the ordinary universal magisterium.[10]

Third, *papal criticism of eiscyclic movements challenged their proponents to reflect on the possible doctrinal inadequacy of their positions, while conversely, criticism of eccyclic movements challenged the ordinary papal magisterium to the same.* Thus Leo XIII challenged Catholics to work out an internally coherent doctrine on the social question before incorporating it into *Rerum novarum*. And Pius XII in *Mystici corporis* effectively challenged Catholics involved in the incipient ecumenical movement of the day to reflect on the nature of the Church's unity, not to neglect to pay due attention to its visible nature, rejecting as far as the spiritual life is concerned anything which smacked of quietism. Yet in regard to the *beta* movements with which we have been concerned in part two, "talking back" to the ordinary papal magisterium was an ultimately successful attempt to ask the ordinary papal magisterium to rethink its position on these doctrinal issues.

Fourth, it may be said that *the* alpha *movements were characterized by* (1) *a Petrine function element,* (2) *associative elements,* (3) *occasional corrections by the Petrine minister followed by subsequent approval resulting in* (4) *more adequately formulated doctrine.*

Fifth, *the* beta *movements may be said to have been characterized by* (1) *a Petrine function element,* (2) *a withstanding-Cephas element,* (3) *a mutual dependence element, resulting in* (4) *more adequately formulated doctrine.*

Associative elements manifested themselves in different ways; in the *alpha* movements, as cooperation; in the *beta* movements, as mutual dependence. The former is sufficiently clear from what preceded the teaching of the ordinary papal magisterium; e.g., much of what Leo XIII said in *Rerum novarum* was an eiscyclic movement before it became eccyclic. It is mutual dependence in the *beta* movements that needs further clarification.

This element becomes less obscure if one introduces a distinction between doctrinal development considered as in a state of becoming (*in fieri*) as opposed to the same concept considered as in a state of being terminated (*in facto esse*). On the one hand, it is beyond doubt that in the *beta* movements under discussion, "talking back" on the part of a minority of theologians was reflected during the Antepreparatory Period in the reports of bishops and theological faculties, in the debates of the Preparatory Period, in those of the Council in session, and finally in the conciliar texts prior to their being promulgated by Paul VI. This aspect of development has to do with development considered as in a state of becoming.

But it is equally clear that had not the doctrinal positions taken by the Council been approved by the Roman Bishop, they would not today be Catholic teaching.[11] At best they would be like those left hanging by the First Vatican Council, a suggestion of what might have been. This aspect of development has to do with development considered as in a state of being terminated. The element of mutual dependence merges when both aspects of development are taken into account.

Sixth, *in doctrinal development considered* in fieri, *cooperation (as in the* alpha *movements) and respectful, responsible "talking back" (as in the* beta *movements) were the constants; in doctrinal development considered* in facto esse, *the constant was the Petrine function both in the* alpha *and in the* beta *movements.*

Seventh, regarding the *alpha* movements, *a partial parallel in the New Testament is discernible between* (1) *the Petrine function* (Matt. 16:18-19; Luke 22:31-33; John 21:15-17; Acts 15:6-12a), (2) *associative elements* (Matt. 18:18-19; Acts 15:12b-21) *and* (3) *more adequately formulated doctrine* (Acts 15:23-29). *There is no parallel to* (4) *correction by the Petrine function.* Here those who judge that the ordinary papal magisterium (as distinct from the manner of its exercise) is a legitimate development of the Petrine ministry as discernible in the New Testament documents would answer that a corrective role by the Petrine function is implicitly affirmed in principle since the power of the keys in Matt. 16:18 is given to Peter alone and that there is no evidence to suggest that the *Sitz im Leben in der Kirche* as reflected in the New Testament amounted to a denial that the Petrine function might have a doctrinally corrective role.[12] Indeed, recent dialogues between Catholics and some non-Catholic Christians have recognized that possibility under certain conditions, specifically in regard to the Roman Bishop.[13] Yet it must be conceded that though in Gal. 2:11 Paul called Peter "Cephas" (the Aramaic term for "Rock") not "Simon" thereby reflecting the oral tradition that later came to be written in Matt. 16:18, Paul cannot be said on the basis of that text to be speaking of the Petrine function as currently understood by the Catholic Church.

Eighth, regarding the *beta* movements, *a partial parallel in the New Testament is discernible between* (1) *the Petrine function* (Matt. 16:18-19; Luke 22:31-33; John 21:15-17; Acts 15:6-12a), (2) *a withstanding-Cephas element* (Gal. 2:11), (3) *a mutual dependence element* (1 Cor. 12:21) *and* (4) *more adequately formulated doctrine* (Acts 15:23-29). The withstanding-Cephas element however is somewhat problematic. Paul in Gal. 2:11 does not withstand Cephas because of the latter's doctrine but because of the latter's conduct.[14] By contrast, in the *beta* movements isolated above, it was the doctrine, not the conduct of the ordinary papal magisterium, that was subjected to criticism.

Despite the fact that the parallels are not perfect, and that they do not by themselves establish Roman claims relative to the function of the Roman Bishop within Christianity, they do suggest that what had happened in development in the seven issues with which I have dealt in parts one and two is not totally outside the limits of New Testament thinking.

Ninth, *reception was a reciprocal movement.* It was not only a question of how the rest of the Catholic Church received the teaching of its Petrine minister; it was also a question of how the Petrine minister received the teaching of the rest of the Catholic Church. For certainly—to recall just two of the issues with which we have dealt—in the case of *Rerum novarum,* Leo XIII listened carefully to what the local Churches were saying before accepting the basic thrust of that eiscyclic movement, just as the Roman Bishop had to approve the modification of the teaching of his predecessors in the religious freedom question before that new position could become Catholic doctrine. It should be fairly obvious that reception is not a one-way street, a point frequently overlooked in contemporary discussion.[15]

Tenth, *associative elements (as cooperation) isolated in the* alpha *movements and associative elements (as mutual dependence) isolated in the* beta *movements suggest that Catholicism as an institution, inasmuch as it had to do with doctrinal development, exhibited characteristics of the Church considered as* κοινωνία. It remains to show the sense in which this seems to have been the case.

The Church as *Κοινωνία*

Enough work has been done on the Church as κοινωνία to dispense with my having to write a miniature treatise on that subject.[16] Though I do not intend to show that such is the basic model of the Church, my findings as I shall indicate below have something to say about the work of those theologians who have so argued.[17] I merely intend to clarify the sense in which, as stated in the tenth conclusion, the Catholic Church in the case of the seven doctrinal issues explored above manifested the characteristics of that fundamental Biblical concept.[18] It will first be necessary to enter into a few general considerations.

PHILOLOGICAL CONSIDERATIONS
AND THEIR CONTEXTS

To express the idea of sharing-in (or participation), the New Testament authors commonly used two groups of words, (namely κοινωνία and μετέχειν) and their prefixal variants. The latter in its cognate nominal form, occurs only twice in the New Testament; the former in its cognate nominal form, eighteen times: thirteen in Paul, one in Acts, one in Hebrews, and three in 1 John. Scholarly consensus no longer maintains that the difference between κοινωνεῖν and μετέχειν is that the former connotes sharing or participation in the sense that each receives a part but that the latter suggests participation or sharing in the sense that each "possesses" or shares the whole. Granted that both groups of words mean substantially the same thing, one may however ask whether in the Church of Christ sharing-in (or participation) implies the notion of sharing in the sense of each possessing or sharing the whole. The contexts in which the cognate nominal form of κοινωνεῖν occurs suggest an affirmative answer. For though in 1 Cor. 10:16 ("The cup of blessing which we bless, is it not a participation [κοινωνία] in the blood of Christ? The bread which we break, is it not a participation [κοινωνία] in the body of Christ?") could mean sharing in the sense of each possessing a part, [19] there are other contexts, and they constitute the vast majority, where κοινωνία means "participation" or "sharing" in the sense of each "possessing" or "sharing" the whole. These are the contexts where the term refers to a reality that cannot be divided; either it is possessed (albeit perhaps in varying degrees) as a whole, or it is not possessed at all. Examples are those passages that refer to κοινωνία with the Father (1 John 1:3), with the Son (1 Cor. 1:9) and with the Holy Spirit (2 Cor. 13:13).[20] I find nothing to indicate that Christian sharing-in as the state of affairs resulting from *x the whole of which is shared or "possessed" by each* is not part of its usual meaning.[21] That however is not to contrast κοινωνία with μετοχή. When philological matters are studied in their contexts, *x the whole of which is shared by each* though perhaps in different degrees may be the more fundamental connotation of Christian sharing-in, participation, and/or communion.[22] Within the nuances of these philological considerations I shall henceforth for the most part refer to Christian sharing-in, participation and/or communion as κοινωνία.[23]

The Marks of Κοινωνία

General Characteristics

Lionel Thornton has shown that κοινωνία language covers a great variety of ideas, all of which can be seen to be closely interrelated in a well-defined pattern of common spiritual life.[24] That life transcends the community because in essence it is communion with the Godhead.[25] Thus all characteristics of κοινωνία in the New Testament are manifestations of two fundamental factors, "...of this one complex yet simple whole with two fundamental aspects, the human and the divine."[26] That Christians are partakers of Christ, of the Spirit, of God's life; that they partake of Christ's victory; that the Church is the bride of Christ and his fullness: All of these relations are aspects of that same complex yet simple whole called κοινωνία. Κοινωνία is the result of two relations, the one vertical consisting in communion with the Godhead, the second horizontal consisting in communion among Christians.[27] It is the vertical relation that grounds everything else.

The ultimate cause of κοινωνία is of course God's grace; paramount among its proximate causes are Baptism and Eucharist. Indeed, from the point of view of causality, it is κοινωνία on the level of sacrament that is usually stressed by Catholic ecclesiologists. The kind of doctrinal development that manifested itself in the seven issues studied in parts one and two suggests κοινωνία on a level to which both Thornton and George Panikulam allude but do not develop.[28] This is κοινωνία on the level of word; it is primarily a Johannine emphasis.[29]

Κοινωνία *in 1 John 1: 1-3*

Text A. That which was from the beginning, which we have heard, which we have seen with our eyes, which we have looked upon and touched with our hands, concerning the Word of Life—the Life was made manifest, and we saw it, and testify to it, and proclaim to you the Eternal Life which was with the Father and was made manifest to us....

Text B. that which we have seen and heard we proclaim [α'παγγέλλομεν] to you also

Text C. so that you may have communion [κοινωνία] with us;

Text D. and our communion [κοινωνία] is with the Father and with his son Jesus Christ.[30]

In this passage from 1 John *word* functions in two senses. The first is explicit. The subject of proclamation is the Word of Life, which was with the Father and was made manifest (Text A). The second is implicit and has to do with what is proclaimed about the Word of Life (Text B). What is proclaimed about the Word of Life, and what has been seen and heard, is not simply the historical circumstances surrounding the manifestation of the Word of Life, which circumstances might serve as *praemabula fidei.*

What is proclaimed has to do with eternal life itself (Text A). The word κήρυγμα does not appear in the Johannine corpus, but what is proclaimed about the Word of Life is functionally equivalent to τὸ κήρυγμα Ἰησοῦ Χριστοῦ of Rom. 16:25 where that term has to do not simply with the act of preaching but with its content. The ὁ ἀπαγγέλλομεν is thus synonymous with the Word of God as kerygma. Though the author's language in the passage cited above is not sufficiently nuanced to be able to determine whether his purpose is to plant the seed of κοινωνία where it does not yet exist or to deepen an already existing κοινωνία, subsequent passages indicate that he meant the latter.[31] It is word as *that which... we proclaim* which has for its purpose κοινωνία in the latter sense both horizontally (Text C) and vertically (Text D).

Whereas Paul usually deals with κοινωνία on other levels including the sacramental, the author of 1 John 1:1-3, in identifying the purpose of *that which...is proclaimed* employs the same concept on the level of word. It is on this level that the Catholic Church, inasmuch as in the period under discussion it had to do with doctrinal development, manifested characteristics of κοινωνία.

But in what sense was that the case? What was the κοινόν *the whole of which was shared by each*?

Growth in Understanding the Word

What is proclaimed, word in the second of the two senses distinguished above, is not really distinct from what a later generation was to call *fides quae*.[32] *Fides quae* is nothing else but word as content (not to be identified simply with a series of propositions[33]) embraced on the authority of God revealing (*fides qua*). In the development of doctrine that I have analyzed in parts one and two, *fides quae* was the κοινόν, the whole of which was shared by each, for *fides quae* was both the *terminus a quo* of development and its *terminus ad quem*. That is to say: From a Catholic point of view, under the guidance of the Spirit, reflection on the content of faith (*terminus a quo*) resulted in growth in understanding of the Word of God and its exigencies (*terminus ad quem*).

But a problem seems to arise, for there does not seem to be any connection between sharing *in the sense of the whole being shared by each* and mutual dependence isolated in the *beta* movements. The solution to this difficulty consists in realizing that whoever exercises the Petrine function has the same *fides quae* as the rest of the Church and vice-versa—hence the κοινόν the whole of which is shared by each;[34] and in realizing that, as shown above, mutual dependence emerges when development is considered both *in fieri* and *in facto esse.* Associative elements as mutual dependence and κοινωνία converged precisely here, in that becoming which begins with *fides quae* and ends with it as the Word of God more adequately understood.[35]

Word and sacrament are the two pillars on which the Church rests, as Ratzinger pointed out in the context of *communio.*[36] The manner of doctrinal development as it emerges from an analysis of the *alpha* and *beta* movements, the basis of the pivotal conclusion drawn above, suggests that while κοινωνία continued as sacrament it was also operative on the level of word.[37] But here, as I have suggested, the thrust was Johannine rather than Pauline.

My findings thus tend to confirm the work of those theologians who have argued that the Catholic Church is, or at least functions essentially as κοινωνία[38] and further suggest that the view of those who doubt that any one model can be truly adequate in expressing what the Church is may be overly cautious.[39] Whatever eventual consensus in this regard may turn out to be, the various ways in which the Church manifests itself as κοινωνία in the New Testament fully allow in principle for the possibilities that seem to have been realized (*réalisé, verwirklichtet*) in regard to the manner in which doctrine seems to have developed within the context of the seven issues under discussion.[40] Among those realized possibilities, that stated in the pivotal conclusion above is fundamental to everything else, for it shows in Troeltsch's terms that associative elements were integrated into the Catholic Church as institution, a fact highly disclosive of what the Catholic Church really is.

The non-Catholic Christian will no doubt observe that the blend of Church as association with Church as institution on the level of doctrine and the ordinary papal magisterium is all well and good. But he or she will almost certainly ask whether this blending ever occurs where it really counts; namely, on the level of dogma and the extraordinary papal magisterium. It thus remains to determine whether associative elements were significantly present in the process that culminated in the definition of the two Marian dogmas. Within that limited context I shall deal, then, with aspects of the extraordinary papal magisterium and what is commonly called papal infallibility.

PART FOUR
"UNIVERSITAS FIDELIUM. . .
IN CREDENDO. . ."†

---

† The body of the faithful [as a whole, anointed as they are by the Holy One. . . *cannot err] in matters of belief. . . ."* (AG, p. 29, emphasis mine).

Chapter VIII
THE EXTRAORDINARY PAPAL MAGISTERIUM: CHURCH AS ASSOCIATION AND THE MARIAN DOGMAS

Mary is only intelligible in terms of Christ. If someone does not hold with the Catholic faith that the Word of God became man in Adam's flesh so that the world might be taken up redemptively into the life of God, he can have no understanding of Catholic dogma about Mary either. It may indeed be said that a sense of Marian dogma is an indication of whether Christological dogma is being taken really seriously; or whether it is being regarded (consciously or unconsciously) merely as a rather outmoded, problematic, mythological expression of the fact that in Jesus (who is basically just a religious man) we undoubtedly feel God (here again a cipher for an unexpressed mystery) particularly close to us. No, this Jesus Christ, born of Mary in Bethlehem, is at once, as One and Indissoluble, true man and true Word, consubstantial with the Father. And so Mary is in truth the Mother of God.

It is only to someone who truly and unreservedly confesses this that the Catholic Church can continue to speak meaningfully about her other Marian dogmas.[1]

The purpose of this long quotation from an earlier essay by Karl Rahner is simply this: Whether or not the non-Catholic Christian agrees with Catholic theologizing about the mother of Jesus, it is essential that he or she grasp the fact that Catholic dogma on this matter (and, one might add, other matters) can be understood only as part of a whole. In the pages that follow I have no intention of delineating that whole, much less of attempting to ground the credibility of Catholic dogma. My purpose is simply to sustain the argument stated below.

Before I proceed it will be good to note that associative elements stand in tension with what I call *the determinative factors in the Petrine function* inasmuch as they have to do with so-called papal infallibility. I mean by that the view expressed by Bishop Gasser during the First Vatican Council that in exercising the extraordinary papal magisterium the Roman Bishop does not need *in any strict or absolute sense* the prior or subsequent agreement of the rest of the Catholic Church.[2] That is to say: *In the exercise of the extraordinary papal magisterium, the Roman Bishop does not have to agree with the rest of the Catholic Church but the rest of the Catholic Church must agree with the Roman Bishop* as far as the definition goes.[3] Of these two factors, prior and subsequent agreement, it is the former that, as we shall see, is the more crucial. In the context of determinative factors in the Petrine function inasmuch as they have to do with papal infallibility, associative elements may be said to have to do with mutual cooperation, not with mutual dependence. I shall return below to these considerations and the ecumenical problems they pose. It will be sufficient here to note further that although the extraordinary papal magisterium is exercised only in the actual moment in which a doctrine is defined, nonetheless associative elements present in the process that culminates in such definitions may be said to be present *on the level of the extraordinary papal magisterium* or what is commonly called papal infallibility. I suggest this manner of speaking is justified in that the meaning of a process is discerned primarily in relation to its *terminus ad quem*.

These preliminary clarifications and remarks having been made, I shall argue as follows:

I.   *Associative elements were significantly present in the process that culminated in the definition of the doctrines of the Immaculate Conception and the Assumption.*

II. In that process, the more crucial factor in the Petrine function was not operative; hence, associative elements present in the process which culminated in the definition of the two Marian dogmas suggest that the determinative factors in the Petrine function, inasmuch as they have to do with so-called papal infallibility, are for official Catholicism a value having to do more with principle than with practice.

This chapter comprises two parts, corresponding to each part of the argument stated above. The first consists in examining associative elements operating prior to the definitions of the doctrine of the Immaculate Conception as well as the Assumption and constitutes the major thrust of this chapter; the second, in showing the relevance of these findings for Catholicism's external problem and so-called papal infallibility.

A word must be said about the sources, as they affect both method and style. The principal sources for documenting associative elements present in the process that led to the definition of the Immaculate Conception are threefold: (1) the *Pareri dell'Episcopato cattolico*; [4] (2) Augustine de Roskovany's collection;[5] and (3) Vincenzo Sardi's two massive tomes.[6] These were more than ample for my purpose. But when one comes to the Assumption, such documentation is largely inaccessible. Extant material exists primarily in the Vatican Library where sources relating to the Petrine ministry of Pius XII will not usually be available for another generation. Thus the method for grounding the first part of my argument inasmuch as it has to do with the dogma of the Assumption will be different from that employed in regard to the dogma of the Immaculate Conception.

Associative Elements and the Extraordinary Papal Magisterium

THE DOGMA OF THE IMMACULATE CONCEPTION *in fieri*

This part of my inquiry begins with the request of Pius IX that the Catholic episcopacy inform him about the definability of the doctrine of the Immaculate Conception, frequently referred to in the theological writings of the period as the *pia sententia*, though technically its proper theological note seems at that time to have been much higher. The effort to highlight associative elements as cooperation and as significantly present in the process that ended in the proclamation of the new dogma will then take the following form: I shall examine Laborde's Protest, the subsequent assessment of its grounds consisting of a study of reports from two French dioceses. This section will close with a general overview of the data, with a careful eye to those who expressed dissent.

Pius IX

Ubi primum of February 2, 1849 (not to be confused with *Ubi primum* of December 17, 1847), a document of some 750 words and in Sardi's text comprising two and a half pages in folio,[7] had for its principal purpose the solicitation of prayers and the expressed judgment of the bishops on the matters discussed below in Texts B and C. Pius began by stating that upon taking office he had been consoled by the fact that during the previous pontificate there had existed throughout the Catholic world an ardent desire for a solemn judgment by the Apostolic See on the *pia sententia*, something to which the many requests made to his predecessor and himself bore witness.[8] Indeed, many learned men had been amazed that the doctrine had not been defined already.[9] All this was very satisfying to the Pope, as from his earliest years he had had a special devotion to the Blessed Virgin Mary.[10] He had every confidence that she would protect the Christian people (*Christianum populum*) in those troubled times. Everyone knew that the Pope had placed all his trust in her. Pius then stated:

> *Text A.* Wherefore we are writing this letter to you, Venerable Brothers, by which we [intend to] move deeply your great piety and episcopal concern and we exhort you again and again each in his own diocese according as he judges prudent, to announce and to conduct services so that the most kind Father of lights may deign to fill us with the heavenly light of his divine Spirit . . .[11]

> *Text B.* Moreover, we strongly desire that as quickly as possible you take it upon yourselves to make known to us the quality of devotion whereby your clergy and your faithful people venerate the Conception of the Immaculate Virgin and the degree to which they desire that the matter be decided by the Apostolic See . . .[12]

Text C. . . . in the first place we desire especially to learn, Venerable Brothers, how according to your consummate wisdom you your-selves feel about this very question and what you earnestly desire.[13]

Texts A, B, and C follow closely upon one another and manifest the same florid style we have noted in other documents from Pius IX. The first reflects the seriousness with which Pius approached the subject at hand; the second and third, the need he seems to have felt for help from the rest of the Church in coming to a decision. The Pope did not ask for reasons why the doctrine should be defined, though as we shall see, some dioceses were to supply them. The Pope merely wanted to know (1) how the bishops themselves viewed the matter (Text C) and (2) what in fact was the belief of their people (Text B). While the bishops were preparing their reply, a few Catholics were to voice violent objections against any such definition.

Laborde's Protest

Jean-Joseph Laborde, a priest of the Archdiocese of Paris, strongly opposed the definition, doing so not only in his own name but in that of a certain number of Catholics of the Archdiocese—he did not say how many. Dated November 21, 1854, his objections as found in Sardi's folio edition were limited to one and a half pages and comprised nineteen theses.[14] Yet they had not constituted Laborde's first sally. As early as 1850, four years before the actual definition, he had made his views known in a work that, in the revised edition of 1851, comprises 164 pages.[15] Though the first edition was condemned by the Holy Office in a decree dated July 10, 1850, and the second by the Sacred Congregation of the Index in a decree dated September 6, 1852, these events did not prevent Laborde from submitting further remonstrances. The protest addressed to the Pope and bishops in 1854, seventeen days before the definition, may therefore be regarded as a compendium of the Abbé's views. Of the nineteen theses stated in that document, only six are of interest to us here. Listed according to Laborde's enumeration, they may be translated as follows:

> I. The teaching of the Church is that which, having been taught by Jesus Christ or to the apostles under the inspiration of the Holy Spirit, has been preached by the same apostles and has come from them to us by a tradition which has been handed down [*une tradition de main en main*].[16]

II. The Church does not make new dogmas of faith.[17]

III. It is a sin to announce new dogmas; it is a sin to accept them. . .[18]

VI. The doctrine of the Immaculate Conception does not come from Jesus Christ and the Apostles through the channel of tradition.[19]

VII. In everything done up to now in order to turn the opinion about the Immaculate Conception into a dogma of faith, the canonical rules have not been observed.[20]

X. A great number of bishops have answered that the clergy and faithful of their dioceses met with them to express to Our Holy Father the Pope the wish that the question be defined; whereas, as a matter of fact, neither clergy nor the faithful had been consulted; there were educated people among the faithful and priests in good standing who rejected the Immaculate Conception even as an opinion. There was moral pressure and even violence used in order to prevent them from manifesting their feelings.[21]

Since my purpose in these pages is not to defend the credibility of the dogma of the Immaculate Conception but simply tò show that associative elements were present in the process that led up to the definition, I shall pass over theses I, II, III, and VI. They are translated here merely to illustrate the tone of Laborde's objections. My attention will be focused on theses VII and X, which may be restated as follows:

(A) The canonical rules of procedure in the matter were not being observed.

(B) Neither the clergy nor the faithful had been consulted.

(C) There were educated people among the faithful and priests in good standing who rejected the Immaculate Conception even as an opinion.

(D) There was moral pressure and even violence used in order to prevent them from showing how they felt.

If Laborde's charges were sustainable, the matter would be serious indeed. They would remove completely any ground from under the first part of my argument inasmuch as it pertains to the doctrine of the Immaculate Conception. The place to begin an evaluation of Laborde's protest is with the report submitted by his own bishop.

The Archdiocese of Paris

Though Sardi did not hesitate to include Laborde's protest, he did not, strangely enough, include that of his Archbishop, Marie-Dominique-Auguste Sibour (1793-1857), who was generally sympathetic to the views expressed by the Parisian Abbé. I must therefore turn to the *Pareri dell'Episcopato cattolico*. This collection in eleven volumes contains the Catholic bishops' responses to the request of February 2, 1849, as published under Pius IX's direction from 1851 to 1854. The first eight volumes were published in 1852 and contain the reports of most of the bishops, thus manifesting two years before the actual definition that an affirmative consensus existed among the magisterial officers of the Catholic Church. Therein one finds from the Archbishop at Paris three documents dated August 25, 1849, July 26, 1850, and December 17, 1850, respectively.[22] Only the first is of central importance.

Sibour's initial response to the Pope's request as it appears in the *Pareri* consists of forty-two pages and logically may be considered as comprising four parts; namely:

1. The letter and judgment of Sibour as Archbishop at Paris
2. The *dubia*
3. The report of the Committee set up by Sibour to examine the question
4. A paper by a biologist writing on the Immaculate Conception

Sibour submitted the last mentioned item not because of its intrinsic value but in order to show why scientists themselves were interested in the matter.[23] The document is of no theological significance; I shall therefore not refer to it again. The *dubia* were thirty-eight problems concerned with various aspects of the question. These Sibour discussed and in some cases answered, though many of his answers were further questions. Together with the letter, the whole comprises about five thousand words and a total of twenty pages. Both documents were written in Latin, the style of the *dubia* being different (not to say somewhat awkward) from that of the letter, a fact which suggests that they had different authors though both appear above Sibour's signature. The report of the Committee was shorter, consisting of sixteen pages and about 3,800 words.[24]Since Sibour's letter was ultimately based on that of his Committee, I shall begin with the latter.

Written in French, the report distinguished two questions, the one pertaining to doctrine, the other to prudence. The first was subdivided; it was one thing for the Church or the Holy See to make a dogmatic judgment that resulted in an article of faith; it was quite another to make a judgment that a particular doctrine is certain.[25] In the first case, all the faithful would be required to believe the doctrine in such a way that those who refuse to do so would be heretical in the strict sense of the term; in the second, the doctrine so defined would not be a truth of the Catholic faith (*De fide catholica*) but one that is certain and as such taught by the infallible authority of the Church.[26] What the Committee was getting at but failed to make sufficiently clear is that the former is believed on the authority of God revealing; the second, however certain, is not believed under that modality. Now to reject a doctrine so defined (i.e., in the second sense) would not, properly speaking, be heretical; but for Catholics it would be rash to say the least. The Committee mentioned several examples of truths defined in this second sense.

As one reads the report, one is struck by a certain confusion cleared up since by the First Vatican Council. On the one hand the cited examples of papal definitions in this second sense were doctrinal pronouncements of the ordinary papal magisterium; on the other, conciliar speeches and particularly Gasser's reports, which came to a climax in the definition of papal infallibility as stated in *Pastor Aeternus*, mean that the ordinary papal magisterium does not define.[27] But twenty-one years before the First Vatican Council and its stormy debates, confusion on the part of the Paris Committee was no doubt understandable. Regarding the matter of doctrine as opposed to that of prudence, the Committee stated its position in the form of propositions or theses and then proceeded to demonstrate them. The propositions were twofold:

1. It seems that the doctrine of the Immaculate Conception of the Blessed Virgin can be absolutely decided by a decree of the Church or the Holy See that establishes the doctrine as certain without elevating it to the level of an article of faith[28]
2. It is more difficult to say whether the doctrine of the Immaculate Conception of the Blessed Virgin can be defined as an article of faith or as a truth of the Catholic faith (*De fide catholica*) by a decree of the Church or the Holy See[29]

Attention will be focused on the Committee's reasoning presented in support of its second proposition. It began by clarifying the meaning of certain terms as the Committee understood them. By *a truth of the Catholic faith* was understood one that the Church proposes as immediately revealed by God and that is consequently contained in scripture or in tradition.[30] All the faithful, stated the Committee, are obliged to accept such a doctrine as having always been the faith of the Church *at least implicitly*. Conversely, however firmly established by human reasoning, a teaching about one or more revealed doctrines can never become a truth of the Catholic faith in the technical sense of that term.[31] Thus to paraphrase what the Committee seems to have been trying to state: The doctrine of the Divine Maternity was a truth of the Catholic faith but the doctrine of the Immaculate Conception, which is a truth about that truth, is not, because its formal object is not the authority of God revealing but a "deduction" by human reasoning from the truth about the Divine Maternity. It is clear that the Committee was embracing an opinion the application of which was even more questionable. Be that as it may, these distinctions were the basis for its position that a point of doctrine, even one generally admitted from the beginning, could never be put on the level of a truth of the *Catholic* faith (*De fide catholica*), if it had not first been regarded as a truth of *divine* faith (*De fide divina*).[32] Such a doctrine can be respected as a teaching of the Church and might not be denied without temerity.[33] This applied to a number of doctrines taught in the Catholic Church, such as the Assumption. Thus the doctrine of the Immaculate Conception, for all its certainty as a doctrine in this second sense, could not be defined.

The Committee then summarily discussed the reasons of those theologians who held the contrary. The principal difficulties seemed to have been that in the early patristic period many texts adduced as "proofs" of the implicit belief of the Church in the Immaculate Conception of Mary as associated with Christ in the act of redemption could be taken as referring to her personal sinlessness, and did not necessarily refer to her freedom from original sin. And even if it could be demonstrated that belief in the Immaculate Conception had indeed been implicit, it was something else again to show that it had been believed as a truth of divine faith.[34]

As the second proposition related to the matter of opportuneness also, the Committee, after some discussion of the advantages and disadvantages of a definition, concluded that a definition would not be opportune even in the sense of the first proposition.[35] This is the background for Sibour's response:

> And I myself, most Holy Father, like my theological consultants, think that very serious difficulties and perhaps great calamity will come upon the Church from the Promulgation of such a decree.
> And I myself judge [*censeo*] with them that it is not lawful in any case for the Church and the Holy See to number the doctrine of the Immaculate

Conception among the articles of faith or, if you will, among the truths of the Catholic faith.

Nay, most Holy Father, going further than the aforementioned theologians, I doubt whether the Church or the Holy See can in a solemn decree decide that the doctrine is certain and to be embraced by all under the pain of mortal sin and eternal damnation.[36]

Thus it is clear that Sibour's own personal position was even more conservative than that of his advisors, since he rejected the possibility that the Committee had attempted to sustain in the first of the two propositions quoted above. But he went beyond it in another sense. The Committee had not stated that refusal to accept the doctrine defined in the second sense (i.e., as a doctrine that was certain but that could nonetheless not be believed on divine and Catholic faith [De fide divina et catholica]) could be a cause for eternal damnation; it had simply said that henceforth to deny a doctrine so defined would be rash. There is thus some evidence to suggest that Sibour had not really grasped the distinction that the Committee had made between the two different kinds of definitions.

As to the important matter of the belief of his people, Sibour approached it in the answer to the thirty-eighth and last dubium, which asked: Will not deciding the question turn without any compensation to the ruin of a great number of souls?[37] Sibour answered:

The wishes of the faithful are incessantly offered to us as a definitive reason [for the definition] because of which they hope that the opinion [opinionem] about the Immaculate Conception will be numbered among the dogmas of faith or at least among the truths which have been defined as certain.

Holy Father, those who put forth these things exceed the limits of the truth. The faithful seem to us to be almost unconcerned about the definition; it is sufficient for them devoutly to pray to the Immaculate Virgin. If pious souls more eager for the faith have in some way expressed the wish that the doctrine be defined, they are certainly few in number. Nevertheless, compared to unbelievers, heretics, or the indifferent, let them be considered not one out of a thousand but, I should say, one out of a hundred; the faith or the piety of this [one] faithful will reap no advantage from that definition while for unbelievers, heretics, and the indifferent, it will, as has just been said, be a calamity.[38]

Sibour's response to the papal request of February 2, 1849, was thus unambivalent. Most of the other dubia had to do with theoretical questions; e.g., the seventh asked whether the Church could propose as obligatory a doctrinal opinion which was not necessarily connected with a revealed dogma. Sibour's answers to a number of them suggest that Laborde's protest must have been entirely exceptional and representative of only a few, something borne out indirectly in the answer to the last of the *dubia* where Sibour stated that the faithful of his diocese were unconcerned about the forthcoming definition and simply went about their devotion to the *Immaculate* Virgin. He seems to have been aware of the difficulties of people like Laborde, however, as a subsequent letter to Pius IX attests.[39] That belief in the doctrine of the Immaculate Conception was indeed the coin of the realm in his diocese seems further confirmed by Sibour's answer to the fifth *dubium*, which asked whether the Church without evident necessity should ever define a question of doctrine *about which, here and now, there is no controversy*. Sibour answered by asking another question:

> The Church [has] never [defined] a point of doctrine from the cold, if I may so speak, without the heat of controversy or of urgent necessity, or in one word, if I may, by reason of the sole desire of defining it, has it?[40]

I shall not analyze Sibour's report further, the foregoing being sufficient to understand its general tenor. In his closing remarks, the Archbishop expressed his own personal belief in the doctrine and then stated:

> If Your Holiness should define this pious opinion by a solemn decree, we will change our private view about the definability of the matter, joining our voice to the voice of the Catholic world, and exclaim from our heart: Peter has spoken through the mouth of Pius IX.[41]

The Diocese of Arras

In stark contrast to the report submitted by Sibour, that produced by Charles-Aimable Cardinal (prince de) la Tour d'Auvergne-Lauraguais exhibited a very different judgment. De la Tour d'Auvergne, from one of the most distinguished families of the old French nobility, later Archbishop at Bourges, was in 1849 Bishop at Arras. The five-man Committee he set up in order to respond to the Pope's request met ten times between March 26, 1849, and May 1 of the same year. Its report as found in Sardi's text spans thirty-nine pages in folio and comprises almost twenty thousand words.[42]

The work of its first session consisted essentially in taking cognizance of its legal standing and of determining the method with which it would approach its task. There were to be five steps, only the first three of which are relevant to this point of my inquiry. Each of the members was to study the questions in private and produce the results of his findings in the early sessions; after taking a position on the most difficult part of the assignment, the Committee was to sum up all aspects necessary for discerning as responsibly as possible the dispositions and desires of both clergy and people; it would then formulate in Latin the report to be sent to the Pope at the Cardinal's request.[43]

In the session of April 2, the Committee discussed the general principles that were to guide its work; e.g., Mary, as a daughter of Adam, was subject to the general law of original sin; if she was entirely freed from the application of that law in her regard, this could only be by way of a glorious exception; if it could be affirmed that there were sufficient theological grounds for affirming the doctrine of the Immaculate Conception, this could only refer to conception in the passive sense; i.e., to that moment of conception when a substantial union between body and soul takes place. There could be no question of conception *sine macula* in the active sense; i.e., in the matter from which her body was to be formed.[44] The Committee then listed the principal objections against the definability of the doctrine, among which were the following:

1. The silence of scripture
2. The fact that early tradition does not seem to make up for this silence
3. If a virtually unanimous agreement exists between clergy and people on definability, does not this agreement come upon the scene rather late? Does a consensus which manifests itself only after fifteen centuries of incertitude offer a very solid basis for an affirmative answer to this serious question?[45]

There were still further objections, of course. Thus one could cull from the Fathers certain statements that seem to militate against the very notion of the doctrine. Cyril, for example, maintained that only Jesus had never sinned, while Leo and Ambrose used similar expressions. The further one went into the history of the Church, the more did the Church's doctors, Bernard and Aquinas among them, seem opposed. The Committee summed up its deliberations by stating:

Whence we conclude that an opinion which is rooted neither in scripture nor in early tradition but which rests only on a pious belief cannot be sanctioned by dogmatic definition.[46]

The Committee spent the remaining sessions up to that of April 23 facing these and other difficulties. Its first analysis and its weakest was an attempt to find some basis for the belief in scripture. The silence of scripture, it was said, was not as absolute as it might seem. Thus the angelic salutation of Luke 1:28 ("Hail, O highly favored one . . .") and Elizabeth's greeting in Luke 1:42 ("Blessed are you among women . . ."), together with Gen. 3:15 ("I will put enmity between you and the woman, and between your seed and her seed . . ."), suggest that the scriptures were not entirely mute.[47] Though these texts did not "prove" the doctrine of the Immaculate Conception, so continued the Committee, they were nonetheless not unfavorable to it.[48] (Here the members of the Committee seemed to have overstepped the limits of careful exegesis. It would have kept within its bounds if it had simply stated, particularly in regard to the New Testament, that nothing in the end seemed to militate against the doctrine and that while the scriptures cannot be said to affirm it, nonetheless certain passages in the New Testament suggest that in the primitive Church Mary seems to have been regarded as a woman of exalted holiness.)

More impressive was the Committee's analysis of patristic data and of later tradition. Beginning with the fifteenth century and proceeding backwards, its work, while not exhaustive in a brief compendium of thirty-nine pages, was nonetheless marked by a certain thoroughness that only an unfair critic could call into question. Its principal emphasis however was on the teaching of those Fathers whose remarks were sometimes used against the doctrine. Thus Cyril (d. 444) in his commentary on the Gospel of John:

All of us human beings, with the exception of him born of the Virgin and with the exception also of the most Holy Virgin, from whom the God-man came forth into the world, are born with original sin . . . .[49]

And Augustine (354-430) in *De Natura et Gratia*:

With the exception of the Holy Virgin Mary, about whom when it is a matter of sin, I wish for the honor of the Lord there be absolutely [*prorsus*] no question; for we know indeed that in order to conquer sin from every source [*ex omni parte*] more grace was conferred on her who was [found] worthy to conceive and bring forth Him who, as is evident, had no sin.[50]

The Committee was not so naive as to suggest that these Fathers spoke explicitly of the doctrine of the Immaculate Conception. But terms like *prorsus* and *ex omni parte* in authors like Augustine suggested, so it seemed to the Committee, that a belief functionally equivalent to the total sinlessness of Mary was interwoven into the faith-structure of the Church at that time. There was confirmation in Jerome; one could even find traces in Origen (185-c. 254) and somewhat earlier in Tertullian (160-c. 225).[51] Some Fathers were of course more explicit than others. In his commentary on Psalm 118 Ambrose referred to the *Virgo per gratiam ab omni integra labe peccati* and a Bishop like Amphilocus used terms like *sine macula et sine peccato.*[52]

In the following session (April 12) the Committee turned to evidence of the Church's belief insofar as it was discernible in other sources. When it came to different liturgies—*lex orandi lex credendi*—it reversed its movement, beginning with the earliest liturgies and proceeding to the later. Here the evidence tended to the affirmative.[53] But when it was a question of the Councils, the Committee had to admit that the evidence was sparse in the sense that the most that could be said was that Basel and Trent had left the question open.[54] Analysis of the papal decrees was superficial in the extreme and consisted in hardly more than the evidence Perrone had uncovered from the time of Gregory XVI. When it came to the witness of the theologians, the Committee highlighted the fact that in 1496 the University of Paris had obliged its faculty under oath to swear it would defend the doctrine of the Immaculate Conception whenever appropriate occasion arose.[55]

Eleven days later, the Committee took up further objections, this time of a more theoretical nature, and having solved them to its satisfaction, came to the conclusion that in its judgment the doctrine of the Immaculate Conception could indeed be defined.[56] The Church in centuries past had defined other doctrines not explicitly found in the scriptures. Whether or not the definition was opportune was another matter best left for the Pope and bishops to decide.

The Committee's work was not yet terminated, for in the following session (April 24) it summarized a detailed analysis of the belief of clergy and people in the diocese of Arras. It was the Committee's judgment that belief in the Immaculate Conception was of long standing.[57] As evidence, it pointed to the fact that the University of Douai, which came under the jurisdiction of the diocese of Arras, had in 1660 adopted the same practice that the University of Paris had adopted much earlier; i.e., a condition for academic advancement was a commitment to defend the doctrine of the Immaculate Conception.[58] But belief in the doctrine seemed to go back earlier. Here the Committee brought out a missal printed in Arras in 1517. The orations for the Mass of the Conception clearly suggested belief in the Immaculate Conception as currently understood.[59] But in addition to instances that had to do with the past, evidence of contemporary belief was plentiful. An example pointed out by the Committee was the fact that once the Archconfraternity of the Heart of Mary had been established in the capital, the diocese continued to receive frequent requests to authorize affiliation with it in every parish of the diocese. The number of medals with the invocation "Mary, conceived without sin . . ." asked for and given out in the Cathedral alone was incalculable, and the same situation obtained everywhere in the diocese. The clergy's attitude was no different.[60] One could therefore affirm that in the diocese of Arras a definition of the doctrine would be received with great satisfaction.[61] The Committee ended its work by expressing the hope that the initiative that Pius IX was undertaking would meet with complete success.

Now in the session of April 26, a surprising thing happened. Cardinal de La Tour d'Auvergne, having apparently read the Committee's report, took it upon himself to raise further difficulties, saying that the question before the Committee was very difficult and delicate, for it was not merely a question of honoring Mary but of imposing a new article of faith upon the faithful.[62] If that was to be done, then the reasons for it must be beyond dispute. The Cardinal then enumerated his difficulties, the more significant of which were as follows:

1. The silence of the Church when it came to teaching this doctrine as an article of faith was very weighty[63]
2. The penalty for Adam's disobedience was universal and without exception[64]
3. The power of God to purify the instruments he uses is so great that at the moment of Mary's *fiat* she could have been completely sanctified; there was thus no need for her to be sanctified in the moment of her conception[65]
4. Up to the present, the Church has believed in the Immaculate Conception as a *pia sententia*; why go further without a sign from heaven?[66]
5. It was to be feared that a new article of faith would become the object of ridicule, disdain and insult against the Catholic Church[67]

The Committee then responded to the Cardinal's objections, suggesting that a solid argument for definability was to be found in its detailed report.[68] As to the silence of the Church that had for so long a time allowed belief in the Immaculate Conception only as a pious option—this seemed to be de La Tour d'Auvergne's principal objection—this long silence merely proved that the Church had not judged the question to be ripe for definition; it did not prove that belief in the doctrine was not sufficiently grounded in revelation and that it was not ready for definition now.[69] As for the universal need of redemption, nothing in scripture requires one to believe that there could not be an exception to the law of original sin. That God could have sanctified Mary completely at the moment of the Incarnation is beyond dispute. But in that case she would have been less favored than John the Baptist who had been sanctified in his mother's womb.[70] And if up to the present the doctrine of the Immaculate Conception had been permitted only as a pious belief, that could be explained by the fact that circumstances required a certain reserve. Finally, if the Catholic Church were to be subject to ridicule because of this definition, this would merely provide the occasion for it to show its love of God.[71]

The record as it is contained in Sardi's text gives no indication of how on this occasion de La Tour d'Auvergne responded to the Committee's answers to his objections. That the response may be presumed to have been favorable may be gathered from the fact that in the following session the Committee drew up a projected answer to the papal request of the previous February. This response was essentially a summary of all the foregoing and highlighted the present belief of people and clergy and its basis in the tradition. Indeed, belief in the doctrine of the Immaculate Conception was universal in the Catholic Church and was at the time shared even by those who once opposed it most (e.g., the Dominicans).[72] The penultimate paragraph had to do with de La Tour d'Auvergne himself:

> As the oldest bishop in Christendom and as a member of the sacred College devoted more than any other to the interests of the Church and to the veneration of Mary its most powerful protectress, it will be for our advanced years and our long episcopate a crown which will fill us with joy, as well as the clergy and people of our diocese.[73]

The final paragraph stated that if the definition were put off at this point, the result would bring harm to the Church and would perhaps give rise to doubts ". . . all the more painful as the belief in this doctrine is today the more deeply rooted in our hearts."[74] The last session was spent in translating this response into Latin, at the end of which the signatures of the five members of the Committee appear. At the bottom of the page appears this cryptic sentence:

> Vu et après sérieux examen approuvé dans tout son contenu. Arras, 12 mai 1849. Ch. Card. de La Tour d'Auvergne Lauraguais Ev. d'Arras.[75]

OVERVIEW

The foregoing reports from two French dioceses suffice, I suggest, to show that the Abbé Laborde's protest was devoid of foundation. Certainly it could not be maintained—recall the summary of his objections stated above—that the canonical rules were not being observed (A), nor that priests and people had not been consulted (B), unless Laborde meant that an actual plebiscite had not been taken. Each bishop simply testified to his own views, those of his priests and people. I have come upon no evidence to suggest that violence or pressure had been put on anyone (C); indeed, although Laborde seems to have been unaware of it, his own bishop had already expressed to the Pope views not unlike his own, and in a subsequent letter alluded to Catholics like Laborde.[76] That there were educated people among both priests and faithful who stood opposed to the doctrine even as a pious opinion (D) cannot be seriously doubted; but the evidence suggests that they were very few. Stances like those taken in Laborde's Protest seem to have been very exceptional.

For the position taken by Sibour was not at all typical of his peers among Catholicism's magisterial officers. Le Bachelet reported that 603 bishops had responded to the request of 1849 and that all but fifty-six or fifty-seven of those were in favor of a solemn definition.[77] Among this small number, opinion tended to vary: Twelve asked to abstain from judgment; twelve did not wish to see a direct definition in the sense that the contradictory would be labeled heresy; twenty-four did not think the definition opportune; four or five were frankly opposed, among them the Archbishop at Paris.[78] Le Bachelet did not account for the remaining four or five. But it matters little, for the vast majority had responded positively to the questions raised in Texts B and C.

To say that a bishop was opposed to the definition does not mean however that he necessarily was so in the sense that Sibour had been. I cite one example, from the diocese of Evreux. Dated April 16, 1849, and signed simply with the bishop's Christian name (Nicolas) as was the custom of the time, the response to the papal request stated in part:

1. I hardly judge opportune to treat the question of the Immaculate Conception at the present time [*moderno tempore*] for (a) *no Catholic contests it; indeed at no time has it been so generally accepted as in our day;* (b) many Protestants reconciled to the papacy [*Pontificatui*] through our beloved and holy Pontiff Pius IX would go back to where

they were before, nor would anything be more repelling than that an obligation be imposed, by force of which it would no longer be permitted to consider pious faith in the Immaculate Conception as an opinion.[79]

2. I do not think the texts of Holy Scripture are sufficiently precise nor the language of tradition sufficiently explicit or sufficiently consistent through the course of the centuries for this opinion, *though it seems certain to me*, to be proposed as a dogma of faith. The rules established by all theologians militate against this intention.[80]

This letter is useful in that it shows the sense in which a bishop could be against a definition: the doctrine was disputed by no one—he was obviously unaware of *Laborde's protest*—and was considered certain by the Bishop; yet the data were not sufficient to consider it a *dogma* with everything that implied about divine revelation. Arguments against opportuneness were primarily pastoral in orientation. When therefore one says that a particular bishop was against the definition, some care must be exercised in determining precisely what one means.

As one peruses the documentation in the *Pareri*, in Roskovany's collection or in Sardi's tomes, there can be no doubt on the one hand that responses like those from the dioceses of Paris and Arras were not typical in length and on the other that the bishops had not taken their commission lightly. The average response from a bishop totaled about six hundred words, was written usually in Latin of varying quality, and simply addressed itself to the questions posed by the Roman Bishop. There is no way whatsoever in which it could be maintained on the basis of the data that the vast majority of Catholic bishops did not judge that the doctrine of the Immaculate Conception was indeed the belief of their priests and people and that it could and should be defined. That fact is not surprising, since theological discussion had intensified between the years 1830 and 1854, as studies by such authors as Luigi Cardinal Lambruschini, widely read and translated, and that by the Jesuit G. Perrone attest.[81]

The doctrine of the Immaculate Conception was thus an eiscyclic movement long before it ever became eccyclic.[82] But to demonstrate that fact would take me considerably beyond the historical period I have set out to deal with. Within that time-span, it should be considered beyond dispute that associative elements as mutual cooperation between the ordinary papal magisterium and the rest of the Catholic Church, primarily bishops and theologians, were significantly present. While this establishes the first part of my argument inasmuch as it has to do with the dogma of the Immaculate Conception, it remains to determine the extent to which the same assessment applies to the other Marian dogma with which we are concerned.

THE DOGMA OF THE ASSUMPTION *in fieri*

The request made by Pius XII that his brother bishops or fellow magisterial officers inform him about the faith of the people in their dioceses and the bishops' own judgment relative to the doctrine of the Assumption was ultimately published but seems to have been originally a private communication.[83] Except for a breakdown of figures subsequently analyzed in the *Osservatore romano*, detailed results of the survey have not been promulgated by the Holy See, as far as I know. This is contrary, as we have seen, to what obtained under Pius IX in the case of the Immaculate Conception. Hence my approach must take a different tack. I shall begin with an analysis of the petitions addressed to the Holy See that the doctrine of the Assumption be defined. I shall then describe the role of the theologians and the extent of episcopal consensus inasmuch as the latter is known from a secondary source published by Hentrich, the whole of which is sufficient, I suggest, to establish the first part of my argument inasmuch as it has to do with the dogma of the Assumption. This section like the former will close with a brief overview.

The Petitions

The Work of Hentrich and De Moos

A source that must not be overlooked are the two massive tomes edited by G. Hentrich and R. De Moos, assistants (*qualificatori*) in what was formerly called the Holy Office. Entitled *Petitiones de Assumptione Corporea B.V. Mariae in Caelum Definienda ad Sanctam Sedem Delatae*, they were published in 1942,[84] four years before Pius XII formally requested a judgment from the Catholic episcopate. This work, which had its remote origin in Leo XIII's directive that all requests for a definition of the doctrine of the Assumption be deferred to the Holy Office for scrutiny, had for its purpose an analysis of those submitted between 1869 and 1941. *Petitiones* is divided into two parts unequally distributed throughout the two tomes, the first and second of which comprise 1061 and 1108 pages, respectively. Part one has to do with an analysis and classification of requests considered in a descending hierarchical order (i.e., proceeding from requests by Cardinals, Patriarchs to bishops, superiors general, etc.), spanning pages 4-1058 of tome I and pages 1-658 of tome II; part two has to do with an analysis of dogmatic, geographic and historical factors. In the very beginning of part one, the authors reproduce the various forms of petitions in use during the period. Whenever a petitioner wrote a personal letter, the integral text is provided; when the petitioner used one of the current forms, only a summary analysis of its content is presented, the purpose in this latter case being the omission of needless repetition. I cannot hope to reproduce here the exhaustive analysis that the work of Hentrich and De Moos entailed. I shall instead be content with three examples.

Typical of a request submitted by way of a form is that represented by the following schema:

Mardensis Syrorum ab. a 1888 sedes unitae "Mardensis et Amidensis Syrorum (Mardin ed Amidi, dei Siri)" diocesem patriarchalem constituunt (Marden, dei Siri)—Reipublicae Turcarum pars Asiatica.

Ignatius Philippus *Harcus*. Episc. Resid. (dioeceseos Patriarchalis). Patriarchus Syrorum—1870, feb. 23.

Analysis:
  Descr.: 1° Corpore, 2° postmortem ("resurrectio").
  Qualif.: "Definire."
  Unitus cum Episcopo Murano in Concilio Vaticano.
  Litt. *individ.*: Subscr. postulato Vatic g. (p. 108)
  Prob.: 1° Utriusque Ecclesiae perpetuus,—2°   veneranda traditio
  Pro. opp.: 1° Nova gloria B.V.M.,—2° praesidium ad interimendas haereses nunc grassantes,—3° desiderium fidelium.[85]

This verbatim reproduction from *Petitiones* is not particularly revealing except in the total context of Hentrich and De Moos' work. The second paragraph identifies the petitioner, a residential bishop who was Patriarch of the Syrians; the first paragraph indicates the diocese. The second paragraph mentions the date of the request (February 23, 1870). Hentrich and De Moos note that from 1888 onwards, the diocese of Mardin had been amalgamated with that of Amidi; hence at the time, the patriarch was not the bishop at both dioceses. The fourth line of the *Analysis* identifies the form (*g*) used by the petitioner (who was not alone—he was joined by his auxiliary who had accompanied him to the First Vatican Council, as the preceding line indicates). The reference (p. 108) is to tome I, where the reader is informed that the form *g* is verbatim the same as form *d*. As the reader looks at the data more closely, it becomes apparent that the forms *a* through *k* are those that circulated during the First Vatican Council, and that while forms *d* and *g* are verbally the same, all the others contain significantly different theological nuances. Thus form *k* contained a request that the Fathers of Vatican I define the doctrine of the Assumption and that they do so by acclamation—only one bishop signed it(!); form *f* was more sober, and contained a request that the Fathers of Vatican I study the matter and that if they deemed it wise, proceed to a definition. That particular form was signed by thirteen bishops. The theological reasoning within the various forms is likewise different, one form stressing the almost universal belief of the people, another stressing the Assumption as a consequence of the Immaculate Conception. In choosing form *g* (or as the case may be *d*), Harcus and his auxiliary were opting for a particular theological slant. Thus in the *Analysis* provided by Hentrich and De Moos, *Descr* indicates that the term *Assumption* is to be understood in a bodily sense and that it presupposed Mary's physical death; *Qualif* is the theological note; i.e., form *g* (or as the case may be *d*) does not suggest that the doctrine had already been defined by the ordinary universal magisterium but that it could be defined (either by Pope or Council); *Prob* means that the theological basis was the constant judgment (*sensus*) of the Churches both in the East and the West (*utriusque Ecclesiae*) and venerable tradition; finally, *Pro opp* means that the reasons why a definition was considered fitting were threefold: the honor of the Blessed Virgin; defense against growing heresies; and the desire of the people.

Of some seven hundred Council Fathers present at Vatican I, only 187 presented petitions for a definition.[86] That fact in itself is susceptible of a number of different interpretations. Careful reading of Mansi reveals however that on May 8, 1870, the Holy Office let it be known that such requests should not be discussed at the Council. That fact more than the fact that the Council came to a premature close may explain why the requests were not more numerous.

Petitions expressed by way of signing one of the current forms were however only one way in which associative elements manifested themselves. Another was that of personal letters often representing a national hierarchy, an example of which is the request submitted by the Austrian bishops on November 10, 1917. In the Latin text, it comprises fifteen pages and almost six thousand words. It is divided into three sections. In section I the bishops presented their request; in section II, the grounding of the doctrine of the Assumption in tradition; and in section III the reasons why they considered it opportune. I quote only from the first section:

> Wherefore we also [the preceding paragraph indicates that the bishops considered themselves in continuity with those Fathers of Vatican I who had requested a similar definition], the Cardinals, Archbishops and Bishops of all parts of the Austrian Empire, by reason of our own and our people's devotion to the Blessed Mother of God and our Mother . . . beseech and ardently ask that Your Holiness, by reason of the supreme authority of the infallible magisterium which you possess [*pollet*] in the Church of Christ, for the ineffable consolation of all Christ's faithful, define and declare that the doctrine which holds that the Mother of God is alive body and soul in heaven is a doctrine revealed by God and is therefore firmly and constantly to be held by all the faithful.[87]

The Latin is slightly ambiguous,[88] but the thinking of the bishops then at their annual meeting in Vienna is unmistakable. Though most of the petitions individually drafted are not as lengthy as that of the Austrian hierarchy, the Austrian request was similar to the thrust of most. That Hentrich and De Moos had exercised at least reasonable caution is suggested by this third and final example presented here as illustrative of their work:

> Bernard I. *Otten* in the book entitled "*Instititiones Dogmaticae*, Tomus III, De Verbo Incarnato" (Chicago, Illinois, 1922) affirms on p. 412, n. 533: "A few years ago the Bishops of North America humbly asked the Pope finally to define this doctrine (sc. of the Assumption of the B.V. Mary). Since we have not been able to find anything either in the files of the Holy Office or in other sources, we abstract from it in this book.[89]

Further indication of the authors' thoroughness may be found in part two, where the dogmatic content of the petitions is studied along with their geographical distribution. An analysis of the theological notes employed by the bishops itself covers some forty-nine pages. The results of the study could be looked at from a variety of perspectives. Of the Cardinals, Patriarchs, Bishops, Prelates *Nullius* (q.v.) Chapters and Faculties of Theology there were during the years 1869-1941 no less than 3,018 petitions; of these 2,917 (or between 96 percent and 97 percent of the total) were that the Assumption be defined as the revealed word of God. Or one could look simply at the residential sees. In that case the results of Hentrich and De Moos' inquiry were that in the same period 820 sees (or 73 percent of the residential sees) asked for a definition. The following paragraph may be taken as a synthesis of the authors' findings:

> . . . it is evident that residential patriarchs, archbishops, bishops of all nations and all Sees spread throughout the world in "moral" agreement as authentic teachers of the Church teach that the doctrine which holds that the Blessed Virgin Mary has been taken up body and soul into heaven is a doctrine revealed by God and therefore can be defined as a dogma of faith . . . at the same time [it is evident] that with the same agreement they declare . . . that the definition is opportune.[90]

I wish to note here two inconsistencies, the first of which may be only apparent. As it stands, the above quotation seems to conflict with the previous one relative to the American bishops. However, the authors meant they could locate no petition from the American bishops as a group, though individual American bishops had made petitions. Given the care with which they seem to have gone about their research, and given the fact that elsewhere their conclusions are stated more precisely, the statement recorded in the passage just cited may be regarded as a slip of the pen. Second, if the majority of bishops were teaching in union with the Pope that the doctrine was one revealed by God, then it was already defined by the ordinary universal magisterium and had no need of a further definition. Be that as it may, it is quite clear that Hentrich and De Moos' primary concern was the teaching of the bishops, not the belief of the people. That is to say, they record but do not analyze petitions sent in by others in the Church. There were 32,291 petitions from priests and religious men; 50,975 from religious women, and 8,086,396 from the people.[91]

Hentrich and De Moos' work produced two reactions, the first of which was critical scrutiny by their peers; the second was widespread support by the Catholic Church at large.

Critique

A number of theologians expressed doubt about the validity of Hentrich and De Moos conclusions. Such were the difficulties raised by Martin Jugie in a book for which Bernard Lonergan was to have both praise and blame, and about which I shall have more to say below.[92] Jugie's principal objection seems to have been that it had not been established that the ordinary universal magisterium had been teaching the doctrine of the

Assumption as a doctrine revealed by God. Though in these pages Jugie did not explicitly refer to the book by its title nor to its authors (he directly refers to Hentrich in another context[93]), there can be no doubt it was the monumental work of Hentrich and De Moos that he had in mind when he questioned its principal thesis. Jugie's critique consisted of nine points, of which the ninth is a partial restatement of the fifth. The second and eighth deserve special attention.

In his second objection, Jugie questioned the real significance of Hentrich and De Moos findings, pointing out that the total of 820 Sees requesting a definition was spread over a period of seventy years from 1870 to 1940.[94] It was not established that at any given time (for example, in 1870, 1900, 1925 or 1950) 75 percent of the bishops were teaching that the doctrine of the Assumption was a revealed truth. Bishops die, are replaced, their successors do not always have the same convictions as their predecessors. But Jugie overlooked an important point stressed by F. S. Mueller two years later, which was fully documented in *Petitiones*.[95] Can it be seriously maintained, Mueller asked in effect, that in the case of a request submitted by a national hierarchy—that cited above from the Austrian hierarchy was only one of many—a man who at the time was only a priest, when subsequently chosen as bishop did not share the view, at least on important points, of the national hierarchy? Mueller thought this very unlikely. His argument may have had some probability, for if the bishop-elect did not in important matters share the views of those instrumental in appointing him, it is rather improbable, though not entirely impossible, that he would have been chosen as bishop in the first place. Thus the fact that during his term of office the said bishop did not make a personal request over and above that previously submitted by a national hierarchy may not have been as significant as Jugie suggested. Furthermore, Mueller claimed it could be shown with certainty that at least 512 residential bishops repeated the requests of their predecessors.[96]

Jugie's eighth objection was the contention that requests for a definition by the bishops did not prove that they themselves taught the doctrine of the Assumption as a formally revealed truth; what the requests show is a virtually unanimous desire on the part of the episcopate to see the doctrine defined by the solemn magisterium of the Church.[97] The requests therefore could not be considered as equivalent to *placets* given by bishops in a Council.[98] In coming to Hentrich and De Moos' defense, Mueller was quick to point out that careful reading of the requests submitted during the period suggested that the bishops already considered the doctrine to be revealed truth.[99] Mueller's assessment was correct if judged on the basis of the documentation then available; it was an understatement if judged by an event unforeseen even by the strongest supporters of the definition.

Reaction by the Catholic Church at Large

Critique by Jugie and others had not been typical, for *Petitiones* unleashed a flood of support for the definition, as Hentrich was to show five years after Jugie's attack.[100] In a long report that comprises two sections, Hentrich (unlike *Petitiones* this report was not co-authored) in section I ("De Recenti Theologorum Motu Assumptionistico") described the Catholic world's reaction to the former work. The response of the theologians had been almost overwhelming, support coming not only from individuals but also from whole faculties of theology, including the Institut Catholique de Paris, a fact worthy of note given its former archbishop's (Sibour's) refusal to encourage definition of the Immaculate Conception.[101] There were however very few from German and Dutch faculties. It is certain that most of the better Catholic theological minds of the time were in favor of a dogmatic definition. But more than that: Many bishops who had not personally made a petition for definition began to make one, and this well before Pius XII's formal polling of the Catholic episcopate in 1946. Thus at the time of the publication of *Petitiones* (1942), only 5.5 percent of the English hierarchy had asked that the doctrine be defined, but as soon as *Petitiones* was released, the whole English hierarchy petitioned. Hentrich called this a classical case since there had not been lacking those who pointed to the apparent reticence of certain national hierarchies as an indication that these bishops entertained some doubt on the matter.[102] But the English bishops did more than that. At their invitation, requests (*subscriptiones*) were gathered from the people and priests of every English diocese, were collated into huge volumes and sent to the Holy See.[103]

These facts and much more were reported in section II ("Circa Momentum Dogmaticum 'Petitionum De Assumptione Definienda ad S. Sedem Delatarum'"), the title of which was somewhat inaccurate. What Hentrich was about in that section had more to do with answering his critics than with the dogmatic importance of the petitions. I must limit myself here to one example. The Franciscan, Angelo a Roc, taking up the criticism leveled earlier by Jugie, demanded that a strict mathematical proportion of residential bishops asking for the definition be determined. According to a Roc's analysis, in the period 1900-1920, only 20 percent of the residential bishops had petitioned; in that of 1920-1940, only 30 percent; in those of

1927-1940 and 1900-1940, only 32 percent.[104] Hentrich easily isolated a mistake in a Roc's method. The Franciscan had indeed compared the numbers of requests by residential bishops with the number of residential bishops during each period, but he had not asked himself whether bishops who had not made a petition in the period 1900-1920 were not to make one, say, in 1921 or 1922, and so on, for each of the periods a Roc had examined.[105] In the year 1929, for example, Hentrich showed there were 1031 residential bishops; 532 made a petition for definition (or more than 50 percent); in the year 1933, there were 1053 residential bishops of whom 539 (or 51 percent) had made a petition.[106]

At the very least it may be maintained that the analysis published by Hentrich and De Moos showed that as of 1942 an existing episcopal consensus seemed probable. In the meantime another kind of consensus had been forming and was to reach a climax about a year before the definition.

The Role of the Theologians

An adequate history of the theological discussion relative to the doctrine of the Assumption, as it evolved from the First Vatican Council to the definition of November 1, 1950, has not been written.[107] I do not intend to supply for this lack. My attempt to show the presence of associative elements in the process that culminated in the definition will here take the form of describing the kind of argument that took place and of providing a general indication of its extent.

The Nature of the Debate

This will perhaps be grasped more clearly if the reader thinks of a stream with a perceptible undercurrent. The more forceful flow tended to begin from the fact that within the Catholic Church belief in the doctrine of the Assumption was beyond doubt and sought in the tradition or in the *sensus fidelium* an explanation of how it could have materialized; the undercurrent found basis in the tradition (i.e., the scriptures and the Fathers) insufficient and tended to argue that therefore the doctrine could not be defined. Both currents are splendid examples of associative elements present in the process that ended in the definition. Illustration thereof will consist in an examination of the work of three theologians. Indeed, the difference between the two currents may be more sharply perceived in the following contrast.

1. *Martin Jugie and Berthold Altaner.* The principal purpose of Jugie's book had been to show that (1) the doctrine of the Assumption was not yet a truth of divine and Catholic faith, that (2) it could be defined, but that the basis of the definition lay in (3) neither the implicit witness of scripture and tradition nor in the *sensus fidelium* (*sentiment commun des fidèles*)—however suggestive, the evidence in the end was inconclusive—but in (4) speculative theological reasoning.[108] Thus were excluded the principle of *lex orandi lex credendi* and the fact that the feast of the Assumption had been celebrated both in the East and the West for many centuries; [109] excluded also was the teaching of the ordinary universal magisterium in that it had not been proven that the bishops in union with the Roman Bishop had taught the doctrine as formally (though implicitly) revealed.[110] Jugie's reason for urging definition was precisely this: The doctrine of the Assumption was implicitly contained in another dogma, that of the Immaculate Conception. That is to say: If original sin had never occurred, a human being would have had the "right," after a time of testing, to the immediate glorification of the body; but since original sin had no part in Mary, one must acknowledge that Mary had the "right" to the immediate glorification of hers.[111]

In advancing this argument, Jugie admitted that his position was close to that taken some twenty years earlier by P. Jalaber.[112] Be that as it may, the former's conclusions did not win the universal support of his peers and were in fact subjected to probing criticism. One of these critiques deserves particular attention not only because of its incisiveness but also because it came from the pen of a well-known patrologist, Berthold Altaner, and represents the counter-current in the debate.

Altaner's remarks were published in two articles that appeared in the *Theologische Revue*.[113] Considering this bipartite article as a whole, one should distinguish central concerns (lack of sufficient evidence from the scriptures and the Fathers) from peripheral ones. I shall begin with the latter, which had to do with (1) the petitions addressed to the Holy See that the doctrine be defined, (2) the fact that much earlier the doctrine had been considered only a *pia sententia* but that it had begun to be considered as *certa*, (3) the fact that theologians were now favorable to a definition, (4) the effects of a definition on relations with non-Catholic Christians, and (5) theology as a discipline (*Wissenschaft*). On these matters, Altaner's comments, though much to the point, were somewhat loosely organized; I shall therefore not treat them in the order presented above.

Jugie had addressed himself to the question of petitions sent to the Roman Bishop and, as we have seen, had not been impressed. Altaner went further. Without documenting his case, he indicated the source of the petitions, stating that when the Vatican Council had been convoked, the Benedictine, A. Vaccari and the Franciscan R. Buselli had begun to collect signatures from the Council Fathers.[114] Altaner mentioned that 187 Spanish, Latin American, and Near Eastern bishops had submitted petitions but only with great difficulty could one give that fact any particular theological significance. And although some ten years later, on February 19, 1880, the Holy Office characterized as unbecoming the international movement organized by Vaccari for the definition of the Assumption[115] (a "censure" of which Altaner seems to have been totally unaware) Altaner conceded that from 1899 onwards the number of petitions increased, in many cases because of Eucharistic and Marian congresses.[116] He then alluded approvingly to Jugie's statement that from 1870 onwards theology as a discipline had made no progress in the matter.[117] As to theologians favorable to a definition, Jugie had maintained that contrary to what had happened in the development of the doctrine of the Immaculate Conception, that of the Assumption had been denied by no theologian but that certain theologians had refrained from judgment (". . . sont restés en suspens à son sujet . . .").[118] On this point Altaner simply mentioned that the number of theologians favorable to a definition were cited at least in recent times as the basis for the necessity and usefulness of a definition;[119] he then indulged in an extended parenthesis.

Altaner asked how many Catholics really desired this definition.[120] For many it would make no difference and in the end would only tend to obscure more important Marian dogmas like that of the *Theotokos*. Indeed, the definition would only puzzle that group of people, not to be underestimated, who, brought up in a modern scientific world-view, would simply not understand it.[121] He then launched into a theme which Jugie had not treated at length, namely the effect of such a definition on non-Catholic Christians. Surely love for the separated brethren should suggest some restraint.[122] At this point, Altaner took up again the theme he had left dangling, that of the consensus among theologians, and distinguished three groups among them:

(1)   Those who thought that definability could be *shown* from (a) the scripture, (b) tradition, (c) speculative theology, and (d) the *sensus fidelium* (*Glaubenssinn der Kirche*)[123]

(2)   Those who thought that scripture and tradition provided no usable

proof but who nonetheless thought that definability might be considered on the basis of (a) speculative theology and (b) the *sensus fidelium*[124]

(3) Those who based their approach to definability only on the *sensus fidelium*[125]

None of these reasons were sufficient, Altaner maintained, and therefore in the name of theology as a discipline no more petitions should be sent to the highest magisterium in the Church.[126] Only the magisterium could settle the question, and until it did, theologians should remain opposed to a definition. Though reasons based on theology as a discipline and the *sensus fidelium* had to do with what I have called Altaner's peripheral concerns, in the latter context he had much to say. Jugie had admitted that in its present state the *sensus fidelium* was insufficient to ground a definition; Altaner went still further, as he had in other matters. A distinction must be made between *quaestio juris* and *quaestio facti*. In the former case, what the whole Catholic Church believes as a matter of faith (*Glaubensatz*) must indeed have its origin in divine revelation and tradition, even when scripturally and historically there are lacunae.[127] Otherwise, the Church would have fallen into doctrinal error, something which would be contrary to the promise of Christ himself.[128] But when one comes to the question of fact, these conditions could not be said to have materialized in the case of the Assumption, for the Church does not teach this as dogma nor do her people understand it as such.[129] The doctrine of the Assumption in the Church had the status of a *pia opinio* and nothing more. To attempt to define the doctrine on the basis of the *sensus fidelium* would amount to *petitio principii*.[130] Indeed, a definition in such a state of affairs would contribute to the erosion of theology as a discipline.[131]

As to possible grounding in speculative theology (which had in the end constituted Jugie's only argument), Altaner stated that this kind of a proof could be considered valid only if it flowed from strict logical necessity.[132] If a parallel between Jesus and Mary is maintained (i.e., just as Jesus had conquered sin and death and so entered into glory, so Mary as intimately associated with the work of redemption and as one free from the effects of original sin must be considered as having been proleptically raised as was Jesus), why is it, Altaner asked, that Jesus was raised on the third day but that Mary was not?[133]

These considerations led Altaner to discuss another of the concerns listed above, namely that what had been a *pia sententia* was now considered by the majority of theologians as a *sententia certa*. There were no sufficient grounds for this change in the theological note attributed to the doctrine of the Assumption; the change was due to the "Marian atmosphere" of the day, or more precisely, to the lack of theological reflection in which time-conditioned piety and attitudes played their part.[134] What Jugie advanced as a conclusion from speculative reasoning was, upon analysis, nothing else but reasons of fittingness (*Konvenienzbeweise*). So much for speculative theology, stated Altaner: *Tantum valet quantum probat*.[135]

We come now to what seem to have been Altaner's central concerns, lack of sufficient evidence from scripture and the Fathers. While Jugie had allowed that Rev. 12 might have some indirect reference to Mary as associated with the work of the one mediator between God and humankind, the evidence was inconclusive; but Jugie had scarcely considered Gen. 3:15 as suggestive of a similar notion. Yet it was upon that text that Altaner focused his attention in regard to the Old Testament. The argument went, so Altaner stated, that since the victory of the Messiah over sin, and over death as the effect of sin, was complete, then, given the Eve-Mary parallel, the victory of Mary over sin, and the effect of sin, must have been complete too. Hence the basis for some suggestion in the Old Testament of Mary's proleptic glorification, if one reads the text in its total context. Against this interpretation, Altaner maintained that only the original text was inspired and that in the original the word *seed* meant a collectivity.[136] Regarding the New Testament Jugie had allowed that the term *Mother of My Lord* (Luke 1:43) might have some implications about Mary's dignity and privileges of grace but for Jugie even that was inconclusive.[137] Altaner seems to have not understood Jugie's reservations on the proper use of scripture, and launched into an attack against the *Ave, gratia plena* of the Vulgate. This was a clear misrepresentation of the Greek, which read simply κεχαριτωμένη. This term gradually came to be read as *plena* and then as *plenissima*. If κεχαριτωμένη means *full* of grace, then of course one could certainly consider that for Mary all graces and privileges were promised, including her Assumption. But such a reading does violence to the Greek, for κεχαριτωμένη means only *graced*.[138]

Altaner now advanced to his forte, Patristics. Jugie had examined at some length the two texts from the Patristic period, one from Epiphanius of Salamis, the other, a sermon reportedly preached by a Christian priest named Timothy who had ministered in Jerusalem. I shall cite these texts below, it being sufficient here to point out that Epiphanius seems to have left open the possibility of the Assumption whereas Timothy seems to have unquestionably affirmed it. The case of the priest Timothy was perhaps the more striking: Here one had, at the beginning of the fifth century, in

Jerusalem itself, an apparent affirmation of the Assumption and no evidence that the preacher was aware of a contrary tradition. Because Timothy had not mentioned the *Theotokos*, Jugie had suggested that the text probably dates from about 400.[139] Altaner responded by saying that he had already pointed out in an earlier study that the text in question belonged to a later period.[140] Indeed, he said, the evidence suggested that it was written by an anonymous author somewhere between the sixth and eighth centuries. Furthermore, the text had nothing to do with the Assumption. (Altaner probably meant that the text might be taken to refer to an ascent into heaven after the manner of Elias, and hence lacked the element of the body's being "changed," as according to the Pauline witness [1 Cor. 15:51] resurrected bodies are.) When one comes to Epiphanius, the extant documents show that this Church Father was unaware of any historical tradition about the Assumption.[141]

While this summary does not do full justice to Altaner's acerbic criticism, it may nonetheless be sufficient for an adequate grasp of the kind of theological debate that took place prior to the definition and of the self-criticism Catholic theologians subjected each other to. Upon reading Altaner's articles it is clear that he was out not only to review Jugie's book but also to voice once again his own deeply rooted objections to a definition. Nothing else seems to explain his sallies into matters that Jugie had not treated or into reasons Jugie himself had admitted were insufficient to ground a definition. Indeed, Altaner's criticisms of Jugie were themselves not above criticism. Thus regarding the petitions, the fact that only 187 of the Fathers at the First Vatican Council had signed them could on the surface be taken to mean that the majority either did not think the question sufficiently mature or that they refused to be pressured; the data suggest another reason that I have indicated above. And when he maintained that many doctrines formerly believed by the faithful were no longer believed, he should have asked, believed *how*? As pertaining to the substance of the faith? As probable? As a pious opinion subject to further scrutiny by the magisterial officers of the Church? Altaner was sensitive enough to the question of theological notes as certain passages of his bipartite article attest. His failure to make appropriate distinctions when such distinctions might militate against his own position suggest that he himself, for all his claim that theology must be a discipline, was not without a certain *parti pris*.

2. *Fulbert Cayré*. A further example of the main current was Fulbert Cayré. Professor at the Institut Catholique de Paris, Cayré's principal contribution consisted of a paper given at the *Journées d'Etudes.mariales*

in Montreal (August, 1948).[142] In an extended introduction in which he discussed the notion of the Assumption and acknowledged it as a dogmatic fact (he used the term loosely in the sense of a belief shared by virtually all Catholics and Orthodox) which however could not be grounded historically, Cayré attempted to clarify the conditions in which doctrinal development could take place. Absolutely central to his endeavor was the relation between history and the *sensus fidei* (or in my language, the *sensus fidelium*). Though Cayré did not speak explicitly in these terms, such seems to have been his meaning when he suggested that development comes about from a seed planted within Catholic consciousness.[143] The French scholar thought that seed was discernible in the scriptures.[144]

Thus in the first of the three stages of his analysis, Cayré pointed to a number of scriptural passages. There were the classical ones of course— Gen. 3:15-16 and Luke 1:42. But then he went on to certain passages in Romans (5:12-21) where the whole of humanity is described as united in the new Adam and in the freedom promised to all the redeemed. Taken up again in 1 Cor. 15:20-23, the doctrine of the fullness of the redemption may be summed up in the $\dot{\alpha}\nu\alpha\kappa\epsilon\phi\alpha\lambda\alpha\iota\dot{\omega}\sigma\alpha\sigma\theta\alpha\iota$ of Eph. 1:10, the recapitulation of all things in Christ. To these texts may be added that of Rev. 12.

Now Cayré was quite careful in what he was about. He did not say that these texts "proved" the Assumption. He merely said that all these texts taken together may have suggested to Catholic consciousness that the fullness of redemption brought about by Christ may have been applied in advance to his mother.[145] I shall for the moment pass over the second stage of Cayré's analysis. Part of the problem in coming to a theologically grounded consensus about the definability of the doctrine was the lateness with which explicit belief in the Assumption seems to have manifested itself. Because evidence for explicit belief in that doctrine prior to the seventh century could not be shown, many theologians considered that, though the doctrine of the Assumption was a fact of Catholic consciousness, it was nonetheless not definable as dogma. Taking Jugie as a model, Cayré analyzed two texts, one of which was clearly from the fourth century. This was the *Panarion* of Epiphanius, written between 374 and 377, the relevant passages of which had to do with certain theological excesses in regard to Mary, the Mother of Jesus. On the one hand, there were those who denied her virginity; on the other, there were those whose Marian devotion bordered on adoration. Epiphanius thought he was steering a course between two extremes. In order to refute the second group, it would have been sufficient to say that Mary had died. But he did not do so; instead he advanced three hypotheses without excluding any:

If the Blessed Virgin had died and was buried, her falling asleep was surrounded by honors; death found her pure and her crown was that of virginity. If she was killed, according to what was written, "And a sword will pierce your soul," she shines among the martyrs and her holy body was proclaimed blessed; indeed, through her, the dawn of light had risen on the world. Or else, she continued to live, for to God nothing is impossible and he can do anything he wants. In fact, no one knows what her end was like.[146]

Elsewhere in the same treatise, Epiphanius added: "If it appears to some that we are mistaken, let them search the scriptures. There they will find neither Mary's death, nor whether she died; neither will they find whether she was buried or not."[147] But the Bishop had more to say on the matter of Mary's end:

Scripture has kept complete silence because of the greatness of the miracle, in order not to strike the human mind with excessive surprise. As for myself, I dare not speak of it; I keep it in my thoughts and keep my own counsel. Perhaps we have even found somewhere a trace of this holy blessed woman, such as the fact that it is impossible to discover whether she died. On the one hand, Simeon indeed said of her: "And as for you, a sword shall pierce your soul, so that thoughts hidden in the hearts of many may be revealed . . . ."[148] On the other hand, the Apocalypse of John says that the dragon will jump on the woman who had given birth to the male child . . . and that she was taken into the desert so that the dragon could not get her. It is possible that that was acomplished in Mary. I do not however affirm this in any absolute manner, and I do not say that she remains immortal. But neither do I say she died.[149]

Cayré subsequently quoted Epiphanius as stating "*Scripture . . . has left this* [last] *point in doubt.*"[150] The second source cited by the French theologian was a sermon preached by a Christian priest in Jerusalem. The relevant text as translated is as follows:

"And as for you, a sword shall pierce your soul . . ." From that some have concluded that the mother of the Savior, put to death by the sword, had obtained the glorious end of the martyrs. But such is not the case. A metal sword pierces the body but it does not rend the soul. It was not so because the Virgin, to this day, is immortal. *He who made his stay in her having taken her to the place of his ascension.*[151]

Though Cayré did not say so, the second text was somewhat problematic in that the likely dates of its composition span a considerable period, from about 350 to 550; indeed, Altaner had suggested a much later date.

Following Jugie, Cayré thought it more likely to have been written about 400 since the term *Theotokos* does not appear in it. In any case, though neither text could be taken as the basis for grounding the doctrine of the Assumption, they did suggest that evidence for an evolving belief in that doctrine could be found before the seventh century. Thus it was not the apographa, the various *Transitus Mariae* which began to spring up around the seventh century which brought about belief in the Assumption, but an evolving belief in the Assumption which brought about the apographa. Indeed, had he cared to, Cayré might have provided texts which suggest that some bishops of the seventh century were "editing" some of the apographa, removing the extravagances but leaving the kernel of the doctrine intact, a fact difficult to explain if belief in the doctrine had not begun to be formed before that time. Cayré concluded that the doctrine was definable, his principal reason seeming to be that it was certainly the belief of the Church for many centuries.

But he seemed to have gone beyond the data when he asserted that early historical foundation might be sufficient to authorize a definition.[152] This last assessment was one of the weaknesses of his argument. All that history could be said to establish was a twofold point: (1) there was no clear historical evidence that indicated early Christian belief denied the doctrine and (2) there was some historical evidence that as early as the fourth century and thus clearly before Ephesus, Catholic consciousness may have been evolving toward a doctrine of the Assumption. But that was all that history could affirm. If the doctrine was definable, then in Catholic terms it was definable because it was embedded in Catholic consciousness as somehow pertaining to salvation brought about by the Christ. That the seeds of the doctrine may have been planted by the scriptures remained a possibility, as the *Panarion* of Epiphanius suggests.

The Extent of Theological Discussion

The foregoing should suffice to show the nature of the theological debate illustrative of Church as association, a factor radically constitutive of the process that ended as a dogmatic definition. In general terms it may be said that theological reflection on the Assumption increased markedly after the First World War, particularly in the mid-twenties, reaching a climax about a year before the actual definition. And it was the major current that was to win out. The principal vehicle was undoubtedly the Marian Congresses that under strong Franciscan influence took place with increasing frequency. Indeed, Martin Jugie himself acknowledged his indebtedness to a paper read at the Marian Congress held at Nancy in 1924 while Bernard Lonergan at that held at Montreal in 1948 was to argue for definability.[153] A list of Mariological literature on the Assumption during the brief span from 1948 to 1950 just prior to the definition would itself fill several pages.

An indication that all this discussion was having its effect may be seen from a comparison of two articles on the Assumption as found in two well-known Catholic encyclopedias. If one compares the article by J. Bellamy in the *Dictionnaire de Théologie catholique* as found in its first volume published in 1909 with the article by J. Demahuet in *Catholicisme: Hier, Aujourd'hui, Demain* in the relevant volume published in 1948, the difference is remarkable. In the former, Bellamy asked whether the doctrine was definable and seemed to incline to an affirmative answer, but not without some hesitation;[154] in the latter, Demahuet stated the doctrine was ". . . une vérité proche de la foi;"[155] i.e., he considered its proper theological note to be *fidei proximum* (q.v.).

The discussion had indeed been international in scope and had involved the best Catholic theological minds of the day.

Episcopal Consensus

The request of Pius XII that his fellow magisterial officers inform him of their judgment on the definability of the doctrine of the Assumption and the faith of their people in that regard had been made in the Apostolic Constitution (privately circulated but later promulgated) *Deiparae Virginis* of May 1, 1946.[156] In *Munificentissimus Deus*, he indicated that the response had been almost unanimously in favor of a definition.[157] Several months earlier, in the *Osservatore romano* of August 16 and 17, G. Hentrich published a breakdown of the figures.[158] The proportion of bishops whose responses had arrived was 94 percent; i.e., 1,191 *residential* bishops, including Cardinals and Patriarchs, had responded; the answers of eighty-six sees in missionary territories difficult of access had not yet arrived. Exactly 1,169 responses were affirmative to both questions, only twenty-two bishops expressing doubts about the matter. That is to say: Most of the twenty-two simply thought the definition was inopportune but six of them doubted the doctrine could be defined. This amounted to only 0.4 percent of the total. Among Abbots and Prelates *nullius*, fifty-seven out of fifty-nine had answered affirmatively; among Vicars apostolic, 203

out of 206, but twelve responses had not yet arrived; one of fifty-four
Eastern bishops had answered negatively. On the basis of Hentrich's
analysis, affirmative consensus among Catholic bishops clearly approached
100 percent, an event that the critics of the earlier *Petitiones* had not
anticipated, nor indeed had Jugie and Altaner.

OVERVIEW

In the end the doctrine of the Assumption was defined primarily because
of the *sensus fidelium*, perceived as it was to be intimately linked to other
dogmas relating to Christ the Redeemer. Just as the dogma of the Immaculate Conception was understood as a de facto result of the Divine Maternity and thence of the Incarnation and the Redemption, so the dogma of
the Assumption was seen as an aspect of Christian belief about the resurrection of the body, itself a further effect of the redemptive work of Christ.
Further speculation about the Assumption after the definition led to the
view of Mary as the Archtype of the Church, a concept which *mutatis
mutandis* was later assimilated by the Second Vatican Council.

The data uncovered above suggest that, like those pertaining to the
dogma of the Immaculate Conception, associative elements were significantly present on the way to the definition subsequently made by the
Roman Bishop. While from a non-Catholic point of view this in no way
grounds the credibility of the dogmas, it does, I submit, ground my
argument as advanced thus far in this chapter and suggests that, even on
the level of the extraordinary papal magisterium, *Church as association*
was intimately involved with *Church as institution*. It is thus time to ask a
further relevant question; namely, what significance do associative elements have for at least a partial solution to Catholicism's external
problem?

Associative Elements
and Papal Infallibility

At a deeper level the central issue in Catholicism's external problem lies,
as everyone knows, in the claim to infallibility on the part of the Roman
Bishop. Within that central issue is a core difficulty, a kind of knot that, to

change the metaphor, the ecumenical dialogues have so far not succeeded in loosening. Such is the matter I wish now to address. I shall first quote and explain the relevant paragraph from *Pastor Aeternus* and in the context of the antecedent conciliar debates identify the cause of the impasse at the First Vatican Council. It is virtually the same as that experienced in present ecumenical relations inasmuch as they have to do with the issue of authority. I shall then suggest how my findings in the first part of this chapter and below may, perhaps, contribute to a partial solution.

THE CORE DIFFICULTY

Promulgated on July 18, 1870, the Dogmatic Constitution *Pastor Aeternus* stated in part:

> *Text D.* .... the Roman Pontiff, when he speaks *ex cathedra*, that is when acquitting himself of his task as pastor and teacher of all Christians, defines in virtue of his supreme authority a doctrine of faith or morals to be held by the whole Church, through the divine assistance promised him in the Blessed Peter, possesses that infallibility with which the Divine Redeemer wished his Church to be provided in defining a doctrine of faith or morals; and therefore, *these kinds of definitions of the Roman Pontiff are irreformable of themselves, not from the consent of the Church.*[159]

There are two kinds of language functioning in the text, the one theological (pertaining to infallibility-under-certain-circumstances of the Roman Bishop as exercising the Petrine ministry within Catholicism), the other legal or canonical (pertaining to conditions for validity in law). The *ex sese* does not refer to the Roman Bishop but to *definitiones*, a point frequently overlooked by commentators. What the decree excludes by the *ex sese, non autem ex consensu Ecclesiae* is the notion that once the Roman Bishop under the circumstances envisaged by the decree has come to and has actually promulgated a decision, the rest of the Catholic Church must agree with him in order for the definition to be binding. That is to say: What the *ex sese* excludes is the necessity of post-definitional consent in the sense of ratification. Thus for example, after the definition of the Immaculate Conception Bishop Dupanloup published a very long pastoral letter explaining to his people why the definition should be accepted, a treatise similar to the report submitted by the diocese of Arras prior to the definition.[160] And Archbishop Sibour, in highly polished Latin, did likewise, approaching the question from the viewpoint of a theory of doctrinal development reminiscent of that espoused earlier by Newman.[161] What the *ex sese* was saying in effect was that, however commendable such efforts were, the Pope's infallibility-under-certain-circumstances is not dependent on the modalities of its reception. But that does not mean that the Council Fathers thought the Pope was infallible in and of himself. Such a view constitutes a false reading of the *ex sese*, a point to which I shall return below.

But what about pre-definitional assent? This is a much more difficult matter. In the debates themselves, the Council Fathers do not seem to have addressed the question in these terms but tended to speak of the necessity for prior consultation of and cooperation with the rest of the Church, particularly of and with bishops and theologians. The fact that the Council Fathers tended to see the matter from this angle poses an initial problem that I shall attempt to resolve below; that is, canonically a person may be obliged to prior consultation (*votum consultativum*) without being obliged to have the agreement (*votum deliberativum*) of his consultors. This distinction in Canon Law is of long standing. In view of the documentation, at least four questions should be distinguished:

(A)   Is the Roman Bishop obliged to consult the rest of the Church prior to a definition?
(B)   What is the nature of the obligation?
(C)   Does failure to consult jeopardize the Roman Bishop's infallibility?
(D)   What relevance do the answers to these questions have for the necessity of pre-definitional assent?

Though various aspects of these matters had been treated much earlier by Bishop Pie, then bishop at Poitiers, and Cardinal Guidi of Bologna,[162] a vitally important speech was that given by Bishop Gasser on July 11, 1870, one week before the voting on *Pastor Aeternus* (Text D). Within the limits of the caution suggested above, Gasser was clearly a spokesman for the majority;[163] the "we" of his speech was not an editorial one, a fact that must be kept in mind as we proceed. Regarding Questions (A), a relevant passage in Gasser's speech is as follows:

Text E.   This cooperation of the Church is not at that point [*tum*] therefore excluded, for the infallibility of the Roman Pontiff does not come to him by way of inspiration and revelation but by way of the divine

assistance. Hence the Pope by reason of his office and the seriousness of the question is bound [*tenetur*] to use means apt for correctly investigating and stating the truth in a suitable manner; and
these means are councils, or even the advice of bishops, cardinals
and theologians, etc. These means certainly differ according to
circumstances and we must [*debemus*] devoutly believe that in the
divine assistance given [*facta*] to Peter and to his successors by
Christ the Lord there is at the same time contained the promise of
the means which are necessary and suitable for affirming the
infallible judgment of the Pontiff.[164]

The context in which Text E occurs is that wherein Gasser envisaged the
Church in serious theological dissension or a case where the bishops
themselves have fallen into error (as in the Arian crisis, though Gasser did
not allude to specific instances). The *tum* of Text E thus takes on added
significance, for even in those circumstances cooperation from the rest of
the Church is not excluded. Indeed the first sentence seems to imply that
Gasser envisaged the possibility that the divine assistance might well come
to the Roman Bishop through the rest of the Catholic Church. The
importance of Text E lies however in the second sentence, which is relevant
to the question of pre-definitional assent. The Pope by reason of his office
(*pro officio suo*) is obliged to consult the rest of the Church prior to a
definition. But what is the nature of the obligation? Seeking an answer to
Question (B) will bring us closer to Gasser's (and the majority's) thinking:

> *Text F.* Some very reverend Fathers . . . go further and wish to introduce
> into the dogmatic constitution conditions which are found in var-
> ious theological tracts and which have to do with the good faith
> and diligence of the Pontiff in investigating and propounding truth
> and which therefore must be accounted [as belonging] *to the moral
> rather than to the dogmatic realm* [*ordini*]. For our Lord Jesus
> most considerately [*piissime*] willed that the charism of truth
> depend not on the conscience of the Pontiff, which is a private,
> indeed very private affair of each individual known only to God,
> but on the Pontiff's public relation to the universal Church. . . [165]

Gasser then went on to add:

> *Text G.* There is therefore no reason to fear, as though through the bad
> faith and negligence of the Pontiff the whole Church could be led
> into error about the faith. For the protection of Christ and the
> divine assistance promised to Peter's successors is so efficacious a

cause that the judgment of the Sovereign Pontiff, if it were erroneous and destructive of the Church, would be impeded; or if the
Pontiff in fact comes to a definition, it is infallibly true.[166]

The larger context in which Text G occurs is that of Text E, which has to
do with the obligation of prior consultation. When Texts F and G are read
in that frame of reference, the brunt of Gasser's (and the majority's)
position seems to have been that the Roman Bishop, prior to an eventual
definition, is morally obliged to seek out the faith of the Catholic Church in
cooperation with others. What Gasser meant by the distinction between
the moral and dogmatic realm seems to become less obscure as one
ponders other passages in his speech. Against the opinion of those who
maintained that the Roman Bishop can define nothing without the advice
and help of his fellow bishops, Gasser's response was unrelenting:

Text H. Before I answer this objection, it helps to recall that in the opinion
of those who object it is a question of a strict and absolute necessity
of the advice and help of the bishops in any infallible judgment of
the Roman Pontiff, with the result that it ought to have its place in
the very definition of our dogmatic constitution. *In this strict and
absolute necessity consists the whole difference between us, not in
the opportuneness* or in some relative necessity which must be left
to the judgment of the Roman Pontiff weighing the circumstances.
This therefore cannot have any place in the definition [contained]
in the dogmatic constitution.[167]

A dogmatic obligation thus seems synonymous with *the strict and
absolute necessity* of Text H, which in turn suggests what the core difficulty was. And it was that *strict and absolute necessity* which the majority
of the Council Fathers rejected.

The answers to Questions (A), (B), and (C) should now be clear. The
majority understood that the Roman Bishop prior to a definition is obliged
to consult the rest of the Catholic Church; the obligation is moral, not
dogmatic; failure to do so may be sinful (the "bad faith and negligence" of
Text G) but the Roman Bishop's failure in this regard would not lead the
rest of the Catholic Church into theological error (Text G).

But since the obligation of prior consultation is conceptually distinct
from the obligation of prior assent, Question (D) must now be faced. It
may first be stated that Gasser sometimes used the term *auxilium Ecclesiae*
synonymously with *assensus Ecclesiae*.[168] Second, although the necessity
of prior consultation does not logically (or canonically) imply the necessity
of prior agreement or assent, nonetheless he who rejects the dogmatic

necessity of prior consultation or cooperation probably intends to reject the dogmatic necessity of prior agreement or assent. But it must be asked, does this probability have a basis in the documents? Not so much in the debates themselves as in other of the conciliar records. The question of pre-definitional assent had been brought to the attention of the Committee on Faith (the *Deputatio de rebus ad fidem pertinentibus*) as early as April 27, 1870, but it decided not to add anything to the section on papal infallibility itself.[169] It intended to come at the matter by stating in another section of the draft on the Church that the Council rejected any appeal from the Pope to a Council.[170] It is clear then that the Committee had at least considered the question but also that the issue does not seem to have been debated explicitly on the Council floor except in the context of prior consultation, in which speakers like Gasser sometimes used "help" interchangeably with "assent." The historian is not left however with a deduction from the rejection of the necessity of prior consultation and the way some speakers used certain terms. On July 14, 1870, three days after Gasser's crucial speech and only four days prior to the actual voting of *Pastor Aeternus*, a letter that seems to have reflected the view of the majority was sent to Pius IX. Written in Italian, it stated in part:

> The Gallicans and especially Bishop Maret admit that the definitions of the Popes are infallible if there is the previous, concomitant, or subsequent consent of the bishops. In order to stop [*ferire*] this error head on, it is necessary to put the contradictory into the definition . . . .
>
> Therefore, according to the feeling even of Bishop Freppel and a few other good French bishops, it would be necessary to make a slight addition to the formula which would read as follows: and *therefore these kinds of definitions of the Roman Pontiffs are irreformable of themselves, without the previous, concomitant, or subsequent consent of the bishops being necessary. . . .*[171]

It is beyond doubt that Pius IX approved this move and that he instructed Cardinal Bilio to make the appropriate change in the draft to be subsequently presented for vote by the Council Fathers.[172] In fairness, however, it should be noted that the Pope did not make the suggestion on his own but that the matter had been brought to his attention by representatives of the majority. The form that the change was to take was the addition of the *ex sese, non autem ex consensu Ecclesiae* of Text D. While the phrase itself as it stands seems to refer only to post-definitional consent, the letter to Pius IX, which was the occasion of Cardinal Bilio's introduction of the change in the text to be voted on, suggests that its target was the exclusion of the necessity for pre-definitional assent as well. Thus the thinking of the majority on the matter is not merely a deduction from what they through their spokesman had had to say on prior consultation or from their occasional manner of using certain terms but has further basis in the conciliar records.

That the Pope should (*tenetur* in Gasser's speech,[173] *debet* in Guidi's[174]) consult the rest of the Church, particularly bishops and theologians, prior to a definition was clearly the thinking of all the Council Fathers; that he must do so, that he could not define unless the rest of the Catholic Church agreed with him was clearly rejected by the majority. Thus the necessity of pre-definitional assent was deliberately kept out of the decree. The reason behind this emphasis-by-omission is further illustrated by Luke 22:31-32 as explained by Gasser. For in that text as an indication of how the New Testament witness understood the function of Peter in the Church, the *you* in "...Satan demanded to have *you* that he might sift *you* as wheat..." is a plural ($\dot{\upsilon}\mu\hat{\alpha}$s) whereas the *you* in "... but I have prayed for *you* that your faith might not fail ..." is a singular ($\pi\epsilon\rho\grave{\iota}\ \sigma o\hat{\upsilon}$). Gasser suggested the implications were that the rest of the Church might fall into doctrinal error—Gasser speaking of course in the context of the extraordinary papal magisterium—but that Peter would not because of special help from Christ.

From the explicit exclusion of the dogmatic necessity of post-definitional consent and the emphasis (by omission) of no dogmatic need for pre-definitional assent by the rest of the Catholic Church (particularly by the bishops) emerge what I have called *the determinative factors in the Petrine function inasmuch as they have to do with so-called papal infallibility*. It is the second of these factors that is the more crucial of the two, for obviously if there is pre-definitional assent, then post-definitional consent will take care of itself. A further question arises, however:

(E)   Do the determinative factors in the Petrine function inasmuch as they have to do with so-called papal infallibility mean that the Council understood the Roman Bishop's infallibility-under-certain-circumstances to be an infallibility separate from the Church?

The answer to this question has considerable implications for ecumenical advance. For Gasser was to respond that the Roman Bishop's infallibility could be said to be separate if *separate* meant *distinct*; i.e., it results from a special promise of Christ.[175] But papal infallibility was not separate if *separate* meant one separates the Pontiff from a very ordered union with the Church.[176] Gasser continued:

> *Text I.*   Furthermore, from the cooperation and help of the Church we do
> not separate a pope who infallibly defines, at least in the sense that
> we do not exclude cooperation and help by the Church.[177]

Other members of the majority had already powerfully expressed what Gasser was trying to say.[178] The Pope, according to Catholic understanding in this regard is not infallible of himself—this would be a complete misreading of the *ex sese* (Text D). According to Catholic dogma his judgment can be infallible under certain circumstances only because of his relation to the universal Church. As it stands Text D of *Pastor Aeternus* is considerably less encompassing than the extremists among the infallibilists desired.[179]

But however benignly one interprets it, so-called papal infallibility is the chief stumbling block in ecumenical relations inasmuch as they have to do with the function of authority. Though pre-definitional assent is the more fundamental, both factors constituted the core difficulty at the First Vatican Council. And it is that core difficulty that in the present context remains the dominant concern of ecumenically minded non-Catholic Christians.

POSSIBILITIES OF A PARTIAL SOLUTION?

When one examines with some care what happened in the process that culminated in the definition of the two Marian dogmas, *it is clear that the more crucial factor in the Petrine function inasmuch as it has to do with so-called papal infallibility was simply not operative.* The Roman Bishop did not define the Marian dogmas without the previous assent of the rest of the Catholic Church; *hence associative elements present in that process suggest that the determinative factors in the Petrine function inasmuch as they have to do with so-called papal infallibility as understood by official Catholicism are for that body a value having to do more with principle than with practice.* The second part of the argument in this chapter is thus largely a corollary of the first and may, I suggest, be considered as grounded on the basis of the foregoing analysis. For as in the case of the development of doctrine, so in that of dogma the Catholic Church seems to have manifested characteristics of the Church considered as κοινωνία.

The data suggest further observations. The determinative factors in the Petrine function as they concern so-called papal infallibility stand in creative tension with another equally fundamental principle in the Catholic heritage, namely, ". . . universitas fidelium . . . in credendo . . . falli nequit . . ."[180] Though Pius IX in a heated argument with Cardinal Guidi is reported to have exclaimed, "La tradizione son'io," the instinctive insight of the Roman Bishops whenever a concrete, definitively binding doctrinal decision was to be made was that the *sensus fidelium* as a guide to the faith of the Church was to be found in the whole Catholic Church. Nothing else seems to explain the care with which they sought to determine, in the case of the two Marian dogmas, what the faith of the Catholic Church really was. Here again praxis not only illumines theory but transforms it, not in the sense that it removes the determinative factors in the Petrine function as they have to do with so-called papal infallibility, but in a wholly unexpected way. *For the study of praxis reveals that whatever authoritarianism the Roman Bishops may have exhibited in the period under discussion was manifested on the level of the ordinary papal magisterium, not on the extraordinary.* When one adds to these considerations the fact that on that level, indeed in several significant instances explored in part two, *modalities of reception by the rest of the Church were a decisive factor in developing, modifying and/or rejecting certain doctrinal stances or positions taken by the Roman Bishops and that these changes were subsequently accepted and approved by one of their successors,* then the basis of Karl Barth's charge should be considered significantly diminished.[181] To be sure, the issues that separate the Catholic Church from non-Catholic Christian churches, at least as far as Protestantism is concerned, go far deeper than the exercise of authority. They have to do with a particular theology of grace, as Troeltsch pointed out, [182] and ultimately, perhaps, with the role of reason in grounding the credibility of the Christian kerygma. If what happened in the *beta* movements has important implications for Catholic ecclesiology, then surely what happened in the process that culminated in the definition of the two Marian dogmas has something to say to those Christians who feel that the way authority functions within Catholicism constitutes reasons for rejecting the Petrine function as exercised by the Roman Bishop. For in the context of the exercise of that authority, is there in the end a very solid basis for speaking of "the Vatican crime" if both in the development of doctrine and dogma the Catholic Church exhibited characteristics of the Church as κοινωνία, and that precisely on the level of word?

PART FIVE
AND "...THE HEAD [CANNOT SAY] TO THE FEET, 'I HAVE NO NEED OF YOU' "
(1 Cor. 12:21)

Chapter IX
CONCLUDING ASSESSMENT
AND WIDER REFLECTIONS

> Where can the succession of his [i.e., Paul's] teaching office be realized today alongside a magisterium in the Petrine succession? In our ecumenical situation this is not only a matter of collegiality among bishops. Does the medieval model of a double magisterial succession of prelate and theologian have a chance today?[1]

The study of praxis as illuminating and transforming theory suggests, perhaps, a new approach to these concerns. For besides those notes—by far the majority—that confirm impressive guidance by its captain, the ship's log contains a number of revealing ones whose significance proves that members of the crew have had to suggest occasional modification in the direction their captain had initially decided as more suitable for the

347

voyage. If most of the foregoing (Chaps. II-VI) have drawn prolonged attention to these "negatives," it is not only because their meaning has either been neglected (as in the case of the maximalists) or distorted (as in the case of the minimalists); the reason is also that these "negatives" are an indispensable factor in that *Aufhebung* which results in synthesis, and which it is to be hoped, will provide a fresh thrust to the ecumenical dialogue.

The inquiry that I have pursued overflows into certain related questions that were not the principal object of this investigation, but upon which some comment, however brief, may be called for, in view of the present state of Catholic ecclesiology. I shall therefore distinguish between areas of indirect and direct concern. This chapter is thus divided into three sections, the first two of which deal with those concerns respectively; the third constitutes a concluding overview.

Areas of Indirect Concern

First, regarding the nature of reception, the data suggest that *a clear distinction must be made between reception as obedience and reception as functionally equivalent to an active* sensus fidelium[2] (*and/or* sensus fidei). At first sight, there appears to be nothing new in this assessment, as for a number of years before the promulgation of *Lumen gentium* theologians of high repute had argued for an active tradition fundamentally equivalent to an active *sensus fidelium*.[3] Though in principle the reflections of these writers could be said to embrace the professional theologian, they nonetheless tended to limit themselves to the hierarchical magisterium[4] as "over against" the so-called laity.[5] Vatican II itself seems to have sanctioned this development when it ascribed to the whole People of God (in a context, to be sure, that seems to refer primarily to the so-called laity) a role in the discernment of the faith that is not purely passive.[6] Where my findings may take us beyond these considerations, however, consists in this; namely, *that if the distinction between doctrinal development* in fieri *and* in facto esse *is legitimate, then in the context of the former the distinction between* ecclesia docens *and* ecclesia discens *may not be as clear-cut as has traditionally been supposed.*[7] Hence, the statement in *Dei Verbum* that the task of "...authentically interpreting the word of God...has been entrusted *exclusively* to the teaching office of the Church..."[8] is true primarily of doctrinal development *in facto esse*. In the case of the doctrinal issues with which we have been concerned in Chaps. II-VI, the initiative did not come from the bishops. The initiative came from a handful of theologians, some of whom had earlier been harshly treated by the former Holy Office. It was their work that influenced the bishops in the Antepreparatory and Preparatory Sessions, thence in conciliar debate, and finally in the conciliar documents as promulgated by the Roman Bishop. Thus the sentence quoted from John Chrysostom that "...he who occupies the See of Rome knows that the people of India are his members..."[9] may have a ring of truth far different from that originally intended by the Council Fathers or for that matter by Chrysostom himself.[10] I shall return to this theme below.

Second, *the conditions described in* Lumen gentium *according to which the rest of the Catholic Church may judge that the ordinary universal magisterium has infallibly taught a particular doctrine may have to be revised by a future ecumenical Council.* Number 25 of *Lumen gentium* stated in part:

> *Text A.* Although the individual bishops do not enjoy the prerogative of infallibility, they can nevertheless proclaim Christ's doctrine infallibly. This is so, even when they are dispersed around the world, provided that while maintaining the bond of unity among themselves and with Peter's successor, and while teaching authentically on a matter of faith or morals, they concur in a single viewpoint as the one which must be held conclusively [*tamquam definitive tenendam*].[11]

The phrase *tamquam definitive tenendam*, which might have been better rendered as *to be held definitively* rather than as *to be held conclusively*, constitutes a marked change from the manner of speaking adopted by the First Vatican Council. The relevant text from *Dei Filius* reads:

> *Text B.* Furthermore all those things are to be believed with divine and Catholic faith which are contained in the Word of God as written or as handed down and which are proposed by the Church either in a solemn judgment or by way of the ordinary universal magisterium to be believed as divinely revealed [*tamquam divinitus revelata credenda*].[12]

Text B recalls the language of Pius IX in 1863 to the German bishops.[13] In comparing the two texts, a clear distinction should be made between the object of divine and Catholic faith (Text B) and the scope of infallibility

(Text A). The questions are distinct yet connected, for both are concerned with the function and infallibility of the ordinary universal magisterium. While the Fathers of the First Vatican Council wished to correct the growing opinion of some theologians, especially in Germany, who held that a Catholic was obliged to accept as of divine and Catholic faith only what was so proposed by an ecumenical Council, they did not decide the question whether divine and Catholic faith includes the virtually revealed (q.v.).[14] By contrast, the Fathers of Vatican II intended to complete the teaching of the previous Council by pointing out that, whatever be the proper theological note involved, the infallibility of the ordinary universal magisterium, when operative, is not limited to revealed truths.[15] Thus Text A embraces both primary and secondary objects of infallibility (q.v.).

The point at issue here is whether Text A as it stands (as distinguished from the intent of those who composed and voted for it) adequately expresses Catholic teaching on those conditions that must be realized before it may be judged that the ordinary universal magisterium has infallibly taught a particular doctrine. I submit that Text A borders on being incoherent when measured against the Church's praxis.

The crux of the problem is the phrase *tamquam definitive tenendam* as applicable to the teaching of the Roman Bishop in the light of the data analyzed in part two. Undoubtedly the subcommittee responsible for the wording of Text A thought it was sufficient to say that in a matter of faith and morals when the ordinary universal magisterium concurs in one view as the one to be held definitively, the charism of infallibility should be judged to be operative. But a further relevant question remains: to be held definitively *how*? At first sight, this may seem paralogistic, for to say something must be held *definitively* (or *conclusively*) should imply that the matter is settled once and for all. But in any doctrinal stance taken by the Roman Bishop in the exercise of his ordinary magisterium, at least seven possibilities present themselves to his fellow magisterial officers (I shall limit myself for the moment to the first three); namely, the said doctrine is (1) to be held irrevocably, (2) it is to be held definitively as pertaining to the substance of the faith, or (3) it is to be held definitively as the authentic, authoritative teaching of the Roman Bishop. The first is the meaning the phrase has in Salaverri's treatise, from which it was probably borrowed[16] and is not really distinct from the second. For in Catholic theology, to say that a particular doctrine must be held irrevocably by the whole Church is functionally equivalent to saying that it must be held definitively as pertaining to the substance of the faith. In these first two cases, the bishops receive the Roman Bishop's teaching, and perceiving that it pertains to the substance of the faith, so teach it to their people, the Roman Bishop either initially or subsequently concurring in this interpretation. From a Catholic point of view, the charism of infallibility should then be considered operative. It is something very much like this which the subcommittee that drafted Text A and the bishops who voted for it seem to have had in mind, as the references listed under footnote 40 in number 25 of *Lumen gentium* attest. Regarding the issues discussed in part two of this book, I have come upon no evidence to suggest that the majority of Catholic bishops received papal teaching in this way. The third meaning is susceptible of a maximalist interpretation. In that case, the position of the Roman Bishop would be received as infallible merely because it is the doctrine of the ordinary papal magisterium and on that account alone would be considered as pertaining to the substance of the faith. Virtually none of the maximalist positions discussed above hold a view so extreme.[17]

But the third meaning need not be maximalist. Thus a moderate infallibilist (q.v.) might hold that the position of the ordinary papal magisterium is (4) to be held definitively as the authentic, authoritative teaching of the Roman Bishop without being thereby logically constrained to mean that the Pope's teaching is to be held as pertaining to the substance of the faith. That is so because the fourth meaning encompasses at least three others; namely (5) the papal position must be considered *theologice certum* (q.v.); (6) the contradictory of the Roman Bishop's teaching cannot be licitly held or taught by Catholics; or (7) the question is no longer open to discussion within Catholicism. These last three meanings, it is true, come close to implying that the teaching of the Roman Bishop pertains to the substance of the faith. But to make that judgment requires a further movement of the mind which the data in a particular case may not call for. Even *theologice certum* does not necessarily imply infallibility. Unless the bishops are actually polled, it may be impossible to determine over the short haul (and the short haul may entail a couple of centuries) just what is happening. That is to say, the *tamquam definitive tenendam* of Text A is rather ambiguous, for some bishops may be holding and teaching papal doctrine according to one of the first two meanings, others according to one of the last four. It is not entirely clear from the conciliar records just what the phrase must be taken to mean, as the references listed under footnote 40 refer (in the Latin) to the whole of Text A, not to the phrase *tamquam definitive tenendam* as such. Furthermore, the fact that theologians like Salaverri understood the term *definitive* as the equivalent of *irrevocabiliter* does not solve the problem for the obvious reason that no manual can substitute for a conciliar text.[18] The Catholic Church is bound by what the Council said, not by what it might have said.[19]

Recall that in a number of significant instances—the Church-state and religious freedom issues being perhaps the most outstanding—the Fathers of Vatican II reversed the teaching of the ordinary papal magisterium in some significant respect. But if the ecclesiology of Text A is an adequate expression of Catholic faith inasmuch as it has to do with the infallibility-under-certain-circumstances of the ordinary universal magisterium, then with the possible exception of John XXIII the position of Pius IX and his successors on religious freedom had already been defined by the ordinary universal magisterium with the consequence that the distinctive contribution of *Dignitatis humanae* could not, or at least should not, have materialized. For it is beyond doubt that during a period of almost one hundred fifty years the majority of Catholicism's magisterial officers upheld the papal teaching in these matters, and though there is no evidence that they held or taught it as pertaining to the substance of the faith, they surely maintained it as *definitive tenendum* if one of the meanings is equivalent to one of the last four.[20] Thus in terms of the last possibility: If on the one hand the data indicate that the majority of Catholic bishops upheld this particular teaching of the Roman Bishops over such a long period; that they did so *tamquam definitive tenendum* at least in the sense that the question was no longer open to discussion within Catholicism; and if on the other hand several generations later, Catholicism's magisterial officers with the approval and consent of the Roman Bishop significantly reversed the same doctrine, then to say that Text A taken at face value is an inadequate expression of Catholic dogma concerning the infallibility-under-certain-circumstances of the ordinary universal magisterium is to put things rather mildly.

It is here that Salaverri's distinction between *doctrina catholica* in the strict sense as distinguished from *doctrina catholica* in the generic sense is entirely germane. In the last four of the possibilities mentioned above, bishops may not be too certain about the theological status of the Pope's teaching. In that case, positive reception even over several generations may amount to no more than obedience while in the long run the *sensus fidelium* may eventually head in another direction, modification of the original papal position being fully approved by a subsequent Roman Bishop. Admittedly, such cases are rare; that they have occurred in the *beta* movements seems beyond dispute. Only time and prayerful discernment will tell whether a viewpoint held definitively in the sense of one of the last four meanings is ultimately going to be held as something more; that is, irrevocably, or definitively as pertaining to the substance of the faith. For "...the body of the faithful...cannot err in matters of belief."[21]

The text from the First Vatican Council was written in great haste;[22] that from the Second does not seem to have been given the attention it deserves.[23] Though hindsight is easy, perhaps the ambiguity that I believe I detect in Text A may someday be removed by adding a phrase to the effect that in teaching a matter pertaining to faith and morals to the whole Church, Catholicism's magisterial officers do so infallibly when *in unam sententiam tamquam* **ad fidei substantiam spectantem** *ac definitive tenendam conveniunt*. That distinction is crucial, for everything depends on the kind of judgment that the bishops make in union with the Church's Petrine minister. In the meantime, while the apparent dilemma with which Küng believes the Catholic Church is faced (either to repudiate infallibility or accept as factual that Catholicism's official position on the morality of artificial contraception has been infallibly taught by the ordinary universal magisterium) is in the end the tyranny of a false alternative, the use of Text A as it stands can lead to obfuscation of the very issue to which Küng alludes.[24]

Areas of Direct Concern

THE INTERNAL PROBLEM

I come now to those matters central to my endeavor. Recall the pivotal conclusion drawn in Chap. VII; namely, that one of the ways in which doctrine seems to have developed within the Catholic Church from the time of Pius IX up to the end of the Second Vatican Council was through the interplay of two forces: the authentic, authoritative, non-infallible doctrinal pronouncements of the ordinary papal magisterium and the modalities whereby these pronouncements were received by the rest of the Catholic Church. That inference has further implications bearing directly upon the contentions of both minimalists and maximalists as described earlier in this study.[25]

First, regarding those whom I have called minimalists: Given that pivotal conclusion, then *tension between the ordinary papal magisterium and the rest of the Catholic Church, particularly between the former and its theologians, was merely one of the factors in doctrinal development.* If such was the case, then it is at best an oversimplification to cite modification and/or reversal because of the modalities whereby the teaching of the ordinary papal magisterium was sometimes received as evidence against the dogma of so-called papal infallibility. In taking this tack, Küng, Tierney and their followers seem to have made what Gilbert Ryle called a category mistake somewhat analogous to a situation where, say in a Third World country, natives having been granted their independence were to ask whether they should go to the bank to collect it. The question whether the Petrine function can be infallibly exercised arises in a very different context.

Now minimalists will undoubtedly argue that since I have spoken of authentic, authoritative, non-infallible doctrinal pronouncements of the ordinary papal magisterium I have begged the question. *Ganz im Gegenteil*, for the distinction is based on an a posteriori, not an a priori judgment. That is to say: Outside the context of the two Marian dogmas, my characterizing as non-infallible the doctrinal positions of the papal magisterium discussed in this book is the result of an induction inasmuch as it is an inference based on the data. Take the case of Pius IX and the Syllabus. It is demonstrably clear that this Roman Bishop, however authoritarian he may appear in retrospect, was on the one hand aware of the difference between insisting that the rest of the Catholic Church accept his judgment (which may imply no more than obedience) and on the other hand binding it to assent in such a way that henceforth to depart from the papal judgment is to fall away from the Catholic and apostolic faith. In the latter case, the infallibility of the Church itself is somehow involved. The reader has only to compare the language used in *Quanta cura* with that used ten years earlier in *Ineffabilis Deus*:

> *Text C.* Therefore, given the perversity of such morally wrong opinions [lit.:... in such great perversity of morally wrong opinions...] rightly aware of our apostolic office and concerned about our most holy religion, sound doctrine, the salvation of souls divinely committed to our care and especially the good of human society itself, we have judged it [necessary] again to raise our apostolic voice. And so with our apostolic authority we disapprove of, declare unlawful and condemn each and every wrong opinion and doctrine referred to one by one in this letter and we wish and command that they be considered by the sons of the Catholic Church as wholly disapproved of, declared unlawful, and condemned.[26]

> *Text D.* ...by the authority of Our Lord Jesus Christ, the blessed apostles Peter and Paul and by our own, we declare, pronounce and define *the doctrine* which holds that the most Blessed Virgin Mary in the first moment of her conception was, by a singular grace and

privilege of Almighty God and in view of the merits of Jesus Christ the Savior of the human race, preserved immune from every stain of original sin *to be revealed by God* and therefore to be firmly and constantly believed by all the faithful.[27]

Wherefore, if any, which may God forbid, presume to feel in their hearts otherwise than we have defined, let them be aware and furthermore know that they have been condemned by their own judgment, that they have suffered shipwreck regarding the faith, and that they have fallen away from the unity of the Church...[28]

The two different levels of theological discourse in Text D (*Ineffabilis Deus*) and in Text C (*Quanta cura*) should be evident. With all due allowance for mid-nineteenth century Italian oratorical style, there can be no doubt that in *Quanta cura* and the Syllabus the Roman Bishop insisted that the rest of the Church accept his judgment regarding the condemned propositions; but I find nothing anywhere in the documents that suggests that he intended to define their contradictories as pertaining to the substance of the faith. Nothing of the sort can be maintained about Text D. Its meaning is so obvious that further comment can be dispensed with. Whether or not one acknowledges infallibility as a meaningful and/or sustainable theological concept applicable to the Church as a whole and/or to its Petrine minister under certain circumstances does not change the fact established by Texts C and D. Hence, reference to authentic, authoritative, *non-infallible* doctrinal pronouncements of the ordinary papal magisterium cannot reasonably be ascribed to *parti pris* or labeled Pickwickian but is grounded in the papal documents themselves. Furthermore, it should not be forgotten that the question whether the ordinary papal magisterium can be infallibly exercised is after the First Vatican Council affirmatively answered only by a particular current of thought beginning with Vacant. The minimalist argument as defined herein is thus more properly with those I have called maximalists than it is with moderate infallibilists (q.v.).

Now if these considerations obtain in the case of Pius IX and the Syllabus, which is the more difficult of the problems I have attempted to address, then they do so a fortiori in cases of lesser moment involving his successors. Minimalists would have a point if they could adduce a single instance—the case of Boniface VIII in *Unam sanctam* notwithstanding— in which three conditions were fulfilled; namely, (1) a Roman Bishop defining a particular doctrine as pertaining to the substance of the faith; (2) this definition being reversed or rejected; and (3) the reversal or rejection being subsequently approved by the same or a later Roman Bishop.[29] Until minimalists produce an example of such an event, they have no case; if such a case ever occurs, it will be the end of Catholic Christianity.[30]

Second, regarding the maximalists, *the fact of the* beta *movements demolishes all basis for the viability of that claim.* Previous attempts to refute it have been limited chiefly to showing that it rested on an unfounded interpretation of documents and debates surrounding the First Vatican Council.[31] While such endeavors are justified, they have never succeeded in establishing as factual that a number of Council Fathers may not have voted for *Pastor Aeternus* as a last resort, leaving to another generation the task of carrying forward the papal cause as they saw it. The study of praxis, I suggest, provides a definitive bulwark against the various currents that flow into the maximalist stream.

Recall that for Arthur Peiffer the infallibility-under-certain-circumstances of the ordinary papal magisterium was said to result from a constellation of two circumstances; namely, (1) the majority of Catholicism's magisterial officers' teaching p as *doctrina catholica* in Scheeben's sense (which means that they teach p as revealed by God or so closely connected with a revealed truth that to deny p amounts to denying the revealed truth itself) and (2) the Roman Bishop's concurring, so expressing himself to the whole Church.[32] But the example Peiffer cites as illustrative of his case (the teaching of Pius XII on the identity between the [Roman] Catholic Church and the Mystical Body of Christ) is an unfortunate choice. Where, to begin with, is the evidence that the first of these circumstances ever materialized? An unpromulgated draft of the First Vatican Council spoke in terms of the Church as the Mystical Body of Christ but did not explicitly make an equation between that and the (Roman) Catholic Church.[33] Though theologians as we have seen subsequently developed the theme well before Pius XI in *Mortalium animos*, there is no evidence to suggest that a consensus existed either among the theologians or the bishops themselves to the effect that the relation was one of identity and that the doctrine on identity was Catholic doctrine in Scheeben's sense (q.v.). Thus even though Pius XII himself seems to have thought that the doctrine pertained to the substance of the faith (and therefore was Catholic doctrine in Scheeben's sense),[34] the conditions under which Peiffer considers that the ordinary papal magisterium is infallibly exercised are not verifiable. Recall too that Salaverri in his first phase had argued that the ordinary papal magisterium is infallibly exercised when the Roman Bishop in a doctrinal matter makes known his intention to bind the Church to absolute assent and that despite the fact that Salaverri himself has subsequently become somewhat more cautious, the current of maximalist think-ing representative of his first phase has by no means died out. Recall finally that Nau and Gallati attempted to sustain the thesis that when a series of Roman Bishops teach *p* over an extended period, their teaching is infalli-ble, or, in Nau's later language, faithful to revelation. I submit that these and similar views are utterly shattered when they come up against the rock of Catholicism's praxis, as are those espoused much earlier by Vacant, Billot, and Dublanchy. Whereas the old Gallican thesis still reflected in the latest ARCIC report[35] cannot be harmonized with Catholic dogma on the level of the extraordinary papal magisterium, there may be some truth to it on the level of the ordinary. That is to say: *From a Catholic point of view it may be possible to argue that the teaching of the ordinary papal magiste-rium may be judged to be unerring only when it has been so received by the rest of the Catholic Church.*[36]

It is of course undoubtedly true that if the only clear case within our period were that of papal teaching on the identity question as propounded in *Mortalium animos, Mystici corporis* and *Humani generis,* then it might be argued that papal teaching on this point had not been long enough to qualify for the criteria set up by Nau and Gallati. At most only two Roman Bishops were involved, there being only about thirty-four years between the promulgation of *Mortalium animos* by Pius XI on January 6, 1928, and the opening of the Second Vatican Council. But papal teaching on religious freedom is an entirely different matter. If all the papal magiste-rium had done was to insist on a negative answer to Question (F) of Chap. IV (Does a human being have an *objective* right to worship God in a way other than the way God is worshiped in the Roman Church and those other local Christian Churches in union with it?), I would have no case, for in this matter the Fathers of Vatican II stand firmly with the Roman Bishops and indeed with the whole of Catholic tradition. But Catholicism's Petrine ministers did more than that. In order to deal with a situation in which non-Catholics were living in a so-called Catholic state, they embraced a theory that non-Catholics were to be allowed religious freedom on the basis of the toleration of error for the common good, a position that the Popes insisted on unquestionably as a matter of doctrine, not merely of policy, for well over one hundred fifty years. Yet the fact that the Council Fathers in effect answered affirmatively to Question (E) of Chap. IV (Does a human being in the present economy of salvation have the *objective* right to worship God in the manner in which a responsible use of intellect indicates he or she should?) means that the religious freedom of non-Catholics could no longer be said to be enjoyed on the basis of toleration of error for the common good but on the basis of the dignity of the human person which cannot seek the truth effectively unless he or she is free. In taking that tack, the Second Vatican Council overturned in this respect the teaching of Catholicism's Petrine ministers, a teaching the latter had maintained for several generations.

Now it will undoubtedly appear to many a working Catholic ecclesiologist that my pivotal conclusion is distressingly obvious. *Dato sed non concesso*: Nothing suggests it is obvious to official Catholicism. Nor does it seem obvious to Hans Küng, Brian Tierney, and their followers. And it seems even less obvious to the intellectual heirs of Alfred Vacant, Louis Billot, and Edmond Dublanchy. It is true that Joaquín Salaverri de la Torre in his first phase along with Paul Nau and Fidelis Gallati could not have foreseen the turn that Catholicism was to take at Vatican II, though Arthur Peiffer and Petrus Bilaniuk should have seen it in retrospect. But even in the case of Salaverri, Nau and Gallati, surely there was enough in Catholicism's long history to have suggested some measure of caution. In any case, there is no excuse for those who in the postconciliar period doggedly persist in propagating maximalist views. Henceforth, any attempt to defend a maximalist position can be made only with one's eyes closed to history. Indeed, the implications of my pivotal conclusion may transcend both minimalist and maximalist theses along with their variants in that the *beta* movements may be constitutive, a theme to which I shall return below.

On the basis, then, of these considerations and on the basis of the analyses pursued in the foregoing chapters, I submit that the first part of my central argument as stated in the Introduction has been grounded; namely, that *the way doctrine has in fact developed within the Catholic Church beginning with the Petrine ministry of Pius IX up to the end of the Second Vatican Council requires a correction of the understanding of how the ordinary papal magisterium functions within Catholicism.* In the name of historical and theological coherence, both minimalists and maximalists must modify their views. But as we shall see, the Roman Bishops can and should do likewise.

The External Problem

Third, the data uncovered on the level of dogma bring additional factors into consideration. Associative elements discernible in the years prior to the definition of the two Marian dogmas were sufficient to establish the conclusion stated in the preceding chapter and partially recalled here; namely, that the determinative factors in the Petrine function, inasmuch as they have to do with papal infallibility, are for official Catholicism a value having to do more with principle than with practice. That conclusion grounds, I suggest, the second part of the central argument stated in the Introduction; that is to say: *The same associative elements may provide a partial solution to the ecumenical impasse brought about by the common understanding of so-called papal infallibility, for in the exercise of their extraordinary magisterium, the Roman Bishops did not "...lord it over them..."* (Matt. 20:25). On the contrary, the data suggest that they went out of their way to be more than certain that what they defined was indeed the faith of the Catholic Church.[37]

Though this may provide a partial solution on the level of praxis, the core difficulty within the central issue remains on the level of theory; i.e., the determinative factors in the Petrine function are not a matter on which official Catholicism can compromise. According to this view, *the Roman Bishop in the exercise of the extraordinary papal magisterium does not have to agree with the rest of the Catholic Church but the rest of the Catholic Church must agree with the Roman Bishop.* Well-disposed ecumenically minded non-Catholic Christians maintain that it is precisely that principle that they can never accept.[38] This is a matter to which I hope to return in another book wherein I shall attempt to deal with the infallibility question as such. In the meantime, perhaps it is not too sanguine to hope that relevant parts of the present inquiry may nudge Christian Churches closer to reconciliation and subsequent reunion.

Besides the care that the Roman Bishops exercised in consulting the rest of the Catholic Church prior to the definition of the two Marian dogmas, the basis for that hope is, in the main, threefold. First, to the extent that reasons advanced by ecumenically minded Protestants against the infallibility-under-certain-circumstances of the Roman Bishop are substantially the same as those of the minimalist charge (with the consequence that eventual full reconciliation and reunion does not seem possible as long as Roman claims persist), then my remarks about the minimalists may apply *mutatis mutandis* to this Protestant difficulty. Second, if, as I have suggested in the preceding chapter, (1) whatever authoritarianism the Roman Bishops may have exhibited during the period under discussion was manifested on the level of their ordinary magisterium, not the extraordinary; and if (2) respectful and responsible "talking back" to the Roman Bishops on the level of the ordinary papal magisterium succeeded in bringing about desired adjustments in official Catholic teaching; and if (3) in that process the Catholic Church exhibited characteristics of the Church as κοινωνία on the level of word, then perhaps the ecumenical dialogue on the function of authority can be viewed in a new perspective. Third, I stated above that if in the name of theological coherence both minimalists and maximalists must modify their understanding of how the ordinary papal magisterium functions within Catholicism, then the pivotal conclusion drawn in Chapter VII and repeated above suggests that the Roman Bishops should do likewise. From what happened in the *beta* movements it does not seem inappropriate to conclude that the Roman Bishops learn from the rest of the Church in a manner that they have so far been unwilling to admit. Were they to admit that their teaching on the level of their ordinary magisterium at times had to be revised, on rare occasions even reversed, great ecumenical advances might follow. At the very least it should remove much of the basis for misgiving tactfully expressed in previous ecumenical dialogues.

Concluding Overview

What, it may be asked in Lonergan's terms, was going forward that contemporaries for the most part were unaware of?[39] Interplay between the ordinary papal magisterium and the rest of the Catholic Church on the level of doctrine together with the debates among theologians and consultation by the Popes of the rest of the Catholic Church prior to the definition of the two Marian dogmas suggest that in the development of doctrine and dogma *Church as association* was intimately linked with *Church as institution.* That is to say: In that *Aufhebung* that both takes away and preserves, Church as institution (*Anstaltskirche*) and Church as association (*Vereinskirche*) blended into Church as κοινωνία on the level of word. The import of that *Aufhebung* for Catholicism's internal and external problems may be incalculable. For if it is true that *agere sequitur esse,* then not only the *alpha* movements (as is to be expected) but also the *beta* movements (which are, to be sure, exceptional) result from the very nature of the Church. This was already implied in the great encyclical *Mystici corporis.* But whoever drafted that document for the Pope did not foresee (or at least did not suggest) the implications of 1 Cor. 12:14-27 for theory of doctrinal and dogmatic development. Associative elements as constitutive of the Catholic Church as institution are pertinent not only to that body's ecumenical relations with Protestants; they are also pertinent to its relations with Orthodoxy, for official Catholicism's stand on the

Petrine ministry has been overly dominated by law and insufficiently attentive to the Church as κοινωνία.[40] Yet paradoxically in the issues studied above, κοινωνία on the level of word is precisely what characterized its praxis. The implications are considerable.[41]

The underlying idea, the condition whereby that *Aufhebung* was possible, seems to have been not only an active *sensus fidelium* (and/or *sensus fidei*) but an active *sensus fidelium* of a different kind. The difference may perhaps be grasped by a comparison of the kind of *sensus fidelium* uncovered above with that described by Newman in the so-called Rambler article.[42] It may be said that in this essay Newman distinguished both an active and a passive *sensus fidelium*, though the distinction is not explicit. Thus in the case of the dogma of the Immaculate Conception the persistent belief of the people was the principal factor in development[43] while in the case of the Arian crisis the role of the laity was reductively passive. That is to say, the people rejected the Arian christology because it was contrary to the *paradosis* they had received. In our period, something very different seems to have occurred. With the exception of Dupanloup, whose role, as I indicated in Chap. VI, was somewhat different, the theologians (who, after all, must be numbered among the faithful) spoke back to the ordinary papal magisterium, saying in effect, "We fully acknowledge your right to teach and our duty to listen. But we have problems with what you are saying; before you make up your mind, hear us out." The honest probing of theologians, whose brotherly submission to the Popes as exercising the Petrine ministry within Catholicism was and is beyond dispute, came at last to have its effect in *Lumen gentium* and *Dignitatis humanae*. Unlike, say, the question of the relation of the Catholic Church to non-Christian religions as expressed in *Nostra aetate* and *Ad gentes*; those of religious freedom and the correlative matter of ideal Church-state relations, together with the identification of the Mystical Body of Christ with the Catholic Church and the theology of Church membership—the context of the *beta* movements—for those questions the way had *not* been prepared at least in part by the teaching of the ordinary papal magisterium. Nor had the path been blazed by those who simply presumed that because the ordinary papal magisterium had spoken it was therefore beyond question. Rather the path had been blazed by those members of the Catholic Church who accepted the papal teaching for what it was; namely, the authentic, authoritative, non-infallible teaching of the Roman Bishop as succeeding to certain functions of Peter within the Catholic Church, and who in the name of fidelity respectfully and responsibly "talked back." In the context of eccyclic and eiscyclic movements, the *beta* movements could not have had the effect they had unless the *sensus fidelium* in relation to the ordinary papal magisterium was not only active but active in a way very different from what has so far been put forth.[44]

In the case of the theologians, this phenomenon is not the same as that which is admitted in even the most conservative manuals of Catholic theology. That position states that the unanimous consensus of theologians on a particular doctrinal matter is a reliable index of the faith of the Catholic Church. What happened in the case of the *beta* movements was very different. There a relatively small minority was ultimately influential in persuading the majority that papal teaching on certain important matters left something to be desired; these modifications of papal teaching were subsequently approved by the ordinary papal magisterium. Though associative elements were present in both *alpha* and *beta* movements the key factor is not so much the former movements as the latter. For official Catholicism has no difficulty in admitting that the Roman Bishop learns from the rest of the Church in the sense that Leo XIII prior to *Rerum novarum* and Pius XII prior to *Mystici corporis* listened to what the local Churches were saying, and after having made appropriate modifications, exercised the Petrine ministry within Catholicism by formulating their respective doctrinal positions. What official Catholicism has never admitted is that the teaching of the ordinary papal magisterium has sometimes had to be modified and/or reversed because of the modalities of its reception.

Papal teaching on the social question from Leo XIII on, and the teaching of Pius XII in *Fidei donum* and its suggestions pregnant with meaning for the evolving concept of collegiality were only two of the many instances of the positive effects of papal teaching within Catholicism. But the story does not end there. Eccyclic and eiscyclic movements as further manifest in the *alpha* and *beta* movements seem to correspond to a number of triads that continuously interpenetrated each other until in each movement they came to relative rest and the Catholic Church was disclosed for something it is not usually taken to be, at least by those outside it. For it stood revealed as a Church stamped with the marks of κοινωνία on the level of word. Non-Catholic Christians should perhaps take another look at the way authority functions within it; the Roman Bishops and their advisers should perhaps ask themselves whether their theory about the function of the ordinary papal magisterium is fully in harmony with Catholicism's praxis. For the image that corresponds to the data is not that of a pyramid in which the action is from the top to the base but that of series of concentric circles in which eccyclic and eiscyclic movements are both mutually influential and mutually beneficial.

Now if one of the ways in which doctrine has developed in the period we have dealt with was through an interplay between the authentic, authoritative, non-infallible doctrinal pronouncements of the Roman Bishops as exercising the Petrine ministry within Catholicism and the modalities of their reception by the rest of the Catholic Church, and if that interplay included what I have called the *beta* movements, then one should not be surprised either that similar events may have transpired in the more distant past or that they may do so again. This calls for two parenthetical but nonetheless important remarks.

First, regarding the past, was something analogous operative, say, during the time of Honorius and the Monothelite controversy and still further back in the dispute between Cyprian and Stephen? Perhaps. It would not be difficult to find additional examples throughout the long history of the Catholic Church. Sporadic tension between Catholicism's Petrine minister and the rest of the Catholic Church, particularly her theologians, may not only be "normal"; on the level of word it may also flow from the very nature of the Church as κοινωνία and as such be no more than a catalyst for growth in the understanding of doctrine (which in some cases may become dogma). In the first of the cases mentioned above, that of Honorius, the Roman Bishop may indeed have been "corrected";[45] in the second, that of the dispute between Stephen and Cyprian, it was the Roman Bishops who were ultimately vindicated, with unforeseen benefit for the Church. Who could have foreseen, for example, in the far-off days of Stephen and Cyprian, that insistence on the validity of baptism performed by a heretic (from a Catholic point of view) was to become many centuries later a factor in the ecumenical rapprochement of a divided Christendom? In terms of Hermann Josef Sieben's groundbreaking analysis, not only *alpha* but also *beta* movements may be factors in achieving that horizontal and vertical consensus which constitutes the basis of authentic reception.[46]

Second, regarding the future, it can hardly have escaped the reader's notice that interplay between the teaching of the ordinary papal magisterium and the rest of the Catholic Church, particularly her theologians, is relevant to at least two ongoing concerns. I refer to official Catholicism's stance on artificial contraception and the ordination of women to the ministerial priesthood. But before one too quickly assumes that "talking back" on these issues must necessarily result in their modification and/or reversal, one might do well to recall not only that an oft-repeated papal doctrinal position in the period with which we have dealt did not "take" if it was contrary to a deeply imbedded Catholic tradition—the *sensus fidelium* was able to eventually sniff out the difference—but also that before a subsequent Roman Bishop approved a shift in the official Catholic position he had to be convinced that the teaching of his predecessors was logically inconsistent with a fundamental Catholic doctrine and/or dogma. Thus, to recall only two instances, the negative attitude of Pius IX on possible truth or good in non-Christian religions did not "take" probably because it was contrary to John 1:9 and the *Logos spermatikos* concept while the equation made by Pius XII between the Mystical Body of Christ and the (Roman) Catholic Church had to be modified because it could not be harmonized with Catholic teaching on baptism. It is not only a question of theological consistency, however. Shifts in teaching may come about for other reasons; e.g., if the question changes because of new information, one should not be surprised that the "answer" changes accordingly. But whatever be the ultimate result of respectful and responsible "talking back" on these and other matters, and despite the fact that failure to "talk back" responsibly may be pusillanimous, it is not less true to say—and I wish this to be gently stated—the very least one might expect from a Catholic theologian is that he or she spend as much time asking why the teaching of Catholicism's Petrine minister may be right as he or she may be willing to spend in trying to show why it is wrong.† For just as in the quarrel between Cyprian and Stephen, so in the dispute, say, between a number of Catholic theologians and the Roman Bishops on the morality of artificial contraception and the ordination of women to the ministerial priesthood, the Roman Bishops may in the end be completely vindicated. Only time, study, and prayerful discernment will tell. But if the past is in any way paradigmatic, perhaps the more urgent task for official Catholicism is to determine not so much whether it has the "right answers" as whether or not in matters of this kind it has been asking the right questions.

My concern in the foregoing pages has not however been directly with postconciliar tensions but rather with larger ecclesiological matters. If I have dwelt for the most part on those data that show that given the weather conditions other members of the crew have had to suggest a shift in the direction their captain had originally charted, it is not because in the history of this period the captain's failings were the dominant motif. Quite the contrary. The performance of the Roman Bishops as exercising the Petrine ministry within Catholicism has been on the whole quite impressive. What is needed is a change in attitude reflected, for example, in the theologizing of a modern Pope whose brilliance and service to the Church are largely beyond dispute. Thus in a speech given on September 14, 1956, to the Sixth Convention of the Italian Clergy, Pius XII expressed concern about the role of theologians in the Church.[47] In those cases where theolo-

---

† Thus persistent "talking back" is not necessarily responsible, as the truly great know when silence is called for, convinced that *if* they are right, they will ultimately be vindicated.

gians advance scientific arguments for their positions, what is the guarantee of truth, the Pope asked, the teaching of the theologians? Or that of the magisterium?[48] The answer for Pius was obvious, otherwise the theologians would end up teaching the magisterium.[49] Though in this speech the context indicates that Pius was thinking primarily of the ordinary universal magisterium, it is difficult to see, given his complaint in *Humani generis*, why his remarks should not, *mutatis mutandis*, be taken to apply to the ordinary papal magisterium. It is here that the oversimplification lies. While from a Catholic point of view there can be no doubt that regarding doctrinal and dogmatic development *in facto esse* the Petrine function was and will remain the constant; regarding doctrinal and dogmatic development *in fieri*, the theory espoused by Pius XII does not harmonize with the Catholic Church's praxis. Regarding dogma, exactly who was teaching whom when prior to the definitions of the two Marian dogmas the Roman Bishops carefully sounded out the rest of the Catholic Church? Regarding doctrine, the *beta* movements are decisive. *In those cases, it was not the ordinary papal magisterium that taught the rest of the Church so much as it was the rest of the Church that taught the ordinary papal magisterium in a way that so far seems to have escaped official Catholicism's notice.* Though the *beta* movements were not an everyday event, they have nonetheless occurred. They are a massive fact which may no longer be wrapped in a blanket of silence.

That Paul VI, as Giovanni Battista Cardinal Montini, was in the context of these matters on the side of the so-called progressives at the beginning of the Council does not alter the fact that, as one later exercising the Petrine ministry within Catholicism, he confirmed doctrinal positions contrary to the teaching of Pius IX and his successors up to but possibly excluding John XXIII. Given the nature of theological discussion propaedeutic to that climax, the facts suggest that there is a sense in which Paul's sentence in Gal. 2:11 ("...but when Cephas came to Antioch, I withstood him to the face ...") is, or at least can be under certain circumstances, a perfectly normal Catholic response, something of far-reaching implications for Catholic ecclesiology. In doctrinal development considered *in fieri*, cooperation (as in the *alpha* movements) and respectful, responsible "talking back" (as in the *beta* movements) were the constants, not the Petrine function. Thus the data suggest that an approach to the persistent malaise within Catholicism and its relevance to a slowdown in ecumenical progress is likewise to be found rooted in the New Testament. For equally Pauline and not less Catholic is the fact that in the body of Christ "...the head [cannot say] to the feet, 'I have no need of you' " (1 Cor. 12:21).

On the eve of the Second Vatican Council, few things indeed seemed so secure as the ordinary papal magisterium. It is still secure; it is no longer self-sufficient, if indeed it ever really was. My findings do not suggest that the Catholic Church is or even can be a democracy as that term is commonly understood. Much less do they suggest that within Catholicism dissent should be a way of life; they suggest that within that world-wide body there is room for a "loyal opposition," that though within the body of Christ there are people of different rank, there are nonetheless no second-class citizens. Whether the assessment presented above will in the end win the support of my peers and those who are more than my peers remains to be seen. Whether in the end it will contribute to orienting Catholic and non-Catholic Christian Churches toward new ecumenical horizons will depend on the extent to which my conclusions, particularly as they have to do with the function of the Roman Bishop as exercising the Petrine ministry within Catholicism, can be integrated into official Catholic teaching.

For the problems that beset Catholicism are not simply the result of changing paradigms of authority, though they are that.[50] Failure to come to grips with the implications of the *beta* movements is not so much an abuse as it is a state of affairs (*état de choses*) to employ the language Yves Congar used some thirty years ago.[51] To correct an abuse it is sufficient to recall and to apply existing norms; to correct a state of affairs, it is necessary that the Catholic Church renew its way of thinking by returning once again to the sources.[52] In this case, one of those sources is lived experience, the praxis that illumines and transforms theory. Just as Troeltsch following Schleiermacher found in a deeper study of Protestantism a way to correct the exaggerated tendencies of the sect-type (Church as association) resulting in a new concept of the Church as organism (*Lebenszusammenhang*[53]), so it may be possible from a deeper study of Catholicism to find a way to correct the exaggerations of the Church-type (Church as institution), a correction resulting in a renewed concept of the Catholic Church and hence in a revised view of the function of authority within that body. The authentic Catholic senses that the Petrine ministry as claimed by the Roman Bishop is part of the whole and that the Catholic Church is somehow not "whole" without it; that without its captain the ship will eventually founder. It is evident that for the authentic Catholic the Roman Bishop ultimately has no human peer. But if the fundamental thrust of my argument is at all viable; if praxis not only illumines theory but transforms it, then it may be time for the ship's captain to admit that he needs his crew in a sense far different than he so far seems to have realized.

Indeed, the past may yet be prologue.

NOTES

Preface

[1]   For a pertinent example, see the statement by the so-called Concilium group of theologians as reported in *The New York Times*, Monday, June 25, 1984, sec. A, pp. 1 and 8. The context is Vatican critique of Liberation Theology.

[2]   See below, pp. 287-88.

[3]   See my article, "*Humanae vitae* Re-examined: A Response," *Homiletic and Pastoral Review* 73 (July 1973), pp. 57-64, especially pp. 62-63.

[4]   Thus among others, see J[ean]-M[arie]-R[oger] Tillard, "A propos du *'sensus fidelium*,' " *Proche-Orient chrétien* 25 (1975): 113-34, and Antonio Cañizares Llovera, "El Magisterio de la Iglesia," *Iglesia viva* 79 (1979): 357-75.

[5]   See Hans Küng, *Unfehlbar? Eine Anfrage* (Zurich, Einsiedeln and Cologne: Benziger Verlag, 1970). English translation: *Infallible? An Inquiry*, trans. Edward Quinn (Garden City, N.Y.: Doubleday & Co., 1971 and 1983).

[6]   See pp. 31-39

[7]   See pp. 30-31

Glossary

[1]   See Francis A. Sullivan, *Magisterium: Teaching Authority in the Catholic Church* (New York and Ramsey: Paulist Press, 1983), p. 123. Contrary to Sullivan's claim, I do not believe this usage is grounded in the Dogmatic Constitution *Dei Filius* (q.v.) See ibid., p. 122.

[2]   See the article, "Magisterium" in Karl Rahner and Herbert Vorgrimler, *Dictionary of Theology*, second edition, trans. Richard Strachan, David Smith, Robert Nowell and Sarah O'Brien Twohig (New York: Crossroad, 1981), pp. 285-87, esp. p. 287.

[3]   See the article, "Definition," ibid., p. 115. Rahner and Vorgrimler do not use the term *substance of the faith*, but their meaning is the same.

[4]   It is a matter of some dispute whether truths pertaining to the natural law can be defined. I would be prepared to argue that they can, provided they can be shown to pertain to the secondary object of infallibility. Further comment is beyond my present scope.

[5]   Karl Rahner and Herbert Vorgrimler, *Dictionary of Theology*, p. 285.

[6]   See *Lumen gentium* in *The Documents of Vatican II*, ed. Walter M. Abbott and Joseph Gallagher (New York: America Press, 1966), p. 48.

[7]   See the discussion pp. 349-53.

[8]   Rahner and Vorgrimler, *Dictionary of Theology*, p. 342. For some of the problems, see P. Fransen, "Einige Bemerkungen zu den theologischen Qualifikationen," in *Die Interpretation des Dogmas*, ed. Piet Schoonenberg (Düsseldorf: Patmos Press, 1969), pp. 111-37.

Introduction

[1]   See Langdon Gilkey, *How the Church Can Minister to the World without Losing Itself* (New York: Harper & Row, 1964), p. 129. Southern Baptists are accustomed to working within a gigantic centralized organization, but that is different from their theory about themselves as autonomous, covenanted congregations of regenerate, adult, biblically loyal Christians who recognize no spiritual authority but their Bibles. Southern Baptist praxis has thus "Catholicizing" implications that have yet to be faced on the level of theory.

[2]   Thus at least one contemporary ecclesiologist points to a certain "solitude" within which the Roman Bishops in the post-Vatican II era still act. See J[ean]-M[arie]-R[oger] Tillard, *L'Évêque de Rome* (Paris: Les Editions du Cerf, 1982), pp. 236-38.

[3]   See Yves Congar, *Diversités et communion* (Paris: Les Editions du Cerf, 1982), pp. 235-40.

[4]   See Ernst Troeltsch, *The Social Teachings of the Christian Churches*, trans. Olive Wyon, 2 vols. (New York: Harper & Row, Harper Torchbooks, 1960), 2: 461.

[5]   See ibid.

[6]   See ibid.

[7]   Troeltsch's translator uses the English word *fellowship*, whereas I prefer to use the Greek word κοινωνία because at least in American English *fellowship* loses

the nuance of the Greek and its connotations in the New Testament. I regard κοινωνία as fundamentally equivalent to *communio*. Whatever be the advantages of using the latter term as a statement about what the Church is (see Herwi Rikof, *The Concept of Church: A Methodological Inquiry into the Use of Metaphors in Ecclesiology* [London: Sheed & Ward, and Shepherdstown, West Virginia: Patmos Press, 1981], p. 233) for reasons alluded to (see pp. 293-97 and p. 455, n. 37), I regard κοινωνία as the deeper reality and hence as foundational to everything else.

   8   Troeltsch, *The Social Teachings of the Christian Churches*, 2: 461.

   9   See ibid.

   10   These are not Troeltsch's words but they seem to be his meaning. See ibid., 1: 338-39.

   11   In the 1912 edition of vol. 3 of *Die Religion in Geschichte und Gegenwart*, Troeltsch describes the Church-type as *Anstaltskirche* (*Church as institution*) and the sect-type as *Vereinskirche* (*Church as association*). See Ernst Troeltsch, "Kirche III: Dogmatisch," in *Die Religion in Geschichte und Gegenwart*, 5 vols. (Tübingen: J.C.B. Mohr, 1909-13), 3 (1912): 1150 and 1152. I am grateful to B.A. Gerrish (oral communication) for pointing out that fact and for suggesting *Church as association* as an appropriate translation of *Vereinskirche*. Since I shall be concerned with the difference in function of authority rather than with other differences between the Church-type and the sect-type, it is this latter set of terms (*Church as institution* and *Church as association*), which, for the most part, will constitute my frame of reference. In the pages that follow, then, the term *associative elements* and / or *participation* means the part played particularly by bishops and theologians in the development of doctrine and dogma within Catholicism. For my understanding of the *sensus fidelium*, see p. 44.

   12   See Giuseppe Alberigo, "New Frontiers in Church History," in *Church History in Future Perspective*, ed. Roger Aubert, Concilium, vol. 57 (New York: Herder & Herder, 1970), pp. 68-84, especially p. 73.

   13   It has been noted that the distinction between *divine* and *human right* is not entirely satisfactory. See Lutherans and Catholics in Dialogue V, *Papal Primacy and the Universal Church*, ed. Paul C. Empie and T. Austin Murphy (Minneapolis: Augsburg Publishing House, 1974), p. 31. A recent study by Michael J. Miller seems particularly helpful in this regard. According to this view, the Petrine function itself is regarded as of *institutione divina* (divine or dominical institution) as contrasted with its embodiment in the concrete, historical papacy, which is considered of *ordinatione divina* (divine design), coming under the general aegis of God's providence. See Michael J. Miller, *The Divine Right of the Papacy in Recent Ecumenical Theology* (Rome: Università Gregoriana Editrice, 1980), p. 281. For a wider discussion, see Karl Rahner, "Reflection on the Concept of 'Ius Divinum'' in "Catholic Thought," in *Theological Investigations*, 20 vols. (London: Darton, Longman & Todd, and New York: The Seabury Press, 1961-) 5 (1966): 219-43. Volume 5 is translated by Karl-H. Kruger. For an older view, which, at least until recently considered the traditional terms theologically adequate while at the same time admitting their ecumenical awkwardness, see Avery Dulles, "*Ius Divinum* as an Ecumenical Problem," *Theological Studies* 38 (1977): 681-708.

[14]   On the various kinds of conciliarism, see Francis Oakley, *Council over Pope?* (New York: Herder & Herder, 1969), pp. 61-74. For a balanced approach to the question but one that is not without its problems, see Giuseppe Alberigo, *Chiesa conciliare: identità e significato del conciliarismo* (Brescia: Paideis, 1981).

[15]   Hans Küng, *Infallible? An Inquiry*, trans. Edward Quinn (Garden City, New York: Doubleday & Co., 1971), p. 31.

[16]   See ibid., p. 33.

[17]   See inter alia Karl Rahner, ed., *Zum Problem Unfehlbarkeit: Anworten auf die Anfrage von Hans Küng*, Quaestiones Disputatac, no. 54 (Freiburg im Breisgau, Basel, and Vienna: Herder, 1971), and the much later Edmund Schlink, Erich Grässer, Josef Blank, Otto Hermann Pesch, Heinrich Ott, Jürgen Moltmann, and Heinrich Stirnimann, *Papsttum als ökumenische Frage*, ed. Arbeitsgemeinschaft ökumenischer Universitätsinstitute (Munich: Kaiser, and Mainz: Grünewald, 1979).

[18]   See Hans Küng, *Infallible? An Inquiry*, trans. Edward Quinn (Garden City, New York: Doubleday & Co., 1983), p. 37. With the exception of the first sixteen pages, entitled "Introduction to the New American Edition," this 1983 edition seems to be verbally the same as the English translation of 1971. References henceforth will be to the 1983 edition.

[19]   Leonard Swidler, "The Ecumenical Problem Today: Papal Infallibility," *Journal of Ecumenical Studies* 8 (1971): 755 (first emphasis mine).

[20]   Though long implicit in Catholic theologizing, the distinction between the ordinary papal magisterium and the extraordinary was not, as far as I know, current before the First Vatican Council. (Pius IX, in a letter to the German Hierarchy in 1863, referred to the ordinary magisterium, but the context meant the ordinary universal magisterium [q.v.]. See *Enchiridion Symbolorum Definitionum et Declarationum de Rebus Fidei et Morum*, ed. Henricus Denzinger and Adolfus Schönmetzer, 26th corrected ed. [Barcelona, Freiburg im Breisgau, and Rome: Herder, 1976], no. 2789.) I find somewhat baffling the suggestion that this distinction as used by modern Catholic theologians is Pickwickian. (See Brian Tierney, *Origins of Papal Infallibility: 1150-1350* [Leiden: E.J. Brill, 1972], p. 3.) For surely there is a difference between (1) proposing a doctrine as clearly binding upon the Church, in which case the proper theological note might "only" be *doctrina catholica* in Salaverri's strict sense (q.v.), and (2) proposing a doctrine in such a way that to reject it is henceforth to fall away from the Catholic faith, in which case the proper theological note might be *de fide catholica* (q.v.). The question of infallibility arises only in the latter case; to say it arises in the former is, as I have said, a maximalist position which, as I shall attempt to show, cannot be sustained. For further considerations, see pp. 356-58 above.

[21]   See Tierney, *Origins of Papal Infallibility*, pp. 2-3.

[22]   For an overview of the various currents that flow into the maximalist stream of thought up to 1960, see Arthur Peiffer, *Die Enzykliken und ihr formaler Wert für die dogmatische Methode* (Freiburg [Switzerland]: Universitätsverlag, 1968), pp. 72-100.

23 See Jean-Michel-Alfred Vacant, *Etudes théologiques sur les Constitutions du Concile du Vatican*, 2 vols. (Paris and Lyons: Delhomme et Briguet, éditeurs, 1895), 2: 91-92. (A book to which I have never been able to have direct access but which is frequently cited in the literature is Vacant's *Le Magistère ordinaire de l'Eglise et ses organes* [Paris and Lyons: n.p., 1887]).

24 "Nor must it be thought that what is expounded in Eycyclical Letters does not of itself demand consent, since in writing such letters the Popes do not exercise the supreme power of their Teaching Authority.... But if the Supreme Pontiffs in their official documents purposely pass judgment on a matter up to that time under dispute, it is obvious that the matter, according to the mind and will of the same Pontiffs, cannot be any longer considered a question open to discussion among theologians" (Pius XII, *Humani generis*, in AAS 42 [1950]: 561-78). (National Catholic Welfare Conference translation [Boston: Daughters of St. Paul, n.d.], pp. 1-17. The passage cited here may be found on p. 8 of the English translation. Henceforth, references are to the translation unless stated to the contrary.

25 For reasons stated above, I prefer to speak of the bishop *at* rather than *of* a particular place. See p. 43

26 "... auctoritate papatus pontifex est semper supremus iudex in rebus fidei et morum, et omnium christianorum pater et doctor; sed assistentia divina ipsi promissa, qua fit, ut errare non possit, *solummodo tunc* gaudet, cum munere supremi iudicis in controversiis fidei et universalis ecclesiae doctoris *reipsa* et *actu* fungitur" (*Sacrorum Conciliorum Nova et Amplissima Collectio*, 53 vols. [Arnheim and Leipzig: Société nouvelle d'édition de la collection Mansi, curantibus Ludovico Petit et Ioanne Baptista Martin, 1748-], 52 [1927]: 1213 AB, emphasis mine). All translations are mine unless indicated to the contrary. Cited henceforth as MPM. For an account of how the maximalist tendency continued despite the exposition given by Gasser, see Gustave Thils, *L'Infaillibilité pontificale: source, conditions, limites* (Gembloux: Editions J. Duculot, 1969), pp. 179-82.

27 "Hinc sententia: Romanus pontifex est infallibilis, non quidem ut falsa debet traduci, cum Christus personae Petri et personae successoris eius illam promiserit; sed est solummodo incompleta, *cum papa solummodo sit infallibilis quando solemni iudicio pro universa ecclesia res fidei et morum definit*" (ibid., emphasis mine).

28 See Paul Nau, "Le magistère pontifical ordinaire au premier concile du Vatican," *Revue thomiste* 62 (1962): 341-97, especially p. 354.

29 See p. 376, n.63.

30 See Edmond Dublanchy, "Infaillibilité du Pape," in *Dictionnaire de Théologie catholique*, 15 vols, 22 tomes (Paris: Letouzey et Ané, 1909-) 7 (1927): 1638-1717, especially pp. 1705-6; and Ioachim Salaverri de la Torre, *De Ecclesia Christi* in *Sacrae Theologiae Summa*, 4 vols. (Madrid: La Editorial católica [Biblioteca de Autores cristianos] 1950-53), 1 (2d ed., 1952): 497-953, especially pp. 692-93 (no. 647); "Valor de las Encíclicas a la luz de 'Humani generis,'" *Miscelánea Comillas* 17 (1952): 135-72.

31 In addition to those already cited, see, for example, J. Bellamy, who

thought *Pastor Aeternus* rightly interpreted meant that the Pope could speak *ex cathedra* in two ways; in that of the extraordinary magisterium and that of the ordinary. See J. Bellamy, *La Théologie catholique au XIXᵉ siècle*, 3rd ed. (Paris: Gabriel Beauchesne, 1904), p. 241, and, much later, Joseph Clifford Fenton, who thought that the very fact the Pope wishes to put an end to all discussion on a theological point was sufficient to judge that the charism of infallibility is operative. See Joseph Clifford Fenton, "The Doctrinal Authority of Papal Encyclicals," *American Ecclesiastical Review* 121 (1949): 210-20, especially pp. 212 and 214.

[32]   See Salaverri, *De Ecclesia Christi.*

[33]   See ibid.

[34]   See Salaverri, "Valor de las Encíclicas a la luz de '*Humani generis*,'" p. 163.

[35]   "... iuxta Conc. Vaticanum, Romanus Pontifix 'ea infallibilitate pollet qua Divinus Redemptor Ecclesiam suam instructam esse voluit.' Atqui Ecclesia instructa est infallibilitate quam exercet modis extraordinario et ordinario. Ergo iisdem modis Romano Pontifici concedendum est suam infallibilitatem exercere" (Salaverri, *De Ecclesia Christi*, pp. 692-93 [no. 647]).

[36]   Referring to the canon with which Chap. III of *Pastor Aeternus* (q.v.) ends (that those are to be considered anathema who deny that the Roman Pontiff has full and supreme power of jurisdiction over the whole Church, etc.), Salaverri uses what might be called a wedge argument, as paraphrased above: "...Summus Pontifex habet potestatem infallibilitatis modo etiam *ordinario*. Secus enim concludendum esset, supremam potestatem infallibilitatis, saltem in modo quo exercetur, esse in Romano Pontifice magis restrictam quam in Ecclesia..." (ibid. p. 693).

[37]   For Dublanchy, it would be necessary that the truth taught by the Pope *be proposed as already defined*; or *as having always been believed or admitted* by the Church; or finally, as having been attested by the Church's theologians unanimously and constantly as a Catholic truth. See Dublanchy, "Infaillibilité du Pape," p. 1705.

[38]   See inter alios J. Beumer, "Sind päpstliche Enzykliken unfehlbar?," *Theologie und Glaube* 42 (1952): 262-69; B. Brinkmann, "Gibt es unfehlbare Äusserungen des '*Magisterium ordinarium*,' des Papstes?," *Scholastik* 18 (1953): 202-21; H. Stirnimann, "Magisterio enim ordinario haec docentur . . . ," *Freiburger Zeitschrift für Philosophie und Theologie* 1 (1954): 17-47.

[39]   See Ioachim Salaverri de la Torre, *De Ecclesia Christi* in *Sacrae Theologiae Summa*, 1 (5th ed., 1962): 488-976, esp. pp. 700-1 (no. 647). As far as I know, there has been, as of this writing, no subsequent edition.

[40]   Joaquín Salaverry [*sic*] "Encyclicals," *Sacramentum Mundi: An Encyclopedia of Theology*, 6 vols. (New York: Herder & Herder, and London: Burns & Oates, 1968-70), 2 (1968): 229-30. (For some unaccountable reason, the author's name is herein spelled *Salaverry*.) The sentence: "Though encyclicals do not represent infallible pronouncements of the magisterium, they present authentic teaching . . ." [ibid., p. 230] which follows the above quotation is obviously somewhat inconsistent, since Salaverri had just allowed that they may under certain circumstances.

There is some indication that in the 1950s Salaverri was thinking along the lines later adopted in the *Sacramentum Mundi* article quoted above. Thus in an article published in *Estudios eclesiásticos* he stated that ". . . the various forms which the Popes use or may use in the exercise of their supreme magisterium differ very greatly and one may not say that the exercise of this power is tied to any one particular form. Rather it has been left completely to the free choice of the same Pontiff. . . . His teaching authority having been clearly established, one must further keep in mind that within his supreme magisterium there can be two principal degrees of authority: the highest degree of infallibility, as when he speaks *ex cathedra*, and the other, lower degree of the merely authentic magisterium, which is the kind he exercises ordinarily in all the other cases in which he does not indicate his intention of engaging the same infallibility." [*Las diversas formas* de que se valen o pueden valer los Papas para ejercer su supremo Magisterio sabemos que son muy varias, y no se puede decir que el ejercicio de esa potestad esté vinculado a forma particular alguna, sino que ha sido dejado plenamente a la libre elección del mismo Pontífice . . . Comprobada claramente su autoridad magisterial, se ha de tener presente además que dentro de su Magisterio supremo se pueden dar dos grados principales de autoridad: el grado sumo de infalibilidad, como cuando habla *ex cathedra*, y el otro grado inferior de Magisterio meramente auténtico, cual es el que ejerce ordinariamente en todos los demás casos en los que no manifiesta su intención de empeñar la misma infalibilidad] (Joaquín Salaverri de la Torre, "La Potestad de Magisterio Eclesiástico y asentimiento que le es debido," *Estudios eclesiásticos* 29 [1955]: 177). But this apparent shift, already discernible in 1955, was not incorporated into the 1962 edition of Salaverri's *De Ecclesia Christi*.

[41] "Must one conclude that the Syllabus and the other acts of the ordinary magisterium are definitions *ex cathedra*? Most theologians think so, and rightly, if one understands by an *ex cathedra* definition every pontifical act that fulfills the conditions the Vatican Council asked [be fulfilled] in order for the Pope to be infallible. But then it seems appropriate to distinguish two kinds of *ex cathedra* definitions: those made in solemn judgments and those which are the work of the ordinary magisterium of the sovereign pontiff." [Faut-il en conclure que le Syllabus et les autres actes du magistère ordinaire sont des définitions *ex cathedra*? La plupart des théologiens le pensent, et avec raison, si l'on entend par définition *ex cathedra* tout act pontifical qui remplit les conditions demandées par le concile du Vatican pour que le pape soit infaillible. Mais alors il convient de distinguer deux sortes de définitions *ex cathedra*: celles qui sont portées par des sentences solennelles, et celles qui sont l'oeuvre du magistère ordinaire du souverain pontife] (Bellamy, *La Théologie catholique au XIXᵉ siècle*, p. 241).

[42] See Salaverri, "Valor de las Encíclicas a la luz de *Humani generis*," p. 163.

[43] See Petrus Boris Bilaniuk, *De Magisterio Ordinario Summi Pontificis* (Toronto: Apud Auctorem, 1966). In this dissertation, written under the direction of Michael Schmaus, the author maintains that the ordinary papal magisterium teaches infallibly when, with the intention of teaching a [theological] truth to the

whole Church, it obliges it to full, sincere, and internal assent. See ibid., p. 97. In this I perceive no discernible difference from the position of Salaverri in his first phase. Bilaniuk's position relative to the Syllabus, however, is more nuanced. See ibid., p. 231.

[44]   See Joseph F. Costanzo, "Academic Dissent: An Original Ecclesiology," *The Thomist* 34 (1970): 636-53; and more recently, Edward J. Capestany, "McCormick and the Erosion of the Magisterium." *Catholicism in Crisis* 1, no. 7 (June 1983), pp. 23-28, especially pp. 24 and 26.

[45]   Besides those mentioned below [see p. 378, n.73], see Luigi (now Cardinal) Ciappi in "Il magistero vivo di S.S. Pio XII: norma prossima e universale di verità," *Sapienza* 7 (1954): 125-51, especially pp. 143-46. After having distinguished the secondary from the primary teaching mission of the Church and of the Roman Pontiff, Ciappi maintained that the authority of the Pope in the case of the former (secondary mission) is prudential. (See ibid., p. 144.) Ciappi then went on to ask what ought to be the attitude of the believer toward such teaching of the ordinary [papal] magisterium. His answer was that the authority of the Church is the *immediate* foundation [the *mediate* foundation, said Ciappi, is God, who rules the Church] of an assent that can be either mediated divine faith, obedience, ecclesiastical faith, or religious assent, etc., depending on whether the papal magisterium appears to be infallible or not. (See ibid., p. 146.) The basis for judging that the ordinary [papal] magisterium has been infallibly exercised is whether the Roman Pontiff intends to engage the fullness of his prudential authority, addressing the whole Church as its supreme head, intending to determine that which is conducive to drawing minds toward or away from divine truth. (See ibid., p. 145) Examples given here are some of the positions taken by Pius XII in *Humani generis*. (See ibid.) In these cases it is a question of infallible security [*infallibile sicurezza*] rather than infallible truth [*infallibile verità*], the latter expression being reserved by Ciappi for dogmatic definitions of the extraordinary papal magisterium. Though it seems to me that Ciappi here makes a distinction without a difference, there can be no doubt that as of 1954 he held that the ordinary papal magisterium can be infallibly exercised under conditions similar to those described by Salaverri in his first phase. I have come upon no indication that Ciappi has since changed his mind.

[46]   See Fidelis Gallati, *Wenn die Päpste sprechen: das ordentliche Lehramt des apostolischen Stuhles und die Zustimmung zu dessen Entscheidungen* (Vienna: Verlag Herder, 1960). Gallati seems to have misunderstood Ciappi's position in that he interpreted Ciappi as meaning that encyclicals do not lay claim to infallibility. (See ibid., p. 57, n. 40.) Quite clearly Ciappi means that they can, in certain circumstances, as I have shown above in the preceding note.

[47]   See Paul Nau, "L'autorité doctrinale des Encycliques," *La Pensée catholique*, no. 15 (1950), pp. 45-63; no. 16, (1950): pp. 42-59; and especially no. 19 (1951), pp. 63-84. For essentially the same thesis put somewhat more succinctly, see his *Une Source doctrinale: les Encycliques. Essai sur l'autorité de leur enseignement* (Paris: Les Editions du Cèdre, 1952), and "Le Magistère pontifical ordinaire, lieu théologique," *Revue thomiste* 56 (1956): 389-412.

48   See Gallati, *Wenn die Päpste sprechen*, p. 199.

49   See ibid.

50   See ibid.

51   See ibid.

52   "Wenn aber mehrere Päpste immer wieder durch längere Zeiträume hindurch nicht-endgültige Lehrkundgebungen erlassen, welche inhaltlich und der Sache nach dieselbe Lehre verkünden, entsteht eine Uberlieferung des Apostolischen Stuhles; diese ist klare Regel für den Glauben der ganzen Kirche. Eine solche Uberlieferung besitzt darum die umbedingte Bürgschaft der Wahrheit, sie ist unfehlbar wahr. Somit ist unter den angeführten Bedingungen nicht bloss das ausserordentliche, sondern auch das ordentliche Lehramt des Apostolischen Stuhles mit dem Charisma der Unfehlbarkeit ausgestattet" (ibid.).

53   See Paul Nau, *Une Source doctrinale: les Encycliques*.

54   In a review of Nau's *Une Source doctrinale: les Encycliques* Yves Congar paraphrased Nau's position and concluded, "Cette analyse nous semble très exacte" (see Yves Congar, review of *Une Source doctrinale: les Encycliques. Essai sur l'autorité de leur enseignement*, by Paul Nau, in *Revue de Sciences philosophiques et théologiques* 37 [1953]: 734-35). However, in fairness to Congar two factors should be highlighted. First, Congar's paraphrase of Nau's thesis may have amounted to an intended attenuation; i.e., whereas in the book under review Nau claimed infallibility for a doctrinal position consistently maintained by a series of Roman Bishops (see Nau, *Une Source doctrinale: les Encycliques*, pp. 75 and 80), Congar, in paraphrasing Nau's position and asking whether the teaching of encyclicals might share in the privilege of infallibility, answered: ". . . each affirmation in encyclicals is not in itself an infallible judgment; but when there is a convergence, an insistence, we find ourselves in the presence of a firm and, at the very least, virtually unanimous teaching of the ordinary magisterium which excludes the possibility of a doubt about the authentic content of that teaching." [. . . chaque affirmation des enc. (*sic*) prise à part n'est pas, de soi, un jugement infaillible; mais quand il y a convergence, insistence, on se trouve en présence d'un enseignement ferme, et, virtuellement tout au moins, unanime, du magistère ordinaire, qui exclut la possibilité d'un doute sur l'authentique contenu de cet enseignement] (Congar, review of *Une Source doctrinale: les Encycliques*). To say that the content of a teaching is authentic is not to say it is infallible. Second, while the reasons for this apparent attenuation may have been syntactical (i.e., infallibility has to do with the judgment, not with a teaching; viz., if the *judgment* that makes it is *infallible*, a particular *teaching* is *certainly true* as far as it goes), Congar's language may have been intended to suggest less than full endorsement. For he went on to point out some reasons for caution, one of which is the fact that encyclicals are frequently meant to address particular circumstances, a case in point being John Courtney Murray's assessment of the teaching of Leo XIII on Christian democracy. (See ibid.) I shall treat these and related matters at some length in Chaps. III, IV, and VI.

55   See Paul Nau, "Le Magistère pontifical ordinaire au premier Concile du Vatican," *Revue thomiste* 62 (1962): 341-97.

[56]   See M. Caudron, "Magistère ordinaire et infaillibilité pontificale d'après la constitution *Dei Filius*," *Ephemerides Theologicae Lovanienses* 36 (1960): 393-431, especially p. 431.

[57]   "... that tradition of the Roman Church ... to which unfaithfulness has no access ..." MPM 52 (1927): 1217A. The context suggests, of course, that *perfidia* [unfaithfulness] refers to a definitive but erroneous judgment pertaining to the substance of the faith, not to moral conduct. Clearly the Roman Church in its leadership has sometimes sinned.

[58]   See ibid.

[59]   Bishop d'Avanzo is recorded to have spoken as follows: "The way in which infallibility in the Church is exercised is twofold. The first is through the ordinary magisterium of the Church ... Whether they have been defined, whether they are explicitly contained in the treasury of revelation but have not yet been defined, or whether in the end they are implicitly believed: All these moreover the Church teaches *daily*, sometimes through the Pope as head [*principaliter*], sometimes through bishops as individuals in union [*adhaerentes*] with the Pope. All, both Pope and bishops, are infallible in this ordinary magisterium and that from the infallibility of the Church itself. They differ only in this way: The bishops by themselves are not infallible but need to be in communion with the Pope, by whom they are strengthened. But the Pope needs only the help of the Holy Spirit promised him. *Therefore, he teaches and is not taught; he strengthens, but is not strengthened.*" [Duplex ergo est modus infallibilitatis in ecclesia; primus exercetur per magisterium ordinarium ecclesiae . . . Docet autem ea omnia quae sive sunt definita, sive in thesauro revelationis explicite continentur, sed nondum sunt definita, sive tandem quae implicite creduntur: ista docet *quotidie* ecclesia, tum per papam principaliter, tum per singulos episcopos papae adhaerents. Omnes et papa et episcopi in isto ordinario magisterio sunt infallibiles ex ipsius ecclesiae infallibilitate: in hoc tantummodo differunt, quod episcopi per se non sunt infallibiles sed indigent communione cum papa, a quo confirmentur; papa vero non indigeat nisi assistentia sancti Spiritus illi promissa: *ideo docet et non docetur, confirmat, et non confirmatur*] (ibid., p. 764AB, emphases mine).

[60]   "Leur conclusion aussi est la même: Si le pape peut et doit parfois recourir à une consultation des évêques, cette consultation ne saurait être posée comme condition de l'exercice infaillible du souverain magistère. Un critère suffit, toujours à la disposition du pape, a rappelé Mgr Gasser . . . la seule tradition de l'Eglise de Rome" (Nau, "Le Magistère pontifical ordinaire au premier Concile du Vatican," p. 354.)

[61]   See ibid., p. 397.

[62]   See ibid., p. 397.

[63]   Though because of his paraphrase of and partial dependence on Irenaeus (". . . ad quam [ecclesiam romanam] propter potentiorem illius principalitatem omnem oportet convenire ecclesiam . . ." [MPM 52 (1927): 1217A]) the internal logic of Gasser's speech may have been open to Nau's own view, to suggest that Gasser's position was the same as Bartolomeo d'Avanzo's constitutes, I believe, a

serious distortion of the data. It must not be forgotten that in the context of the *ordinary* magisterium d'Avanzo is recorded to have maintained that the Church daily (*quotidie*) teaches infallibly, sometimes through the Pope as head (*principaliter*), sometimes through the bishops united with him. According to d'Avanzo's view, one could therefore in principle be dealing not simply, say, with a series of Roman Bishops but with an individual. In order for the internal logic of Gasser's statements to have been the same as that expressly articulated by d'Avanzo on June 20, 1870, Gasser's meaning would have to have been that, on the level of the *ordinary* papal magisterium, an individual Roman Bishop (*sedens*) in teaching the whole Church that p is the tradition of his predecessors (*sedes*) invariably interprets correctly the tradition of the Roman Church. *But that is precisely the move Gasser did not make*, as is borne out, I suggest, by Texts A and B quoted above. Nowhere in the article cited does Nau quote these texts.

  64   See Paul Nau, "Le Magistère pontifical ordinaire au premier Concile du Vatican," in *De Doctrina Concilii Vaticani Primi*, by Alexander Kerrigan, Robert Schlund, Roger Aubert, Marc Caudron, Paul Nau, Georges Paradis, Lambert Beauduin, Umberto Betti, Wilfrid F. Dewan, Walter Kasper, Giuseppe Colombo, Jérôme Hamer, Ursicino Dominiques del Val, J.P. Torrell, Georges Dejaifve, Gustave Thils, and Antoine Chavasse (Rome: Libreria Editrice Vaticana, 1969), pp. 161-220.

  65   See Arthur Peiffer, *Die Enzykliken und ihr formaler Wert für die dogmatische Methode.*

  66   *Doctrina catholica* in Scheeben's sense means for Peiffer that p has been revealed by God [primary object of infallibility] or that p is so closely connected with a revealed truth that to deny p is to put a revealed truth in doubt [secondary object of infallibility]. See ibid., p. 140.

  67   "In diesem lehramtlichen '*testimonium*' liegt die ureigene, für die Glaubenserkenntnis und die theologische Erkenntnis so eminent wichtige Bedeutung der Enzykliken, insofern sie ein matierielles Dogma klar und deutlich als formales Dogma erkennbar machen und authentisch bezeugen, dass eine bestimmte Lehre auf der Offenbarung gründet und durch das lebendige Lehramt der Gesamtkirche übereinstimmend verkündet wird. Bei dieser mehr deklarativen Lehrvermittlung handelt es sich natürlich noch nicht um eine eigentliche und *spezifische Glaubensentscheidung*. Doch darf man sagen, dass hiermit die letzte Phase der prädefinitorischen Dogmenentwicklung abgeschlossen ist . . . .

  "Ein sehr rezentes Beispiel solcher vertieften Glaubenserkenntnis vermittels einer Enzyklika haben wir im Rundschreiben Pius XII. '*Mystici corporis*' . . . ." (ibid., p. 196).

  68   See ibid., p. 195.

  69   See ibid., p. 196.

  70   See ibid., p. 141.

  71   See ibid., pp. 193-94. Though Peiffer published his dissertation in 1968, he does not seem to have been aware of the shift in Salaverri's opinion. I say this despite the fact that Salaverri's *Estudios eclesiásticos* article and that (in the

German edition, 1967) of *Sacramentum Mundi* is listed in Peiffer's bibliography. See ibid., p. xvi.

[72]   See ibid., p. 196.

[73]   See, for example, Joseph F. Costanzo, "Papal Magisterium and *Humanae vitae*," *Thought* 44 (1969): 377-412, especially pp. 393-97; Vincent P. Miceli, "A Forgotten Encyclical," *Homiletic and Pastoral Review* 76 (June 1976): 19-28; Edward J. Berbusse, "Infallibility in the Ordinary Teaching of the Supreme Pontiff," *Homiletic and Pastoral Review* 76 (July 1976): 26-32.

[74]   "With authentic definitions, which are conclusive judgments, one can speak of an infallibility *in facto esse*; with preceding judgments, which can belong to the ordinary magisterium [*Lehramt*] of the Pope, one can speak of infallibility *in fieri*" [Bei den eigentlichen Definitionen, die abschliessende Urteile sind, kann man von einer Unfehlbarkeit *in facto esse* sprechen, bei den vorausgehenden Urteilen, die zum ordentlichen Lehramt des Papstes gehören können, von einer Unfehlbarkeit *in fieri*] (Heinrich Stirnimann, "Magisterio enim ordinario haec docentur . . . ," *Freiburger Zeitschrift für Philosophie und Theologie* 1 [1954]: 39. See also ibid., p. 40.)

[75]   *LCD V*, p. 13.

[76]   See Karl Rahner, "Open Questions in Dogma Considered by the Institutional Church as Definitely Answered," *Journal of Ecumenical Studies* 15 (1978): 221. The translation is by Michael A. Fahey.

[77]   See *Agreement on Authority: The Anglican-Roman Catholic Statement*, with commentary by Julian W. Charley (Bramcote: Grove Books, 1977), p. 15.

[78]   Rahner, "Open Questions in Dogma," p. 221.

[79]   For a recent treatment of the various aspects of the question, see Terry J. Tekippe, ed., *Papal Infallibility: An Application of Lonergan's Method* (Washington, D.C.: University Press of America, 1983).

[80]   Let me say in passing, however, that I find unpersuasive any strict conciliarist interpretation of the *Haec sancta* of April 6, 1415 and the decree *Frequens* of October 9, 1417. Thus I have never ceased to be puzzled by the fact that, in his treatment of the Council of Constance, Hans Küng omits all mention of the *Laetentur coeli* of the Council of Florence. At first sight this may not appear to be relevant until one recalls that the latter decree is fully in harmony with certain paragraphs of *Inter cunctas* of February 22, 1418 wherein suspected followers of Wyclif and Hus were to be asked *inter alia* whether they believed a canonically elected Pope, for the length of time that he is Pope, is in his own name the successor of Peter, having supreme power over the Church of God. (See DS, no. 1264) Data of this kind are highly suggestive of the way in which the *Haec sancta* of April 6, 1415 was understood by Martin V. I have already alluded to Alberigo's recent work and have added a further comment below (see pp. 394-95, n.156). For an earlier study providing an analysis of the events that led up to that particular *Haec sancta* and the ecclesiological stance it seems to reflect, see August Franzen, "The Council of Constance: Present State of the Problem," in *Historical Problems of Church Renewal*, edited by Roger Aubert, Concilium vol. 7 (Glen Rock, New Jersey: Paulist Press, 1965), pp. 29-68.

⁸¹   See Oakley, *Council over Pope?*, pp. 176-78.

⁸²   "If the popes have always been infallible in any meaningful sense of the word . . . then all kinds of dubious consequences ensue. Most obviously, twentieth century popes would be bound by a whole array of past papal decrees reflecting responses of the Roman Church to the religious and moral problems of former ages. . . . To defend religious liberty would be 'insane' and to persecute heretics commendable. . . . Unbaptized babies would be punished in Hell for all eternity. Maybe the sun would still be going round the earth" (Brian Tierney, *Origins of Papal Infallibility*, p. 2).

⁸³   See the remarks of Antonio Jannucci, Bishop at Penne-Pescara (Italy), in *Acta Synodalia Sacrosancti Concilii Oecumenici Vaticani Secundi*, 4 vols., 26 tomes (Rome: Typis Polyglottis Vaticanis, 1971-80), 2, pt. 2: 176. This collection is henceforth referred to as *Acta Syn.*

⁸⁴   It is a truism in Catholic theology that the Petrine function and/or ministry could in principle be exercised by the bishop of another see and that, in a fully united Christendom, such may one day be the case. Thus the "presidency" of the Church could rotate. In that sense, there is nothing sacred about Rome. As far as I can see, the fundamental questions are (1) whether the Petrine ministry and/or function as exercised by an individual is *normative* for authentic Christianity and (2) whether authentic Christianity is free to abolish that norm as it sees fit. Though the implication of the circumstances surrounding, say, the Council of Constance must be honestly assessed, I would be prepared to argue for an affirmative answer to the first question and for a negative answer to the second. To enter into this kind of discussion beyond these few remarks would, however, carry me too far afield. Let me simply note that I find somewhat enigmatic the following statement by Avery Dulles: "The inevitability that there be a certain division of labor in the papacy could at some future time call for changes that would make the papacy more like a 'constitutional' government, with a legally sanctioned separation of powers. The Catholic Church might experience a constitutional evolution some- what similar to that of Great Britain, for example, in modern times" (Avery Dulles, "Papal Authority in Roman Catholicism," in *A Pope for All Christians?*, ed. Peter J. McCord [New York, Paramus, N.J., Toronto: Paulist Press, 1976], p. 56). Does this mean that the role of Catholicism's (or as the case may one day be, Christiani- ty's) Petrine minister would be analogous to that presently played by the English sovereign? If so, I do not believe such a view of the Petrine ministry can be sustained within the limits of Catholic ecclesiology.†

⁸⁵   Thus applied to the First Vatican Council, the term refers to vols. 49-53 of the so-called Mansi-Petit-Martin (MPM) collection. Applied to the Second Vati- can Council, it refers to the *Acta et Documenta Concilio Oecumenico Vaticano Secundo apparando* Series I (Antepraeparatoria), 5 vols., 16 tomes (Rome: Typis Polyglottis Vaticanis, 1960-61) and Series II (Praeparatoria), 3 vols., 7 tomes (Rome: Typis Polyglottis Vaticanis, 1964-69); the *Acta Syn.*; the promulgated Latin text, *Sacrosanctum Oecumenicum Concilium Vaticanum Secundum: Con- stitutiones, Decreta, Declarationes* (Rome: Typis Polyglottis Vaticanis, 1966), and the English translations of the last mentioned, *Documents of Vatican II*, ed. Walter

†   This book was written before the appearance of Dulles' *The Catholicity of the Church* (Oxford: The Clarendon Press, 1985). See ibid., p. 143.

M. Abbott and Joseph Gallagher (New York: America Press, 1966). Occasional reference is made to the so-called Flannery edition. See Austin Flannery, general ed., *Vatican II: The Conciliar and Post-Conciliar Documents* (Wilmington, Delaware: Scholarly Resources Inc., 1975).

[86]   See AG, pp. 29-30.

[87]   For a brief description of some usages prior to the Council, see p. 348 above.

[88]   Though I intend to touch on this matter more fully when treating an area of indirect concern (i.e., the position taken at Vatican II on the infallibility of the ordinary universal magisterium), I would like to point out here that I find the treatment by Elmar Klinger oversimplified when that writer seems to restrict infallibility, when it is operative, to proclamation of a given truth as revealed. See Elmar Klinger, "Die Unfehlbarkeit des ordentlichen Lehramtes," in *Zum Problem Unfehlbarkeit: Anworten auf die Anfrage von Hans Küng*, Quaestiones Disputatae no. 54. ed. Karl Rahner (Freiburg im Breisgau, Basel and Vienna: Herder, 1971), pp. 278-79.

[89]   Gerald O'Collins, *The Case against Dogma* (New York, Paramus, N.J., and Toronto: Paulist Press, 1975), p. 96. While I agree with O'Collins that the term *dogma* is not a univocal one and may not be treated as an *ultimate* norm of faith (see ibid.) if *ultimate* is meant to rule out complementary pluralism, I must reject completely his view that "No dogma can say to us: 'Set your mind . . . at rest about this truth' "(ibid., p. 17).

[90]   Likewise I must reject the contention of Josef Nolte when he asserts that the concept of "dogma" in the New Testament is not characterized by "irreformability" or "infallibility." See Josef Nolte, *Dogma in Geschichte: Versuch einer Kritik des Dogmatismus in der Glaubensdarstellung* (Freiburg, Basel and Vienna: Herder, 1971), p. 266. It is difficult to see how Nolte's position can be harmonized with Gal. 1: 8-9. Nolte would like dogmatic statements limited to what he calls *metadogmata* (e.g., brief symbols which sum up the faith [as in scripture] or brief symbols which sum up and defend it [as in the early Councils]) but considers undesirable any explicitly partisan broadening of belief (such as in the Marian dogmas). For reasons that would take me too far afield to state here, I cannot accept Nolte's position since the Marian dogmas fit into the whole of which Rahner speaks. See Karl Rahner, "The Immaculate Conception," in *Theological Investigations*, 20 vols., various translators (London: Darton, Longman & Todd, and New York: Seabury Press, 1974), 1: (1961): 202-3.

[91]   For a view more in harmony with my own, see Paul Schrodt, *The Problem of the Beginning of Dogma in Recent Theology* (Frankfurt am Main, Bern, Las Vegas: Peter Lang, 1978), pp. 337-38. For an insightful discussion of the wider issues, see William E. Reiser, *What Are They Saying about Dogma?* (New York and Ramsey, N.J.: Paulist Press, 1978), and "Dogma and Heresy Revisited: A Heideggerian Approach," *The Thomist* 46 (1982): 509-38.

[92]   Here I must disassociate myself from the interpretation of Newman expounded by my friend, professor, and former mentor at the Sorbonne, Henri Gouhier, who, for a number of reasons, seems to have misunderstood him. (See

Henri Gouhier, "Tradition et développement à l'époque du modernisme," in *Ermeneutica e Tradizione*, Archivio di filosofia, ed. Enrico Castelli [Padua: Celam, 1963], nos. 1-2, pp. 75-99, and the record of the discussion [as edited by Castelli] which followed Gouhier's paper, ibid., pp. 100-4.) I shall limit myself here to one of the reasons why this misunderstanding seems to have come about. It comes down to this: Newman's theory of doctrinal development risks being misunderstood if one reads only his *Essay on the Development of Christian Doctrine*. His thinking must be approached within the broader context of his epistemology, which, unfortunately, is not located in any one work, though an important part of it is to be found in *An Essay in Aid of a Grammar of Assent*. For an example of how complex Newman's epistemology seems to have been (and which incidentally answers the question with which Owen Chadwick's book ends [see Owen Chadwick, *From Bossuet to Newman: The Idea of Doctrinal Development* (Cambridge: Cambridge University Press, 1957), p. 195]) see what I have called the *Letter to Ryder* in H. de Achával, "An Unpublished Paper by Cardinal Newman on the Development of Doctrine," *Gregorianum* 39 (1958): 585-96. But even if one limits oneself to the *Grammar of Assent*, Newman's thinking must be followed very closely. Therein the illative sense is functionally equivalent to Pascal's *connaissance par le coeur* and has to do with the judgment. That the degrees of knowledge in Pascal have been misunderstood by thinkers like Nietzsche and those who have commented on Nietzsche should not be allowed to obscure that fact. It is through the illative sense that the Church, ultimately through its magisterial officers, judges whether or not a particular doctrine fits in or does not fit in with the Idea of the Incarnation *as a concrete whole*. While Gouhier admitted that Newman explicitly distinguished development of ideas from organic development, he nonetheless interpreted Newman as thinking organic development (*l'imagerie vitaliste*) analogously conducive to an understanding of intellectual (*spirituel*) development (by which I take Gouhier to have meant growth in understanding by the rest of the Church; see Gouhier, "Tradition et développement à l'époque du modernisme," p. 95). But Newman's theory is not dependent on an organic model, and though it predominates in the *Essay on Development*, he mentions other possible models. (See John Henry Newman, *An Essay on the Development of Christian Doctrine* [Westminster, Md.: Christian Classics, Inc., 1973], pp. 41-54). Furthermore, it should not be forgotten that Newman evolved his theory as the result of having realized that the Vincentian canon, when applied to the early Christological and Trinitarian controversies, simply does not work. If Newman was right, then Gouhier's attempt to substitute a theory (based on an interpretation of Bergson) of rediscovery of the Word [*ré-invention des "paroles divines"*] (see Gouhier, "Tradition et développement à l'époque du modernisme," pp. 97-98) does not work either. I believe Gouhier was correct when he pointed out that development conceived according to an organic model must be discarded; I believe he was wrong in presuming that Newman's theory is, in effect, inseparably linked thereto. It is interesting to note that in the discussion which followed Gouhier's paper, only Henri (now Cardinal) de Lubac seems to have been aware that Newman's theory cannot be disposed of so easily. See ibid., pp. 100-1.

[93] Gouhier's rejection (see ibid.) of an organic model had, of course, been anticipated much earlier (see, for example, M.M. Tuyaerts, *L'Evolution du dogme: étude théologique* [Louvain: Imprimerie "Nova et Vetera," 1919]), but Gouhier seems to have come to the same conclusion independently. In this regard, his thinking was unquestionably in line with what was to become the present scholarly consensus. (See Nicholas Lash, *Change In Focus: A Study of Doctrinal Change and Continuity* [London: Sheed & Ward, 1973], p. 133.) Unfortunately, Tuyaerts too thought Newman's theory was necessarily bound up with an organic model (see *L'Evolution du dogme: étude théologique*, p. 31) and seems to have judged that development takes place only according to a strictly logical process (*procédé logique* [see ibid., p. 251]).

[94] Karl Rahner was undoubtedly correct when he stated that no one theory is sufficient to account for the labyrinthine paths development of doctrine has taken. (See Karl Rahner, "Dogmenentwicklung," in *Lexicon für Theologie und Kirche: Das Zweite Vatikanische Konzil*, 3 vols. [Freiburg: Verlag Herder, 1966-68], 3 [1968]: 461.) It is a truism, of course, to say that all development of doctrine and dogma has been culturally conditioned to some extent, for manifestly it has made a difference—a difference coming, to be sure, under the aegis of divine providence—that the kerygma went toward Greece before it went toward India. This, it hardly need be said, does not mean that intrareligious dialogue is not possible. Among pioneering works in this regard, see some of those by Raymond Panikkar, e.g., *The Unknown Christ of Hinduism* (London: Darton, Longman & Todd, 1964), and *The Intrareligious Dialogue* (New York and Ramsey, N.J.: Paulist Press, 1978); R.C. Zaehner, *Christianity and Other Religions*, Twentieth Century Encyclopedia of Catholicism, vol. 140 (New York: Hawthorn Books, 1964); and most recently, Mariasusai Dhavamony, *Classical Hinduism* (Rome: Gregorian University Press, 1982).

[95] Though Jean-Pierre Jossua subsequently provided an analysis that seems more susceptible to being harmonized with the historical data (see Jean-Pierre Jossua, "Signification des confessions de foi," *Istina* 17 [1972]: 48-56, especially p. 54), he has never, as far as I know, explicitly modified the position he attempted to sustain in 1968. It is to this kind of structural approach to doctrinal (and dogmatic) development that I refer. At the risk of some oversimplification, Jossua's thought-provoking article (see Jean-Pierre Jossua, "Immutabilité, progrès ou structurations multiples des doctrines chrétiennes," *Revue des sciences philosophiques et théologiques* 53 [1968]: 175-200) may be reduced to the following central points:

1. First there is the kerygma (see ibid., p. 182) followed by an ensemble of key-concepts (*idées-force*) which are clearly distinguished from partial or global structures (see ibid.). An example of a key-concept is the true humanity and the true divinity of Jesus Christ (see ibid., p. 191).

2. Christians grow in understanding what the kerygma implies (see ibid., p. 197).

3. The kerygma is structured differently according to various cultural contexts (see ibid.).

4. There are developments, even homogeneous developments (see ibid., p. 196). But the developments are of structures, not of doctrine or dogma.
5. Hence, the idea of doctrinal development in the sense of continued growth (*progrès continu*) is incompatible with the historical facts (see ibid., p. 180) and must be replaced by a structural approach.
6. Development of structure does not take place except according to the rules of structural balance (*règles d'équilibre structural*); i.e., an immutable truth is not maintained except by a simultaneous and correlative evolution of all notions which keep among themselves the same relation (*rapport*; see ibid., p. 184).

Space does not permit me to comment on Jossua's interesting thesis except to point out a few of the reasons why I do not think he has proved it. Jossua maintains an ensemble of key concepts clearly distinguished from their structures; even if the given is never grasped in a pure state but is always the result of a reformulation of some sort, the fact that it is taken up again attests to its existence, while comparison of the reformulation with the given reveals its permanence in the mind which had grasped the given. (See ibid., p. 182.) I find this unbelievable precisely in view of the historical data on which Jossua claims his position is based. Where is the *idée-force* of three *equal* persons in the Godhead in the earliest stages of Christianity? Even the baptismal formula with which Matthew's gospel (see Matt. 28: 19-20) ends is susceptible of a subordinationist interpretation. Can it be legitimately argued that subordinationist texts in Justin Martyr's *First Apology*, in Tertullian's *Adversus Praxeam* or Origen's *De Principiis* are simply restructuralizations of a primitive *idée-force* about the divinity of Christ and the nature of the Trinity? As for the so-called rules of structural balance, they are, I suggest, even more difficult to sustain. If I understand Jossua correctly, the theandric nature of Christ is a common structure, composed of three partial structures: the divine nature, the divine person, and the human nature. Let us say that the *homoousios* of Nicea is a partial structure occurring some 125 years before Chalcedon. Where is the evidence that this concept moves along together with the other two ([divine] person and human nature) *keeping the same relationship* with them in the mind of the Church until it is restructured at Chalcedon? I submit that Newman's theory, though only seminal as proposed in the *Essay on Development*, faces the problem more felicitously. It seems unfortunate that Jossua, seeing the success with which Henri Bouillard (see Henri Bouillard, *Conversion et grâce selon S. Thomas d'Aquin* [Paris: Aubier, Editions Montaigne, 1944]) illustrated what Jossua calls the rules of structural balance at work within the theological system of Aquinas, seems to have presumed that the same principle (which incidentally has its roots in the work of Jean Piaget) is operative precisely in those areas where the lack of system was the very cause of difficulty. For a more plausible account of what seems to have happened at least up to the time of Nicea, see Bernard Lonergan, *The Way to Nicea: The Dialectical Development of Trinitarian Theology*, trans. Conn O'Donovan (Philadelphia: Westminster Press, 1976). For a report on a wider discussion of the structuralist approach to doctrinal and dogmatic development, see L. Fontaine-de Visscher, "Une rencontre sur 'Structuralisme et dogmatique chrétienne,' " *Revue théologique de Louvain* 4 (1973): 257-61; Regnier Pirard, and Adolphe Gesché, two separate reports on "Structuralisme et dogmatique: intégration et dépassement," ibid., pp. 384-89.

[96]   The study of reception is comparatively recent. A selective bibliography would include at least the following: Yves Congar, "La 'Réception' comme réalité ecclésiologique," *Revue des sciences philosophiques et théologiques* 56 (1972): 369-403, and "Quod omnes tangit ab omnibus tractari et approbari debet," *Revue historique du droit français et étranger* 36 (1958): 210-39; Alois Grillmeier, "Konzil als Rezeption: Methodische Bemerkungen zu einem Thema der ökumenischen Diskussion," in *Mit Ihm und in Ihm* (Freiburg, Basel and Vienna: Herder, 1975), pp. 303-34; Franz Wolfinger, "Die Rezeption theologisher Einsichten und ihre theologische und ökumenische Bedeutung: von der Einsicht zur Verwirklichung," *Catholica* 3 (1977): 202-33; Adolf Lumpe, "Zu 'recipere' als 'gültig annehmen, anerkennen,' in Sprachgebrauch des römischen und kanonischen Rechts," *Annuarium Historiae Conciliorum: Internationale Zeitschrift für Konziliengeschichtsforschung* 7 (1975): 118-34; and Miguel M.ª Garijo Guembe, "El concepto de 'Recepción' y su enmarque en el seno de la Eclesiología católica," *Lumen* 29 (1980): 311-31.

[97]   See p. 293 above.

[98]   See pp. 293-97 above where the implications of my findings in this regard are more fully explored.

[99]   Thus Canon 752 of the *Codex Iuris Canonici Auctoritate Joannis Pauli II Promulgatus* (n.p.: Liberia Editrice Vaticana, 1983) speaks of the religious compliance or deference (the text reads *obsequium*, which could be rendered as *obedience*) of mind and will which should· (*praestandum* could also be read as *must*) be given to the authentic teaching of the Supreme Pontiff and the College of Bishops, even when such teaching is not definitive. Though the Canon makes it clear that such compliance or deference is not the assent of faith (see the *Scale of Theological Notes* in the Glossary), nonetheless Canon 1371.1 states that those who pertinaciously reject such teaching are liable to punishment. But "respectful and responsible talking back" is not coterminous with pertinacious rejection. Hence there is a *tertium quid* clearly grounded in the Church's praxis and meticulously documented in part two of this study, a *tertium quid* that the current code of Canon Law neither affirms nor denies. That is to say: Those who drafted the relevant canons of the present code seem to have taken no cognizance of the manner in which doctrine has developed within Catholicism over the past one hundred fifty years. Thus Catholics on the far right, basing their approach on the current code, do not seem to be able to make the distinction just alluded to, while those on the far left tend to exaggerate its significance. If my conclusions are correct, neither position is fully Catholic. In the meantime, those theologians whose fundamental loyalty is beyond dispute but who in certain cases consider, and in their writings equivalently state, that a given position officially taken by the

Roman Bishop or a particular Vatican Congregation may be oversimplified are made to feel like "bad boys." This, I have argued, is part of Catholicism's internal problem. Its solution in terms of the richness of its unfolding tradition may lead to an ecumenical breakthrough of unforeseen proportions.

100   "Fratres mei, compatimini mecum. Ubi tales inveneritis, nolite occultare, non sit in vobis perversa misericordia: prorsus ubi .tales inveneritis, occultare nolite. Redarguite contradicentes et resistentes ad nos perducite. Jam enim de hac causa duo concilia missa sunt ad Sedem Apostolicam: inde etiam rescripta venerunt. *Causa finita est*" (Aurelius Augustinus, Sermo CXXXI, "De Verbis Evangelii Joannis, cap. vi, 55-66, Nisi manducaveritis carnem, etc., deque verbis Apostoli et Psalmorum contra Pelagianos," *PL* 38 (1845): 734, emphasis mine).

CHAPTER I

1   *Acta Syn* 1, pt. 4: 653-94.

2   See ibid., pp. 653-54.

3   The titles of the chapters as translated are as follows: I. *Knowledge of Truth*; II. *God*; III. *The Creation and Evolution of the World*; IV. *Public Revelation and the Catholic Faith*; V. *The Development of Doctrine*; VI. *Private Revelation*; VII. *The Natural and Supernatural Order*; VIII. *Original Sin*; IX. *The Last Things*; X. *The Satisfaction Brought About by Christ*. See ibid., pp. 654-90.

4   See ibid., p. 653.

5   See ibid., pp. 654-55.

6   See ibid., pp. 657-58.

7   See ibid., p. 660.

8   See ibid., p. 661.

9   See ibid., p. 662.

10   See ibid., p. 663.

11   See ibid., p. 672-73.

12   See ibid., p. 674.

13   See ibid., p. 678.

14   See ibid., p. 681.

15   See ibid., pp. 687-88.

16   See ibid., p. 691.

17   See ibid., p. 659, n. 1.

18   See ibid., p. 656, n. 12.

19   See ibid., p. 670, n. 11.

20   See ibid., p. 659, n. 6.

21   See ibid., p. 655, n. 2.

22   See ibid., p. 655, and p. 656, n. 8.

23   See ibid., p. 670, n. 11, where H. Duméry is singled out for special "censure."

[24]   See ibid., p. 678.

[25]   See ibid., pp. 695-717.

[26]   As translated, the titles of the chapters are as follows: I. *The Foundations of the Christian Moral Order*; II. *Christian Conscience*; III. *Ethical Subjectivism and Relativism*; IV. *Sin*; V. *The Natural and Supernatural Dignity of the Human Person*. See ibid., pp. 695-713.

[27]   See ibid., p. 696.

[28]   See ibid., p. 697.

[29]   See ibid., p. 696.

[30]   See ibid., p. 703.

[31]   See ibid.

[32]   See ibid., p. 706.

[33]   See ibid.

[34]   See ibid., p. 707.

[35]   See ibid.

[36]   See ibid., p. 710.

[37]   See ibid., pp. 713-14.

[38]   See ibid., p. 714.

[39]   See ibid., p. 713.

[40]   See ibid., p. 715.

[41]   "Omnino a mente Ecclesiae est dicere Christianos ob spem et amorem rerum aeternarum temporalia bona aestimare non posse, ut oportet, et falso quodam indifferentismo laborare ad mala physica, dolores, famem bellumque quod spectat" (ibid., p. 716).

[42]   Ibid.

[43]   See discussions related to the natural law: Joseph Ratzinger. "Naturrecht, Evangelium und Ideologie in der katholischen Soziallehre. Katholische Erwägungen zum Thema," in *Christlicher Glaube und Ideologie*, eds. Klaus von Bismark and W. Dirks (Stuttgart and Berlin: Kreuz Verlag and Mainz: Matthias Grünewald, 1964), pp. 24-30. For a wider discussion of the literature on this subject, see Richard A. McCormick, "Notes on Moral Theology," *Theological Studies* 28 (1967): 760-69.

[44]   See *Acta Syn* 1, pt. 4: 700, nn. 5 and 6.

[45]   See ibid., nn. 8 and 9.

[46]   See ibid., p. 704, n. 4.

[47]   See ibid., p. 705, n. 5.

[48]   See ibid., for example, p. 717, nn. 7 and 8 passim.

[49]   See Roger Aubert, *Le Pontificat de Pie IX (1846-1878)* (Paris: Bloud & Gay, 1952), pp. 486-87. For a much fuller treatment, see Lillian Parker Wallace, *Leo XIII and the Rise of Socialism* (Durham: Duke University Press, 1966), especially pp. 254-68 passim; Alcide de Gasperi, *I Tempi et gli Uomini che prepararono la "Rerum Novarum"* (Milan: Società Editrice "Vita e Pensiero," 1945), p. 6; and Henri Rollet, "Les Origines de *Rerum Novarum*," *La Vie intellectuelle* 19 (1951): 4-21.

⁵⁰   See Aubert, *Le Pontificat de Pie IX*, p. 487, n.2.

⁵¹   See Pius XI, *Quadragesimo anno*, in Acta Apostolicae Sedis (Rome: Typis Polyglottis Vaticanis, 1908-), 23 (1931): 197-228 (English translation, Boston: St. Paul Editions, n.d.). Reference is to the English translation, p. 20.

⁵²   See Leo XIII, *Rerum novarum*, in Acta Sanctae Sedis, 42 vols. (Rome: Ex Typographia Polyglotta, 1865-1908), 23 (1890-91): 641-70.

⁵³   See Etienne Gilson, ed., *The Church Speaks to the Modern World: The Social Teachings of Leo XIII* (Garden City, N.Y.: Image Books, 1954), p. 20.

⁵⁴   See Pius XI, *Quadragesimo anno*, p. 8.

⁵⁵   See ibid., p. 34.

⁵⁶   See Pius XII, *La solennità*, radio address of June 1, 1941, in AAS 33 (1941): 195-205.

⁵⁷   See John XXIII, *Mater et Magistra*, in AAS 53 (1961): 401-64 (English translation, Boston: St. Paul Editions, n.d.). References are to the English translation.

⁵⁸   See ibid., pp. 6-16.

⁵⁹   See ibid., p. 17.

⁶⁰   Ibid., p. 18.

⁶¹   Ibid., p. 19.

⁶²   See ibid., pp. 37-43.

⁶³   This was a theme powerfully developed by Paul VI in *Populorum Progressio* (March 26, 1967). That encyclical, along with *Octogesima adveniens* (May 14, 1971), which marked the eightieth anniversary of *Rerum novarum*, is beyond my present scope.

⁶⁴   See, for example, Angel Berna Quintana, *Doctrina social de la Iglesia* (Madrid: Instituto Social León XIII, 1969), p. 29; Rafael Gonzalez Moralejo, "Enseñanzas de la Encíclica 'Rerum Novarum,' y opportuno desarollo en el Magisterio de Pío XI y Pío XII," in *Comentarios a la Mater et Magistra*, ed. M. Brugarolo, trans. José Luis Gutierrez García and Luis Ortiz Muños (Madrid: Biblioteca de Autores cristianos, 1963), p. 123; Lucien Guissard:

> But what is said, as one could not realize, does not necessarily meet with spontaneous much less with unanimous approval among Christians.... In order to be convinced of this fact, it is sufficient to re-read the history of Catholic reaction to *Rerum novarum*. [Mais la parole, on n'a pu s'en rendre compte, ne rencontre pas nécessairement une approbation spontanée, ni surtout unanime, chez les chrétiens...il suffit, pour s'en convaincre, de relire l'histoire des réactions catholiques autour de *Rerum Novarum*] (Lucien Guissard, "Postface: Paroles pour un temps de crise," in *Les Evêques français prennent position*, ed. Pierre Toulet [n.p.: Le Centurion, 1972], p. 262).

These authors do not document their remarks in this regard, however. That is why contemporary witnesses like Georges Goyau are all the more valuable:

When the encyclical *Rerum novarum* appeared in May, 1891, an immense shudder shook the Christian world: the kind of amazement which one experiences in the face of an event which changes one's manner of seeing and perceiving. With certain very rare characters, whose prejudices and interests were offended, emotional reaction took on the nuance of bad feeling; in the majority of cases, admiration was unclouded. [Lorsque parut l'encyclique *Rerum Novarum*, au mois de mai 1891, un immense frisson secoua le monde chrétien: cette sorte de stupeur que l'on éprouve devant un événement qui change notre manière de voir et de sentir. En quelques esprits, bien rares, dont les préjugés ou les intérêts se trouvèrent heurtés, l'émoi se nuança de mauvaise humeur; chez le plus grand nombre, l'admiration fut sans nuage] (Georges Goyau, ed., *L'Eglise et la démocratie chrétienne* [Liège: Imprimerie centrale, 1901], p. 1).

65   Besides the works mentioned above, a very selective bibliography would include at least the following: L'Abbé J.B. Boudignon, *L'Encyclique sur la question sociale avec commentaire historique et littéral* (Paris: P. Lethielleux and LePuy: Chez l'Auteur, 1891); Rudolf Hausleithner, *Der Geist der neuen Ordnung: Einblicke in das päpstliche Gesellschaftsrundschreiben* "Quadragesimo Anno" (Vienna; Verlag und Druck Typographische Anhart, 1937); Joseph Pieper, *Thesen zur sozialen Politik: Die Grundgedanken des Rundschreiben* Quadragesimo Anno, 4th ed. (Frankfurt am Main: Verlag Josef Knecht, 1947); José Luis Gutierrez García, *Conceptos fundamentales en la doctrina social de la Iglesia* (Madrid: Centro de Estudios sociales del Valle de los Caîdos, 1971); Georges Guitton, *1891: Une date dans l'histoire des travailleurs* (Paris: Aux Editions Spes, 1930); Vincenzo Mangano, *Il Pensiero sociale e politica di Leone XIII* (Isola del Liri: Società tipografica Macioce e Pisane, 1931); Fernand Mourret, *Les Directions politiques intellectuelles et sociales de Léon XIII* (Paris: Bloud & Gay, 1920); Jakob Strieder and Johannes Messner, *Die Soziale frage und der Katholizismus: Festschrift zum 40. jährigen Jubiläum der Enzyklika* "Rerum Novarum" (Paderborn: Verlag von Ferdinand Schöningh, 1931); Oswald von Nell-Breuning, *Reorganization of Social Economy*, English ed. prepared by Bernard W. Dempsey (New York, Milwaukee and Chicago: Bruce Publishing Co., 1936); Jean-Yves-Perrin Calvez, *The Church and Social Justice*, trans. J.B. Kirwan (Chicago: Henry Regnery Co., 1961); John A. Ryan and Joseph Husslein, *The Church and Labor* (New York: Macmillan Co., 1920); Joseph Husslein, *The Christian Social Manifesto* (New York, Milwaukee and Chicago: Bruce Publishing Co., 1931).

66   See AG, p. 276.

67   See ibid., p. 277.

68   See ibid., p. 280.

69   Pius XI, *Quadragesimo anno*, p. 60.

70   " '. . . ciascun Vescovo nell'atto ed in vigore della sua ordinazione, entra ad essere membro del corpo episcopale, e per consequenza entra in diritto di governare e ammaestrare tutta la Chiesa, quando sarà in unione con tutti gli altri, e formerà corpo cogli altri'. . .' " (Mauro Cappellari, *Il Trionfo della Santa Sede e della Chiesa* [Venice: Nella Casa del Tipografo Editore Giuseppe Ballaggia, 1832],

p. 119.). The first edition of this work appeared in 1799 and was written as a defense of papal infallibility against the "innovators" who were denying it.

71 This does not mean that Cappellari himself was always consistent: "As I have already suggested, *il Trionfo* contains on the one hand a full and formal adherence to teaching on the communion between papacy and episcopacy but on the other manifests a passive adherence to it, or really, a carelessness about the truly theological premises of such a system, indulging in the suggestion of an analogy with monarchy. In Cappellari these two elements not only coexist but succeed in harmonizing and balancing themselves . . ." [Como ho già accennato, *il Trionfo* contiene da un lato una adesione formale e piena alla dottrina della communione tra papato ed episcopato, ma da un altro lato manifesta una adesione passiva o addirittura una trascuratezza per le premesse propriamente teologiche di tale systema, indulgendo alla suggestione dell'analogia con la monarchia. Nel Cappellari questi due elementi non solo coesistono ma riescono a comporsi e ad equilibrarsi . . .] (Giuseppe Alberigo, *Lo Sviluppo della dottrina sui poteri nella Chiesa universale. Momenti essenziali tra il XVI e il XIX secolo* [Rome, Freiburg, Basel, Barcelona, Vienna: Herder, 1964], pp. 366-67).

72 Thus distortion in practice cannot be laid exclusively at the door of the Popes: ". . . but when later the influence [*suggestione*] of authoritarian currents became stronger throughout the whole of European culture, it was not difficult even for many theologians to lose sight of the organic complexity of ecclesiology and to shift it completely in favor of an exclusive papal authority" [...ma quando più tardi la suggestione delle correnti autoritarie diverrà più forte in tutto il campo della cultura europea non sarà difficile che anche molti teologi perdano di vista l'organica complessità dell'ecclesiologia e si spostino completamente a favore di una esclusiva autorità del papa] (ibid., p. 367).

73 For an examination of the thinking of the bishops at the First Vatican Council relative to collegiality, see J[ean]-P[ierre] Torrell, *La Théologie de l'épiscopat au premier concile du Vatican* (Paris: Les Editions du Cerf, 1961) and Jérôme Hamer, "Le Corps épiscopal uni au pape, son autorité dans l'Eglise," *Revue des Sciences philosophiques et theologiques* 45 (1961): 21-31.

74 See Pius XII, *Fidei donum*, in AAS 49 (1957): 225-48.

75 See ibid., p. 227.

76 See ibid., p. 227 and 230.

77 See ibid., p. 231.

78 See ibid.

79 See ibid., p. 236.

80 "...quae Nostros aggravat umeros" (ibid.).

81 "Procul dubio uni Petro Apostolo eiusque Successoribus, Romanis nempe Pontificibus, Iesus Christus gregis sui universitatem concredidit: 'Pasce agnos meos, pasce oves meas' " (ibid., pp. 236-37).

82 "Quodsi unusquisque Episcopus portionis tantum gregis sibi commissae sacer pastor est, tamen qua legitimus Apostolorum successor ex Dei institutione et praecepto apostolici muneris Ecclesiae una cum ceteris Episcopis sponsor fit, secundum illa verba, quae Christus ad Apostolos fecit: 'Sicut misit me Pater, et ego

mitto vos.' Haec quae 'omnes gentes . . . usque ad consummationem saeculi' amplectitur missio, cum Apostoli de mortali vita decesserunt, minime decidit; immo in Episcopis communionem cum Iesu Christi Vicario habentibus, adhuc perseverat" (ibid., p. 237).

83   See ibid., pp. 243 and 246.

84   See ibid.

85   See ibid., p. 247.

86   ". . . together with the rest of the bishops [he] *becomes responsible for* the apostolic task of the Church . . ." (ibid., p. 237, emphasis mine).

87   For examples of those who seem to have interpreted Pius XII's position (see Texts C and D) as militating against the concept of collegiality, see among others Cardinal Browne, *Acta Syn* 3, pt. 1: 629-30; Bishop Luigi Carli (Segni), ibid., p. 660; and Aniceto Fernández, Superior General of the Dominicans, ibid., p. 697.

88   See Pius XII, *Mystici corporis*, in AAS 35 (1943): 193-248. English trans., *Encyclical Letter of His Holiness Pius XII on the Mystical Body of Christ and Our Union in It with Christ* (Boston: St. Paul Editions, n.d.). Unless indicated to the contrary, references are to the English translation.

89   See ibid., p. 8.

90   See ibid., p. 6.

91   See ibid., p. 13.

92   Ibid., p. 26, emphasis mine.

93   Ibid., emphasis mine.

94   See DS, no. 3112-117.

95   "Sacris enim canonibus dilucide et expresse sancitum est ut ad unam Sedem Apostolicam pertineat iudicare, num quis ad dignitatem et munus Episcopi idoneus sit, utque Romani Pontificis sit Episcopos libere nominare. . . Hoc posito, efficitur, ut Episcopi nec nominati nec confirmati a Sede Apostolica, immo contra expressas eius ordinationes electi et consecrati, nulla fruantur potestate magisterii et iurisdictionis, cum iurisdictio Episcopis per unum Romanum Pontificem obtingat, quemadmodum in Litteris Encyclicis *Mystici Corporis* . . . monuimus . . ." (Pius XII, *Ad Apostolorum Principis sepulcrum*, in AAS 50 [1958]: 610).

96   ". . . the result is [that such bishops illicitly consecrated] do not *enjoy* any power to teach nor to govern . . ." (ibid., emphasis mine).

97   The distinction between *in actu primo* and *in actu secundo* is analogous but not reducible to that between potency and act; it differs from the latter in that *in actu primo* refers to the existence of a capacity as distinguished from its use (*in actu secundo*).

98   ". . . you desire to share that concern for all the Churches . . ." (Pius XII, *Fidei donum*, p. 236).

99   See *ADOC* II, 2, pt. 3: 986-1083.

100   See *Acta Syn* 1, pt. 4: 12-121.

101   See ibid., 2, pt. 1: 215-35.

102   See ibid., 3, pt. 1: 158-233.

103   See ibid., pt. 8: 784-811. Unless specified to the contrary, references will be to the Abbott and Gallagher (AG) edition.

104 "Corpus Episcopale seu Collegium Episcoporum quod Collegio Apostolorum in magisterio et regimine pastorali succedit, immo in quo Corpus Apostolicum continuo perseverat, una cum capite suo Romano Pontifice, et numquam sine hoc capite, unum subiectum plenae et supremae potestatis in universam Ecclesiam creditur. Potestas tamen huius Corporis nonnisi modo extraordinario et iussu solius Capitis et ad nutum exclusivum eiusdem exercetur" (*ADOC* II, 2 pt. 3: 1041).

105 ". . . is not exercised except in an extraordinary way . . ." (ibid.).

106 See ibid., p. 1046.

107 See ibid., p. 1047.

108 See ibid., p. 1048.

109 See above, pp. 74-78

110 ". . . ex iussu solius Capitis et ad nutum exclusivum eiusdem . . ." (*ADOC* II, 2, pt. 3: 1048).

111 See ibid., p. 1052.

112 See ibid.

113 ". . . Pius XI in Littera Encyclica [*sic*] *Rerum Ecclesiae* et Pius XII in Littera [*sic*]*Fidei donum* non potuerunt [*sic:* the speaker meant *potuissent*] sese referre ad obligationem collaborationis pro omnibus episcopis in labore evangelisationis. Non est quaestio tatummodo sollicitudinis sed etiam responsabilitatis . . ." (ibid.).

114 On König, see ibid., pp. 1053-55; on Döpfner, see pp. 1055-58; on Bea, see p. 1058; and on Lienart, see p. 1066.

115 "Quoad Cap. IV, par. 3; Item noto omnes Episcopos habere debere responsabilitatem et sollicitudinem pro universa Ecclesia, sed non video in quo consistere posset iurisdictio Collegii Episcoporum, etiam sub Romano Pontifice, extra Concilium Oecumenicum" (ibid., p. 1078). Much later in the third session, Browne was to come back to the same theme. See *Acta Syn* 3, pt. 1: 629-30.

116 See *ADOC* II, 2, pt. 3: 1070.

117 "Detur exacta et ordinata doctrina de Episcopatu, uno schemate magis organico et completo. Hac de re Concilium silere nequit; expectatio enim totius Ecclesiae catholicae et fratrum dissidentium ad hoc maxime intendit argumentum.

"Ne pigeat hunc coetum neve Concilium cras pavescat hanc pertractare doctrinam, quae illam de primatu et infallibilitate pontificia a Concilio Vaticano primo definitam integrat et coronat . . .

"Votum denique Em.m. Card. Confalonieri magna mihi auctoritate pollere videtur . . ." (ibid.).

118 See ibid., pp. 1059-66.

119 See ibid., p. 1072.

120 ". . . the College of Bishops exists in some way and fruitfully even outside a Council. And this must be said. It is self-evident that the bishops have a concern for the whole Church. And this in some way is said in this draft. The duty to be concerned entails, like all duties, responsibility. And this can be said . . ." [. . . Collegium Episcoporum aliquomodo et fructuose vivit etiam extra Concilium. Quod dici debet. Sollicitudinem Episcopos habere erga totam Ecclesiam eo ipso patet. Et hoc aliquomodo dicitur in hoc schemate. Officium sollicitudinis inducit, sicut omnia officia, responsabilitatem. Et hoc potest dici . . .] (ibid., p. 1067). The

seeds of Siri's ultimate disagreement with the direction which the Council was to take are to be found in the concluding lines of his remarks where he stated that this college exists wherever the conditions for its existence can be verified. That is to say: for the *exercise of authority*, conditions in the present case are verified only with difficulty. See ibid:, p. 1068.

121   See ibid., pp. 1066-83.

122   On this point Karl Rahner's assessment must be regarded as overly generous: ".. the code of canon law, apropos of an ecumenical council, already affirms what is said here [i.e., in *LG*-c], and merely expresses something that the Catholic mind had long since taken for granted . . . This also follows from the fact *that the draft of 10 November 1962 [AU-*b] *composed by Roman theologians, propounds in effect the same doctrine.* Some of its formulae are unhappy, as when it suggests that the ordinary power of the college of bishops can only be exercised in an extraordinary way . . ." (Karl Rahner in *Commentary on the Documents of Vatican II,* ed. Herbert Vorgrimler, 5 vols., various translators [London: Burns & Oates, and New York: Herder & Herder, 1966-69], 1[1966]: 195-96, emphasis mine). There is no real discrepancy between the date Rahner assigns to the draft and the one I have assigned. The decision to distribute the draft was signed November 10, 1962; the date of its actual distribution to the Council Fathers was November 23 of the same year. See *Acta Syn* 1, pt 4: 12. I have preferred to identify it by the latter date.

123   "Collegium Episcoporum quod Collegio Apostolorum in magisterio et regimine pastorali succedit, immo in quo Collegium Apostolorum continuo perseverat, quoque missionem Iesu Christi eiusdemque doctrinam et leges continuo testatur, una cum capite suo, Romano Pontifice et numquam sine hoc capite, unum subiectum plenae et supremae potestatis in universam Ecclesiam creditur. Potestas tamen huius Collegii, etsi ordinaria, utpote officio inhaerens, nonnisi modo extraordinario et in devota subordinatione Iesu Christi Vicario in terris, quando, quomodo et quousque eidem id in Domino videtur expedire, legitime exercetur" (ibid., p. 27).

124   See Jérôme Hamer, "Note sur la Collégialité épiscopale," *Revue des Sciences philosophiques et théologiques* 44 (1960): 40-50; Karl Rahner and Joseph Ratzinger, *The Episcopate and the Primacy,* trans. Kenneth Barker et al., (New York: Herder & Herder, 1962); Y[ves] Congar and B. D. Dupuy ed., *L'Episcopat et L'Eglise universelle* (Paris: Les Editions du Cerf, 1962).

125   The ease with which Albino Cardinal Luciani, the future John Paul I, seems to have produced it in his argument for collegiality attests to this fact. See *Acta Syn* 2, pt. 2: 801. Luciani does not seem however to have noted that Cappellari was quoting Bolgeni.

126   Of special interest is the brilliant defense of collegiality by the future John Paul I. See ibid., pp. 798-802.

127   See especially ibid., 1, p. 4: 409.

128   See ibid.

129   See ibid.

130   ". . . ut solemniter declaravit Littera Encyclica [*sic*] *Fidei donum,* post multa alia documenta pontificalia . . ." (ibid.).

[131] "Sicut in Evangelio, statuente Domino, sanctus Petrus et alii Apostoli unum collegium apostolicum constituunt, eadem ratione successor Petri, Romanus Pontifex, et Episcopi, successores Apostolorum, inter se coniunguntur.

"Romanus Pontifex habet in Ecclesia per se plenam et universalem potestatem; collegium Episcoporum autem, quod collegio Apostolorum in magisterio et regimine pastorali succedit, imo in quo corpus apostolicum continuo perseverat, una cum Capite suo Romano Pontifice, et numquam sine hoc capite, indivisum subiectum plenae et supremae potestatis in universam Ecclesiam creditur" (ibid. 2, pt. 1: 235).

[132] See among others Angel Temiño Saiz, Bishop at Orense, ibid., pt. 2: 473; Vicente Enrique y Tarancón, then Bishop at Solsona, ibid., p. 737; Giuseppe Fenacchio, Bishop at Pontremoli, ibid., p. 742.

[133] Thus for example Bishop José Pont y Gol, Bishop at Segorbe-Castellón de la Plana, ibid., p. 480; Vincenzo Jacono, Bishop at Nicasto, ibid., p. 502; Pablo Gúrpide Beope, Bishop at Bilbao, ibid., p. 771.

[134] See ibid., p. 223.

[135] See ibid., pp. 223-24.

[136] "Tandem, et semper relate ad collegialitatem, proponere vellem ut accuratius exprimeretur munus episcoporum erga Ecclesiam universalem. Pag. 28, lin. 15, schema hoc munus definit dicendo episcopos 'ex officio sollicitudinem' habere debere erga totam Ecclesiam. Optarem ut schema non tantum in notula 39 sed in ipso textu revocet, saltem quoad sensum, verba magis vigorosa et profunda Papae Pii XII in Litteris Encyclicis *Fidei donum* adhibita. In hoc documento praesentatur episcopus particularis ut 'sponsor' totius Ecclesiae cum aliis episcopis . . ." (ibid., p. 224).

[137] "Sed ut membrum collegii, pro universa Ecclesia ea sollicitudine ex officio tenetur, quae, licet actus iurisdictionis non sit, summopere tamen confert ad Ecclesiae universalis emolumentum" (ibid., p. 236).

[138] ". . . from the institution and command of Christ" (ibid. 3, pt. 1: 217).

[139] See ibid., p. 248

[140] AG, p. 42.

[141] Ibid., p. 43.

[142] Ibid., p. 41.

[143] See *CDD*, pp. 129-30.

[144] See ibid.

[145] AG, p. 100.

[146] Ibid., p. 101.

[147] This does not mean, of course, that there are no unresolved tensions. If a central conclusion stated in chap. VIII is correct [see p. 343], then the blending of *Church as association* with *Church as institution* on the level of praxis has much to say about Catholicism on the level of theory.

[148] Thus it would be doubtful that the infallibility-under-certain circumstances of the ordinary universal magisterium constitutes a collegial act. There seems to have been a divergence of views at the Council, some holding that, since the bishops individually do not teach infallibly, the infallibility of the ordinary universal

magisterium, when operative, derives from the College itself. (See Umberto Betti, *La Dottrina sull'episcopato nel capitolo III della constituzione dommatica* Lumen Gentium [Rome: Città Nuova Editrice, 1968], p. 401.) Others held that such infallibility cannot be a collegial act, for in the case supposed each bishop teaches what he himself believes to be the faith of the Church. (See ibid.) Betti himself in 1968 accepted the view of the *Nota Explicativa* (see ibid., p. 402).† Against that position I would advance an argument *ad hominem*; namely, that in an ecumenical council, in the case, say, of a dogmatic definition, each bishop votes for what he himself thinks the truth of the faith is. Yet the act of the bishops in such a case is clearly collegial. It is only *ex post factum* that consensus emerges. I shall have more to say about the ordinary universal magisterium in Chap. IX.

[149]   "... maintaining the collegial bond ..."

[150]   "... maintaining the bond of unity among themselves and Peter's successor ..." AG, p. 48.

[151]   "... only at intervals ..." AG, p. 100.

[152]   "... only with the consent of its head ..." Ibid.

[153]   While it must be assumed that the *Nota explicativa praevia* had the full endorsement of the Pope—it is difficult to interpret the phrase "Superiore dein Auctoritate ... communicatur ..." [From higher authority there is communicated (to the Fathers)] (AG, p. 98) otherwise—there are, of course, charitable ways of interpreting the Pope's action; e.g., under the pressure of the moment, in order to forestall a deadlock, thinking "half a loaf of bread is better than none," Paul VI, though clearly on the side of the new emphasis as his speech quoted above attests, succumbed to the opposition. It is however to be regretted that in this instance he did not exercise the same firmness which in the post-conciliar period he was to exhibit on other issues.

[154]   "... it operates through collegial actions only at intervals and only with the consent of its head ..." AG, p. 100.

[155]   This seems to be the meaning of *LG*-c (number 22). See AG, pp. 42-43. The statement by the National Lutheran-Roman Catholic Dialogue on Peter's relation to the Twelve is however more reserved:

> *Peter was the most important of the Twelve* in Jerusalem and its environs ... That Peter served as spokesman for the Twelve is clear in Acts, perhaps implied in Gal. 1:18, and certainly implied in the Gospel accounts of Peter's having this function during Jesus' ministry. Yet in reference to the Twelve, Peter's position was nuanced; and special authority over the others is not *clearly* attested (Raymond E. Brown, Karl P. Donfried, and John Reumann, eds., *Peter in the New Testament* [Minneapolis: Augsburg Publishing House, and New York: Paulist Press, 1973], emphasis mine), p. 161.

[156]   "In fact it is evident that the theological principles operative in the decree at Constance transcend circumstances in a way analogous to the fact that Trinitarian or Christological principles elaborated at Nicaea or Chalcedon transcend the situation which necessitated them in relation to which they were respectively formulated ... To think that the doctrinal import and the historical force of the

---

†   Betti's position remains the same in the revision of this book. See his *La Dottrina sull'Episcopato del Concilio Vaticano II* (Rome: n.p., 1984), p. 418.

decisions at Constance can be reduced from their theological note to a disciplinary decree or alternatively increased to a definition seems naive. It is certain that *Haec sancta* was approved by a general council, that it regulated its life [*esistenza*] for three years and that it constitutes the coming [*prossimo*] foundation of the modern papacy." [Infatti è evidente che i principi teologici messi in opera nel decreto costantiense trascendono la circonstanza analogamente al fatto che i principi trinitari o cristologici elaborati a Nicaea o a Calcedonia trascendono la situazione di necessità in ordine alla quale furono rispettivamente formulati . . . Pensare che la portata dottrinale e la forza storica delle decisioni constantiensi possa essere ridotta o accresciuta dalla loro qualificazione teologica come definizione oppure come decreto disciplinare appare ingenuo. Certo è che *Haec sancta* è stata approvata da un concilio generale, ne ha retto l'esistenza per tre anni e costituisce il fondamento prossimo del papato moderno] (Giuseppe Alberigo, *Chiesa conciliare*, pp. 352-53). I have rendered Alberigo's Italian somewhat freely here, but I believe this is his meaning.

The informed reader will be struck by the fact that Alberigo's position on the *Haec sancta* of April 6, 1415 is markedly different from that of A[lfred] Baudrillart (see A[lfred] Baudrillart, "Constance [Concile de]," *DTC* 3 [1938]: 1200-1223]. Despite further probing over the past twenty some years no one, as far as I can see, has succceeded in demonstrating that Baudrillart's position is not substantially correct. This assessment includes the work of Paul De Vooght. See *inter alios* P[aul] De Vooght, "Les controverses sur les pouvoirs du concile et l'autorité du pape au Concile de Constance," *Revue théologique de Louvain*, (1970): 45-75.

CHAPTER II

1   See Pius XII, *Evangelii praecones*, in AAS 43 (1951): 497-528. The reference to Tertullian is found on p. 522. English translation by The National Catholic Welfare Conference (Washington, D.C.: n.d.), pp. 3-30. The reference to Tertullian is on p. 24. Henceforth, unless indicated to the contrary, reference will be to the English translation.

2   See ibid., p. 24.

3   See M. l'Abbé Bruls, "L'Attitude de l'Eglise devant les cultures non-chrétiennes," in *Missions et Cultures non-chrétiennes* (n.p.: Desclée de Brouwer, 1959), p. 54.

4   See among others Joseph Ratzinger, "Der christliche Glaube und die Welt-religionen," in *Gott in Welt: Festgabe für Karl Rahner*, ed. Johannes Baptist Metz, 2 vols. (Freiburg im Breisgau: Herder, 1964), 2: 287-305; Walter Kasper, "Are Non-Christian Religions Salvific?" in *Evangelization, Dialogue and Development: Selected Papers of the International Theological Conference* (Nagpur, India), 1971, ed. Mariasusai Dhavamony (Rome: Università Gregoriania Editrice, 1972) pp. 157-68; J. López-Gay, "Evolución histórica del concepto de 'Evangelisación,'" in *Evangelization*, ed. Mariasusai Dhavamony (Rome: Università Gregoriana Editrice, 1975), pp. 161-90; Walter Kasper, *Absolutheit des Christentums* (Frei-

burg: Herder, 1977); and the extensive bibliography in Joseph J. Spae, *Buddhist-Christian Empathy* (Chicago: Institute for Theology and Culture; and Tokyo: Oriens Institute for Religious Research, 1980), pp. 245-52.

⁵   "It is necessary to recall and to reprove a very serious error in which some Catholics are unfortunately involved . They hold that human beings, living in error and separated from the true faith and Catholic unity can be saved, something which, to be sure, cannot be more opposed to Catholic doctrine. *You and I know that those who labor under invincible ignorance about our most holy religion and who carefully keep the natural law and its precepts engraved by God on the heart of all human beings and are prepared to obey God and who live a good upright life, can through the working of divine light and grace obtain eternal life.* But very well known also is the Catholic dogma, namely, that no one outside the Catholic Church can be saved . . ." [Iterum commemorare et reprehendere oportet gravissimum errorem quo nonnulli catholici misere versantur, qui homines in erroribus viventes et a vera fide atque catholica unitate alienos ad aeternam vitam pervenire posse opinantur. Quod quidem catholicae doctrinae vel maxime adversatur. *Notum Nobis vobisque est, eos, qui invicibili circa sanctissimam nostram religionem ignorantia laborant, quique naturalem legem eiusque praecepta in omnium cordibus a Deo insculpta sedulo servantes ac Deo oboedire parati, honestam rectamque vitam agunt, posse, divinae lucis et gratiae operante virtute aeternam consequi vitam* . . . Sed notissimum quoque est catholicum dogma, neminem scilicet extra catholicam Ecclesiam posse salvari . . .] (DS nos. 2865, 2866, and 2867, emphasis mine). In the original, the three numbers in DS follow consecutively in the same paragraph and are so rendered here.

⁶   The standard way of resolving this tension was to claim that those outside the Catholic Church through no fault of their own could be saved if they belonged to the Soul of the Church, i.e., if because of their sincere intentions, they were in fact in a state of favor with God, these dispositions being ultimately the effect of God's grace, an indirect reference to John 1:9. But that was not to be taken as endorsing the concept of an invisible Church. For just as body and soul in a living human being constitute one existent, so those belonging to the Soul of the Church did not form an invisible Church separate from the visible. Thus the axiom, *outside the Church there is no salvation*, took on the meaning not as it is found in Cyprian but as propounded by the Roman Bishop Stephen with whom Cyprian was in conflict, and by extension came to be applied to non-Christians.

⁷   "Homines in cuiusvis religionis cultu viam aeternae salutis reperire, aeternamque salutem assequi possent" (Pius IX, *Syllabus*, in Pii IX Pontificis Maximi Acta, 9 vols. [Rome: Ex Typographia Bonarum Artium, 1854-78], 3: 704-5).†

⁸   See pp. 240-43 above where Bishop Dupanloup's role in interpreting the Syllabus for the Church in France is described at some length.

⁹   See Pius IX, *Qui pluribus*, in PIXA 1: 4-24.

¹⁰   See ibid., p. 4.

¹¹   Thus within the very first paragraph of this encyclical the Pope refers on the one hand to his brother bishops as associates and helpers (*socios et adjutores*) and on the other as sheep (*oves*) whom he as Pope is to shepherd. This in itself however

†   Claudia Carlen's *The Papal Encyclicals: 1740-1981*, 5 vols (n.p.: McGrath Publishing Co., 1981) would have been immensely helpful had they been published when this book was being written.

is not necessarily opposed to the direction which Vatican II was to take. For the "definition" of collegiality in *Lumen gentium* unambiguously states that the episcopal college separated from the Roman Pontiff is no longer an exercise of collegiality. For a brief discussion of some remaining problems, see Karl Rahner's comments in Herbert Vorgrimler, ed., *Commentary on the Documents of Vatican II*, 1: 195-207.

¹²   See Pius IX, *Qui pluribus*, pp. 5-6.

¹³   See ibid., p. 7.

¹⁴   See ibid., p. 8.

¹⁵   See ibid., p. 9.

¹⁶   See ibid., p. 11.

¹⁷   "Huc spectat horrendum, ac vel ipsi naturali rationis lumini maxime repugnans de cujuslibet religionis indifferentia systema, quo isti veteratores, omni virtutis et vitii, veritatis et erroris, honestatis et turpitudinis sublato discrimine, homines in cujusvis religionis cultu aeternam salutem assequi posse comminiscuntur, *perinde ac si ulla umquam esse posset participatio justitiae cum iniquitate, aut societas lucis ad tenebras, et conventio Christi ad Belial*" (ibid., pp. 12-13, emphasis mine).

¹⁸   See ibid., p. 15.

¹⁹   See ibid., p. 14.

²⁰   See ibid.

²¹   "Neque minori animi firmitate in omnibus fovete unionem cum Catholica Ecclesia, *extra quam nulla est salus*, et obedientiam erga hanc Petri Cathedram, cui tanquam firmissimo fundamento tota sanctissimae nostrae religionis moles innititur" (ibid., p. 15, emphasis mine).

²²   In *Multiplices inter* of September 25, 1865, Pius spoke at length about this plot, which he claimed had been uncovered by the Holy See. See Pius IX, *Multiplices inter*, PIXA 4: 23-28, especially p. 23.

²³   See Pius IX, *Ubi primum*, in PIXA 1: 70-71.

²⁴   ". . . Nos ita benevole sentire de quocumque hominum genere, ut nedum Ecclesiae filios, sed *ceteros etiam utut a Catholica unitate alieni permaneant, esse pariter in salutis via, atque ad aeternam vitam pervenire posse arbitremur*" (ibid., p. 75, emphasis mine).

²⁵   See ibid.

²⁶   See ibid., p. 76.

²⁷   See Pius IX, *Singulari quidem*, in PIXA 2: 510-30.

²⁸   See ibid., p. 512.

²⁹   See ibid., p. 517.

³⁰   "A qua turpissima sane *indifferentisimi* forma haud admodum distat illud de religionum *indifferentia* systema e tenebris eruptum, quo a veritate alienati, veraeque confessionis adversarii, suaeque salutis immemores, et inter se pugnantia docentes, et numquam stabilitam sententiam habentes, *nullum inter diversas fidei professiones discrimen admittunt, et pacem cum omnibus miscent, omnibusque aternae* [sic] *vitae portum ex qualibet religione patere contendunt*" (ibid., pp. 512-13, emphasis mine).

³¹   See ibid., p. 513.

³²   ". . . extra quam nec vera fides, nec aeterna invenitur salus . . ." (ibid.).

³³   See ibid., pp. 514-15.

³⁴   ". . . aside from the excuse of invincible ignorance" (ibid., p. 517).

³⁵   Some recent writers have argued that the Catholic Church should relinquish the use of this axiom, since it cannot be taken literally. See, for example, Jerome Theisen, *The Ultimate Church and the Promise of Salvation* (Collegeville, Minnesota: St. John's University Press, 1976), p. 153. This suggestion, however, may be premature, for if my analysis below is correct, the axiom may still retain its essential meaning. See pp. 202-5.

³⁶   Thus in *In Apostolicae Sedis fastigio* of December 19, 1853, a private speech to the Cardinals, Pius mentions among his concerns the failure of the missions in Haiti. His language here is limited to the purpose of the mission ("expeditionibus ad animarum tantum lucra susceptis, hominibus ad veram fidem adducendis" [Pius IX, *In Apostolicae Sedis fastigio*, in PIXA 1: 559]). And much later, *Iamdiu factum est* of January 30, 1877, refers to a vicariate apostolic to be set up in the diocese of Brisbane "pro convertendis potissimum indigenis" (ibid. 7: 284). In neither case does one encounter the negative stance of Text A in *Qui pluribus*.

³⁷   Thus Edmond Dublanchy in those aspects of his work that bear upon our question, concluded that in non-Christian religions there is no means of salvation other than perfect contrition. (See Edmond Dublanchy, *De Axiomate* Extra Ecclesiam Nulla Salus [Barri-Ducis: Constant-Laguerre, 1895] pp. 361-62). It should be noted that Dublanchy's words were carefully weighed. He did not state there is no religious truth or good in non-Christian religions (Question [A]). He avoided that matter entirely. He merely affirmed that nothing in such religions is salvific (Question [C]). Thus there is, perhaps, an implied departure from the view of Pius IX. Given the fact, as we shall see, that the author of *Supremi pastoris* had used 2 Cor. 6:14-16 as supporting evidence for his interpretation of the axiom *extra Ecclesiam nulla salus* (which interpretation constituted a negative answer to Question [A]), it is highly unlikely that Dublanchy was unaware of either Text A itself or of its use in this unpromulgated draft of the First Vatican Council. Thus his treatment is all the more surprising in that on the ordinary papal magisterium he represents what I have called a maximalist position. (See pp. 31-39.) Dublanchy's implicit departure from the papal optic in this regard may suggest that he thought the Pope had spoken parenthetically.

³⁸   In commentaries on the Syllabus a negative outlook on possible truth or good in non-Christian religions was not infrequent, though not always with reference to Text A. See among others Lodovico di Castelplanio, *Pio IX e gli errori moderni* (Velletri: Tipografia Colonensi, 1865), pp. 45-64; the anonymous *Apologia Popolare del Sillabo per un Dottore in S. Teologia* (Rome: dalla Tipografia Salvucci, 1867), pp. 72-73; Pierre Gual, *Oracula Pontificia praesertim Encyclicae Quanta cura et Syllabi Errorum a Ss. D. N. Pio Papa IX Damnatorum* (Paris: Adrianus Le Clere et Soc., 1869), p. 232; and Pietro Rota, *Il Sillabo di Pio IX* (Milan: La Scuola Cattolica, 1884), p. 117. Damian McElrath reports the case of a Catholic member of the British Parliament who attempted to defend the Pope in

the aftermath of *Quanta cura* and the Syllabus by explaining that Pius IX's stand on *extra ecclesiam nulla salus* (the context in which number 16 of the Syllabus was frequently discussed) was not any more narrow-minded than number 18 of the Articles of the Established Church of England, and that the only relevant question was: Which Church is the true Church? See Damian McElrath, *The Syllabus of Pius IX: Some Reactions in England* (Louvain: Publications Universitaires de Louvain, 1964), pp. 66-70, especially p. 68.

[39] "The Encyclical and the Syllabus," *Dublin Review* 56, n.s., no 4 (1865): 441-529. The quoted paragraph is on p. 445.

[40] The tendency to view negatively non-Christian religions was sometimes implicit in that Catholic apologists of the period were inclined to attempt to demonstrate the necessity of revelation by showing (1) the baseness of all religions prior to Christianity and (2) the de facto incapacity of human nature to come to a knowledge of the natural law in regard to its secondary precepts, Judaism of course excepted. In most cases the tendency during the first half of the nineteenth century was to omit comment on contemporary non-Christian religions. As an indirect result of (1) and (2), the implication was that there was nothing noteworthy relative to possible truth or good in these religions. Typical of this attitude was J.B. Bouvier, whose book by 1865 had already gone through twelve editions. See J.B. Bouvier, *Institutiones Theologicae ad usum Seminariorum*, 6 vols., 12th ed. (Paris: Apud Mequignon Juniorem, 1865), 1: 34-44. Occasionally there is a directly stated negative judgment as in Ignatius Ottiger, *Theologia Fundamentalis*, 2 vols. (Freiburg im Breisgau: Sumptibus Herder, 1897), 1: 905-21; J.B. Heinrich, *Dogmatische Theologie* 9 vols. (Mainz: Verlag von Franz Kircheim, 1882), 2: 646; and J. Hermann, *Institutiones Theologiae Dogmaticae,* 2 vols. (Rome: Ex Typographia Pacis Philippi Cuggiani, 1897), 1: 176-79. The trend was to continue well into the early decades of this century and beyond. See Hermann Dieckmann, *De Revelatione Christiana* (Freiburg im Breisgau: Herder & Co., 1930), pp. 223-29. Dieckman's attitude, while directed primarily at pagan religions contemporary with the rise of Christianity, was occasionally directed explicitly at modern non-Christian religions, thus following the path of Ottiger. And as late as 1966 Emmanuel Doronzo was to state: "In modern cultures which have voluntarily withdrawn from the very light of revelation, the state of religious knowledge is not any better, although their ethical knowledge seems better than that of ancient [cultures] because of the influence of revealed morality which [influence] those cultures have not yet been able to shake off easily and completely." [Apud modernas culturas, quae ab ipso lumine revelationis voluntarie recesserunt, non melior est conditio cognitionis religiosae, quamvis ipsa ethica generaliter melior quam antiqua videatur, ob influxum ipsius revelatae moralitatis, quem nondum facile ac totaliter illae culturae excutere valuerunt] (Emmanuel Doronzo, *Theologia Dogmatica*, 2 vols. [Washington, D.C.: Catholic University of America, 1966, 1: 175). Doronzo seems to have been highly dependent on Dieckmann's much earlier study (see Hermann Dieckmann, "Die religiösen Anschauungen eines Gebildeten im ersten nachchristlichen Jahrhundert," in *Stimmen aus Maria Laach* 53 [1912]: 287-95, 438-49, and 508-15). Though Dieckmann was concerned primarily with a *lex degenerationis*

that he saw as built into the religions of antiquity, Doronzo seems to apply it to modern non-Christian religions. Thus, if I understand Doronzo's remark correctly, when cultures formerly Christian lose the light of revelation, the same law of degeneration becomes operative again. I refer to Doronzo's remark only because it illustrates the fact that in Catholicism shortly after Vatican II traces of a negative outlook on possible truth or good in non-Christian religions were still to be found. Most post-conciliar writing by Catholics is, however, preponderantly the reverse.

[41]   See MPM 51 (1926): 539-52.

[42]   See ibid., pp. 553-636.

[43]   See ibid., p. 541.

[44]   See Roger Aubert, *Vatican I* (Paris: Editions de l'Orante, 1964), p. 153.

[45]   See Gerald McCool, *Catholic Theology in the Nineteenth Century* (New York: The Seabury Press, 1977), p. 134-45.

[46]   I have omitted a lengthy sentence that restates the position expressed by the Pope in *Quanto conficiamur moerore* relative to so-called invincible ignorance and the possibility of salvation for non-believers.

[47]   The Latin reads ". . . qui claudunt regnum caelorum ante homines . . ." MPM 51 (1926): 542.

[48]   "Porro dogma fidei est, extra ecclesiam salvari neminem posse . . . .
. . . .
Quare reprobamus et detestamur impiam aeque ac ipsi rationi repugnantem de religionum indifferentia doctrinam, qua filii huius sàeculi, veritatis et erroris sublato discrimine, dicunt, omnibus aeternae vitae portum ex qualibet religione patere . . . .
Pariter reprobamus impietatem illorum, qui claudunt regnum caelorum ante homines, falsis praetextibus affirmantes indecorum vel ad salutem minime necessarium esse, deserere religionem, etsi falsam, in qua quis natus vel educatus ac institutus est; nec non ecclesiam ipsam, quae se religionem esse unice veram profitetur, omnes autem religiones et sectas a sua communione separatas proscribit et damnat, criminantur, *perinde ac si ulla unquam esse posset participatio iustitiae cum iniquitate, aut societas lucis ad tenebras, et conventio Christi ad Belial*" (ibid., pp. 541-42, emphasis mine).

[49]   See ibid., pp. 569-70.

[50]   See ibid., p. 572.

[51]   "Ab indifferentia speciali omnium *christianae religionis societatum* delapsi plurimi sunt in indifferentiam generalem *omnium simpliciter religionum* . . ." (ibid., p. 571).

[52]   See ibid., p. 574.

[53]   See ibid., pp. 732-1059. I make this assessment with some measure of caution, as the data in MPM may not be complete.

[54]   See F.-L. M. Maupied, *Le Syllabus et l'Encyclique* Quanta cura *du 8 décembre 1864: Commentaire* (Tourcoing: Bibliothèque de Tout le Monde, 1876), pp. 60-94.

[55]   See ibid., pp. 86-87.

[56]   Similar attitudes were sometimes reflected in the periodical literature of the day but without explicit reference to Text A. An interesting example is the dispute

between Canon Léon Joly and Alexandre Brou. The former had attacked the adequacy of Catholic missionary effort in the Far East. (See Léon Joly, *Le Christianisme et l'Extrême Orient*, 2 vols. [Paris: P. Lethielleux, n.d.], 2: 390-404.) The brunt of Joly's critique was the failure of the missionaries to develop independent indigenous Churches; Joly thus anticipated the stance of Benedict XV and Pius XI in *Maximum illud* and *Rerum Ecclesiae* respectively. Joly's remarks had little to do with truth or good in non-Christian religions; yet, in his defense of the missionary effort, Alexandre Brou pointed out, among other things, that one of the reasons why missionaries had made so little headway in the Far East was error and degeneracy of non-Christian religions in those areas. (See Alexandre Brou, "Le Péché des missionnaires," *Etudes* 111 [1907]: 743-44.)

⁵⁷ See *L'Ami du Clergé* 29 (1907): 313-15.

⁵⁸ See ibid., p. 313.

⁵⁹ See ibid.

⁶⁰ See ibid.

⁶¹ See Lucien Choupin, *Valeur des décisions doctrinales et disciplinaires du Saint-Siège*, 3rd ed. (Paris: Gabriel Beauchesne, 1928), p. 236.

⁶² "Sans doute, il peut arriver qu'un homme, attaché à un culte faux, puisse se sauver. Là n'est pas la question. Mais, oui or non, ce culte faux est-il la *voie* qui *conduit au salut éternel?*

"Cet homme, pendant qu'il appartient à une fausse religion, trouve-t-il en elle le chemin du salut éternel et le moyen d'y arriver? Assurément non. Le culte faux dans lequel il est engagé, loin d'être pour lui un secours, *n'est qu'un obstacle*" (ibid., p. 236, final emphasis mine).

⁶³ See pp. 202-5, where I take up this question at some length.

⁶⁴ Choupin's words are to the effect that while the Syllabus is not infallible, the contradictory of some of its condemned propositions may be *de fide*. See ibid., pp. 155-56.

⁶⁵ Evidence for positive reception of the papal perspective does not of course end with Choupin's book, a fact illustrated by a dispute reported by Louis Capéran, rector of the diocesan major seminary of Toulouse. It seems that a certain abbé Glorieux had been arguing that the reason for the missionary activity of the Catholic Church is not so much a matter of (spiritual) life or death for the pagan as it is a question of fullness, a view thoroughly in harmony with the ancient *logos spermatikos* concept and indeed anticipatory of Catholic missionary thrust in the last quarter of this century. Attacked by Dominican Father Hugueny, who quoted the Syllabus against him, Glorieux subsequently reversed his position, referring explicitly to numbers 16 and 17 of that document. (See Louis Capéran, *Le Problème du salut des infidèles: essai historique* [Toulouse: Grand Séminaire, 1934] pp. 137-38.) Capéran himself seems to have interpreted the sense of *Qui pluribus* as reproving religious indifference, not as denying possible truth or good in non-Christian religions. It is significant, however, that Capéran omitted any mention of Text A of *Qui pluribus* and the interpretation given it by Choupin, something of which he could hardly have been unaware. See Capéran, *Le Problème du salut*, pp. 138-42.

⁶⁶ This conclusion is further confirmed by global endorsements of the whole

Syllabus. Thus, in addition to the studies mentioned above, one might add *inter alia* the work of A. Giron, *L'Infaillibilité pontificale: étude historique.* (Brussels: Société belge d'édition, 1908), p. 139, where the author treats expressly of the Syllabus.

67 A similar assessment seems applicable to documents not promulgated during this pontificate. Thus in the draft on the missions (*Dum Dominicum*) as prepared for debate at the First Vatican Council, one finds attention being given to (1) the benevolent manner in which missionaries should approach non-Christian peoples, (2) the need to adapt to their customs, (3) no suggestion that there may be some truth or good in non-Christian religions but (4) at least two direct references to (a) darkness wherein these peoples live and (b) the necessity to keep free of their superstitions. See "Schema Constitutionis super Missionibus Apostolicis Patrum examini Propositum," in *Acta et Decreta Sacrorum Conciliorum Recentiorum: Collectio Lacensis*, 7 vols. (Freiburg im Breisgau: Sumptibus Herder, Typographi Editoris Pontificii, 1890), 7: 682-94, especially pp. 686b and d and 692c.

68 See Leo XIII, *Sancta Dei civitas*, in *Leonis XIII Pontificis Maximi Acta*, 23 vols. (Rome: Ex Typographia Vaticana, 1887-1905), 2 (1882): 169-78.

69 "The people *who walked in darkness* have seen a great light . . ." (Isa. 9:1, emphasis mine).

70 See Leo XIII, *Humanae salutis*, in *Sanctissimi Domini Nostri Leonis Papae XIII: Allocutiones, Epistolae, Constitutiones, Aliaque Acta Praecipua*, 7 vols. (Bruges and Lille: Desclée de Brouwer et Soc., 1887-1906), 2 (1887): 229-39.

71 See ibid., p. 232.

72 See ibid.

73 See Leo XIII, *Tametsi*, in SDNL 7 (1906): 439-443; the reference to this passage in John's gospel is to be found on p. 438.

74 See Pius X, *Lacrimabili statu Indorum* as found in *Sylloge: Praecipuorum Recentium Summorum Pontificum et S. Congregationis de Propaganda Fide necnon aliarum S. Congregationum Romanarum ad usum Missionariorum* (Rome: Typis Polyglottis Vaticanis, 1939), pp. 64-68.

75 ". . . his praesidiis quae, divino beneficio, Nobis praesto sunt . . . uti *ad Indos e Satanae hominumque perversorum servitute liberandos* . . ." (ibid., p. 68, emphasis mine).

76 See Benedict XV, *Maximum illud*, in AAS 11 (1919): 440-55. English trans. by National Catholic Welfare Conference (n.p:: n.d.), pp. 31-46. References are to the English translation.

77 Benedict XV, *Maximum illud*, p. 38.

78 Ibid., p. 44, emphasis mine.

79 Ibid., emphasis mine.

80 See Pius XI, *Rerum Ecclesiae*, in AAS 18 (1926): 65-83. English trans. by National Catholic Welfare Conference (Washington, D.C.: n.p., n.d.), pp. 1-19. References are to the English translation.

81 Ibid., p. 15.

82 Ibid., p. 4., emphasis mine.

83 See for example the *Collectanea S. Congregationis de Propaganda Fide seu*

Decreta Instructiones Rescripta pro Apostolicis Missionibus (Rome: Typographia Polygotta, eds. 1893 and 1907). The latter edition comprises two tomes.

84 Caveat autem missionarius ne tam subtilibus argumentis quam petitis ex communi omnium sensu rationibus et exemplis vulgaribus, in proponendis hisce fundamentis utatur; persuasus utique in religionis schola Dei esse, qui interius docet, intellectum dare, et intelligentiam. *Caveat ne his agendo cum Gentilibus, videatur novam inferre doctinam; sed quasi constaret eos aliqua veritatum illarum notitia tinctos esse, de illarum pulchritudine disserens . . ."* (*Monita ad Missionarios Sacrae Congregationis de Propaganda Fide*, editio altera [Rome: n.p., 1840], p. 64, emphasis mine). The Latin is gauche, not to say problematic; e.g., *persuasus* makes more sense if read as the French *persuadé* and *constaret* would make better sense if read in the sense of the French *constater*. Latin is flexible enough to allow for the first but not the second. I have had no choice but to translate *quasi constaret* as "let it be known."

85 See Josef Metzler, "Die Synode von Ajuthia (Siam [Thailand]) 1664-1665," *Annuarium Historiae Conciliorum: Internationale Zeitschrift für Konziliengeschichtsforschung* 11 (1979): 397-424, esp. pp. 401-12.

86 See ibid., p. 419.

87 Written communication from my friend and colleague, Jean Coste.

88 See Metzler, "Die Synode von Ajuthia," p. 405.

89 See ibid.

90 ". . . as items we do not need . . ." (ibid.).

91 As I have intimated above when dealing with Pius XI, there was during his Petrine ministry a tendency on his part toward a more open attitude on indigenous cultures. On the question of non-Christian religions as such, however, I have come upon no evidence that his outlook was any more positive than that of his predecessors.

92 If my analysis is correct, the author of the article in the *Lexicon für Theologie und Kirche* overstates his case when he says that *Akkommodation* has been expressly taught in the Mission encyclicals of the recent Popes. As of 1957, when vol. 1 of the *Lexicon* was published, *Akkommodation* as applicable to truth or good in non-Christian religions as such had been expressly taught only by Pius XII. See "Akkommodation III: Missionarische," in *Lexicon für Theologie und Kirche*, 11 vols. (Freiburg: Verlag Herder, 1957-68), 1 (1957): 243.

93 *Declaration on the Relationship of the Church to non-Christian Religions*, in AG, p. 662, emphasis mine.

94 *Decree on the Missionary Activity of the Church*, in AG pp. 595-96, emphasis mine.

95 "Quidquid veri, quidquid boni, quidquid honesti, ac pulchri habet unaquaeque natio ex propria indole proprioque ingenio, Ecclesia praecipit ut servetur, et pro munere suo ad altiorem ordinem evehit" [Whatever truth, good, honor and beauty each nation has from its own character and temperament, that the Church commands to be preserved and by virtue of her task elevates to a higher order] (*Acta Syn* 1, pt. 4: 76).

96 "Opera autem sua efficit ut quidquid boni in corde menteque hominum vel in

propriis ritibus et culturis populorum seminatum invenitur, non tantum non pereat, sed sanetur, elevetur et consummetur ad gloriam Die, confusionem daemonis et beatitudinem hominis" [By her work (of preaching) moreover, (the Church) brings it about that, whatever good already sown [and] found in the hearts and minds of human beings or in indigenous (*propriis*) rites and cultures of peoples, not only does not perish, but is healed, sublimated, and perfected for the glory of God, the confounding of the demon, and the happiness of mankind] (ibid. 3. pt. 1: 191).

[97]   See ibid., 2, pt. 5: 412-41.

[98]   See ibid., 2, pt. 5: 431-32.

[99]   See ibid., 3, pt. 2: 327-29.

[100]   See ibid., pt. 8: 637-43.

[101]   See ibid., 4, pt. 4: 690-96.

[102]   See ibid., pt. 5: 616-20. Henceforth references to this text will usually be cited in the Abbott-Gallagher edition (AG).

[103]   See ibid., 2 pt. 5: 431-32.

[104]   "Hac caritate erga fratres nostros compulsi, magna cum observantia consideremus opiniones et doctrinas quae quamvis a nostris in multis discrepent, *tamen in multis referunt radium illius Veritatis quae illuminat omnem hominem venientem in hunc mundum*" (ibid. 3, pt. 2: 329 , emphasis mine).

[105]   See ibid. 2, pt. 5: 540.

[106]   ". . . ostendatur quod Ecclesia catholica debito modo aestimat germina veritatis in iisdem contenta quibus nempe secundum consilia Providentiae ad Christum praeparare videntur . . ." (ibid).

[107]   See ibid.

[108]   See ibid., p. 556.

[109]   ". . . *Quidquid verum, quidquid bonum est super terram et in corde hominum, Christi est, semen Verbi est*, et possumus addere: *iam in patrimonium Ecclesiae a Christo ipso introducitur*" (ibid.).

[110]   "In hoc textu redigendo, statui deberent haec tria: (1) unicam esse oeconomiam salutis pro toto genere humano; (2) *omnes religiones generis humani includi in hac unica oeconomia salutis*; (3) has religiones, [praesertim perantiquissimae culturae] tamquam praeparationem esse evangelicam ad perfectam Dei revelationem in Christo" (ibid., p. 745, emphasis mine; the brackets indicate that the phrase was spoken *ad libitum* and does not constitute a part of the text submitted to the Secretariat).

[111]   See ibid. 3, pt. 2: 799. Lokuang's remarks here are essentially the same as those he made earlier on the draft as a whole. See ibid. 2, pt. 5: 799.

[112]   See ibid., 3, pt. 3: 621.

[113]   See ibid., 3, pt. 2: 790.

[114]   See ibid., pp. 786-87.

[115]   See ibid.

[116]   See ibid., p. 787.

[117]   At least one bishop (John B. Gahamanya of Butare, Rwanda) suggested that besides indicating relationships between Christianity, Judaism and Islam, the draft should touch upon elements common to Christianity and animism. This suggestion

was not however adopted, the reason being as later explained (see ibid. 4, pt. 4: 700) that animism was not mentioned in the draft because animism is not one religion but rather a type of several religions among different peoples.

[118] "Et ita feliciter reiicitur ille modus iudicandi et condemnandi a priori, et sub unico vocabulo 'paganismi,' omnia quae inveniuntur in religionibus non christianis, tanquam pagana et proinde religioni nostrae contraria, et positive affirmatur habitudo nostra fraterne amplectendi sincera conamina non christianorum quaerentium *quidem* ipsam Veritatem necnon inveniendi vestigia Veritatis ab iisdem possessa tanquam praeparatio [*sic*] quaedam [*sic*] ad Evangelium. Deest tamen in nostro texto mentio de alio modo quo concrete christiani cum non christianis convivere et cooperari possint et debeant" (ibid. 3, pt. 3: 21. The editors indicate that *quidem* is underlined because while spoken in the aula it is lacking in the written text handed in to the Committee.)

[119] "Videtur tamen nos ulterius progredi posse et vera fundamenta quae Christi revelationem postulant in libris sacris religionum non-christianarum invenire . . .

"Hoc autem verum est specialiter de sinceris ac devotis sectatoribus religionum maiorum non-christianarum sicut Hinduismi. Libri enim eorum sacri vere documenta sunt horum gemituum ad Christum . . . ." (ibid., p. 44).

[120] See *ADOC* II, 2, pt. 3: 144-62 and 441-43.

[121] See *Acta Syn* 3, pt. 6: 659-76.

[122] See ibid., pp. 327-32.

[123] See ibid., 4, pt. 3: 663-92.

[124] See ibid., pt. 6: 207-61.

[125] See ibid., pt. 7: 673-704. References to this document will usually be to the Abbott-Gallagher edition (AG).

[126] "Hoc ministerium veritatis quae personas singulas liberat, populis quoque reddit Ecclesia, cum Christus cui inservit, sit 'desiderium gentium, 'expectatio creaturae,' et omnium recapitulatio" (ibid 3, pt. 6: 662).

[127] "Cum autem Ecclesia vim et capacitatem habeat omne quod humanum est, praeter peccatum assumendi et in Christum transformandi, oportet ut quaecumque sunt vera, quaecumque sancta, quaecumque amabilia ipsi Christo integrentur" (ibid.).

[128] "Gentis evangelizandae patrimoniun religiosum et culturale, linguam et mores intimius callere studebunt et in eorum magna varietate providentiam Dei quae vias ad Evangelium praeparat, agnoscent . . ." (ibid., pp. 664-65).

[129] "Animis bene dispositis Christus, mundi Salvator, proclamari oportet utpote qui culturam et spirituales exigentias earum complet, imo longe superat . . ." (ibid., p. 665).

[130] "Etenim Ecclesia Christi, utpote catholica, nullam apud gentem vel nationem extranea appareat oportet, sed uniuscuiusque populi usui vitae consentanea, ita ut 'quaecumque bonae famae, si qua virtus, si qua laus disciplinae' assumantur ad aedificationem populi Dei qui facit omnia recapitulari in Christo . . ." (ibid., p. 667).

[131] "In patrimonio praesertim religioso cuiusque populi ea quaerantur quae a Divina Providentia disposita clarificationem et plenitudinem in Evangelio Christi

inveniunt" [In the patrimony, especially the religious one let those things be sought which as dispositions of Divine Providence find their clarification and fullness in the Gospel of Christ] (ibid., p. 329).

[132] "Non enim per verbum praedicationis et celebrationem sacramentorum Christum salutis auctorem praesentem reddit tantum, sed quidquid veritatis et gratiae iam apud gentes quasi secreta Dei praesentia inveniebatur, *a contagiis malignis liberat et Auctori suo Christo restituit*, ut per Ipsum omnibus notum et amatum efficiatur, et *quidquid boni in corde menteque hominum vel in propriis ritibus et culturis populorum seminatum invenitur, non tantum non pereat, sed sanetur, elevetur et consummetur ad gloriam Dei, confusionem daemonis et beatitudinem hominis*" (ibid. 4, pt. 3: 669, emphasis mine).

[133] Ibid.

[134] Ibid., 3, pt. 6: 677. Gracias submitted this report in English.

[135] Ibid., p. 680.

[136] Ibid., p. 678.

[137] See ibid., pp. 357-58.

[138] See ibid., pp. 403 and 422, respectively.

[139] See ibid., p. 422.

[140] See ibid., p. 438.

[141] Zoghby's thought here is more clearly expressed in his written speech than it was in the words actually spoken in the aula. Cf. ibid., p. 440.

[142] "Primum commodum in eo consistit quod nulla fit scissura inter Verbum redemptorem et genus humanum creatum et Verbum creatorem vel inter genus humanum redemptum. In missione, tamquam epiphania descripta, irruit in mundum ipsa divina lux quae hominibus communicata est cum vita in die creationis: 'In principio erat Verbum . . . In ipso vita erat, et vita erat lux hominum' " (ibid., pp. 438-39).

[143] "Secundum commodum istius Patrum descriptionis de missione in eo consistit quod Ecclesia missionalis invitatur maximi momenti facere illius germinis Verbi in unoquoque homine conditi . . . Ecclesia in populis evangelizandis illud divinum semen detegere primum debet, atque divitias naturales quas idem semen produxit" (ibid., p. 439).

[144] See ibid. 4, pt. 7: 30.

[145] Ibid., pt. 6: 218 (". . . who overturns the power of the devil and prohibits the manifold evil of his crimes").

[146] See ibid., pt. 7: 30.

[147] ". . . aliquid de destruendo regno Satanae et de sceleribus, quae ex eo sequuntur, dicitur, ne species falsi optimismi foveatur" [. . . something about destroying the kingdom of Satan and the evils which follow from him is said lest a kind of false optimism be favored] (ibid., pt. 6: 274).

[148] See *LG*-b, numbers 13, 16, and 17 (*Acta Syn* 3, pt. 1: 186-87, 190, and 191, respectively).

[149] "(1) Fundamentale principium enuntiatur, religiones alias non simpliciter esse spernendas, sed quidquid valoris ethici et religiosi in eis invenitur, agnoscendum et servandum esse. (2) Fundatur haec habitudo in mysterio Christi, quod sub

duplici aspectu consideratur: Christus est tota et universalis revelatio Patris, est via, veritas, et vita; ita tamen venit ut in eo creatura non destruatur, sed assumatur, et Deo reconcilietur. (3) Hinc Ecclesia, secundum traditionem antiquam cuius testis Irenaeus affertur, in diiudicandis religionibus et in practica relatione imprimis ea respicit, quae sunt falsa; in earum valoribus positivis veritatem agnoscit, quae ex Deo oritur, scl. radium luminis aeterni illuminantis omnes homines" (ibid., pt. 8: 645-46).

[150] There is a reference to Pius IX, however, but in a different context. Thus Archbishop Armand Fares (Catanzaro, Italy) in a written critique desired that the draft (*ECF*) treat more clearly of the necessity of the Church for salvation on the one hand and on the other that the draft state, according to the teaching of Pius IX in *Quanto conficiamur* of August 10, 1863, that those who are inculpably unaware of the Church can attain salvation. See ibid., pt. 6: 535.

[151] In the various critiques submitted, Bishop da Veiga Coutinho seems to have come the closest to affirming the potentially salvific value of non-Christian religions.

[152] See among others Walter Kasper, "Are Non-Christian Religions Salvific?"

[153] See pp. 233-34 above.

[154] See A. Knöpfler, "Die Akkommodation im altchristlichen Missionswesen," *Zeitschrift für Missionswissenschaft* 1 (1911): 41-51.

[155] See ibid., p. 41.

[156] See ibid., pp. 49-50.

[157] See Johannes Thauren, *Die Akkommodation im katholischen Heidenapostolat: eine Missionstheoretische Studie* (Münster im Westfalen: Verlag der Achendorffschen Verlagsbuchhandlung, 1927).

[158] See Thauren, *Die Akkommodation*, pp. 46-107.

[159] See ibid., p. 105.

[160] "Bei genauerer Betrachtung des Religiösen in Heidentum entdecken wir selbst unter den Primitiven viel Licht und Wahrheit. Das Wesen des Logos Spermatikos verspürt man noch in allen heidnischen Religionen. In diesem Sinne gilt auch das Wort Christi: 'Ich bin nicht gekommen, das Gesetz aufzuheben, sondern es zu erfüllen.' Das Christentum soll und will den Heiden nicht trennen von seiner ganzen geschichtlichen und religiösen Vergangenheit. Es ist ein Fehler, wenn der Missionar auf den einseitigen Standpunkt steht, dass er dem Volke etwas *absolut* Neues bringe, daher einen scharfen Trennungsstrich zwischen seinem religiösen Besitz und dem Heidentum zieht" (ibid., p. 91, emphasis mine). *Property* or *possession* is the usual meaning of *Besitz*; I prefer to render it here by *domain*.

[161] Thauren misquoted it (reading *notitiam* for *notitia*) and apparently thought the text dates from the nineteenth century. See ibid., p. 16.

[162] See ibid., pp. 144-45. Thauren is careful in his statements: It is not that the Holy See reneged on *Akkommodation*; it judged, incorrectly, that *Akkommodation* could not be applied in the circumstances and in Thauren's words preferred to forego the conversion of China than to depart a hair's breadth from what it deemed to be the truth. See ibid., p. 144.

[163] Thus Thauren's frequent use of Wilhelm Schmidt's *Der Ursprung der Gottes-*

idee, 12 vols. (Münster: Verlag der Aschendorffschen Verlagsbuchhandlung, 1926-55). Schmidt's central thesis has long been discarded in comparative religious studies.

¹⁶⁴   See Joseph Schmidlin, *Catholic Mission Theory* [Katholische Missionslehre im Grundriss; translator not indicated] (Techny, Ill.: Mission Press, S.V.D., 1931), pp. 229-52, especially pp. 246-48; also J. P. Steffes, "Akkommodation und Synkretismus als Missionsproblem," *Zeitschrift für Missionswissenschaft und Religionswissenschaft* 23 (1933): 1-11; K. Müller, "Das christliche Menschenbild als Aufgabe missionarischer Akkommodation," *Orientierung* 19 (1955): 249-54; Thomas Ohm, *Machtet zu Jüngern alle Völker* (Freiburg im Breisgau: Erich Wewel Verlag, 1962), especially pp. 691-709; Louis J. Luzbetak, *The Church and Cultures* (Techny, Ill.: Divine Word Publications, 1963), pp. 342-53.

¹⁶⁵   See Pius XII, *Summi pontificatus*, in AAS 31 (1939); 413-53 [The Encyclical Letter of Pius XII on the Function of the State in the Modern World, Official Vatican Text (Derby, N.Y.: Daughters of St. Paul, n.d.), pp. 3-48]. References are to the English translation.

¹⁶⁶   Ibid., p. 15.

¹⁶⁷   Ibid.

¹⁶⁸   "Nor can we pass over in silence the profound impression of heartfelt gratitude made on Us by the good wishes of those who, though not belonging to the visible body of the Catholic Church, have given noble and sincere expression to their appreciation of all that unites them to Us in love for the Person of Christ or in belief in God. We entrust them one and all to the protection and guidance of the Lord . . ." (ibid., pp. 9-10).

¹⁶⁹   See ibid., pp. 17 and 23.

¹⁷⁰   Ibid., p. 22.

¹⁷¹   Ibid., p. 29.

¹⁷²   See ibid., p. 23.

¹⁷³   Ibid., p. 21.

¹⁷⁴   Pius XII, *Evangelii praecones*, p. 24, emphasis mine.

¹⁷⁵   Ibid.

¹⁷⁶   Ibid.

¹⁷⁷   See Thauren, *Die Akkommodation im katholischen Heidenapostolat*, pp. 144-45.

¹⁷⁸   "Do not express a desire and in no way persuade those peoples to change their rites, customs and morals, provided they not be *most clearly* opposed to religion and good morals" [Nullum studium ponite, nullaque ratione suadete illis populis ut ritus suos, consuetudines et mores mutent, si non sint *apertissime* Religioni et bonis moribus contraria] (*Collectanea S. Congregationis de Propaganda Fide seu Decreta Instructiones Rescripta pro Apostolicis Missionibus*, 1[1907]: 42, emphasis mine).

¹⁷⁹   Pius XII, *Evangelii praecones*, p. 25, emphasis mine.

¹⁸⁰   See ibid.

¹⁸¹   See Pius XII, *Summi pontificatus*, p. 20. For the Latin text see *AAS* 31 (1939): 429.

¹⁸² See Pius XII, *Summi pontificatus*, English translation, p. 21.

¹⁸³ See pp. 289-90 and 363.

CHAPTER III

1 See p. 145 (Text F) above.

2 See pp. 233-34 above.

3 See pp. 147-94 above.

4 'Ecclesia a Statu, Statusque ab Ecclesia seiungendus est" (Pius IX, *Syllabus*, in PIXA 3: 712).

5 See Pius IX, *Acerbissimum*, in PIXA 1: 383-95.

6 See ibid., p. 383.

7 See ibid.

8 See ibid., p. 385.

9 See ibid., p. 386.

10 *"Itaque nihil dicimus de illis conceptis decretis, quibus proponebatur, ut Ecclesia nempe a Statu sejungeretur,* ut Regularium Ordinum, piorumque Legatorum bona oneri mutuum dandi omnino subjiceretur, ut omnes abrogarentur leges, quae ad Religiosarum Familiarum statum tutandum, earumque jura, et officia tuenda pertinent, ut civili auctoritati tribueretur jus erigendi, et circumcribendi Dioeceses, et Canonicorum Collegia, ut ecclesiastica iis conferretur jurisdictio, qui a Gubernio nominati fuissent" (ibid., p. 392; emphasis mine).

11 See ibid.

12 See Aubert, *Le Pòntificat de Pie IX*, p. 444.

13 "Quae falsae ac perversae opiniones eo magis detestandae sunt, quod eo potissimum spectant, ut impediatur et amoveatur salutaris illa vis, quam catholica Ecclesia ex divini sui Auctoris institutione, et mandato libere exercere debet usque ad consummationen saeculi non minus erga nationes, populos summosque eorum Principes . . ." (Pius IX, *Quanta cura*, in PIXA 3: 689).

14 ". . . utque de medio tollatur mutua illa inter Sacerdotium et Imperium consiliorum societas et concordia, quae rei cum sacrae tum civili fausta semper extitit ac salutaris" (ibid., pp. 689-90).

15 ". . . *contra sacrarum Litterarum, Ecclesiae, sanctorumque Patrum doctinam* asserere non dubitant, 'optimam esse conditionem societatis, in qua Imperio non agnoscitur officium coercendi sancitis poenis violatores catholicae religionis, nisi quatenus pax publica postulet' " (ibid., p. 690, emphasis mine).

16 See Leo XIII, *Immortale Dei*, in ASS 18 (1885): 161-79 (English translation, *Leo XIII: The Great Encyclicals of Pope Leo XIII*, ed. John J. Wynne [New York, Cincinnati, and Chicago: Benziger Bros., 1903], pp. 107-34. References are to the English translation only, unless indicated to the contrary.).

17 See Leo XIII, *Immortale Dei*, in *The Great Encyclicals of Pope Leo XIII*, pp. 125-26.

[18]   See ibid.

[19]   See ibid., pp. 111-12.

[20]   See ibid., pp. 110-11.

[21]   "Itaque inter utramque potestatem quaedem intercedat necesse est ordinata *colligatio*: quae quidem *coniunctioni* non immerito comparatur, per quam anima et corpus in homine copulantur" (Leo XIII, *Immortale Dei*, in ASS 18: 166, emphasis mine).

[22]   See Leo XIII, *Immortale Dei*, in *The Great Encyclicals of Pope Leo XIII*, p. 125.

[23]   See ibid., p. 114.

[24]   Ibid., p. 115.

[25]   See *ADOC* II, 2, pt. 4: 661-71.

[26]   See *Acta Syn* 1, pt. 4: 68-74.

[27]   Aubert warns against this danger while admitting a difference of nuance in Leo XIII as compared with Pius IX. See Roger Aubert, "L'Enseignement du Magistère ecclésiastique au XIXe siècle sur le libéralisme," in *Tolérance et Communauté humaine* (Tournai and Paris: Casterman, 1951), pp. 94-95.

[28]   See Pius X, *Vehementer Nos*, in ASS 39 (1906): 3-16, especially pp. 5-6; Pius XI, *Quas primas*, in AAS 17 (1925): 593-610, especially p. 609; Pius XII, *Mediator Dei*, in AAS 39 (1947): 521-45, especially pp. 525-26.

[29]   See p. [175 below].

[30]   Besides John Courtney Murray's contribution as treated above, see George W. Shea, "Catholic Doctrine and 'The Religion of the State,'" *American Ecclesiastical Review* 123 (1950): 161-74; Francis J. Connell, "The Theory of the 'Lay State,'" *AER* 125 (1951): 7-18; Joseph Clifford Fenton, "Principles Underlying Traditional Church-State Doctrine," *AER* 126 (1952): 452-62. Regarding the secondary literature, two studies should not be overlooked. See Donald Pelotte, *John Courtney Murray: Theologian in Conflict* (New York: Paulist Press, 1976), and Reinold Sebott, *Religionsfreiheit und Verhältnis von Kirche und Staat* (Rome: Università Gregoriana, 1977).

[31]   See pp. 166-67 above.

[32]   There are in fact a fourth and a fifth document; the first draft of *Homo a Deo Destinatus* is reproduced in ADOC II, 3, pt. 1: 176-191 and the draft on church-state relations (*In nova salutis oeconomia*) is reproduced in ADOC 3, pt. 2: 436-41. In these cases, there is the simple statement that the documents were debated by the Preparatory Commission on June 19 and 20, 1962. The record of the debates is reproduced elsewhere, as I have indicated below.

[33]   See ibid., 2. pt. 4; 657-72.

[34]   See ibid., pp. 680-84.

[35]   See *Acta Syn* 1, pt 4: 65-74.

[36]   See *ADOC* II, 2, pt. 4: 657.

[37]   See ibid., p. 658.

[38]   See ibid.

[39]   See ibid.

[40]   See ibid., p. 659.

⁴¹ See ibid.
⁴² See ibid.
⁴³ See ibid.
⁴⁴ See ibid.
⁴⁵ See ibid.
⁴⁶ See ibid.
⁴⁷ See ibid., p. 681.
⁴⁸ See ibid., p. 680.
⁴⁹ See ibid.
⁵⁰ See ibid., p. 681.
⁵¹ See ibid.
⁵² See ibid.
⁵³ See ibid., p. 689.
⁵⁴ See ibid., p. 690.
⁵⁵ The *Adnotationes* do however quote Cardinal Roncalli before his election as Pope (see ibid., p. 682). And Bea in his report refers to the much celebrated speech of Pius XII to the Union of Italian Catholic lawyers on December 6, 1953 (*Ci riesce*). This document applies the traditional doctrine to a new situation; it does not hint at a change in the traditional doctrine. It is therefore difficult for me to understand why *Ci riesce* has been given so much attention. See my analysis above, pp. 162-65.
⁵⁶ See *ADOC* II, 2, pt 4: 691.
⁵⁷ "Quid sit bonum commune humanum auctoritati civili manifestatur lumine *rationis humanae* (ergo legibus naturae); Status autem *quo talis* existentiam et vim ordinis supernaturalis non cognoscit" (ibid., p. 689).
⁵⁸ See ibid., p. 690.
⁵⁹ As far as I am aware, John Courtney Murray was not at this point directly involved with the draft *INS*. However, in his report, Bea explicitly mentioned a certain Weigel, S.J., from the United States, as among those who contributed to it. See *ADOC* II, 2, pt. 4: 691. Presumably this was Murray's friend, Gustave Weigel, S.J.
⁶⁰ See ibid., p. 692.
⁶¹ See ibid., p. 695.
⁶² See ibid., pp. 695-96.
⁶³ See ibid., p. 696.
⁶⁴ See ibid., pp. 701-6.
⁶⁵ See ibid., p. 702.
⁶⁶ See ibid.
⁶⁷ See ibid., p. 703.
⁶⁸ ". . . inter officia potestatis civilis plura hic recensentur, de quibus hucusque disputant auctores catholici . . . ita v. gr. non consentiunt Theologi catholici, an omnis civitas absolute et per se, vi boni communis, obligata sit ad actus civiles cultus publici ponendos, ad explicite amplectendam fidem catholicam, ad limitandam libertatem exercendi cultum non-catholicum. Inter illos, qui tenent sententiam negativam, sunt viri clarissimi et de doctrina sociali Ecclesiae bene meriti, uti

Gundlach, Pavan, Lecler, De la Brière, Rouquette, Murray, A. Hartmann, M. Pribilla. Non videtur opportunum has res hucusque controversas in Concilio decidere" (ibid., p. 704).

⁶⁹   See ibid., p. 715.

⁷⁰   See ibid., pp. 715-16.

⁷¹   See ibid., p. 716. Here Hurley's thought became somewhat obscure. He went on to say (1) that his analysis did not mean that those in state government are not subject to the Church in regard to the morality of their acts; (2) that the Church remained the teacher of consciences; (3) that the Church must form, direct, and in some cases correct the consciences of those in the state (*hominum in potestate civili constitutorum*); but (4) that at most, the indirect power of the Church is to be exercised through the conscience of the Christian politician. It is not entirely clear from Hurley's critique just what some of these assertions were to mean or how they could be harmonized with others by the same speaker (see ibid., pp. 716-17).

⁷²   "... non video cur mutatio haec fieri non possit. *Nam doctrina de obligatione Status colendi Deum in Ecclesia Catholica non est infallibiliter definita* et ipsa argumentatio theologica potuit in praeterito aliquomodo minus recte procedere" (ibid., p. 716, emphasis mine).

⁷³   See ibid., p. 716.

⁷⁴   See ibid., pp. 718-19. Another significant critique was that made by Archbishop Alter of Cincinnati (see ibid., pp. 713-15). Speaking in the frame of reference of Church-state relations in the United States, Alter said a distinction must be made between *societas civilis* and *potestas civilis*. It is possible to deny to the latter jurisdiction, competency and the right to embroil itself in Church affairs, not because it is indifferent or secularistic but because the total civil community has reserved to itself that right and obligation lest the state rashly and incompetently make a judgment about the truth of religion, frequently falling into error in that regard. The obligation to acknowledge and worship God falls on civil society rather than on the state. (Here there was a verbal disagreement with what Hurley was to say in the critique referred to above. Hurley was to subdistinguish *societas civilis* from *societas*. For him, it was on *societas*, not on *societas civilis*, that the obligation to worship God rested.) Civil society, Alter went on, in the United States had already vindicated in various ways its right and obligations to religion by way of military chaplains, tax exemption for works of religion and charity, and exemption of seminarians from military service. Alter's critique was significant in itself and also in that Ottaviani in his reply at the end of the debate said he admitted everything Alter had said, and that it would perhaps be better to distinguish public authority (*publicam auctoritatem*) from civil society (*societatem civilem*). It would thus be better to speak of the obligation of civil society to worship or not worship God. This distinction admitted by Ottaviani found its way into the second draft *HAD*-b , but not without some confusion. See below, p. 413, nn.92 and 95.

⁷⁵   See ibid., pp. 710-12. Besides Browne, there should be mentioned among others Cardinal Ruffini who categorically rejected Bea's positions as stated in the report. But Ruffini seems to have misunderstood Bea. The latter had not said, as Ruffini interpreted him to say, that the state qua state knows nothing of *religion*

but that the state qua state knows nothing of the *supernatural*. For Ruffini's remarks, see ibid., p. 694. Indeed, Bea had explicitly stated that the state recognizes the transcendent value of religion. See ibid., pp. 690-91.

[76] "Quantum ad doctrinam, per quantum ego scio, primum schema quasi impeccabile est; et ego nullo modo possum intelligere quomodo Encyclica *Immortale Dei*, quae scripta fuit a Leone XIII ad tuendam philosophiam et theologiam de praesenti quaestione, umquam possit mutari. Mihi videtur infantilismus quidam supponere quod doctrina exposita in Enc. Litt. *Immortale Dei*, sit doctrina contingens" (*ADOC* II, 2 pt. 4: 710-11).

[77] See ibid., p. 711.

[78] See ibid.

[79] See ibid., pp. 711-12.

[80] See ibid., p. 712.

[81] See ibid., p. 719.

[82] "Hoc semper in Magisterio ecclesiastico fuit" (ibid., p. 720).

[83] See ibid.

[84] See ibid.

[85] See ibid., p. 721.

[86] "Igitur inutile est dicere, sicut dixit aliquis Episcopus: 'salva reverentia erga Magisterium ecclesiasticum'; Magisterium ecclesiasticum fuit hoc, quod datum est, et non possumus dicere: sumus reverentes et postea agere contra hoc Magisterium" (ibid., p. 721).

[87] See ibid., p. 737.

[88] "It would be acceptable if the Theological Commission and the Secretariat for Christian Unity would agree" (ibid., p. 725).

[89] "It is acceptable, within the limits of my observations set forth in the attached pages" (ibid., p. 733).

[90] See ibid., p. 729. Montini's reference to Browne must therefore be taken in the sense of the latter's suggestion that the Pope be asked what kind of a document he wished the Commission to prepare for debate by the Council Fathers.

[91] See *Acta syn* 1, pt. 4: 65.

[92] To be sure, the document here (number 42) reads *communitas civilis*; yet the context indicates that the term is used as synonymous with *potestas civilis*. See ibid., p. 67.

[93] See ibid.

[94] See ibid.

[95] See ibid., p. 67. Here (number 43), however, in contrast to the preceding number, the term *communitas civilis* is used as distinct from *potestas civilis*.

[96] See ibid., p. 67.

[97] "Quae officia Deo debita divinae Maiestati praestanda sunt non tantum a singulis civibus, sed etiam a Potestate civili quae in actis publicis Societatis civilis personam gerit" (ibid., p. 67).

[98] In this section, reference is made to the documents *DH*-a, *DH*-b, *DP* and *ME*, which are more directly related to the issue of the religious freedom. For a description of this material see pp. 172-80 above.

[99]   AG, p. 685.

[100]   See *Acta Syn* 4, pt. 1: 152.

[101]   See ibid., p. 606, pp. 637-38, and p. 633, respectively. It should be borne in mind that these critiques had to do with the draft *Dignitatis personae humanae* (*DP*) presented at the end of but not discussed during the third session. The previous drafts on religious freedom from *ME* onwards had simply omitted the matter of Church-state relations.

[102]   That this is much less than the more conservative elements in the Council would have wished is beyond dispute.

De Smedt's report on number 6 of *DH*-b, which remains fundamentally the same in the promulgated text and which differs only slightly from its first appearance in *DH*-a, is instructive on the form which Text F finally took: ". . . on the special recognition of one religious community in the juridical set-up of the state, many Fathers ask for a number of things; nevertheless some for some things, others for others, certainly contradictory. And of these Fathers' positions *sufficiently defined* there are considered to be four: (a) let not even a word be said on the matter in the Declaration on Religious Freedom; (b) let it be clearly affirmed in the juridical set-up of the state that as soon as possible special recognition be given to the true religion; (c) *if* in the Declaration this matter is treated, let it be in a hypothetical form; (d) let the matter be treated but in a hypothetical way. The Secretariat has considered that the hypothetical form is to be chosen as a *via media*" [. . . de speciali unius Communitatis religiosae agnitione in iuridica civitatis ordinatione multi Patres pluria [*sic*]petunt; tamen alii aliter et quidem contradictoria. Quorum Patrum positiones *sufficienter definitae* putantur esse praesertim quattuor: a) de hac re in declaratione de Libertate Religiosa ne verbum quidem fiat, b) clare affirmetur in iuridica civitatis ordinatione specialem agnitionem verae Religioni tribuendam esse statim ac id est possible, c) si in Declaratione de hac re agitur, de ea in forma hypothetica agatur, d) de hac re agatur, sed in forma hypothetica. Secretariatus censuit formam hypotheticam tamquam viam mediam eligendam esse] (ibid., pt. 5: 153. In the English , the first emphasis is that of the editor, the second is mine; in the Latin, the emphasis is the editor's.).

CHAPTER IV

[1]   John Courtney Murray, Introduction to the *Declaration on Religious Freedom*, in AG, p. 673.

[2]   See Owen Chadwick, *From Bossuet to Newman: The Idea of Doctrinal Development* (Cambridge: Cambridge University Press, 1957), pp. 1-20.

[3]   See Jaroslav Pelikan, *Development of Christian Doctrine: Some Historical Prolegomena* (New Haven: Yale University Press, 1969), p. viii.

[4]   John XXIII, *Pacem in terris*, in AAS 55 (1963): 260. (English translation, National Catholic Welfare Conference [Boston: Daughters of St. Paul, n.d.], p. 10). Unless stated to the contrary, references will henceforth be to the English translation.

⁵   Illustrative of this line of reasoning during the Council are the remarks of Archbishop Pedro Cantero Cuadrado (see *Acta Syn* 4, pt. 1: 302-3); those of Archbishop Garrone (see ibid., 3, pt. 2: 533-35); those of Lawrence Cardinal Shehan (see ibid. 4, pt. 1: 396-97). Illustrative of the same trend after the Council is the commentary by Jérôme Hamer, who in a book co-authored with Clemente Riva (*La libertà religiosa nel Vaticano II* [Torino-Leumann: Elle di Cie, 1966]), paraphrased uncritically and one may assume approvingly Bishop De Smedt's first report (see Hamer and Riva, *La libertà religiosa*, pp. 52-56); and Enrique Torres Rojas, *La libertad religiosa en León XIII y en el Concilio Vaticano II* (Victoria, Spain: Editorial Eset, 1968), who argued (1) for absence of contradiction between the doctrine of Leo XIII and Vatican II on religious freedom (see ibid., p. 193) and (2) that the teaching of Vatican II, far from being opposed to Leo's stance, completes and explains it. It will become clear below that I find this and kindred views untenable.

⁶   Sancti Thomae Aquinatis, *Summa Theologiae*, 5 vols. (Madrid: Biblioteca de Autores cristianos, 1961), Iᵃ IIᵃᵉ, q. 19, a. 5; Iᵃ IIᵃᵉ, q. 21, a. 1.

⁷   See Francisci Suarez, "De Bonitate et Malitia Humanorum Actuum," *Opera Omnia*, 27 vols. (Paris: Apud Ludovicum Vivès, 1856-78), 4(1856): tractatus 3, disputatio 12, quaestio 2, paragraphus 5, pp. 440-41.

⁸   See Pius IX, *Multiplices inter*, in PIXA 1: 280-84.

⁹   See ibid., p. 281.

¹⁰   See ibid.

¹¹   See ibid.

¹²   See ibid.

¹³   See ibid., pp. 281-82.

¹⁴   Ibid., p. 281.

¹⁵   See ibid., pp. 283-84.

¹⁶   See Pius IX, *Maxima quidem laetitia*, in PIXA 3: 451-61.

¹⁷   See ibid., p. 451.

¹⁸   "Cum autem omnes religionis veritates ex nativa humanae rationis vi perverse derivare audeant, tum cuique homini quoddam veluti primarium ius tribuunt, ex quo possit libere de religione cogitare et loqui, eumque Deo honorem et cultum exhibere, quem pro suo libito meliorem existimat" (ibid., p. 454).

¹⁹   ". . . amplecti ac profiteri religionem, quam rationis lumine quis ductus veram putaverit" (ibid., p. 704).

²⁰   See Pius IX, *Quanta cura*, in PIXA 3: 689.

²¹   See ibid., p. 690.

²²   This I take to be the Pope's meaning when in describing *naturalism* he says it is claimed by its proponents that the best setup for civil society requires that human society be constituted and governed with no regard for religion, as though it did not exist or at least with no distinction between true and false religions. See ibid., p. 690.

²³   ". . . libertatem conscientiae, et cultuum esse proprium cuiuscumque hominis ius, quod lege proclamari et asseri debet in omni recte constituta societate . . ." (ibid., p. 690). The Pope is quoting *Mirari vos* of Gregory XVI.

²⁴   See ibid., p. 691.

[25]   See ibid.

[26]   See ibid., p. 693.

[27]   See ibid., pp. 696 and 697.

[28]   This is inferred from the Pope's positive argument as summarized in the preceding chapter. See chap. III, pp. 127-31, especially p. 128.

[29]   In a specifically Catholic context the terms seem to have occurred for the first time in an unsigned article in the *Civiltà Cattolica* 8, ser. 5 (October 2, 1863): 149.

[30]   "It is also agreed that questions are either *definite* or *indefinite*. *Indefinite* questions are those which may be maintained or impugned without reference to persons, time or place or the like. The Greeks call them *theses*, Cicero *propositions*. . . . *Definite* questions involve facts, persons, time and the like. The Greeks call them *hypotheses*, we call them *causes*" (Marcus Fabius Quintillian, *Institutio Oratoria*, 4 vols., trans. H.E. Butler, Loeb Classical Library [Cambridge: Harvard University Press, and London: William Heinemann, 1958], 3: vv. 5 and 7. The difference between the two concepts is explained somewhat more clearly a few lines later: "These persons distinguish a *thesis* from a *cause* as follows: A *thesis* is theoretical while a *cause* has a relation to actual facts, since in the former case we argue merely with a view to abstract truth, while in the latter we have to deal with some particular act" [ibid., v. 11].).

[31]   Thus Maurice Bévenot seems to have missed the complexity of the issue in his dispute with Joseph Lecler when the former concluded: "To turn back now to the distinction between thesis and hypothesis. To apply it to the Catholic doctrine as traditionally formulated would seem in the last analysis to be little better than opportunism: 'absolute' principles being 'mitigated' because of adverse circumstances. But if the distinction is applied to *false* theories, it is a perfectly legitimate one" (Maurice Bévenot, "Thesis and Hypothesis, " *Theological Studies* 15 [1954]: 445). Bévenot seems not to have grasped the fact that thesis/hypothesis language admits of more than two variables.

[32]   See Aubert, "L'Enseignement du Magistère ecclésiastique au XIXᵉ siècle sur le libéralisme," pp., 78-79.

[33]   In addition to the criticism made above, I believe I detect an ambivalence in Bévenot's analysis. On the one hand, Bévenot maintained that the condemnation of theoretical extravagances was the main purpose of the Pope's condemnations, Catholic outlook being formulated only as a means to that end. (See Bévenot, "Thesis and Hypothesis," pp. 445-46.) I take this remark to refer to thesis/hypothesis (γ). On the other hand, he maintained that the author of the unsigned article in *Civiltà Cattolica*, who seems to have been the first to use the terms in Catholic theological language, introduced an innovation in their meaning by subtly slipping from thesis/hypotheses (γ) to thesis/hypothesis (β). This, as I have shown in the preceding chapter, was no innovation but a reflection of papal theory, the proponents of which did not hesitate to state what the ideal situation was.

[34]   See Joseph Lecler, "A propos de la distinction de la 'thèse' et de l'hypothèse," *Recherches de Science religieuse* 41 (1933): 530-34.

[35]   See Gregory XVI, *Mirari vos*, in Acta Gregorii Papae XVI, 4 vols. (Rome: Ex Typographia Polyglotta, S.C. de Propaganda Fide, 1901-4), 1 (1901): 172, and

the notorious sentence of Gregory XVI: "And from this most fetid source of indifferentism flows that absurd error or rather mental delirium, namely that freedom of conscience be affirmed and guaranteed for everyone" [*Atque ex hoc putidissimo indifferentismi fonte absurda illa fluit ac erronea sententia, seu potius deliramentum, asserendam esse ac vindicandam cuilibet libertatem conscientiae*]. Pius XI was later in *Non abbiamo bisogno* to distinguish between freedom of consciences (the right of individuals) and freedom of conscience (implying that a human being has rights against God). See AAS 23 (1931): 301-2. But while the papacy increasingly refined its position, it did not see the logical implications of what it was maintaining. Thus the error-has-no-rights stance remained its official position, making it unable to see the distinction between Questions (E) and (F).

36   This is not to say that there are no differences of nuance. See Aubert, "L' Enseignement du Magistère ecclésiastique au XIXᵉ siècle sur le libéralisme," pp. 94-95.

37   See Leo XIII, *Libertas praestantissimum*, in ASS 20 (1887): 593-613. There is some confusion in the volumes of the then newly created *Acta Sanctae Sedis*: The encyclical, dated July 20, 1888, is found in vol. 20 of 1887. (English translation, *The Great Encyclicals of Pope Leo XIII*, ed. John J. Wynne [New York, Cincinnati and Chicago: Benziger Bros., 1903], pp. 135-63. References are to the English translation unless stated to the contrary.)

38   See Leo XIII, *Libertas praestantissimum*, p. 136.

39   See ibid.

40   See ibid., p. 137.

41   See ibid., p. 138.

42   Ibid., p. 139, emphasis mine.

43   See ibid.

44   See ibid., p. 140.

45   See ibid., p. 142.

46   Ibid., p. 145.

47   Ibid., p. 142.

48   Ibid., p. 147, emphasis mine.

49   Ibid., pp. 149-50.

50   Ibid., p. 155.

51   Ibid., p. 157.

52   See ibid.

53   See Aubert, "L'Enseignement du Magistère ecclésiastique au XIXᵉ siècle sur le libéralisme," p. 95 (where Aubert notes an identity of views between the two popes) and p. 97 (where he allows an undeniable difference of accent).

54   See above, [p. 415, n.5].

55   Leo XIII, *Libertas praestantissimum*, pp. 155-56. The translation is somewhat too free. The Latin phrase in brackets reads ". . . which most nobly upholds the dignity of the human person. . . ." It is of course sentences such as these that to some Council Fathers seemed to hint of continuity between Leo XIII and *Dignitatis humanae* as it was developing in the successive drafts.

56   Ibid., p. 156.

[57]   See Pius XI, *Non abbiamo bisogno,* in AAS 23 (1931): 295-312 (English translation, Vatican Press [Washington, D.C.: National Catholic Welfare Conference, 1931] sixth printing). References are to the English translation.

[58]   Ibid., p. 21.

[59]   See Pius XI, *Mit brennender Sorge,* in AAS 29 (1937): 145-67 (English translation, Vatican Press [Washington, D.C: National Catholic Welfare Conference, 1937]). References are to the English translation.

[60]   See ibid., p. 10.

[61]   See ibid., pp. 9, 10, 22 and passim.

[62]   See ibid., pp. 25, 28 and 30.

[63]   Ibid., pp. 24-25.

[64]   See Bishop De Smedt's first report, *Acta Syn* 2, pt. 5: 493.

[65]   See Alaphridus Ottaviani, *Compendium Iuris Publici Ecclesiastici ad Usum Auditorum S. Theologiae* (Rome: Typis Polyglottis Vaticanis, 1936), pp. 322-31. The Latin equivalent of the phrase "error-has-no-rights" does not occur in these pages, but such was clearly Ottaviani's view: ". . . nothing is more evident in a Catholic society than the obligation of citizens commanding the prohibition of heterodox cults" [. . . nihil magis evidens est quam civilium imperantium, in societate catholica, obligatio circa heterodoxorum cultuum prohibitionem] (ibid., p. 326). Ottaviani wrote here on the level of principle, and in the following pages treated the conditions under which toleration is called for.

[66]   Besides the Christmas message of December 24, 1942, other documents from the pontificate of Pius XII are frequently cited. Among them are the Christmas messages of 1941 and 1944. In the former, the Pope listed as the fifth presupposition of a just international order the principles that henceforth there could be no place for persecution of religions and of the Church (see Pius XII, *Nell'alba,* radio address of December 24, 1941, in AAS 34 [1942]: 18) for the believer in God is a support of a sound society (see ibid., p. 19); in the latter the more relevant statements pertain to the place of Christianity in a democracy and in that context the Pope stated that the battles that the Church, constrained by the abuse of power (*forza*), had to wage in the past to defend freedom received from God were at the same time battles for the true freedom of a human being. (See Pius XII, *Benignitas,* radio address of December 24, 1944, in AAS 37 [1945]: 22.) But nothing in the text suggests that this true freedom (*vera libertà dell'uomo*) of a human being is anything else than an application of John 8:32 ("The truth shall make you free . . .") as applied to Catholic Christianity.

[67]   See Pius XII, *Con sempre,* radio address of December 24, 1942, in AAS 35 (1943): 9-24.

[68]   See ibid., p. 10.

[69]   "Chi vuole che la stella della pace spunti e si fermi sulla società concorra da parte sua a ridonare alla persona umana la dignità concessale da Dio fin dal principio . . . .

"Sostegna il rispetto e la pratica attuazione dei seguenti fondamentali diritti della persona: il diritto a mantenere e sviluppare la vita corporale, intellettuale e morale, e particolarmente il diritto ad una formazione ed educazione religiosa; il diritto al culto di Dio privato e pubblico, compresa l'azione caritativa religiosa . . ." (ibid., p. 19).

⁷⁰ See, for example, John Courtney Murray, "Contemporary Orientations of Catholic Thought on Church and State in the Light of History," *Theological Studies* 10 (1949): 177-234.

⁷¹ See among others Alfredo Cardinal Ottaviani, "Church and State: Some Present Problems in the Light of the Teaching of Pope Pius XII," *AER* 128 (1953): 321-34; Joseph Clifford Fenton, "Toleration and the Church-State Controversy," *AER* 130 (1954): 330-43; Giuseppe di Meglio, "*Ci riesce* and Cardinal Ottaviani's Discourse," *AER* 128 (1953): 384-85.

⁷² See Pius XII, *Ci riesce*, in AAS 45 (1953): 794-802, especially p. 795.

⁷³ See ibid., p. 797.

⁷⁴ See ibid., p. 798.

⁷⁵ See ibid.

⁷⁶ See ibid.

⁷⁷ "Primo: ciò che non risponde alla verità e alla norma morale, *non ha oggettivamente alcun diritto nè all'esistenza nè alla propaganda, nè all'azione.* Secondo: il non impedirlo per mezzo di leggi statali e di disposizioni coercitive può nondimeno essere giustificato nell'interesse di un bene superiore e più vasto" (ibid., p. 799, emphasis mine).

⁷⁸ See ibid., p. 800.

⁷⁹ See ibid.

⁸⁰ ". . . out of regard for those who in good conscience (although erroneous but invincible) are of a different opinion" (ibid., p. 801).

⁸¹ As far as I have been able to determine, however, Pius does not say that it is a question of a subjective right. Thus Cardinal Döpfner seems to have been incorrect when he implied (see *ADOC* II, 2 pt. 4: 703) that in the allocution to the Italian Jurists (the reference was to AAS 45 [1953]: 801 and therefore to *Ci riesce*) Pius XII spoke of the freedom of the erroneous conscience as a natural right.

⁸² Thus in the context of Church-state relations: "She [i.e., the Church] by way of principle or, if you will, as *thesis*, cannot approve the complete separation of the two powers" [Essa per principio, ossia in *tesi*, non può approvare la completa separazione fra i due Poteri] (AAS 45 [1953]: 802).

⁸³ See Pius XII, *Con sempre*, in AAS 35 (1943): 19.

⁸⁴ See ibid.

⁸⁵ See ibid., p. 20.

⁸⁶ See ibid., p. 21.

⁸⁷ See ibid., p. 22.

⁸⁸ See, for example, pp. 172-92.

⁸⁹ John XXIII, *Pacem in terris*, p. 10.

⁹⁰ John XXIII, *Pacem in terris*, in AAS 55 (1963): 260.

⁹¹ Janssens seems to have attempted to interpret John XXIII's meaning in the former sense (see L. Janssens, *Liberté de conscience et liberté religieuse* [Paris: Desclée de Brouwer, 1964], p. 25) by distinguishing the Thomist view of *recta conscientia* from the later one espoused by Suarez. (See ibid., pp. 15-25.) It is this

latter view, Janssens seems to mean, which is behind the encyclical *Pacem in terris:* why else would John XXIII have said ". . . ad rectam conscientiae *suae* normam . . .?" Given John XXIII's quotation of Lactantius and Leo XIII in the two sentences that immediately follow upon Text K, I find Janssens' view unpersuasive. For further comments relevant to Janssens' interpretation, see Guy de Broglie, *Le Droit naturel à la liberté religieuse* (Paris: Beauchesne, 1964), pp. 183-88.

⁹² See Jérôme Hamer's commentary on this ambiguity in Hamer and Riva, *La Libertà religiosa nel Vaticano II*, pp. 57-60.

⁹³ See John XXIII, *Pacem in terris*, p. 10.

⁹⁴ See ibid.

⁹⁵ This was noted at the time. See de Broglie, *Le Droit naturel à la liberté religieuse*, pp. 183-88.

⁹⁶ Ottaviani's remark was a concession made in the third session only after the heat of debate. Interestingly enough, when making this remark Ottaviani did not single out a particular papal document to support it. (See *Acta Syn* 3, pt. 2: 377).

⁹⁷ See ibid., pp. 66-67.

⁹⁸ "Quae officia Deo debita divinae Maiestati praestanda sunt non tantum a singulis civibus, sed etiam a Potestate civili quae in actis publicis Societatis civilis personam gerit. Deus enim est auctor Societatis civilis et fons omnium bonorum quae per ipsam in omnia membra profluunt. Licet autem, in hoc ordine a Christo volito, cultus liturgicus unice spectet veram Dei Ecclesiam, tamen etiam communitas civilis modo quodam sociali Deum colere debet. Quod autem, spectata eius indole, tunc maxime praestabit, si in procurando bono communi fideliter servabit leges Dei, pro hac oeconomia salutis a divina Maiestate conditas. Quod ante omnia postulat, ut plena libertate Ecclesiae concessa, excludantur a legislatione, regimine et actione publica omnia ea quae assecutionem finis aeterni impedire Ecclesia iudicet . . ." (ibid. 1, pt. 4: 67).

⁹⁹ For a fuller description of both *HAD*-a and *HAD*-b, see above, pp. 134-37 and 144-45 respectively.

¹⁰⁰ "Quod autem non impedit, quominus potestas civilis conditiones intellectuales, sociales et morales procurare debeat quibus fideles etiam scientia minus exculti in fide accepta facilius perseverent. Quam ob rem, sicut Potestas civilis publicam moralitatem tueri a se alienum non putat, ita ad tutandos cives ab errorum seductionibus, ad ipsam Rempublicam in unitate fidei conservanda, quod est bonum summum, et beneficiorum plurium etiam temporalium fons, Potestas civilis de se aliorum cultuum publicas manifestationes temperare potest, et contra difusionem falsarum doctrinarum quibus, iudicio Ecclesiae, salus aeterna in periculum vocatur, cives suos defendere" (*ADOC* II, 2, pt. 4:660).

¹⁰¹ Pietro Pavan's comment on the orientation of *HAD*-a and *HAD*-b is as follows: "Hence, if almost all members of the majority profess the true, that is to say, the Catholic religion, the State, too, has the duty to profess it. Those citizens who belong to other religions *do not have the right not to be prevented from professing these religions* . . . If, on the other hand, almost the whole community or the majority is non-Catholic, it is the duty of the state to follow the natural law in every respect. Hence it must leave Catholics completely free to profess their own

religion. . . . ." (Pietro [now Cardinal] Pavan, "Declaration on Religious Freedom" in *Commentary on the Documents of Vatican II*, ed. Herbert Vorgrimler, vol, 4, trans, Hilda Graef, W.J. O'Hara, and Ronald Walls [London: Burns & Oates, and New York: Herder & Herder, 1969], p. 50). The German edition, from which the translation of Pavan's article was made by Hilda Graef, reads the same. Pavan's comment goes beyond the text but is faithful to the intended meaning of its author(s), as I have pointed out in my comment on Luigi Taparelli d'Azeglio's work. See above, p. 170.

[102]   See Luigi Taparelli d'Azeglio, *Essai théorique de droit naturel*, 2 vols, translated from the last Italian ed., 3rd ed. (Paris: Librairie Internationale Catholique, Leipzig: L.-A. Kittler, and Tournai: Vve H. Casterman, 1883): "If the acceptance of revelation has been reasonable or based on reason, society has the right *and the duty* to repress any innovation . . . ." [Si l'acceptation de la révélation a été raisonnable ou fondée en raison, la société a le droit *et le devoir* de repousser toute innovation . . . .] (1: 390, emphasis mine).

[103]   AG, p. 677; *CDD*, pp. 512-13; emphasis mine.

[104]   AG, p. 682; *CDD*, also pp. 516-17.

[105]   Actually, there are nine documents, if one includes *Mater Ecclesia* as found in *ADOC* II, 3, pt. 2: 433-41. Since it is verbally the same as *Mater Ecclesia* of *ADOC* II, 2, pt. 4: 676-79, minus the critical apparatus, I have not considered it here as a separate document.

[106]   See ibid., 2, pt. 4: 676-79.

[107]   See *Acta Syn*, 2, pt. 5; 433-41.

[108]   See ibid., 3, pt. 2: 317-27.

[109]   See ibid., pt. 8: 426-49.

[110]   See ibid., 4, pt. 1: 146-67.

[111]   See ibid., pt. 5: 77-98.

[112]   See ibid., pt. 6: 703-18.

[113]   See ibid., pt. 7: 663-73. Unless indicated to the contrary references to the text will be cited from the Abbott-Gallagher edition.

[114]   See pp. 137-38.

[115]   *ADOC* II, 2 pt. 4: 678.

[116]   See ibid., p. 677.

[117]   See *Acta Syn* 2, pt. 5: 433.

[118]   See ibid.

[119]   See ibid., p. 435.

[120]   See ibid., 3, pt. 2: 317.

[121]   See ibid., p. 319.

[122]   See ibid.

[123]   An acerbic criticism of the view that only the Catholic religion had the right to be coin of the realm was made by Bishop Leo Lemay, then Vicar apostolic of the North Solomon Islands. He said that only those who had the Catholic faith could be expected to see this. Why expect this from non-Catholics, since God (in not seeing to it so far that they had the Catholic faith) had not done so? See Lemay's written comments in ibid., pp. 713-16.

124   Karol Wojtyla was to emphasize the necessity of this orientation. See ibid. 4, pt. 2: 11, in the context of *DH*-a.

125   "... secundum quod homines debent liberi seu immunes esse a coercitione ex parte hominum et cuiusvis potestatis mere humanae, non solum in sua conscientia efformanda de re religiosa, sed etiam in religionis libero exercitio" (ibid. 3, pt. 8: 427).

126   See ibid.

127   See ibid., p. 438.

128   See ibid., p. 439.

129   See the six questions ([A]-[F]) listed above, p. 148. This movement seems to have been largely due to an effort to do justice to the complaint of a strong minority (probably about 10 percent) in the Council who persistently brought to the attention of the Fathers that the doctrine evolving in the drafts was not in continuity with the teaching of the ordinary papal magisterium.

130   See ibid., 4, pt. 5: 77.

131   Ibid., p. 78.

132   Ibid.

133   See ibid.

134   "*Itaque, quum libertas religiosa, quam homines, in exequendo officio Deum colendi, exiguunt ... immunitatem a coercitione in societate civili respiciat, constat eam integram* relin*quere* doctrinam catholicam de unica vera religione, de unica Christi Ecclesia *et de morali* hominum erga ipsam officio" (ibid.). The purpose of the editor's emphasis in this case is to highlight the additions wherein *DP* differed from the previous draft.

135   See ibid., pt. 1: 146-62. See especially p. 147, lines 16-24, and p. 148, lines 25-28, of the *Textus reemendatus*.

136   See ibid., pt. 6: 703.

137   See ibid., p. 704.

138   See ibid., p. 704.

139   See ibid.

140   "*Secundum dignitatem enim suam homines omnes, quia personae sunt, ratione, scilicet et libera voluntate praediti ideoque personali responsabilitate aucti, sua ipsorum natura impelluntur necnon morali tenetur obligatione ad veritatem quaerendam, illam imprimis, quae religionem spectat. Tenentur quoque veritati cognitae adhaerere atque totam vitam suam iuxta exigentias veritatis ordinare*" (ibid., pt. 5: 79. The emphasis is the editor's, its purpose being to indicate passages that did not appear in the previous draft).

141   "*Huic autem obligationi satisfacere homines, modo suae propriae naturae consentaneo, non possunt nisi libertate psychologica simulatque immunitate a coercitione externa fruantur.* **Non tamen in dispositione subjectiva sed in ipsa natura personae humanae libertas religiosa fundatur.** *Quamobrem ius ad immunitatem perseverat etiam in iis qui obligationi quaerendi veritatem eique adhaerendi non satisfaciunt, dummodo legitimo ordine publico servato, aliorum iura non laedant*" (ibid. The emphasis is the editor's, with the same purpose as stated in n. 140 above, except for the second sentence, where the emphasis is mine).

[142] E.g., "Non tamen in dispositione subiectiva sed in ipsa natura personae humanae libertas religiosa fundatur . . ." of *DH*-b (ibid.) becomes "Non ergo in subiectiva personae dispositione sed in ipsa eius natura ius ad libertatem religiosam fundatur . . ." of *DH*-c (ibid., pt. 6: 704).

[143] "Patet igitur libertatem religiosam hodie non eodem modo ac olim considerari. Revera saeculo decimo nono in multis nationibus invalere coepit ideologia, laicismus nuncupata. Nitebatur in placito rationalistico de absoluta autonomia individualis rationis humanae, secundum quod homo est sibi ipsi lex et Deo nullatenus subiicitur. Ex hoc placito philosophico derivata est quaedam notio libertatis religiosae, in quo omnimodus relativismus atque indifferentismus in re religiosa latebat. Hanc libertatis religiosae notionem eiusque praemissam philosophicam Ecclesia reprobavit. Componi enim non potest notio haec cum dignitate humana, quae maxime consistit in eo, quod homo, ad imaginem Dei factus, Deum vivum et verum cognoscat Eique soli serviat" (ibid. 3 pt. 8: 427-28).

[144] See ibid., p. 428.

[145] "Utraque haec damnatio, olim lata, hodie manet integra et immutabilis. Mutantur tamen tempora et ideologiae. Etenim his nostris diebus hoc rude rationalismi genus, quod saeculo decimo nono proprium fuit, iam gravioribus erroribus locum fere cessit. Quod maius est, ex eo tempore totalitarismus status libertati humanae prorsus infensus, in multis orbis regionibus praevalere coepit. Praeterea Ecclesia, novis problematibus exsurgentibus et perspectis, *e principiis, quae semper eadem manent in suo sensu et sua sententia*, ampliorem doctrinam de re sociali et civili continuo evolvit, de thesauro suo proferens nova et vetera. In hac doctrina firmius in dies persona humana asseritur esse . . . totius vitae socialis fundamentum, finis, subiectum. Itemque in luce ponitur hominem, prout est persona, officiis teneri iuribusque gaudere, quae exsurgunt e suiipsius natura. Hoc valet in omnibus partibus vitae atque activitatis humanae, ac praecipue in iis, quae ad religionem spectant. Tandem clarius in dies affirmatur, praecipuum potestatis publicae munus in eo esse quod omnium civium naturalia iura tueatur, colat, vindicet" (ibid., pp. 428-29).

[146] See ibid., p. 429.

[147] Thus in regard to *ME*, see the remarks of, among others, Cardinals Ruffini (see *ADOC* II, 2, pt. 4: 695), Micara (see ibid., pp. 722-23), Garibi y Rivera (see ibid, p. 731), His Beatitude Paul II Cheikko (see ibid., p. 738), and Bishop Lefebvre (see ibid., p. 740). This last mistakenly attributed to Pius IX the notorious expression "*deliramentum*" (as applied to religious freedom understood as an objective right to worship God in a way other than the way God has determined), whereas the expression originates in *Mirari vos* of Gregory XVI (see *Acta Gregorii Papae XVI*, 1: 172). In regard to *HC*, see the remarks of Bishops Ubaldo Evaristo Cibrián Fernández (see *Acta Syn*, 3, pt. 2: 817), Raphael García de Castro (see ibid., p. 825), Pablo Gúrpide Beope (see ibid., p. 829), and Antonio Pildáin y Zapiáin (see ibid., p. 835). In regard to *HD*, see the speech of Cardinals Browne (see ibid., pp. 470-71), and Roberti (see ibid., p. 515), Bishops Antonio de Castro Mayer (see ibid., pp. 485-86), Angel Temiño Saiz (see ibid., p. 500), Anastasio Granados García (see ibid., pp. 508-9), Cibrián Fernandez (see ibid., pp. 520-21), Frederico Melendro, S.J., (see ibid., p. 526), Xaverio M. Ariz Huarte (see ibid., pp. 620-21), Laureano

Castán Lacoma (see ibid., p. 642), Benigno Chiriboga (see ibid., pp. 648-49), Abilio del Campo y de la Bárcena (see ibid., p. 659), Flores Martin and Hervás y Benet (see ibid., pp. 680-81), Angel Ocampo Berrio (see ibid., p. 722), Antonio Pildáin y Zapiáin (see ibid., p. 729), Most Reverend Aniceto Fernández, Superior General of the Dominicans (see ibid., pp. 546-47), Most Reverend Jean Prou, Superior General of the French Benedictines (see ibid., p. 734). It is obvious that the voices articulating concern for continuity with the teaching of the ordinary papal magisterium were increasing in volume well before the draft *DP* along with the *Quaestio historica* was presented for debate. It would have been surprising, then, if something like the *Quaestio historica* of *DP* had not been attempted.

[148]   This occurs as early as *HC*. See *Acta Syn*, 2, pt 5: 437-38, n. 1. In addition, it had been pointed out more than once that in this regard the authors of the drafts tended to cite papal documents out of context, making it appear that the doctrine evolving in the drafts was continuous with that of the ordinary papal magisterium. See on this point the critique by twelve bishops in the document entitled *Quidam Patres Conciliares* (see ibid., 3, pt. 2: 839-46).

[149]   See ibid., pt. 8: 428.

[150]   "Optandum esset novum caput: '*Doctrina libertatis religiosae sub luce magisterii Summorum Pontificum.*'

"Nempe, quid de libertate religiosa sentierunt Leo XIII, S. Pius X, Benedictus XV, Pius XI, Pius XII? Mirandum sane est nolle hunc doctrinalem aspectum debito studio considerare. Quia huiusmodi libertatem religiosam prout in schemate proponitur, praefati Pontifices non admittunt eamque reiiciunt? Hoc silentium circa constans Magisterium Summorum Pontificum nostri temporis Concilium Oecumenicum admittere non potest" (ibid. 4, pt. 1: 815-16).

[151]   "Ad n. 2 . . . Omnino hic numerus omittendus est. Imprimis, quia hi excursus historici-doctrinales sunt valde periculosi, interpretationibusque personalibus ansam praebent . . .

"Praeterea, quia, etsi expresse non dicatur, intentio huius numeri dirigitur ad imminuendam vim Magisterii Ecclesiae, vel melius, Romanorum Pontificum, praesertim Leonis XIII, valorem mere occasionalem eius doctrinae tribuendo" (ibid., p. 812).

[152]   "N. 2: Vel omittatur totus textus inde a verbis no. 2 pag. 4 'patet igitur libertatem' usque ad verba 'colat, vindicet' versus finem pag. 5; cetera huius numeri adaptentur secundum infra dicenda. Vel: pag 4. lin. 5 n. 2 loco 'laicismus nuncupata' dicatur sic vel simili modo 'quae quidem germina quoque veritatis continebat, sed tandem illum errorem protulit, qui laicismus nuncupatur.' Pag. 5 . . . post 'ideologiae' addatur 'Ecclesia vero novis quaestionibus exortis mota est, ut ex fonte Evangelii profundiorem intelligentiam libertatis religiosae inquirat et doctrinam suam de hac libertate aptiori modo exprimat.' *Rationes* . . . Continuitas historica, quam conspectus historicus in n. 2 exhibitus monstrare intendit, de facto hoc modo non existit. *Expositio prout datur historice teneri nequit.* Iamvero veracitas historica tum pro catholicis tum pro lectoribus non-catholicis maximi momenti et officium pastorale Ecclesiae est. *Intentio apologetica salvandi principium continuitatis non debet nos inducere, ut facta historica secundum beneplacitum nostrum adaptemus*" (ibid., pp. 612-13, second and third emphases mine).

153 See the remarks of Cardinal Quiroge y Palacios (*Acta Syn* 4, pt. 1: 638-39), Bishop Carli (ibid., p. 685), Bishop Raphael García y García de Castro (ibid., p. 750), Bishop Jubany Arnau (p. 787).

154 See ibid., pp. 302-3.

155 "His explicitationibus stabilitis, salva semper doctrina catholica de unica vera religione et de unica Ecclesia Christi, humiliter puto quod non in plano simplicis tolerantiae sed in plano iuridico civili, agnitio et affirmatio positiva veri et obiectivi iuris civilis personae et communitatum ad exercitium limitatum praedictae liberatatis religiosae, potest defendi ut propositio vera et consona . . . cum principiis fundamentalibus Magisterii ecclesiastici, quae principia in sua orientatione et evolutione doctrinali sunt plene cohaerentia ab Encyclica *Mirari vos* usque ad *Pacem in terris* et *Ecclesiam suam* nostri Sanctissimi Patris Papae Pauli VI" (ibid., p. 303).

156 See ibid., p. 304.

157 See ibid.

158 Ibid., p. 305.

159 For Garrone's remarks in regard to *HD*, see ibid. 3, pt. 2: 533-35; for Shehan's, see ibid., 4, pt. 1: 396-97.

160 Regarding the future Paul VI, see his remarks made during the preparatory period in *ADOC* II, 2 pt. 4: 729.

161 See *Acta Syn* 3, pt. 2: 531.

162 See ibid.

163 See ibid., pp. 838-39.

164 See ibid. 4, pt. 2: 12.

165 See ibid. 3, pt. 2: 531.

166 See ibid.

167 "Oportet, ut persona humana appareat in reali sublimitate suae naturae rationalis, religio autem ut culmen istius naturae. Consistit enim in libera mentis humanae ad Deum adhaesione, quae est omnino personalis et conscientiosa, *et ex appetitu oritur veritatis*" (ibid., pp. 531-32, emphasis mine).

168 See ibid., p. 532.

169 See ibid., pp. 554-57. The difference is that Colombo based his position on a combination of three principles: (1) the natural right of every human being to inquire into the truth, especially in religious and moral matters (Question [A]); (2) the obligation, whence the right, to follow conscience (Question [C]); and (3) the freedom and supernaturalness of Catholic Christian faith. On this last point, Colombo meant that faith is not the province of the state. See ibid., p. 555.

170 See ibid., where Colombo alludes to *Pacem in terris*, and p. 556, where he makes clear that the freedom in question is *in societate civili* not *in dogmatica materia*.

171 For an insightful account of the events dubbed with this title, see Ralph M. Wiltgen, *The Rhine Flows into the Tiber* (New York: Hawthorn Books, 1967), pp. 234-43.

172 See, for example, the devastating speech by Joseph Buckley, Superior General of the Society of Mary (Marist), *Acta Syn* 3, pt. 2: 493-94.

173 "Aliqui Patres affirmant Declarationem non sufficienter ostendere quomodo

nostra doctrina non opponatur documentis ecclesiasticis usque ad Summum Pontificem Leonem XIII. Ut in ultima relatione iam diximus, in futuris studiis theologicis et historicis haec materia in plena luce ponenda erit" (ibid. 4, pt. 6: 719).

174   See ibid., pt. 7: 96.

175   See Roger Aubert, "La liberté religieuse du Syllabus de 1864 à nos jours," in *Essais sur la liberté religieuse*, Recherches et débats du Centre Catholique des intellectuels français, no. 50 (Paris: Librairie Arthème Fayard, March, 1965), pp. 13-25.

176   See *Acta Syn* 2, pt. 5: 485-95.

177   See ibid., p. 490.

178   See ibid., p. 491.

179   See ibid., pp. 491-92.

180   "Certamen igitur committendo contra laicismi placita cum philosophica tum politica, Ecclesia pro dignitate personae humanae et pro eius vera libertate omni ratione dimicabat" (ibid., p. 492).

181   "Ex quo sequitur, quod Ecclesia iuxta regulam continuitatis cum olim tum hodie, quantumvis mutatis rerum condicionibus, sibi plane consentiat" (ibid.).

182   See ibid.

183   See ibid., p. 492.

184   See ibid., pp. 493-94.

185   See ibid., p. 494.

186   "Hunc textum nunc vestris cogitationibus submittimus. In historico conspectu huius doctrinae ostendimus quod in pontificiis documentis praeter continuitatem notanda est progressiva doctrinae explicitatio. Manifestum est schemati nostro obici posse quasdam citationes pontificales materialiter aliter sonantes. Sed quaeso, venerabiles Patres, ne faciatis textus loqui extra contextum historicum et doctrinalem, ne faciatis piscem natare extra aquam" (ibid., p. 494).

187   It is noteworthy that, in his penultimate report, De Smedt no longer refers to the Popes he referred to in his first. His sole example, besides the remark made by Paul VI during a visit to the Roman catacombs and reported in the *Osservatore romano* of September 13, 1965, was that of Benedict XIV, who in 1745 by the instruction *Eo quamvis tempore* had overturned the long-standing tradition whereby anyone forced into sacred orders or religious life was obliged to remain in that state. Benedict's reasons were the rights of nature and of free will (*liberi arbitrii*). With this tenuous grounding of papal concern for the human person, De Smedt then stated that papal exigencies of objective truth and those of regard for the personal subject seemed to be reconciled in the contemporary doctrine (presumably of the draft *DH*-b) and to be there reduced to a synthesis. See *Acta Syn* 4, pt. 5: 101.

188   See Aubert, "L'Enseignement du Magistère ecclésiastique au XIXᵉ siècle sur le libéralisme."

189   See Aubert, "La Liberté religieuse du Syllabus de 1864 à nos jours," p. 25.

190   "Mais alors se pose immédiatement une question assez grave: l'Eglise a-t-elle donc changé de doctrine depuis un siècle? Le Magistère qui a présenté aux fidèles le Syllabus a-t-il fait erreur et a-t-il dû depuis lors redresser sa position au contact des faits ou sous la pression de l'opinion?" (ibid., pp. 13-14).

[191] "On pourrait donc déclarer après examen qu'il représente un faux-pas du Saint-Siège, sans que les bases du système catholique s'en trouve plus ébranlées que lorsque les historiens nous prouvent qu'à l'époque du monophysisme le pape Honorius est tombé dans l'hérésie ou tout comme. Mais faut-il vraiment aller jusque-là? Je crois que la résponse est plus nuancée . . ." (ibid., p. 14).

[192] See ibid., p. 25.

[193] See ibid., p. 16.

[194] See ibid.

[195] See ibid., p. 24.

[196] See E. Amann, "Honorius Ier."

[197] Aubert unquestionably implies this; see "La Liberté religieuse du Syllabus de 1864 à nos jours," p. 15. See (1) numbers 77-80 of the Syllabus, which deal with the then urgent contemporary aspects of religious freedom and (2) number 15, which had to do with the principle of religious freedom itself.

[198] "Cette interprétation historique des documents pontificaux du XIXe siècle, que j'avais esquissée il y a une bonne dizaine d'années . . . a été depuis lors reprise de divers cotés pour montrer qu'il n'y a pas d'objection fondamentale de ce point de vue, notamment par le Cardinal Lercaro dans un discours qui fut remarqué, et plus récemment par Mgr De Smedt en 1963 dans le premier rapport . . . Mgr De Smedt pouvait du reste invoquer désormais des affirmations très nettes de Jean XXIII dans son encyclique *Pacem in terris*" (ibid., p. 25). Actually the article to which Aubert refers was a conference given at the 1951 *Rencontres Doctrinales* held at La Sarte à Huy in October of 1951 and hence fourteen years earlier.

[199] I am not, moreover, alone in this interpretation. Besides the remarks of Cardinal König as quoted above and the sizable minority who, during the Council, tended to reject any draft on religious freedom at variance with the teaching of the ordinary papal magisterium, one may cite, for example, the penetrating analysis of Etienne Borne, "Le problème majeur du Syllabus: vérité et liberté," in *Essais sur la liberté religieuse*, Recherches et débats du Centre Catholique des intellectuels français, no. 50 (Paris: Librairie Arthème Fayard, March, 1965), pp. 26-42, especially p. 42.

[200] See John Courtney Murray, "Vers une intelligence du développement de la doctrine de l'Eglise sur la liberté religieuse," in *Vatican II: la liberté religieuse*, ed. Jérôme Hamer and Yves Congar (Paris: Les Editions du Cerf, 1967), pp. 111-12, 138, and 145.

[201] Besides Aubert and Murray (as of 1967), there are of course others. Thus for example, Torres Rojas, *La libertad religiosa*, especially p. 193, and Joaquín Lopez de Prado, with C. Corral, *La libertad religiosa: analysis de la declaración* "Dignitatis humanae" (Madrid: Editorial Razón y Fe, n.d.), pp. 323-24.

[202] To the extent that *Dignitatis humanae* is discontinuous with the teaching of the ordinary papal magisterium within the period with which I am dealing, to an even greater extent is it discontinuous with that of the earlier Councils; viz., the Fourth Lateran (1215). Nonetheless, contrary to the situation that obtains in the correlative matter of ideal Church-state relations, the reversal was not complete. Thus to the reasons suggested above, one might add a passage frequently overlooked in the same conciliar document: "Nor is anyone to be restrained from acting

in accordance with his own beliefs, whether privately or publicly, whether alone or in association with others, *within due limits*" (AG, p. 679, emphasis mine). Given the tragic events surrounding the cult leader Jim Jones and Peoples' Temple in Georgetown, Guyana and widely reported in the press (see, for example, *The New York Times* [e.g., sec. A, pp, 1, 16 and 17 of November 21, 1978 and secs. 1 and 4 of the Sunday edition, November 26, 1978]), it is not difficult to imagine what the phrase "within due limits" might mean. Let it be supposed that a state and/or religious group has good reason to suspect that something may be seriously wrong with a particular religion and/or cult. Must the state and/or religious group in the name of religious freedom stand by helplessly until several hundred people have been induced to commit mass suicide? The Council's reversal of Catholicism's official position on religious freedom is not total, a point that some critics seem to have missed. See, for example Brian Tierney, *The Origins of Papal Infallibility*, p. 277.

[203]   See pp. 64-78.

CHAPTER V

[1]   Pius XI, *Mortalium animos*, in AAS 20 (1928): 5-16. (National Catholic Welfare Conference translation [Washington, D.C.: Rasdell, 1928], pp. 1-18. The passage cited here may be found on p. 15 of the English translation.)

[2]   Pius XII, *Mystici corporis*, p. 5.

[3]   Ibid., p. 12.

[4]   Pius XII, *Humani generis*, in AAS 42 (1950): 561-78. (National Catholic Welfare Conference translation [Boston: Daughters of St. Paul, n.d.]), pp. 1-17. The passage cited here may be found on p. 10 of the English translation. Henceforth, references are to the translation unless stated to the contrary.)

[5]   See Jérôme Hamer, *L'Eglise est une communion* (Paris: Editions du Cerf, 1962), pp. 16-19.

[6]   See ibid., pp. 21-22.

[7]   Pius XII, *Mystici corporis*, p. 16.

[8]   Ibid., p. 17.

[9]   Ibid.

[10]   See Pius XII, *Cleri sanctitati*, in AAS 49 (1957): 433-600.

[11]   See *Acta Syn* 2, pt. 2: 11.

[12]   See DS, no. 1314.

[13]   See *Canons and Decrees of the Council of Trent*, ed. and trans. H. J. Schroeder (St. Louis and London: B. Herder Book Co., 1941), p. 53.

[14]   "Baptismate homo constituitur in Ecclesia Christi persona cum omnibus christianorum iuribus et officiis, *nisi, ad iura quod attinet, obstet obex ecclesiasticae communionis vinculum impediens*, vel lata ab Ecclesia censura" (*Codex Iuris Canonici* [Rome: Typis Polyglottis Vaticanis, 1918], c. 87, emphasis mine).

[15]   "1° Baptismate homo constituitur in Ecclesia Christi persona.

"2° Persona in Ecclesia Christi omnibus christianorum iuribus fruitur et officiis adstringitur, *nisi, ad iura quod attinet, obstet obex ecclesiasticae communionis vinculum impediens,* vel lata ab Ecclesia censura" (Pius XII, *Cleri sanctitati,* p. 440, emphasis mine).

16   See DS, no. 2568.

17   Pius XII, *MC,* p. 61.

18   Pius XI, *Mortalium animos,* p. 15.

19   Bea advanced this argument as early as the Preparatory Period but without direct reference to *Mystici corporis.* See *ADOC* II, 2, pt. 3: 1016.

20   See the analysis above, pp. 203-8 and 276-79.

21   Pius XII, *MC,* p. 35.

22   Ibid., emphasis mine.

23   Ibid.

24   Ibid., p. 33.

25   Ibid., p. 17.

26   Ibid.

27   Ibid.

28   See Michael Schmaus, "Das Weltrundschreiben '*Mystici corporis*' Pius XII. 1943," in *Wort der Päpste,* ed. Wilhelm Sandfuchs (Würzburg: Echter-Verlag, 1965), p. 147-48.

29   See ibid., p. 144.

30   Pius XII, *Mystici corporis,* p. 12.

31   See Troeltsch, "Kirche III: Dogmatisch," p. 1151.

32   See Heribert Schauf, ed., *De Corpore Christi Mystico sive de Ecclesia Christi Theses: Die Ekklesiologie des Konzilstheologen Clemens* [sic] *Schrader, S.J.* (Freiburg: Verlag Herder, 1959).

33   See MPM, 51: 539BCD.

34   See ibid., p. 541D. .

35   I find little basis in the documents. See ibid., pp. 731-46 and 751-63.

36   See Karl Rahner, "Membership of the Church According to the Teaching of Pius XII's Encyclical '*Mystici corporis Christi,*'" in *Theological Investigations,* 20 vols., various translators (London: Darton, Longman and Todd, New York: Seabury Press, 1961-), 2 (1963): 65.

37   For a general description of the theological trends that *MC* was meant to correct and/or channel into other directions, see Hamer, *L'Eglise est une communion,* pp. 16-21.

38   AG, p. 374.

39   Ibid.

40   Ibid.

41   See *Acta Syn* 1, pt. 3: 528-45.

42   See ibid., pt. 4: 12-91.

43   See ibid. 3, pt. 5: 743-58.

44   See ibid. 2, pt. 1: 215-30.

45   See ibid. 3, pt. 1: 158-233.

46   See ibid., pt. 4: 485-93, for the draft itself. The first sentence of number 2 is verbally same as Text H, except that the latter adds *seu ritus.*

⁴⁷ See ibid., pp. 485-93, and ibid., pt. 1: 158-233, respectively.

⁴⁸ See ibid. 1, pt. 3: 528.

⁴⁹ See ibid.

⁵⁰ "Hoc Corpus Christi est Ecclesia . . . societas electorum qui cum Christo uniuntur et ab eo salutem consequuntur" (ibid.).

⁵¹ See John Calvin, *Institutes of the Christian Religion*, 2 vols., ed. John T. McNeill, trans. Ford Lewis Battles (Philadelphia: Westminster Press, 1960), bk. 4, chap. 1, par. 2.

⁵² See *Acta Syn* 1, pt. 3: 528.

⁵³ See ibid., p. 529.

⁵⁴ See ibid.

⁵⁵ See ibid., p. 530.

⁵⁶ "Itaque, ob fidelitatem erga Christi voluntatem, profitemur et declaramus unam tantum esse Ecclesiam, etiam secundum conditionem eius terrestrem, et istam veram Ecclesiam eam esse quae a Petri successore gubernatur. Alia proinde non datur Ecclesia quae seipsam veram et unicam profiteri valeat. Necessaria est communio cum sede Petri, ita ut quaecumque Ecclesia terrestris ab hac Sede separata, non certe eodem modo ad eamdem Ecclesiam invisibilem et caelestem vere pertineat" (ibid.).

⁵⁷ ". . . neminem latet omnes qui bona fide in separatis Ecclesiis vivunt et a Vicario Christi materialiter tantum et quasi per traditionem seiunguntur, ab Ecclesia vera quodam modo alienos non esse. Privantur tamen multis mediis salutis quae in vera Ecclesia inveniuntur . . ." (ibid., p. 531).

⁵⁸ "Imprimis a redeuntibus nihil plus exigatur quam quod necessarium revera est, ut membra unius, sanctae, catholicae et apostolicae Ecclesiae Christi *reapse* fiant" (ibid., p. 543, emphasis mine).

⁵⁹ See ibid.

⁶⁰ See especially the speeches by Cardinal Liénart, ibid., pp. 554-55; His Beatitude Maximos IV Saigh, pp. 616-18; and Bishop Michel Darmancier, pp. 671-72.

⁶¹ "Tandem haec Oecumenica Synodus, animo considerans non ingens esse discrimen, quo Orientales seiunguntur, atque conspiciens eos quotidie nova et iusta incitamenta invenire ut ad catholicam unitatem accedant, atque de plenitudine Revelationis participent, iubet non plus ab iis convenientibus exigi, quam necessarium revera sit, ut membra unius, sanctae, catholicae et apostolicae Ecclesiae Christi *reapse* fiant . . ." (ibid. 3, pt. 5: 756-57).

⁶² See p. 228.

⁶³ See *Acta Syn* 3, pt. 4: 528-29.

⁶⁴ See ibid., p. 532.

⁶⁵ See ibid., pt. 5: 772.

⁶⁶ See ibid.

⁶⁷ See ibid., p. 853.

⁶⁸ See Joannes M. Hoeck, "Decree on the Eastern Catholic Churches," in *Commentary on the Documents of Vatican II*, vol. 4, pp. 307-31. This omission is particularly strange in Baudoux's case, given his incisive criticisms of *A U*-a and

LG-a on these very points. (*LG*-a has been identified above; *AU*-a is the document on the Church presented to the Preparatory Commission in the Spring of 1962. See pp. 276-81.) On Baudoux's earlier critique, see *Acta Syn* 2, pt. 1: 477 and pt. 2: 71.

[69] See *Acta Syn* 3, pt. 8: 556.

[70] "Commissio iam de hoc expresse egit, et standum est pro eius decisione" (ibid., p. 564).

[71] See ibid., p. 635.

[72] See ibid., p. 653.

[73] See Giuseppe Alberigo and Franca Magistretti, *Constitutionis Dogmaticae Lumen Gentium Synopsis Historica* (Bologna: Istituto per le Scienze Religiose, 1975), pp. ix-x.

[74] See *Acta Syn* 1, pt. 4: 12-34.

[75] See ibid. 2, pt. 1: 215-55.

[76] See ibid. 3, pt. 1: 158-233.

[77] See ibid., pt. 8: 784-859. References are to the Abbot and Gallagher (AG) edition unless specified to the contrary.

[78] "Docet igitur Sacra Synodus et sollemniter profitetur non esse nisi unicam veram Iesu Christi Ecclesiam, eam nempe quam in Symbolo unam, sanctam, catholicam et apostolicam celebramus, quam Salvator sibi in Cruce acquisivit sibique tamquam corpus capiti et sponsam sponso coniunxit, quamque post resurrectionem suam S. Petro et Successoribus, qui sunt Romani Pontifices, tradidit gubernandam; ideoque sola iure Catholica Romana nuncupatur Ecclesia" (ibid. 1, pt. 4: 15).

[79] "Docet autem Sacra Synodus et sollemniter profitetur non esse nisi unicam Iesu Christi Ecclesiam quam in Symbolo unam, sanctam, catholicam et apostolicam celebramus, quam Salvator post resurrectionem suam Petro et Apostolis eorumque successoribus pascendam tradidit, et super illos in salutis sacramentum, 'columnam et firmamentum veritatis' erexit ... Haec igitur Ecclesia, vera omnium Mater et Magistra, in hoc mundo ut societas constituta et ordinata, est Ecclesia catholica a Romano Pontifice et Episcopis in eius communione directa, licet extra totalem compaginem elementa plura sanctificationis inveniri possint, quae ut res Ecclesiae Christi propriae, ad unitatem catholicam impellunt" (ibid. 2, pt. 1: 219-20).

[80] See Calvin, *Institutes of the Christian Religion*, bk. 4, chap. 2, par. 11.

[81] See *Acta Syn* 1, pt. 4: 17, n. 49, and ibid. 2, pt. 1: 225, n. 20. This explicitly stated reference to the position of Pius XII on the identity question was removed from *LG*-b (see ibid. 3, pt. 1: 167; see also above, Text O, p. 228 of this study). In *LG*-b, after the change from *est* to *subsistit in* (see above, Text O, p. 228), the corresponding primary reference is to the Tridentine Profession of Faith, which states: "It is called the Holy, (Catholic, Apostolic) Roman Church" (ibid., p. 170). The former reference to *Mystici corporis* and to *Humani generis* is thus used to refer to the divine and human element in the Church (see ibid., p. 167). This was possible because the paragraphs of these encyclicals are not numbered in the *Acta Apostolicae Sedis*. Since the specific pages cited refer to more than one aspect of

the question, exactly the same page numbers could be cited in other contexts.

[82] "Etsi plures relationes reales existunt in ordine iuridico et sacramentali, immo existere queunt in ordine mystico, quibus omnis omnino baptizatus cum Ecclesia connectitur, tamen ii soli ex antiquissima traditione vero et proprio sensu Ecclesiae membra vocantur, ex quibus ipsa Ecclesia, ut est una et indivisibilis, indefectibilis et infallibilis, in unitate fidei, sacramentorum et regiminis, coalescit. Ii igitur vere et proprie membra Ecclesiae dicendi sunt qui, regenerationis lavacro abluti, veram fidem catholicam profitentes et Ecclesiae auctoritatem agnoscentes, in compagine visibili eiusdem cum Capite eius, Christo videlicet eam regente per Vicarium suum, iunguntur, nec ob gravissima delicta a Corporis Mystici compage seiuncti sunt" (ibid. 1, pt. 4: 18).

[83] (A) "Reapse et simpliciter loquendo Ecclesiae societati incorporantur illi tantum, qui integram eius ordinationem omniaque media salutis in Ea instituta agnoscunt, et in eiusdem compage visibili cum Christo, eam per Summum Pontificem et Episcopos regente, iunguntur, vinculis nempe professionis fidei, sacramenti et ecclesiastici regiminis ac communionis."

(B) "Voto autem cum Ecclesia coniunguntur Catechumeni, qui, Spiritu Sancto movente, cogitate et explicite ut ei incorporentur expetunt . . . Suo modo idem valet de illis, qui nescientes Ecclesiam Catholicam esse veram et unicam Ecclesiam, sincere, adiuvante gratia, voluntatem Christi vel, si distincta cognitione Christi carent, voluntatem Dei Creatoris . . . adimplere satagunt.

(C) "Cum omnibus illis qui, baptizati, christiano nomine decorantur, integram autem fidem vel unitatem communionis sub Romano Pontifice non profitentur, Ecclesia, pia omnium Mater, semetipsam scit plures ob rationes coniunctam" (ibid. 2, pt. 1: 220-21).

[84] See ibid. 1, pt. 4: 21, nn. 6 and 7.

[85] See ibid., p. 20.

[86] "Haec congregatio iustorum a Sanctis Patribus Ecclesia universalis vocatur, 'quae ab Abel iusto usque ad ultimum electum' colligitur" (ibid. 2, pt. 1: 216). The reference given in the text was to p. 1154 in Sancti Gregorii Magni Romani Pontificis, "Quadraginta Homiliarum in Evangeliis Libri Duo," in *Patrologiae Cursus Completus: Patrologia Latina*, ed. J[acques]-P[aul] Migne, 221 vols., (n.p.: 1844-64), 76 (1849): 1075-1312.

[87] See *Acta Syn* 2, pt. 1: 216.

[88] Thus Bishop Francis Franic, who gave the report upon the presentation of *A U-b*, said that it was left for debate whether others (presumably non-Catholics) were members of the Church in an analogous sense but that regarding members in the proper sense the Commission had been divided, and that finally it was decided by vote to stand by the position of Pius XII in *Mystici corporis*. See ibid. 1, pt. 4: 122-23.

[89] See ibid., p. 122. This was of course already an implicit attenuation of the position of Pius XII, which as we have seen was one of identity. It should be noted that had Pius XII in *Mystici corporis* and *Humani generis* merely stated that there is no real distinction between the Mystical Body of Christ and the Catholic Church there would have been no problem. Such was and is the position of the Second

Vatican Council even after the change from *non esse nisi* to *subsistit in* of Texts M-1 and O respectively. The position of Pius XII was much stronger and on the basis of *Humani generis* (Text [B]) must be regarded as one of strict identity. It was that position the Council Fathers challenged and eventually overturned.

⁹⁰ The question may in fact be more complex than presently available documentation suggests. Thus Father (now Bishop) Bonaventura Kloppenburg, present at the Council, stated:

"Another explanation [given by R. Gagnebet in the name of Cardinal Ottaviani] ran along similar lines: 'The main purpose is to emphasize the real identity of the Mystical Body of Christ, as this is found on earth, and the catholic [*sic*] apostolic, Roman Church.' Gagnebet went on to insist: "If, then, the Council rejects this doctrine, it will be casting doubt on the doctrinal value of encyclicals and thus of the ordinary teaching authority of the Church. For almost all bishops of the world now teach this doctrine." (Bonaventura Kloppenburg, *The Ecclesiology of Vatican II* [A Ecclesiologia do Vaticano II] [Rio de Janeiro: Vozes Limitada; and Chicago: Franciscan Herald Press, 1974], p. 64).

I have been unable to verify the statement made by Kloppenburg and which seems to contradict the report found in the *Acta Synodalia*. Indeed, the *Acta Synodalia* state that Bishop Franic, not Father Gagnebet, gave the report preliminary to the debates. It has been shown that as Franic described the Commission's outlook, it intended to present the view that there was no real distinction between the Mystical Body of Christ and the Catholic Church, a position much less strong than one of strict identity. While Kloppenburg's analysis may eventually in the context of fuller documentation prove accurate—the *Acta Synodalia* may not be complete—I must in the meantime stand by the record as contained in the *Acta Synodalia*.

⁹¹ See *Acta Syn* 1, pt. 4: 126.
⁹² See ibid.
⁹³ See ibid.
⁹⁴ See ibid. The term used by Liénart was *Ecclesia romana*, not *Ecclesia Catholica et romana*. From that point of view his words, if taken at face value, were somewhat beside the point. The context seems to suggest that he meant the latter, not the former.
⁹⁵ See Pius XII, *Humani generis*. I have quoted the text above, p. 197 (Text B).
⁹⁶ See *Acta Syn* 1, pt. 4: 126.
⁹⁷ See ibid.
⁹⁸ See ibid., p. 130.
⁹⁹ See ibid.
¹⁰⁰ See ibid.
¹⁰¹ See ibid., p. 131.
¹⁰² See *ADOC* I, 2, pt. 2: 509-10.
¹⁰³ See ibid. II, 2, pt. 3: 1031.
¹⁰⁴ See *Acta Syn* 1, pt. 4: 134.
¹⁰⁵ See ibid., p. 159.

[106]   See ibid., p. 160.

[107]   See ibid. 2, pt. 1: 626-43.

[108]   See ibid., p. 631.

[109]   "Docet Sancta Synodus . . . *unice* Ecclesiam catholicam, a Deo per Iesum Christum conditam *et super Petrum aedificatam*, esse institutum necessarium ad salutem . . ." (ibid.).

[110]   See ibid.

[111]   See ibid., p. 632.

[112]   See ibid., p. 631.

[113]   The reference here is not to the *Acta Synodalia* but to the page of the draft as presented to the Fathers for discussion. See Text N-2 above, p. 218.

[114]   "Quapropter Ecclesiae societati reapse, sicut Christo ipsi, incorporantur omnes valide baptizati qui ab Ecclesiae societate reapse non recesserunt per formale peccatum ab eius communione excludens, quamvis forsan ignorantia invincibili nesciunt Ecclesiam catholicam Romanam solam esse veram Christi Ecclesiam, et alii Ecclesiae vel communitati, christiano nomine decoratae, sed ab Ecclesia Romana seiunctae, bona fide adhaereant . . .

"In praxi tamen, cum solus Dominus intuetur cor (1 Reg. 16:7) ii soli inter adultos baptizatos externe haberi possunt ut Ecclesiae societati incorporati qui integram illius Ecclesiae ordinationem omniaque media salutis in ea constituta agnoscunt, et in compagine visibili eiusdem Ecclesiae cum Christo, eam per Summum Pontificem et episcopos regente, iunguntur, vinculis nempe non tantum baptismi, sed et externae et explicitae professionis fidei, et sacramenti ecclesiastici regiminis ac communionis.

"Non salvatur tamen, licet ad Ecclesiam quoquo modo pertineat, qui in fide, spe et caritate non vivit, sed peccans in sinu Ecclesiae 'corpore' quidem, sed non 'corde' remanet . . ." (ibid. 2, pt. 1: 701).

[115]   "Rationes huius emendationis: cum modo dictum est homines per baptismum tamquam per ianuam Ecclesiam intrare, omne validum baptismum, sive adulti bonae fidei, sive alicuius usu rationis carentis, in veram Christi Ecclesiam eum introducit. Quomodo ergo talis baptizatus ab hac Ecclesia egredi posset sine formali eius culpa? Membrum ergo huius Ecclesiae Romanae semper remanet, etiam si hoc ipse ignoret" (ibid.).

[116]   Since the Council did not distinguish between the Catholic Church and the Roman Catholic Church, it is good to insist on this distinction here. Despite ecumenical progress made since the close of the Council on December 8, 1965, every Protestant body I know of would explicitly reject any notion of belonging to the *Roman* Church. This does not prejudice the possibility that some Protestant bodies may one day opt for communion with the Roman Church on a basis similar to that of the Uniate Churches of the Eastern rites.

[117]   See ibid., p. 467.

[118]   Interesting in retrospect is the written critique of Karol Wojtyla, then vicar capitular of the Archdiocese of Krakow. Though the specific context that he addressed was the question then disputed in the Council whether the chapter on Mary should be part of the Dogmatic Constitution on the Church or whether it

should be a separate document (Wojtyla argued for the former), he took the occasion to address the matter of Church membership without using that term. His argument comprised three points, the third of which is especially important. The draft under discussion highlighted the Church as teacher at the expense of the Church as mother. Since Mary is the spiritual mother of each and every cell in the Mystical Body of Christ, the draft should emphasize the motherhood of the Church, for the Church must be believed and confessed as the spiritual mother of *all* souls. By reason (*ope*) of the universal motherhood of the Blessed Virgin, human beings in the Church are joined together in a special way. See ibid. 1, pt. 4: 598-99.

119   See ibid. 2, pt. 1: 785-86.

120   See ibid., pt. 2: 9.

121   See ibid., p. 10.

122   See ibid., pt. 1: 785-86.

123   See ibid., pt. 2: 10.

124   This was a minor misquotation; Carli had said "*plene,*" not "*plene et perfecte*": ". . . non intelligitur quid significat illud 'simpliciter loquendo.' Aut auferendum aut substituendum per 'plene' " [the meaning of that "*simpliciter loquendo*" is not clear. It should either be removed or "*plene*" put in its place] (ibid., pt. 1: 632).

125   See ibid., pt. 2: 10-11.

126   See ibid., p. 10.

127   See ibid.

128   "In ossequio alla feconda enciclica *Mystici corporis* dovrebbe essere espresso meglio nello schema il concetto di 'membro della Chiesa.'

"Certamente va rispettato il concetto bellarminiano, giustificato dalla polemica protestantica, che mette in prevalente evidenza l'elemento visibile, sociale, giuridico della Chiesa, quale segno inequivocabile per la incorporazione piena e vera alla Chiesa.

"Nello stesso tempo, però, oggi si dovrebbe fare risaltare di più l'elemento ontologico, che rende realmente 'membra della Chiesa;' e cioè il battesimo valido, comunque ricevuto" (ibid., p. 176).

129   "1. Il cattolico è membro della Chiesa in senso reale, pieno e vero.

"2. Il cristiano non cattolico è membro della Chiesa in senso reale, però nè pieno nè pienamente vero.

"3. L'uomo di buona volontà in cerca di salvezza, . . . è membro della Chiesa in senso reale, ma solo rudimentale, . . ." (ibid., p. 177).

130   "Haec Ecclesia, in hoc mundo ut societas constituta et ordinata, *subsistit in* Ecclesia catholica, a *successore Petri* et Episcopis in eius communione gubernata, licet extra eius compaginem elementa plura sanctificationis *et veritatis inveniantur,* quae ut *dona* Ecclesiae Christi propria, ad unitatem catholicam impellunt" (ibid. 3, pt. 1: 167-68).

131   Gérard Philips rightly remarked that the change from *est* to *subsistit in* would cause much ink to flow. See Gérard Philips, *L'Eglise et son mystère au deuxième Concile du Vatican,* 2 vols. (Paris: Desclée et Cie, 1966), 1:119. He himself would have been tempted to translate: "That is where we find the Church of Christ in all its fullness and all its force, as Saint Paul says of the resurrected Christ, that he had

been established Son of God *en dynamei*, in power ("... c'est là que nous trouvons l'Eglise du Christ dans toute sa plénitude et toute sa force, comme saint-Paul dit du Christ ressuscité qu'il est établi Fils de Dieu *en dynamei*, avec puissance ..." (ibid., emphasis mine). Philips' remark of course refers to the promulgated text and constitutes a paraphrase, not a translation. Nonetheless, his comment is highly significant in view of his intimate involvement in the evolution of a number of drafts on the Church. On this point, see Alberigo and Magistretti, *Constitutionis Dogmaticae*, p. x.

[132]   See *Acta Syn* 3, pt. 1: 177.

[133]   See ibid., pt. 6: 78.

[134]   See ibid., pt. 6: 81.

[135]   "Illi *plene* Ecclesiae societati incorporantur qui *Spiritum Christi habentes* integram eius ordinationem omniaque media Salutis in ea instituta *accipiunt*, et in eiusdem compage visibili cum Christo, eam per Summum Pontificem atque Episcopos regente, iunguntur, vinculis nempe professionis fidei, *sacramentorum* et ecclesiastici regiminis ac communionis ... Memores autem sint omnes Ecclesiae filii condicionem suam eximiam non propriis meritis sed peculiari gratiae Christi esse adscribendam ..." (ibid., pt. 1: 188).

[136]   "Cum omnibus illis qui, baptizati, christiano nomine decorantur, *integram autem fidem* non profitentur vel unitatem communionis *sub Successore Petri non servant*, Ecclesia semetipsam novit plures ob rationes coniunctam ... baptismo signantur, *quo Christo coniunguntur* ..." (ibid., p. 189, first emphasis mine).

[137]   See ibid., p. 202. The term used is *Christiani rudiores*.

[138]   See Troeltsch, "Kirche III: Dogmatisch," p. 1151.

[139]   See *Acta Syn* 3, pt. 1: 204.

[140]   See ibid., p. 202.

[141]   "Hi enim qui in Christum credunt et baptismum rite receperunt, in quadam cum Ecclesia catholica communione, etsi non perfecta, constituuntur. Profecto, ob discrepantias variis modis vigentes inter eos et Ecclesiae catholicae fideles tum in re doctrinali et quandoque etiam disciplinari tum circa structuram Ecclesiae, plenae ecclesiasticae communioni opponuntur impedimenta non pauca, quandoque graviora, ad quae superanda tendit motus oecumenicus. Nihilominus, *iustificati per fidem in baptismate*, Christo *incorporantur*, ideoque christiano nomine iure decorantur et a filiis Ecclesiae catholicae ut fratres in Domino merito agnoscuntur" (ibid., pt. 2: 298-99, emphases mine). Regarding the first emphasis, the Latin is poorly constructed and literally reads "those who are justified by faith in baptism," whereas the Latin should have read "Iustificati baptismate per fidem" and thereby have better paraphrased Trent's meaning when it spoke of baptism as "... sacramentum *fidei sine qua* nulli unquam contigit justificatio" (Schroeder, *Canons and Decrees of the Council of Trent*, p. 312, emphasis mine).

[142]   "Pag. 7, lin. 27-28 loco 'Christo incorporantur' dicatur 'Christo uniuntur,' ne videatur contradici doctrinae Encyclicae 'Mystici corporis' Pii XII et theologorum, secundum quam etiam professio verae fidei requiritur, ut quis fiat reapse membrum Corporis Christi mystici, quod est Ecclesia. Appellatio ad Decretum pro Armenis ... dubia est ..." (*Acta Syn* 3, pt. 7: 30).

[143] "In textu dicitur tantum 'Christo,' non vero 'Corpori Christi Mystico,' quod est Ecclesia, *quo evitatur quaestio controversa de membris Ecclesiae*" (ibid., emphasis mine).

[144] "Ad hanc igitur catholicam Populi Dei unitatem, quae pacem universalem praesignat et promovet, omnes asciscuntur homines, ad eamque variis modis pertinent vel ordinantur sive fideles catholici, sive alii credentes in Christo, sive denique omnes universaliter homines, gratia Dei ad salutem vocati" (ibid., pt. 1: 187).

[145] See ibid., p. 188.

[146] See ibid., p. 189.

[147] See ibid., pp. 189-90.

[148] See AG, p. 345, n. 12.

[149] In this respect I must consider inaccurate the assessment by Riudor when he claims that the Council spoke in terms of *degrees* of membership. See Ignacio Riudor, 'La pertenencia a la Iglesia en los dos primeros capítolos de la constitución '*Lumen Gentium*' del Concilio Vaticano II,' *Estudios eclesiásticos* 40 (1965): 317.

[150] *LG*-b and the promulgated *LG*-c keep the orientation of Texts E and F, and though they do not call the Holy Spirit the Soul of the Church as did Pius XII in *Mystici corporis*, the Council Fathers come close to doing so: "[there is] . . . a certain real union in the Holy Spirit who certainly with his gifts and graces works also in them with his sanctifying power" [accedit . . . vera quaedam in Spiritu Sancto coniunctio, quippe qui donis et gratiis etiam in illis sua virtute sanctificante operatur]. I quote from *LG*-b, *Acta Syn* 3, pt. 1: 189).

[151] See Michael Schmaus, "Das Weltrundschreiben *Mystici corporis*," p. 139.

CHAPTER VI

[1] See Chap. II, pp. 92-98 and 103-116.

[2] See Chap. VII, pp. 288-90.

[3] See pp. 135-44.

[4] See pp. 127-34 and 150-67, respectively.

[5] See Aubert, *Le Pontificat de Pie IX*, p. 255.

[6] See ibid.

[7] See ibid., p. 256, where Aubert states that even some members of the Roman Curia were taken aback by the rigidity of the encyclical.

[8] On the manner wherein Dupanloup's was received, see Roger Aubert, "Les réactions suscitées par la publication du Syllabus," *Collectanea Mechliniensia*, n.s. 9 (1949): 309-17.

[9] Félix-Antoine-Philibert Dupanloup, *La Convention du 15 septembre et l'Encyclique du 8 décembre* (Paris: Charles Douniol, Libraire-éditeur, 1865).

[10] Thus for example in part one, Dupanloup speaks of two divisions to be followed by a few remarks on what people expect from the Pope (see ibid., p.10). Actually, there are four divisions, numbered one, two, three and five, respectively.

[11]   Dupanloup's French is stronger; he speaks of *contre bons sens*. See ibid., p. 45.

[12]   See ibid., pp. 45-46.

[13]   See ibid., p. 51.

[14]   See ibid., p. 52.

[15]   See ibid.

[16]   See ibid., p. 53.

[17]   "Dans l'interprétation des propositions condamnées, il faut remarquer tous les termes, toutes les plus légères nuances; car le vice d'une proposition ne tient souvent qu'à cela, à une nuance, à un mot, qui seul fait l'erreur. Il faut distinguer les propositions absolues et les propositions relatives; *car, ce qui pourrait être admissible en hypothèse, sera souvent faux en thèse*" (ibid., p. 54, emphasis mine).

[18]   "Faut-il le redire pour la centième fois? (Ce que l'Eglise) ce que le Pape condamnent, c'est l'indifférentisme religieux . . . cette absurdité, plus absurde peut-être encore qu'elle n'est impie, qu'on nous répète aujourd'hui de tous côtés, sur tous les tons, savoir que la Religion, Dieu, l'âme, la vérité, la vertu, l'Evangile ou l'Alcoran, Boudha ou Jésus-Christ, le vrai et le faux, le bien et le mal, tout cela est égal" (ibid., p. 62, parenthetical phrase omitted in the English translation. The phrase "qu'on nous répète aujourd'hui de tous côtés, sur tous les tons" has been rendered by the English "constantly clanging in our ears").

[19]   "En fait, jamais les Papes n'ont entendu condamner les gouvernements qui ont cru devoir, selon la nécessité des temps, écrire dans leurs constitutions cette tolérance, cette liberté. Que dis-je? Le Pape lui-même la pratique à Rome . . . Et c'est ce que Pie IX voulait bien me dire lui-même l'hiver dernier. 'Les Juifs et les protestants,' me disait-il, sont libres et tranquilles chez moi. Les Juifs ont leur synagogue dans le gettho [*sic*], et les protestants leur temple à la porte du peuple' " (ibid., pp. 62-63).

[20]   Number 16 of the Syllabus deals with the question of religious indifferentism as justifiable in principle.

[21]   Both the letter of Pius to Dupanloup as well as that of the future Leo XIII are reproduced in the third part of Roger Aubert's "Monseigneur Dupanloup et le Syllabus," *Revue d'Histoire ecclésiastique* 51, no. 4 (1956): 913 and 915, respectively.

[22]   By his first rule Dupanloup understood that the contradictory of a condemned proposition is affirmed. (See Dupanloup, *La Convention*, p. 52). But this does not always remove the problems it was meant to solve. Thus number 63 of the Syllabus condemned the proposition that it is permitted to refuse obedience to legitimate rulers. The contradictory according to Dupanloup is what is affirmed; namely it is *not* permitted to do so. But this raises the problem of what to do with a legitimate ruler who is misusing his authority. Here Dupanloup was less than successsful. See ibid.

Ironically, the Old Catholic, Leopold Karl Goetz, was to apply the same method (without an attempt to refute Dupanloup, however), and come up with conclusions that would have made the Bishop at Orléans blush. By applying the principle that the contradictory of a condemned proposition is affirmed, Goetz analyzed the

Syllabus and arrived at the conclusion that the theory of culture behind it was that of the Ultramontanes, one of the groups in nineteenth-century France with whom Dupanloup was *aux prises*, to put it mildly. See Leopold Karl.Goetz, *Der, Ultramontanismus als Weltanschauung auf Grund des Syllabus quellenmässig dargestellt* (Bonn: Carl Georgi Universitäts-Buchdruckerei und Verlag, 1905), pp. 51, 79 passim.

[23] It would not be difficult, but it would be too long given my limited scope to chart the general course of this discussion. Works contemporary to the encyclical *Quanta cura* and the Syllabus abound; thus the *Lettre pastorale de Monseigneur l'Archevêque de Paris relative à la récente encyclique du souverain pontife et mandement pour le carême et le jubilé de l'année* (Paris: A. Le Clere et Cie, 1865); L'Abbé Pelage, *La Bulle* Quanta cura *et la civilisation moderne, ou le Pape les Evêques, les gouvernements et la raison* (Paris: Garnier Frères, 1865); B. de Rénusson, *L'Encyclique expliquée par un catholique libéral (Paris: Librairie Catholique Martin-Beaupré Frères, 1865).* Later on in this *prise de conscience collective* which was taking place in France, the exchange between Pierre Bouvier (*Etudes* 102 [1905]: 235-67, in an article entitled "L'infaillibilité du Pape et le Syllabus") and Paul Violet (*Etudes* 103 [1905]: 250-57, in an article entitled "Controverse sur le 'Syllabus' ") is interesting. The former seemed inclined to consider the Syllabus as in effect an *ex cathedra* position; the latter that the Syllabus did not have the authority people seemed to attribute to it, an interesting comment for a professor of both canon and civil law at the Ecole des chartes. A classic study, which went through several editions, is Lucien Choupin's *Valeur des décisions doctrinales et disciplinaires du Saint-Siège.* Choupin was taken up in good measure with the Syllabus, saw it as an authentic, authoritative but non-infallible doctrinal pronouncement. See ibid., p. 156, and earlier, p. 141.

[24] See Dupanloup, *La Convention*, p. 56.

[25] See Donald E. Pelotte, *John Courtney Murray: Theologian in Conflict*, p. 51. I would like to draw attention to other aspects of Murray's development. Before being silenced, he kept abreast of developments that were taking place elsewhere, as seen for example in the article "On Religious Freedom," *Theological Studies* 10 (1949): 409-32. And on one (as far as I am aware, the only) occasion Murray dealt with the problem as it existed near the end of the other side of the spectrum. I am referring to the article "The Political Thought of Joseph de Maistre," *Review of Politics* 2 (1949): 63-86. De Maistre's views were so far removed from those of, say, a Montalembert that one wonders why Murray bothered with De Maistre. After he was silenced, Murray occasionally dealt with the issue of religious freedom but in a way that could not get him into difficulty with the Roman authorities. Thus in *We Hold These Truths* (New York: Sheed & Ward, 1960), he held that American Catholic assent and commitment to the American Constitution were based on moral grounds (see ibid., p. 78) and that the freedom of the church was conceived as a key to the Christian order of society (see ibid., p. 205). Finally, it should be noted that at the height of the conciliar debate Murray intervened but in a way very different from that of Roger Aubert as indicated above. Murray's contribution here (as distinguished from his actually working at the Council) was limited to

isolating the issues that seemed to prevent two divergent views from arriving at a consensus. See Murray, "The Problem of Religious Freedom," *Theological Studies* 25 (1964): 503-75. See also the exhaustive study by Reinhold Sebott, *Religionsfreiheit und Verhältnis von Kirche und Staat.*

[26] See John Courtney Murray "Freedom of Religion: I. The Ethical Problem," *Theological Studies* 6 (1945): 229-86.

[27] See John Courtney Murray, "Current Theology: Religious Freedom," *Theological Studies* 6 (1945): 85-113, especially pp. 98 and 99-100.

[28] See Murray, "Freedom of Religion: I. The Ethical Problem," p. 235.

[29] See ibid.

[30] See ibid.

[31] See ibid., p. 249. It should be noted that Murray at this time treated elsewhere of the natural law. But his treatment was general and not provided with the explicit view of founding the basis for religious freedom. See Murray, "The Natural Law," in *Great Expressions of Human Rights*, ed. R.M. MacIver (New York and London: Harper & Bros., 1950), pp. 69-103. It is not that Murray in that article is not concerned at all with the issue of religious freedom; his concern is to examine the basis of human rights in general, and under that rubric, the right to religious freedom is thus placed in a broader context. See ibid., p. 72.

[32] See Murray, "Freedom of Religion: I. The Ethical Problem," p. 251.

[33] See ibid.

[34] Ibid., p. 254.

[35] Ibid., p. 258.

[36] This is my example to illustrate the case. That given by Murray is the case of polygamy. See ibid., p. 261.

[37] Ibid., p. 262. Emphasis mine.

[38] See ibid., pp. 263-73.

[39] See ibid., pp. 273-78.

[40] Ibid., p. 273.

[41] Ibid.

[42] Ibid., p. 274.

[43] Ibid.

[44] See ibid., p. 276.

[45] Thus, as will become clear from Murray's analysis of the problem on the theological plane, Catholic consciousness of being the one true religion does not entail the logical necessity of setting up Catholicism as a state religion. And on the basis of his analysis on the ethical plane, in those cases where Catholicism does exist as the state religion, Catholicism has no right to violate religious freedom as grounded in natural law. Grace does not destroy nature but perfects it, in Catholic theology.

[46] See ibid., p. 242.

[47] Ibid., p. 278.

[48] Ibid., p. 266, n. 9b.

[49] See John Courtney Murray, "Governmental Repression of Heresy," *The Catholic Theological Society of America: Proceedings* (1948): 26-98.

50 See John Courtney Murray, "The Problem of State Religion," *Theological Studies* 12 (1951): 158-59.

51 ". . . the state is not society nor is government the state. Society in shortest definition, is man in the full flowering of all the social aspects of his nature. It is the prepolitical 'matter' to which the state imparts a particular, limited 'form,' a political form" (Murray, "Governmental Repression," p. 28).

52 See Murray, "The Problem of State Religion, " p. 177.

53 Ibid., emphasis mine.

54 Ibid., p. 158.

55 Ibid.

56 See Murray, "Governmental Repression," pp. 52-62.

57 See ibid., p. 97.

58 See ibid., p. 55-57.

59 See ibid., p. 59-60.

60 See Murray, "Contemporary Orientations of Catholic Thought on Church and State in the Light of History," p. 233.

61 Ibid., p. 224, emphasis mine.

62 One of Murray's later conclusions was that the precise form of the Church-state problem had continually undergone change; being set by the particular kind of state with which Catholicism sought an orderly relationship. See John Courtney Murray, "For the Freedom and Transcendence of the Church," *AER* 126 (1952): 43. Given the direction of Murray's thought, he probably used the term Catholic *thesis* (*re* the old thesis/hypothesis frame of reference) somewhat tongue-in-cheek in the "Contemporary Orientations of Catholic Thought" article.

63 Murray, "Contemporary Orientations of Catholic Thought," p. 233.

64 See Murray, "Freedom of Religion: I. The Ethical Problem," p. 266, n. 9b.

65 See Murray, "Governmental Repression of Heresy," p. 82.

66 See ibid., p. 71.

67 Ibid.

68 See ibid., p. 77.

69 See ibid., p. 78.

70 Ibid.

71 Ibid., p. 79.

72 Ibid., p. 82.

73 See Murray, "Contemporary Orientations of Catholic Thought," p. 226.

74 See for example, ibid., pp. 186-87.

75 See ibid., p. 189.

76 See John Courtney Murray, "Leo XIII on Church and State: The General Structure of the Controversy," *Theological Studies* 14 (1953): 4.

77 See ibid., p. 22.

78 See ibid.

79 See ibid., p. 20.

80 See also Murray, *We Hold These Truths*, pp. 45-78, and "The Problem of Pluralism in America," *Thought* 29 (1954): 165-208.

81 See also p. 442, n.90.

⁸²   Referring to Msgr. Ryan's reason for governmental right to repress heresy (namely that heresy could become a source of injury to true believers) Murray stated: "This statement goes beyond the text of *Immortale Dei* on which the author Ryan is commenting. Nor can this motivation of governmental repression of heresy claim support in Catholic political philosophy . . ." ("Governmental Repression," p. 91). That a well-known contemporary of Leo XIII was at that time associated with the Gregorian University and attempting to support precisely that motivation for governmental repression of heresy is beyond dispute. See Taparelli d'Azeglio, *Essai théorique de droit naturel*, 1: 388-90. Murray seemed unaware of this fact.

⁸³   See above, p. 421, n. 102.

⁸⁴   This oversimplification in Murray's work still finds an echo today in some of his interpreters: "Indeed, Leo condemned 'separation of Church and state,' but he also frequently referred to and developed the doctrine that there are two distinct jurisdictions. One cannot legitimately conclude, then, that he was doctrinally rejecting the Gelasian formula for a theological 'ideal' of union of Church and state." Clifford G. Kossel, "Religious Freedom and the Church: J.C. Murray," *Communio* 11, no. 1 (Spring 1984), pp. 60-74. The quotation is to be found on p. 71. The fact of the matter is that Leo held on to the Gelasian *Duo sunt* and at the same time insisted that ideally there should be a union between Church and state. See my analysis, pp. 132-33.

⁸⁵   See Leo XIII, *Longinqua oceani*, in ASS 27 (1894): 390.

⁸⁶   Thus in *Ci riesce* the old thesis/hypothesis frame of references continues, without, as I said earlier, its explicit label: ". . . that which does not correspond to the truth and to the norm of morality has objectively no right either to exist or to propagandize or to activity . . . not interfering with it however through laws of state and coercive measures can nevertheless be justified in the interests of a broader, higher good" (". . . ciò che non risponde alla verità e alla norma morale, non ha oggettivamente alcun diritto nè all'esistenza nè alla propaganda, nè all'azione . . . il non impedirlo per mezzo di leggi statali e di disposizioni coercitive può nondimeno essere giustificato nell'interesse di un bene superiore e più vasto" (AAS 45 [1953]: 799).

⁸⁷   See p. 148.

⁸⁸   Aubert in the 1951 article (not to be confused with the orientation in the 1965 article [for the differences, see pp. 189-90 of this study])was close to affirming what Murray was affirming, without dependence on Murray, as far as I can determine. But the Belgian and the French contributions are too long to summarize here. Suffice it to say that already in 1959 they were bearing fruit. See, for example, the brilliant treatment of the central points by the Archbishop at Cambrai, Emile Guerry, in his report to the Antepreparatory Commission, *ADOC* I, 2, pt. 1: 255-59. For a summary of Guerry's critique, see pp. 255-56 of this study.

⁸⁹   See the reports to the Antepreparatory Commission of Bishop Flanagan of Worcester, Massachusetts, in *ADOC* I, 2, pt. 6: 468; of Archbishop Alter of Cincinnati, ibid., pp. 296-97; and of Richard Cardinal Cushing, ibid., p. 279.

⁹⁰   See Arthur Vermeersch, *Tolérance* (Louvain: Librairie Universitaire Uystpruyst-Dieudonné; and Paris: Gabriel Beauchesne, 1912), who argued that though

the Catholic Church is dogmatically intolerant it does not have a built in *précepte persécuteur* (ibid., pp. 40 and 390-91). As early as 1942 the posthumously published class lectures of Yves de Montschueil, tortured to death by the Gestapo because of his part in the French Resistance, reveal that their author was approaching a position not unlike that which John Courtney Murray was later to adopt. See Yves de Montscheuil, *L'Eglise et le monde actuel*, 2nd ed. (Paris: Editions Témoignage chrétien, 1945), pp. 144-47. Some ten years later Yves M. Congar was to state: "To know in what measure one must speak of an acknowledgement of God's sovereignty by the state as such is a problem the solution of which would require further elaboration regarding the very notion of the state and the spiritual status of societies divided as ours are" [C'est un problème, dont la solution demanderait des élaborations nouvelles concernant la notion même d'Etat et le statut spirituel de sociétés diviseés comme sont les nôtres, que de savoir dans quelle mesure il faut parler d'une reconnaissance de la souveraineté de Dieu par l'Etat comme tel . . .] (Yves M. Congar, "Eglise et Etat," in *Catholicisme: hier, aujourd'hui, demain*, 8 vols. [Paris: Letouzey et Ané, 1948-], 3: 1439. The imprimatur of this volume is dated 1952.). It is not however entirely clear whether at the time Congar meant that (a) it was not clear according to Catholic doctrine whether the state as such must recognize the Catholic Church as its official religion or whether (b) it was not clear according to Catholic doctrine whether the state may be *officially* indifferent to religion. If the latter ([b]), Congar seems to have gone beyond Murray, to whom he refers (ibid.). Further contributions during this period were made by Jacques Leclercq, "Etat chrétien et liberté dans l'Eglise," *La Vie intellectuelle* 17 (1949): 99-111; Joseph Lecler, "La papauté moderne et la liberté de conscience," *Etudes* 249 (1946): 287-309; Max Pribilla, "Dogmatische Intoleranz und bürgerliche Toleranz," *Stimmen der Zeit* 144 (1948-49): 27-40; and E. Guerrero, "Con la libertad del acto de fe no es incompatible el Estado católico," *Razón y Fe* 151 (1955): 465-78.

A full discussion of the debate as it was then affecting Catholicism is to be found in Teodoro Ignacio Jiménez Urresti's *Estado e Iglesia: laicidad y confesionalidad del Estado y del derecho*, Victoriensia, no. 6 (Victoria, Spain: Editorial del Seminario, 1958), especially pp. 441-45, where Jimenez Urresti seems to have come down on the side of Maritain and Murray. See also Jacques Maritain, *Man and the State*, ed. Richard O'Sullivan (London: Hollis & Carter, 1954).

⁹¹ See C. Constantin, "Le Libéralisme catholique," in *Dictionnaire de Théologie catholique*, 15 vols, 22 tomes (Paris: Letouzey et Ané, 1909-) 9 (1926): 506-629.

⁹² See for example Patriarch Leopoldo Eijo y Garay ([West Indies] *ADOC* 1, 2, pt. 2: 215), Bishops Santos Moro Briz ([Avila] ibid., p. 134), Enrique Pla y Deniel ([Toledo] ibid., p. 358), Eugenio Beitia Aldazubal ([Badajoz] ibid., p. 429), Roberto Massimiliani ([Città Castellana Orte e Gallese] ibid., pt. 3: 217-18), and Augusto Salinas Fuenzalida ([Linares] ibid., pt. 7: 367). Some of the reports sent in by Italian Bishops do not as they stand in the texts necessarily mean that the respective authors wished to see the Council reaffirm the traditional stand rather than change it. However, given the orientation of the Italian hierarchy in general, the former seems more likely. See for example the report submitted by Bishop Guiseppe Piazzi ([Bergamo]) ibid., pt. 3: 102).

[93]   See the remarks submitted by Bishop James McManus, Bishop at Ponce (Puerto Rico) in a report drafted by Francis Connell, John Courtney Murray's principal antagonist in the Church-state controversy in the United States. See ibid., pt. 6: 648.

[94]   See ibid., pt. 1: 255.

[95]   See ibid., p. 256.

[96]   See ibid., p. 257.

[97]   "Notio haec positiva laicitatis, in natione divisa, quoad fidem apparet tunc ut salvans, reverensque conscientiarum et fidei formarum libertatem, in nomine boni communis, et quamvis omnino doctrinae Ecclesiae non conformis appareat" (ibid.).

[98]   See ibid., p. 258.

[99]   See ibid.

[100]   See ibid.

[101]   "De habitudine Ecclesiae ad Statum quod dicitur modernum et saeculare, et de utriusque facultate vel competentia quoad varias vitae humanae provincias, exortae sunt controversiae valde perturbantes. Quas ut practice dirimantur, expositio perspicua prodest illorum principiorum fundamentalium, tam theologicorum quam iuridicorum, quae novum conceptum suppeditent illius habitudinis, quum veteres conceptus hucusque vigentes radicentur in rebus politicis amplius non vigentibus" (ibid., pt. 6: 279). I translate according to the sense which Cushing's Latinist seems to have intended. Better Latinity might have rendered Cushing's thought as "Ad quas practice dirimendas . . . expositio *prodesset* . . . quae novum conceptum *suppeditarent* . . ."

[102]   See for example the reports submitted by Archbishop Alter (Cincinnati) and Bishop Flanagan (Worcester), ibid., pp. 296 and 468, respectively.

[103]   See *ADOC* 1, 3: 7-8 and 302-4, respectively.

[104]   "Multi auctores his ultimis annis recesserunt a doctrina in documentis Magisterii ecclesiasticis contenta, et a probatis auctoribus edicta quae sese refert ad officia religiosa status catholici. Eis videtur non ex fine essentiali utriusque societatis profluens, sed nihil aliud nisi synthesis theoretica relationum olim existentium inter Ecclesiam et potestatem monarchicam 'vigente sacra christianitate.' Opportuna videtur affirmatio solemnis istius doctrinae dummodo cum ea proponatur doctrina de legitima tolerantia cuius elementa inveniuntur in litteris Encyclicis Leonis Papae XIII et in allocutionibus Pii Papae XII" (ibid., 4, pt. 1, sec. 2: 15-16).

Yet the position of the faculty at the Angelicum was more nuanced than appears from the text I have just quoted. On the very page on which it took a position on the duty of a Catholic state, the faculty added: "For the objective principle according to which 'Only the truth has rights, but error has none,' is to be substituted the subjective principle [according to which] the subject of a right is not something abstract like truth but is a human person either individual or moral whose right of acting *always and everywhere* according to conscience, even when erroneous, is to be acknowledged" [Principio obiectivo, iuxta quod "iura soli veritati competunt, minime vero errori," substituendum est principium subiectivum, "iuris subiectum non est res quaedam abstracta ut veritas, sed persona humana sive individualiter, sive collective sumpta, cui agnoscendum est *ubique et semper* ius agendi secundum suam conscientiam, etiam erroneam"] (ibid., 4, pt. 1, sec. 2: 16, emphasis mine).

I would like to make two remarks about this text. First, it did not involve its authors in contradiction with what they had stated concerning the duties of a Catholic state. Second, the subjective principle as it stands was somewhat over-stated. The right to act *ubique et semper* according to even an erroneous conscience has of its very nature built-in limits. Thus, to give an extreme example, one who because of his or her religious convictions would exterminate all non-believers would be rightly prosecuted by the state.

[105] "Propter motiva eadem ac ea, quae in capite praecedenti relata sunt, inspectis insuper non tantum adiunctis hodiernis in quibus vix detur natio homogenee catholica et in quibus modus sese gerendi catholicorum erga non-catholicos in natione ubi catholici maiorum partem civium constituunt necessario influit in modum sese gerendi non-catholicorum erga catholicos in nationibus ubi non-catholici maiore numero exstant, sed inspectis etiam, et quidem praesertim, princi-piis catholicis de obligatione sese conformandi conscientiae bonae fidei ac de libertate et charactere supernaturali fidei, exoptatur ut Concilium publice et sol-lemniter proclamet fidem catholicam non-posse imponi vel conservari quavis coercitione quae integritatem conscientiae et libertatem fidei laedat, ita ut mani-feste appareat dignitatem personae humanae, quam Dominus Noster Iesus Chris-tus per Incarnationem suam mundo plene revelavit, ab Ecclesia Catholica in omnibus hominibus perfecte agnosci" (ibid., 4, pt. 2: 169).

[106] "Let the Council defend real tolerance, not simply as a concession for the moment by way of fittingness, but let it take stock of the rights of conscience and the dignity of the human person" [Concilium veram tolerantiam propuget quae non sit tantum concessio ad tempus respectu opportunitatis, sed iurium conscien-tiae et personae humanae dignitatis rationem habeat] (*ADOC* I, 4, pt. 2: 499). The recommendation of the faculty at the Institut Catholique of Paris was along the lines which Vatican II was to adopt. I cannot see the faculty's attempt to ground this position in the allocution delivered to the Union of Italian Jurists of December 6, 1953 (*Ci riesce*). For my reasons, see the analysis above, pp. 162-65.

[107] See pp. 135-44.

[108] On Joseph Clifford Fenton, see, for example, "The Extension of Christ's Mystical Body," *AER* 110 (1944): 124-30. On Karl Rahner, "Membership of the Church According to the Teaching of Pius XII's Encyclical '*Mystici corporis Christi*.'"

[109] Besides the studies indicated above and those discussed below, a selected bibliography would include at least the following: Jérôme Hamer, "Le Baptême et l'Eglise," *Irénikon* (1952): 142-64; L. Richard, "Une thèse fondamentale de l'oecuménisme: le baptême, incorporation visible à l'Eglise," *Nouvelle Revue théo-logique* 74 (1952); 485-92; L. Malevez, "Quelques enseignements de l'encyclique '*Mystici corporis*,'" *Nouvelle Revue théologique* vol. 67 (1945): 385-407; A. Liégé, "L'Appartenance à l'Eglise et l'encyclique '*Mystici corporis*,'" *Revue des Sciences*

philosophiques et théologiques 32 (1948): 351-57 and J. Brinktrine, "Was lehrt die Enzyklika '*Mystici corporis*' über die Zugehörigkeit zur Kirche?," *Theologie und Glaube* 38 (1947-48): 290-300. See also the items listed in the Bibliography.

[110]   "Tel qu'il existe sur terre, le Corps mystique du Christ ne comprend-il, au sens strict du mot, que les membres de l'Eglise catholique romaine? C'est à chercher une solution de ce problème que les pages qui suivent sont consacrées. L'encyclique de Sa Sainteté Pie XII, *Mystici corporis Christi*, identifie couramment, il est vrai, l'Eglise catholique et le Corps mystique; mais il incombe à la théologie de scruter, dans un esprit d'entière soumission au magistère ecclésiastique, les enseignements du même magistère et de les traduire en langage théologique technique, en particulier de préciser le sens et le degré de la dite identification" (Valentin Morel, "Le Corps mystique du Christ et l'Eglise Catholique romaine," *Nouvelle Revue théologique* 70 [1948]: 703).

[111]   See ibid., p. 708.
[112]   See ibid.
[113]   See ibid., p. 718.
[114]   See ibid., p. 719.
[115]   See ibid., p. 723.
[116]   See ibid., p. 725.
[117]   See ibid.
[118]   See ibid., p. 722.
[119]   See above, chap. V, Text B, p. 197.
[120]   On the Pontifical Theological Faculty of Milan, see *ADOC* I, 4, pt. 2: 680, n. 7; on Karl Rahner, see ibid., p. 65.
[121]   See P. Michalon, "Eglise, Corps mystique du Christ glorieux," *Nouvelle Revue théologique* 74 (1952): 673-87.
[122]   See ibid., p. 674.
[123]   See ibid., p. 679-80.
[124]   See ibid., p. 684.
[125]   "Nous saisissons par là combien ce serait fausser notre vision de considérer à part l'organisme de l'Eglise. On se vouerait à ne la plus comprendre et à la défigurer" (ibid., p. 687).
[126]   "Peut-être le lecteur saisira-t-il aussi pourquoi l'Eglise catholique romaine s'affirme comme étant à strictement parler le Corps mystique, à cause de la plénitude des liens qui en elle lient les membres de ce Corps. Mais je souligne également que, pour l'Eglise romaine, tous les chrétiens non-catholiques sont ordonnés à ce Corps invisiblement, mais aussi *par certains éléments visibles* qui, à son regard catholique, manifestent leur relative appartenance à l'unique Eglise et fait d'eux, dans une perspective unioniste, 'des membres potentiels de ce Corps'" (ibid., emphasis mine).
[127]   See *ADOC* I, 2, pt. 9: 68-69.
[128]   See ibid., p. 69.
[129]   See ibid.
[130]   The Council had more than 2,100 members, the majority of whom were bishops. As the Council progressed, it is clear that a certain educational process

was taking place, particularly among the bishops, with whom I am here principally concerned. Though the vast majority of bishops in the end voted to modify the teaching of Pius XII on the identity question and the correlative of membership, I have found it impossible to determine the views of the bishops as a whole prior to the Council. The fact that the majority did not bring up the question of *Mystici corporis* may indicate that the majority had no real problem with it; but this silence cannot be taken to indicate that they therefore had received the doctrine of the Roman Bishop as pertaining to the substance of the faith and had so taught their people, as subsequent events at the Council were to prove. On this point, see above, pp. 276-81.

[131]   See *ADOC* I, 2, pt. 1: 429.
[132]   See ibid., pt. 2: 509.
[133]   See ibid., pt. 1: 298-306.
[134]   See ibid., p. 76.
[135]   See ibid., p. 77.
[136]   See ibid., pp. 617-18.
[137]   Wojtyla's report is to be found in ibid., 2, pt. 2: 741-48. One of his many concerns as reflected in this document was the wish that the Council take up the question of the laicization of priests who had been unsuccessful in combining priesthood and celibacy. See ibid., pp. 744-45.
[138]   "Concilium ab omnibus summo studio expectatur, praesertim autem a separatis ab Ecclesiae unitate ratione haerseos vel schismatis. Videntur et ipsi aliqualem possidere amorem Christi Domini, unde spes reconciliationis eorum cum vera Ecclesia Christi, amor enim parit unitatem. Unitas autem Ecclesiae in nullo alio sic exponitur, ut in doctrina de Corpore Christi Mystico: si Ecclesia est Corpus Christi, non potest esse nisi una et unica, unum enim et unicum est etiam hoc Corpus" (ibid., pp. 742-43).
[139]   "In quo membra diversa, sana et aegrota—haec quidem etiam ratione haerseos, quae est contra fidem peccatum, et schismatis, quod est contra caritatem. *Atqui aegrota etiam non desinunt esse aliquo modo membra Corporis Christi,* quod in coelis tantum gloriosum est, in terra tamen vulneratum erat et exinanitum—unde similiter et Corpus Eius Mysticum, quod est in terra, aegrotat et languores patitur. *Languores Eius in nobis omnibus,* qui proinde obligamur de sanitate eius omnes solliciti esse" (ibid., p. 743, emphasis mine).
[140]   "Concilium simul ac tota ecclesiologia theologica haec omnia exponere possunt, minorem accentum praebendo his omnibus, quae separant, quaerendo autem omnia quae conciliant. Sic praeparabitur forsan quaedam conversio in mentibus . . ." (ibid.).
[141]   See ibid., 4, pt. 1, sec. 1: 147.
[142]   See ibid., p. 15.
[143]   See ibid.
[144]   On St. Patrick's, see ibid., 4, pt. 2: 430-38. On the Catholic University, see ibid., pp. 619-21. The report from the former was, however, highly nuanced.
[145]   See ibid., 4, pt. 1, sec. 2: 337-49.
[146]   "1. Si quis affirmaverit mysticum Christi Corpus (quod est sancta, apostol-

ica, catholica atque Romana Ecclesia) non esse unum atque indivisum; a.s." (ibid., p. 343).

[147] "2. Si quis dixerit varios christianorum coetus, etsi fide et regimine inter se dissidentes, mystici Corporis Christi membris adnumerandos esse; a.s. . . ." (ibid).

[148] 6. Si quis affirmaverit in Ecclesiae membris reapse non eos solos adnumerandos esse qui lavacrum regenerationis receperunt atque veram fidem profitentur eidemque regimini subduntur; a.s." (ibid.).

[149] See ibid., pt. 2: 243.

[150] See ibid., p. 477.

[151] See ibid., p. 486.

[152] See ibid.

[153] See ibid.

[154] On the faculty of Bonn, see ibid., p. 773; on that of Fribourg, see ibid., pg. 784.

[155] See ibid., pp. 678-83.

[156] See ibid., p. 679.

[157] See ibid.

[158] See ibid., p. 680, n. 7.

[159] See ibid.

[160] See ibid., p. 682, n. 14.

[161] See ibid.

[162] There is evidence however of a few French bishops endorsing the position of Pius XII. Thus besides Garrone, mentioned above, one might mention among others Bishop Jean Girbeau of Nîmes (see *ADOC* I, 2, pt. 1: 356); Cardinal Richaud of Bordeaux (see ibid., p. 230); Bishop Gaudron, but with some hesitation (see ibid., p. 285); and Bishop Marmottin of Reims (see ibid., p. 397).

[163] See Karl Rahner, "Die Gliedschaft in der Kirche nach der Lehre der Enzyklika Pius XII. '*Mystici corporis Christi*,' " *Schriften zur Theologie* 20 vols. (Einsiedeln, Zürich, Cologne: Benziger Verlag, 1954-) 2 (1962): 7-94. Unless indicated to the contrary, references are to the English translation. (For the bibliographical data, see Chap. V, p. 429, n.36.)

[164] See Rahner, "Membership in the Church," pp. 3-4.

[165] See ibid., p. 65.

[166] See ibid.

[167] See ibid., p. 69.

[168] See ibid., pp. 70-71.

[169] Ibid., p. 73, emphasis mine.

[170] Ibid., p. 76, emphasis mine.

[171] See ibid., p. 79.

[172] Ibid., p. 81, emphasis mine.

[173] See ibid.

[174] See ibid.

[175] Ibid., p. 82.

[176] Ibid., p. 83.

[177] Ibid.

[178] Ibid., p. 84.

179   Ibid., p. 85.

180   Ibid., pp. 85-86.

181   Ibid., p. 75.

182   See ibid., pp. 77 and 86.

183   See ibid., p. 66.

184   Ibid., p. 87.

185   In the German text, Rahner used the term *Wesenschichten* when describing the relation to the Church enjoyed by two justified persons, one of whom is a Catholic and the other not, thereby implying that for him (at least at the time) the difference was not one of degree but of kind. See Karl Rahner, "Die Gliedschaft in der Kirche nach der Lehre der Enzyklika Pius XII. '*Mystici corporis Christi*,' " p. 93

186   See *ADOC* II, 2, pt. 3: 986-93.

187   The difference has however no direct relation to ecclesiology. *AU*-a reaa: "... quam [Ecclesiam] que redivivus S. Petro et Succesoribus tradidit gubernandam...." whereas *AU*-b substituted "post resurrectionem suam" for "redividus." See ibid., p. 988, and *Acta Syn* 1, pt. 4: 15, respectively.

188   See *ADOC* II, 2, pt. 3: 994.

189   See ibid.

190   "Aliud principium est nullam esse distinctionem realem inter Ecclesiam Catholicam Romanam visibilem et inter Corpus Christi Mysticum quod est Ecclesia. Hac de re non solum edocemur dilucide a s. m. Pio Papa XII in duabus epistolis Encyclicis dogmaticis, sed insuper a permultis eius praedecessoribus, quorum unus, Sanctus Pius Papa X . . ." (ibid., pp. 994-95).

191   See ibid., p. 997.

192   See ibid., p. 998.

193   See ibid.

194   See above, pp. 220-21.

195   See *ADOC* II, 2, pt. 3: 1012.

196   See ibid.

197   See ibid., p. 1014.

198   See ibid.

199   See ibid.

200   See ibid., pp. 1014-15.

201   See ibid., p. 1015.

202   See ibid.

203   See ibid.

204   See ibid.

205   See ibid., p. 1016.

206   " 'Qui ex toto et in re adhaerent Ecclesiae catholicae ut est medium salutis, sensu pleno et proprio dici possunt eius membra.' Ipsa autem elementa, illa, quibus aliquis secundum plenam rationem vocis constituitur membrum Ecclesiae visibilis, non pertinent exclusive ad solos catholicos. Multi enim non catholici etiam regenerationis lavacro sunt abluti, et veram fidem christianam profitentur quamvis non integre, atque etiam sese submittunt pastoribus secundum ministerium quod ipsis

legitimum apparent. Immo nec desunt apud non catholicos multa elementa ordinis supernaturalis invisibilis quibus constituitur, nutritur et perseverat communio spiritualium bonorum cum vera Ecclesia Christi. Omnes enim qui in gratia divina vivunt et fidem, spem, caritatem theologicam profitentur, in uno eodem Spiritu manent qui est anima Corporis Christi mystici. Recte igitur vocantur 'fratres' nostri, etsi 'separati,' et 'filii' Ecclesiae, sicut Summus Pontifex in Const. Apost. *Humanae salutis* eos vocat" (ibid.).

[207]   Cardinal Browne was to follow Bea and expressed some difficulty at having to follow up on Bea's remarks. Browne apparently spoke impromptu whereas Bea had obviously spoken from a prepared text. That may explain the intrinsic inconsistency of two of Browne's remarks. On the one hand, he expressed difficulty in accepting Bea's criticism (i.e., Bea had challenged the notion contained in *Mystici corporis* that non-Catholics belong to the Church by desire). Browne said that such was the only way one had to express the reality involved. On the other hand, Browne suggested that a possible solution was to return to the former way of speaking prior to *Mystici corporis* and to say that non-Catholics belong to the Mystical Body of Christ in that they belong to its Soul and Will. See ibid., p. 1017.

[208]   See ibid., p. 1023.

[209]   See ibid.

[210]   See ibid.

[211]   See ibid., p. 1024.

[212]   See ibid.

[213]   See ibid., p. 1025.

[214]   There was a slight anachronism in Ottaviani's remarks in that he referred to the Cardinal at Boston in the context of the so-called Feeney case whereas in fact Cushing was not made a cardinal until some years later.

[215]   See pp. 202-8 above.

[216]   See *ADOC* II, 2, pt. 3: 1028.

[217]   Siri voted *iuxta modum* because of the remarks made by Bea, König and Browne. Referring specifically to the identity question he said: ". . . let it certainly be affirmed that the Mystical Body of Christ converges with the Roman Catholic Church, but let it also be suggested that its extension is wider than the Church on pilgrimage and let it be clear how wide the extension is" [. . . affirmetur utique corpus Christi mysticum convenire cum Ecclesia Catholica Romana, sed insinuetur etiam ipsum latius patere quam Ecclesia quae peregrinatur . . . et quomodo latius pateat] (ibid., p. 1027).

[218]   A very salient exception is the *Nota explicativa* in the context of collegiality. See pp. 76-78.

CHAPTER VII

[1] See Friedrich Schleiermacher, *The Christian Faith*, trans. and ed. H. R. Macintosh and J. S. Stewart from 2nd German ed. (Edinburgh: T. & T. Clark, 1968), pp. 525-28.

[2] For reasons too long to outline here, I do not believe that insights from literary theory developed by Hans Robert Jauss are fully applicable to the kinds of data I have examined or to the conclusions that flow from them. Much more apposite for the theology of reception is the work of Herman Josef Sieben. See my remark above, p. 363.

[3] Outstanding in this context were the excesses of certain trends in Mariology. One example was the attempt to establish theologically the position that the Virgin Mary was a priest because she could be said to have had the spiritual dispositions of one. See Jules Grimal, *With Jesus to the Priesthood*, trans. Gerald Shaughnessy from 6th French ed. (Philadelphia: Dolphin Press, 1946), p. 102.

[4] See, for example, John Boyle, "The Natural Law and the Magisterium," *Catholic Theological Society of America: Proceedings* 34 (1979): 189-210, esp. pp. 202-3 and 210.

[5] While I share the concern of Thomas Dubay as expressed in "The State of Moral Theology: A Critical Appraisal," *Theological Studies* 35 (1974): 482-506, I cannot accept the implications of a later article, "Does Dissent Have a Future?," *Homiletic and Pastoral Review* 83 (January 1983): 10-18. Is there no place in the Catholic Church for a "loyal opposition" in the context of the ordinary papal magisterium? But see p. 364.

[6] See pp. 92-98.

[7] See pp. 99-119.

[8] Roger Aubert stated in 1952 that vol. 22 of the collection *Histoire de l'Eglise depuis les origines jusqu'à nos jours* (Paris: Bloud et Gay, n.d.) was to treat missionary activity during the pontificate of Pius IX. See Aubert, *Le Pontificat de Pie IX*, p. 500, n. 2. As far as I know, that book has never appeared. Two articles by Johannes Beckmann, "The Missions between 1840 and 1870" and "The First Vatican Council and the Missions," are especially helpful in this regard. They may be found in Hubert Jedin, ed., *History of the Church*, 10 vols., various translators (New York: Crossroad, 1965-1981), 8 (1981): 175-98 and 199-206, respectively.

[9] See the table of theological notes in the Glossary, p. 24.

[10] See pp. 349-53.

[11] The reader has correctly divined that my conclusions do not confirm recent trends in the theology of *consensus fidelium* (in my terms, the *sensus fidelium* and/or *sensus fidei*) sometimes found in recent polemical literature. I refer *inter alia* to the article by Leonard Swidler, "*Demo-Kratia*, the Rule of the People of God, or *Consensus Fidelium*," in Leonard Swidler and Piet F. Fransen, ed., *Authority in the Church and the Schillebeeckx Case* (New York: Crossroad, 1982), pp 226-43. Is dialogue on a specific issue endless? Or does it come to an end only when the side opposed to a theological position embraced by Catholicism's Petrine minister has seemingly "won out"?

[12]   Thus the Catholic participants in the Lutheran-Catholic dialogue judged that the papal and episcopal form of ministry as it concretely evolved is a ". . . divinely-willed sequel to the functions exercised respectively by Peter and other apostles according to various New Testament traditions" ("Papal Primacy and the Universal Church," in *LCD V*, pp. 34-35).

[13]   "Both groups can acknowledge that as the forms of the papacy have been adapted to changing historical settings in the past, it is possible that they will be modified to meet the needs of the Church in the future more effectively" (*LCD V*, p. 19). And the members of the Anglican-Roman Catholic International Commission: "It seems appropriate that in any future union a universal primary such as has been described should be held by that see [i.e., the See of Rome]" (*Agreement on Authority: The Anglican-Roman Catholic Statement*, p. 14).

[14]   See Joseph A. Fitzmyer, "The Office of Teaching in the Christian Church According to the New Testament," in *LCD VI*, p. 191.

[15]   See Georg Denzler, "The Authority and Reception of Conciliar Decisions in Christendom," in *The Ecumenical Council—Its Significance in the Constitution of the Church*, ed. Peter Huizing and Knut Walf, Concilium, vol. 167, various translators (Edinburgh: T. & T. Clark, and New York: The Seabury Press, 1983), pp. 13-18. Denzler's concerns go beyond the historical period with which I deal here. It should be obvious that unless a distinction is made between *sedens* and *sedes*, my remarks in the context of reception could not be taken to apply to certain moments in Church history—one has only to think of the Three Chapters Controversy and Bishop Vigilius. The question as I see it is whether, as the Church's understanding of the nature and function of its Petrine ministry has been progressively clarified, it is possible to do justice to all the data and, within the limits of Catholic theology, to treat the nature of reception as though it were a movement in one direction only. This is the distinction that Denzler and others fail to make.

[16]   See, among others, Lionel Thornton, *The Common Life in the Body of Christ*, 3rd ed. (London: Dacre Press, A. & C. Black, 1950); P. C. Bori, Koinonia: *l'idea della communione nell'Ecclesiologia recente e nel Nuovo Testamento* (Brescia: n.p., 1972); J. Y. Campbell, "*Koinonia* and Its Cognates in the New Testament," *Journal of Biblical Literature* 51 (1932): 352-82; Yves Congar, *Vraie et fausse réforme dans l'Eglise* (Paris: Les Editions du Cerf, 1969), avertissement, pp. 15-23 and 241-76, and "Confession," "Eglise," "Communion," *Irénikon* 23 (1950): 3-26; J. Coppens, "La *koinonia* dans l'Eglise primitive," *Ephemerides Theologicae Lovanienses* 46 (1970): 116-21 E. Cothenet, "La *Communio* nel Nuovo Testamento," *Communio* 1 (1972): 13-21; G. D. Fischer, "Zum *Koinonia*-Charakter christlicher Gemeinden," *Theologie und Glaube* 61 (1971): 39-44; A. George, "La Communion fraternelle des croyants dans les Epîtres de Saint-Paul, *Lumière et Vie* 16 (1967): 3-20; M. McDermott, "The Biblical Doctrine of *Koinonia*," *Biblische Zeitschrift* 19 (1975): 64-77 and 219-33; M.-J. LeGuillou, "Eglise et Communion: essai d'Ecclésiologie comparée," *Istina* 7 (1959): 33-82; George Panikulam, Koinonia *in the New Testament: A Dynamic Expression of Christian Life* (Rome: Biblical Institute Press, 1979); Oskar Saier, "*Communio*" *in der Lehre des Zweiten Vatikanischen Konzils* (Bamberg: St. Otto-Verlag, 1973); Antonio Acerbi, *Due*

Ecclesiologie: ecclesiologia giurdica ed ecclesiologia di communione nella "Lumen gentium" (Bologna: Edizioni Dehoniane, 1975); Antonio Cañizares Llovera, "El magisterio de la Iglesia," *Iglesia viva* 79 (1979): 357-75, especially pp. 366-68; J[ean]-M[arie]-R[oger] Tillard, "L'Eglise de Dieu est une communion," *Irénikon* 53 (1980): 451-68; Joseph Komonchak, "The Church Universal as the Communion of Local Churches," in *Where Does the Church Stand?*, Concilium, vol. 146, ed. Giuseppe Alberigo and Gustavo Gutierrez (Edinburgh: T. & T. Clark, and New York: Seabury Press, 1981), pp. 30-35; Yves Congar, *Diversités et communion: dossier historique et conclusion théologique* (Paris: Les Editions du Cerf, 1982), especially pp. 19-68; Piet Fransen, "La Communion ecclésiale, principe de vie," in *Les Eglises après Vatican II: dynamisme et prospective*, Actes du Colloque international de Bologne, 1980, ed. Giuseppe Alberigo (Paris: Beauchesne, 1981), pp. 185-206; Giuseppe Alberigo, "Institutions exprimant la communion entre l'épiscopat universel et l'évêque de Rome," in *Les Eglises après Vatican II*, pp. 259-89; Joseph Lécuyer, "Institutions en vue de la communion entre l'épiscopat universel et l'évêque de Rome," in *Les Eglises après Vatican II*, pp. 297-301; and Herwi Rikof, *The Concept of Church*, pp. 229-36.

[17] See Avery Dulles, *Models of the Church* (Garden City, N.Y.: Doubleday, Image Books, 1971), who at least at that writing was skeptical of the possibility of finding any one model of the church that would be truly adequate to express what the Church is. See ibid., pp. 202-3.

[18] It is well known that H. Seesemann almost fifty years ago maintained that analysis of the function of κοινωνία in the New Testament reveals that the term is not used as parallel to ἐκκλησία. See Heinrich Seesemann, *Der Begriff* Koinonia *im Neuen Testament* (Giessen: Verlag von Alfred Topelmann, 1933), p. 99. On this point, see the critique of Seesemann by Jérôme Hamer, *L'Eglise est une communion*, pp. 173-78. Hamer agreed with Seesemann in the sense that κοινωνία as used in the New Testament does not mean a social entity; he disagreed in the sense that the concept expressed by this word means a way of life, i.e., of being and of acting, resulting from a relation with God and humankind characteristic of the Christian collectivity. Hamer's conclusions coincide with Lionel Thornton's, whose work however is not cited by Hamer. See Thornton, *The Common Life in the Body of Christ*, p. 76.

[19] It is interesting to note however that when Paul speaks of partaking of the bread (1 Cor. 10:17) he uses μετέχομεν but when speaking of its effects (1 Cor. 10:16) he uses κοινωνία. This is not sufficient however to ground the now discarded distinction mentioned above.

[20] There is a scholarly dispute concerning the third of the examples given here (2 Cor. 13:13), which constitutes the closing lines of the epistle. Some read ἡ κοινωνία τοῦ ἁγίου πνεύματος as a subjective, others as an objective genitive. In the former case, κοινωνία is the social entity brought about through the Holy Spirit; in the latter, the "object" in which all share. Seesemann himself inclined to the latter view (see Seesemann, *Der Begriff* Koinonia *im Neuen Testament*, pp. 56-57). On this point, see George Panikulam, who concluded: ". . . any inclusion of the *koinonia tou Pneumatos hagiou* into a subjective or into an objective genitive

exclusively is a wrong interpretation" (Panikulam, Koinonia *in the New Testament*, p. 70).

²¹   See Friedrich Hauck, "κοινός. . .κοινόω," in *Theological Dictionary of the New Testament*, 10 vols., vols. 1-4 ed. Gerhard Kittel, vols. 5-9 ed. Gerhard Friedrich, vol. 10 (Index) compiled by Ronald E. Pritikin, trans. Geoffrey W. Bromiley (Grand Rapids and London: William B. Eerdmans Publishing Co., 1964-76), 3 (1965): 789-809.

²²   Here Thornton seems to have ceded the ground too easily to those who discard the former distinction between μετέχειν and κοινωνεῖν as consisting respectively in the two senses of sharing-in or participation mentioned above. See Thornton, *The Common Life in the Body of Christ*, pp. 449-50. One can agree with those who no longer find grounds for the distinction between the μετέχειν group and the κοινωνεῖν group and at the same time ask the further question whether or not Christian sharing-in or participation, whether expressed by μετέχειν or κοινωνεῖν, does imply sharing in the sense of each having the whole, because of the indivisible nature of what is shared. It is obvious of course that Thornton inclines toward this view but seems to have been too hesitant in affirming it, being content to state: ". . . the view that κοινωνεῖν 'implies more distinctly the idea of community with others' appears to have some support in N.T. usage . . .' (ibid., p. 450). It is not clear whom Thornton is quoting.

²³   I have already indicated that I do not find the word "fellowship" as used in American English a suitable translation of either μετοχή or κοινωνία. Thornton, who occasionally uses the term, acknowledges this difficulty. See ibid., p. 157.

²⁴   See ibid., p. 76.

²⁵   See ibid.

²⁶   Ibid.

²⁷   See ibid, pp. 158-59.

²⁸   See ibid., pp. 156-64, and Panikulam, Koinonia *in the New Testament*, p. 136.

²⁹   There is one example in Paul, however. See Philm. 1:6, where ἡ κοινωνία τῆς πιστεώς σου seems better read as an objective genitive. On this point, see Panikulam, Koinonia *in the New Testament*, p. 88.

³⁰   1 John 1:1-3.

³¹   This is clear from 1 John 2: 12-17 and such phrases as "I write to you, young men . . . because the Word of God [ὁ λόγος τοῦ θεοῦ] remains in you . . .," (1 John 2: 14).

³²   To my knowledge, the distinction between *fides quae* and *fides qua* occurs for the first time in Augustine (*De Trinitate*[*PL* 42 (1841): 819-1098], XIII. 2.5). Augustine is less clear on *fides qua* and sometimes uses it in that treatise as synonymous with motives of credibility. See ibid.

³³   See Sancti Thomae Aquinatis, *Summa Theologiae* IIª, IIᵃᶜ, q. 1, a. 2, *ad secundum*, where Aquinas maintains that believing does not end with the proposition in which the content of faith is expressed but with the reality expressed by the proposition.

³⁴   This idea is beautifully expressed in a related context by Leonardo Boff in

"Is the Distinction between *Ecclesia docens* and *Ecclesia discens* justified?," *Who Has the Say in the Church?*, Concilium, vol. 148, ed. Jürgen Moltmann and Hans Küng (Edinburgh: T. & T. Clark, and New York: Seabury Press, 1981), pp. 47-48.

[35] This fact responds, I believe, to a concern frequently expressed by non-Catholic Christians. See, for example, Karlfried Froelich, "Fallibility instead of Infallibility? A Brief History of the Interpretation of Galatians 2:11-14," in *LCD VI*, p. 269. I feel, along with Joseph Fitzmyer ("The Office of Teaching in the Christian Church According to the New Testament," in *LCD VI*, pp. 186-212, especially p. 191) that Gal. 2:11-14 has to do with Peter's conduct, not with his doctrine, and is hence inappropriately cited in the context of the infallibility debate. Nonetheless, the issue that Froelich raises is completely consistent with responsible "talking back" to the ordinary papal magisterium and to the theory of doctrinal development that I shall attempt to sustain.

[36] "H. Schauf . . . critical of Rahner, suggests a solution [to the problem of the relation between episcopacy and primacy] based on the biblical idea of multiple witnesses and is thus closer to a theology of 'word' and an interpretation that I also favor. Yet I would like to point out, against Schauf, that besides his notion, and indeed prior to it, the development of the question from the notion of *communio* is possible and justified. The question has two aspects, which, *in accordance with the dual structure of the Church arising from sacrament and word*, do not exclude each other" (Karl Rahner and Joseph Ratzinger, *The Episcopate and the Primacy*, p. 45, n. 16, emphasis mine). My findings, if correct, suggest that any opposition between κοινωνία and word is in effect a *faux problème*.

[37] Herwi Rikof writes: "*Communio* is the translation of *koinonia* and both are interchangeable. Our ultimate option for *communio* is based upon an initial understanding due to the links with terms like 'community,' 'communion,' 'communication'; *koinonia* lacks this . . . To express clearly the quintessential approach the complete basic statement should then be: *the church is the* communio *of the faithful*" (Rikof, *The Concept of Church*, p. 233). I have no fundamental quarrel with this conclusion. I simply prefer the term κοινωνία because I regard it as fundamental to everything else; e.g., that which is (or can be) κοινόν between God and humankind on the level of grace and that which is (or can be) κοινόν between Christians in regard to *fides quae*.

[38] In addition to the bibliographical data noted above, consider the following remark by Ratzinger: "Father Rahner has tried to explain this relationship between primacy and episcopacy more exactly in the light of the notion of *communio*. This remains undoubtedly the central point of the attack since the Church by her inmost nature is communio, *fellowship with and in the body of the Lord*" (Rahner and Ratzinger, *The Episcopacy and the Primacy*, p. 45, emphasis mine).

[39] See *inter alios* Dulles, *Models of the Church*, pp. 202-3.

[40] Non-Catholic Christians should not interpret this last phrase as meaning that either Marian dogma is directly attested to in the New Testament documents, and in the case of the Assumption, in the early patristic period. It would be interesting to respond to Richard Boeckler's criticism in this regard (see his *Der moderne römisch-katholische Traditionsbegriff* [Göttingen: Vandenhoeck & Ru-

precht, 1967], especially pp. 225-29), but to do so would carry me well beyond even an extended footnote.

CHAPTER VIII

[1]   Karl Rahner, "The Immaculate Conception," in *Theological Investigations*, 1: 202-3.

[2]   See MPM 52 (1927): 1215 CD.

[3]   See ibid., p. 1215 C. There is always room, however, for complementary as opposed to contradictory pluralism. Some thought must be given to what the equivalent of the Nicene-Constantinopolitan Creed would sound like if the Christian kerygma had gone toward India before it went toward Greece. See the glossary under the heading *Philosophico-Cultural Limits of a Definition*.

[4]   *Pareri dell'Episcopato cattolico, di Capitoli, di Congregazioni, di Università, di Personaggi ragguardevoli*, 11 vols. (Rome: coi tipi della Civiltà Cattolica, 1851-54).

[5]   *Beata Virgo Maria in suo conceptu Immaculata ex monumentis omnium seculorum* (sic) *demonstrata*, ed. Augustine de Roskovány, 9 vols. (Budapest: Typis Athenaei, 1873-81).

[6]   *La Solenne Definizione del Dogma dell'Immaculato Concepimento*, ed. Vincenzo Sardi, 2 vols., Atti e Documenti pubblicati nel cinquantesimo anniversario della stessa definizione (Rome: Tipografia Vaticana, 1904).

[7]   See ibid., 1: 571-74.

[8]   See ibid., pp. 571-72.

[9]   See ibid., p. 572.

[10]   See ibid.

[11]   "Quamobrem has vobis, Venerabiles Fratres, scribimus Litteras, quibus egregiam vestram pietatem atque episcopalem sollicitudinem magnopere excitamus, Vobisque etiam atque etiam inculcamus, ut quisque vestrum pro suo arbitrio atque prudentia in propria Diocesi publicas preces indicendas, ac peragendas curet, quo clementissimus luminum Pater nos superna divini sui Spiritus luce perfundere . . . dignetur . . ." (Pius IX, "Ubi primum," in Sardi, *La Solenne Definizione*, 1: 573.)

[12]   "Optamus autem vehementer, ut maiore qua fieri potest celeritate Nobis significare velitis, qua devotione vester Clerus, Populusque fidelis erga Immaculatam Virginis Conceptionem sit animatus, et quo desiderio flagret, ut eiusmodi res ab Apostolica Sede decernatur . . ." (ibid.).

[13]   ". . . atque in primis noscere vel maxime cupimus quid Vos ipsi, Venerabiles Fratres, pro eximia vestra sapientia de re ipsa sentiatis quidque exoptetus" (ibid.).

[14]   See ibid. 2: 250-52.

[15]   See Jean-Joseph Laborde, *De la Croyance à l'Immaculée Conception de la Sainte Vierge* (Toulouse: Privat, 1851).

[16]   "I. La doctrine de l'Eglise est ce qui, ayant été enseigné par Jésus-Christ ou inspiré par le Saint-Esprit aux Apôtres, a été prêché par les mêmes Apôtres, et est

venu d'eux jusqu'à nous par une tradition de main en main" (Sardi, *La Solenne Definizione*, 2: 250).

[17] "II. L'Eglise ne fait point de nouveaux dogmes de foi" (ibid.).

[18] "III. C'est un péché d'annoncer de nouveaux dogmes; c'est un péché d'en recevoir . . ." (ibid.).

[19] "VI. La doctrine de l'Immaculée Conception ne vient pas de Jésus-Christ et des Apôtres par le Canal de la Tradition" (ibid., p. 251).

[20] "VII. Dans tout ce qui s'est fait jusqu'ici pour parvenir à ériger l'opinion de l'immaculée conception (*sic*) en dogme de foi, les règles canoniques n'ont pas été observées" (ibid.).

[21] "X. Un grand nombre d'évêques ont répondu que le Clergé et les fidèles de leur diocèse se réunissaient à eux pour exprimer à N.S.P. le Pape le voeu, que la question fut [*sic*] définie; tandisque, par le fait, ni le Clergé ni les fidèles n'avaient été consultés; tandisque qu'il y avait des fidèles instruits et des prêtres recommandables qui repoussaient l'Immaculée Conception, même comme opinion. Il y a eu pression morale et même violence, pour empêcher ceux-ci de manifester leur sentiment" (ibid.).

[22] See *P* 2: 26-46, 3: 310-11, and 3: 338, respectively.

[23] See ibid. 7: 337-43.

[24] See ibid., p. 319-35.

[25] See ibid., p. 320.

[26] See ibid.

[27] Recall however the nuance flowing from the internal logic of Gasser's explicit statements and their relation to the maximalist position embraced by Paul Nau. See above, pp. 38 and 376, n.63

[28] See *P* 7: 321.

[29] See ibid., p. 326.

[30] See ibid.

[31] See ibid., p. 327.

[32] See ibid.

[33] See ibid.

[34] See ibid., p. 329.

[35] See ibid., pp. 330-35.

[36] "Et ego ipse, Sanctissime Pater, ut theologi consultores, arbitror ex huiusmodi decreti promulgatione gravissima incommoda et magnas forsitan Ecclesiae calamitates orituras esse.

"Et ego ipse, cum eis censeo nec Ecclesiae nec Sanctae Sedis [*sic*] licere in ullo casu doctrinam de Immaculata Conceptione *inter Articulos fidei seu fidei Catholicae veritates* enumerare.

"Imo, Sanctissime Pater, longius quam dicti theologi progrediens, dubito an possit Ecclesia vel Sancta Sedes solemni decreto statuere doctrinam hanc esse *certam* et ab omnibus sub peccati mortalis et aeternae damnationis poena amplectendam" (ibid. 2: 27).

[37] "Nonne magno animarum numero, absque compensatione ulla in ruinam vertetur quaestionis decisio?" (ibid., p. 44).

[38]   "Incessanter nobis proferuntur quasi definitiva ratio fidelium vota, quibus exoptant piam immaculatae Conceptionis opinionem inter fidei dogmata, vel saltem inter veritates quae ut certae definitae sunt annumerari [sic].

"Veritatis limites excedunt, Beatissime Pater, qui ista iactitant. Imo nullam fere definitionis curam habere nobis videntur fideles; *satis est illis devotas ad immaculatam Virginem preces effundere*, si qua in fidem propensiores piae animae votum illud emiserunt procul dubio numero paucissimae sunt. Sint tamen, si libet, respectu incredulorum, haereticorum, aut indifferentium quasi unum, non pro mille, dixerim sed pro centum; nihil proficiet ex illa definitione, huius fidelis animae pietas aut fides, dum centum illis incredulis, haereticis, indifferentibus, ut modo dictum est, in perniciem vertetur" (ibid., emphasis mine).

[39]   This was the letter of July 26, 1850. See ibid. 3: 310-11.

[40]   "Numquid unquam Ecclesia doctrinae punctum quodlibet, ex frigido ut ita dicam, nulla fervente controversia, nulla urgenti necessitate, et, uno verbo dicam, sola definiendi voluptate?" (ibid. 2: 29-30). The sentence as found in the *Pareri* is elliptical.

[41]   "Si piam hanc opinionem solemni decreto definierit Sanctitas Vestra, privatum de definibilitate quaestionis iudicium reformabimus, vocem nostram cum Orbis Catholici voce coniungentes, et ex corde clamantes: Petrus per Pium IX locutus est" (ibid., p. 46).

[42]   See Sardi, *La Solenne Definizione*, 1: 631-70.

[43]   See ibid., pp. 632-33.

[44]   See ibid., p. 633.

[45]   See ibid., p. 635.

[46]   "D'où l'on conclue qu'une opinion qui n'a sa racine ni dans l'Ecriture ni dans la tradition primitive, mais qui ne repose que sur une pieuse croyance n'est pas susceptible de recevoir la sanction d'une définition dogmatique" (ibid.).

[47]   See ibid., p. 637.

[48]   See ibid., p. 638.

[49]   "Omnes homines, excepto illo qui de Virgine natus est, Sanctissima etiam Virgine, ex qua Deus homo prodiit in mundum, excepta, cum peccato originali nascimur . . ." (ibid., p. 639).

[50]   "Excepta sancta Virgine Maria, de qua propter honorem Domini, nullam prorsus, cum de peccatis agitur, haberi volo quaestionem; inde enim scimus, quod ei plus gratiae collatum fuerit ad vincendum ex omni parte peccatum, quae concipere ac parere meruit quem constat nullum habuisse peccatum" (ibid.).

[51]   See ibid., p. 640.

[52]   See ibid.

[53]   See ibid., pp. 643-45.

[54]   See ibid., pp. 645-46.

[55]   See ibid., p. 647.

[56]   See ibid., p. 651.

[57]   See ibid., p. 653.

[58]   See ibid.

[59]   See ibid., p. 654.

60 See ibid.
61 See ibid.
62 See ibid., p. 655.
63 See ibid.
64 See ibid., p. 656.
65 See ibid.
66 See ibid.
67 See ibid.
68 See ibid., pp. 656-57.
69 See ibid., p. 657.
70 See ibid.
71 See ibid., p. 660
72 See ibid., p. 664.
73 "Evêque le plus ancien de la·chrétienté, dévoué plus que tout autre comme membre du Sacré Collège, aux intérêts de la Sainte Eglise et au culte de Marie qui en est la plus puissante protectrice, ce sera pour notre grand âge et notre long Episcopat, un couronnement qui nous comblera de joie, ainsi que notre clergé et tous nos fidèles diocésains" (ibid., p. 665).
74 ". . . la croyance en cette doctrine est aujourd'hui plus profondément enracinée dans les coeurs" (ibid., p. 665).
75 "Seen and after serious study approved in its entirety. Arras, May 12, 1849. Charles Cardinal de la Tour d'Auvergne. Lauraguais, Bishop at Arras" (ibid., p. 670).
76 See *P* 3: 310.
77 See X. Le Bachelet, "L'Immaculée Conception," *DTC* 7 (1927): 1198.
78 See ibid.
79 "Opportunum haud censeo, quaestionem de immaculata Conceptione moderno tempore pertractare; nam (a) *nullus catholicorum illam oppugnat*; *quin imo nullo tempore tam generatim recepta fuit, quam seculo* [*sic*] *nostro*. (b) Quia multi protestantium, per desideratissimum nobis et sanctum Pontificem Pium IX Pontificatui reconciliati, ad priora reverterentur, nec quidquam eos magis repellendo esset, quam imponenda obligatio, vi cuius piam fidem immaculatae conceptionis non amplius instar opinionis considerare liceret" (*Beata Virgo Maria*, 4: 915-16, emphasis mine).
80 "Non puto textus S. Scripturae satis praecisos, nec linguam traditionis satis explicitam esse, aut per decursum seculorum [*sic*] sibi sufficienter constare, ut haec opinio, *quantumvis certa mihi videatur*—tanquam fidei dogma proponatur. Regulae, ab omnibus Theologis stabilitae, huic intentioni adversari videntur" (ibid., p. 916, emphasis mine).
81 See the detailed bibliography in Edward Dennis O'Connor, *The Dogma of the Immaculate Conception: History and Significance* (Notre Dame: University of Notre Dame Press, 1958), pp. 537, 544-45, 560-62, 571-74, 585-89 and 596-97.
82 That is to say: There is no evidence to suggest that belief in this doctrine began to take root in the Catholic Church because of prior action on the part of the Roman Bishops.

[83]   See Pius XII, *Deiparae Virginis* in AAS 42 (1950): 782-83.

[84]   See *Petitiones de Assumptione Corporea B.V. Mariae in Caelum Definienda ad Sanctam Sedem Delatae*, eds. G[uilhelmus] Hentrich and R[udolfus] G[ualterus] De Moos, 2 vols. (Rome: Typis Polyglottis Vaticanis, 1942).

[85]   HD, 1: 649.

[86]   HD, 2: 880.

[87]   "Quare et nos Cardinales, Archiepiscopi, Episcopi omnium Austriae Imperii partium pro nostra et populorum nostrorum erga benedictam Dei Matrem ac Matrem nostram devotione, ad pedes Sanctitatis Vestrae humillime provoluti supplicamus et perardenter postulamus, ut Sanctitas Vestra pro suprema qua in Ecclesia Christi pollet, infallibilis magisterii auctoritate, solemni iudicio ad maiorem Dei Filii atque Deiparae gloriam, ad ineffabilem omnium Christifidelium consolationem declarare ac definire velit et dignetur: Doctrinam, quae tenet Deiparam anima et corpore in coelis adesse gloriose viventem, esse a Deo revelatam ac proinde ab omnibus fidelibus firmiter constanterque tenendam" (HD, 1: 188).

[88]   The Pope is addressed in the second person plural while the corresponding verb is in the third person singular.

[89]   "Bernardus I. *Otten* in libro qui inscribitur '*Institutiones Dogmaticae*, Tomus III: De Verbo Incarnato' (Chicago, Illinois, 1922), affirmat p. 412, no. 533: 'Paucis abhinc annis episcopi Americae Septentrionalis Papam suppliciter rogaverunt, ut vellet hanc doctrinam (scl. Assumptionis B.V. Mariae) demum definire.' Cum neque in tabulariis S.O. neque aliis in fontibus quidquam de tali postulato collectivo reperiri potuerit, in hoc libro ab eo abstrahitur" (ibid., p. 968).

[90]   ". . . constat Residentiales Patriarchas, Archiepiscopos, Episcopos omnium nationum et omnium Sedum [sic] per orbem dispersos 'moraliter' concordes tanquam Magistros authenticos Ecclesiae docere: doctrinam, quae tenet B.V. Mariam anima et corpore in Caelum esse assumptam, esse a Deo revelatam ideoque tamquam dogma fidei divinae definiri posse: simulque eos cum eadem concordia declarare . . . hanc definitionem esse opportunam" (ibid., pp. xxi-xxii).

[91]   Ibid., p. xxiii.

[92]   See Martin Jugie, *La Mort et l'Assomption de la Sainte Vierge: étude historico-doctrinale* (Vatican City: Biblioteca Apostolica Vaticana, 1944). Lonergan stated: "This monumental work is an invaluable source of historical information. However, the author's scholarship is frequently put to the service of theological opinions of little or no probability. The latter tendency in the work unfortunately has led to not a little obscuration of its great merit and utility" (Bernard J.F. Lonergan, "The Assumption and Theology," in *Vers le Dogme de l'Assomption* [Montreal, São Paulo, Paris, South Bend: Fides Publishers, 1948], p. 411, n. 1). Lonergan was to argue that the doctrine could be defined because it was implicitly revealed: "The Assumption of our Lady to heaven could be defined as a dogma of divine and Catholic faith. Though not explicitly revealed in Holy Scripture nor as far as we know with certitude, in any explicit, oral apostolic tradition, still it is revealed implicitly. That implication is grasped as human understanding, illumined by faith and aided by grace, penetrates the economy of man's Fall and Redemption and settles our Lady's place in it" (ibid., p. 424).

93 See Jugie, *La Mort et l'Assomption*, p. 471, n. 1.
94 See ibid., p. 596.
95 See F. S. Mueller, "Petitiones de Assumptione corporea B.V. Mariae in caelum definienda," *Gregorianum* 27 (1946): 110-35.
96 See ibid.
97 See Jugie, *La Mort et l'Assomption*, p. 599.
98 See ibid., p. 600.
99 See Mueller, "Petitiones," p. 130.
100 See Guilhelmus Hentrich, "De Definibilitate Assumptionis B.M.V.," *Marianum* 11 (1949): 259-311.
101 See ibid., p. 277.
102 See ibid., pp. 302-3.
103 See ibid.
104 See ibid., pp. 300-1.
105 See ibid., p. 301.
106 See ibid..
107 The reader will however find much information in the work of Clément Dillenschneider, *Le Sens de la foi et le progrès dogmatique du mystère marial* (Rome: Academia Mariana Internationalis, 1954).
108 See Jugie, *La Mort et l'Assomption*, pp. 623-24.
109 See ibid., pp. 608-9.
110 See ibid., pp. 595-600.
111 See ibid., p. 624.
112 See ibid., p. 639.
113 See Berthold Altaner, "Zur Frage der Definibilität der Assumptio B.M.V. [I], "*Theologische Revue* 45 (1949): 129-42, and "Zur Frage der Definibilität der Assumptio B.M.V. [II]," *Theologische Revue* 46 (1950): 5-20.
114 See Altaner, "Zur Frage der Definibilität der Assumptio B.M.V. [I]," p. 138.
115 See Hentrich, "De Definibilitate Assumptionis B.M.V.," p. 299.
116 See Altaner, "Zur Frage der Definibilität der Assumptio B.M.V. [I]," p. 139.
117 See ibid.
118 See Jugie, *La Mort et l'Assomption*, p. 595.
119 See Altaner, "Zur Frage der Definibilität der Assumptio B.M.V. [II]," p. 15.
120 See ibid.
121 See ibid., p. 16.
122 See ibid.
123 See ibid., p. 18.
124 See ibid.
125 See ibid.
126 See ibid.
127 See ibid., pp. 10-11.
128 See ibid., p. 11.
129 See ibid.
130 See ibid., p. 20.
131 See ibid., p. 19.

[132] See ibid., p. 13.

[133] See ibid.

[134] See ibid., p. 14.

[135] See ibid., p. 13.

[136] See Altaner, "Zur Frage der Definibilität der Assumptio B.M.V. [I]," p. 132.

[137] See Jugie, La Mort et l'Assomption.

[138] See Altaner, "Zur Frage der Definibilität der Assumptio B.M.V. [I]," p. 134.

[139] See Jugie, La Mort et l'Assomption, p. 74.

[140] See Altaner, "Zur Frage der Definibilität der Assumptio B.M.V. [I]," p. 135.

[141] See ibid.

[142] See Fulbert Cayré, "L'Assomption aux quatre premiers siècles: état embryonnaire de la doctrine," in Vers le Dogme de l'Assomption (Montreal, São Paulo, Paris, South Bend: Fides Publishers, 1948), pp. 123-49.

[143] See ibid., pp. 125-26.

[144] See ibid., pp. 128 and 131-32.

[145] This, for Cayré, may have been suggested by the Pauline corpus taken as a whole. See ibid., p. 132.

[146] Ibid., p. 143.

[147] Ibid., p. 143.

[148] Ibid., p. 144.

[149] Ibid.

[150] Ibid., p. 153 (emphasis and interpolation mine).

[151] Ibid., p. 146.

[152] See Cayré, "L'Assomption aux quatre premiers siècles," p. 149.

[153] See Lonergan, "The Assumption and Theology," pp. 411-24, especially p. 424.

[154] See J. Bellamy, "Assomption de la Sainte Vierge," in DTC 1 (1909): 2139-40.

[155] See J. Demahuet, "Assomption," in Catholicisme: Hier, Aujourd'hui, Demain 1 (1948): 951.

[156] See Pius XII, Deiparae Virginis in AAS 42 (1950): 782-83.

[157] See Pius XII, Munificentissimus Deus in AAS 42 (1950): 753-71. English translation by the National Catholic Welfare Conference (Boston: Daughters of St. Paul, n.d.). The statement relative to the results of the survey appears on p. 7 of the English translation.

[158] See Guilhelmus Hentrich, "Alla vigilia della definizione dogmatica dell'Assunzione corporea di Maria Santissima," in Osservatore romano 90 (16-17 agosto 1950), no. 191, p. 1.

[159] ". . . Romanum Pontificem, cum ex cathedra loquitur, id est, cum omnium Christianorum pastoris et doctoris munere fungens pro suprema sua Apostolica auctoritate doctrinam de fide vel moribus ab universa Ecclesia tenendam definit, per assistentiam divinam ipsi in beato Petro promissam, ea infallibilitate pollere, qua divinus Redemptor Ecclesiam suam in definienda doctrina de fide vel moribus instructam esse voluit; ideoque eiusmodi Romani Pontificis definitiones ex sese, non autem ex consensu Ecclesiae, irreformabiles esse" (DS, no. 3074).

[160] See Sardi, La Solenne Definizione, 2: 561-625.

[161] See Beato Virgo Maria, 6: 107-23.

[162] For Pie, see MPM (1927) 52: 36D; for Guidi, see ibid., p. 742CD.

[163] See the Introduction, pp. 38 and 376, n.63.

[164] "Hanc cooperationem ecclesiae tum ideo non excludimus, quia infallibilitas pontificis Romani non per modum inspirationis vel revelationis, sed per' modum divinae assistentiae ipsi obvenit. Hinc papa pro officio suo et rei gravitate tenetur media apta adhibere ad veritatem rite indagandam et apte enuntiandam; eiusmodi media sunt concilia vel etiam consilia episcoporum, cardinalium, theologorum etc. Haec media pro diversitate rerum utique sunt diversa, et pie debemus credere quod in divina assistentia Petro et successoribus eius a Christo Domino facta, simul etiam contineatur promissio mediorum, quae necessaria aptaque sunt ad affirmandum infallibile pontificis iudicium" (MPM 52 [1927]: 1213D).

[165] "Sed nonnulli ex reverendissimis patribus . . . ulterius progrediuntur, et volunt etiam in hanc constitutionem dogmaticam inducere conditiones, quae in tractatibus theologicis diversae in diversis inveniuntur, et quae bonam fidem et diligentiam pontificis in vertitate indaganda et enuntianda concernunt; quae proinde, cum non relationem Pontificis, sed conscientiam ipsius ligent, *ordini potius morali quam dogmatico accensendae sunt*. Piissime enim Dominus noster Iesus Christus charisma veritatis non a conscientia pontificis, quae est uniuscuiusque res privata immo privatissma, soli Deo cognita, sed a relatione pontificis publica ad universalem ecclesiam dependens voluit . . ." (ibid., p. 1214CD, emphasis mine).

[166] "Sed ideo nil timendum, ac si per malam fidem et negligentiam pontificis universalis ecclesia in errorem circa fidem induci posset. Nam tutela Christi et assistentia divina Petri successoribus promissa est causa ita efficax, ut iudicium summi pontificis, si esset erroneum et ecclesiae destructivum, impediretur; aut, si reapse pontifex ad definitionem deveniat, illa infallibiliter vera existat" (ibid., p. 1214D).

[167] "Antequam ad hanc obiectionem respondeam, meminisse iuvat agi hic in sententia adversariorum de stricta et absoluta necessitate consilii et auxilii episcoporum in quovis infallibili iudicio dogmatico Romani pontificis, ita ut in ipsa definitione nostrae dogmaticae constitutionis suum locum occupare debeat. *In hac stricta et absoluta necessitate consistit tota differentia quae inter nos versatur, et non in opportunitate* aut aliqua relativa necessitate, quae iudicio Romani pontificis rerum circumstantias ponderantis prorsus remittenda est. Haec proinde in definitione constitutionis dogmaticae locum habere non potest" (ibid., p. 1215CD, emphasis mine).

[168] "But they [the opposition] still insist and say: Whatever the case may be about those human means, the help of the Church, the assent of the Church, that is the witness and advice of the bishops not only may not be excluded from the definition of infallibility but should [*debet*] in the definition itself be put among the conditions which are of faith . . ." [Sed adhuc instant et dicunt: quidquid sit de illis mediis humanis, auxilium ecclesiae, assensus ecclesiae, id est testimonium et consilium episcoporum non solummodo non potest excludi a definitione infallibilitatis, sed debet inter conditiones quae sunt de fide in ipsa definitione poni] (ibid., p. 1215BC).

[169] See the suggestion by Canon Maier of Ratisbon (ibid., 53 [1927]: 238C).

[170]   See ibid.

[171]   "I gallicani, e specialmente monsignor Maret ammettono, che le definizioni dei papi sono infallibili se vi è il consenso dei vescovi o antecedente, o concomittante, o sussequente. Per ferire direttament tale errore e necessario mettere nella definizione la contradittoria . . .

"Quindi anche a sentimento di monsignor Freppel, e di alcuni altri buoni vescovi Francesi sarebbe necessario fare alla formola una piccola aggiunta, che sarebbe la seguente, cioè; *ideoque eiusmodi Romani pontificis definitiones esse ex sese irreformabiles, quin sit necessarius consensus episcorporum sive antecedens, sive concomitans, sive subsequens . . .*" (MPM 52 [1927]: 1262BC).

[172]   The editors of MPM state that on this letter was written in Pius IX's handwriting: "Let Cardinal Bilio read the observations all together [*unite*] and see to it that they are used . . ." [Il card. Bilio legga le unite osservazioni e procuri di farne uso . . .] (ibid., p. 1262C).

[173]   See above, Text E, p. 338.

[174]   Like the view expressed by Gasser, that by Guidi as well reflected the perspective of the majority: "The Roman Pontiff in defining questions of faith or morals may be said and understood to be dependent in another way on the Church or if you will on the advice and cooperation of the bishops in that he ascertains from them what the sense of the universal Church is, what tradition about the controverted truth is contained in the local and distant churches . . . In one word, the Pontiff must [*debet*] before he expresses his supreme and decisive [*decretorium*] judgment have information from the Church, to know what is the faith of the daughter churches; whether it agrees with the Roman Church, which is the mother, teacher, and head of all . . ." [Alio modo dependens ab ecclesia, seu ab episcoporum consilio aut cooperatione Romanus pontifex in definiendis fidei et morum quaestionibus dici et intelligi potest ita, ut ab eis resciat quinam universalis ecclesiae sit sensus, quaenam traditio in ecclesiis particularibus dissitisque contineatur de controversa veritate . . . Uno verbo debet pontifex antequam iudicium suum supremum et decretorium proferat, ecclesiae, ut aiunt, informationes habere, ecclesiarum filiarum scire quae sit fides; an cum sua Romana ecclesia, quae est omnium mater et magistra et caput, concordet] (ibid., p. 742CD). Guidi then went on to add that what is believed in Rome and everywhere, and at all times, must be believed by all. See ibid., p. 742D.

[175]   See ibid., p. 1213C.

[176]   ". . . non separamus pontificem ab ordinatissima coniunctione cum ecclesia" (ibid., p. 1213B).

[177]   "Non separamus porro papam infallibiliter definientem a cooperatione et concursu ecclesiae, saltem id est in eo sensu, quod hanc cooperationem et hunc concursum ecclesiae non excludimus" (ibid., p. 1213C).

[178]   Besides Cardinal Guidi's speech given on June 18, 1870 (see ibid., pp. 740-42), see among others that by Bishop Pie given the previous May 13 (see ibid., pp. 29-38).

[179]   See John T. Ford, "Infallibility: Who Won the Debate?," *Catholic Theological Society of America: Proceedings* 31 (1976): 179-92.

[180] "The . . . body of the faithful . . . cannot err in matters of belief" (AG, p. 29).
[181] See Karl Barth, *Die kirchliche Dogmatik*, 4 vols, 13 tomes (Munich: C. Kaiser, 1932-67), I, pt. 2: 634.
[182] See Troeltsch, "Kirche III: Dogmatisch," in *Religion in Geschichte und Gegenwart*, 3 (1912): 1151. For a Catholic view, see W[illem] H[endrick] van de Pol, *The Christian Dilemma: Catholic Church—Reformation*, trans. G. Van Hall (New York: The Philosophical Library, 1952), pp. 285-93. Areas of interconfessional dispute have narrowed significantly in this regard. See Lutherans and Catholics in Dialogue VII, *Justification by Faith*, ed. H. George Anderson, T. Austin Murphy, and Joseph A. Burgess (Minneapolis: Augsburg Publishing House, 1985), pp. 58-74.

CHAPTER IX

[1] Froelich, "Fallibility instead of Infallibility?," p. 269.
[2] For my meaning of the term, see the Introduction, p. 44.
[3] See Otto Semmelroth, "Uberlieferung als Lebensfunktion der Kirche," *Stimmen der Zeit* 148 (1950-51): 1-11; Joseph Ternus, "Vom Gemeinschaftsglauben der Kirche," *Scholastik* 10 (1935): 1-30, and "Beiträge zum Problem der Tradition," *Divus Thomas* (Freiburg) 16 (1938): 35-56 and 197-299; Heinrich Bacht, "Tradition als menschliches und theologisches Problem," *Stimmen der Zeit* 159 (1956-57): 285-300; and "Tradition und Lehramt um das Assumpta-Dogma," in *Die mündliche Uberlieferung: Beiträge zum Begriff der Tradition*, ed. Michael Schmaus (Munich: Max Hueber Verlag, 1957), especially pp. 60-61; Clément Dillenschneider, *Le Sens de la foi et le progrès dogmatique du mystère marial*; J[ames] P. Mackey, *The Modern Theology of Tradition* (New York: Herder & Herder, 1963), pp. 200-5; Gustave Thils, *L'Infaillibilité du peuple chrétien "in credendo,"* (Paris: Desclée de Brouwer, and Louvain: E. Warny, 1963), pp. 54-55.
[4] I have borrowed this distinction from a recent publication by Avery Dulles. See his *A Church To Believe In: Discipleship and the Dynamics of Freedom* (New York: Crossroads, 1982), pp. 118-32.
[5] See, for example. Josef Rupert Geiselmann, *The Meaning of Tradition*, trans. W.J. O'Hara (Freiburg, Herder, and London: Burns & Oates, 1966), p. 22; and Michael Schmaus, *Katholische Dogmatik*, 4 vols., 7 tomes (Munich: Max Hueber Verlag, 1958), 3, pt. 1: 779-80; and much earlier Matthias Joseph Scheeben, *Gesammelte Schriften*, 8 vols., 9 tomes (Freiburg im Breisgau: Verlag Herder, 1948-1967) 3 (1948): 98-99. Vol. 3 of this collection is Vol. 1 of the *Handbuch der katholischen Dogmatik* edited by Martin Grabmann. It had originally appeared in three parts between 1873 and 1875.
[6] See "*Lumen gentium*" and "*Dei Verbum*," AG, pp. 20-30 and 116, respectively.
[7] My conclusions in this regard were reached independently of Leonardo Boff's in the article cited above. Boff states: "We need a two-track way, from the

learners to the teachers as well as from the teachers to the learners" (Boff, "Is the Distinction between *Ecclesia docens* and *Ecclesia discens* justified?" p. 51). He then goes on to mention three rules that must be observed in order for this to work: (1) open dialogue on both sides; (2) an attitude of mutual criticism; and (3) a point of reference "outside ourselves" (see ibid.). While I fully concur with this, there is, I believe, a fourth value that Boff does not deny but in my judgment should be equally highlighted: "*No matter how much the Church stands in need of reformation (and it always will be to some extent), separation from the body of the Church is never an acceptable means of reform.* Reformation must always take place within the Body of the Church; one must suffer the injustice, the pride, the narrow-mindedness, while expending every effort to make the Church be truly a community of love. Even if the Church should excommunicate a reformer for his efforts, his faith, if it is Catholic, will not allow him to acquiesce in that situation. He will do everything he can, accepting injustice and misunderstanding if necessary, to be restored to visible unity with the Body of Christ. He will consider this a redemptive price for the healing of the Church, and will trust to the power of the Holy Spirit for ultimate vindication" (John H. Wright, "The Meaning and Structure of Catholic Faith," *Theological Studies* 39 [1978]: 710, emphasis mine). By his conduct subsequent to his having been criticized, indeed "punished" by the Roman authorities, Boff has shown where his true sentiments lie.

[8]   AG, pp. 116-17, emphasis mine. The Latin reads ". . . soli vivo Ecclesiae Magisterio . . . ," *CDD*, pp. 431-32.

[9]   "*Lumen gentium*," AG. p. 31.

[10]   Perhaps my findings may contribute to the efforts of those who in the postconciliar period have worked to clarify the relation between the laity and the hierarchical magisterium (see B. Sesboüé, "Autorité du magistère et vie de foi ecclésiale," *Nouvelle Revue théologique* 93 [1971]: 337-62, especially pp. 357-59; Heinrich Bacht, "Vom Lehramt der Kirche und in der Kirche," *Catholica* 25 [1971]: 144-67, especially pp. 149-50; J[ean]-M[arie]-R[oger] Tillard, "A propos du *sensus fidelium*," *Proche-Orient chrétien* 25 [1975]: 115-34; and Antonio Cañizares Llovera, "El Magisterio de la Iglesia," *Iglesia viva* 79 [1979]: 357-75, especially pp. 366-68); that between the theological and hierarchical magisteria (see A.L. Descampes, "Théologie et magistère," *Ephemerides Theologicae Lovanienses* 52 [1976]: 82-133; Robert Coffy, "Magisterium and Theology," *Irish Theological Quarterly* 43 [1976]: 247-59; and Cahal B. Daly, "Theologians and the Magisterium" in *Who Has the Say in the Church:*, Concilium, vol. 148, ed. Jürgen Moltmann and Hans Küng [Edinburgh: T. & T. Clark, and New York: Seabury Press, 1981], pp. 225-45; Dulles, *A Church To Believe In*, pp. 118-32; and Gabriel Daly, "Which Magisterium Is Authentic?", in *Who Has the Say in the Church*," pp. 52-55); the extent to which Catholicism can and should integrate the notion of reception into its theologizing (see Bacht, "Tradition und Lehramt und das Assumpta-Dogma"; Yves Congar, "La 'Réception' comme réalité ecclésiologique." *Revue des sciences philosophiques et théologiques* 56 [1972]: 369-401; Franz Wolfinger, "Die Rezeption theologischer Einsichten und ihre theologische und ökumenische Bedeutung: von der Einsicht zur Verwirklichung," *Catholica* 3

[1977]: 202-33; and Miguel M.ᵃ Garijo Guembe, "El concepto de 'recepción' y su enmarque en el seno de la Eclesiología católica," *Lumen* 29 [1980]: 311-31).

¹¹ "*Lumen gèntium*," AG, p. 48. Austin Flannery translated this phrase as follows: "... when ... they are in agreement that a particular teaching is tó be held definitely *and absolutely*." See Austin Flannery, gen. ed., *Vatican II: The Conciliar and Post-Conciliar Documents* (Wilmington, Del.: Scholarly Resources Inc., 1975), p. 379, emphasis mine. While Flannery's rendition is a better expression of Catholic belief in this regard, it states more than the text of *Lumen gentium* states.

¹² "Porro fide divina et catholica ea omnia credenda sunt, quae in verbo Dei scripto vel tradito continentur et ab Ecclesia sive solemni iudicio sive ordinario et universali magisterio tamquam divinitus revelata credenda proponuntur" (DS, no. 3011).

¹³ Pius IX, *Tuas libenter*, DS, no. 2897.

¹⁴ See Roger Aubert, *Le Problème de l'acte de foi* (Louvain: E. Warny and Publications Universitaires, 1950), p. 187.

¹⁵ See the report on *LG*-b: "For the words '*in revelata fide tradenda*' ... have been put the words '*res fidei et morum docentes*' lest the infallibility of the body of bishops seem to be limited only to those matters which are proposed by the same [body] as divinely revealed" [Pro verbis "in revelata fide tradenda" ... ponuntur verba "*res fidei et morum* docentes," ne videatur infallibilitas corporis episcopalis coarctari tantum ad ea quae ab eodem ụt divinitus revelata credenda proponuntur]' (*Acta Syn* 3, pt. 1: 251). For the identification of *LG*-b, see above, p. 216.

¹⁶ See Salaverri, *De Ecclesia Christi* in *Sacrae Theologiae Summa* 1 (1952): 659 (no. 543). According to the conciliar records Salaverri was not a member of the subcommittee responsible for this section of the draft. It is difficult to believe, however, that his book was not consulted by Carlo Colombo and Umberto Betti who constituted the subcommittee. See *Acta Syn* 3, pt. 1: 269-70.

¹⁷ See pp. 31-38.

¹⁸ I must therefore disagree with Francis Sullivan in this respect. See Francis A. Sullivan, *Magisterium: Teaching Authority in the Catholic Church* (New York and Ramsey: Paulist Press, 1983), p. 125.

¹⁹ The manner in which Gerard Philips translated the relevant phrases removes the ambiguity. His translation reads in part: "... lọrsque les évêques ... s'accordent pour enseigner authentiquement qu'une doctrine concernant la foi et les moeurs s'impose *de manière absolue* . . ." Philips' *L'Eglise et son mystère*, 1:324-25, emphasis mine). Philips' translation suggests how he himself and perhaps a number of the Committee understood the troublesome phrase. There is no evidence, however, as I have pointed out below, that the Council Fathers themselves, who were more concerned with the issue of collegiality as such, had thought the matter through. In any case, the only text of reference is the promulgated Latin text.

²⁰ I have come upon no manual of theology published from the time of the Syllabus that had an *imprimatur* and that also maintained a position at variance with the official papal doctrine. But this does not mean that individuals did not argue against it. See, for example, Ernest Naville, *L'Eglise de Rome et la liberté des cultes* (Geneva: A. Cherbuliez et Cie and Paris: G. Fischbacher, 1878), pp. 25-9,

29-32, 32-39. In this long pamphlet of ninety-eight pages, a discourse given in Geneva on December 20, 1877, the author, as far as his conclusions were concerned, anticipated the position which John Courtney Murray was later to champion. Nor is it a question of whether a particular bishop here and there may have been somewhat more tolerant than others. The state of the question has to do with the attitude of the *corpus episcoporum*.

21   *Lumen gentium*, AG, p. 29.

22   See Aubert, *Le Problème de l'acte de foi*, p. 186.

23   As one peruses the conciliar documents, it is clear that the vast majority of bishops did not seem to be aware of the problem and that those who were could have been counted on the fingers of one hand. I limit myself here to the Council in session. A conservative coalition consisting of Bishops de la Chanonie, Lefebvre, Grimault, and Morilleau and Abbot Prou seemed to wish to keep the more stringent formulation of the First Vatican Council (see *Acta Syn* 2, pt. 1: 317) while Francis Simons, bishop at Indore (India) seems to have been one of the very few to have sensed the issue I have raised. (See *Acta Syn* 2, pt. 1: 727.) Although his criticism of *LG*-a was reflected in the report on suggested amendments thereto (see ibid., p. 317), the Council Fathers unfortunately did not follow through with his suggestions. In attempting to solve the problem it is indeed unfortunate that Carlo [Bishop] Colombo and Umberto Betti, who seem to have been principally responsible for the reworking of the desired change (*Acta Syn* 3, pt. 1: 270) did no more than borrow a phrase from Salaverri. (See Salaverri, *De Ecclesia Christi*, p. 658 [reference here is to the second edition of 1952].) Since the Council, there seems to have been little reflection on the underlying difficulties, Umberto Betti in his commentary remaining, so it seems, as unaware of the problem then as he seems to have been during the Council itself. (See Umberto Betti, *La Dottrina sull'episcopato nel capitolo III della costituzione dommatica* Lumen gentium: *sussudio per la lettura del testo* [Rome: Città Nuova Editrice, 1968], pp. 399-402, and "Magistero episcopale e magistero pontificio nel Vaticano II," *L'Ecclesiologia dal Vaticano I al Vaticano II* [Brescia: Editrice La Scuola, 1973], pp. 206-51.)† There is, however, an occasional happy exception. See Joseph A. Komonchak, "*Humanae Vitae* and Its Reception," *Theological Studies* 39 (1978): 246.

24   Thus it has been argued that the received Catholic teaching on contraception has been infallibly proposed by the ordinary universal magisterium. See John C. Ford and Germain Grisez, "Contraception and the Infallibility of the Ordinary Magisterium," *Theological Studies* 39 (1978): 258-312. By *ordinary magisterium* the authors mean what I have called the ordinary universal magisterium. The thesis is initially plausible because from a Catholic point of view, whatever truth Text A of *Lumen gentium* contains was always true. When Text A is looked at through a microscope instead of through a telescope, however, other data become apparent. I shall limit myself here to one. Prior to Vatican II, consensus among theologians relative to the ordinary universal magisterium and the secondary object of infallibility was far from complete. (Needless to say, it is still not complete.) Compare in this regard Salaverri, *De Ecclesia Christi* (1952), pp. 662-67 and pp. 712-19 with J.

---

†   The 1984 edition (see pp. 416-17) of the former work by Betti is here verbally the same as the edition of 1968. For the bibliographical data, see below, p. 511.

M. Hervé, *Manuale Theologiae Dogmaticae*, 4 vols. (Paris: Apud Berche et Pagis [1951-53]), 1 (1952): 491-92 and pp. 499-500. Both manuals were widely used in seminary training. When compared, they attest to the ongoing uncertainty after *Dei Filius* (Text B). And though manuals were not the usual staple of the 'Roman faculties, the differences could not have been passed over unnoticed.

Hervé tended to speak of the infallibility of the magisterium in the context of truths taught as *revealed*. But neither Hervé nor Salaverri considered the thesis relative to infallibility and the secondary object to be *de fide* (nor, may I add, does Vatican II, since the Council Fathers did not intend to define anything). The upshot of the matter comes down, then, to this: Since there is no evidence that the majority of Catholic bishops proposed the doctrine of *Casti conubii* as revealed, can it reasonably be affirmed, without more data, that they intended to propose it as infallibly true *if there is evidence sufficient to suggest they may have been in doubt whether infallibility extended to the very kind of question being addressed?* Proponents of the Ford-Grisez thesis seem to be inattentive to matters of this kind. In upholding the teaching of the Roman Bishops, the majority of the Catholic bishops could have done so according to meanings (4), (5), (6), or (7) of the phrase *tamquam definitive tenendam* as described above. While the Catholic should be grateful for whatever clarity Vatican II may have produced, he should not allow it to be read back into the minds of the bishops in the thirty-three year period between *Casti conubii* and the promulgation of *Lumen gentium*. For another view critical of the Ford-Grisez thesis, but which does not locate the source of the problem in the phrase *tamquam definitive tenendam* (Text A), see Francis A. Sullivan, *Magisterium*, pp. 142-148. Grisez responded to Sullivan. See Germain Grisez, "Infallibility and Specific Moral Norms: A Review Discussion," *The Thomist* 49 (April 1985), no. 2, pp. 248-87. I have no further comment here except to say that I remain unconvinced by Grisez's argument.

25 See pp 29-39.

26 "In tanta igitur depravatarum opinionum perversitate, Nos Apostolici nostri officii probe memores, ac de sanctissima nostra religione, de sana doctrina, et animarum salute Nobis divinitus commissa, ac de ipsius humanae societatis bono maxime solliciti, Apostolicam Nostram vocem iterum extollere existimavimus. Itaque omnes et singulas pravas opiniones ac doctrinas singillatim hisce Litteris commemoratas auctoritate Nostra Apostolica reprobamus, proscribimus atque damnamus, easque ab omnibus catholicae Ecclesiae filiis, veluti reprobatas, proscriptas atque damnatas omnino haberi volumus et mandamus" (*Quanta cura*, PIXA 3: 695).

27 ". . . auctoritate Domini nostri Iesu Christi, beatorum Apostolorum Petri et Pauli ac Nostra declaramus, pronuntiamus et definimus, *doctrinam*, quae tenet, beatissimam Virginem Mariam in primo instanti suae conceptionis fuisse singulari omnipotentis Dei gratia et privilegio, intuitu meritorum Christi Iesu Salvatoris humani generis, ab omni originalis culpae labe praeservatam immunem, esse *a Deo revelatam atque idcirco ab omnibus fidelibus firmiter constanterque credendam"* (DS, no. 2803, emphasis mine).

28 "*Quapropter, si qui secus ac a Nobis definitum est, quod Deus avertat, praesumpserint corde sentire, ii noverint, ac porro sciant, se proprio iudicio*

condemnatos, naufragium circa fidem passos esse, et ab unitate Ecclesiae defecisse
. . ." (DS, no. 2804, emphasis mine).

[29]   Brian Tierney has stated: "The one papal definition made since 1870 which
has been commonly accepted as infallible is Pope Pius XII's proclamation of the
dogma of the Assumption. But if, in due course, Catholic theologians find it
desirable to retreat from the view that this late-blooming dogma forms an intrinsic
part of the Christian faith, there will be no lack of theological argumentation
devoted to proving that Pius XII (in spite of his best efforts) did not succeed in
making an infallible pronouncement after all" (Tierney, *Origins of Papal Infallibility: 1150-1350*, p. 4). In all candidness, I must say this statement seems to smack of
the very Alice-in-Wonderland logic of which Tierney complains when he attacks
the infallibilist position (see ibid., p. 5).

[30]   Avery Dulles remarked some years ago: "Many Catholic theologians contend that Divine Providence will never permit the pope to fall into error in making a
solemn judgment. We may piously believe this to be so, but there is no strict proof.
In fact, there are several objections. For one thing, it is always dangerous to set
limits to what Divine Providence will permit. God has allowed many things to go
awry, even in the Church." Avery Dulles, "Papal Authority in Roman Catholicism," pp. 63-64. If infallibility is a viable theological concept, and if the Roman
Bishop under certain circumstances can and should be judged to be endowed with
that charism—a question with which I am not directly concerned in this book—
then I do not see how Dulles' statement, which seems to refer to what I have called
the extraordinary papal magisterium, can be reconciled with Catholic dogma.† It is
true that somewhat later in the same paragraph, Dulles states that he does not think
that the medieval opinion (held down to the time of Albert Pighius) that the Popes
in their public teaching can fall into heresy is irreconcilable with the teaching of the
First Vatican Council. I take it that in this case Dulles refers to what I have called
the ordinary papal magisterium.

[31]   See J. Beumer, "Sind päpstliche Enzykliken unfehlbar?," *Theologie und
Glaube* 42 (1952): 262-69; B. Brinkmann, "Gibt es unfehlbare Äusserungen des
'Magisterium ordinarium' des Papstes?," *Scholastik* 18 (1953): 202-21; H. Stirnimann, "Magisterio enim ordinario haec docentur . . ." *Freiburger Zeitschrift für
Philosophie und Theologie* 1 (1954): 17-47; M[arc] Caudron, "Magistère ordinaire
et infaillibilité pontificale d'après la constitution *Dei Filius*," *Emphemerides Theologicae Lovanienses* 36 (1960): 393-420; Umberto Betti, *La Costituzione dommatica* "Pastor aeternus" *del Concilio Vaticano I* (Rome: Pontificio Ateneo "Antonianum," 1961), pp. 646-47.

[32]   In terms of Catholic theology, the conditions described by Peiffer are more
correctly ascribed to what Catholic theologians call the ordinary universal
magisterium.

[33]   See *Supremi pastoris*, MPM 51 (1926): 539.

[34]   The Pope stated that the doctrine is based on the sources of revelation. For
the Pope to have made that judgment is not, of course, the same as to have defined
the doctrine. Compare the language used in *Humani generis* (see p. 197-98 above,
Text B) with that used in the definition of the Assumption, in *Munificentissimus*

---

†   I believe this is true of Dulles' statement *tel quel*. Be that as it may, his
position seems to be significantly modified in *The Catholicity of the Church* (see
pp. 143-44), which appeared after this book was written.

Deus, p. 25. Therein the Pope states that those who do not accept the dogma as defined have fallen away completely from divine and Catholic faith. Language of this kind does not occur in *Humani generis*.

[35] "In spite of our agreement over the need of a universal primacy in a united Church, Anglicans do not accept the guaranteed possession of such a gift of divine assistance in judgment necessarily attached to the office of the bishop of Rome by virtue of which his formal decisions can be known to be wholly assured before their reception by the faithful." (Anglican-Roman Catholic International Commission: *The Final Report* [Cincinnati: Forward Movement Publications and Washington, D.C.: U.S. Catholic Conference, 1982]pp. 96-97).

[36] The basic thrust of Miguel Nicolau's assessment may be correct when he states that one may speak of a consequent (*consiguiente*) infallibility of the ordinary papal magisterium; i.e., a doctrinal position taken by the same may be regarded as infallible once it has entered into the consciousness of the faithful and has been accepted by them. See Miguel Nicolau, "Magisterio 'ordinario' en el Papa y en los obispos," *Salmanticenses* 9 (1962): 455-78, esp. p. 468. Nicolau does not mean, of course, nor do I, that the teaching of the ordinary papal magisterium should be considered dubious until proved correct. Quite the contrary. The question is what are the criteria by which Catholics can and should judge that a particular teaching of the *ordinary* papal magisterium is *certainly* true. (See Nicolau's remarks on pp. 469-70 where he implies that the authentic Catholic will not dissent lightly from the teaching of the Roman Bishop even as a diocesan bishop.) I would like however to make two comments. First, I presume that when Nicolau speaks of the teaching of the ordinary papal magisterium's having entered the consciousness of the faithful (*fieles*) he means the rest of the Catholic Church, not simply the so-called laity. Second, I find Nicolau's manner of speaking somewhat oversimplified. When one speaks of the teaching of the ordinary papal magisterium's being accepted (in Nicolau's terms) by the faithful, one must ask, *accepted how*? As probable? As certain? As pertaining to the substance of the faith? Given the present state of confusion, I do not think one can insist too much on the fact that everything depends on the nature of the judgment made.

[37] I thus find it difficult to understand the basis for Anglican demurral in this matter: "For many Anglicans, the teaching authority of the bishop of Rome, independent of a council, is not recommended by the fact that through it these Marian doctrines were proclaimed as dogmas binding on all the faithful" (*Anglican-Roman Catholic International Commission: The Final Report*, p. 96). Comment on the observation in the preceding sentence of the same report (to the effect that neither Marian dogma is sufficiently supported by scripture) is beyond my present scope.

[38] This concern is reflected in the most recent ARCIC Report quoted above. I stated in the Introduction that I do not intend to deal here with the issue of infallibility per se, whether papal or of the Church as a whole. See, however, the highly interesting study by Jesús Sancho Bielsa, *Infalibilidad del Pueblo de Dios. "Sensus fidei" e Infalibilidad orgánica de la Iglesia en la Constitución "Lumen gentium" del Concilio Vaticano II* (Pamplona: Ediciones Universidad de Navarra,

1979), esp. pp. 266-67. One of Sancho's conclusions is that there is only one infallibility in the Church; that is, the *sensus fidei* has three subjects: people, bishops, and the Roman Pontiff. See ibid., p. 187. This is not to say, of course, that infallibility, to the extent that it is a viable theological concept, has three subjects. Even in those relatively rare cases where the claim is made that the Roman Bishop, in exercising the Petrine function, has expressed an infallible judgment, it is always the infallibility of the Church as a whole that has come into play.

[39]   See Bernard J.F. Lonergan, *Method in Theology* (New York: Herder & Herder, 1972), p. 179.

[40]   See Alexander Schmemann, "The Idea of Primacy in Orthodox Ecclesiology," in John Meyendorff, Alexander Schmemann, Nicolas Afanassief, and Nicolas Koulomzine, *The Primacy of Peter* (Wing Road, Leighton Buzzard, and Bedfordshire: The Faith Press, second edition, 1973) pp. 30-56, esp. p. 49. The translator of this article is not indicated.

[41]   Thus in a somewhat different context: "The function and identity of religions are uncovered only by attending to the self-reflection and praxis of the religion itself. Ecclesiastic identity cannot be defined in isolation from the other dimensions of life but only in its interaction with them. The search for self-understanding as it evolves through praxis is part of Catholicism's pressing agenda as it cautiously moves toward the end of a century that has opened it to radical change." Stephen Duffy, "Catholicism's Search for a New Self-Understanding," in *Vatican II: Open Questions and New Horizons*, ed. Gerald M. Fagin (Wilmington, Delaware: Michael Glazier, Inc., 1984), pp. 9-27. The quotation begins on p. 26. Depending on what one means by "radical," I may be able to concur completely.

[42]   See John Henry Newman, *On Consulting the Faithful in Matters of Doctrine*, edited with an introduction by John Coulson (New York, Sheed and Ward, n.d.).

[43]   See ibid., pp. 103-4.

[44]   Newman, as far as I know, nowhere explicitly discusses this possibility. Yet it may not be inconsistent with what he describes as the interplay between priestly, prophetical and kingly offices in the Church. See John Henry Newman, Preface to 3rd ed. of *The* Via Media *of the Anglican Church*, 2 vols. (London: Basil Montagu Pickering, 1877), 1: xl-xciv.

[45]   For a view somewhat different from that of E. Amann's ("Honorius Ier" *Dictionnaire de Théologie catholique*, 15 vols., 22 tomes [Paris: Letouzey et Ané, 1909—]7[1927]: 93-132), see Jaroslav Pelikan, *The Christian Tradition: A History of the Development of Doctrine*, vol. 2: *The Spirit of Eastern Christendom* (Chicago and London: University of Chicago Press, 1974), pp. 67-68 and 150-53.

[46]   See Hermann Josef Sieben *Die Konzilsidee der Alten Kirche* (Paderborn, Munich, Vienna, and Zurich: Ferdinand Schöningh, 1979), pp. 313-14 and 511-16.

[47]   See Pius XII, *Di gran cuore*, AAS 48 (1956): 699-727, especially p. 709.

[48]   See ibid.

[49]   See ibid.

[50]   See Thomas Howland Sanks, *Authority in the Church: A Study in Changing Paradigms* (Missoula, Montana: Scholars' Press, 1971), pp. 140-61.

51   See Congar, *Vraie et fausse réforme dans l'Eglise*, pp. 171-74. At this writing the first edition of this book was not accessible to me.

52   See ibid.

53   See Troeltsch, "Kirche III: Dogmatisch," p. 1153.

SELECTED BIBLIOGRAPHY

Texts

Acta Apostolicae Sedis. Rome: Typis Polyglottis Vaticanis, 1908-.

Pius XI. *Non abbiamo bisogno.* Washington, D.C.: National Catholic Welfare Conference, 1931.

_____. *Mit brennender Sorge.* Washington, D.C.: National Catholic Welfare Conference, 1937.

_____. *Mortalium animos.* National Catholic Welfare Conference translation. Washington, D.C.: Rasdell, Inc., 1928.

_____. *Quadragesimo anno.* Boston: St. Paul Editions, n.d.

_____. *Rerum Ecclesiae.* National Catholic Welfare Conference translation. Washington, D.C.: n.p., n.d.

Pius XII. *Evangelii praecones.* National Catholic Welfare Conference translation. Washington, D.C.: n.p., n.d.

_____. *Humani generis.* National Catholic Welfare Conference translation. Boston: Daughters of St. Paul, n.d.

_____. *Munificentissimus Deus.* National Catholic Welfare Conference translation. Boston: Daughters of St. Paul, n.d.

————. *Mystici corporis.* Boston: St. Paul Editions, n.d.

————. *Summi pontificatus.* Official Vatican Text. Derby, N.Y.: Daughters of St. Paul, n.d.

John XXIII. *Mater et Magistra.* Boston: St. Paul Editions, n.d.

————. *Pacem in terris.* National Catholic Welfare Conference translation. Boston: Daughters of St. Paul, n.d.

Acta et Decreta Sacrorum Conciliorum Recentiorum: Collectio Lacensis. 7 vols. Freiburg im Breisgau: Sumptibus Herder, typographi Editoris Pontificii, 1890.

Acta et Documenta Concilio Oecumenico Vaticano Secundo apparando. Series I (Antepraeparatoria). 5 vols., 16 tomes. Rome: Typis Polyglottis Vaticanis, 1960-61.

Acta et Documenta Concilio Oecumenico Vaticano Secundo apparando. Series II (Praeparatoria). 3 vols., 7 tomes. Rome: Typis Polyglottis Vaticanis, 1964-69.

Acta Gregorii Papae XVI. 4 vols. Rome: Ex Typographia Polyglotta S.C. de Propaganda Fide, 1901-04.

Acta Sanctae Sedis. 42 vols. Rome: Ex Typographia Polyglotta, 1865-1908.

Leo XIII. *The Great Encyclicals of Pope Leo XIII.* Translations from approved sources. Edited by John J. Wynne. New York, Cincinnati and Chicago: Benziger Bros., 1903.

Acta Synodalia Sacrosancti Concilii Oecumenici Vaticani Secundi. 4 vols., 26 tomes. Rome: Typis Polyglottis Vaticanis, 1971-80.

Beata Virgo Maria in suo Conceptu Immaculata ex Monumentis Omnium Seculorum [sic] *Demonstrata.* 9 vols. Edited by Augustine de Roskovány. Budapest: Typis Athenaei, 1873-81.

Canons and Decrees of the Council of Trent. Edited and translated by H.J. Schroeder. St. Louis and London: B. Herder Book Co., 1941.

Codex Iuris Canonici. Rome: Typis Polyglottis Vaticanis, 1918.

Codex Iuris Canonici. Auctoritate Ioannis Pauli PP. II Promulgatus. N.p.: Libreria Editrice Vaticana, 1983.

Collectanea S. Congregationis de Propaganda Fide Seu Decreta, Intructiones, Rescripta pro Apostolicis Missionibus. Rome: Typographia Polyglotta, eds. 1893 and 1907. The latter edition comprises two tomes.

Constitutionis Dogmaticae Lumen Gentium *Synopsis Historica.* Edited by Giuseppe Alberigo and Franca Magistretti. Bologna: Istituto per le Scienze Religiose, 1975.

Documents of Vatican II. Edited by Walter M. Abbott and Joseph Gallagher. New York: America Press, 1966.

Enchiridion Symbolorum Definitionum et Declarationum de Rebus Fidei et Morum. Edited by Henricus Denzinger and Adolfus Schönmetzer. 26th corrected ed. Barcelona, Freiburg im Breisgau and Rome: Herder, 1976.

Leonis XIII Pontificis Maximi Acta. 23 vols. Rome: Ex Typographia Vaticana, 1887-1905.

Monita ad Missionarios Sacrae Congregationis de Propaganda Fide. Editio altera. Rome: n.p., 1840.

Pareri dell'Episcopato cattolico, di Capitoli, di Congregazioni, di Università, di Personaggi ragguardevoli. 11 vols. Rome: coi tipi della Civiltà Cattolica, 1851-54.

Petitiones de Assumptione Corporea B.V. Mariae in Caelum Definienda ad Sanctam Sedem Delatae. 2 vols. Edited by G[uilhemus] Hentrich and R[udolfus] G[ualterus] De Moos. Rome: Typis Polyglottis Vaticanis, 1942.

Pii IX Pontificis Maximi Acta. 9 vols. Rome: Ex Typographia Bonarum Artium, 1854-78.

Sacrorum Conciliorum Nova et Amplissima Collectio. 53 vols. Arnheim and Leipzig: Société nouvelle d'édition de la collection Mansi, curantibus Ludovico Petit et Ioanne Baptista Martin, 1748-1927.

Sacrosanctum Oecumenicum Concilium Vaticanum Secundum: Constitutiones, Decreta, Declarationes. Rome: Typis Polyglottis Vaticanis, 1966.

Sanctissimi Domini Nostri Leonis Papae XIII: Allocutiones, Epistolae, Constitutiones, Aliàque Acta Praecipua. 7 vols. Bruges and Lille: Desclée, de Brouwer et Soc., 1887-1906.

La Solenne Definizione del Dogma dell'Immacolato Concepimento. 2 vols. Edited by Vincenzo Sardi. Atti e Documenti pubblicati nel cinquantesimo anniversario della stessa definizione. Rome: Tipografia Vaticana, 1904.

Sylloge: Praecipuorum Recentium Summorum Pontificum et S. Congregationis de Propaganda Fide necnon aliarum S. Congregationum Romanarum ad usum Missionariorum. Rome: Typis Polyglottis Vaticanis, 1939.

Vatican II: *The Conciliar and Post-Conciliar Documents.* Edited by Austin Flannery. Wilmington, Del.: Scholarly Resources, Inc., 1975.

General Sources

Agreement on Authority: The Anglican-Roman Catholic Statement. With commentary by Juliañ W. Charley. Bramcote, Notts.: Grove Books, 1977.

Anglican-Roman Catholic Dialogues: The Work of the Preparatory Commission. Edited by Alan C. Clark and Colin Davey. London and New York: Oxford University Press, 1974.

Anglican-Roman Catholic International Commission: The Final Report. Windsor, September 1981. North American ed. Cincinnati: Forward Movement Publications, and Washington, D.C.: Office of Publishing Services, U.S. Catholic Conference, 1981.

Baraúna, Guilherme, and Congar, Yves. *L'Eglise de Vatican II.* 3 vols. Paris: Les Editions du Cerf, 1966.

Caprile, Giovanni. *Il Concilio Vaticano II.* 5 vols. Rome: Edizioni "La Civiltà Cattolica," n.d.

Catholicisme: hier, aujourd'hui, demain. 8 vols. Paris: Letouzey et Ané, 1948-.

Dictionnaire de Théologie catholique. 15 vols., 22 tomes. Paris: Letouzey et Ané, 1909-.

Die Religion in Geschichte und Gegenwart. 5 vols. Tübingen: J.C.B. Mohr, 1909-13.

Encyclopedia of Theology. The Concise Sacramentum Mundi. Edited by Karl Rahner. New York: Crossroad, 1982.

History of the Church. Edited by Hubert Jedin. 10 vols. Various translators. Vols. 1-4, published under the title *Handbook of Church History.* New York: Herder and Herder, 1965-70. Vols. 5-10 published under the title *History of the Church.* New York: Crossroad, 1980-81.

Lexicon für Theologie und Kirche. 11 vols. Freiburg: Verlag Herder, 1957-67.

Lexicon für Theologie und Kirche: Das Zweite Vatikanische Konzil. 3 vols. Freiburg: Verlag Herder, 1966-68.

Lutherans and Catholics in Dialogue. Vol. 1: *The Status of the Nicene Creed as the Dogma of the Church.* Vol. 2: *One Baptism for the Remission of Sins.* Vol. 3: *The Eucharist as Sacrifice.* Edited by Paul C. Empie and T. Austin Murphy. Minneapolis: Augsburg Publishing House, n.d. Vol. 4: *Eucharist and Ministry.* N.p., 1970. Vol. 5: *Papal Primacy and the Universal Church.* Edited by Paul C. Empie and T. Austin Murphy. Minneapolis: Augsburg Publishing House, 1974. Vol. 6: *Teaching Authority and Infallibility in the Church.* Edited by Paul C.

Empie, T. Austin Murphy and Joseph A. Burgess. Minneapolis: Augsburg Publishing House, 1978. Vol. 7: *Justification by Faith*. Edited by H. George Anderson, T. Austin Murphy and Joseph A. Burgess. Minneapolis: Augsburg Publishing House, 1985.

Ministry and Ordination: A Statement of the Doctrine of the Ministry Agreed by the Anglican/Roman Catholic International Commission, Canterbury, 1973. London: S.P.C.K., 1973.

Mysterium Salutis. Edited by Johannes Feiner and Magnus Löhrer. 5 vols., 7 tomes. Zurich, Einsiedeln and Cologne: Benziger Verlag, 1965-76.

The New Catholic Encyclopedia. 17 vols. New York: McGraw-Hill, 1967-78.

Rahner, Karl, and Herbert Vorgrimler. *Dictionary of Theology*. Trans. Richard Strachan, David Smith, Robert Nowell, and Sarah O'Brien Twohig. Second Edition. New York: Crossroad, 1981.

Sacramentum Mundi: An Encyclopedia of Theology. 6 vols. Edited by Karl Rahner. New York: Herder & Herder, and London: Burns & Oates. Ltd., 1968-70.

Schmidlin, Joseph. *Papstgeschichte der Neuesten Zeit*. 3 vols. Munich: Verlag Joseph Kösel and Friedrich Pustet, 1933-36.

Theological Dictionary of the New Testament. 10 vols. Translated by Geoffrey W. Bromiley. Vols. 1-4 edited by Gerhard Kittel, vols. 5-9 edited by Gerhard Friedrich, vol. 10 (Index) compiled by Ronald R. Pritikin. Grand Rapids, Mich., and London: William B. Eerdmans Publishing Co., 1964-76.

Vorgrimler, Herbert, ed. *Commentary on the Documents of Vatican II*. 5 vols. London: Burns & Oates, and New York: Herder & Herder, 1966-69.

Treatises

Augustinus, Aurelius. *De Trinitate*. In *Patrologiae Cursus Completus*. Edited by J[acques]- P[aul] Migne. Paris: n.p., 1844-64. *Patrologia Latina*, 221 vols. 42 (1845): 819-1098.

Barth, Karl. *Die kirchliche Dogmatik*. 4 vols., 13 tomes. Munich: C. Kaiser, 1932-67.

Bellarmine, Robert Francis Romolo. *Opera Omnia*. 8 vols. Editio nova iuxta Venetam anni MDCCXXI. Naples, Panormi and Paris: C. Pedone Lauriel, 1872.

Billot, Louis.   *Tractatus de Ecclesia Christi.*   2 vols. Rome: Apud Aedes Universitatis Gregorianae, 1927.

Bouvier, J.B.   *Institutiones Theologicae ad usum Seminariorum.*   6 vols. 12th ed. Paris: Apud Mequignon Juniorem, 1865.

Calvin, John.   *Institutes of the Christian Religion.*   2 vols. Edited by John T. McNeill. Translated by Ford Lewis Battles. Philadelphia: Westminster Press, 1960.

Cappellari, Mauro.   *Il Trionfo della Santa Sede e della Chiesa.*   1st ed. 1799. Venice: Nella Casa del Tipografo Editore Giuseppe Ballaggia, 1832.

Dieckmann, Hermann.   *De Revelatione Christiana.*   Freiburg im Breisgau: Herder & Co., 1930.

Doronzo, Emmanuel.   *Theologia Dogmatica.*   2 vols. Washington, D.C.: Catholic University of America, 1966.

Franzelin, Joannis Baptista.   *Tractatus de Divina Traditione et Scriptura.*   3rd edition. Rome: Ex Typographia Polyglotta, 1872.

Heinrich, J.B.   *Dogmatische Theologie.*   9 vols. 2nd ed. Mainz: Verlag von Franz Kirchheim, 1882.

Hermann, J.   *Institutiones Theologiae Dogmaticae.*   2 vols. Rome: Ex Typographia Pacis Philippi Cuggiani, 1897.

Hervé, J.M.   *Manuale Theologiae Dogmaticae.*   4 vols. Paris: Apud Berche et Pagis, 1951-53.

Ottaviani, Alaphridus.   *Compendium Iuris Publici Ecclesiastici ad Usum Auditorum S. Theologiae.*   Rome: Typis Polyglottis Vaticanis, 1936.

Ottiger, Ignatius.   *Theologia Fundamentalis.*   2 vols. Freiburg im Breisgau: Sumptibus Herder, 1897.

Quintilian, Marcus Fabius.   *Institutio Oratoria.*   4 vols. Translated by H.E. Butler. Loeb Classical Library. Cambridge: Harvard University Press, and London: William Heinemann, Ltd., 1958.

Salaverri de la Torre, Ioachim.   *De Ecclesia Christi.*   In *Sacrae Theologiae Summa.* 4 vols. Madrid: Biblioteca de Autores cristianos, 1950-53. 1 (2d ed., 1952): 497-953 and 1 (5th ed., 1962): 488-976.

Sancti Thomae Aquinatis.   *Summa Theologiae.*   5 vols. Madrid: Biblioteca de Autores cristianos, 1961.

Scheeben, Matthias Joseph.   *Gesammelte Schriften.*   8 vols., 9 tomes. Freiburg im Breisgau: Verlag Herder, 1948-67.

Schleiermacher, Friedrich.   *The Christian Faith.*   Edited and translated by H.R. Mackintosh and J.S. Stewart from 2nd German ed. Edinburgh: T. & T. Clark, 1968.

Schmaus, Michael.   *Katholische Dogmatik.*   4 vols., 7 tomes. Munich: Max Hueber Verlag, 1958.

Suarez, Francisci, *Opera Omnia.*   27 vols. Paris: Apud Ludovicum Vivès, 1856-78.

Taparelli d'Azeglio, Luigi.   *Essai théorique de droit naturel.* . 2 vols. Translated from the last Italian ed. 3rd ed. Paris: Librairie Internationale Catholique, Leipzig: L.-A. Kittler, and Tournai: Vve H. Casterman, 1883.

Theses on the Relationship between the Ecclesiastical Magisterium and Theology.   The International Theological Commission (June 6, 1976). Including "A Commentary on the Theses of the International Theological Commission on the Relationship between the Ecclesiastical Magisterium and Theology," by Otto Semmelroth and Karl Lehmann. Washington, D.C.: United States Catholic Conference, 1977.

Studies

BOOKS

Acerbi, Antonio.   *Due Ecclesiologie: ecclesiologia giurdica ed ecclesiologia di communione nella* "Lumen gentium."   Bologna: Edizione Dehoniane, 1975.

Actes du Colloque international d'histoire religieuse de Grenoble des 30 septembre-3 octobre 1971: Les Catholiques libéraux au XIXe siècle. Grenoble: Presses Universitaires de Grenoble, 1974.

Alberigo, Giuseppe.   *Lo Sviluppo della dottrina sui poteri nella Chiesa universale. Momenti essenziali tra il XVI e il XIX secolo.*   Rome, Freiburg, Basel, Barcelona, Vienna: Herder, 1964.

————. *Chiesa conciliare: identità e significato del conciliarismo.* Brescia: Paideia, 1981.

Anger, Joseph.   *La doctrine du Corps mystique de Jésus-Christ d'après les principes de la théologie de Saint-Thomas.*   Paris: Beauchesne, 1946.

Apologia popolare del Sillabo per un Dottore in S. Teologia.   Rome: dalla Tipografia Salvucci, 1867.

Aubert, Roger.   *Le Problème de l'acte de foi.*   Louvain: E. Warny and Publications Universitaires, 1950.

————. *Le Pontificat de Pie IX (1846-1878).*   Paris: Bloud et Gay, 1952.

————. *Vatican I.*   Paris: Editions de l'Orante, 1964.

Aufhauser, J.B. *Umweltsbeeinflussung der christlichen Mission.* Munich: Max Hueber, 1932.

Augustin, Pius. *Religious Freedom in Church and State: A Study in Doctrinal Development.* Baltimore: Helicon, 1966.

Balic, Carolus. *Testimonia de Assumptione ex omnibus saeculis.* Rome: Academia Mariana, 1948.

Baltasar, Hans Urs von. *Der antirömische Affekt.* Freiburg im Breisgau: Verlag Herder KG, 1974.

Bandera, Armando. *La Iglesia, misterio de comunión en el corazón del Concilio Vaticano II.* Salamanca: San Esteban, 1965.

Bellamy, J. *La Théologie catholique au XIXᵉ siècle.* 3rd ed. Paris: Gabriel Beauchesne et Cie, 1904.

Bergeron, Richard. *Les Abus de l'Eglise d'après Newman. Etude de la Préface à la troisième édition de La* Via Media. Tournai: Desclée et Cie, and Montreal: Bellarmin, 1971.

Berna Quintana, Angel. *Doctrina social de la Iglesia.* Madrid: Instituto Social León XIII, 1969.

Bertrams, Wilhelm. *The Papacy, the Episcopacy and Collegiality.* Trans. Patrick T. Brennan. Westminster, Maryland: The Newman Press, 1964.

Betti, Umberto. *La costituzione dommatica "Pastor Aeternus" del Concilio Vaticano I.* Rome: Pontificio Ateneo "Antonianum," 1961.

——— *La dottrina sull'episcopato nel capitolo III della costituzione dommatica* Lumen gentium: *sussidio per la lettura del testo.* Rome: Città Nuova Editrice, 1968.†

Betz, Johannes, and Fries, Heinrich, eds. *Kirche und Überlieferung.* Freiburg, Basel and Vienna: Herder, 1960.

Biemer, Günter. *Überlieferung und Offenbarung: die Lehre von der Tradition nach John Henry Newman.* Freiburg: Herder, 1961.

Bilaniuk, Petrus Boris. *De Magisterio Ordinario Summi Pontificis.* Toronto: Apud Auctorem, 1966.

Botte, B., ed. *Le Concile et les Conciles: contribution à l'histoire de la vie conciliaire de l'Eglise.* N.p.: Editions de Chevetogne du Cerf, 1960.

Boudignon, L'Abbé J.B. *L'Encyclique sur la question sociale avec commentaire historique et littéral.* Paris: P. Lethielleux and LePuy, Chez l'Auteur, 1891.

Bouillard, Henri. *Conversion et grâce selon S. Thomas d'Aquin.* Paris: Aubier, Editions Montaigne, 1944.

Bouyer, Louis. *The Church of God: Body of Christ and Temple of the Spirit.* Trans. Charles Underhill Quinn. 3 vols. Chicago: Franciscan Herald Press, 1982.

---

† For the bibliographical data relative to the 1984 revision of this book, see below, p. 511.

Bovis, André de. *What Is the Church?* Translated by R.F. Trevett. New York: Hawthorn Books, 1961.

Brandmüller, Walter, ed. *Synodale Strukturen der Kirche. Entwicklung und Probleme.* DonauwPorth: Verlag Ludwig Auer, 1977.

Brière, Yves de la. *Les Luttes présentes de l'Eglise.* Paris: Editions des "Questions actuelles," 1913.

Broglie, Guy de. *Le droit naturel à la liberté religieuse.* Paris: Beauchesne, 1964.

Brown, Raymond E., Donfried, Karl P., and Reumann, John, eds. *Peter in the New Testament.* Minneapolis: Augsburg Publishing House, and New York: Paulist Press, 1973.

Bungener, Laurence Louis Félix. *Pape et Concile au XIXᵉ siècle.* Paris: Michel Lerry Frères, 1870.

Calvez, Jean-Yves-Perrin. *The Church and Social Justice.* Translated by J.R. Kirwan. Chicago: Henry Regnery Company, 1961.

Capéran, Louis. *Le problème du salut des infidèles: essai historique.* Toulouse: Grand Séminaire, 1934.

Casali, Giuseppe. *La dottrina del Corpo mistico.* Lucca: Edizioni "Regnum Christi," 1962.

Castelli, Enrico, ed. *L'Ermeneutica della libertà religiosa.* Archivio di Filosofia. Padua: Casa Editrice Antonio Milani, 1968.

_____, ed. *L'Infaillibilité. Son Aspect philosophique et théologique.* Paris: Editorial Montaigne, 1970.

Castelplanio, Lodivoco di. *Pio IX e gli errori moderni.* Velletri: Tipografia Colonensi, 1865.

Chadwick, Owen. *From Bossuet to Newman: The Idea of Doctrinal Development.* Cambridge: Cambridge University Press, 1957.

Choupin, Lucien. *Valeur des décisions doctrinales et disciplinaires du Saint-Siège.* 3rd ed. Paris: Gabriel Beauchesne, 1928.

Congar, Yves. *Lay People in the Church: A Study for a Theology of the Laity.* Translated by Donald Attwater. Westminster, Md.: Newman Press, 1957.

_____. *La Tradition et les traditions.* 2 vols. Paris: A. Fayard, 1960-63

_____. *Situation et tâches présentes de la théologie.* Paris: Les Editions du Cerf, 1967.

_____. *Vraie et fausse réforme dans l'Eglise.* Paris: Les Editions du Cerf, 1969.

_____. *Diversités et communion.* Paris: Les Editions du Cerf, 1982.

Corbin, Adrien Mangaux. *Dernier coup d'oeil sur l'Encyclique de N.S.P. le Pape Pie IX du 8 décembre 1864.* Paris: C. Douniol, 1865.

Coriden, James A. *The Case for Freedom: Human Rights in the Church.* Washington, D.C., and Cleveland: Corpus Books, 1969.
———, ed. *The Once and Future Church.* Staten Island, N.Y.: Alba House, 1971.
———, ed. *Who Decides for the Church? Studies in Co-Responsibility.* Hartford, Conn.: Canon Law Society of America, 1971.
Coste, René. *Théologie de la liberté religieuse.* Gembloux: Editions J. Duculot, 1969.
Delacrois, S., ed. *Histoire universelle des Missions catholiques.* 4 vols. Paris: Librairie Grund, 1957-59.
Denzler, Georg; Christ, Felix; Trilling, Wolfgang; Stockmeier, Peter; De Vries, Wilhelm; Lippert, Peter. *Petrusamt und Papsttum.* Stuttgart: Verlag Katholisches Bibelwerk, GmbH, 1970.
Dhavamony, Mariasusai. *Classical Hinduism.* Rome: Gregorian University Press, 1982.
Dillenschneider, Clément. *Le sens de la foi et le progrès dogmatique du mystère marial.* Rome: Academia Mariana Internationalis, 1954.
Dóriga, Enrique. *Jerarquía, Infalibilidad y Comunión intereclesial.* Barcelona: Editoral Herder, 1973.
Drane, James F. *Authority and Institution: A Study in Church Crisis.* Milwaukee: Bruce Publishing Co., 1969.
Dublanchy, Edmond. *De Axiomate* Extra Ecclesiam Nulla Salus. Barri-Ducis: Constant-Laguerre, 1895.
Ducos, Marcel, *Gouvernement et efficacité dans l'Eglise: analyse et prospective.* Paris: Editions Fleurus, 1969.
Dulles, Avery. *The Survival of Dogma.* Garden City, N.Y.: Doubleday, 1971.
———. *Models of the Church.* Garden City, N.Y.: Doubleday, Image Books, 1978.
———. *A Church To Believe In: Discipleship and Dynamics of Freedom.* New York: Crossroad, 1982.
Dupanloup, Félix-Antoine-Philibert. *La convention du 15 septembre et l'Encyclique du 8 décembre.* Paris: Charles Douniol, Libraire-éditeur, 1865.
Dupont, Jacques, and Lécuyer, Joseph, eds. *La Collégialité épiscopale: histoire et théologie.* Paris: Les Editions du Cerf, 1965.
Edelby, Neophytos, and Dick, Ignace. *Vatican II: les Eglises orientales catholiques.* Paris: Les Editions du Cerf, 1970.
Ellard, Gerald. *The Mystical Body and the American Bishops.* N.p.: The Queen's Work, 1939.
Falconi, Carlo. *L'umanità e il Cristo: il corpo mistico in Adamo e in Cristo.* Milan: Edizioni di Communità, 1949.

Femiano, Samuel D. *Infallibility of the Laity: The Legacy of Newman.* New York: Herder & Herder, 1967.

Finlay, James Charles. *The Liberal Who Failed.* Washington, D.C.: Corpus Books, 1968.

Gallati, Fidelis. *Wenn die Päpste sprechen: das ordentliche Lehramt des apostolischen Stuhles und die Zustimmung zu dessen Entscheidungen.* Vienna: Verlag Herder, 1960.

Gaspari, Alcide de. *I tempi et gli uomini che prepararono la* "Rerum Novarum." Milan: Società Editrice "Vita e Pensiero," 1945.

Geiselmann, Josef Rupert. *Die lebendige Überlieferung als Norm des christlichen Glaubens.* Freiburg: Herder Verlag, 1959.

_____. *The Meaning of Tradition.* Translated by W. J. O'Hara. Freiburg: Herder, and London: Burns & Oates, 1966.

Gerrish, B. A. *Tradition and the Modern World: Reformed Theology in the Nineteenth Century.* Chicago and London: University of Chicago Press, 1978.

_____. *The Old Protestantism and the New: Essays on the Reformation Heritage.* Chicago: The University of Chicago Press, and Edinburgh: T. and T. Clark, Limited, 1982.

Gilkey, Langdon. *How the Church Can Minister to the World without Losing Itself.* New York: Harper & Row, Publishers, 1964.

Gilson, Etienne, ed. *The Church Speaks to the Modern World: The Social Teachings of Leo XIII.* Garden City, N.Y.: Image Books, 1954.

Giron, A. *L'Infaillibilité pontificale: étude historique.* Brussels: Société belge d'édition, 1908.

Goetz, Leopold Karl. *Der Ultramontanismus als Weltanschauung auf Grund des Syllabus quellenmässig dargestellt.* Bonn: Carl Georgi Universitäts-Buchdruckerei und Verlag, 1905.

Gomez-Heras, J. J. G. *Temas dogmáticos del Concilio Vaticano I: Aportación de la Comisión teológica preparatoria a su obra doctrinal.* 2 vols. Victoria, Spain: Editorial Eset, 1971.

Goyau, Georges, ed. *L'Eglise et la démocratie chrétienne.* Liège: Imprimerie centrale, 1901.

Gracchi, Orio. *Libertà della Chiesa e Autorità dello Stato.* Milan: Giuffré, 1963.

Granfield, Patrick *Ecclesial Cybernetics: A Study of Democracy in the Church.* New York: Macmillan, 1973.

Grimal, Jules. *With Jesus to the Priesthood.* Translated by Gerald Shaughnessy from 6th French ed. Philadelphia: Dolphin Press, 1946.

Gual, Pierre. *Oracula Pontificia praesertim Encyclicae Quanta cura et Syllabi Errorum a Ss. D. N. Pio Papa IX Damnatorum.* Paris: Adrianus Le Clere et Soc., 1869.

Guerry, Emile Maurice. *In the Whole Christ*. Translated by M. G. Carroll. Staten Island, N.Y.: Alba House, 1963.

Guitton, Georges. *1891: Une date dans l'histoire des travailleurs*. Paris: Aux Editions Spes, 1930.

Gutierrez García, José Luis. *Conceptos fundamentales en la doctrina social de la Iglesia*. Madrid: Centro de Estudios sociales del Valle de los Caïdos, 1971.

Hamer, Jérôme. *L'Eglise est une communion*. Paris: Editions du Cerf, 1962.

————, and Riva, Clemente. *La libertà religiosa nel Vaticano II*. Torino-Leumann: Elle di Cie, 1966.

Hausleithner, Rudolf. *Der Geist der neuen Ordnung: Einblicke in das päpstliche Gesellschaftsrundschreiben* "Quadragesimo Anno." Vienna: Verlag und Druck Typographische Anhart, 1937.

Hégy, Pierre. *L'Autorité dans le Catholicisme contemporain du Syllabus à Vatican II*. Paris: Beauchesne, 1975.

Helmreich, Ernst Christian. *A Free Church in a Free State. The Catholic Church: Italy, Germany, France, 1864-1914*. Boston: Heath, 1964.

Hocedez, Edgar. *Histoire de la théologie au XIX siècle*. 3 vols. Paris: Desclée, 1948.

Hoensbroech, Paul Kajus Graf von. *Der Syllabus, seine Authorität und Tragwerte*. Munich: J. F. Lehmann, 1904.

Hourat, P. *Le Syllabus, étude documentaire*. 3 vols. Paris: N.p.: n.p., 1904.

Husslein, Joseph. *The Christian Social Manifesto*. New York, Milwaukee and Chicago: Bruce Publishing Co., 1931.

Janssens, L. *Liberté de conscience et liberté religieuse*. Paris: Desclée de Brouwer, 1964.

Jimenez Urresti, Teodoro Ignacio. *Estado e Iglesia: laicidad y confesionalidad del Estado y del derecho*. Victoriensia, no. 6. Victoria, Spain: Editorial del Seminario, 1958.

Joly, Léon. *Le Christianisme et l'Extrême Orient*. 2 vols. Paris: P. Lethielleux, n.d.

Jugie, Martin. *La Mort et l'Assomption de la Sainte Vierge: étude historico-doctrinale*. Vatican City: Biblioteca Apostolica Vaticana, 1944.

Kasper, Walter. *Dogma unter dem Wort Gottes*. Mainz: Matthias Grünewald Verlag, 1965.

————. *Glaube und Geschichte*. Mainz: Matthias Grünewald Verlag, 1970.

_____. *Absolutheit des Christentums.* Freiburg: Herder, 1977.

Kerrigen, Alexander; Schlund, Robert; Aubert, Roger; Caudron, Marc; Nau, Paul; Paradis, Georges; Beauduin, Lambert; Betti, Umberto; Dewan, Wilfrid F.; Kasper, Walter; Colombo, Giuseppe; Hamer, Jérôme; Dominiques del Val, Ursicino; Torrell, J.P.; Dejaifve, Georges; Thils, Gustave; Chavasse, Antoine. *De Doctrina Concilii Vaticani Primi.* Rome: Libreria Editrice Vaticana, 1969.

Kilmartin, Edward J. *Toward Reunion: The Roman Catholic and the Orthodox Churches.* New York, Ramsey, and Toronto: The Paulist Press, 1979.

Kloppenburg, Bonaventura. *The Ecclesiology of Vatican II* [A Ecclesiologia do Vaticano II]. Rio de Janeiro: Vozes Limitada, and Chicago: Franciscan Herald Press, 1974.

Küng, Hans. *Structures of the Church.* Trans. by Salvator Attanasio. Notre Dame, Ind., and London: University of Notre Dame Press, 1964.

_____. *The Church.* Trans. Ray and Rosalen Ockenden. New York: Sheed and Ward, 1967.

_____. *Infallible? An Inquiry.* Trans. Edward Quinn. Garden City, N.Y.: Doubleday & Co., 1971 and 1983.

_____. *The Church—Maintained in Truth: A Theological Meditation.* Trans. Edward Quinn. New York: The Seabury Press, 1980.

Laborde, Jean-Joseph. *De la croyance à l'Immaculée Conception de la Sainte Vierge.* Toulouse: Privat, 1851.

Lash, Nicholas. *Change in Focus: A Study of Doctrinal Change and Continuity.* London: Sheed and Ward, 1973.

_____. *Newman and Development: The Search for an Explanation.* Shepherdstown, West Virginia: Patmos Press, 1975.

Latourette, K. S. *A History of the Expansion of Christianity.* 7 vols. New York and London: Harper & Bros., 1936-45.

Lee, D., ed. *Vatican II: The Theological Dimension.* N.p.: Thomist Press, 1963.

Lengsfeld, Peter, ed. *Ökumenische Theologie.* Stuttgart, Berlin, Cologne, Mainz: Verlag W. Kohlhammer, 1980.

Lesourd, Paul. *Histoire des Missions catholiques.* Paris: Librairie de l'Arc, 1937.

Lettre pastorale de Monseigneur l'Archevêque de Paris relative à la récente encyclique du souverain pontife et mandement pour le carême et le jubilé de l'année 1865. Paris: A. Le Clere et Cie, 1865.

Lindbeck, George A. *Infallibility.* The 1972 Père Marquette Lecture. Milwaukee: Marquette University Press, 1972.

Lombardi, Riccardo. *The Salvation of the Unbeliever.* Westminster,

Maryland: The Newman Press, 1956.

Lonergan, Bernard J. F.   *Method in Theology*. New York: Herder & Herder, 1972.

―――.   *The Way to Nicaea: The Dialectical Development of Trinitarian Theology*. Trans. Conn O'Donovan. Philadelphia: Westminster Press, 1976.

López de Prado, Joaquín, with C. Corral.   *La libertad religiosa: analysis de la declaración* "Dignitatis humanae." Madrid: Editorial Razón y Fe, n.d.

Lubac, Henri de (Cardinal).   *The Splendour of the Church*. Trans. Michael Mason. Glen Rock, N.J.: The Paulist Press, 1963.

Mackey, J[ames] P[atrick].   *The Modern Theology of Tradition*. New York: Herder & Herder, 1963.

―――.   *Tradition and Change in the Church*. Dayton: Pflaum Press, 1968.

Malmberg Felix.   *Ein Leib, Ein Geist: vom Mysterium der Kirche*. Freiburg, Basel, Vienna: Herder, 1960.

Mangano, Vicenzo.   *Il Pensiero sociale e politica di Leone XIII*. Isola del Liri: Società tipografica Macioce e Pisane, 1931.

Marín-Sola, Francisco.   *L'Evolution homogène du dogme catholique*. Fribourg: n.p., 1924.

Maritain, Jacques.   *Man and the State*. Edited by Richard O'Sullivan. London: Hollis & Carter, 1954.

Maupied, F.-L. M.   *Le Syllabus et l'Encyclique* Quanta cura *du 8 décembre 1864: commentaire*. Tourcoing: Bibliothèque de Tout le Monde, 1876.

Maurier, Henri.   *The Other Covenant: A Theology of Paganism*. Trans. Charles McGrath. Glen Rock, N.J. and New York: The Newman Press, 1968.

McBrien, Richard P.   *Do We Need the Church?* New York and Evanston: Harper & Row, 1969.

McCool, Gerald A.   *Catholic Theology in the Nineteenth Century: The Quest for a Unitary Method*. New York: Seabury Press, 1977.

McElrath, Damian.   *The Syllabus of Pius IX: Some Reactions in England*. Louvain: Publications Universitaires de Louvain, 1964.

Mencacci, Paolo.   *Gli errori moderni confutati nel Sillabo*. Rome: Libreria Cattolica Internazionale, Desclée, Lefebre et Cie, 1885.

Mersch, Emile.   *La Théologie du Corps mystique*. 2 vols. Paris: Desclée de Brouwer, 1946.

―――.   *Le Corps mystique du Christ: études de théologie historique*. Louvain: Museum Kessianum, 1953.

Metz, Johannes Baptist, ed. *Gott in Welt: Festgabe für Karl Rahner.* 2 vols. Freiburg, Basel and Vienna: Herder, 1964.

Meuzelaar, J. *Der Leib des Messias.* Assen: Van Corcum, 1961.

Meyendorff, J.; Afanassieff, N.; Schmemann, A.; and Koulomzine, N. *The Primacy of Peter in the Orthodox Church.* Various translators. Wing Road, Leighton Buzzard, and Bedfordshire (Eng.): The Faith Press. Second Edition. 1973.

Miller, Michael J. *The Divine Right of the Papacy in Recent Ecumenical Theology.* Rome: Università Gregoriana Editrice, 1980.

Minnerath, Roland. *Le Pape, évêque universel ou premier des évêques?* Paris: Editions Beauchesne, 1978.

_____. *Le Droit de l'Eglise à la liberté. Du Syllabus à Vatican II.* Paris: Editions Beauchesne, 1982.

Misner, Paul. *Papacy and Development: Newman and the Primacy of the Pope.* Leiden: E.J. Brill, 1976.

Montscheuil, Yves. *L'Eglise et le monde actuel.* 2nd ed. Paris: Editions Témoignage chrétien, 1945.

Mourret, Fernand. *Les Directions politiques intellectuelles et sociales de Léon XIII.* Paris: Bloud et Gay, 1920.

Mühlen, Heribert. *Una Mystica Persona: die Kirche als das Mysterium der Identität des Heiligen Geistes in Christus und in Christen: eine Person in vielen Personen.* Munich: F. Schöning, 1964.

Müller, Alois. *Das Problem von Befehl und Gehorsam im Leben der Kirche: eine Pastoraltheologische Untersuchung.* Einsiedeln: Benziger Verlag, 1964.

Mura, Ernest. *The Nature of the Mystical Body.* Translated by M. Angeline Bouchard. St. Louis: B. Herder Book Co., 1963.

Murray, John Courtney. *We Hold These Truths.* New York: Sheed & Ward, 1960.

_____, ed. *Freedom and Man.* New York: P.J. Kenedy & Sons, 1965.

_____, ed. *Religious Liberty: An End and a Beginning.* New York: Macmillan & Co., 1966.

Nau, Paul. *Une Source doctrinale: les Encycliques. Essai sur l'autorité de leur enseignement.* Paris: Les Editions du Cèdre, 1952.

Naville, Ernest. *L'Eglise romaine et la liberté des cultes.* Geneva: A. Cherbuliez, and Paris: G. Fischbacher, 1878.

Nédoncelle, Maurice, ed. *L'Ecclésiologie au XIX siècle.* Paris: Les Editions du Cerf, 1960.

Nell-Breuning, Oswald von. *Reorganization of Social Economy.* English ed. prepared by Bernard W. Dempsey. New York, Milwaukee and Chicago: Bruce Publishing Co., 1936.

Newman, John Henry.   *The* Via Media *of the Anglican Church.* 2 vols. London: Basil Montagu Pickering, 1877.

————. *An Essay on the Development of Christian Doctrine.* Westminster: Christian Classics, Inc., 1878.

————. *On Consulting the Faithful in Matters of Doctrine.* Edited and with an introduction by John Coulson. New York: Sheed & Ward, n.d.

Nolte, Josef. *Dogma in Geschichte: Versuch einer Kritik des Dogmatismus in der Glaubensdarstellung.* Freiburg, Basel, and Vienna: Herder, 1971.

Oakley, Francis. *Council over Pope? Towards a Provisional Ecclesiology.* New York: Herder and Herder, 1969.

O'Collins, Gerald. *The Case against Dogma.* New York, Paramus, N.J., and Toronto: Paulist Press, 1975.

O'Connor, Edward Dennis. *The Dogma of the Immaculate Conception: History and Significance.* Notre Dame: University of Notre Dame Press, 1958.

Ohm, Thomas. *Machtet zu Jüngern alle Völker.* Freiburg im Breisgau: Erich Wewel Verlag, 1962.

Ommen, Thomas B. *The Hermeneutic of Dogma.* Missoula, Montana: Scholars Press, 1975.

Panikkar, Raymond. *The Unknown Christ of Hinduism.* London: Darton, Longman & Todd, 1964.

————. *The Intrareligious Dialogue.* New York and Ramsey, N.J.: The Paulist Press, 1978.

Panikulam, George. Koinonia *in the New Testament: A Dynamic Expression of Christian Life.* Rome: Biblical Institute Press, 1979.

Pannenberg, Wolfhart. *The Church.* Trans. Keith Crim. Philadelphia: The Westminster Press, 1983.

Papa, Egidio. *Il Sillabo di Pio IX e la Stampa francese, inglese, italiana.* Rome: Cinque Lune, 1968.

Peiffer, Arthur. *Die Enzykliken und ihr formaler Wert für die dogmatische Methode.* Freiburg: Universitätsverlag, 1968.

Pelage, L'Abbé. *La Bulle* Quanta cura *et la civilisation moderne ou le Pape, les Evêques, les gouvernements et la raison.* Paris: Garnier Frères, 1865.

Pelikan, Jaroslav. *Development of Christian Doctrine: Some Historical Prolegomena.* New Haven: Yale University Press, 1969.

————. *The Christian Tradition: A History of the Development of Christian Doctrine,* vol. 2: *The Spirit of Eastern Christendom.* Chicago and London: University of Chicago Press, 1974.

Pelotte, Donald. *John Courtney Murray: Theologian in Conflict.* New York: Paulist Press, 1976.

Pepe, Gabriele. *Il Sillabo e la Politica dei Cattolici.* Rome: Capriotti, 1945.

Petitalot, R. P. *Le Syllabus, base de l'Union catholique.* Paris: Bray et Retaux, 1877.

Philippe, M.-D. *Mystère du Corps mystique du Christ.* Paris: Editions du Vieux Colombier, 1960.

Philips, Gerard. *L'Eglise et son mystère au deuxième Concile du Vatican.* 2 vols. Paris: Desclée et Cie, 1966.

Pieper, Joseph. *Thesen zur sozialen Politik: Die Grundgedanken des Rundschreiben* Quadragesimo Anno. 4th ed. Frankfurt am Main: Verlag Josef Knecht, 1947.

Pottmeyer, H. J.*Unfehlbarkeit und Souveränität: die päpstliche Unfehlbarkeit im System der ultramontanen Ekklesiologie des 19. Jahrhunderts.* Mainz: Matthias-Grünewald-Verlag, 1975.

Przywara, Erich. *Katholische Krise.* Düsseldorf: Patmos-Verlag, 1967.

Quacquarelli, A. *La Crisi della Religiosità contemporanea dal Sillabo al Concilio.* The Vatican: Bari, 1946.

Rahner, Karl. *The Dynamic Element in the Church.* Trans. W.J. O'Hara. Quaestiones Disputatae no. 12. Freiburg: Herder, and London: Burns and Oates, 1964.

―――――. *The Shape of the Church to Come.* Trans. Edward Quinn. New York: Crossroad, 1983.

―――――― and Ratzinger, Joseph. *The Episcopate and the Primacy.* Translated by Kenneth Barker. New York: Herder & Herder, 1962.

―――――― and Schlier, Heinrich, ed. *Vorfragen zu einem ökumenischen Amtsverständnis.* Quaestiones Disputatae no. 65. Freiburg, Basel, and Vienna: 1974.

Ratzinger, Joseph. *Das neue Volk Gottes. Entwürfe zur Ekklesiologie.* Dusseldorf: Patmos Verlag, 1969.

―――――― and Neumann, Johannes, ed. *Theologie im Wandel. Festschrift zum 150. jährigen Bestehen der Katholisch-Theologischen Fakultät an der Universität Tübingen 1817-1967.* Munich and Freiburg im Breisgau: Erich Wewelverlag, 1967.

Regan, Richard J. *Conflict and Consensus: Religious Freedom and the Second Vatican Council.* New York: Macmillan, 1967.

Reiser, William E. *What Are They Saying about Dogma?* New York and Ramsey, N.J., Paulist Press, 1978.

Renusson, B. de. *L'Encyclique expliquée par un catholique libéral.* Paris: Librairie Catholique Martin-Beaupré Frères, 1865.

Rétif, André. *Introduction à la Doctrine pontificale des Missions.* Paris: Editions du Seuil, 1953.

————. *Les papes contemporains et la Mission.* Paris: Apostolat des Editions, 1965.

Reumann, John. *Righteousness in the New Testament.* With Responses by Joseph A. Fitzmyer and Jerome D. Quinn. Philadelphia: Fortress Press, and New York/Ramsey, N.J.: The Paulist Press, 1982.

Rikof, Herwi. *The Concept of Church: A Methodological Inquiry into the Use of Metaphors in Ecclesiology.* London: Sheed and Ward, and Shepherdstown, West Virginia: Patmos Press, 1981.

Rinaldi, C. G. *Il Valore del Sillabo: studio teologico e storico.* Rome: n.p., 1888.

Rota, Pietro. *Il Sillabo di Pio IX.* Milan: La Scuola cattolica, 1884.

Ryan, John A., and Husslein, Joseph. *The Church and Labor.* New York: Macmillan Co., 1920.

Saier, Oskar. *"Communio" in der Lehre des Zweiten Vatikanischen Konzils.* Bamberg: St. Otto Verlag, 1973.

Sancho Bielsa, Jesús. *Infalibilidad del Pueblo de Dios. "Sensus fidei" e Infalibilidad orgánica de la Iglesia en la Constitución "Lumen gentium" del Concilio Vaticano II.* Pamplona: Ediciones Universidad de Navarra, 1979.

Sancti Gregorii Magni Romani Pontificis. *Quadraginta Homiliarum in Evangeliis Libri Duo.* In *Patrologiae Cursus Completus.* Edited by J[acques]- P[aul] Migne. Paris: n.p., 1844-64. *Patrologia Latina,* 221 vols. 76 (1849): 1075-1312.

Sanks, Thomas Howland. *Authority in the Church: A Study in Changing Paradigms.* Missoula, Montana: Scholars Press, 1974.

Satgé, John de. *Peter and the Single Church.* London: SPCK, 1981.

Sauras, Emilio. *El Cuerpo mistico de Cristo.* Madrid and Valencia: Biblioteca de Autores cristianos, 1956.

Schauf, Heribert, ed. *De Corpore Christi Mystico sive de Ecclesia Christi Theses: Die Ekklesiologie des Konzilstheologen Clemens* [sic] *Schrader, S.J.* Freiburg: Verlag Herder, 1959.

Schlink, Edmund; Grässer, Erich; Blank, Josef; de Vries, Wilhelm; Ott, Heinrich; Moltmann, Jürgen; Stirnimann, Heinrich. *Papsttum als ökumenische Frage.* Munich: Kaiser, and Mainz: Grünewald, 1979.

Schmidlin, Joseph. *Catholic Mission Theory* [Katholische Missionslehre in Grundriss]. Techny, Ill.: Mission Press, S.V.D., 1931.

Schmidt, Wilhelm. *Der Ursprung der Gottesidee.* 12 vols. Münster: Verlag der Aschendorffschen Verlagsbuchhandlung, 1926-55.

Schoonenberg, Piet, ed. *Die Interpretation des Dogmas*. Düsseldorf: Patmos Verlag, 1969.

Schrodt, Paul. *The Problem of the Beginning of Dogma in. Recent Theology*. Frankfurt am Main, Bern, and Las Vegas: Peter Lang, 1978.

Sebott, Reinold. *Religionsfreiheit und Verhältnis von Kirche und Staat*. Rome: Università Gregoriana, 1977.

Seesemann, Heinrich. *Der Begriff* Koinonia *im Neuen Testament*. Giessen: Verlag von Alfred Topelmann, 1933.

Semmelroth, Otto. *Die Kirche als Ursakrament*. Frankfurt am Main: J. Knecht, 1953.

Sieben, Hermann Josef. *Die Konsilsidee der Alten Kirche*. Paderborn, Munich, Vienna, Zürich: Ferdinand Schöningh, 1979.

_____. Traktate und Theorien zum Konzil. Frankfurt am Main: Verlag Josef Knecht, 1983.

Silva-Tarouca, C. *Institutiones Historiae Ecclesiasticae*. Rome: Pontificia Universitas Gregoriana, 1933.

Skydsgaard, K. E. *The Church as the Body of Christ*. Notre Dame: University of Notre Dame Press, 1963.

Spae, Joseph. *Buddhist-Christian Empathy*. Chicago: Institute of Theology and Culture, and Tokyo: Oriens Institute for Religious Research, 1980.

Stangetti, G. *Prassi della S. Congregazione di Propaganda Fide*. Rome: Officium Libri Catholici, 1943.

Strieder, Jakob, and Messner, Johannes. *Die soziale Frage und der Katholizismus: Festschrift zum 40. jährigen Jubiläum der Enzyklika* "Rerum Novarum." Paderborn: Verlag von Ferdinand Schöningh, 1931.

Suenens, Léon-Joseph (Cardinal). *Coresponsibility in the Church*. Trans. Francis Martin. New York: Herder & Herder, 1968.

Sullivan, Francis A. *Magisterium: Teaching Authority in the Catholic Church*. New York. Ramsey, N.J.: The Paulist Press, 1983.

Tekippe, Terry J., ed. *Papal Infallibility: An Application of Lonergan's Method*. Washington, D.C.: University Press of America, 1983.

Ternus, J. *Der gegenwärtige Stand der Assumptafrage*. Regensburg: J. Habbel, 1948.

Thauren, Johannes. *Die Akkommodation im katholischen Heidenapostolat: eine missionstheoretische Studie*. Münster im Westfalen: Verlag der Aschendorffschen Verlagsbuchhandlung, 1927.

Theisen, Jerome. *The Ultimate Church and the Promise of Salvation*.

Collegeville, Minnesota: St. John's University Press, 1976.

Thils, Gustave. *L'Infaillibilité du peuple chrétien* "in credendo." Paris: Desclée de Brouwer and Louvain: E. Warny, 1963.

_____. *L'Infaillibilité pontificale: source, conditions, limites*. Gembloux: Editions J. Duculot, 1969.

_____. *La primauté pontificale. La doctrine de Vatican I: les voies d'une révision*. Gembloux: Editions J. Duculot, 1972.

Thornton, Lionel. *The Common Life in the Body of Christ*. 3rd ed. London: Dacre Press, A. & C. Black, 1950.

Tierney, Brian. *Origins of Papal Infallibility: 1150-1350*. Leiden: E.J. Brill, 1972.

Tillard, J[ean]-M[arie]-R[oger]. *L'Evêque de Rome*. Paris: Les Editions du Cerf, 1982.

Torrel. J[ean]-P[ierre]. *La Théologie de l'épiscopat au premier concile du Vatican*. Paris: Les Editions du Cerf, 1961.

Torres Rojas, Enrique. *La libertad religiosa en León XIII y en el Concilio Vaticano II*. Victoria, Spain: Editoral Esset, 1968.

Tracy, David; Küng, Hans; and Metz, Johann, ed. *Toward Vatican III: The Work That Needs To Be Done*. New York: The Seabury Press, 1978.

Troeltsch, Ernst. *The Social Teachings of the Christian Churches*. Translated by Olive Wyon. 2 vols. New York: Harper & Row, Harper Torchbooks, 1960.

Tromp, Sebastian. *Corpus Christi quod est Ecclesia*. 3 vols. Rome: Apud Aedes Universitatis Gregorianae, 1946-60.

Tuyaerts, M. M. *L'Evolution du dogme: étude théologique*. Louvain: Imprimerie "Nova et Vetera," 1919.

Vacant, Jean-Michel-Alfred. *Etudes théologiques sur les Constitutions du Concile du Vatican*. 2 vols. Paris and Lyons: Delhomme et Briquet, éditeurs, 1895.

Van de Pol, W[illem] H[endrik]. *The Christian Dilemma*. Trans. G. Van Hall. New York: The Philosophical Library , 1952.

Vander Gucht, Robert, and Vorgrimler, Herbert. *Bilan de la théologie du XXe siècle*. 2 vols. Paris: Casterman, 1970.

Vermeersch, Arthur. *Tolérance*. Louvain: Librairie universitaire Uystpruyst-Dieudonné, and Paris: Gabriel Beauchesne, 1912.

Viering, Fritz. *Christus und die Kirche in römisch-katholischer Sicht: ekklesiologische Probleme zwischen dem Ersten und Zweiten Vatikanischen Konzil*. Göttingen: Vandenhoeck & Ruprecht, 1962.

Villain, Maurice, and Baciocchi, Joseph de. *La vocation de l'Eglise: étude biblique*. Paris: Librairie Plon, 1954.

Vincent, André. *La liberté religieuse: droit fondamental.* Paris: Editions P. Téqui, 1976.

Violet, Paul. *L'Infaillibilité du Pape et le Syllabus: étude historique et théologique.* Besançon: Jacquin, and Paris: Lethielleux, 1904.

Virgo Immaculata: Acta congressus Mariologici-Mariani Romae Anno MCMLIV celebrati. 18 vols. Rome: Academia Mariana Internationalis, 1956.

Wainwright, Geoffrey. *The Ecumenical Moment: Crisis and Opportunity for the Church.* Grand Rapids: William B. Eerdmans Publishing Company, 1983.

Walgrave, Jan Hendrik. *Unfolding Revelation: The Nature of Doctrinal Development.* Philadelphia: Westminster, 1972.

Wallace, Lillian Parker. *Leo·XIII and the Rise of Socialism.* Durham: Duke University Press, 1966.

Wiltgen, Ralph M. *The Rhine Flows into the Tiber.* New York: Hawthorn Books, 1967.

Zaehner, R.C. *Christianity and Other Religions.* Twentieth Century Encyclopedia of Catholicism, vol. 140. New York: Hawthorn Books, 1964.

ARTICLES

Alberigo, Giuseppe. "New Frontiers in Church History." In *Church History in Future Perspective*, pp. 68-84. Edited by Roger Aubert. Concilium, vol. 57. New York: Herder & Herder, 1970.

_____. "L'Unité de l'Eglise dans le service de l'Eglise romaine et de la papauté (XIe—XXe siècles)." *Irénikon* 51 (1978): 46-72.

_____. "Institutions exprimant la communion entre l'épiscopat universel et l'évêque de Rome." In *Les Eglises après Vatican II: dynamisme et prospective*, pp. 259-90. Actes du Colloque international de Bologne (1980). Edited by Giuseppe Alberigo. Paris: Beauchesne, 1981.

Altaner, Bertold. "Zur Frage der Definibilität der Assumptio B.V.M." *Theologische Revue* 45 (1949): 129-42 and 46 (1950): 5-20.

Amann, E. "Honorius I." In *Dictionnaire de Théologie catholique* 7 (1927): 93-132. 15 vols., 22 tomes. Paris: Letouzey et Ané, 1909-.

Aubert, Roger. "Les réactions suscitées par la publication du Syllabus." *Collectanea Mechliniensia*, n.s. 19 (1949): 309-17.

_____. "L'Enseignement du Magistère ecclésiastique au XIXe siècle sur le libéralisme." In *Tolérance et Communauté humaine*, pp. 75-103. Tournai and Paris: Casterman, 1951.

————. "Monseigneur Dupanloup et le Syllabus." *Revue d'Histoire ecclésiastique* 51 (1956), no. 1, pp. 79-142, nos. 2-3, pp. 471-512, no. 4, pp. 837-915.

————. "L'Ecclésiologie au Concile du Vatican." In *Le Concile et les Conciles: contribution à l'histoire de la vie conciliaire de l'Eglise*, pp. 245-84. Edited by B. Botte. N.p.: Editions de Chevetogne and Editions du Cerf, 1960.

————. "Un centenaire: le Syllabus de décembre 1864." *La Revue nouvelle* 40 (1964): 369-85 and 481-99.

————. "La liberté religieuse du Syllabus de 1864 à nos jours." In *Essais sur la liberté religieuse*, pp. 13-25. Recherches et débats du Centre Catholique des intellectuels français, no. 50. Paris: Librairie Arthème Fayard, March 1965.

Augustinus, Aurelius. Sermo CXXXI, "*De Verbis Evangelii Joannis, cap. vi*," 55-56, *Nisi manducaveritis carnem*, etc. *deque verbis Apostoli et Psalmorum, contra Pelagianos*." In *Patrologiae Cursus Completus.* Edited by J[acques]-P[aul] Migne. Paris: n.p., 1844-64. *Patrologia Latina*, 221 vols. 38 (1845): 729-34.

Bacht, Heinrich. "Tradition und Lehramt um das Assumpta-Dogma." In *Die mündliche Überlieferung: Beiträge zum Begriff der Tradition*, pp. 3-62. Edited by Michael Schmaus. Munich: Max Hueber Verlag, 1957.

————. "Tradition als menschliches und theologisches Problem." *Stimmen der Zeit* 159 (1957): 285-300.

————. "Vom Lehramt der Kirche und in der Kirche." *Catholica* 25 (1971): 144-67.

Balic, Dragutin. "De Assumptione B.V. Mariae quatenus in Deposito Fidei continetur." *Antonianum* 24 (1949): 153-82.

Baudrillart, A[lfred]. "Constance, [Concile de]." In *Dictionnaire de Théologie catholique*. 3 (1938): 1200-1223. 15 vols., 22 tomes. Paris: Letouzey et Ané, 1909-.

Beinert, Wolfgang. "Bedeutung und Begründung des Glaubenssinnes (*Sensus Fidei*) als eines dogmatischen Erkenntniskriteriums." *Catholica* 25 (1971): 271-303.

Bellamy, J. "Assomption de la Sainte Vierge." In *Dictionnaire de Théologie catholique*, 1 (1909): 2139-40. 15 vols., 22 tomes. Paris: Letouzey et Ané, 1909-.

Berbusse, Edward J. "Infallibility in the Ordinary Teaching of the Supreme Pontiff," *Homiletic and Pastoral Review* 76 (June 1976): 26-32.

Betti, Umberto. "Magistero episcopale e magistero pontificio nel

Vaticano II." In Thils, Gustave; Antón, Angel; Dejaifve, George; Vagaggini, Cipriano; Betti, Umberto; De Vries, Guglielmo; Hamer, Jérôme. *L'Ecclesiologia dal Vaticano I al Vaticano II*, pp. 199-208. Brescia: Editrice La Scuola, 1973.

Beumer, J. "Sind päpstliche Enzykliken unfehlbar?" *Theologie und Glaube* 42 (1952): 262-69.

Bévenot, Maurice. "Thesis and Hypothesis." *Theological Studies* 15 (1954): 440-46.

Boff, Leonardo, "Is the Distinction between *Ecclesia docens* and *Ecclesia discens* Justified?" *Who Has the Say in the Church?*, pp. 47-51. Concilium, vol. 148, Edited by Jürgen Moltmann and Hans Küng. Edinburgh: T. & T. Clark, and New York: The Seabury Press, 1981.

Borne, Etienne. "Le problème majeur du Syllabus: vérité et liberté." In *Essais sur la liberté religieuse*, pp. 26-42. Recherches et débats du Centre Catholique des intellectuels français, no. 50. Paris: Librairie Arthème Fayard, March, 1965.

Bouesse, Humbert. "De la Maternité de Marie à sa glorieuse assomption." *Nouvelle Revue théologique* 70 (1948): 923-34.

Bouvier, Pierre. "L'Infaillibilité du Pape et le Syllabus." *Etudes* 102 (1905): 250-57.

Bouyer, Louis."Où en est la théologie du Corps mystique?" *Revue des Sciences religieuses* 22 (1948): 313-33.

Bover, José Maria. "Proceso historico-teologico de la creencia asuncionista." *Revista española de Teologia* 8 (1948): 601-16.

Boyle, John. "The Natural Law and the Magisterium." *The Catholic Theological Society of America: Proceedings* 34 (1979): 189-210.

Bracken, Joseph A. "Toward a Grammar of Dissent." *Theological Studies* 31 (1970): 437-59.

Brinkmann, J. "Gibt es unfehlbare Äusserungen des Magisterium ordinarium' des Papstes?" *Scholastik* 28 (1953): 202-21.

Brinktrine, J. "Was lehrt die Enzyklika '*Mystici corporis*' über die Zugehörigkeit zur Kirche?" *Theologie und Glaube* 38 (1947-48); 290-300.

Brou, Alexandre. "Le Péché des missionaires." *Etudes* 111 (1907): 737-73 and 112 (1907): 161-87.

Bruls, M. "L'Attitude de l'Eglise devant les cultures non-chrétiennes." In *Missions et cultures non-chrétiennes*, pp. 45-57. N.p.: Desclée de Brouwer, 1959.

Caffrey, Thomas A. "Consensus and Infallibility: The Mind of Vatican I." *Downside Review* 88 (1970): 107-31.

Campbell, J. Y. "*Koinonia* and Its Cognates in the New Testament." *Journal of Biblical Literature* 51 (1932): 352-82.

Cañizares Llovera, Antonio. "El Magisterio de la Iglesia." *Iglesia viva* 79 (1979): 357-75.

Capestany, Edward J. "McCormick and the Erosion of the Magisterium," *Catholicism in Crisis* 1, no. 7 (June 1983), pp. 23-28.

Carol, Juniper. "The Definability of Mary's Assumption." *American Ecclesiastical Review* 118 (1948): 161-77.

Caudron, M[arc]. "Magistère ordinaire et infaillibilité pontificale d'après la constitution *Dei Filius*." *Ephemerides Theologicae Lovanienses* 36 (1960): 393-431.

Cayré, Fulbert. "L'Assomption aux quatre premiers siècles: état embryonnaire de la doctrine." In *Vers le Dogme de l'Assomption*, pp. 123-49. Montreal, São Paulo, Paris, South Bend: Fides Publishers, 1948.

Chavasse, A. "Ordonnés au Corps mystique." *Nouvelle Revue théologique* 70 (1948): 703-26.

Chenu, M.-D. "Pour une lecture théologique du Syllabus." In *Essais sur la liberté religieuse*, pp. 43-51. Recherches et débats du Centre Catholique des intellectuels français, no. 50. Paris: Librairie Arthème Fayard, March, 1965.

Ciappi, Luigi. "Magistero della Chiesa e teologia." *Sapienza* 16 (1963): 505-516.

―――. "Il magistero vivo di S. S. Pio XII: norma prossima e universale di verità," *Sapienza* 7 (1954): 125-51.

Coffy, Robert. "Magisterium and Theology." *Irish Theological Quarterly* 43 (1976): 247-59.

Colombo, Carlo (now Bishop). "La Definibilità dell'Assunzione di Maria SS. nella teologia recente." *La Scuola cattolica* 75 (1947): 265-81.

―――. "Obedience to the Ordinary Magisterium." In Rahner, Karl; Labourdette, Michel; Nicholas, Marie Joseph; Lefèbvre, Joseph (Cardinal); Lécuyer, Joseph; Colombo, Bishop Carlo; Oggioni, Mgr. Giulio; Pellegrino, Michele (Cardinal); Martil, Germán; Corallo, Gino; Suenens, Leo Josef (Cardinal); Dezza, Paolo; Fromm, Ferdinand; Jáchym, Bishop Franziskus. *Obedience and the Church*, pp. 75-93. Washington and Cleveland: Corpus Books, 1968.

Congar, Yves. "Confession," "Eglise," "Communion," *Irénikon* 23 (1950): 3-26.

―――. "Le Peuple fidèle et la fonction prophétique de l'Eglise," *Irénikon* 24 (1951): 289-312 and 440-466.

―――. Review of Paul Nau's *Une Source doctrinale: les Encycliques*.

Essai sur l'autorité de leur enseignement. (Paris: Les Editions du Cèdre, 1952.) In *Revue des Sciences philosophiques et théologiques* 37 (1953): 734-35.

_____. "Eglise et Etat." In *Catholicisme: hier, aujourd'hui, demain*, 3 (1954): 1430-41. 8 vols. Paris: Letouzey et Ané, 1948-.

_____. "Quod omnes tangit ab omnibus tractari et approbari debet." *Revue historique du droit français et étranger* 36 (1958): 210-39.

_____. and B.-D. Dupuy, ed., *L'Episcopat et l'Eglise universelle*. Paris: Les Editions du Cerf, 1962.

_____. "La Collégialité épiscopale." In *Histoire et Théologie*. Paris: Unam Sanctam, 1965.

_____. "La 'Reception' comme réalité ecclésiologique." *Revue des Sciences philosophiques et théologiques* 56 (1972): 369-401.

_____. "Bref historique des formes du 'Magistère' et de ses relations avec les docteurs," *Revue des Sciences philosophiques et théologiques* 60 (1976): 98-112.

_____. "Pour une histoire sémantique du terme 'Magisterium.'" *Revue des Sciences philosophiques et théologiques* 60 (1976): 85-97.

_____. "*Jus divinum*." In *Droit ancien et structures ecclésiales*, no. 2, pp. 88-112. London: Variorum Reprints, 1982.

Connell, Francis J. "The Theory of the 'Lay State.'" *American Ecclesiastical Review* 123 (1950): 161-74 and 125 (1951): 7-18.

_____. "Reply to Father Murray." *American Ecclesiastical Review* 126 (1952): 49-59.

Constantin, C. "Libéralisme catholique." In *Dictionnaire de Théologie catholique*, 9 (1926): 506-629. 15 vols., 22 tomes. Paris: Letouzey et Ané, 1909-.

Coppens, J. "La *koinonia* dans l'Eglise primitive." *Ephemerides Theologicae Lovanienses* 46 (1970): 116-21.

_____. "La Définibilité de l'Assomption." *Ephemerides Theologicae Lovanienses* 26 (1950): 309-12.

Costanzo, Joseph F. "Papal Magisterium and *Humanae Vitae*," *Thought* 44 (1969): 377-412.

_____. "Academic Dissent: An Original Ecclesiology." *The Thomist* 34 (1970): 636-53.

Cothenet, E. "La *Communio* nel Nuovo Testamento." *Communio* 1 (1972): 13-21.

Daly, Cahal B. "Theologians and the Magisterium." *The Irish Theological Quarterly* 43 (1976): 225-45.

Daly, Gabriel. "Which Magisterium Is Authentic?" *Who Has the Say in the Church?* Concilium, vol. 148, pp. 52-55. Edited by Jürgen Molt-mann and Hans Küng. Edinburgh, T. & T. Clark, and New York: The Seabury Press, 1981.

Dejaifve, Georges. "L'Ecclesiologia del Concilio Vaticano II," in Thils, Gustave; Antón, Angel; Dejaifve, Georges; Vagaggini, Cipriano; Betti, Umberto; De Vries, Guglielmo; Hamer, Jérôme; *L'Ecclesiologia dal Vaticano I al Vaticano II*, pp. 87-98.

Demahuet, J. "Assomption." In *Catholicisme: hier, aujourd'hui, demain*, 1 (1948): 949-53. 8 vols. Paris: Letouzey et Ané, 1948-.

Denzler, Georg. "The Authority and Reception of Conciliar Decisions in Christendom." In *The Ecumenical Council—Its Significance in the Constitution of the Church*, pp. 13-18. Concilium, vol. 167. Edited by Peter Huizing and Knut Walf. Various translators. Edinburgh: T. & T. Clark, and New York: The Seabury Press, 1983.

Descamps, A.L. "Théologie et magistère," *Ephemerides Theologicae Lovanienses* 52 (1976): 82-133.

Dieckmann, Hermann. "Die religiösen Anschauungen eines Gebildeten im ersten nachchristlichen Jahrhundert." In *Stimmen aus Maria Laach* 53 (1912): 287-95, 438-49, and 508-15.

Diet, Marcel. "Eglise et Etat selon Vatican II.". *Ephemerides Theologicae Lovanienses* 54 (1978): 145-60.

Dionne, Robert J. "*Humanae vitae* Re-examined: A Response." *Homiletic and Pastoral Review* 73 (July 1973): 57-64.

Dubay, Thomas. "The State of Moral Theology: A Critical Appraisal," *Theological Studies* 35 (1974): 482-506.

———. "Does Dissent Have a Future?" *Homiletic and Pastoral Review* 83 (January 1983): 10-18.

———. "Theologians in the New Canon Law." *Homiletic and Pastoral Review* 84 (May 1984): 10-15.

Dublanchy, Edmond. "Infaillibilité du Pape." In *Dictionnaire de Théologie catholique* 7 (1927): 1638-1717. 15 vols., 22 tomes Paris: Letouzey et Ané, 1909-.

Duffy, Stephen. "Catholicism's Search for a New Self-Understanding." In *Vatican II: Open Questions and New Horizons*, pp. 9-37. Edited by Gerald M. Fagin. Wilmington, Delaware: Michael Glazier, Inc., 1984.

Dulles, Avery. "Papal Authority in Roman Catholicism." In *A Pope for All Christians?* pp. 48-70. Edited by Peter J. McCord. New York, Paramus, Toronto: Paulist Press, 1976.

———. "*Ius Divinum* as an Ecumenical Problem." *Theological Studies* 38 (1977): 681-708.

"The Encyclical and the Syllabus." *Dublin Review* 56, n.s. 4 (1865): 441-529.

Fenton, Joseph Clifford. "The Extension of Christ's Mystical Body." *American Ecclesiastical Review* 110 (1944): 124-30.

――――. "The Doctrinal Authority of Papal Encyclicals." *American Ecclesiastical Review* 121 (1949): 210-20.

――――. "The Relation of the Christian State to the Catholic Church According to the *Pontificale Romanum.*" *American Ecclesiastical Review* 123 (1950): 214-18.

――――. "The State of a Controversy." *American Ecclesiastical Review* 124 (1951): 451-58.

――――. "Principles Underlying Traditional Church-state Doctrine." *American Ecclesiastical Review* in 126 (1952): 452-62.

――――. "Toleration and the Church-State Controversy." *American Ecclesiastical Review* 130 (1954): 330-43.

Filograssi, Giuseppe. "De Definibilitate Assumptionis Beatae Mariae Virginis."*Gregorianum* 29 (1948): 7-41.

――――. *"Traditio divino-apostolica et assumptio B.V.M."* *Gregorianum* 30 (1959): 443-89.

Fischer, Gerd-Dieter. "Zum *Koinonia*-Charakter christlicher Gemeinden." *Theologie und Glaube* 61 (1971): 39-44.

Fitzmyer, Joseph A. "The Office of Teaching in the Christian Church According to the New Testament." In *Lutherans and Catholics in Dialogue.*Vol. 6: *Teaching Authority and Infallibility in the Church,* pp. 186-212. Edited by Paul C. Empie, T. Austin Murphy and Joseph A. Burgess. Minneapolis: Augsburg Publishing House, 1978.

Fontaine-de Visscher, L. "Une rencontre sur 'Structuralisme et dogmatique chrétienne.' " *Revue théologique de Louvain* 4 (1973): 257-61.

Ford, John C., and Grisez, Germain. "Contraception and the Infallibility of the Ordinary Magisterium." *Theological Studies* 39 (1978): 258-312.

Ford, John T. "Infallibility: Who Won the Debate?" *The Catholic Theological Society of America: Proceedings* 31 (1976): 179-92.

Fransen, P[iet]. "Einige Bemerkungen zu den theologischen Qualificationen." In *Die Interpretation des Dogmas,* pp. 111-37. Edited by Piet Schoonenberg. Düsseldorf: Patmos Verlag, 1969.

――――. "La Communion ecclésiale, principe de vie." In *Les Eglises après Vatican II: dynamisme et prospective,* pp. 185-206. Edited by Giuseppe Alberigo. Actes du Colloque international de Bologne (1980). Paris: Beauchesne, 1981.

Franzen, August. "The Council of Constance: Present State of the Problem." In *Historical Problems of Church Renewal,* pp. 29-68. Concilium, vol. 7. Edited by Roger Aubert. Various translators. Glen Rock, New Jersey: Paulist Press, 1965.

Fries, Heinrich. *"Ex sese, non ex consensu Ecclesiae."* In *Volk Gottes: Festgabe für Joseph Höfer*, pp. 480-500. Edited by R. Bäumer and H. Dolch. Freiburg, Basel and Vienna: Herder, 1958.

Froelich, Karlfried. "Fallibility instead of Infallibility? A Brief History of the Interpretation of Galatians 2:11-14." In *Lutherans and Catholics in Dialogue*. Vol. 6: *Teaching Authority and Infallibility in the Church*, pp. 259-69. Edited by Paul C. Empie, T. Austin Murphy and Joseph A. Burgess. Minneapolis: Augsburg Publishing House, 1978.

Garijo Guembe, Miguel M.ª "El concepto de 'Recepción' y su enmarque en el seno de la Eclesiología católica." *Lumen* 29 (1980): 311-31.

Garrigou-Lagrange, R. "La Définibilité de l'Assomption." *Divus Thomas* 50 (1958): 81-86.

George, A. "La Communion fraternelle des croyants dans les Epîtres de Saint-Paul." *Lumière et Vie* 16 (1967): 3-20.

Glaser, John W. "Authority, Connatural Knowledge, and the Spontaneous Judgment of the Faithful." *Theological Studies* 29 (1968): 742-51.

Gonsalez Moralejo, Rafael. "Enseñanzas de la Encíclica 'Rerum Novarum,' y opportuno desarollo en el Magisterio de Pio XI y Pio XII." In *Comentarios a la* Mater et Magistra, pp. 120-33. Edited by M. Brugarolo. Translated by José Luis Gutierrez García and Luis Ortiz Muños. Madrid: Biblioteca de Autores cristianos, 1963.

Gouhier, Henri. "Tradition et développement à l'époque du modernisme." In *Ermeneutica e Tradizione*, pp. 75-104. Archivio di filosofia, nn. 1-2. Edited by Enrico Castelli. Padua: Cedam, 1963.

Grillmeier, Alois. "Konzil und Rezeption: methodische Bemerkungen zu einem Thema der ökumenischen Diskussion." In *Mit Ihm und in Ihm*. pp. 303-34. Freiburg, Basel, and Vienna: Herder, 1975.

Guerrero, E. "Con la libertad del acto de fe no es incompatible el Estado católico." *Razón y Fe* 151 (1955): 465-78.

Grisez, Germain. "Infallibility and Specific Moral Norms: A Review Discussion." *The Thomist* 49 (1985): 248-78.

Guissard, Lucien. "Postface: Paroles pour un temps de crise." In *Les Evêques français prennent position*, pp. 262-72. Edited by Pierre Toulet. N.p.: Le Centurion, 1972.

Hallett, Garth L. "Contraception and Prescriptive Infallibility." *Theological Studies* 42 (1982): 629-50

Hamer, Jérôme. "Le Baptême et l'Eglise." *Irénikon* 25 (1952): 142-64.

————. "Le Corps épiscopal uni au pape, son autorité dans l'Eglise." *Revue des Sciences philosophiques et théologiques* 45 (1961): 21-31.

_____. "Note sur la Collégialité épiscopale." *Revue des Sciences philosophiques et théologiques* 44 (1960): 40-50.

Hauck, Friedrich. "κοινός...κοινόο." In *Theological Dictionary of the New Testament*, 3 (1965): 789-809. 10 vols. Vols. 1-4 ed. Gerhard Kittel, vols. 5-9 ed. Gerhard Friedrich. vol. 10 (Index) compiled by Ronald E. Pritikin. Trans. Geoffrey W. Bromiley. Grand Rapids and London: William B. Eerdmans Publishing Co., 1964-76.

Hentrich, Guilhelmus. "De Definibilitate Assumptionis B.V.M." *Marianum* 11 (1949): 259-311.

_____. "Alla vigilia della definizione dogmatica dell'Assunzione corporea di Maria Santissima." *Osservatore romano* 90, no. 191 (16-17 agosto 1950): 1.

Hernandez, A.S. "Salvación y paganismo." *El problema teológico de la salvación de los infieles.* Santander: Sal Terrae, 1960.

Hoeck, Joannes M. "Decree on the Eastern Catholic Churches." In *Commentary on the Documents of Vatican II*, 1 (1966): 307-31. Edited by Herbert Vorgrimler. Translated by Lalit Adolphus, Kevin Smyth and Richard Strachan. 5 vols. London: Burns & Oates, and New York: Herder & Herder, 1966-69.

Hryniewicz, Waclaw. "Die ekklesiale Rezeption in der Sicht der orthodoxen Theologie." *Theologie und Glaube* 65 (1975): 250-66.

Hughes, Gerard J. "Infallibility in Morals." *Theological Studies* 34 (1973): 415-28.

Jossua, Jean-Pierre. "Immutabilité, progrès ou structurations multiples des doctrines chrétiennes." *Revue des sciences philosophiques et théologiques* 53 (1968): 175-200.

_____. "Signification des confessions de foi." *Istina* 17 (1972): 48-56.

Kasper, Walter. "Are Non-Christian Religions Salvific?" In *Evangelization, Dialogue and Development: Selected Papers of the International Theological Conference* (Nagpur, India), *1971*, pp. 157-68. Edited by Mariasusai Dhavamony. Rome: Università Gregoriana Editrice, 1972.

Kerkevoorde, A. "La théologie du Corps mystique au XIXe siècle." *Nouvelle Revue théologique* 67 (1945): 417-30.

Klinger, Elmar. "Die Unfehlbarkeit des ordentlichen Lehramtes." In *Zum Problem Unfehlbarkeit: Antworten auf die Anfrage von Hans Küng.* Quaestiones Disputatae no. 54, pp. 274-88. Edited by Karl Rahner. Freiburg im Breisgau, Basel, and Vienna: Herder, 1971.

Knöpfler, A[lois]. "Die Akkommodation in altchristlichen Missionswesen." *Zeitschrift für Missionswissenschaft* 1 (1911): 41-51.

Komonchak, Joseph A. "Ordinary Papal Magisterium and Religious

Assent." In Charles E. Curran, ed., *Contraception: Authority and Dissent*, pp. 101-26. New York: Herder & Herder, 1969.

―――. *"Humanae vitae* and Its Reception." *Theological Studies*, 39 (1978); 221-57.

―――. *"The Universal Church and the Communion of the local Churches."* In *Where Does the Church Stand?* Concilium, vol. 146, pp. 30-35. Ed. Giuseppe Alberigo and Gustavo Gutierrez. Edinburgh: T & T. Clark, New York: The Seabury Press, 1981.

Koninck, Charles de. "La Personne de Marie dans le Culte de l'Eglise et la définibilité de l'Assomption." *Laval théologique et philosophique* 5 (1949); 25-32.

Kossel, Clifford, G. "Religious Freedom and the Church: J. C. Murray." *Communio* 11, no. 1 (Spring 1984), pp. 60-74.

Küng, Hans. "The World Religions in God's Plan of Salvation." in *Christian Revelation and World Religions* pp. 25-66. Edited by J. Neuner. London: Burns and Oates, 1967.

―――. "Im Interesse der Sache: Antwort an Karl Rahner." *Stimmen der Zeit* 187 (1971); 43-64 and 105-122.

Laurentin, René. "L'Action dur Saint-Siège par rapport au problème de l'Immaculée Conception." In *Virgo Immaculta: Acta congressus Mariologici-Mariani Romae Anno MCMLIV celebrati*, vol. 2: 6-98. 18 vols., Rome: Academia Mariana Internationalis, 1956.

Le Bachelet, X. "L'Immaculée Conception." In *Dictionnaire de Théologie catholique*, 7 (1927); 979-1218, 15 vols., 22 tomes. Paris: Letouzey et Ané, 1909-.

Lecler, Joseph. "La papauté moderne et la liberté de conscience." *Etudes* 249 (1946); 289-309.

―――. "A propos de la distinction de la 'thèse' et de l''hypothèse.' " *Recherches de Science religieuse* 41 (1953): 530-34.

Leclercq, Jacques. "Etat chrétien et liberté de l'Eglise." *La Vie intellectuelle* 17 (1949): 99-111.

Lécuyer, Joseph. "Institutions en vue de la communion entre l'épiscopat universel et l'évèque de Rome." In *Les Eglises après Vatican II: dynamisme et prospective*, pp. 297-301. Actes du Colloque international de Bologne (1980). Edited by Guiseppe Alberigo. Paris: Beauchesne, 1981.

LeGuillou, M.J. "Eglise et communion: essai d'ecclésiologie comparée." *Istina* 7 (1959): 33-82.

Levie, Jean. "L'Encyclique '*Humani generis.*' " *Nouvelle Revue théologique* 72 (1950): 785-93.

Lialine, C. "Une étape en ecclésiologie: réflexions sur l'encyclique '*Mystici corporis.*' " *Irénikon* 19-20 (1946-47): 54-83.

Liégé, A. "L'Appartenance à l'Eglise et l'encyclique '*Mystici corporis*.' " *Revue des Sciences philosophiques et théologiques* 32 (1948): 351-57.

Lonergan, Bernard J. F. "The Assumption and Theology." In ,*Vers le Dogme de l'Assomption*, pp. 411-24. Montreal, São Paulo, Paris, South Bend: Fides Publishers, 1948.

López-Gay, J. "Evolución histórica del concepto de 'Evangelisación.' " In *Evangelization*, pp. 161-90. Edited by Mariasusai Dhavamony. Rome: Università Gregoriana, 1975.

Lumpe, Adolf. "Zu 'recipere' als 'gültig annehmen, anerkennen,' im Sprachgebrauch des römischen und kanonischen Rechts." *Annuarium Historiae Conciliorum: Internationale Zeitschrift für Konziliengeschichtsforchung* 7 (1975): 118-34.

Malevez, L. "Quelques enseignements de l'encyclique '*Mystici corporis*.'" *Nouvelle Revue théologique* 67 (1945): 385-407.

Martina, Giacomo. "Osservazioni sulle varie redazioni del Sillabo." In *Chiesa e Stato nell'Ottocento II*, pp. 419-523. Padua: Editrice Antinare, 1962.

McBrien, Richard P. "Is the Papacy Worth Defending?" In Richard P. McBrien, *Has the Church Surrendered?*, pp. 100-03. Denville, New Jersey: Dimension Books, Inc., 1974.

McCormick, Richard A. "Notes on Moral Theology." *Theological Studies* 28 (1967): 760-69.

_____. "Notes on Moral Theology." *Theological Studies* 45 (1984): 80-138.

McDermott, M. "The Biblical Doctrine of *Koinonia*." *Biblische Zeitschrift* 19 (1975): 64-77 and 219-33.

McSorley, Harry J. "Some Ecclesiological Reflections on *Humanae Vitae*."*Tijdschrift voor philosophie en theologie* 30 (1969): 3-8.

Meglio, Giusepe di. "*Ci riesce* and Cardinal Ottaviani's Discourse." *American Ecclesiastical Review* 128 (1953): 384-85.

Metzler, Josef. "Die synode von Ajuthia (Siam, [Thailand]) 1664-1665." In *Annuarium Historiae Conciliorum: Internationale Zeitschrift für Konziliengeschichtsforchung* 11 (1979): 397-424. Edited by Walter Brandmüller and Remigius Bäumer.

Miceli, Vincent. "A Forgotten Encyclical." *Homiletic and Pastoral Review* 76 (June 1976): 19-28.

Michalon, P. "Eglise, Corps mystique du Christ glorieux." *Nouvelle Revue théologique* 74 (1952): 673-87.

Misner, Paul. "The Papacy: Three Schools of Thought." *The Ecumenist* 11 (May, June, 1973), no. 4, pp. 52-55.

Morel, Valentin. "Le Corps mystique du Christ et l'Eglise catholique romaine." *Nouvelle Revue théologique* 70 (1948): 703-26.

Moulard, A., and Vincent, F.   Letter to the Editors, *L'Ami du clergé* 29 (1907): 313-15.

Mueller, F. S.   "Petitiones de Assumptione corporea B.V. Mariae in caelum definienda." *Gregorianum* 27 (1946): 110-35.

Müller, K.   "Das christliche Menschenbild als Aufgabe missionarischer Akkommodation." *Orientierung* 19 (1955): 249-54.

Murray, John Courtney.   "Current Theology: Freedom of Religion." *Theological Studies* 6 (1945): 85-113.

———.   "Freedom of Religion: I. The Ethical Problem." *Theological Studies* 6 (1945): 229-86.

———.   "A Review of *Religious Liberty: An Inquiry*, by M. Searle Bates." *Theological Studies* 7 (1946): 151-63.

———.   "St. Robert Bellarmine on the 'Indirect Power." *Theological Studies* 9 (1948): 491-535.

———.   "Governmental Repression of Heresy." *The Catholic Theological Society of America: Proceedings* (1948): 26-98.

———.   "The Political Thought of Joseph de Maistre." *Review of Politics* 2 (1949): 63-86.

———.   "Contemporary Orientations of Catholic Thought on Church and State in the Light of History." *Theological Studies* 10 (1949): 177-234.

———.   "On Religious Freedom." *Theological Studies* 10 1949): 409-32.

———.   "The Natural Law." In *Great Expressions of Human Rights*, pp. 69-101. Edited by R.M. MacIver. New York and London: Harper & Bros., 1950.

———.   "The Problem of the State Religion." *Theological Studies* 12 (1951): 155-78.

———.   "The Problem of the 'Religion of the State.' " *American Ecclesiastical Review* 124 (1951): 327-52.

———.   "For the Freedom and Transcendence of the Church." *American Ecclesiastical Review* 126 (1952): 28-48.

———.   "Leo XIII on Church and State: The General Structure of the Controversy." *Theological Studies* 14 (1953): 1-30.

———.   "Leo XIII: Separation of Church and State." *Theological Studies* 14 (1953): 145-214.

———.   "Leo XIII: Two Concepts of Government." *Theological Studies* 14 (1953): 551-67.

———.   "The Problem of Pluralism in America." *Thought* 29 (1954): 165-208.

———.   "The Problem of Religious Freedom." *Theological Studies* 25 (1964): 503-75.

———. "The Issue of Church and State at Vatican II."*Theological Studies* 27 (1966): 580-606.

———. "Vers une intelligence du développement de la doctrine de l'Eglise sur la liberté religieuse." In *La liberté religieuse*, pp. 111-47. Edited by Jérôme Hamer and Yves Congar. Paris: Les Editions du Cerf, 1967.

Nau, Paul. "L'autorité doctrinale des Encycliques." In *La Pensée catholique*, no. 15 (1950), pp. 45-63; no. 16 (1950), pp. 42-59; no. 19 (1951), pp. 63-84.

———. "Le Magistère pontifical ordinaire, lieu théologique." *Revue thomiste* 56 (1956): 389-412.

———. "Le magistère pontifical ordinaire au premier concile du Vatican." *Revue thomiste* 62 (1962): 341-97.

The New York Times. November 21, 1978, Sec. A, pp. 1, 16 and 17; November 26, 1978, secs. 1 and 4; June 25, 1984, sec. A., pp. 1 and 8.

Newman, John Henry. Letter to Ryder, quoted in "An Unpublished Paper by Cardinal Newman on the Development of Doctrine." Edited by H. de Achával. *Gregorianum* 39 (1958): 585-96.

Nicolau, Miguel. "Magisterio 'ordinario' en el Papa y en los obispos." *Salmanticenses* 9 (1962): 544-78.

Nothomb, M. "L'Eglise et le Corps du Christ: dernières encycliques et doctrine de saint-Thomas." *Irénikon* 25 (1952): 226-48.

Ottaviani, Cardinal Alfredo. "Church and State: Some Present Problems in the Light of the Teaching of Pope Pius XII." *American Ecclesiastical Review* 128 (1953): 321-34.

Pavan, Pietro [now Cardinal]. "Declaration on Religious Freedom." In *Commentary on the Documents of Vatican II*, 4 (1969): 49-86. Edited by Herbert Vorgrimler. Translated by Hilda Graef, W. J. O'Hara and Ronald Walls. 5 vols. London: Burns & Oates, and New York: Herder & Herder, 1966-69.

Pereira, José. "Fallible?" *Thought* 47 (1972): 362-414.

Philips, G. "Autour de la définibilité d'un dogme." *Marianum* 10 (1948): 81-111.

———. "Quelques publications récentes autour du problème de l'Assomption." *Ephemerides Theologicae Lovanienses* 26 (1950): 365-82.

———. "La Constitution dogmatique sur l'Eglise '*Lumen Gentium*.'" *Ephemerides Theologicae Lovanienses* 42 (1966): 5-39.

Pirard, Regnier, and Gesché, Adolphe. Two separate reports on "Structuralisme et dogmatique, intégration et dépassement," *Revue théologique de Louvain* 4 (1973): 384-89.

Poma, Antonio. "The Mission of Bishops as *Diakonia* of the Faith."

The Irish Theological Quarterly 43 (1976): 274-92.

Pribilla, Max. "Dogmatische Intoleranz und bürgerliche Toleranz." *Stimmen der Zeit* 144 (1948-49): 27-40.

Rahner, Karl. "Membership of the Church According to the Teaching of Pius XII's Encyclical, '*Mystici corporis Christi*.'" In *Theological Investigations*, 2 (1963): 1-88. Translated by Karl-H. Kruger. 20 vols. London: Darton, Longman and Todd, and New York: Seabury Press, 1961-. German original: "Die Gliedschaft in der Kirche nach der Lehre der Enzyklika Pius XII. '*Mystici corporis Christi*.'" In *Schriften zur Theologie* 2 (1962): 7-94. 20 vols. Einsiedeln, Zürich and Cologne: Benziger Verlag, 1954.

―――. "Christianity and the Non-Christian Religions." In *Theological Investigations* 5 (1966): 115-34. Trans. Karl-H. Kruger. 20 vols. London: Darton, Longman, and Todd and New York: The Seabury Press, 1961-.

―――. "Reflections on the Concept of '*Ius Divinum*' in Catholic Thought." In *Theological Investigations* 5 (1966): 219-43. Trans. Karl-H. Kruger. 20 vols. London: Darton, Longman, and Todd, and New York: The Seabury Press, 1961-.

―――. "Dogmenentwicklung." In *Lexicon für Theologie und Kirche*: *Das Zweite Vatikanische Konzil*, 3 (1968): 457-63. 3 vols. Freiburg: Verlag Herder, 1966-68.

―――. "The Hierarchical Structure of the Church with Special Reference to the Episcopate." Commentary on nos. 18-27 of *Lumen gentium*. In *Commentary on the Documents of Vatican II*, 1 (1966): 186-218. Edited by Herbert Vorgrimler. Translated by Lalit Adolphus, Kevin Smith and Richard Strachen. 5 vols. London: Burns & Oates, and New York: Herder & Herder, 1966-69.

―――. "Kritik an Hans Küng." *Stimmen der Zeit* 186 (1970): 361-77.

―――. "Zum Begriff der Unfehlbarkeit in der katholischen Theologie." *Stimmen der Zeit* 186 (1970): 18-31.

―――. "Replik. Bemerkungen zu: Hans Küng, Im Interesse der Sache." *Stimmen der Zeit* 187 (1971): 145-60.

―――. "The Development of Dogma." In *Theological Investigations*, 1 (1961): 39-77. Translated by Cornelius Ernst. 20 vols. London: Darton, Longman & Todd, and New York: Seabury Press, 1961-.

―――. "Open Questions in Dogma Considered by the Institutional Church as Definitively Answered." *Journal of Ecumenical Studies* 15 (1978): 211-26. Trans. Michael A. Fahey.

―――. "Theologie und Lehramt." *Stimmen der Zeit* 198 (1980): 363-75.

Ratzinger, Joseph. "Naturrecht, Evangelium und Ideologie in der katholischen Soziallehre. Katholische Erwägungen zum Thema." In

Christlicher Glaube und Ideologie, pp. 760-69. Edited by W. von Bismarck and W. Dirks. Stuttgart: n.p., 1964.

Ratzinger, Joseph. "Der christliche Glaube und die Weltreligionen." In *Gott in Welt: Festgabe für Karl Rahner*. 2 (1964): 287-305. Edited by Johannes Baptist Metz. 2 vols. Freiburg im Breisgau: Herder, 1964.

Reiser, William E. "Dogma and Heresy Revisited: A Heideggerian Approach." *The Thomist* 46 (1982): 509-38.

Richard, L. "Une thèse fondamentale de l'oecuménisme: le baptême, incorporation visible à l'Eglise." *Nouvelle Revue théologique* 74 (1952): 485-92.

Riudor, Ignacio. "La pertenencia a la Iglesia en los dos primeros dos capítulos de la constitución '*Lumen Gentium*' del Concilio Vaticano II." *Estudios eclesiásticos* 40 (1965): 301-18.

Robichaud, J. Armand. "The Immaculate Conception and the Magisterium of the Church before 1954." *Marian Studies* 5 (1954): 73-144.

Rollet, Henri. "Les Origines de *Rerum Novarum*." *La Vie intellectuelle* 19 (1951): 4-21.

Salaverri de la Torre, Joaquín. "Valor de las Encíclicas a la luz de '*Humani generis*.'" *Miscelánea Comillas* 17 (1952): 135-72.

———. "La Potestad de Magisterio Eclesiástico y asentimiento que le es debido." *Estudios eclesiásticos* 29 (1955): 155-95.

———. "La Obediencia debida a la potestad magisterial de la Iglesia." *Sal Terrae* 43 (1955): 26-30 and 86-91.

———. [Salaverry] "Encyclicals." *Sacramentum Mundi: an Encyclopedia of Theology*; 6 vols. 2 (1968): 228-30. New York: Herder & Herder, and London: Burns & Oates, 1968-70.

Sartori, Luigi. "What is the Criterion for the *Sensus Fidelium*?" *Who Has the Say in the Church*? Concilium, vol. 148, pp. 56-60. Ed. Jürgen Moltmann and Hans Küng. Edinburgh: T. & T. Clark, and New York: The Seabury Press, 1981.

Sauras, E. "El misterio de la asunción y la firmeza teológica que ha alcanzado." *Ciencia tomista* (1948): 57-97.

Scheffczyk, Leo. "Die theologische Diskussion um des Unfehlbarkeitsdogma." *Münchener Theologische Zeitschrift* 22 (1971): 282-95.

Schmaus, Michael. "Das Weltrundschreiben '*Mystici corporis*' Pius XII. 1943." In *Wort der Päpste*. Edited by Wilhelm Sandfuchs. Würzburg: Echter-Verlag, 1965.

———. "Das gegenseitige Verhältnis von Leib Christi und Volk Gottes im Kirchenverständnis." In *Volk Gottes: Festgabe für Josef Höfer*, pp. 13-27. Edited by R. Bäumer and H. Dolch. Freiburg, Basel and Vienna: Herder, 1967.

Schmemann, Alexander. "The Idea of Primacy in Orthodox Ecclesiology." In Meyendorff J.; Schmemann, A.: Afanassieff, N.; and Koulomzine, N., *The Primacy of Peter*, pp. 30-56. Wing Road, Leighton Buzzard, and Bedfordshire: The Faith Press, second edition, 1973.

Schnackenburg, Rudolf. "Wesenszüge und Geheimnis der Kirche nach dem Neuen Testament." In *Mysterium Kirche* 1 (1962): 89-199. Edited by Ferdinand Holböck and Thomas Sartory. 2 vols. Salzburg: Otto Müller Verlag, 1962.

Schüller, Bruno. "Bemerkungen zur authentischen Verkündigung des kirchlichen Lehramtes." *Theologie und Philosophie* 42 (1967): 534-51.

Semmelroth, Otto. "Mariens leibliche Himmelfahrt heilsgeschichtlich gesehen." *Geist und Leben* 41 (1948): 440-48.

_____. "Überlieferung als Lebensfunction der Kirche." *Stimmen der Zeit* 148 (1950-51): 1-11.

Sesboüé, J. "Autorité du Magistère et vie de foi ecclésiale." *Nouvelle Revue théologique* 93 (1971): 337-62.

Steffes, J. P. "Akkommodation und Synkretismus als Missions problem." *Zeitschrift für Missionswissenschaft und Religionswissenschaft* 23 (1933): 1-11.

Stephenson, Anthony A. "The Development and Immutability of Christian Doctrine." *Theological Studies* 19 (1958): 481-532.

Stirnimann, H. "Magisterio enim ordinario haec docentur . . ." *Freiburger Zeitschrift für Philosophie und Theologie* 1 (1954): 17-47.

Swidler, Leonard. "The Ecumenical Problem Today: Papal Infallibility." *Journal of Ecumenical Studies* 8 (1971): 751-67.

_____. "*Demo-Kratia*, the Rule of the People of God, or *Consensus Fidelium*." In *Authority in the Church and the Schillebeeckx Case*, pp. 226-43. Edited by Leonard Swidler and Piet F. Fransen. New York: Crossroad, 1982.

Taymans, F. "L'Encyclique '*Humani generis*' et la théologie." *Nouvelle Revue théologique* 73 (1951): 3-20.

Ternus, Joseph. "Vom Gemeinschaft der Kirche." *Scholastik* 10 (1935): 1-30.

_____. "Beiträge zum Problem der Tradition." *Divus Thomas* 16 (1938): 33-56 and 197-229.

Tierney, Brian. "Infallibility in Morals: A Response," *Theological Studies* 34 (1973): 507-17.

Tillard, J[ean]-M[arie]-R[oger]. "A propos du *sensus fidelium*.' " *Proche-Orient chrétien* 25 (1975): 113-34.

_____. "La primauté romaine." *Irénikon* 50 (1977): 291-325.

_____. "La Jurisdiction de l'évêque de Rome." *Irénikon* 51 (1978): 358-73 and 508-20.

_____. "The Jurisdiction of the Bishop of Rome." *Theological Studies* 40 (1979): 3-22.

_____. "L'Eglise de Dieu est une communion," *Irénikon* 53 (1980): 451-68.

_____. "Eglise catholique romaine et Eglises unies." *Irénikon* 55 (1982): 19-23.

Troeltsch, Ernst. "Kirche III: Dogmatisch." In *Die Religion in Geschichte und Gegenwart* 3 (1912): 1147-55. 5 vols. Tübingen: J. C. B. Mohr, 1909-13.

Violet, Paul. "Controverse sur le Syllabus." *Etudes* 103 (1905): 250-57.

Vooght, P[aul] De. "Les controverses sur les pouvoirs du concile et l'autorité du pape au Concile de Constance." *Revue théologique de Louvain* 1 (1970): 45-75.

Wojtyla, Karol. "Bishops as Servants of the Faith." *The Irish Theological Quarterly* 43 (1976): 260-73.

Wolfinger, Franz. "Die Rezeption theologischer Einsichten und ihre theologische und ökumenische Bedeutung: von der Einsicht zur Verwirklichung." *Catholica* 3 (1977): 202-33.

Wright, John W. "The Meaning and Structure of Catholic Faith." *Theological Studies* 39 (1978): 701-18.

Zalba, Marcellinus and Díez Alegría, Josephus. "Declaratio Concilii Vaticani II '*Dignitatis humanae*' de libertate religiosa." In Antón, A.; Bertrams, W.; and Beyer, J. *De Concilio Oecumenico Vaticano II Studia*, pp. 18-45. Rome: Libreria Editrice dell' Università Gregoriana, 1966.

Addenda

Betti, Umberto. *La Dottrina sull'Episcopato del Concilio Vaticano II. Il capitolo III della Constituzione dommatica* Lumen gentium. Rome: n.p., 1984.

Bravo Ugarte, José. *Diocesis y Obispos de la Iglesia Mexicana 1519-1939*. Mexico, D.F.: "Buena Prensa," 1941.

Dulles, Avery. *The Catholicity of the Church*. Oxford: Clarendon Press, 1985.

Jauss, Hans Robert. "Literary History as Challenge to Literary Theory." In *Toward an Aesthetic of Reception*, pp. 3-45. Trans. Timothy Bahti. *Theory and History of Literature* vol. 2. Minneapolis: University of Minnesota Press, 1982.

DETAILED
TABLE OF CONTENTS

513

INDEX

517